Torts and Personal Injury Law

THIRD EDITION

DELMAR CENGAGE Learning

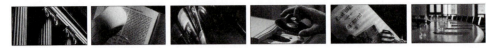

Options.
Over 300 products in every area of the law: textbooks, online courses, CD-ROMs, reference books, companion websites, and more – helping you succeed in the classroom and on the job.

Support.
We offer unparalleled, practical support: robust instructor and student supplements to ensure the best learning experience, custom publishing to meet your unique needs, and other benefits such as Delmar Cengage Learning's Student Achievement Award. And our sales representatives are always ready to provide you with dependable service.

Feedback.
As always, we want to hear from you! Your feedback is our best resource for improving the quality of our products. Contact your sales representative or write us at the address below if you have any comments about our materials or if you have a product proposal.

Accounting and Financials for the Law Office • Administrative Law • Alternative Dispute Resolution • Bankruptcy Business Organizations/Corporations • Careers and Employment • Civil Litigation and Procedure • CLA Exam Preparation • Computer Applications in the Law Office • Constitutional Law Contract Law • Court Reporting • Criminal Law and Procedure • Document Preparation • Elder Law Employment Law • Environmental Law • Ethics Evidence Law • Family Law • Health Care Law Immigration Law • Intellectual Property • Internships • Interviewing and Investigation Introduction to Law • Introduction to Paralegalism • Juvenile Law • Law Office Management Law Office Procedures • Legal Nurse Consulting • Legal Research, Writing, and Analysis Legal Terminology • Legal Transcription • Media and Entertainment Law • Medical Malpractice Law Product Liability • Real Estate Law • Reference Materials • Social Security • Sports Law • Torts and Personal Injury Law • Wills, Trusts, and Estate Administration • Workers' Compensation Law

---

DELMAR CENGAGE Learning
5 Maxwell Drive
Clifton Park, New York 12065

For additional information, find us online at:
www.delmar.cengage.com

DELMAR
CENGAGE Learning™

Torts and Personal Injury Law

◆

THIRD EDITION

William R. Buckley
Cathy J. Okrent

DELMAR
CENGAGE Learning·

Australia • Brazil • Japan • Korea • Mexico • Singapore • Spain • United Kingdom • United States

Torts and Personal Injury Law,
Third Edition
William R. Buckley, Cathy J. Okrent

Vice President, Career Education Strategic
  Business Unit: Dawn Gerrain

Editorial Director: Sherry Gomoll

Acquisitions Editor: Pamela Fuller

Senior Developmental Editor:
  Melissa Reviglia

Editorial Assistant: Sarah Duncan

Production Director: Wendy A. Troeger

Production Manager: Carolyn Miller

Production Editor: Matthew J. Williams

Marketing Director: Donna J. Lewis

Channel Manager: Wendy E. Mapstone

Cover Image: Corbis

Cover Design: Dutton & Sherman Design

For product information and technology assistance, contact us at
Cengage Learning Customer & Sales Support, 1-800-354-9706

For permission to use material from this text or product,
submit all requests online at **www.cengage.com/permissions**
Further permissions questions can be emailed to
permissionrequest@cengage.com

Library of Congress Control Number: 2003051668

ISBN-13: 978-0-7668-4761-3

ISBN-10: 0-7668-4761-6

Delmar
Executive Woods
5 Maxwell Drive
Clifton Park, NY 12065
USA

Cengage Learning is a leading provider of customized learning solutions with
office locations around the globe, including Singapore, the United Kingdom,
Australia, Mexico, Brazil, and Japan. Locate your local office at
international.cengage.com/region

Cengage Learning products are represented in Canada by
Nelson Education, Ltd.

For your lifelong learning solutions, visit **delmar.cengage.com**

Visit our corporate website at **www.cengage.com**

Printed in Canada
6 7 11 10 09 08

DEDICATION

This book is dedicated to my friend Christine Pettica Festine, who was an inspiration to friends, family, and colleagues alike.

Cathy J. Okrent

CONTENTS

Preface xix
Table of Cases xxv

CHAPTER 1   **Introduction to Torts and Legal Analysis 1**

§ 1.1   Introduction 2

§ 1.2   Torts Defined 2
          Sources of Tort Law 3
          Broad Categories of Tort Law 3

§ 1.3   History of Tort Law 4
          The King's Writs 5
          Evolution of Modern Tort Law 5

§ 1.4   Public Policy Objectives in Tort Law 5
          Protecting Persons and Property: Accountability 5
          Minimum Standards of Conduct: Deterrence 6
          Allocating Losses among Different Individuals or Groups 6

§ 1.5   Analyzing Hypothetical Problems 7
          Analytical Framework for Hypotheticals: *IRAC* 7
          Factual Distinctions Result in Different Conclusions 8

§ 1.6   Solving Tort Problems 8
          Tort Analysis: From General to Specific 8
          Hypothetical 9

§ 1.7   Overview of a Civil Case 10
          Complaint 10
          Answer 11
          Discovery 11
          Pretrial Procedures 11
          Trial 11
          Post-Trial Procedures 12

§ 1.8   Case Resolution 12
          Alternate Dispute Resolution 12
          Arbitration 12
          Mediation 12
          Minitrial 12
          Rent-a-Judge 12
          Summary Jury Trial 13

CHAPTER 2   **Negligence 17**

§ 2.1   Introduction 18

§ 2.2   Negligence 18
Negligence Defined: Reasonable Care 18
Acts or Omissions 19

§ 2.3   Elements of Negligence 19

§ 2.4   Scope of Duty and Standard of Reasonable Care 20
Duty Defined 20
Scope of Duty 20
Foreseeability 22
Foreseeable Plaintiffs Theory 23
Standard of Reasonable Care 23
The Reasonable Person Standard 24
Professional Malpractice 25
Matching Skill and Disabilities 25
Medical Malpractice 26
Special Duty Based upon Special Relationship 28

§ 2.5   Causation of Injury 30
Cause-in-Fact 31
Substantial Factor Analysis 31
Joint and Several Liability 33
Contribution 34
Courts and Causation 34

§ 2.6   Proximate Cause 37
Foreseeability of Injury 37
Proximate Cause and Scope of Duty Combined 38
"Taking the Victim as You Find Him" 42

§ 2.7   Damages 45
Compensatory Damages 46
General Damages 46
Special Damages 46
Economical and Non-Economical Damages 46
Verdict 46
Nominal Damages 47
Punitive Damages 47

§ 2.8   Proving Negligence 48
Burdens of Proof and Rejoinder 49
Res Ipsa Loquitur 49

§ 2.9   Violation of a Statute 53

CHAPTER 3   **Special Negligence Actions 59**

§ 3.1   Introduction 60

§ 3.2   Premises Liability 60
Land Owner's Different Duties of Reasonable Care 61
Victim's Status on Land Defines Scope of Duty 61
Modern Judicial Trends 61
Land Owner's "Zero Duty" Toward Trespassers 62
Special Rule for Trespassing Children:
   Attractive Nuisance 62
Licensees Defined 66
Land Owner's Duty of Reasonable Care Toward
   Licensees 66
Invitees Defined 67
Land Owner's Highest Duty of Reasonable Care
   Toward Invitees 68
Invitees and Licensees Distinguished 68
Implicit or Express Invitation 68
Limited Areas of Invitation 68
Using Traditional Negligence Theory in
   Land Owner Cases 70

§ 3.3   Vicarious Liability 73
Vicarious Liability Defined 73
Employment Not an Essential Element 73
Respondeat Superior 74
Coming and Going Rule 74
Frolic and Detour Rule 75
Independent Contractors 75
Motor Vehicle Vicarious Liability 76

§ 3.4   Negligent Infliction of Emotional Distress 78
Extra Elements in the Common Law 78
Impact Rule 78
Physical Manifestations Rule 79
Zone of Danger Rule 79
Family Relationships Rule 81
California Approach 81

§ 3.5   Negligence Per Se 84
Defenses to Negligence Per Se 84
Plaintiff Within Class of Persons Protected by Statute 85
Absolute Liability Mislabeled as Negligence Per Se 85
Toxic Torts as Negligence Per Se 86

CHAPTER 4   **Defenses to Negligence 91**
§ 4.1   Introduction 92
§ 4.2   How Negligence Defenses Are Used 92

§ 4.3   Contributory Negligence and Last Clear Chance 93
Contributory Negligence Defined 93
Last Clear Chance 94

§ 4.4   Comparative Negligence 95
Elements 95
The Balancing Act 95
Criticism of Comparative Negligence 96

§ 4.5   Assumption of Risk 99
Voluntary Assumption of Known Risk 100
Full Appreciation of Danger 100
Proof of Assumption of Risk 101
The Complete Defense 101

§ 4.6   Statutes of Limitations 104

CHAPTER 5   **Intentional Torts: Injuries to Persons 111**

§ 5.1   Intentional Torts in General 112
Intent and Action Together 112
Crime versus Torts 113

§ 5.2   Assault and Battery 113
Assault Defined 114
Battery Defined 116
Transferred Intent 117

§ 5.3   False Imprisonment 122
Confinement 122
Physical Barriers Restricting Movement 124
Express or Implied Threats of Force 125
Captive's Consent to Confinement 125
Intent to Confine 125
Confinement for Appreciable Time Period 126
No Reasonable Means of Escape 126

§ 5.4   Infliction of Emotional Distress 130
Intentional Infliction 130
Outrageous Conduct 130
Reckless Infliction 135
Sexual Harassment 136

§ 5.5   Fraud and Misrepresentation 140
Definitions and Distinctions 140
False Statements Intended to Deceive 141
Knowledge of Falsity of Information 141
Tortfeasor's Profit from Deception 141
Innocent Party's Injury 141

§ 5.6   Malicious Prosecution and Abuse of Process 145
Malicious Prosecution 145

              Groundless Criminal Prosecution 145
              Abuse of Process 146

§ 5.7   Invasion of Privacy 151
              Appropriation 151
              Unreasonable Intrusion 151
              Public Disclosure of Private Facts 156
              False Light in the Public Eye 158

§ 5.8   Defamation: Libel and Slander 160
              Nature of the Statement 160
              Harm to Reputation in the Community 161
              Publication 161
              Public Figures 161
              Slander Per Se 161
              Truth and Privilege as Absolute Defenses 162

CHAPTER 6   **Intentional Torts: Injuries to Property 173**

§ 6.1   Introduction 174

§ 6.2   Trespass to Land 174
              Elements of Trespass to Land 174
              Entry Defined 175
              Unauthorized Entry 175
              No Actual Harm Required 176
              Intentional Interference 176
              Possession: Land Owner's Exclusive Right to Use 176
              Trespass Above and Below Land: Is the Sky the Limit? 179

§ 6.3   Toxic Tort Actions 181
              Nature of the Problem 181
              Toxic Trespass 185
              Importance of Environmental Statutes 188

§ 6.4   Trespass to Chattel 188
              Unauthorized Possession of Another's Chattel 189
              Unauthorized Interference with Use 189
              Intent to Deprive or Interfere 191

§ 6.5   Conversion 194
              History 194
              Elements of Conversion 195
              Depriving of Possession 195
              Extent of Deprivation 195
              Methods of Depriving 195
              Intent to Deprive and Convert to Own Use 196
              Lack of Consent 196
              Conversion as a Crime 198

§ 6.6   Slander of Title, Commercial Disparagement,
              and Defamation by Computer 200

Slander of Title 200
Commercial Disparagement 201
Defamation by Computer 204
Computerized Credit Reporting 204
Creation of a New Tort 209

CHAPTER 7   Defenses to Intentional Torts 219

§ 7.1   Introduction 220

§ 7.2   Self-Defense 221
Reasonable Force 222
Countering an Attacking or Offensive Force 222
Force Necessary to Prevent Injury,
   Offensive Contact, or Confinement 222

§ 7.3   Defense of Persons or Property 224
Defense of Persons: Elements 224
Defense of Property: Elements 225

§ 7.4   Rightful Repossession 228
Retaking Possession of Personal Property 229
Prompt Repossession Efforts 229
Wrongful Denial of Possession 229
Wrongful Dispossession 230

§ 7.5   Consent 233
Informed Consent: Voluntary Acceptance 234
Implied Consent 234

§ 7.6   Mistake 237
Good-Faith Conviction 238
Belief Based upon Inaccurate Information 238
Otherwise Tortious Acts 238
The *Restatement (Second) of Torts* 238

§ 7.7   Privilege 240
Motives and Socially Desirable Goals 240
Less Injurious Alternatives 241
Similarity Between Privilege and Other Defenses 241
The *Restatement (Second)* Position 241

§ 7.8   Necessity 243
Thwarting a More Substantial Harm 243
External Forces 244
Reasonably Necessary Action 244
The *Restatement (Second)* Position 245

§ 7.9   Public Officer's Immunity for Legal Process
   Enforcement 246
Service of Process 247
Execution Sales 247

Attachment or Replevin 247
Arrest by Warrant 248
Prosecutors and Judges 248

§ 7.10 Warrantless Arrest by Law Enforcement Officials or
Citizens 250

§ 7.11 Statutes of Limitations 252

§ 7.12 Workers' Compensation 254

CHAPTER 8   **Strict, or Absolute, Liability 261**

§ 8.1 Introduction 262

§ 8.2 An Overview of Strict Liability 262
Fault Is Irrelevant 262
Limitations to Absolute Liability 263
Public Policy Objectives Behind Strict Liability 263
Insurance Analogy 263
Historical Development 263

§ 8.3 Abnormally Dangerous Activities 264
Restatement (Second) Rule 264
Hazards Outweigh Benefits: Balancing Test 266
Defenses 268
Public Policy Objectives Behind Statutory Immunity 271

§ 8.4 Mass Torts 273

§ 8.5 Animal Owners' Liability 276
Wild Animals Defined 276
Ownership of Wildlife 276
Importance of Wildlife Ownership 276
Comparison with Domesticated Animals 277
Vicious Propensity Rule 277
Defenses in Animal Absolute Liability Cases 277
Dog-Bite Statutes 279

§ 8.6 Scope of Liability: Proximate Cause 281
No Duty of Reasonable Care 282

CHAPTER 9   **Products Liability 287**

§ 9.1 Introduction 288

§ 9.2 Products Liability Theory and History 288
Public Policy Objectives Behind Products Liability 289
Historical Development of Products Liability 289

§ 9.3 Parties 293
Manufacturers and Sellers 293
The Ultimate User 294

§ 9.4   Elements 295
No Privity of Contract Requirement 295
Negligence Is Irrelevant 295
A Typical Products Liability Formula 295
Restatement (Second) Rule 296
Unreasonably Dangerous Products 296
Consumer Contemplation Test 297
Danger/Utility Test 298
Business Requirement 299
Substantially Unchanged Condition Requirement 299
Proximate Cause 300
Proper Use Requirement 300
Foreseeable Plaintiffs Theory 302

§ 9.5   Defenses 306
Contributory or Comparative Negligence
    Not a Defense 307
Ultimate User's Misuse of Product 307
Assumption of Risk 308

§ 9.6   Comparison to Contract Law Warranties 314

§ 9.7   Bad Faith 314

CHAPTER 10   Special Tort Actions 319

§ 10.1   Introduction 320

§ 10.2   Nuisances 320
Private Nuisance Defined 321
Unreasonable and Substantial Defined 321
Community Standard 321
Use and Enjoyment 321
Classic Examples 321
Physical Effects on Land 322
"Coming to the Nuisance Defense" 326

§ 10.3   Public Nuisances 331
Use and Enjoyment of Common Legal Rights 331
Governments as Plaintiffs 331
Types of Public Nuisances 331
Mixed Nuisances 332
Nuisances Per Se 332
"Coming to the Nuisance" Not a Defense 332

§ 10.4   Remedies or Nuisances 336
Abatement 337
Money Damages 337
Injunctions 337
Review of Hypotheticals 341

§ 10.5   Survival Statutes and Wrongful Death Statutes 343
Typical Facts in Wrongful Death Cases 343
Plaintiffs in Wrongful Death Actions 343
Damages 344
Loss of Consortium 344
Defenses 344

§ 10.6   Wrongful Birth 347
Typical Fact Pattern: Genetic Counseling Gone Awry 347
Wrongful Life: The New Tort 348

CHAPTER 11   **Tort Immunities 355**

§ 11.1   Introduction 356

§ 11.2   Governmental, or Sovereign, Immunity 356
History 356
Modern Applications 357
Difficulty with the Governmental/Proprietary
Distinction 358
Modern Steps to Eliminate the Distinction 358
Suits Against States 358

§ 11.3   Public Officers 359
Exceptions 359
Who Is Protected 359
Rationale for Immunity 359

§ 11.4   Children of Tender Years 362
Definition 362
Absolute Immunity for Intentional Torts 362
Immunity from Negligence 362

§ 11.5   Spousal/Family Immunity 365
Spousal Immunity 365
Family Immunity (parent/child) 365

§ 11.6   Workers' Compensation 366

CHAPTER 12   **Paralegal Ethics 371**

§ 12.1   Introduction 372

§ 12.2   NALA Ethics Code and Guidelines 372
Restricted Duties 372
NALA Model Standards and Guidelines for
Utilization of Legal Assistants 373
Paralegal Representation Before
Administrative Agencies 375
Lay Representation in Justice or Small Claims Court 375
Supervised Duties 375

No Independent Legal Judgment 376
Protecting Client Confidences 376
Avoiding the Appearance of Impropriety 376
Integrity and Competency 376
Lawyer Ethics Rule Application 377
Model Standards' List of Permissible Activities 377
Legal Effect of NALA Rules 377

§ 12.3 NFPA Code and Model Rules 379
NFPA Model Rules 380

§ 12.4 ABA Code and Model Rules 380
ABA Code of Professional Responsibility 381

§ 12.5 Hypothetical Problems 385

§ 12.6 Further Ethics Information 389

CHAPTER 13   Tort Investigation 395

§ 13.1 Tort Investigation 396

§ 13.2 Introduction to Investigation 397

§ 13.3 The Importance of Tort Case Investigation 397
Paralegals and Investigators 397
Customizing the Investigation 398
Details, Details, Details! 398
Goals of Tort Case Investigation 398

§ 13.4 Witness Interview Techniques and Questions 398
Client Interview Techniques 402

§ 13.5 Determining and Locating Defendants 403
Using Discovery to Locate Defendants 403
Study Documents Carefully 403
Use Caution When Naming Defendants 406
Using the Telephone as a Research Tool 406
Internet Resources 406
Obtaining Information About Corporations 407
Obtaining Information About Partnerships 408
Obtaining the Names of Sole Proprietors and Partners 409
Ambulance Services and Fire Departments
as Defendants 409
Investigating Licensed or Regulated Businesses 411
Sample Defendant Search 411

§ 13.6 Documenting the Scene 412
Obtaining Visual Documentation, Measurements,
and Other Details 412
Knowing the Evidentiary Rules for One's Jurisdiction 413
Using Proper Evidentiary Form 413

Hearsay Problems 415
Video and Computer Technologies 416

§ 13.7   Public and Private Sector Resources 416
Local Governmental Agencies 416
Newspapers 417
Television and Radio News Reports 417
Computerized Databases 418
Additional Information Regarding Criminal Acts 418

§ 13.8   Additional Areas to Investigate 420
Employment and Lost Wages 420
Expenses Related to the Injury 420
Insurance Coverage and Other Benefits 422
Previous Claims or Lawsuits of Plaintiff 422
Previous Injuries to Plaintiff 423
The Parties' Criminal Histories 423
Driving Records 423

§ 13.9   Investigating Different Types of Tort Cases 424
Automobile Accident Cases 424
Medical Negligence Cases 425
Obtaining Information About Health Care Providers 427
Health Care Facilities that Receive
        Government Funding 430

APPENDICES

Appendix A   Confidential Client Information Form 439
Appendix B   Understanding Appellate Court Opinions 445
Appendix C   Supplementary Cases 449

Glossary 505
Index 517

PREFACE

Focus

Entertainment is a lot to expect from any book, but torts are custom made with something interesting for everybody.

While never intended to amuse, the cases selected to represent legal points demonstrate behavior that has caused some outrageous actions, which is why *Jones v. Clinton* is included. For fans of the Internet, *A&M Records v. Napster* is featured.

Overview

This text is an overview of tort law for the personal injury paralegal. Chapter 1 discusses tort law generally and historically; it also provides an overview of a civil case and alternative dispute resolution (ADR). Chapter 2 summarizes negligence. Chapter 3 discusses special negligence actions, including premises liability, vicarious liability, and negligent infliction of emotional distress. Chapter 4 focuses on the defenses to negligence actions. Chapter 5 considers intentional torts and injuries to persons. Chapter 6 is devoted to intentional torts and injuries to property. Chapter 7 addresses defenses to intentional torts. Chapter 8 covers strict, or absolute, liability. Chapter 9 illustrates product liability cases. Chapter 10 features special tort actions. Chapter 11 discusses tort immunities. Chapter 12 reviews paralegal ethics. Chapter 13 focuses on tort investigation.

Chapter Features

Chapters begin with an outline and introduction. Chapters end with a summary, review questions, additional problems, and a list of key terms that were used throughout the chapter, in addition to chapter-specific Internet resources. Many recent cases have been added.

The running glossary features standard definitions from *Oran's Dictionary* to help students learn or refresh their knowledge regarding these terms. Additional definitions supplied by the author are marked with a dagger.

The text combines theoretical and practical applications. Accompanying each tort topic are hypothetical examples to illustrate how the abstract rules pertain to real life. Illustrative cases are included to portray the actual application of legal principles in appellate court opinions, legal encyclopedia summaries, and the *Restatement (Second) of Torts*.

All cases included are for educational purposes, as examples. The cases have been heavily edited, and citations omitted, so as to include as many cases in the text as possible. The reader should always refer to original sources and verify that there have been no recent changes in the law in a particular jurisdiction. Sample letters, forms, and reports are included for illustrative purposes. The people named in the exhibits and hypotheticals are all fictional; any resemblance to known people is purely coincidental.

New Chapter Additions

What else is new to the third edition? By popular demand, the following:

+ Mass torts and class actions
+ Alternate dispute resolution (ADR)
+ Internet resources for investigation and legal research
+ Bad faith tort liability
+ Overview of a civil case
+ Web site URLs, including state-specific information
+ More in-depth coverage of workers' compensation
+ Computer tort cases
+ Family immunity and spousal immunity

Teaching Aids and Features

+ There is an **Instructor's Manual** with test bank to accompany this text. Also included are answers to the problems in text.

+ The **Test Bank** provided in the Instructor's Manual is also available in computerized format on CD-ROM.

+ There is an **Online Resource** to accompany this book. It contains chapter-by-chapter Web links from the text as well as state-specific links pertinent to torts. These sites are excellent starting points for legal research and tort-case investigation. Also included are the complete appendices A and B from the text.

+ **Web page**—Come visit our Web site at **www.paralegal.delmar.cengage.com**, where you will find valuable information such as hot links and sample materials to download, as well as other West Legal Studies products.

◆ **WESTLAW®**—West's online computerized legal research system offers students "hands-on" experience with a system commonly used in law offices. Qualified adopters can receive ten free hours of WESTLAW®. WESTLAW® can be accessed with Macintosh and IBM PC and compatibles. A modem is required.

◆ **Strategies and Tips for Paralegal Educators**, a pamphlet by Anita Tebbe of Johnson County Community College, provides teaching strategies specifically designed for paralegal educators. A copy of this pamphlet is available to each adopter. Quantities for distribution to adjunct instructors are available for purchase at a minimal price. A coupon on the pamphlet provides ordering information.

◆ **Survival Guide for Paralegal Students**, a pamphlet by Kathleen Mercer Reed and Bradene Moore covers practical and basic information to help students make the most of their paralegal courses. Topics covered include choosing courses of study and note-taking skills.

◆ **West's Paralegal Video Library**—Delmar, Cengage Learning is pleased to offer the followig videos at no charge to qualified adopters:

   ◆ *The Drama of the Law II: Paralegal Issues Video*
   ISBN: 0-314-07088-5

   ◆ *"I Never Said I Was a Lawyer": Paralegal Ethics Video*
   ISBN: 0-314-08049-x

   ◆ *The Making of a Case Video*
   ISBN: 0-314-07300-0

   ◆ *ABA Mock Trial Video—Anatomy of a Trial: A Contracts Case*
   ISBN: 0-314-07343-4

   ◆ *ABA Mock Trial Video—Product Liability*
   ISBN: 0-314-07342-6

   ◆ *Arguments to the United States Supreme Court Video*
   ISBN: 0-314-07070-2

◆ **Court TV Videos**—Delmar, Cengage Learning is pleased to present the following videos from Court TV for a minimal fee:

   ◆ *New York v. Ferguson—Murder on the 5:33:*
   The Trial of Colin Ferguson
   ISBN: 0-7668-1098-4

   ◆ *Ohio v. Alfieri*
   ISBN: 0-7668-1099-2

   ◆ *Flynn v. Goldman Sachs—Fired on Wall Street:*
   A Case of Sex Discrimination?
   ISBN: 0-7668-1096-8

   ◆ *Dodd v. Dodd:—Religion and Child Custody in Conflict*
   ISBN: 0-7668-1094-1

- *In Re Custody of Baby Girl Clausen—Child of Mine:
  The Fight for Baby Jessica*
  ISBN: 0-7668-1097-6

- *Fentress v. Eli Lilly & Co., et al.—Prozac on Trial*
  ISBN: 0-7668-1095-x

- *Garcia v. Garcia—Fighting over Jerry's Money*
  ISBN: 0-7668-0264-7

- *Hall v. Hall—Irretrievably Broken—A Divorce Lawyer Goes to Court*
  ISBN: 0-7668-0196-9

- *Maglica v. Maglica—Broken Hearts, Broken Commitments*
  ISBN: 0-7668-0867-x

- *Northside Partners v. Page and New Kids on the Block—New Kids
  in Court: Is Their Hit Song a Copy?*
  ISBN: 0-7668-9426-7

Please note the internet resources are of a time-sensitive nature
and URL addresses may often change or be deleted.

Contact us at **www.paralegal.delmar.cengage.com**

ACKNOWLEDGMENTS

Torts and Personal Injury Law could not have been produced without the dedication of many people. I thank my editors at Delmar (in particular, Joan Gill, Pamela Fuller, Melissa Riveglia, and Alexis Breen Ferraro) and the American Law Institute, the National Law Journal, and the *Rutgers Computer & Technology Law Journal*, for allowing use of reprinted portions of their materials.

Special thanks to Graphics West and Dan Branagh, project coordinator/editor, for managing the production of this book in a timely, thorough, and professional manner. I truly appreciate your suggested changes, guidance, and assistance.

Additionally, I would like to acknowledge the invaluable contributions of the following reviewers for their suggestions and attention to detail:

Hugh Birgenheier
Pierce College
University Place, WA

Chelsea Campbell
Lehman College
Bronx, NY

Kathy Cook
The University of Central Florida
Orlando, FL

Kenneth Frank
Brenau University
Gainsville, GA

William Goren
MacCormac College
Chicago, IL

Gary Ivanson
Roger Williams University
Tiverton, RI

Ralph Livieri
Branford Hall Career Institute
Branford, CT

Elizabeth Mann
Greenville Technical College
Greenville, SC

Carolynn Smoot
Southern Illinois University
Carbondale, IL

Robin Wertheimer
NYT Career Institute
New York, NY

Angie Williams
The University of Mississippi
University, MS

Alex Yarbrough
Virginia College at Birmingham
Birmingham, AL

Thank you one and all.

TABLE OF CASES

A

A&M Records, Inc. v. Napster, Inc. 205–7
Adger v. Dillard Department Stores 32

B

Babits v. Vassar Brothers Hospital, et. al 51
Bennett v. Stanley 63–4
Boutte v. Nissan Motor Corp. 291–3
Brown v. Hearst Corp. 165–8
Burt v. Beautiful Savior Lutheran Church 177–9

C

Carroll v. W.R. Grace & Co. 345–6
Cereghino v. Boeing Co. 266–7
Csizmadia v. Town of Webb 341–3

D

Dean & a. v. MacDonald 102–3
Decker v. Princeton Packet, Inc. 80–1, 163–4
Delahanty v. Hinckley 272, 305
Deuschle v. Jobe 132–33
Douglas v. Gibson 29–30
Dykeman v. Englebrecht 97–8

E

Egede-Nissen v. Crystal Mountain, Inc. 70–2
Estiverne v. Sak's Fifth Avenue 208–9

F

Fidelity Mortgage Co. v. Cook 141–4
Field v. Philadelphia Electric Co. 118–120

G

Greene County Board of Education v. Bailey 197–8

H

Higgins v. E.I. Dupont De Nemours & Co. 309–11
Hoffman v. Capital Cities/ABC, Incorporated 152–4
Hossler v. Hammel 202–3

J

Jacobs v. City of Jacksonville 333–4
Johnson v. Valu Food, Inc. 123–4
Joint Eastern & Southern Districts Asbestos Litigation, In Re 268–271
Jones v. Clinton 136–8
Jurco v. State 226–7, 249, 251

K

Knight v. Jewett 235–6
Knoller v. City and County of San Francisco 390–2
Koepnick v. Sears, Roebuck & Co. 192–4
Koester v. VCA Animal Hospital 190–1

L

Leo v. Kerr-McGee 182–4
Lineberry v. State Farm Fire & Casualty Co. 156–8

M

Marrs v. Marriott Corp. 154–5
Martin v. Heffelfinger 360–1
McDonald's Coffee, A Burning Issue 48
Mezrah v. Bevis 27
Mitchell v. Globe International Publishing, Inc. 133–5
Moscatello v. University of Medicine and Dentistry of New Jersey 348–50

O

Ohio Casualty Insurance Co. v. Todd 21–2, 84–5

P

Palsgraf v. Long Island Railroad 39–41
Pollicino v. Roemer and Featherstonhaughn P.C. 105–6
Pote v. Jarrell 147–9
Powers v. Palacios 279–80

R

Robinson v. Health Midwest Development Group 252–4
Rogers v. T.J.X. Cos. 127–9

Rosenberg v. Packerland Packing Co. 115
Russell Corporation v. Sullivan et. al., Avondale Mills, Inc. 186–8

S

Sampson v. Zimmerman 42–44
Shehyn v. United States 230–2
Sherk v. Indiana Waste Systems, Inc. 327–9
Shields v. Zuccarini 212–4
Silvester v. Spring Valley Country Club 325–6
Smith v. Scripto-Tokai Corp. 301–2, 377–9
Sparks v. Johnson 382–5

U

United States Environmental Protection Agency v. The Port Authority of New York and New Jersey, et.al. 339–41

V

Vorvis v. Southern New England Telephone Co. 366–7

W

Wells v. Hickman 363–5

CHAPTER 1

INTRODUCTION TO TORTS AND LEGAL ANALYSIS

CHAPTER OUTLINE

§ 1.1 Introduction
§ 1.2 Torts Defined
§ 1.3 History of Tort Law
§ 1.4 Public Policy Objectives in Tort Law
§ 1.5 Analyzing Hypothetical Problems
§ 1.6 Solving Tort Problems
§ 1.7 Overview of a Civil Case
§ 1.8 Case Resolution

⟨ ◆ ⟩

The law often allows what honor forbids.
BERNARD JOSEPH SAURIN

§ 1.1 Introduction

This chapter covers the definition of a tort, the three broad categories of torts, the history of tort law, the public policy objectives behind tort law, and the analytical processes used both to understand appellate court opinions and to solve hypothetical problems.

This chapter includes:

◆ Definitions of torts

◆ An initial description of negligence

◆ The elements of strict (absolute) liability

◆ The historical roots of tort law

◆ The public policy objectives of tort law in terms of compensating injured parties, holding wrongdoers liable, and allocating losses across society

◆ Development of an analytical framework to understand appellate court opinions

◆ Construction of an analytical formula to solve hypothetical problems by applying the legal principles to the facts of the case

◆ Assembly of an analytical formula that allows any tort law problem or question to be continuously narrowed to reveal the answer (IRAC)

◆ Demonstration of how tort law analysis goes from the general to the specific

◆ An overview of a civil case

◆ A discussion of alternate dispute resolution.

§ 1.2 Torts Defined

A **tort** is a wrongful injury to a person or his or her property. The person inflicting the harm is called the **tortfeasor** (*feasor* meaning "doer"). The

tort A civil (as opposed to a criminal) wrong, other than a breach of contract. For an act to be a tort, there must be: a legal duty owed by one person to another, a breach (breaking) of that duty, and harm done as a direct result of the action.

tortfeasor A person who commits a tort.

common law Either all caselaw or the caselaw that is made by judges in the absence of relevant statutes.

negligence The failure to exercise a reasonable amount of care in a situation that causes harm to someone or something.

intentional injury (tort)† An injury *designed* to injure a person or that person's property as opposed to an injury caused by negligence or resulting from an accident.

battery An intentional, unconsented to, physical contact by one person (or an object controlled by that person) with another person.

assault An intentional threat, show of force, or movement that could reasonably make a person feel in danger of physical attack or harmful physical contact.

word *tort* is French, taken from the Latin *torquere* (meaning "to twist") and characterizes behavior that warps or bends society's rules about avoiding causing harm to others. The French phrase *de son tort demesne* (meaning "in his own wrong") was used to describe grievous misconduct between individuals and to assign blame to the responsible party.

Sources of Tort Law

Tort law is derived both from **common law** and statutory law. Legislatures often enact statutes to supplement, modify, or supersede common law tort principles. Courts may turn the tables on the legislature by issuing new common law rulings interpreting the meaning of statutes. In this way the law matures, with both courts and legislatures adjusting the law to meet the changing needs of society.

Broad Categories of Tort Law

Tort law considers the rights and remedies available to persons injured through other people's carelessness or intentional misconduct. Tort law also holds persons in certain circumstances responsible for other people's injuries regardless of blame. Torts are commonly subdivided into three broad categories: negligence, intentional torts, and strict (or absolute) liability.

Negligence

Negligence is the failure of an ordinary, reasonable, and prudent person to exercise due care in a given set of circumstances. It is distinguishable from intentional torts in that negligence does not require an *intent* to commit a wrongful action; rather, the wrongful action itself is sufficient to constitute negligence. Intentional torts, as the name indicates, require the tortfeasor to intend to commit the wrongful act. What makes misconduct negligent is that the behavior was not reasonably careful and someone was injured as a result of this unreasonable carelessness; for example, failing to watch the road ahead when driving a car.

Intentional Torts

Intentional torts are actions designed to injure another person or that person's property. The tortfeasor intends a particular harm to result from the misconduct. There are several different types of intentional torts: intentional, reckless, or negligent. Examples of specific intentional torts are assault and battery, each of which is discussed in detail in later chapters.

Specific Intentional Torts: Brief Definitions **Battery** occurs when a tortfeasor touches another person without consent. **Assault** is an

trespass A wrongful entry onto another person's property. ...

attempted battery. **Trespass** is unlawful or unreasonable interference with the use of someone's property.

Strict (Absolute) Liability

strict (absolute) liability The legal responsibility for damage or injury, even if you are not at fault or negligent.

Strict (absolute) liability is the tortfeasor's responsibility for injuring another regardless of intent, negligence, or fault. The most important type of strict liability is *products liability*, a theory under which the manufacturer or other seller of an unreasonably dangerous or defective product is held liable for injuries the product causes. Strict liability is different from intentional torts in that intent to commit an absolute liability tort is irrelevant. Likewise, strict liability is distinguishable from negligence, because the tortfeasor is responsible under absolute liability regardless of how careful he or she might have been.

These concepts are presented here only to establish basic terminology. Subsequent chapters explore each of these topics in greater detail.

The Unique Elements of Each Tort

Each type of tort contains its own unique elements. While the elements of each are unique, tort analysis in general is the same. In a tort case, one must always ask whether the following exist:

1. Duty
2. Breach of duty
3. Causation
4. Damages.

For instance, battery may be readily distinguished from defamation because it carries its own definition and rules that separate it from other intentional torts. Likewise, the elements of negligence are different from strict liability's components, and so on. The key to understanding tort law is to identify the type of broad tort category involved in the case. Ask whether the problem contains intentional torts (and, if so, which particular one(s)), negligence, or strict liability. Next, apply the appropriate rules of law to the specific facts of the case.

Like all forms of law, torts have undergone a long and interesting period of growth and development. Section 1.3 briefly examines the history of tort law.

§ 1.3 History of Tort Law

Tort law, like all American law, traces its origins to English and Western European history. After the Norman conquest of England in 1066, William the Conqueror brought Norman law (which was heavily influenced by Roman law) to intermingle with Anglo-Saxon and Celtic legal traditions. The result was the common law, which at the time consisted of the underlying legal principles and social attitudes gleaned from generations of judicial decisions by local tribunals. Even today, the bulk of tort law has been derived from our common law heritage.

The King's Writs

During the Middle Ages, much of this common law was passed on orally, although substantial portions were written down by scriveners, who were mostly monks or church clerics. As a result, common law often varied widely among localities—even those separated by only a few miles. To unify these divergent legal ideas, the king eventually established formal procedures by which crown subjects could petition the king's courts for redress. These formal processes were called the *king's writs*.

Evolution of Modern Tort Law

During the eighteenth and nineteenth centuries, English tort law began to shift from the old writs system to torts involving intent and fault, known today as intentional torts and negligence. This evolution was copied in the United States. Gradually, the common law grew to include the modern torts discussed throughout this text. Today's tort law is a combination of English and American common law plus statutory law.

What does tort law seek to accomplish? Section 1.4 examines the social and economic purposes that influence, and are influenced by, tort law.

§ 1.4 Public Policy Objectives in Tort Law

Like every aspect of our legal system, there are several purposes underlying tort principles. These include (1) protecting persons and property from unjust injury by providing legally enforceable rights; (2) compensating victims by holding accountable those persons responsible for causing such harms; (3) encouraging minimum standards of social conduct among society's members; (4) deterring violations of those standards of conduct; and (5) allocating losses among different participants in the social arena.

Protecting Persons and Property: Accountability

Like the king's writs, modern tort law strives to prevent unjustified harm to innocent victims. Tort law enables private citizens to use the legal system to resolve disputes in which one party claims that the other has acted improperly, resulting in harm. The system compels the tortfeasor to compensate the injured party for his or her losses. This *accountability* (or *culpability*) factor is crucial to our legal sense of fair play and equity.

People should be held responsible for their actions, especially when they wreak havoc on others. Redress should be available for innocent victims of carelessness, recklessness, or intentional injury.

Minimum Standards of Social Conduct: Deterrence

To function meaningfully in American society, citizens must understand society's norms and values. One extremely important norm encourages the public to behave in such a manner as to avoid hurting others or their belongings. Tort law is largely composed of *minimum standards of conduct*. Persons functioning below such thresholds are defined as tortfeasors; individuals acting at or above such criteria are acceptable to the community. However, the intent is not to ensure conformity; rather, the ideal is to inspire people to respect the dignity and integrity each individual possesses.

Persons should not infringe heedlessly upon others' activities unless society is willing to accept such interference with its members' lives. Tort law discourages abuses by establishing a clear system of legal rights and remedies enforceable in court proceedings. We know that we can go to court when someone strikes us, invades our privacy, creates a nuisance, or acts negligently toward us. Likewise, we know that we might be hauled into court if we do these things to others. By establishing minimum standards of conduct, tort law sets the rules for living—those "rules of thumb" by which we try to get along with other people.

Allocating Losses among Different Individuals or Groups

It is easy to grasp the idea that an individual tortfeasor should compensate the victim for the tortfeasor's wrongdoing. However, in modern society there are often many different participants in virtually any activity, making it less clear who should be labeled as tortfeasor or victim. For example, at the time of the American Revolution, most Americans were fairly self-sufficient and dealt directly with other individuals for goods or services. If a colonist bought a broken plow or a poorly shod horse from the local blacksmith, he or she knew who to hold responsible. However, as the United States became more industrialized, commercial transactions ceased to be one-on-one interactions. Today, people buy canned fruit from a local grocery that bought it from a wholesaler that bought it from a manufacturer that bought it from a grower. If the fruit is spoiled, perhaps the purchaser's spouse or child, rather than the purchaser, will suffer the injury. The lines of culpability become less clear as the producer of the defective item becomes more removed from the ultimate user.

Tort law has evolved *products liability* to determine who is in the best position to bear the costs of defective products—the innocent user or the sellers and manufacturers. It is an economic decision that courts and legislatures have made by stating that industry can best afford the costs of injuries caused by dangerously made goods. In other words, the burden of shouldering the economic loss is placed upon commercial business instead of the individual suffering the harm. Thus, tort law can be used to assign the expenses associated with misfortune, even when fault is hazy at best. More commonly, though, a single tortfeasor can be identified and saddled with the financial obligation.

§ 1.5 Analyzing Hypothetical Problems

This book poses many hypothetical fact problems (hypotheticals) to help develop analytical talents. Perhaps the most popular analytical framework is discussed here.

Analytical Framework for Hypotheticals: *IRAC*

The analytical framework for hypotheticals sequentially investigates four general elements of a problem: the **i**ssue, **r**ules of law, **a**pplication of the rules to the facts, and **c**onclusions (IRAC). With this approach, legal principles are applied to specific factual scenarios. When analyzing a hypothetical, first decide which *issues* are presented. To accomplish this, one must identify the general area of law involved in the problem. For instance, if John takes Jose's bicycle without permission, then John has committed some type of tort. This identifies the broad area of law (torts).

Next, the different parts of the general legal area must be explored to see which specific tort applies. The particular tort John appears to have engaged in is called conversion. So the issue would be whether or not John converted Jose's property. This question can be answered by referring to the appropriate *rule of law*. To generalize, the rule of law for conversion defines it as the wrongful deprivation of another's property without consent.

This rule must now be *applied* to the facts. John took Jose's property without permission. This means John wrongfully deprived Jose of the use and enjoyment of his property. This constitutes conversion.

The *conclusion* would be that Jose may successfully sue John to recover possession of the bicycle, plus damages, because these legal remedies are appropriate for conversion (as chapter 6 explains).

This analytical formula is a useful tool in applying abstract legal principles to different factual situations.

— HYPOTHETICAL —

Delroy Magnus visited the Gym Dandy Fitness Center to use its weight and steam rooms. As he walked from the locker room into the weight room, he slipped on a puddle of water on the floor and fell. The puddle was caused by leaking water pipes along the wall leading to the steam room. Delroy broke his left arm as a result of the fall. Mary Perrington, another patron, mentioned that she had seen the puddle when she first arrived at the center approximately two hours before Delroy's accident.

Legal Analysis in Action

Would Delroy's negligence lawsuit against Gym Dandy Fitness Center succeed? Applying the rules of law established in other negligence cases, Delroy (the plaintiff) must prove that Gym Dandy (the defendant) either created the hazardous condition or had actual or constructive notice of the danger. The puddle was caused by Gym Dandy's leaking water pipes, so Gym Dandy created the danger that hurt Delroy. Further, Mary testified that the puddle had been visible on the floor for two hours. That was sufficient time for Gym Dandy's employees to observe and correct the problem. Thus, Gym Dandy had constructive notice of the puddle and the danger it posed to customers. The conclusion: Gym Dandy was negligent in creating the puddle upon which Delroy fell and was injured. Accordingly, Delroy's negligence lawsuit against Gym Dandy should be successful.   ∎

Factual Distinctions Result in Different Conclusions

A rule of law may be applied to various factual situations to reach different results. This is exactly what appellate courts do when deciding cases dealing with similar legal issues. It is also what attorneys and paralegals do when applying rules of law to the particular facts of a client's case. In the previous hypothetical, if the puddle of water was there for just two minutes, instead of two hours, Delroy's lawsuit would probably not be successful. A single variation in a factual situation can change the legal outcome.

§ 1.6 Solving Tort Problems

Another approach to tort problem solving is moving from broad subject areas to specific types of torts. This method identifies the exact issues, rules of law, and conclusions in a problem by helping the reader to narrow the analytical focus.

Tort Analysis: From General to Specific

Tort analysis should go from the general to the specific as depicted in Figure 1-1. For example, how can one tell if infliction of emotional distress has occurred unless one is aware that some type of tort law was involved in the problem? Experienced paralegals may appear to readily know the answer. In reality, that paralegal has streamlined the analytical process, but still has moved from the general to the specific. Implicitly, that paralegal recognized a general negligence problem and then narrowed it to the specific defense—assumption of risk—necessary to excuse the negligent conduct.

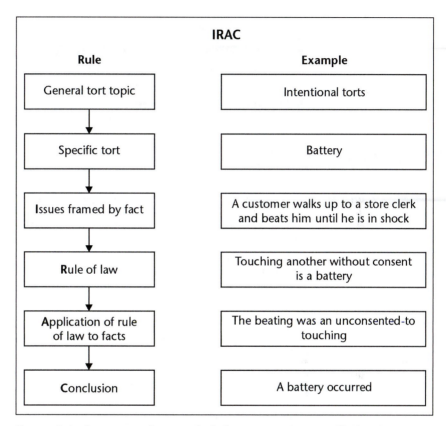

FIGURE 1-1 Sequence of tort analysis from general to specific (IRAC)

Hypothetical

The following hypothetical should more clearly illustrate tort analysis.

─ HYPOTHETICAL ─────────────────────

Jerry lives next to a vacant lot owned by Steven. Jerry dumps his grass clippings onto Steven's lot after mowing his lawn. Eventually, these grass clippings begin to smell and attract rats. Steven never gave Jerry permission to dump grass (or anything else) on Steven's lot. What legal rights does Steven have, if any?

> Jerry's actions appear to fall within the intentional torts category, as Jerry is deliberately discarding his grass clippings onto Steven's lot. The framed issue is: Did Jerry trespass against Steven by dumping grass on Steven's lot without permission? The elements of trespass are, generally, unlawful interference with another person's use of his or her property. Applying this rule to the facts, Jerry's actions (1) were unlawful, in that he did not have Steven's permission to dump grass onto Steven's lot, and (2) interfered with Steven's use of his property, because Steven could not use his lot freely without having to contend with the grass and vermin. The conclusion: Jerry is liable to Steven for the intentional tort of trespass. ■

§ 1.7 Overview of a Civil Case

There are several basic steps that occur in civil cases. However, it is important to note that at any point in the litigation process a plaintiff may decide to drop his or her lawsuit or settle with the defendant out of court. In some instances a plaintiff may not even need to institute a lawsuit to recover damages. Sometimes a simple letter from a law office can promote the necessary exchange, thus settling the claim. However, a civil case generally proceeds in the following manner:

♦ Complaint

♦ Answer

♦ Discovery

♦ Pretrial procedures

♦ Trial

♦ Post-trial procedures

complaint The first main paper filed in a civil lawsuit. It includes, among other things, a statement of the wrong or harm done to the plaintiff by the defendant, a request for specific help from the court, and an explanation why the court has the power to do what the plaintiff wants.

service of process The delivery (or its legal equivalent, such as publication in a newspaper in some cases) of a legal paper, such as a writ, by an authorized person in a way that meets certain formal requirements.

Complaint

After being injured or harmed in some manner, a plaintiff might seek out legal representation. The paralegal and/or attorney will conduct an interview of the client. As the interview progresses, the facts need to be compared with the particular elements needed for the specific type of action alleged. Even though the facts might seem similar to those of a prior case, each case will have slightly different details that could change the results of the case. Accordingly, it is important to get *all* the facts.

Either the paralegal or attorney will then draft a written **complaint** based upon the information provided. The exact procedural steps as to when the complaint needs to be filed with the court vary by jurisdiction, as do the time limits and rules for the **service of process**. Accordingly, it is very important to consult local court rules.

Answer

answer The first pleading by the defendant in a lawsuit. This pleading responds to the charges and demands of the plaintiff's complaint. The defendant may deny the plaintiff's charges, may present new facts to defeat them, or may show why the plaintiff's facts are legally invalid.

The defendant's response (**answer**) to the complaint must be filed with the court and served upon opposing party. The defendant's response must either admit to or deny the allegations and, if denying, must explain the reason for the denial. This is also the opportunity for a defendant to bring counter-claims against the plaintiff.

Discovery

discovery The formal and informal exchange of information between two sides in a lawsuit. Two types of discovery are interrogatories and depositions.

Discovery—the exchange of information and narrowing of the issues in dispute in a case—can be either a simple process or a long and drawn-out one that takes years and involves millions of documents. The nature of discovery depends on the type of claim involved. If a case is clear-cut and there are witness statements and photographs of the scene, it is possible that not much discovery will be needed. In a complex case involving, for example, a defective automobile, the discovery of information can go on for years.

Paralegals are typically involved in preparing discovery requests or gathering information to respond to discovery requests. This might involve the request for documents, setting up a time to question witnesses and parties in a case, or summarizing the contents of documents received in response to a request. Discovery is the point in the case at which a paralegal's communication skills come into play. Clients can become frustrated or confused, not understanding why a court date has not been scheduled immediately after the complaint was filed. The paralegal will need to explain the discovery needed for the particular case and the anticipated time frame. It may be that the defendant has asked for additional time to respond to requests, thus delaying the progress of a case.

Pretrial Procedures

pretrial procedures† Any procedure that immediately precedes trial; for example, the settlement conference.

Depending on the kind of case and your local jurisdiction, various **pretrial procedures** might be scheduled. Generally there is a pretrial conference during which the judge who will preside over the case will encourage the parties to settle the case pretrial. Alternatively, a court date is set and the parties must commence final preparation for trial.

Trial

trial The process of deciding a case (giving evidence, making arguments, deciding by a judge and jury, etc.). It occurs if the dispute is not revoked by pleadings, pretrial motions, or settlement. A trial usually takes place in open court, and may be followed by a judgment, an appeal, etc.

The **trial** is your client's "day in court." This is the client's chance to be heard and explain his or her side of an incident. Few cases actually go to trial; the majority are settled at some point in the litigation proceedings. Because of the time and expense usually required to wait for and actually go to trial, other methods have been sought to streamline or avoid this process.

post-trial procedures†
The procedures that occur after a trial, such as an appeal or the steps that must be taken in order to collect on an award.

Post-Trial Procedures

Post-trial procedures are those that occur after a trial, such as an appeal or the steps necessary to collect on an award.

§ 1.8 Case Resolution

alternate dispute resolution Ways to resolve a legal problem without a court decision; for example, arbitration, mediation, minitrial, rent-a-judge, summary trial, etc.

arbitration Resolution of a dispute by a person (other than a judge) whose decision is binding. This person is called an *arbitrator*. Submission of the dispute for decision is often the result of an agreement (an *arbitration clause*) in a contract. If arbitration is required by law, it is called *compulsory arbitration*.

mediation Outside help in settling a dispute. The person who does this is called a *mediator*. This is different from arbitration in that a mediator can only persuade, not force, people into a settlement.

minitrial Alternative dispute resolution by a panel of executives from two companies engaged in a complex dispute. A neutral moderator helps the two sides sort out factual and legal issues to reach a voluntary settlement.

Not all lawsuits will go to trial; in fact, the majority of cases are informally settled by the parties out of court. A very tiny percentage of cases are actually tried before a judge or jury. When you are initially analyzing a case, you should consider whether the particular case can be resolved early on through **alternate dispute resolution**.

Alternate Dispute Resolution

Alternate dispute resolution is a way to resolve a legal problem without a court decision. This avenue of case resolution is becoming more and more popular as parties wish to avoid costly public court proceedings. Alternate dispute resolution is also a means of avoiding lengthy waits for a case to reach trial—in some jurisdictions the wait can be as long as three to five years. Many plaintiffs, particularly businesses, would prefer to have a lawsuit resolved quickly, rather than waiting years for closure.

There are a variety of different ways to resolve a legal dispute without the formality of a trial; for example, arbitration, mediation, minitrial, rent-a-judge, and a summary jury trial.

Arbitration

Arbitration is a resolution of a dispute by a person other than a judge. This person's decision is binding. The person deciding the case is called the arbitrator. Sometimes parties agree through a written contract that, in the event of a potential dispute, they will resort to arbitration. Some companies routinely include an arbitration clause in their contracts.

Mediation

In **mediation** the parties use outside help in settling a dispute. Mediation differs from arbitration in that the mediator can only persuade the parties to reach a settlement. The mediator does not dictate an actual decision. Through a mediator's intervention and assistance the parties reach a mutually agreeable resolution.

Minitrial

A **minitrial** is a means of alternate dispute resolution by a panel of executives from two companies engaged in complex dispute. A neutral

rent-a-judge Alternative dispute resolution in which two sides in a dispute choose a person to decide the dispute. The two sides may agree to make the procedure informal or formally similar to a real trial, and they may agree to make the decision advisory only or binding and enforceable.

summary jury trial Alternative dispute resolution in which the judge orders the two sides in a complex case to present their most important facts to a small jury, with admission of evidence either agreed to or decided by the jury in advance. The two sides may agree in advance to be bound by the verdict or may interview the jurors and use the results to negotiate a settlement.

moderator helps the two sides sort out factual and legal issues to reach a settlement.

Rent-a-Judge

Rent-a-judge allows the parties to choose a person to decide their dispute. Retired judges often are willing to act in this capacity. The parties can decide the degree of formality of the procedure and whether the decision will be binding or merely advisory.

Summary Jury Trial

In complex cases, the two sides may present important facts and evidence to a small jury, an action referred to as a **summary jury trial**. Either the parties will agree in advance to be bound by the decision or, based on their interview with the jury, to use the jury's advice to aid in settlement negotiations.

Parties can save a lot of time and money if they are willing to consider and abide by one of the many forms of alternate dispute resolution. However, it is to be noted that, despite the many advantages, some claimants will insist on their day in court and their right to be heard by a jury. Accordingly, when alternate dispute resolution is elected, it is very important to obtain the client's consent in writing, having him or her acknowledge that this choice has been knowingly and freely made.

Summary

Tort law involves the study of wrongful conduct. Torts are wrongful injury to another's person or property. The wrongdoer is called the tortfeasor, and tort law provides the injured party with legal rights and remedies that may be enforced in a court of law. Torts may be divided into three general categories: negligence, intentional torts, and strict (absolute) liability. Negligence is the failure to exercise reasonable care to avoid injuring others. Intentional torts consist of misconduct designed to injure another person or that person's property. Strict (absolute) liability holds the tortfeasor liable for injuring another regardless of intent, negligence, or fault.

Much of tort law comes from ancient English and early American court decisions. In medieval England, there were primarily two torts. Both involved breaches of the king's peace. Today, there are many more tort actions because society is much more complicated than it was during the Middle Ages. Tort law has become correspondingly more sophisticated so as to deal with modern legal problems.

Tort law seeks to accomplish several goals. First, it serves to protect innocent persons and their property from careless or intentional injury at the hands of tortfeasors. It also attempts to hold tortfeasors responsible for their misconduct. Second, tort law encourages minimum standards of conduct among the public to avoid injuring others through heedless, reckless, or intentional behavior. It also deters persons from injuring other people and their property by holding tortfeasors liable for such mischief. Third, tort law allocates losses among different groups or individuals, based upon society's decision (as expressed through its legislatures and courts) as to who is best able to bear such losses.

To apply the rules of law to different hypothetical problems, one method breaks down the factual scenario in terms of the issues, the rules of law that must then be applied to each case's specific facts, and the conclusions regarding the probable outcome of the hypothetical case. When analyzing tort law problems, one decides on the general tort topic area, the specific tort involved, the issues framed by the facts, the rules of law for the particular tort involved, and how to apply those rules of law to the facts. Finally, one draws conclusions regarding the hypothetical or problem.

A civil case generally proceeds in the following manner: complaint, answer, discovery, pretrial procedures, trial and post-trial procedures. Parties often look for alternative means to resolve a dispute. These alternatives to trial are referred to as *alternate dispute resolution*. A few of the means of resolving a case without a trial are the use of arbitration, mediation, a minitrial, rent-a-judge, or summary jury trials.

Key Terms

alternate dispute resolution	intentional injury (tort)	strict (absolute) liability
answer	mediation	summary jury trial
arbitration	minitrial	tort
assault	negligence	tortfeasor
battery	post-trial procedures	trespass
common law	pretrial procedures	trial
complaint	rent-a-judge	
discovery	service of process	

Problems

Using the definitions of specific torts discussed in §1.2 of this chapter, answer the following hypotheticals using the analytical approaches discussed earlier.

1. Thomas Casterman is a 12-year-old boy who enjoys climbing trees. The Casterman family just moved into a new house. The electrical wires to Thomas's house run from an electrical pole through the high branches of an oak tree in his backyard. While the rest of the family was moving into the home, Thomas ran to the backyard to climb the tree. As he neared the top, he grabbed the electrical wires with his right hand. The wires were not insulated and Thomas was severely burned from the resulting electrical shock. He also broke both his legs when he fell, unconscious, from the tree. Thomas's father wishes to know if he might successfully sue the utility company for negligence.

2. Shady Acres is a subdivision being developed by Bartholomew Real Estate Management, Inc. (BREM). While bulldozing the lots and streets, BREM's crews created huge piles of dirt. BREM did not erect any barriers to keep these dirt piles in place. Pamela Jovanco owns a house at the bottom of a hill upon which BREM placed several earth piles. During heavy rains, mud would slide down the hill and cover Pamela's entire yard. Some mud even seeped through her basement windows, damaging her basement carpet and furniture. Pamela wonders if trespass has occurred.

3. Samantha Billingsly stood outside her downtown hotel hailing a cab. The driver screeched to a halt alongside the curb. Samantha opened the rear door of the automobile and began to climb

inside. In doing so, she placed her right hand on the roof of the car where the top of the door would close. Suddenly, the cab driver accelerated the automobile, causing the rear door to slam shut onto Samantha's hand. Samantha suffered lacerations and several broken bones in her right hand and wrist. She also suffered a neck injury as she was thrown against the back seat as the taxi lurched forward. The cab driver later explained that he had accelerated suddenly to avoid being struck by a shuttle bus, which he thought was about to collide with his taxi when he saw it approaching very rapidly in his rearview mirror. Using negligence theory, Samantha would like to sue the Blue Cab Company, which owns the taxi.

4. Eddie Peterson owned a coyote, which he captured while hunting the previous summer in the mountains. The coyote had become quite tame and at parties, to entertain guests, Eddie would routinely allow the animal to eat out of his hand. One day Eddie's next-door neighbor, Angela Starlight, a seven-year-old girl, visited Eddie's backyard to play with the coyote. Angela's parents had warned her several times to avoid approaching the coyote, although neither they nor Angela had ever seen the animal bite or growl at anyone. When Angela reached out to pet the coyote, it bared its teeth and snapped at her hand, biting and cutting her severely. Angela's parents sued Eddie under theory of absolute liability. Under most states' common law, owners are strictly liable for injuries caused by wild animals kept as pets.

Review Questions

1. How is a tort best defined? What are the three broad categories of torts? How might you define each variety?

2. What is negligence? How might you distinguish it from intentional torts?

3. What are intentional torts? What are examples of intentional torts?

4. How might you define strict (absolute) liability? What is the most important type of strict liability?

5. Discuss the historical roots of tort law. From what country or countries did torts originate? How have torts changed since their inception?

6. What are the purposes that tort law attempts to accomplish? Do these objectives sometimes conflict? Do they sometimes complement one another?

7. Suggest an analytical formula you might use to answer a hypothetical fact problem. In what order are these steps taken? Why do you think this order is appropriate? Is each step of the technique necessary to reach the next phase?

8. Tort analysis moves from the general to the specific to the general. Why is this best suited to answering tort hypotheticals?

9. Describe the stages of a civil lawsuit.

10. What is the difference between arbitration and mediation?

Project

Read the case of *Frankel v. Warwick Hotel* in Appendix C. Was Adam Frankel's dismissal from the hotel a wrongful discharge? Was the plaintiff successful with his claim for intentional infliction of emotional distress? Explain. Did Frankel's acts constitute an invasion of privacy? Do you agree with the court's decision?

Internet Resources

This chapter provides an introduction to torts and legal analysis. To learn about torts, the following sites can be accessed:

General Legal Information

http://www.law.cornell.edu
http://www.findlaw.com
http://www.washlaw.com
http://www.kentlaw.edu/portals/lawyers.html
http://www.law.indiana.edu

Links to State Courts

http://vls.law.vill.edu/compass
http://www.courts.net

Link to Federal Courts

http://www.uscourts.gov

Information for Paralegals

http://www.nala.org
http://www.paralegals.org

For additional resources, visit our Web site at
www.paralegal.delmar.cengage.com

CHAPTER 2
NEGLIGENCE

CHAPTER OUTLINE

§ 2.1   Introduction
§ 2.2   Negligence
§ 2.3   Elements of Negligence
§ 2.4   Scope of Duty and Standard of Reasonable Care
§ 2.5   Causation of Injury
§ 2.6   Proximate Cause
§ 2.7   Damages
§ 2.8   Proving Negligence
§ 2.9   Violation of Statute

EQUAL JUSTICE UNDER LAW

───────────⟨ ◆ ⟩───────────

When a man points a finger at someone else,
he should remember that four of his fingers
are pointing at himself.
LOUIS NIZER

§ 2.1 Introduction

The field of negligence is the most complex of the torts. What makes negligence enigmatic is its conceptual ambiguity. The elements of negligence
appear to be so broadly defined that it is difficult to discern clear lines for
negligent behavior. Negligence is not a mathematical equation. Instead,
negligence resembles probability theory, in which specific conduct is more
likely than not to be considered negligent under a particular set of circumstances. In this chapter, the following aspects of negligence are discussed:

♦ The elements of negligence

♦ The tortfeasor's duty of reasonable care

♦ The breach of duty, reasonable care, and the reasonable person standard

♦ Causation, substantial factor analysis, and joint and several liability

♦ Damages available in negligence actions

♦ Burdens of proof and rejoinder in negligence cases

♦ Res ipsa loquitur.

§ 2.2 Negligence

Most people equate negligence with carelessness. The phrase conjures up
images of actions that are slovenly, haphazard, heedless, or foolhardy. As a
legal concept, negligence is much more precise, but it embodies all of
these characteristics.

Negligence Defined: Reasonable Care

Negligence may be broadly defined as the failure to exercise reasonable
care to avoid injuring others or their property. Reasonable care depends

negligence The failure to exercise a reasonable amount of care in a situation that causes harm to someone or something. It can involve doing something carelessly or failing to do something that should have been done. Negligence can vary in seriousness from *gross* (recklessness or willfulness), through *ordinary* (failing to act as a reasonably careful person would), to *slight* (not much).

upon the exact circumstances of each case. This is the "shifting sands" aspect of negligence with which legal students—and the legal system—struggle. The key term is *reasonableness*. In any tort case in which negligence might exist, ask the threshold question: Did the tortfeasor act unreasonably under the circumstances? This is essentially all that negligence entails.

Acts or Omissions

A tortfeasor can be negligent either by doing or by not doing something. When courts speak of *negligent acts* or *omissions* by the tortfeasor, they mean that the tortfeasor behaved unreasonably either by doing a specific careless activity or by failing to do something that the tortfeasor should have done.

Negligent actions are positive events; something is done. For instance, if Roger lit a fire in high winds that carried sparks onto a neighbor's roof and set the house ablaze, Roger's action (careless burning) would be deemed unreasonable. Negligent omissions are usually phrased negatively; the tortfeasor failed to do a reasonable act. For example, suppose Marie's front porch has a rotten step that she has failed to repair. A salesperson visiting her home falls through the step and breaks a leg. Marie's omission (failure to repair the step) would be considered unreasonable.

Like all areas of law, negligence has developed discernible elements that can be enumerated and outlined more clearly. Section 2.3 outlines the elements of negligence.

§ 2.3 Elements of Negligence

Negligence can be specifically defined as a tortfeasor's failure to exercise reasonable care, thus causing a foreseeable injury to another person or that person's property. Negligence includes the following elements:

1. Duty of care
2. Breach of the duty by the tortfeasor (unreasonable conduct)
3. Causation of injury to the victim
4. Damages to the victim (actual harm).

Each of these elements is required for negligence to exist, so each element is a threshold question. If "no" answers any single element, negligence does not exist. For example, the first question is: Did the tortfeasor owe a duty of reasonable care to the injured party? If not, then the analysis stops, with the conclusion that no negligence has occurred. If yes, then one must ask: Did the tortfeasor breach the duty of reasonable care? If not, the inquiry is finished, and once again the analyst concludes that there was no negligence. If yes, then one continues querying through causation, and damages. Each element must be satisfied for negligence to exist.

Each of the elements of negligence receives detailed treatment in the following sections.

§ 2.4 Scope of Duty and Standard of Reasonable Care

foreseeability† The notion that a specific action, under particular circumstances, would produce an anticipated result.

duty 1. An obligation to obey a law. 2. A legal obligation to another person, who has a corresponding right. 3. Any obligation, whether legal, moral, or ethical.

due (reasonable) care That degree of care a person of ordinary prudence (the so-called *reasonable person*) would exercise in similar circumstances.

scope of duty† In negligence law, defined in terms of those individuals who might foreseeably be injured as a result of the tortfeasor's actions. This is called *reasonableness of foreseeability*. The scope of duty includes all those foreseeable plaintiffs who could have been hurt because of the tortfeasor's conduct. This is called *foreseeability of the victim*.

Negligence analysis begins with the duty of reasonable care. First, the scope of the duty must be determined. This focuses on the **foreseeability** of the victim.

Duty Defined

In tort law, **duty** is the obligation either to do or not to do something. In negligence, the duty of **due reasonable care** is the responsibility to act reasonably so as to avoid injuring others. This may also be stated negatively: the duty of reasonable care is the obligation *not* to behave *un*reasonably so as to avoid injuring others.

For example, motor vehicle operators owe a duty of reasonable care to drive carefully and avoid injuring other drivers, their vehicles, or pedestrians. Suppose Parker is driving on a four-lane highway and chooses to pass the truck in front of him. He fails to look in the rearview mirror before pulling into the left lane. Unbeknownst to Parker, another vehicle is attempting to pass him, and he pulls directly in front of that driver. This action forces that driver to swerve and collide with a telephone pole. Did Parker violate any duty of reasonable care?

In analyzing this duty hypothetical, the first question is: Did Parker owe the other driver a duty of reasonable care? Parker owed anyone driving or walking upon the street a duty to drive safely. By failing to check his rearview mirror to see if any traffic was approaching from behind in the left lane, Parker breached his duty to the other driver. He acted imprudently by not looking for other traffic before he switched lanes. He failed to see that which was there to be seen.

Scope of Duty

Clearly, one does not owe a duty of reasonable care to everyone else in the universe. **Scope of duty** is a limitation on the persons to whom one owes the duty.

For example, while driving on the four-lane highway in her city, Janet owes no duty of reasonable care to someone driving in another city hundreds of miles away. Janet's actions (i.e., driving her car) could not possibly have any effect on such a person. Janet's scope of duty does not extend to individuals who cannot directly be affected by her carelessness. Scope of duty is often described in terms of reasonable foreseeability.

The Case of Drunken Duty

In negligence litigation, an injured plaintiff always argues that the defendant's scope of duty extends to the injured party. The contention sometimes reaches absurdity. Plaintiffs may attempt to avoid personal responsibility for their own injuries by claiming that a defendant breached some supposed duty of care. In the following case, an intoxicated driver injured himself and then sought damages against the tavern owner for having served alcohol to the plaintiff when he was already visibly drunk. As the Oklahoma Supreme Court observed, negligence law will not assist careless persons in avoiding personal responsibility for their apparent stupidity.

OHIO CASUALTY INSURANCE CO.

v.

TODD

Supreme Court of Oklahoma
813 P2d 508 (Okla. 1991)
June 11, 1991
Summers, Justice

The question certified for our resolution calls upon us to decide whether *Brigance v. Velvet Dove Restaurant, Inc.* [citation omitted], should be extended to create a common law cause of action against a tavern owner for an adult who voluntarily becomes intoxicated and is injured as a result of his own inability to drive a vehicle properly. We decline to extend *Brigance* to this situation, following the reasoning used by a majority of jurisdictions.

* * *

On November 6, 1986, Rick Robertson was injured in a one-car accident after having been served alcohol in Todd's Tavern. ...

Robertson [alleged] that the employees of Todd's Tavern served him alcoholic beverages when he was noticeably intoxicated in violation of [Okla. Stat. tit. 37,] § 537 [1981], and that for this reason Todd is liable for [Robertson's] injuries. Todd moved to dismiss ... .

All agree that the pertinent case is *Brigance* ... . Robertson urges that *Brigance* should be extended to cover the situation at bar. Todd, however, asserts that *Brigance* creates a cause of action for innocent third parties, and should

not be stretched to include a situation wherein the inebriate sues for his own injuries.

In *Brigance* we recognized for the first time a common law "dram shop" action; a third party who was injured in an intoxicated driver's auto accident may now state a cause of action against the restaurant that served liquor to the driver. At common law, such an action was not possible. ...

In changing the common law rule and creating this cause of action, we acknowledged that legal duty and liability are matters of public policy and are therefore subject to the changing attitudes and needs of society. We pointed out that protection must be afforded to the innocent bystander ... .

The creation of this cause of action, therein limited to third parties, served to protect the innocent by allowing liability to be placed not only on the intoxicate drivers but concurrently on those parties who continued to serve alcohol to their customers already noticeably intoxicated.

Left open by *Brigance* was the question of whether the consumer-inebriate would have a cause of action against the vendor for on-premises consumption. ...

The elements of negligence are "(1) the existence of a duty on [the] part of defendant to protect plaintiff from injury; (2) a violation of that duty; and (3) injury proximately resulting therefrom." All three of these elements must exist before the plaintiff has a valid cause of action. Robertson, relying on [Okla. Stat. tit. 37,] § 537(A)(2) [Supp. 1985], urges that a duty exists on the part of a tavern keeper to refrain from serving alcoholic beverages to an adult customer who is noticeably intoxicated. Section 537(A)(2) states in relevant part that no person shall "[s]ell, deliver or knowingly furnish alcoholic beverages to an intoxicated person."

... Because we find that the duty of the tavern owner does not extend to an adult customer who voluntarily consumes intoxicants and is injured, we need not address the question of proximate cause.

* * *

Several states have considered the question. See Annot., 98 A.L.R.3d 1230 (1980). A majority of them have refused to create a cause of action for an adult who voluntarily drinks to the point of intoxication and is thereby injured. These jurisdictions have generally concluded that as a matter of public policy drunken persons who harm themselves are responsible for their condition, and should not prevail either under a common law or statutory basis. Focusing on the "duty" concept, these courts hold the view that no duty should be imposed "upon the tavernkeeper, and protection should not be extended, because the adult voluntarily created the vulnerability that is the problem."

* * *

If this Court were to create a cause of action against the tavern owner, the inebriate could be rewarded for his own immoderation. Such was not the intent of *Brigance,* nor will we allow such a reward. ...

Then there are the practical consequences of recognizing such suits. "Pause, if you will and contemplate the vast number of claims that may be urged by drunks, if they were entitled to every expense and injury that are natural concomitants of their intoxication." In a world where alcohol is readily available for consumption by adults the ultimate accountability should rest on the adult consumer, absent unusual circumstances or injury to an innocent third party. ...

Here, the question is simply whether the intoxicated adult must bear the responsibility for his own injury which occurred due to his voluntary consumption of an excessive amount of alcohol. ...

Accordingly, under the facts as presented to us we find that the tavern owner has no liability to the intoxicated adult who voluntarily consumes alcoholic beverages to excess and sustains injuries as a result of his intoxication.

Case Questions

1. What was the court's public policy justification for its decision? Do you agree or disagree? Explain.
2. Suppose a passenger in Robertson's vehicle had been injured. Would the passenger have a cause of action against the tavern owner under the common law and statute? Explain.

Foreseeability

In tort law, foreseeability is the notion that a specific action, under particular circumstances, would produce an anticipated result. If an injury were foreseeable, then one could take precautions to avoid the behavior that might be expected to cause harm. If a tortfeasor failed to take such precautions, he or she breached the duty of reasonable care.

For instance, in the preceding driving example, Parker did not check his rearview mirror before attempting to pass on a four-lane highway. Is it foreseeable that another vehicle might be passing Parker in the lane he was trying to enter, and that his failure to look behind him could result in a collision? This consequence is clearly foreseeable. Suppose, however, that it is late at night, and that the other driver trying to pass Parker did not have headlights on. Thus, Parker could not see the car approaching as he moved into the left lane to pass the truck. Was it reasonably foreseeable that another driver would come up from behind without headlights? No. So the result (the other driver swerving to avoid hitting Parker's car) was not foreseeable under these facts. A slight difference in the circumstances changes the answer.

Foreseeable Plaintiffs Theory

foreseeable plaintiffs theory[†] A theory used in analyzing negligence cases. Under this theory, if it were reasonably foreseeable that the injured victim would be harmed as a consequence of the tortfeasor's actions, then the tortfeasor's scope of duty includes the victim. This victim is said to be a *foreseeable plaintiff.*

Foreseeability limits the scope (extent) of the duty owed to others. One asks the threshold question: Was it reasonably foreseeable that the person injured would be harmed as a consequence of the tortfeasor's actions? If so, the scope of the duty of reasonable care includes the individual hurt. This is sometimes called the **foreseeable plaintiffs theory**, because it was reasonably foreseeable that the plaintiff (who is suing the tortfeasor for negligence) would be damaged because of the tortious conduct. It is the foreseeability of injury or damage that is of concern, not the degree or amount of injury or damage involved.

unforeseeable plaintiffs[†] Persons whose injuries the tortfeasor could not reasonably have anticipated as a result of the tortfeasor's actions.

Persons outside this range of duty are considered **unforeseeable plaintiffs**, because the tortfeasor could not reasonably have anticipated that they would be harmed by the tortfeasor's actions. People driving several hundred feet in front of Parker would not likely be influenced by either Parker or the swerving other driver. They would be beyond Parker's scope of duty, and so he would not be required to exercise reasonable care toward them. However, persons driving close behind Parker and the swerving driver could reasonably be expected to become involved in the accident. These individuals would be within Parker's scope of duty. His failure to use reasonable care (by not looking in the rearview mirror, which caused him to cut off the swerving driver) violated his duty to them as well as to the swerving driver.

reasonable person test (standard)[†] A means of determining negligence based on what a reasonable person would have done in the same or similar circumstances. Basically, it is a measurement of the failure to do that which a person of ordinary intelligence and judgment would have done in the same circumstances.

Table 2-1 on page 24 outlines scope of duty and the foreseeable plaintiffs theory.

Standard of Reasonable Care

Reasonable care is a most elusive concept in negligence law. It depends upon the particular facts of each problem. Still, tort law has developed an abstract measure of reasonable care, called the **reasonable person test (standard)**.

Scope of Duty	Foreseeable Plaintiffs Theory
The tortfeasor owes a duty of reasonable care to avoid injuring others or their property.	The plaintiff may recover from the defendant only if it were reasonably foreseeable that the defendant's actions would injure the plaintiff.
Duty includes persons for whom it is reasonably foreseeable that injury will occur as a result of the tortfeasor's actions.	Persons outside the defendant's scope of duty are considered unforeseeable plaintiffs.

The Reasonable Person Standard

The *reasonable person* is an imaginary individual who is expected to behave reasonably under a given set of circumstances to avoid harming others. The tortfeasor is alleged to have done something, or have failed to do something, that was unreasonable and that caused the victim's injuries. The tortfeasor's conduct is measured under the reasonable person standard in this fashion: In the same or similar circumstances, would the reasonable person have acted as the tortfeasor behaved? If so, then the tortfeasor did not violate his or her duty of reasonable care. If not, then the tortfeasor breached the duty.

In our previous driving hypothetical, would the reasonable person have looked in his or her rearview mirror before entering the left lane to pass a truck on a four-lane highway, when it was reasonably foreseeable that another vehicle might already be occupying that lane while attempting to pass the reasonable person's car? Checking the rearview mirror when changing lanes seems reasonable, and so the reasonable person could be expected to do so under these conditions. Parker did not, however. Therefore, Parker acted unreasonably in this case. He violated his duty of care to the swerving driver because he did not act as the reasonable person would have behaved in the same situation.

The mythical reasonable person may seem too intangible to compare to real-life persons. Nevertheless, American and English courts have relied on the concept in over 200 years of court decisions (though older opinions refer to the *reasonable man*).

Who Decides How the Reasonable Person Would Have Acted

The trier-of-fact in a negligence lawsuit determines whether the defendant did not act as the reasonable person would have behaved in a specific case. This is usually a jury, but it could be the judge in a bench trial. In effect, the jurors decide what was reasonable by investigating how they, and others they know, would have behaved. Suddenly, the reasonable person standard becomes clear: it is what the jurors conclude was reasonable under the circumstances. This settles the question of whether the defendant breached the duty of reasonable care to the plaintiff.

At first glance, the reasonable person standard seems arbitrary, as each juror determines the defendant's negligence based upon his or her own personal, gut-level response. However, sociologists would remind us that this is precisely how each individual views the world—through the eyes of his or her own experience. The judicial system safeguards against one capricious definition of reasonableness by offering the option of a jury trial, which forces several persons to agree upon an appropriate measure of due care. Although a judge in a bench trial is the sole trier-of-fact, the judge's legal training is presumed to compensate for any bias in defining reasonableness.

Matching Skills and Disabilities

professional community standard of care† The standard of reasonable care used in negligence cases involving defendants with special skills and knowledge.

The reasonable person is supposed to resemble the defendant as closely as possible in terms of special abilities. This enables the trier-of-fact to assess reasonableness more precisely in a specific case. For example, if the defendant were a plumber and was alleged to have negligently installed a leaking water line, the reasonable person would also possess the same training and knowledge as plumbers employed in the defendant's geographical area. This is sometimes called the **professional community standard of care**, which is based on the custom and practice among professionals working in the defendant's community. This measure is determined through expert testimony from members of the defendant's profession. The standard for experts is now national in most jurisdictions.

The defendant's limitations are also important in shaping the reasonable person standard. For instance, if the defendant were physically disabled, then the reasonable person would likewise share identical disabilities. One could hardly decide how a blind defendant should have behaved by comparison with a reasonable person who has normal vision. This forces the trier-of-fact to empathize with the defendant's situation to understand more clearly how the defendant acted. In effect, the jury must conceptualize how the reasonable person would have behaved in a wheelchair or with a hearing disability. The result of this should be a more accurate definition of reasonableness that best fits the defendant and the circumstances of the case. The result, ideally, is a just and equitable outcome in the litigation.

Table 2-2 on page 26 summarizes the reasonable person standard.

Professional Malpractice

A professional's negligent failure to observe the appropriate standard of care in providing services to a client or patient, or misconduct while engaging in the practice of a profession, is considered malpractice. Failure to exercise the degree of care and skill reasonably required of like

TABLE 2-2
Reasonable person
standard

1.	Ask: Would the reasonable person have acted as the defendant did, under the same or similar circumstances?
2.	Match the skills or abilities of the reasonable person to those of the defendant (e.g., plumber, rodeo rider) if these abilities were involved in the alleged negligent actions (professional community or national standard).
3.	Trier-of-fact decides how the reasonable person would have acted in a particular situation.

professionals in similar circumstances, if that failure causes damage or injury, is malpractice. Originally, the precise degree of skill used to judge a professional's actions was the care and skill of other professionals practicing in the same community. Many jurisdictions have now expanded this to include the same community *or* a similar locality. Likewise, a specialist must possess the degree of skill and competence that a specialist in the same or similar community would exercise.

Many jurisdictions have taken this a step further and hold specialists to a national standard, without regard to their location. Some jurisdictions are applying the national standard to general practitioners as well. Professional malpractice cases have been brought against doctors, lawyers, accountants, travel agents, and even priests, depending on the jurisdiction.

Medical Malpractice

To prove a medical malpractice case, generally one or more expert witnesses will be needed for trial. This major expense prevents attorneys from bringing suit for anything but serious and permanent injury cases.

Typically, medical malpractice cases involve one or more of the following:

◆ Abandonment (failure to attend to a patient)
◆ Improper diagnosis
◆ Medical instruments, sponges, needles, or other foreign objects dropped and left in surgical field
◆ Lack of informed consent
◆ Errors in prenatal diagnostic and genetic testing
◆ Failure of hospital to supervise employees
◆ Failure to diagnose
◆ Failure to advise of diagnosis
◆ Medication errors.

The Case of the Late Diagnosis

A physician's negligent failure to observe the appropriate standard of care in providing services to a patient is malpractice. In this case, a medical malpractice action was brought against a gynecologist for failure to diagnose breast cancer.

MEZRAH v. BEVIS

**District Court of Appeal of Florida,
Second District
593 So. 2d 1215
(Fla. Dist. Ct. App. 1992)
February 21, 1992
Lehan, Acting Chief Judge**

In this medical malpractice action the defendants, a gynecologist and his professional association, appeal a final judgment entered on a jury verdict finding them liable to plaintiff for failing to diagnose breast cancer. We affirm.

As to defendants' first argument that the trial court erred in allowing expert testimony from a pathologist that defendants breached the standard of care, we conclude that there was no error. Also, there was additional competent testimony from another expert to that effect.

As to defendants' second argument, we do not agree that the evidence on the issue of causation was merely speculative. There was competent expert testimony which, as we have said, was not improperly allowed that had defendants not breached the standard of care, plaintiff's breast cancer "more likely than not" would have been completely cured.

Noor v. Continental Casualty Co., in which this court affirmed a judgment for defendants in a medical malpractice case based upon the alleged failure to timely diagnose breast cancer, is distinguishable. Damages were sought in that case on the alleged basis that Mrs. Noor's life expectancy had been shortened due to a delay of several months in failing to diagnose her cancer. This court pointed out that her life expectancy had been shortened as a result of the disease even if the disease had been correctly diagnosed by defendant doctor at the first opportunity. The plaintiffs in that case did not prove causation because they did not produce any "nonspeculative evidence as to what extent, if any, [defendant doctor's] failure to immediately diagnose her disease added to Mrs. Noor's decreased life expectancy." On the other hand, plaintiff in this case apparently sought damages on a different basis, i.e., that had the breast cancer been timely diagnosed, she more likely than not would have been cured. As noted above, she produced sufficient evidence in that regard.

Affirmed.

Case Questions

1. How is the *Noor* case distinguishable from the instant case?
2. Can you put a dollar value on a patient's claim of having lost the chance to be cured?

Practical Application

As a practical note, it is important to remember that the mere fact that there is an injury, or the occurrence of a bad result in medicine, does not necessarily mean that there has been malpractice.

The following hypothetical examines another situation in which the standard of care is at issue. Note how scope of duty, foreseeability, and the reasonable person standard are established.

— HYPOTHETICAL

John makes an appointment to see his family physician. John's throat has been hurting him for the past week. The doctor takes a throat culture. John has strep throat, a condition that requires antibiotics. John's doctor calls John with the results and advises that he will call the pharmacy and order medication. Unbeknownst to John, the drug that the doctor orders is one in a category of drugs to which John is highly allergic and should never take. The doctor failed to check John's chart for known allergies before ordering the prescription. Because the drug has a different name than the drug John previously had a reaction to, John assumes that the drug is a different drug that is safe for him to take. Minutes after taking the prescription, John goes into shock and dies. Did the doctor owe John a duty of reasonable care? If so, did the doctor breach that duty?

To establish negligence by a physician, it must be shown that the injury complained of was caused by the physician's failing to act as a family physician would have acted under like circumstances. Failing to check a chart for allergies falls below the standard of care that a family physician of ordinary skill would have used under similar circumstances. The physician did not follow professional practices and failed to comply with the reasonable standard of care owed to John. It was foreseeable that John would be hurt. ■

Special Duty Based upon Special Relationship

The majority of negligence actions are based upon an affirmative duty or act owed to another that is improperly performed. In contrast, if a person fails to act there generally is no liability in negligence, except under certain limited exceptions. An example of a failure to act would be when you are walking down the street and see a stranger about to trip and do not try to prevent the accident. In this example, you would have no duty to stop and warn the stranger. Only if the plaintiff and the defendant have a special relationship between them will the defendant's failure to act lead to a cause of action in negligence.

Just a few of the many special relationships that might create a duty to act are those between an employer and employee, a parent and child, a teacher and student, an innkeeper and guest, and common carriers and passengers. The law imposes a special relationship between these parties and also a duty to act based upon this relationship. For example, if one student injures another student or is about to hurt another student, their teacher has an obligation to intervene and try to help, even though the

◆〈◆〉◆

The Case of Restraint

A patient enters a hospital and leaves in a worse condition than when admitted. Malpractice does not always involve problems with the actual surgery or medication; it could also involve issues such as failure to order appropriate restraints or to properly monitor a patient following surgery.

DOUGLAS

v.

GIBSON

**Supreme Court, Appellate Division,
Third Department
630 N.Y.S.2d 401 (App. Div. 1995)
August 3, 1995
Cardona, Presiding Justice**

On December 1, 1988, defendant Mark D. Gibson surgically removed a previously placed fixation device from plaintiff's left hip. Following the surgery, plaintiff was placed in a vest restraint. Although no doctor ordered that plaintiff be restrained, his wife requested restraints during plaintiff's admission procedures because he had become confused in the past after surgery. Plaintiff was 64 years old at the time and suffering from Parkinson's disease. On the day after the surgery, plaintiff was examined by Gibson's partner, defendant William C. Bishop, who found him to be in stable condition. In the early morning hours of December 3, 1988, it was discovered that plaintiff had fallen between the side rails of his bed and suffered a fracture of his left distal femur.

Plaintiff commenced this medical malpractice action against Gibson and Bishop (hereinafter collectively referred to as defendants) alleging, inter alia, that they were negligent in failing to order that plaintiff be appropriately restrained, in failing to provide him with an adequate restraint and in failing to adequately monitor him. The bill of particulars further alleged that defendants failed to properly supervise staff personnel. Following joinder of issue and examinations before trial, defendants moved for summary judgment dismissing the complaint against

them. Supreme Court granted the motion and plaintiff now appeals.

Initially, we are of the view that defendants made a prima facie showing that no material issues of fact exist as to the alleged malpractice asserted against them in the complaint as amplified by the bill of particulars. In support of their motion, defendants submitted, *inter alia,* their own affidavits, the affidavits of their attorney and Donald Douglas, a physician, as well as hospital records and transcripts of examinations before trial of staff personnel. Through this and other evidence in the record, defendants established that although they did not order plaintiff to be restrained, the vest restraint placed on him was appropriate and would have been the same devise they would have ordered postoperatively. Douglas averred that the vest restraint used was the standard restraint and was not a departure from accepted medical standards of care. Defendants also established that no additional or further restraint prior to the incident was medicallyindicated. Finally, defendants sufficiently rebutted plaintiff's claim of improper supervision.

Given this evidence, the burden shifted to plaintiff to come forward with evidentiary proof sufficient to raise a question of fact. His evidence, in opposition to defendants' motion, consisted of the affidavits of Patricia Newland, a registered nurse, and Miles St. John, a surgeon. These averments, however, lacked the requisite level of proof necessary to defeat defendants' motion. These affidavits state that based on plaintiff's prior medical history, he was a "high risk" patient who needed more secure restraints than those provided and that defendants' failure to do so constituted a deviation from accepted medical practice. They claim that on previous occasions plaintiff had attempted to get out of bed and had fallen or injured himself. Notably absent from the record, however, is any evidence of any such prior incidents to support these allegations. Therefore, the allegations are conclusory, unsupported by competent evidence and fail to raise a question of fact. The affidavits also claim malpractice due to the lack of a physician's order to use a restraint. Defendants, however, averred that, had they ordered a restraining device, it would have been the vest restraint actually used. Thus, insofar as a restraint was in fact used and was the same one that would have been ordered, the failure to so order does not raise an issue of fact.

Plaintiff also failed to offer any competent proof that another physician would have ordered anything other than a vest restraint. Although Newland's affidavit claimed that a more secure device was required, she was giving her professional opinion as to what a physician should have ordered which, in our view, went beyond her professional and educational experience and cannot be considered "competent medical opinion" on this issue. As to St. John's averment that a more secure restraint was warranted, this was based only on his unsupported assertion that plaintiff was a high risk patient. ... There were no medical records submitted to support the specifically disputed factual assertion that there were prior falls, which was the basis for St. John's conclusion that plaintiff was a high risk patient.

We also note that plaintiff failed to offer any proof that the type of security restraint he claims should have been used would have prevented him from falling. He thus failed to establish the requisite nexus between the alleged malpractice and his injury. Finally, plaintiff submitted no adequate proof on the issue of sufficient oversight of plaintiff's case or of staff personnel. We therefore conclude that summary judgment was properly awarded to defendants. Plaintiff's remaining arguments are rejected as unpersuasive.

Case Questions

1. What was the court's reason for denying the plaintiff's medical malpractice claim?
2. What specific kinds of proof did Justice Cardona suggest could have been introduced at trial to prove malpractice that were not offered as proof by this plaintiff's attorneys?
3. If you were the plaintiff in this case, how would you feel upon reading an appellate decision in which numerous suggestions are made to counsel as to what could have been offered at trial?

teacher was not negligent and did not cause the incident. Likewise, employers are responsible for workers injured on the job even if the employer did not harm the employee (see chapter 7 for more information on workplace injuries).

§ 2.5 Causation of Injury

Even if the defendant breaches his or her duty of care owed to the plaintiff, the defendant will not be legally negligent, nor liable for the plaintiff's injuries, unless the defendant's actions proximately caused the harm. To have causation, both "cause-in-fact" and "proximate cause" must be present.

Cause-in-Fact

cause-in-fact[†]
Cause of injury in negligence cases. If the tortfeasor's actions resulted in the victim's injuries, then the tortfeasor was the cause-in-fact of the victim's harm.

Causation is a critical component of negligence. To be liable, the tortfeasor must have caused the victim's injuries. *Causation of injury* relates to the tortfeasor's actions that result in harm to the injured party. Courts frequently refer to this as **cause-in-fact**, meaning that, in negligence litigation, the defendant's misconduct produced the plaintiff's injuries.

The defendant's acts must be the *actual* and *factual* cause of the plaintiff's injuries. The formula is straightforward: but for the tortfeasor's (defendant's) actions, the victim (plaintiff) would not have been harmed. The tortfeasor's behavior is usually the immediate, direct, and dominant cause of the victim's injuries. For example, if Samantha spills a beverage on a stairway and does not clean it up, and Daniel slips on the slick spot and falls down the stairs, Samantha has caused Daniel's injuries. The causation is direct: but for Samantha's failure to clean the drink spill on the stairs, Daniel would not have slipped and fallen.

Consider another illustration. Suppose an automobile mechanic changes the tires on Quinn's car but neglects to tighten the lug nuts properly. While the vehicle is moving, the left rear tire comes loose and flies off. The car skids out of control and crashes into a telephone pole, hurting Quinn. Again, there is causation: but for the mechanic's failure to tighten the nuts sufficiently, the tire would not have come off and Quinn would not have collided with the pole.

Sometimes several forces combine to produce injuries. For example, in the loose tire example, suppose the tire had not come completely off the automobile but was wobbling loosely. However, as Quinn was driving, he encountered broken glass on the highway, which punctured his left rear tire. Because of the flat tire and the looseness of all the tires, Quinn lost control of the car and crashed. Here, two factors resulted in Quinn's injuries: the glass that ruptured his tire and the loose nuts that lessened his control of the vehicle.

Substantial Factor Analysis

substantial factor analysis[†] A test for indirect causation in negligence cases. The tortfeasor is liable for injuries to the victim when the tortfeasor's conduct was a substantial factor in producing the harm.

Substantial factor analysis states that the tortfeasor is liable for injuries to the victim when the tortfeasor's misconduct was a *substantial factor* in producing the harm. In the preceding tire illustration, the broken glass flattened Quinn's tire and made the car difficult to handle. However, had the lug nuts not also been loose, the tires would not have been wobbling. Quinn probably would have been able to control the vehicle better and might not have crashed at all. The mechanic's failure to tighten the nuts was a substantial factor in Quinn's losing control and colliding with the pole. Thus, the mechanic would be liable, even though the broken glass and punctured tire also influenced the accident.

<◆>

The Case of the Quarter-Sized Puddle

One of the more common negligence actions you will encounter is the slip-and-fall case. If the plaintiff is to be successful, causation must be established.

ADGER
v.
DILLARD DEPARTMENT STORES

Court of Appeal of Louisiana
662 So. 2d 864 (La. Ct. App. 1995)
November 1, 1995
Williams, Judge

On the evening of May 11, 1993, the plaintiff and a companion, Beverly Franklin, visited Dillard's Department Store at Pierre Bossier Mall. ... Ms. Franklin was walking slightly ahead of the plaintiff and did not see her slip, but turned and saw her falling to the floor.

Margaret P. Stinson, area sales manager for Dillard's, was notified of the incident. When Ms. Stinson arrived at the young-men's section, plaintiff was standing with Ms. Franklin and David Piazza, a security guard. They helped plaintiff walk to a nearby chair. The security officer questioned the plaintiff and filled out an accident report.

* * *

[P]laintiff testified that she did not know what caused her fall and had not noticed anything on the floor before or immediately after she fell. She apparently did not examine her clothing for dampness or staining, which would have indicated that she slipped in liquid. She testified that her foot slid along the floor, but defense counsel pointed out that plaintiff had not made that claim during a prior deposition.

Ms. Franklin also testified that she did not notice any water on the floor before plaintiff fell, or immediately after the fall, when her attention centered on helping the plaintiff. Ms. Franklin asserted that a short time later, she returned to the place where the plaintiff fell and found a quarter size puddle of water. Ms. Franklin maintained that she told someone standing nearby that plaintiff had slipped in water. However, Ms. Stinson testified that she inspected the area where the accident occurred and found the floor clean and dry.

* * *

Here, the plaintiff has failed to establish that her fall was caused by the quarter-sized puddle of water observed by Ms. Franklin. Moreover, another witness contested the presence of any water in the area of the accident. Even if we were to assume that the small puddle of water was present at the time of the accident, there is no evidence, other than Ms. Franklin's hypothesis, that the water contributed to the plaintiff's fall. After reviewing the record and the trial transcript, we cannot find that the trial court was clearly wrong in granting the defendant's motion for involuntary dismissal.

* * *

AFFIRMED.

Case Questions

1. Do you think the trial court believed the plaintiff's version of the facts? Explain.
2. What kinds of facts would have had to be presented to hold the defendant department store liable for the slip and fall?

A classic substantial factor analysis case is *Summers v. Tice*, 33 Cal. 2d 80, 199 P.2d 1 (1948), which can be found in Appendix C. In this case, the plaintiff was hunting quail with two defendants. When the birds were flushed out, the defendants aimed and fired their shotguns in the plaintiff's direction, striking the plaintiff and causing severe physical injuries. It was unclear which defendant's shot hit the plaintiff, because both defendants used the same gauge shotgun and size of shot. The California Supreme Court applied the substantial factor test in determining causation and liability. Although it could not be conclusively established which defendant's weapon caused the plaintiff's injuries, either defendant's action was sufficient to produce the resulting harm. Quoting a Mississippi Supreme Court case, Justice Carter stated: "We think that … each is liable for the resulting injury …, although no one can say definitely who actually shot [the plaintiff]. To hold otherwise would be to exonerate both from liability, although each was negligent, and the injury resulted from such negligence."

Summers v. Tice resembles another type of case in which multiple forces combine to produce harm. When two or more defendants act together to produce the plaintiff's injury, the courts consider them to have *acted in concert*. All defendants are held liable for their combined conduct in such cases. This is called **joint and several liability**, another form of causation.

Joint and Several Liability

joint and several liability[†] When two or more persons who jointly commit a tort can be held liable both together and individually.

Multiple tortfeasors are each held individually accountable to the victim for the combined negligent behavior of all the tortfeasors. For instance, suppose that a surgical team, composed of two surgeons, three nurses, and an anesthesiologist, loses count of surgical sponges and leaves one in the patient's abdomen. The patient contracts peritonitis as a consequence. Because all of the medical personnel acted together in the operation, they are said to have functioned in concert. Their collective conduct produced harm to the patient. Thus, each individual would be personally liable for the patient's injuries. In other words, all of the personnel would be jointly and severally liable.

Multiple tortfeasors may injure a victim by acting in sequence, rather than simultaneously as in the medical malpractice example. The sequence of combined events produces the harmful results. For example, assume that a shipping company does not refrigerate a shipment of perishable food. As a result, the items spoil in transit. The shipment arrives at a supermarket, which fails to notice the spoiled condition of the products and stocks them on its shelves. Carla's roommate buys some of the goods but does not check them for freshness, despite obvious odors and discoloration. After her roommate cooks dinner, Carla eats the bad food and becomes seriously ill.

Who does Carla sue? Several tortfeasors combined negligent behavior to produce her injury. First the shipper failed to refrigerate the food, and it turned rotten. Next the grocery store failed to notice the spoiled food and stocked it. Then Carla's roommate failed to notice the spoilage and prepared the food for her to eat. All these tortfeasors—the shipping company, the supermarket, and Carla's roommate—contributed to a sequence of events that resulted in her illness. Carla would not have become sick had any of these tortfeasors identified the threat (spoiled food) and taken reasonable precautions to avoid injuring customers. But for the concerted conduct of these tortfeasors, Carla would not have been hurt. Therefore, they are all jointly and severally liable to her for the harm caused.

Table 2-3 outlines the causation-of-injury theories.

TABLE 2-3
Causation of injury theories

Cause-in-Fact (But-For Causation)	Substantial Factor Analysis	Joint and Several Liability
But for the defendant's actions, the plaintiff's injury would not have happened.	When multiple defendants combine to injure the plaintiff, a single defendant is liable if his or her actions were a substantial factor in producing the harm.	When multiple defendants act together to injure the plaintiff, all defendants are liable for the harm.

Contribution

contribution 1. The sharing of payment for a debt (or judgment) among persons who are all liable for the debt. 2. The right of a person who has paid an entire debt (or judgment) to get back a fair share of the payment from another person who is also responsible for the debt.

Contribution is another issue that comes up when multiple defendants are involved in a negligence action. Most jurisdictions permit one tortfeasor to seek contribution from the others. Contribution means that one tortfeasor pays all or part of the liability for a wrong and is then allowed to recover all or part of this amount from the other tortfeasors. Some jurisdictions allow parties to seek contribution only when there was no concert of action, when the wrong was not an intentional one, or when the person seeking contribution was not primarily liable. For example, Marie sues Adam, Bobby, and Cindy and is awarded a judgment for $12,000. Each defendant's share is one-third of $12,000, or $4,000. If Adam pays the entire $12,000 judgment, he can seek contribution of $4,000 from Bobby and $4,000 from Cindy.

Courts and Causation

American Jurisprudence 2d, a legal encyclopedia, provides an excellent and accurate summary of causation analysis.

57A AMERICAN JURISPRUDENCE 2D *Negligence* §§ 431, 434, 436, 464, 471, 474-75, 478 (1989) [All footnotes omitted.]

[§ 431] Cause in fact as an element of proximate cause means that the wrongful act was a substantial factor in bringing about the injury and without which no harm would have been incurred. . . .

[§ 434] There are two steps in analyzing a defendant's tort liability. The first is determining whether he breached his duty of care, the second whether the breach was at least a cause of the accident. Liability for negligence is predicated upon a causal connection between the negligence alleged as the wrong and the injury of which complaint is made, and the common law refers the injury to the proximate, not the remote, cause, and establishes as an essential element of liability for negligence what has traditionally been referred to as proximate cause, or, as it is now frequently denominated, legal cause. ...

[§ 436] The Restatement of Torts 2d says that, in order for a negligent actor to be found liable for another's harm, it is necessary not only that the actor's conduct be negligent toward the other, but also that the negligence of the actor be a legal cause of the other's harm. The Restatement further points out that the conduct of a negligent actor need not be the predominant cause of the harm. The wrongful conduct of a number of third persons may also be a cause of the harm, so that such third persons may be liable for it, concurrently with the actor. ...

[§ 464] It has been recognized that the issue of "causation in fact" is regarded as an aspect of "proximate cause" ... . Traditionally, courts have used the term "proximate cause" as descriptive of the actual "cause in fact" relation which must exist between a defendant's conduct and a plaintiff's injury before there may be liability. Additionally, the courts have used the same term as a shorthand description of various complex legal concepts and principles which have nothing to do with the fact of actual causation, but which define and control the existence and extent of liability ... .

In all cases where proximate cause is in issue, the first step is to determine whether the defendant's conduct, in point of fact, was a factor in causing plaintiff's damage. ... If the inquiry as to cause in fact shows that the defendant's conduct, in point of fact, was not a factor in causing plaintiff's damage, the matter ends there, but if it shows that his conduct was a factor in causing such damage, then the further question is whether his conduct played such a part in causing the damage as makes him the author of such damage and liable therefor in the eyes of the law. ...

[§ 471] Most jurisdictions have historically followed this so-called "but-for" causation-in-fact test. It has proven to be a fair, easily understood and serviceable test of actual causation in negligence actions ... . Where the "but for" test is recognized, it has been said to be useful and generally adequate for the purpose of determining whether specific conduct actually caused the harmful result in question, but that it cannot be indiscriminately used as an unqualified measure of the defendant's liability ... .

[§ 474] The "but-for" test, while it explains the greater number of cases, does not in all instances serve as an adequate test. If two causes concur to bring about an event, and either one of them, operating alone, would have been sufficient to cause the identical result, some other test is needed. ... The response of many courts to this problem has been to apply the "substantial factor" test, either in addition to or in place of the "but for" test. ...

[§ 475] The substantial factor test ... makes the question of proximate or legal cause depend upon the answer to the question, "was defendant's conduct a substantial factor in producing plaintiff's injuries?"

As pronounced in the Restatement, Torts 2d, the test is as follows: The actor's negligent conduct is a legal cause of harm to another if (a) his conduct is a substantial factor in bringing about the harm, and (b) there is no rule of law relieving the actor from liability because of the manner in which his negligence has resulted in the harm. ...

[§ 478] Many courts lump the "but for" and the "substantial factor" tests together and apply them both, with some taking the view that the "but for" standard is only one element of the "substantial factor" standard, and a few holding that in the great majority of cases the two tests amount to the same thing ... .

Causation becomes clearer through an example. The following illustration should lend substance to the analytical formula.

─ HYPOTHETICAL ─

Angel runs a beauty salon. Aspen is one of her regular customers. Angel received a shipment of hair coloring products in unlabeled bottles. Rather than return the shipment, Angel placed the bottles in a storeroom for future use. She applied one bottle to Aspen's hair without carefully checking its contents beforehand. Because of unusually high pH levels in Aspen's hair, the product turned Aspen's hair bright blue. Did Angel cause Aspen's injury?

But for Angel's failure to inspect the bottle's contents prior to treating Aspen's hair, Aspen would not have suffered hair discoloration. Direct causation functions easily and clearly to conclude that Angel caused Aspen's injury.

Suppose instead that Angie, one of Angel's employees, had taken the bottle from the storeroom and applied it to Aspen. Would both Angel and Angie be liable for Aspen's harm and damage? Angel failed to identify the unlabeled bottles before storing them. Angie failed to check the bottle's contents before applying them to Aspen's hair. Both combined in their unreasonable actions to produce the harmful result. Accordingly, Angel and Angie are jointly and severally liable to Aspen.

Suppose the bottles had been mislabeled by the manufacturer. Angel unknowingly stocked the bottles, assuming the labels to be correct. Angie then applied the contents of one bottle to Aspen's hair without observing that the contents were the wrong color and texture (a point that an experienced beautician should reasonably have known). The but-for test does not produce clear results in this case. One cannot say that, but for the manufacturer's mislabeling, Aspen would not have been hurt, because Angie actually misapplied the product to Aspen's hair. Neither may one contend that, but for Angie's use of the improperly labelled product, Aspen would not have been harmed, because Angie was not responsible for the mislabeling. Substantial factor analysis, however, helps to reach an acceptable answer. Angie's failure to inspect the bottle's contents and determine the error before applying the mixture to Aspen's hair was a substantial factor in producing Aspen's injury. Accordingly, Angie would be liable to Aspen. ■

§ 2.6 Proximate Cause

In order to establish liability for negligence, the tortfeasor must be the legal or proximate cause of injury. However, the tortfeasor is not liable for *all* injuries. When a plaintiff suffers unusual injuries or the tortfeasor has started a chain of events causing injury, at some point the tortfeasor's liability might be cut off and limited to those injuries that were foreseeable.

Foreseeability of Injury

proximate cause
The "legal cause" of an accident or other injury (which may have several actual causes). The proximate cause of an injury is not necessarily the closest thing in time or space to the injury and not necessarily the event that set things in motion because proximate cause is a legal, not a physical concept.

Duty is governed by foreseeability. **Proximate cause**, or *legal cause* as it is sometimes called, exists when the tortfeasor's actions cause a foreseeable injury to the victim. If foreseeability is not present, then no duty is owed. Court opinions often refer to the plaintiff's injuries as the natural and probable consequence of the defendant's misconduct. The key to proximate cause is foreseeable injury. Was the victim's injury the reasonably foreseeable result of what the tortfeasor did? If so, then the tortfeasor's actions proximately caused the plaintiff's harm and a duty is owed. If not, then proximate cause did not exist, and the defendant will not be liable to the plaintiff under negligence theory.

Proximate cause is a subcategory of causation. *Causation* is the chain of events linking the tortfeasor's conduct to the victim's injury. *Proximate cause* is the zone within which the plaintiff's injury was reasonably foreseeable as a consequence of the defendant's behavior. Think of proximate cause as a circle. Actions inside the circle cause foreseeable injuries to victims. Actions outside the circle are beyond the zone of danger. Figure 2-1 illustrates this concept.

Consider a hypothetical. Patrick is building an additional garage and workshop in his backyard. As he is excavating to install the foundation, he hits an underground natural gas pipeline that services his neighborhood. The pipe ruptures and disrupts gas supplies to the other houses in the area. As a result, those houses with gas heat cannot use their furnaces. It is

FIGURE 2-1
Proximate cause
zone of danger

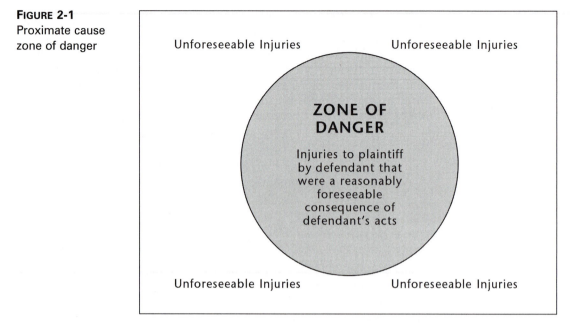

January, and outside temperatures fall well below freezing at night. With no heat, the water pipes in the neighbors' homes freeze and burst, causing substantial water damage to the structures and furnishings. Did Patrick proximately cause the harm to the neighbors' houses?

It was reasonably foreseeable that an underground utility line might be severed. If this line were carrying a heating source, such as natural gas, it would likewise be reasonably foreseeable that neighboring homes would lose their heat service. Because it was winter, it was also reasonably foreseeable that temperatures could go below freezing and cause water pipes in unheated buildings to freeze and burst. Water damage to structures and furnishings is a natural and inevitable consequence of broken pipes. Clearly, Patrick's actions proximately caused the injury to his neighbors' homes, because the harm was reasonably foreseeable as a result of Patrick's breaking the natural gas pipeline.

Proximate Cause and Scope of Duty Combined

Some legal scholars have included scope of duty as an aspect of proximate cause. This seems logical, as both include the element of foreseeability, but there is a subtle distinction. Scope of duty examines whether it was reasonably foreseeable that the plaintiff would be injured as a result of the defendant's actions. Proximate cause focuses upon whether the injury itself was reasonably foreseeable.

Thus, it is possible for the tortfeasor to owe a duty of reasonable care to the victim but not proximately cause the injury if the harm was unforeseeable. For instance, suppose that Shannon, who manages a shoe store,

◆◇◆

The Case of the Scale that Shook Tort Law

In this landmark case, a man waiting for a train was carrying a package wrapped in newspaper with fireworks inside. The railroad guards were unaware of the contents of the parcel and helped the man board the moving train. As the guards tried to help, the package was dislodged, fell to the tracks, and exploded. This caused the platform to shake, which in turn caused a scale to fall. The scale seriously injured Helen Palsgraf, who was waiting on the platform. Was a duty owed to the plaintiff? Where does one draw the line?

PALSGRAF
v.
LONG ISLAND RAILROAD
Court of Appeals of New York
162 N.E. 99 (N.Y. Ct. App. 1928)
May 29, 1928
Cardozo, C.J.

Plaintiff was standing on a platform of defendant's railroad after buying a ticket to go to Rockaway Beach. A train stopped at the station, bound for another place. Two men ran forward to catch it. One of the men reached the platform of the car without mishap, though the train was already moving. The other man, carrying a package, jumped aboard the car, but seemed unsteady as if about to fall. A guard on the car, who had held the door open, reached forward to help him in, and another guard on the platform pushed him from behind. In this act, the package was dislodged, and fell upon the rails. It was a package of small size, about fifteen inches long, and was covered by a newspaper. In fact it contained fireworks, but there was nothing in its appearance to give notice of its contents. The fireworks when they fell exploded. The shock of the explosion threw down some scales at the other end of the platform many feet away. The scales struck the plaintiff, causing injuries for which she sues.

The conduct of the defendant's guard, if a wrong in its relation to the holder of the package, was not a wrong in its relation to the plaintiff, standing far away. Relatively to her it was not negligence at all. Nothing in the situation gave notice that the falling package had in it the potency of peril to persons thus removed. Negligence is not actionable unless it involves the iinvasion of a legally protected interest, the violation of a right. "Proof of negligence in the air, so to speak, will not do." "Negligence is the absence of care, according to the circumstances." ... If no hazard was apparent to the eye of ordinary vigilance, an act innocent and harmless, at least to outward seeming, with reference to her, did not take to itself the quality of a tort because it happened to be a wrong, though apparently not one involving the risk of bodily insecurity, with reference to some one else.

* * *

One who jostles one's neighbor in a crowd does not invade the rights of others standing at the outer fringe when the unintended contact casts a bomb upon the ground. The wrongdoer as to them is the man who carries the bomb, not the one who explodes it without suspicion of the danger. ... What the plaintiff must show is "a wrong" to herself; i.e., a violation of her own right, and not merely a wrong to some one else, nor conduct "wrongful" because unsocial, but not "a wrong" to any one. ... The risk reasonably to be perceived defines the duty to be obeyed, and risk imports relation; it is risk to another or to others within the range of apprehension. This does not mean, of course, that one who launches a destructive force is always relieved of liability, if the force, though known to be destructive, pursues an unexpected path. "It was not necessary that the defendant should have had notice of the particular method in which an accident would occur, if the possibility of an accident was clear to the ordinarily prudent eye." Some acts, such as shooting as so imminently dangerous to any one who may come within reach of the missile however unexpectedly, as to impose a duty of prevision not far from that of an insurer. Even to-day, and much oftener in earlier stages of the law, one acts sometimes at one's peril. Under this head, it may be, fall certain cases of what is known as transferred intent, an act willfully dangerous to A resulting in injury to B. These cases aside, wrong is defined in terms of the natural or probable, at least when unintentional. The range of reasonable apprehension is at times a question for the court, and at times, if varying inferences are possible, a question for the jury. Here, by concession, there was nothing in the situation to suggest to the most cautious mind that the parcel wrapped in newspaper would spread wreakage through the station. If the guard had thrown it down knowingly and willfully, he would not have threatened the plaintiff's safety, so far as appearances could warn him. His conduct would not have involved, even then, an unreasonable probability of invasion of her bodily security. Liability can be no greater where the act is inadvertent.

* * *

One who seeks redress at law does not make out a cause of action by showing without more that there has been damage to his person. If the harm was not willful, he must show that the act as to him had possibilities of danger so many and apparent as to entitle him to be protected against the doing of it though the harm was unintended.

* * *

The law of causation, remote or proximate, is thus foreign to the case before us. The question of liability is always anterior to the question of the measure of the consequences that go with liability. If there is no tort to be redressed, there is no occasion to consider what damage might be recovered if there were a finding of a tort. We may assume, without deciding, that negligence, not at large or in the abstract, but in relation to the plaintiff, would entail liability for any and all consequences, however novel or extraordinary. There is room for argument that a distinction is to be drawn according to the diversity of interests invaded by the act, as where conduct negligent in that it threatens an insignificant invasion of an interest in property results in an unforeseeable invasion of an interest of another order, as, e.g., one of bodily security. Perhaps other distinctions may be necessary. We do not go into the question now. The consequences to be followed must first be rooted in a wrong.

The judgment of the Appellate Division and that of the Trial Term should be reversed, and the complaint dismissed, with costs in all courts.

ANDREWS, J. (dissenting). Assisting a passenger to board a train, the defendant's servant negligently knocked a package from his arms. It fell between the platform and the cars. Of its contents the servant knew and could know nothing. A violent explosion followed. The concussion broke some scales standing a considerable distance away. In falling, they injured the plaintiff, an intending passenger.

Upon these facts, may she recover the damages she has suffered in an action brought against the master? The result we shall reach depends upon our theory as to the nature of negligence. Is it a relative concept—the breach of some duty owing to a particular person or to particular persons? Or, where there is an act which unreasonably threatens the safety of others, is the doer liable for all its proximate consequences, even where they result in injury to one who would generally be thought to be outside the radius of danger?

* * *

Negligence may be defined roughly as an act or omission which unreasonably does or may affect the rights of others, or which unreasonably fails to protect one's self from the dangers resulting from such acts.

* * *

Where there is the unreasonable act, and some right that may be affected there is negligence whether damage does or does not result. That is immaterial.

* * *

The proposition is this: Every one owes to the world at large the duty of refraining from those acts that may unreasonably threaten the safety of others. Such an act occurs. Not only is he wronged to whom harm might reasonably be expected to result, but he also who is in fact injured, even if he be outside what would generally be thought the danger zone.

* * *

But, when injuries do result from our unlawful act, we are liable for the consequences. It does not matter that they are unusual, unexpected, unforeseen, and unforeseeable. But there is one limitation. The damages must be so connected with the negligence that the latter may be said to be the proximate cause of the former.

* * *

The proximate cause, involved as it may be with many other causes, must be, at the least, something without which the event would not happen. The court must ask itself whether there was a natural and continuous sequence between cause and effect. Was the one a substantial factor in producing the other? Was there a direct connection between them, without too many intervening causes?

* * *

When a lantern is overturned, the firing of a shed is a fairly direct consequence. Many things contribute to the spread of the conflagration—the force of the wind, the direction and width of streets, the character of intervening structures, other factors. We draw an uncertain and wavering line, but draw it we must as best we can.

* * *

The act upon which defendant's liability rests is knocking an apparently harmless package onto the platform. The act was negligent. For its proximate consequences the defendant is liable.

Case Questions

1. Did the chain of events stop at a foreseeable point?
2. Was it foreseeable that Helen Palsgraf would be injured as a result of the guards' attempt to assist the man with the package?
3. How does the dissenting opinion explain proximate cause?

gave away free helium balloons to families as a promotional gimmick. One of her customers, Addison, suffered from a rare allergy to helium, but was unaware of this condition. Addison inhaled some helium from the balloon to make himself talk in a high-pitched, funny voice, which is a common side effect of helium inhalation. Instead, Addison went into anaphylactic shock, suffered cardiac arrest, and died. Did Shannon proximately cause Addison's death?

Definitely, Shannon owed a duty of reasonable care to all of her patrons to maintain reasonably safe premises. But Addison's uncommon sensitivity to helium (of which even he was unaware) was not something that Shannon could reasonably have been expected to anticipate. The injury simply was not reasonably foreseeable. The vast majority of the population would not possess this allergy and would suffer no ill effects. Accordingly, Shannon did not proximately cause Addison's injury.

"Taking the Victim as You Find Him"

"taking the victim as you find him" A theory in negligence cases which states that the victim's injuries were reasonably foreseeable even if the tortfeasor was unaware of the victim's peculiar physical, health, or other pre-existing conditions. In effect, the tortfeasor takes the victim as the tortfeasor finds him, and thus proximately causes the harm.

Nonetheless, many appellate courts decide this issue differently. These opinions speak of a tortfeasor's **"taking the victim as you find him."** This means that peculiar health conditions are considered to be reasonably foreseeable, as one must always assume that a victim could suffer from an odd affliction such as a helium allergy. Most of these cases, however, involve more deliberate actions (such as striking the head of a person with "a thin skull" or an "eggshell skull" and killing him or her). Such cases involve more intentional torts than negligence (battery, in the eggshell-skull cases), as is typical with the taking-the-victim cases. Still, taking-the-victim analysis surfaces in pure negligence cases as well.

Taking-the-victim cases make almost any physical injury reasonably foreseeable. This raises proximate cause to the point at which the tortfeasor becomes an insurer of the victim's safety. Such reasoning removes the cases from the realm of negligence and deposits them in the field of strict liability, which is discussed later in this text.

The range of the zone of danger is further explored in the next example, the case of *Sampson v. Zimmerman*.

‹♦›

The Case of the Burning Candle

An owner of land generally knows more about the parcel of land than strangers coming upon the land. Accordingly, an owner must remedy any dangerous condition that might cause foreseeable harm. However, the owner of land has no duty to remedy a condition that presents an obvious risk. This case discusses whether a burning candle presents an obvious risk to a child of four years.

SAMPSON
v.
ZIMMERMAN

Appellate Court of Illinois,
Second District
502 N.W.2d 846 (Ill. App. Ct. 1986)
December 31, 1986
Reinhard, Justice

Plaintiff, Paige Sampson, a minor, by her father and closest friend, Randy S. Sampson, appeals from the order of the circuit court of DuPage County which granted summary judgment for defendants, Dennis L. Zimmerman and Linda C. Zimmerman, upon finding that defendants owed no duty to plaintiff as a matter of law.

The issues plaintiff raises on appeal are: (1) whether summary judgment is a proper and appropriate remedy where factual questions concerning foreseeability and appreciation of danger were for the jury; (2) whether a 4-year-old who cannot be held responsible for her own negligence can be held to have "assumed" the risk presented by fire; and (3) whether the trial court erred in failing to ascertain plaintiff's competency to testify as a witness.

The complaint alleges that on December 4, 1983, plaintiff, then four years and four months old, came in contact with a dangerous condition, that being a lighted and unprotected candle on a bathroom counter shelf, while visiting at defendants' home causing her clothes to catch fire and injuring her; that defendants knew or should have known of this dangerous condition; that defendants were negligent because they failed to warn plaintiff of the dangerous condition, failed to extinguish the lighted candle, and failed to provide a protective cover or other safety device for the candle; and that as a direct and proximate result of these acts plaintiff was injured.

After filing an answer, defendants filed a motion for summary judgment stating that they owed no duty as a matter of law to plaintiff to protect her from an obvious danger. They further asserted that a landowner is never an insurer of a child's safety and has no legal duty to protect against obvious dangers, that fire is an obvious danger recognized by case law as one which any child could be expected to appreciate and avoid, that plaintiff understood, as evidenced by deposition testimony, a lighted candle to be fire which was hot and could injure her, and that the child was of above-average intelligence and knew enough to avoid fire. Attached to the summary judgment motion were excerpts of plaintiff's deposition testimony in which she acknowledged that she knew fire could hurt her and that she could be burned by fire, that she had seen birthday candles before and knew fire was on top of the candle, that she had seen the candle enclosed in glass on the counter on the day

in question, and that she climbed onto the bathroom counter before she got hurt. ...

Plaintiff responded to the motion arguing that this case does not involve a situation where she was engaged in an activity or conduct directly involving the obvious danger, but was merely sitting on the bathroom counter unaware that the candle posed a danger to her, that whether fire was an obvious danger to plaintiff is a question of fact, that any obvious danger should have been recognized by an adult and remedied, that the candle was not such an extreme condition as to allow defendants to not protect against an injury to a child, and that the duty owed to plaintiff is for the jury to decide. Plaintiff, however, did not attach any documents to contradict the deposition excerpts accompanying defendants' motion for summary judgment.

The trial court granted the motion for summary judgment. Thereafter, plaintiff filed a motion for rehearing asserting therein that the trial court improperly granted summary judgment without the entire deposition testimony of plaintiff, that plaintiff's deposition testimony demonstrates that she was confused and upset during the deposition proceedings, and that there were insufficient questions presented during the deposition to establish plaintiff's ability "to appreciate on [sic] oath" which can only be judged in person by the trial court.

* * *

In considering whether defendants owed a duty to plaintiff under the circumstances of this case, the customary principles of ordinary negligence must be applied to determine the liability of owners of premises upon which a child is injured. The common law categories of trespasser, licensee and invitee, as they pertain to an injured child's status, however, are no longer relevant in determining liability. The duty which would be imposed under ordinary negligence is that the law impels an owner or occupier of land to remedy any dangerous condition on the premises where that person in possession or control of the premises knows or should know that children frequent the premises, as harm to the children caused by the dangerous condition is sufficiently foreseeable. A dangerous condition is defined as one which is likely to cause injury to children generally who, by reason of their age and immaturity, would not be expected to comprehend and avoid the attendant risks; however, if the condition complained of presents an obvious risk which under ordinary conditions may reasonably be expected to be fully understood, appreciated and avoided by any child of an age to be allowed at large, there is no duty to remedy that condition as children are expected to avoid dangers which are obvious, negating any reasonably foreseeable risk of harm.

Illinois has acknowledged that fire is a danger which under ordinary conditions may reasonable be expected to be fully understood and appreciated by any child of an age to be allowed at large. Additionally, fire has been found to be an obvious danger. See *Jackson v. City of Biloxi* (a 5-year-old boy was found to be mature and intelligent enough to appreciate the obvious danger of an open fire).

Essentially, plaintiff maintains on appeal that the issues of foreseeability of this injury and plaintiff's appreciation of the danger are questions of fact which should not have been decided by summary judgment. We disagree. The material facts on this record are not in dispute, and the issue before us is whether there is a legal duty owed by defendants under the pleadings and depositions filed.

As our supreme court has acknowledged that a danger such as fire under ordinary circumstances may reasonably be expected to be fully understood by any child of an age to be allowed at large we conclude that the danger of fire from a burning candle is similarly one to be understood and appreciated by a child of an age to be allowed at large. The record shows that plaintiff is of above-average intelligence for her age and has been taught by her mother of the danger of fire and that fire burns at the end of a candle. Plaintiff, too, stated in her deposition that she knew fire could hurt her, that fire burned, and that fire was on top of a candle. Plaintiff saw the candle and no issue is raised in the pleadings that defendants were negligent in where they placed the candle. As there can be no recovery for injury caused by a danger found to be obvious, we hold that defendants owed no duty to plaintiff under these facts as a matter of law.

Although plaintiff appears to argue that the trial judge's decision suggests that plaintiff assumed the risk, it is clear that the court below analyzed the duty issue properly in terms of appreciation of the risk rather than assumption of the risk. There also is no merit to plaintiff's contention that the trial court erred in failing to ascertain whether she, as a 5-year-old at the time of her deposition, was competent to appreciate an oath and give testimony as a witness. No objection was made to her competency during the taking of the deposition or at the time the excerpts were submitted in support of the motion for summary judgment. Any objection was therefore waived. ...

For the foregoing reasons, the judgment of the circuit court of DuPage County is affirmed. AFFIRMED.

Case Questions

1. Do you agree with the court that a burning candle presents an obvious risk, even to a four-year-old child?
2. Would the plaintiffs have been more successful had they argued that the defendants were negligent in where they placed the candle? Explain.

— HYPOTHETICAL —————————————————

Colleen operates a laundromat. Geoffrey often washes and dries his clothes there. One day, while Geoffrey was loading his laundry into the washer, the machine unexpectedly began agitating and injured his arms and hands. Did Colleen proximately cause Geoffrey's injuries?

Foreseeability of injury is the starting point. Was it reasonably foreseeable that the washer Geoffrey used would short-circuit and suddenly begin operating while Geoffrey was loading his clothes? It is not uncommon for electrical, mechanical devices to jump to life by themselves unexpectedly. This often occurs when electrical wiring short-circuits after the wires' insulation has frayed. Because people must insert their hands and arms inside the washing machine drum to load clothing, it is reasonably foreseeable that a shorted machine might start itself while a patron's arms are inside. Thus, Geoffrey's injuries were reasonably foreseeable and Colleen proximately caused the harm suffered.

Suppose, however, that Geoffrey's arms and hands were not trapped inside the machine when it suddenly began agitating. Suppose, instead, that the surprise simply frightened Geoffrey, who was unusually susceptible to sudden, loud noises and suffered a heart attack as a consequence of the shock. Could Colleen have reasonably anticipated this tragedy? Most courts would reverse the reasonable person standard (applying it to the plaintiff) and say that a reasonable person would not be so easily alarmed (to the point of heart failure) by an upstart washing machine. However, a few courts would employ taking-the-victim analysis and say that even this remote and unexpected injury was foreseeable. ■

---

§ 2.7 Damages

damages Money that a court orders paid to a person who has suffered damage (a loss or harm) by the person who caused the injury.

Damages are the injury that the plaintiff suffered as a result of the defendant's tortious conduct. As in all torts, damages must be proven for negligence. Courts will not compensate a victim unless some documentable harm has been done.

With certain intentional torts, such as battery, assault, or trespass, no physical harm is required. With a technical trespass, it is sufficient that the tortfeasor engaged in the unauthorized act. Battery can be achieved merely by unconsented touching. In negligence law, however, some determinable injury must be proven for the tortfeasor to be held liable to the injured party. Normally, this involves monetary losses as a result of harm to a person or the person's property. For instance, if someone loses muscular control in the legs after an automobile accident with a careless driver, then the injured party could demonstrate economic loss as a consequence of the harm. The plaintiff could quantify the losses sustained through lost wages, inability to continue an occupation, loss of bodily function, emotional impairment, and related damages.

This vital element of liability is often glossed over by legal scholars and courts. Following such reasoning, damage is often assumed from the fact that the plaintiff sued the defendant for negligence. Of course, it is always a mistake to assume anything in legal study. The plaintiff must prove actual injury to recover in a negligence action. This harm may be physical or emotional or both, but it must exist.

Compensatory Damages

compensatory damages Damages awarded for the actual loss suffered by a plaintiff.

Compensatory or actual damages are most common in negligence cases. As the name suggests, **compensatory damages** are designed to compensate the victim for the tortfeasor's negligence. Normally, the plaintiff proves monetary losses, such as out-of-pocket expenses (e.g., medical, property repair), lost income, pain and suffering, loss of property value, or loss of bodily function. The policy behind compensatory damages in tort law is to make the plaintiff whole.

General Damages

General damages are those compensatory damages that naturally result from the harm caused by the defendant's actions. For example, in a slip-and-fall action anyone who is injured in this manner might suffer some degree of pain and suffering.

Special Damages

Special damages, unlike general damages, are compensatory damages that are specific to a particular plaintiff. In the above slip-and-fall example, the special damages might include a dry-cleaning bill for a stained suit, lost wages, and (depending on the severity of the fall) medical expenses. Usually special damages must specifically be pleaded and proved. In contrast, general damages need not be pleaded with specificity, as they are presumed by law. Another name used for special damages is *consequential damages*.

Economic and Non-Economic Damages

Compensatory damages are divided into economic and non-economic losses. Economic losses are the out-of-pocket expenses a plaintiff incurs, such as medical expenses and lost earnings. Conversely, non-economic losses, such as pain or humiliation, have no particular objective dollar amount that can be placed on them.

Verdict The trial judge will give the jury instructions in awarding damages in the event a verdict is awarded for the plaintiff. It is often difficult to place an exact dollar figure on pain and suffering. In some states, as a result of recent tort reform, the legislatures have enacted caps on the amount of damages that can be awarded in particular types of cases such as medical malpractice claims.

Nominal Damages

nominal damages[†]
Small or symbolic damages awarded in situations in which no actual damages have occurred, or the right has not been proven even though a right has been violated in an intentional tort action.

Nominal damages are not recoverable in actions for ordinary negligence when damages are an element of the cause of action. Nominal damages are awarded in situations in which no actual damages have occurred, or the amount of injury has not been proven even though a right has been violated in an intentional tort action. The court might then award a dollar to a winning party as a symbolic gesture.

Punitive Damages

punitive (exemplary) damages Extra money [over and above compensatory damages] given to a plaintiff to punish the defendant and to keep a particularly bad act from happening again.

gross negligence[†]
Recklessly or willfully acting with a deliberate indifference to the affect the action will have on others.

Punitive (exemplary) damages, which are often awarded for intentional torts such as fraud or intentional infliction of emotional distress, are almost nonexistent in negligence cases, because negligence involves carelessness rather than wanton or intentionally tortious behavior. The punishment component of punitive damages would be excessive in most negligence cases, although exemplary damages are occasionally used in gross negligence cases. **Gross negligence** involves carelessness that exceeds ordinary, reasonable care standards and approaches willful and wanton misconduct. If the negligence is sufficiently excessive, the court might allow punitive damages for the injured party. For instance, if a surgeon were drunk and left a scalpel inside a patient during an operation, this might be considered gross negligence by the medical community. Such misconduct exceeds that degree of reasonable care ordinarily expected of doctors. Physicians simply are expected to avoid such slipshod surgical efforts.

Table 2-4 summarizes damages in negligence actions.

See Chapter 1 for methods of resolving cases other than by trial.

TABLE 2-4
Damages in negligence cases

Plaintiff must suffer actual loss as a result of injury.
Loss is usually gauged in monetary terms.
Compensatory damages provide the plaintiff with recovery for losses that resulted from the defendant's actions (out-of-pocket expenses, pain and suffering, lost income, lost property value, loss of bodily function).

◄◆►

McDonald's Coffee, A Burning Issue

In Albuquerque, New Mexico, in August 1994, a jury awarded Stella Liebeck $2.7 million in punitive damages and $200,000 in compensatory damages (to be reduced for the plaintiff's being 20 percent at fault) against McDonald's Corporation. Liebeck was riding as a passenger in her grandson's car when she bought a cup of coffee at McDonald's. She tried to hold the cup between her knees when she removed the lid, but the cup tipped over and caused third-degree burns. The ultimate award was reduced substantially below the verdict.

This case caused a sensation when the jury award was first reported. Few people were privy to all the facts. Most people were aware that a woman was burnt while drinking coffee from McDonald's, but few could understand why the woman was suing McDonald's if it was she who spilled the coffee. More puzzling was why a jury would award almost $3 million in punitive damages against McDonald's when the plaintiff was either careless enough or foolish enough to be drinking hot coffee in a car.

The details put a different slant on the case. As a company policy, McDonald's sold coffee at between 180 and 190 degrees Fahrenheit. It takes two to seven seconds for coffee at this temperature to cause third-degree burns, which require skin grafts and debridement. The burns can leave a person in pain and disabled for many months or years, and can result in permanent and disfiguring injuries. Liebeck ended up in the hospital for a week and was disabled for more than two years.

During trial, McDonald's acknowledged having been aware of the risk of serious burn injuries from its coffee for over 10 years. In fact, more than 700 people reported being burnt by McDonald's steaming coffee prior to Liebeck's incident. Witnesses who appeared for McDonald's admitted that consumers were unaware of the risk of serious burns from the coffee and that customers were never warned. Most incredible, witnesses for McDonald's stated that the company had no plans to reduce the temperature of the coffee sold, despite the fact that the coffee was "not fit for consumption" when sold because it could cause scalding burns.

Case Questions

1. Taking the case from McDonald's perspective, are there any possible reasons for selling such hot coffee?

2. Balancing McDonald's need to sell hot coffee versus the possible risk of serious injury posed, could there be any reason that McDonald's did not have a plan to reduce the coffee's temperature in the future, despite the prior incidents?

§ 2.8 Proving Negligence

Proof is an essential aspect of all litigation. A cynic might suggest that what is true or false is irrelevant; rather, what can be proven during a lawsuit is all that matters. Negligence claims are normally proven through the typical evidentiary processes. These include oral testimony, written transcripts of discovery depositions, documentary evidence, and demonstrative evidence (such as photographs or computer simulations).

Affirmative defenses must be alleged or proven by the defendant. Unless alleged and proven, the law will presume that no defense exists. These defenses are covered in Chapter 4.

Burdens of Proof and Rejoinder

preponderance of the evidence The greater weight of the evidence, not as to *quantity* (in number of witnesses or facts) but as to *quality* (believability and greater weight of important facts proved). This is a standard of proof generally used in civil lawsuits. It is not as high a standard as *clear and convincing evidence* or *beyond a reasonable doubt.*

The plaintiff has the burden of proving that the defendant was negligent. This forces the plaintiff to prove by a **preponderance of the evidence** that all negligence elements existed (duty, breach, causation, and injury). The evidence must establish that the defendant's actions were negligent and caused the plaintiff's injuries. Burden of proof is sometimes referred to as *burden of production.*

Once the plaintiff has made a **prima facie case** (meaning that proof has been established by or beyond a preponderance), the burden shifts to the defendant, who must then counter the plaintiff's evidence with proof of his or her own. This is sometimes called the defendant's **burden of rejoinder,** persuasion, or rebuttal. The defendant must refute the plaintiff's case against him or her.

prima facie case A case that will be won unless the other side comes forward with evidence to disprove it.

burden of rejoinder [†] The defendant's burden of proof to refute the plaintiff's evidence in a lawsuit.

In some cases, however, the burden of proof is different. What if the plaintiff cannot prove the defendant's negligence? Consider an example. Suppose a patient was unconscious during an operation. Suppose the surgical nurse failed to remove all the sponges from the patient, and later the patient contracted peritonitis. How could the plaintiff prove that the defendants (nurse, surgeon, and hospital) were negligent in leaving the sponge inside the plaintiff? What witnesses could the plaintiff call to testify, other than the surgical team? The plaintiff was unconscious and unaware of the entire procedure. How could the plaintiff meet the burden of proof in such circumstances? Such unusual cases require a special burden of proof, which is called *res ipsa loquitur.*

res ipsa loquitur (Latin) "The thing speaks for itself." A rebuttable presumption (a conclusion that can be changed if contrary evidence is introduced) that a person is negligent if the thing causing an accident was in his or her control only, and if that type of accident does not usually happen without negligence.

Res Ipsa Loquitur

Res ipsa loquitur is Latin meaning "the thing [*res*] speaks [*loquitur*] for itself [*ipsa*]." It is used in negligence cases in which the plaintiff is in a disadvantaged position for proving the defendant's negligence because the evidence is unavailable to the plaintiff, but is or should be available to the defendant. Under the doctrine of res ipsa loquitur, the defendant's negligence is presumed as a result of his or her actions. This shifts the burden of proof to the defendant. In other words, the defendant must disprove his or her negligence from the outset of litigation. The plaintiff's burden of proof is converted into the defendant's burden of rejoinder.

Elements of Res Ipsa Loquitur

The plaintiff must prove only certain essential facts, such as what injury occurred, what the defendant was doing, and how the defendant's action (or inaction) related to the plaintiff's harm. To use res ipsa loquitur, whatever occurred must not ordinarily occur without someone acting negligently. Court opinions often quote the following elements:

1. The defendant (or his or her employee[s]) must have been in exclusive control of the object or action that produced the plaintiff's injury.
2. The plaintiff's injury must be of a type that ordinarily would not have happened unless negligence were involved.
3. The defendant must be in a better position to prove his or her lack of negligence than the plaintiff is to prove the defendant's negligence.

Certain courts and legal scholars add a fourth element, which states that the plaintiff cannot have contributed to his or her own injuries. This, however, simply states contributory and comparative negligence, which are two similar defenses to negligence.

Defendant's Exclusive Control

For res ipsa loquitur to apply, the events that led to the plaintiff's injury must have been under the defendant's exclusive control. This includes the defendant's employees. For example, suppose the plaintiff was walking through the defendant's warehouse. Suppose the defendant's employees had stacked many crates of merchandise, and the stacks rose thirty feet high. If a top crate fell upon and injured the plaintiff, but nobody except the plaintiff was present in that part of the building, who could the plaintiff point the finger toward as having been negligent? Using res ipsa loquitur, the plaintiff would shift the burden of proof to the defendant (warehouse owner) to show that the crates had been safely stowed. Because the crates were under the defendant's exclusive control, and one crate fell and hurt the plaintiff, the first element of res ipsa loquitur would be satisfied.

Presumption of Negligence

Res ipsa loquitur insists that the plaintiff's injury be one that normally would not have happened unless negligence were involved. Consider the preceding illustration. Crates usually do not fall over in warehouses unless they are improperly stacked. Negligence may be presumed in this case because the box fell. This would not normally occur if ordinary, reasonable care were used to store the crates. Because the box did fall on the plaintiff, then the defendant must not have exercised reasonable care in stacking the crates. At least the court will make this presumption and allow the defendant to refute it by proving that reasonable care was used when storing the boxes.

The Case of the Unexpected Burn

Normally, bunrs do not occur during surgery. In the following case, the court allowed the plaintiff to prove the defendant's negligence by using the doctrine of res ipsa loquitur. The defendant's negligence was presumed and the defendant had to disprove its negligence.

BABITS

v.

VASSAR BROTHERS HOSPITAL, et.al.,

287 A.D.2d 670, 732 N.Y.S.2d 46

Supreme Court, Appellate Division, Second Department, New York

October 29, 2001

The plaintiff sustained a third-degree burn on the rear area of her right upper thigh while anesthetized and undergoing surgery on her right knee. The defendants could not conclusively state what caused the injury. ... The defendants presented an alternative theory as to the cause of the burn which did not involve any negligence on their part.

The defendants separately moved to dismiss the complaint at the close of the plaintiff's case, arguing, *inter alia*, that the plaintiff failed to establish the necessary elements of the doctrine of res ipsa loquitur.

* * *

... To rely on the doctrine, a plaintiff must submit sufficient proof that (1) the injury is of a kind that does not occur in the absence of someone's negligence, (2) the injury is caused by an agency or instrumentality within the exclusive control of the defendants, and (3) the injury is not due to any voluntary action on the part of the plaintiff.

* * *

Infliction of a third-degree burn on the rear area of the plaintiff's right upper thigh during orthoscopic knee surgery is an event that the jury could reasonably infer would not occur in the absence of negligence ... . Further, any potential cause of the burn identified in the plaintiff's proof was within the exclusive control of the defendants. Finally, it is undisputed that the plaintiff was unconscious at the moment of injury, and thus could not have contributed to its cause ... . Although the defendants presented an alternative theory as to the cause of the accident that did not involve any negligence on their part, trial testimony nevertheless established that the event was of a kind that ordinarily does not occur in the absence of negligence, and the plaintiff need not conclusively eliminate the possibility of all other causes of the injury. The evidentiary and procedural consequence of res ipsa [is] that of a creation of a permissible inference or deduction of negligence from the facts and circumstances of the case.

* * *

Its effect is to make out a prima facie case permitting submission to the jury, which may, but which is in no way bound to, infer negligence.

* * *

Moreover, the plaintiff's evidence established a prima facie case sufficient to place the matter before the jury even without relying on the doctrine of res ipsa loquitur. Testimony by the plaintiff's expert giving two possible causes for the injury, both of which he described as a departure from accepted medical practice, was sufficient for a reasonable person to conclude that it is more probable than not that the injury was caused by the defendants.

Case Questions

1. Why was the plaintiff permitted to use the doctrine of res ipsa loquitur in ths case?
2. Could a patient develop a burn on their thigh, after surgery on the knee, without any negligence on the part of the physician?

Defendant's Superior Proof Position

Under res ipsa loquitur, the defendant must be in a better position to prove that he or she was not negligent than the plaintiff is to establish the defendant's negligence. In the warehouse example, the plaintiff did not see how the crate fell. None of the defendant's employees were present or nearby when the accident occurred. No witnesses actually saw why the crate fell. But the defendant originally stacked the crates. This makes it easier for the defendant to prove that reasonable care was used in stacking the boxes. The plaintiff is at a disadvantage to prove the defendant's negligence. However, the defendant can more easily show that safeguards were used in stacking the crates (such as ropes tied to support beams and crates, or walls and doors surrounding the stacked boxes). In this fashion, the defendant could prove that reasonable care was used when stacking the crates and therefore no negligence occurred.

Res ipsa loquitur cases often involve medical malpractice, particularly surgery. However, the doctrine is not restricted to such negligence cases, as the following hypothetical illustrates.

― HYPOTHETICAL

Eugene supervises a road-repair crew employed by Pavement Plus, Inc. The county contracts road construction and renovation to Pavement Plus. Eugene's crew was filling potholes on Elm Avenue one spring day. One of Eugene's employees, Everest, improperly mixed the asphalt so that it would not harden adequately. This bad asphalt was used to fill the Elm Avenue holes. Rutherford, who lives on Elm Avenue, drove over the patched potholes a few days later. The asphalt collapsed and the front right tire of Rutherford's automobile wedged in a hole, bending the front axle. Rutherford discovered that Pavement Plus had repaired the street, but had kept no record of the asphalt mixtures used.

Could Rutherford use res ipsa loquitur to shift the burden of proof? Evaluate the elements under these facts. Pavement Plus's foreman, Eugene, and an employee were under exclusive control of the weak asphalt used to fix the street. Asphalt does not normally collapse under vehicular weight unless it is improperly prepared or applied. The defendant is in the best position to prove that the mixture was suitable, as its employees prepared and applied the asphalt. Thus, res ipsa loquitur applies in this case, and the plaintiff need only prove what happened (i.e., his car was damaged when it fell through an asphalted hole that the defendant repaired). The defendant must now establish that its employees used reasonable care in preparing and applying the asphalt. As an aside, this problem also illustrates the value of retaining written records (in this case, of asphalt mixture) to document reasonable care. ∎

Table 2-5 summarizes proof of negligence and res ipsa loquitur.

TABLE 2-5 Burden of proof, burden of rejoinder (rebuttal), and res ipsa loquitur

Burdens of Proof and Rejoinder (Rebuttal)	Res Ipsa Loquitur
Plaintiff must generally prove the defendant's negligence beyond a preponderance of the evidence.	"The thing speaks for itself." This doctrine shifts the burden of proof to the defendant, who must disprove the presumed negligence.
	Elements: (1) the defendant's exclusive control over acts or objects that injured the plaintiff; (2) the plaintiff's injury must be one that ordinarily does not occur without negligence; and (3) the defendant is in the best position to prove that he or she was not negligent.

§ 2.9 Violation of a Statute

Sometimes there will be an allegation in a negligence claim that the defendant also violated a particular statute. For example, there might be a local ordinance requiring all outdoor swimming pools to be fenced. A couple in the area affected by the statute had a pool party for their child and the neighbors. The homeowners took down the fence when they bought the house and had not yet decided the kind of fence they would replace it with. One of the children dove into the pool, struck the bottom, and was severely injured. The question then arises as to what affect the possible violation of the statute might have upon the negligence action. In analyzing the case, you must look to see if the statute was in fact violated and, if so, whether this caused the accident or played a significant role in the accident. It is also important to see if the person injured was the kind of person the statute was designed to protect and whether the statute covers the kind of harm suffered by the plaintiff. In this example, the fact that there was no fence had nothing whatsoever to do with the accident.

However, if the facts had been different and a neighbor's child wandered into the unfenced backyard, fell into the pool, and drowned, this statute would have a direct bearing on the negligence case. In most states, the violation of such a statute would be considered *negligence per se*. This would mean that the proof of the violation of the statute would be sufficient enough to show that there was negligence; the defendant would thus be prevented from introducing evidence as to the degree of care or reasonableness used.

Summary

Negligence is the failure to use reasonable care to avoid injuring others or their property. Reasonable care is dependent upon the particular facts of each case. The key is the reasonableness or unreasonableness of the tortfeasor's actions under the circumstances.

There are four elements of negligence: duty of reasonable care, breach of duty, causation, and injury. The elements are considered sequentially. If any one is missing, then no negligence occurred.

The duty of reasonable care is the tortfeasor's obligation to act reasonably to avoid injuring others. The tortfeasor does not owe this duty to everyone in the world; however, the injured party must fall within the scope of the tortfeasor's duty. This means that it must have been reasonably foreseeable that the plaintiff would be harmed as a consequence of the defendant's actions. This is called the *reasonable plaintiffs theory*. Only foreseeable plaintiffs (who were actually injured as a result of the defendant's conduct) may recover damages in a negligence lawsuit. Reasonable care is defined by the standard of the mythical reasonable person. Would a reasonable person have acted in the same way the defendant did, under the same or similar circumstances? The trier-of-fact decides how the reasonable person would have behaved. The reasonable person standard is adjusted to reflect the defendant's special skills or limitations.

In professional malpractice actions, professionals such as physicians are held to exercise the degree of care and skill reasonably required of like professionals in similar circumstances. Depending on the jurisdiction, the professional will be judged by the skills of professionals in the same community, a similar locality, or (as is the trend) nationally.

The tortfeasor's actions must cause the victim's injuries. Causation under negligence is usually shown through cause-in-fact. But for the defendant's misconduct, the plaintiff would not have been harmed. When multiple tortfeasors are involved in producing the victim's injuries, however, but-for causation does not function well. An alternative causation theory, substantial factor analysis, states that each defendant is liable for the plaintiff's injuries if that defendant was a substantial factor in producing the harm. Joint and several liability holds multiple defendants liable for a plaintiff's injuries when those defendants combine to create the harm.

Proximate cause is an element of causation. Proximate cause declares the line at which injuries are reasonably foreseeable. Inside the boundary are tortfeasors' actions that could reasonably have been anticipated to produce the victim's harm. Outside the perimeter are injuries that were not reasonably foreseeable as a consequence of the tortfeasor's behavior. This circle is sometimes called the *zone of danger*. Some courts speak of proximate cause in terms of foreseeability and scope of duty. Other courts state that tortfeasors take their victims as they find them, which means that the particular injury the plaintiff suffered (usually due to some peculiar physical condition) is always considered foreseeable. While a person failing to act to stop a harm from happening to another is often not held liable for their inaction, under certain specific relationships, such as employer/employee or teacher/student, a person might have an obligation or special duty to act and may be held liable if they do not.

Damages must be proven in every negligence case. The plaintiff must prove that he or she suffered some actual loss as a result of the defendant's actions, whether physical injury, emotional injury, or harm to property. This loss is normally quantified in monetary terms as consequential damages.

Most often, the plaintiff must prove that the defendant was negligent in causing the plaintiff's injuries. This burden of proof calls for a preponderance of the evidence. Once established, the defendant has the burden of rejoinder, or rebuttal, to counter the plaintiff's prima facie case. In certain cases, however, the plaintiff is at a disadvantage in proving the defendant's negligence. Res ipsa loquitur allows the plaintiff to shift the burden of proof to the defendant. Thus, the defendant must disprove the plaintiff's allegations of negligence. Res ipsa loquitur applies in cases in which the defendant exclusively controlled the object or action that hurt the plaintiff; that the plaintiff's injury was one that ordinarily would not happen without negligence; and the defendant is in the better position to prove that he or she was not negligent.

A defendant's violation of a statute might have an affect on the outcome of a negligence case. This is especially true where the statute was designed to prevent the kind of accident that occurred.

Key Terms

burden of rejoinder	gross negligence	punitive (exemplary) damages
cause-in-fact	joint and several liability	reasonable person test
compensatory damages	negligence	(standard)
contribution	nominal damages	res ipsa loquitur
damages	preponderance of the evidence	scope of duty
due (reasonable) care	prima facie case	substantial factor analysis
duty	professional community	taking the victim as you find
foreseeability	standard of care	him/her
foreseeable plaintiffs theory	proximate cause	unforeseeable plaintiffs

Problems

In the following hypotheticals, determine if negligence exists and if the tortfeasor will be liable to the injured party. Identify the plaintiff(s) and the defendant(s).

1. Carlson Pledsoe operates a tanning salon. Meg McKinley is one of his customers. The salon uses tanning beds that are equipped with ultraviolet lights above and below the customer. These lights are automatically regulated to control radiation exposure. Meg visited the salon and, while lying upon one of the tanning beds, fell asleep. The automatic regulator became stuck at maximum intensity. Meg was severely burned by the radiation.

2. Daniel Miller operates a backhoe for a construction company. Douglas Treefall hired the company to excavate a swimming pool in his backyard. Daniel dug the hole using the backhoe. Unbeknownst to Douglas, Daniel, or the neighbors, the United States Army had used the area during World War II as an undercover training facility for minesweepers and several unexploded land mines remained buried in the ground. Daniel hit one with the backhoe shovel, which detonated the explosive. The shovel was blasted away from the machine, flew several feet into the air, and crashed into Douglas's new truck. The impact pushed the truck into the street, causing Debbie Wiley, a neighbor who was driving a van down the street, to swerve into Douglas's front yard, hitting and felling an oak tree (that had been weakened by termites), which crashed into Robert Farlow's house next door to Douglas's home.

3. Bud Askew is a professional painter. He bought exterior latex paint to apply to Joe Barley's barn. The paint store incorrectly labeled the paint as oil-based when in fact it was water-based. Bud painted the barn without noticing the difference. After several severe summer thunderstorms, the paint wore off.

4. Samantha Jacobs is a chemical dependency counselor. One of her clients, Happy Trevor, has been addicted to alcohol and tobacco for years. He has suffered severe liver damage. Samanthat recommended hypnotherapy as a possible cure. Hypnosis is frequently used to treat chemical addiction, and Samantha is a state-certified hypnotherapist. After hypnotizing Happy, she discovered through regression that he had had a traumatic experience involving alcohol at age seven. She felt certain that this memory was the key to his current addiction. When Samantha attempted to

bring Happy out of his hypnotized state, however, she discovered, much to her dismay, that he had fixated and would not return to consciousness. As a result, Happy remained regressed at seven years of age. Psychiatrists indicated that this condition occurs in only 1 in every 10,000 hypnosis cases.

5. Nellie Stevens plays guitar and sings in a rock-and-roll band at a local tavern, The Whiskey Slick. One of her songs, "Death to Phone Solicitors," contains certain explicit and graphically descriptive details. Josie Aztway, a bartender at the Slick, suffers from paranoid delusions. She found Nellie's lyrics overwhelmingly absorbing, and she took them literally. After hearing Nellie's "Death" song at work one night, Josie returned to her apartment, loaded her revolver, drove downtown to a local telephone solicitation business, entered, and shot six operators.

Review Questions

1. Provide a broad definition of negligence. What key factors are involved in analyzing negligence problems?

2. List the elements of negligence. How do they fit together? How do you apply each part to a particular problem?

3. What is duty? How does it relate to reasonable care? How do you define the scope of duty? What role does foreseeability play in scope of duty? What is the foreseeable plaintiffs theory? What is reasonable care? Who is the reasonable person, and why is he or she important in negligence analysis? Who defines this standard and how? How does the standard vary in different cases?

4. Define *causation*. What is cause-in-fact? But-for causation? What is substantial factor analysis, and when is it used? How does it differ from joint and several liability? How is it similar?

5. Define *proximate cause*. What role does foreseeability play? What is the zone of danger? How is scope of duty involved? What is taking the victim as you find him? How is it applied?

6. How are damages determined in negligence cases? What are consequential damages?

7. How is negligence normally proven? Who generally bears the burden of proof? The burden of rejoinder or rebuttal? When is negligence presumed? What Latin phrase is used to describe this presumption? What are this doctrine's elements, and how are they used?

8. What is medical malpractice? If a needle is left in a patient after surgery, can the doctrine of res ipsa loquitur be used to prove the plaintiff's case? Explain your answer.

9. What effect does the special relationship between a teacher and a student have on a student's claim of negligence?

10. How can the violation of a statute affect the outcome of a negligence case?

Projects

1. Find a recent court opinion in your state that defines the elements of negligence. Do these elements differ from those discussed in this chapter? If so, in what ways?

2. As a class or in study groups, create your own hypotheticals using the negligence formula in this chapter. Then change the facts to alter the outcomes of the cases.

3. An argument has been made that large malpractice awards are driving up the price of health care. Should all jurisdictions impose a cap or ceiling limiting the amount awarded in malpractice cases for pain and suffering, as some jurisdictions already do? Explain.

4. Read the case of *Russell v. Archer Building Centers, Inc.* in Appendix C. Was the store owner negligent? Explain.

5. Read the case of *Stander v. Orentreich* in Appendix C. What difference would it make if the physician's acts were treated as simple negligence rather than malpractice?

6. Read the case of *Summers v. Tice* in Appendix C. Why do you think this case is studied in so many law schools?

Internet Resources

This chapter deals with the field of negligence. To learn more about negligence, the following sites can be accessed:

General Legal Information

http://findlaw.com
http://law.emory.edu/LAW/refdesk/subject/tort.html
http://www.hg.org/litg.html
http://www.dri.org

CHAPTER 3

SPECIAL NEGLIGENCE ACTIONS

CHAPTER OUTLINE

§ 3.1   Introduction
§ 3.2   Premises Liability
§ 3.3   Vicarious Liability
§ 3.4   Negligent Infliction of Emotional Distress
§ 3.5   Negligence Per Se

EQUAL JUSTICE UNDER LAW

---

*To succeed in the other trades, capacity must be
shown; in the law, concealment of it will do.*
MARK TWAIN

§ 3.1 Introduction

Negligence theory has evolved special legal concepts to apply, in certain
circumstances, to particular types of activities.

Special negligence actions are cases involving certain well-defined
activities. Special rules of negligence apply in these instances. The most
common special negligence actions involve property ownership,
employer/employee activities, and motor vehicle use. Theories of vicarious liability, in which someone is held accountable for the negligence of
another person, and negligent infliction of emotional distress add unique
and recognizable elements to the study of torts.

The basic negligence formula applies to all special actions discussed
in this chapter. Negligence includes the following elements: duty of
reasonable care, breach of duty, causation, and damages. Always keep this
approach in mind when examining any negligence problem. However,
each special action has its own peculiar analytical twists and turns that
distinguish it from the other torts. This chapter covers the following:

♦ Premises liability

♦ Distinctions between trespassers, licensees, and invitees

♦ Attractive nuisance

♦ Vicarious liability and respondeat superior

♦ Negligent infliction of emotional distress

♦ Negligence per se.

§ 3.2 Premises Liability

Special negligence rules apply to owners and occupiers of land. **Occupiers**
include individuals who do not own but who do use real estate, including
tenants (lessees). For simplicity's sake, we will speak in terms of the owner.

occupier† An individual who does not own but who uses real estate, including tenants (lessees).

The term *occupier* may always be substituted for *owner,* because negligence theories apply to both.

Land Owner's Different Duties of Reasonable Care

As negligence law developed in the late nineteenth and early twentieth centuries, American courts devised different standards of reasonable care for land owners or land users. The distinctions depended upon who the injured party (plaintiff) was, in terms of the victim's purpose for being on the land where the owner's negligence was alleged to have occurred.

Victim's Status on Land Defines Scope of Duty

For example, under old common law, the land owner owed a different duty of reasonable care to the injured party depending upon whether the victim was a trespasser, a licensee, or an invitee. (These terms are explained later in this section.) Thus, the plaintiff's status as a trespasser, licensee, or invitee determined the scope of duty that the owner owed. These distinctions affect the balance of risk of injury from the tort in question, versus the possible benefits that might be received. Intentional torts involve intentional acts, and as such carry a high degree of risk and usually a low degree of social benefit. That is, the risk greatly outweighs the benefit. Therefore, the duty not to intentionally injure someone or something is great.

Modern Judicial Trends

For decades courts and legal scholars have complained that this three-tier analytical approach is arbitrary and unnecessary. After all, ordinary negligence theory appears adequately equipped to establish the land owner's duty of reasonable care. If an owner acted unreasonably in maintaining his or her realty, and as a result a victim was harmed, then the owner should be liable. Regular negligence theory works well to produce a just result, say these critics.

Many courts have in fact abolished the three-tier land owner standards of care. The landmark case was *Rowland v. Christian*, 69 Cal. 2d 108, 443 P.2d 561, 70 Cal. Rptr. 97 (1968) (superseded by statute, as explained in *Perez v. Southern Pacific Transport Co.*, 218 Cal. App. 3d 462, 267 Cal. Rptr. 100 (1990)), in which the distinctions were eliminated in favor of traditional negligence theory. For instance, in states such as New York, the three-tier approach has been discarded by the courts in favor of a traditional negligence approach, whereby all who come upon property must be treated with the same degree of reasonable care. There is no longer a distinction as to the status of a person, such as guest or invitee, and the reason for which they are upon the land. Many states have followed the California Supreme Court's lead. Still, many courts continue to apply the three-tier system.

Land Owner's "Zero Duty" Toward Trespassers

Land owners owe no duty of reasonable care toward trespassers. The risk to a trespasser should be essentially nonexistent compared to the benefit of keeping the trespasser away. Owners may not intentionally injure trespassers upon their real estate, but they need not search their realty and safeguard it for trespassers' unauthorized uses (*Katko v. Briney*, 183 N.W. 2d 657). Courts favoring this policy reason that a land owner should not be required to exercise ordinary reasonable care to protect a tortfeasor (i.e., trespasser) from harm. Because the trespasser is committing an intentional tort, negligence law insists only that real estate owners avoid intentionally injuring trespassers. Otherwise, the trespasser *assumes the risk* of entering someone else's land without permission.

Special Rule for Trespassing Children: Attractive Nuisance

However, land owners owe a higher duty of reasonable care to trespassing children. The reasoning behind this special rule states that children, especially when young, are so inexperienced and naive that they may not fully appreciate dangers lurking upon the land. Therefore, owners must exercise ordinary, reasonable care to safeguard their realty for trespassing children who are enticed onto the land to investigate the dangerous condition that injured them. Young children are often attracted, out of curiosity, to investigate dangerous conditions on realty, such as abandoned wells, railroad tracks, swimming pools, or unused machinery. These alluring items are often hazardous, a fact that the trespassing child may not understand. The attraction element has given this special rule its name of the **attractive nuisance doctrine** (**attraction theory**) or, more commonly, **attractive nuisance**.

Currently, a four-part test is employed to hold the land owner liable under the attractive nuisance doctrine.

1. The owner must know or have reason to know of the artificial condition on the premises.

2. The structure, instrumentality, or condition must be alluring to children and endanger them. They cannot know or appreciate the danger.

3. The presence of children must reasonably have been anticipated.

4. The danger posed to the children outweighs the cost of making the condition safe.

If a trespassing child is injured as a result of having been enticed onto the land to investigate some dangerous condition, then the land owner is liable for such harm.

attractive nuisance doctrine (attraction theory) A legal principle, used in some states, that if a person keeps dangerous property in a way that children might be attracted to it and be able to get at it, then that person is responsible even if the children are trespassing or at fault when they get hurt.

attractive nuisance† Any item that is dangerous to young children but that is so interesting and alluring as to attract them to the location at which it is kept.

The Case of the Nuisance Pool

Special care is taken to protect children under the law. What is clearly dangerous or foolhardy to an adult might seem like the perfect opportunity for fun and entertainment to a child. Must homeowners survey their homes and remove every item or structure that can be transformed into a dangerous instrumentality and hurt a child? What are the ground rules?

BENNETT

v.

STANLEY

Supreme Court of Ohio
92 Ohio St.3d 35, 748 N.E.2d 41
Submitted October 18, 2000
Decided June 13, 2001

In this case we are called upon to determine what level of duty a property owner owes to a child trespasser. We resolve the question by adopting the attractive nuisance doctrine set forth in Restatement of the Law 2d, Torts (1965), Section 339. We also hold that an adult who attempts to rescue a child from an attractive nuisance assumes status of the child, and is owed a duty of ordinary care by the property owner. ...

The Bennetts had moved next door to defendants-appellees, Jeffrey and Stacey Stanley, in the fall of 1996. The Stanleys had purchased their home the previous June. At the time of their purchase, the Stanleys' property included a swimming pool that had gone unused for three years. After moving in, the Stanleys drained the pool once but thereafter they allowed rainwater to accumulate in the pool to a depth of over six feet. They removed a tarp that had been on the pool and also removed the fencing that had been around two sides of the pool.

* * *

The Stanleys were aware that the Bennetts had moved next door and that they had young children. They had seen the children outside unsupervised. Stacey Stanley had once called Chance onto her property to retrieve a dog.

The Stanleys testified, however, that they never had any concern about the children getting into the pool. They did not post any warning or "no trespassing" signs on their property.

Rickey Bennett testified that he had told his children to stay away from the pool on the Stanleys' property. He also stated that he had never seen the children playing near the pool.

Kyleigh told her father that she and Chance had been playing at the pool on the afternoon of the tragedy. The sheriff's department concluded that Chance had gone to the pool to look at the frogs and somehow fell into the pool. His mother apparently drowned trying to save him.

* * *

Ohio has long recognized a range of duties for property owners vis-a-vis persons entering their property. ... Currently, to an invitee the landowner owes a duty "to exercise ordinary care and to protect the invitee by maintaining the premises in a safe condition." To licensees and trespassers, on the other hand, "a landowner owes no duty ... except to refrain from willful, wanton or reckless conduct which is likely to injure [the licensee or trespasser]." Today, we face the issue of whether child trespassers should become another class of users who are owed a different duty of care.

This court has consistently held that children have a special status in tort law and that duties of care owed to children are different from duties owed to adults:

'Children of tender years, and youthful persons generally, are entitled to a degree of care proportioned to their inability to foresee and avoid the perils that they may encounter.' …

Recognizing the special status of children in the law, this court has even accorded special protection to child trespassers by adopting the "dangerous instrumentality" doctrine:

> The dangerous instrumentality exception [to nonliability to trespassers] imposes upon the owner or occupier of a premises a higher duty of care to a child trespasser when such owner or occupier actively and negligently operates hazardous machinery or other apparatus, the dangerousness of which is not readily apparent to children.

* * *

… [T]his court has never adopted the attractive nuisance doctrine. The doctrine as adopted by numerous states is set forth in Restatement of the Law 2d, Torts (1965), Section 339:

> A possessor of land is subject to liability for physical harm to children trespassing thereon caused by an artificial condition upon land if:
>
> (a) the place where the condition exists is one upon which the possessor knows or has reason to know that children are likely to trespass, and
>
> (b) the condition is one of which the possessor knows or has reason to know and which he realizes or should realize will involve an unreasonable risk of death or serious bodily harm to such children, and
>
> (c) the children because of their youth do not discover the condition or realize the risk involved in intermeddling with it or in

coming within the area made dangerous by it, and

> (d) the utility to the possessor of maintaining the condition and the burden of eliminating the danger are slight as compared with the risk to children involved, and
>
> (e) the possessor fails to exercise reasonable care to eliminate the danger or otherwise to protect the children.

This court has never explicitly rejected the Restatement version of the doctrine, which was adopted in 1965.

* * *

Any failure to adopt attractive nuisance would be to reject its philosophical underpinnings and would keep Ohio in the small minority of states that do not recognize some form of the doctrine.

Adopting the attractive nuisance doctrine would be merely an incremental change in Ohio law, not out of line with the law that has developed over time. It is an appropriate evolution of the common law. …

We therefore use this case to adopt the attractive nuisance doctrine contained in Restatement of the Law 2d, Torts (1965), Section 339. In doing so, we do not abandon differences in duty a landowner owes to different classes of users. In this case we simply further recognize that children are entitled to a greater level of protection than adults are.

Judgment reversed and cause remanded.

Case Questions

1. Was it foreseeable that children might be hurt as a result of the pool being poorly maintained?
2. What conditions must be found for the court to hold that an attractive nuisance exists?
3. Would the case have been decided differently if the fence around the pool was still up and intact?

Restatement (Second) of Torts § 339

Many courts now follow § 339 of the *Restatement (Second) of Torts* and hence have discarded the attraction element to the theory. For these courts, it is sufficient that (1) the injury to the trespassing child was reasonably foreseeable; (2) the danger on the land presented an unreasonable risk of harm to trespassing children; (3) the danger on the land was artificial, meaning manmade rather than natural; (4) because of the child's youth, he or she could not appreciate the risks involved or did not discover (and understand) the threat; (5) the threatening condition was located at a place across which children were likely to trespass; and (6) the land owner failed to exercise reasonable care to protect trespassing children from the danger that caused the harm. Under this version of attractive nuisance, the danger did not have to entice the child onto the land. It is adequate that the child encountered and was hurt by a danger that he or she did not fully discern.

Beneath all its trimmings, *Restatement* § 339 is simply negligence theory applied to trespassing children. The basic negligence elements are there, and the reasoning is identical.

A number of jurisdictions depart from the *Restatement*'s artificial condition element. These courts would include natural dangers, such as streams, quicksand, or rock formations, as risks against which the land owner must take precautions to protect trespassing children.

— HYPOTHETICAL

Maybelline is a student attending the local community college. She occasionally trespasses across Farmer Bob's cattle pasture when she walks from her apartment to campus. One day, while cutting across the land, Maybelline encountered Bob's prize bull, which was in a particularly agitated frame of mind. The bull charged and knocked Maybelline to the ground, injuring her. Is Bob liable?

Because Maybelline was a trespasser, Bob owed her no duty of reasonable care. Accordingly, she took her chances by walking across the pasture without permission. Bob would not be liable for her injuries.

Suppose that Maybelline were five years old and came upon Bob's farm to play on the swing set. The set is rickety and old. Attractive nuisance theory would hold Bob liable when Maybelline cuts her hand on a broken, jagged edge of the swing. Maybelline was enticed onto the realty by the swing set, which, due to her youth, she did not notice was old and in disrepair. Bob failed to exercise reasonable care to protect trespassing children such as Maybelline from the risk of being cut by a sharp edge on the swing. The threat of being hurt on the swing was unreasonable, as a child of Maybelline's age could not be expected to realize that the set was too old to be used safely. Young children are likely to be lured onto land to play on playground equipment. The dangerous condition was artificial because Bob installed the swing set on his property and then failed to repair the set or take it down. Any of the attractive nuisance theories discussed previously would hold Bob accountable under these facts.

Suppose, instead, that Maybelline were a cat burglar who was breaking into Bob's barn late one night. Unbeknownst to Maybelline, Bob had wired a shotgun to the windows inside the barn; anyone raising the window frame would instantly be shot. Maybelline tried to enter through the window and was seriously hurt by the gun blast. Would Bob be liable?

Although Bob owes Maybelline (who was trespassing) no duty of reasonable care, he may not set a lethal trap for would-be burglars. Land owners cannot create an unreasonable danger to injure trespassers. Bob would be liable for Maybelline's injuries in this factual scenario. ■

Licensees Defined

licensee A person who is on property with permission, but without any enticement by the owner and with no financial advantage to the owner; often called a *mere, bare,* or *naked licensee* as opposed to an *invitee* in negligence law.

Licensees are persons who have permission to be upon another's land. They are distinguishable from trespassers in that the land owner has consented to their presence upon his or her realty. This consent may be expressed or implied. Examples of licensees include social guests, such as friends who gather at a person's house to study or neighbors coming over to borrow tools; door-to-door salespersons or charitable solicitors (when the land owner has not prohibited their entry by posting warning signs); and frequent trespassers to whose incursions the land owner implicitly consents (such as when trespassers frequently use shortcuts that the land owner does not discourage through fencing or sign-posting).

Land Owner's Duty of Reasonable Care Toward Licensees

Owners owe licensees a duty of reasonable care in using the real estate, because the risk and the benefit are equal. This includes the owner's obligation to correct known dangers (both artificial and natural) on the land. In other words, if the owner knows (or reasonably should know) that a hazardous condition exists on the realty, then he or she must exercise reasonable care in safeguarding licensees from these risks. For example, if an abandoned well has not been covered, and a travelling salesperson visits and falls into the well (which cannot be seen because of overgrown grass), then the land owner has breached his or her duty of reasonable care to the salesperson, assuming that the owner knew (or should have known) that the well was there and could not be detected.

For licensees, the owner is not required to discover and correct unknown threats on the land. For invitees, however, the owner is obligated to do this, as we shall see later.

— HYPOTHETICAL

Irving owns an apartment building. Fundraisers for a local charity frequently solicit contributions from his tenants. Irving does not object to this solicitation, although he does not encourage it. Sterling is one of the charity's fundraisers. While visiting Irving's apartment complex, Sterling broke his leg when he fell through a rotten wooden stairway. Sterling could not see the rotting from the top of the steps, but the damage was evident if one looked up from below the stairway. Is Irving liable to Sterling?

Sterling is a licensee, because Irving permitted him to come onto the apartment premises. The key in this case is whether the rotten steps were a known hazard. Perhaps Irving did not know that the steps were rotten. However, Irving reasonably should have known that his apartment steps were dangerous. A building owner is expected to be aware of such easily discoverable risks, as it is easily foreseeable that a stairway user might be hurt if rotten steps collapse. Thus, Irving would be liable for Sterling's injuries.

Suppose, instead, that Irving had posted signs clearly warning, "NO SOLICITORS ALLOWED! ALL TRESPASSERS WILL BE PROSECUTED!" Would he be liable for Sterling's injuries? In this version of the facts, Sterling would be a trespasser, and so Irving would not owe a duty of reasonable care to Sterling. Accordingly, Irving would not be liable for the harm to Sterling.

Suppose that Irving had posted such signs but did nothing further to discourage solicitors from coming onto his premises. Suppose that door-to-door salespersons and charitable solicitors, including Sterling, regularly visited the apartments with impunity. Under this set of facts, Irving has implicitly consented to the solicitors' presence, including Sterling's. Thus, Sterling would be a licensee. ■

Invitees Defined

invitee A person who is at a place by invitation.

Invitees, or *business invitees* as older court opinions call them, are persons invited upon the land owner's premises. Originally, the common law restricted the term to individuals invited onto premises for business purposes, such as customers to a grocery, clothing store, amusement park, or tavern. Modern cases, however, state that an invitee need not be involved in any business-related purposes when he or she enters another's real estate. It is sufficient that the land owner encourage the invitee to visit.

Usually, invitees are persons coming onto the land for some purpose that the owner wishes to serve. Commonly, this includes any business, but could also include nonprofit organizations, such as churches, soup kitchens, charitable hospitals, or even colleges.

Land Owner's Highest Duty of Reasonable Care Toward Invitees

Land owners owe the highest duty of reasonable care to invitees, because the risk of injury is greater and the benefit is more personal than social. Owners must not only repair known dangers on the property but also must discover and correct unknown risks. This is a broader standard, requiring the land owner to take extra efforts to render his or her premises reasonably safe for invitees.

The logic underlying this stiffer standard of care suggests that owners who invite someone onto realty should be expected to exercise greater caution to ensure that the premises are reasonably danger-free. After all, the invitee would not be on the land to begin with had it not been for the owners' invitation.

Invitees and Licensees Distinguished

Invitee is a subcategory of *licensee,* yet the terms are distinguishable. All licensees have the owner's implied or expressed permission to be on the land, but the land owner does not have to invite or encourage licensees to visit; rather, the owner may just passively tolerate the licensees' presence. With invitees, however, the owner either implies an invitation or expressly invites them onto the real estate. This reflects the owner's active role in getting the invitees onto his or her land. Usually, the owner seeks customers for business; hence, courts often speak of business invitees.

Implicit or Express Invitation

The land owner's invitation to others to enter the premises may be expressed (e.g., a welcome sign outside a church or a business posting its hours on its door) or implied (e.g., a business leaving its doors open during business hours).

Limited Areas of Invitation

Obviously, most land owners do not invite people into every nook and cranny of their property. Certain regions are off-limits. For example, most businesses have storage rooms, manager's offices, or machinery rooms that patrons are specifically discouraged from entering. Virtually any business has door signs warning "private," "authorized personnel only," "keep out," and similar prohibitions. The owner's invitation to invitees does not include such areas. If an individual were injured while visiting an off-limits zone, then that person would be considered merely a licensee, or perhaps even a trespasser (depending upon how sternly the warning was phrased—such as "no trespassing—keep out!"), rather than an invitee.

From a plaintiff's standpoint, being included as an invitee spells maximum tort relief—at least in terms of monetary damages. The following hypotheticals explore invitee cases.

─ HYPOTHETICALS ────────────────────────

Elvis operates a shelter for homeless persons. Anyone forced to live on the streets is welcome at the facility. Jo Ellen frequently visits the shelter for free meals and a bed for the night. While sleeping one evening, Jo Ellen was stabbed by a loose, rusty wire through the mattress upon which she was lying. She had to undergo precautionary medical treatment for tetanus. Would Elvis be liable for Jo Ellen's injury?

Jo Ellen was an invitee, because she was homeless and Elvis expressly encouraged persons such as her to use his premises. Jo Ellen was injured as a result of a hidden danger (the loose wire) that could have been discovered if Elvis had inspected the mattresses for wear and tear. Thus, Elvis failed to exercise reasonable care to make the shelter reasonably safe for his patrons. As a result, one of his customers, Jo Ellen, was harmed, so Elvis is liable to her.

* * *

Danielle manages a local appliance store. Wayne came in one day to look for a new washer and dryer. Danielle showed Wayne a popular model. Wayne wished to see the units operate, but there were no electrical outlets nearby. Danielle went to her office to get an extension cord. Meanwhile, Wayne wandered through a set of swinging doors labeled "warehouse—employees only," hoping that he might find another salesperson who could locate an extension cord. Instead, he found a fork-loading truck that swerved around a wall and knocked Wayne to the ground, severely injuring him. The truck driver did not expect anyone to be in the area. Is Danielle liable to Wayne?

Wayne was an invitee when he visited the store to look for new appliances. However, he ceased to be an invitee when he entered the restricted area (the warehouse) without permission. Because he had been invited into the store originally, most courts would say that Wayne became a licensee once he entered the storeroom, as it is reasonably foreseeable that customers might mistakenly trespass into such a limited-access area. Danielle owed Wayne a duty of reasonable care to discover and correct known dangers on the premises. In this case, the fork truck was not threatening in and of itself, as a rotten stairway or improperly stacked boxes would be. The danger would be considered unknown, as it was not reasonably foreseeable that a patron would be hurt by a truck moving around a restricted-access warehouse. Accordingly, Danielle would not be liable for Wayne's injury.

Arguably, though, the threat of the fork truck harming a wayward customer *was* foreseeable, because the truck driver reasonably should have anticipated that patrons might enter the warehouse from time to time, looking for salespersons or restrooms. This would make the risk known and, arguably, Danielle breached her duty of reasonable care when her employee failed to watch for patrons while driving the truck through the warehouse. This reasoning is equally sound and persuasive. This case points out the artificial distinctions in classifying people by the reason they are on land. The traditional negligence approach would be much simpler. ■

Using Traditional Negligence Theory in Land Owner Cases

As noted earlier, many courts have eliminated the trespasser/licensee/invitee approach in favor of regular negligence theory. Instead of forcing the injured party into one of these three categories, many courts simply ask the routine negligence questions: Was the injury reasonably foreseeable? Did the land owner's scope of duty include the victim? Did the owner cause the victim's injury? and so forth. Many courts, however, cling tenaciously to the older three-tier analysis. This demonstrates how entrenched precedent becomes; once a rule of law becomes settled, it is difficult to raze the monolith and renovate its concepts. The law changes at a snail's pace. More often than not, this provides valuable stability and predictability in legal problem solving. Nonetheless, it also makes legal principles slow to adapt to the rapid changes of our dynamic society. Table 3-1 on page 73 summarizes the special negligence analysis for land owners and occupiers.

The Case of the Free-Falling Flight Attendant

The outcomes of premises-liability cases often hinge upon subtle factual distinctions that place participants within one of the three familiar categories. Courts adhering to the three-tier approach are hesitant to discard the formula, despite the difficulties in its application, as the following case demonstrates.

EGEDE-NISSEN

v.

CRYSTAL MOUNTAIN, INC.

Supreme Court of Washington
606 P.2d 1214 (Wash. 1980)
February 14, 1980
Hicks, Justice

This is an action for personal injuries sustained by petitioner A. E. Egede-Nissen, a Norwegian national, when she fell from a chairlift at Crystal Mountain ski area. A Pierce County Superior Court jury found Crystal Mountain, Inc., negligent, assessed total damages of $150,000, and found Egede-Nissen "contributorially negligent" to the extent of 55 percent.

Crystal Mountain appealed and the Court of Appeals, Division Two, reversed and remanded for a new trial. We agree with the Court of Appeals, although we base our conclusion on somewhat different grounds.

… Crystal Mountain, Inc., operates recreational ski facilities on public-owned land open to the public for recreational purposes. [On] April 25, 1973, plaintiff Egede-Nissen, a stewardess, and several members of her Scandinavian Airlines System (SAS) flight crew traveled to Crystal Mountain to picnic and sightsee. The ski lodge and chairlifts were not open for business, although the C-4 chairlift was running as an accommodation for three employees of a ski manufacturing company. No lift attendants were present.

From the loading area of the C-4 lift, the SAS group noted two or three skiers on the slopes above. Captain Hartvedt decided to ride the lift up to the skiers and look for and inquire about a picnic site. He boarded a moving chair and Egede-Nissen impulsively decided to accompany him. In her haste to board, she slipped and landed in a precarious position facing and grasping the chair with her lower torso and legs dangling below. Captain Hartvedt, occupying the same chair, attempted to stabilize her without himself falling from the chair.

Crystal Mountain employees working in the C-1 lift area had observed the foregoing situation develop and two of them immediately hastened to the C-4 lift, intending to assist Egede-Nissen. In the course of their efforts, one of the employees stopped the lift, restarted it and then stopped it a second time. The chairs on the lift swayed markedly at each stop.

Following the second stop, Egede-Nissen's hold on the chair became insecure and she fell 30 feet to the ground, sustaining injuries.

Petitioner commenced this negligence action against Crystal Mountain in Pierce County Superior Court in June 1973. The case was not tried until November 1976, at which time it was vigorously, often heatedly, contested. A verdict was returned in favor of the plaintiff in the amount of $67,500.

A major legal question at trial was Egede-Nissen's status (invitee, licensee or trespasser) aboard the chairlift. Her status depended upon a factual determination whether Crystal Mountain had given adequate notice, by signs or barricades, that the C-4 lift was not in public operation. On that issue, the evidence was sharply in conflict.

* * *

We granted Egede-Nissen's petition for discretionary review to consider, *inter alia*, whether we should abandon the traditional common-law categories of entrants upon land and adopt a unified standard of reasonable care under the circumstances.

Petitioner Egede-Nissen and amicus curiae urge this court to discard the categorical approach to landowner liability. Although we have questioned the common-law classification scheme in the past, we are not ready at this time to totally abandon the traditional categories and adopt a unified standard. …

There is no serious dispute that … Egede-Nissen's status upon *entering* the Crystal Mountain area was that of a public invitee. Accordingly, as to her, Crystal Mountain's duty was to maintain its premises in a reasonably safe condition. This duty, however, extends only to the "area of invitation"—that portion of the premises arranged so as to lead an invitee to reasonably believe it is open to her.

Petitioner's status aboard the chairlift turned on the resolution of a factual dispute—whether Crystal Mountain had given adequate notice that the C-4 lift was closed to the public. Initially, Egede-Nissen's status was that of a public invitee, which status she would retain until adequately warned of limits to the area of her invitation. If, however, petitioner unreasonably strayed beyond the area of invitation, her status would change from that of invitee to a licensee or trespasser, with a corresponding change in the duty owed to her by Crystal Mountain.

* * *

In the instant case, it was Crystal Mountain's theory that Egede-Nissen was at best a licensee and more properly a trespasser aboard the C-4 lift, to whom it owed a duty only to refrain from willful or wanton misconduct. While there was substantial evidence to support the trespasser theory, as pointed out by the Court of Appeals, … [a]s previously noted, her [Egede-Nissen's] status was dependent upon factual resolution.

The Court of Appeals also found [trial court jury] instruction No. 18 to be erroneous because it assumed petitioner to be an invitee as a matter of law. …

Egede-Nissen's status aboard the lift was dependent upon the scope of the invitation extended to her by Crystal Mountain. The scope of the invitation was a contested matter to be resolved by the jury. As pointed out by the Court of Appeals, the trial court erred in giving instruction No. 18, which assumed that Egede-Nissen had the status of an "invitee." The resolution of that question was dependent upon facts to be found by the jury. We hold that the trial court was sufficiently apprised of the defect in instruction No. 18 and that the giving of the instruction constituted reversible error for which a new trial is required.

* * *

As modified herein, the Court of Appeals is affirmed.

Case Questions

1. In the Washington Court of Appeals' *Egede-Nissen* opinion, the lower court gave a detailed discussion of the "notice of lift closure" issue. As Acting Chief Judge Reed stated the majority opinion:

   The major factual dispute in the case revolves around the extent of defendant's efforts to cordon off the loading area of the C-4 lift or warn away visitors. Plaintiff's witnesses, the other SAS crew members, testified that the loading area was not blocked and that there were no warning signs present. In fact, Tollef Bakke, the SAS copilot, testified that the only writing he noticed were two phrases written on a blackboard: "400 yards to go" and "You see what you get." Captain Hartvedt also stated that he read the phrase "You see what you get" on the blackboard. In contrast, defendant's witnesses, all employees of Crystal Mountain, stated that the area was surrounded by metal rope and fencing, and that a "Sorry Lift Closed" sign had been posted. (*Egede-Nissen v. Crystal Mountain, Inc.*, 21 Wash. App. 130, 584 P.2d 432 (1978)).

   You can see how sharply the parties' witnesses disagree on this issue. Suppose you were a juror in the case. If you believed the plaintiff's witnesses over the defendant's, what would be the outcome of the liability issue? What if you believed the defendant's witnesses instead? Would the outcome change? Explain.

2. What reversible error did the trial court commit in this case? How did it influence the jury's decision?

3. As you can see from the reprinted opinion, the Washington Supreme Court affirmed the court of appeals' decision to reverse and remand the case for a new trial. Given the facts as presented in the preceding excerpts, how would you decide the plaintiff's status issue? Do you think that Egede-Nissen was a trespasser, licensee, or invitee with regard to the lift chair? Support your conclusion using the legal elements discussed in the opinion and the concepts discussed in this chapter.

TABLE 3-1 Land-owners'/occupiers' negligence liability

Duty to Tresspasser	Land owner/occupier owes no duty of reasonable care; is required only to avoid intentional (or willful and wanton) injury.
Duty to Licensee	Land owner/occupier owes duty of reasonable care to correct known dangers on premises.
Duty to Invitee	Land owner/occupier owes duty of reasonable care to discover and correct unknown dangers on premises.
Traditional Negligence Theory	Applies regular negligence standards to determine land owner/occupier liability.
Duty to Tresspassing Children (Attractive Nuisance Theory)	Land owner/occupier owes duty of reasonable care to protect trespassing children from artificial dangers on premises, when (1) owner knows or has reason to know of the dangerous condition on the premises, (2) the structure, instrumentality, or condition is alluring to children and endangers them, (3) the presence of children can reasonably be anticipated, and (4) the danger posed to the children outweighs the cost of making the condition safe.

§ 3.3 Vicarious Liability

Previous chapters have presented hypotheticals in which someone acting on behalf of the defendant actually caused harm to the plaintiff. These have been employees of defendant businesses, in most problems. This illustrates one aspect of vicarious liability.

Vicarious Liability Defined

vicarious liability
Legal responsibility for the acts of another person because of some special relationship with that person; for example, the liability of an employer for certain acts of an employee.

Vicarious liability is the liability of one person, called the *principal,* for the tortious conduct of another, subordinate individual, called the *agent,* who was acting on the principal's behalf. In negligence law, principal/agent relationships most often involve employers and employees. The situation is simple. The principal is the employer, who hires the agent (employee) to work on the employer's behalf.

Employment Not an Essential Element

The principal/agent relationship, however, need not be that of employer and employee. Nineteenth- and early twentieth-century cases spoke of *master and servant.* This older classification suggested that the servant could work for the master without being paid. Thus, whether the agent is compensated for acting upon the principal's behalf is largely irrelevant to the issue of vicarious liability. Instead, focus upon this inquiry: Was one person acting on behalf of another? If so, a principal/agent relationship is present, and vicarious liability can exist.

Respondeat Superior

The employer is responsible for the negligence (or, for that matter, any torts) that his or her employees commit while working. This doctrine of vicarious liability is called **respondeat superior**, a Latin phrase meaning, "Let the master answer."

Liability Within Scope of Employment

Not every employee activity gives rise to the respondeat superior doctrine, however. An employer is responsible for an employee's actions that fall within the scope of employment. **Scope of employment** can be described as the range of conduct that the employer expects the employee to perform as part of his or her job. For example, a truck driver is expected to make deliveries and pickups for the employer; these actions fall within the scope of employment. But the driver is not expected to rob a liquor store while driving the company truck; this action falls outside the scope of employment.

Outside Scope of Employment: Examples

Employers are not liable for torts committed by employees that fall outside the scope of employment. Thus, in the preceding example, the employer would be responsible if the truck driver negligently crashed into another vehicle while making deliveries. However, the employer would not be accountable for the robbery (which actually involves criminal behavior but illustrates the scope concept).

Suppose the driver used the truck for personal purposes while not working, thereby going against company policy. Assume that the driver then negligently collided with another vehicle. Would the employer be responsible? No. The driver was acting outside the scope of employment by using the truck, not for the employer's business, but for unauthorized personal use.

Coming and Going Rule

Employers are usually not vicariously liable for the negligence of their employees while the employees are coming to or going from work. This is called the **coming and going rule**. The only situation in which an employer would be liable in such circumstances is if the employee were performing work-related activities while on the way to or from the job.

---

respondeat superior (Latin) "Let the master answer." Describes the principle that an employer is responsible for most harm caused by an employee acting within the scope of employment. In such a case, the employer is said to have vicarious liability.

scope of employment The range of actions within which an employee is considered to be doing work for the employer.

coming and going rule[†] Rule used when employees commit torts while coming to or going from work. In respondeat superior cases, this rule helps decide whether an employee's actions fall outside the scope of employment.

Frolic and Detour Rules

Employers are not vicariously liable for the negligence of their employees when employees go off on their own to handle personal matters, even though they might be performing work otherwise. For instance, suppose that, while making deliveries for the employer, the truck driver decided to drive 180 miles to stop by and visit a friend in the next state. The employer probably did not authorize this sidetrack from the employee's assigned duties. Visits to socialize with friends fall outside the employee's scope of employment. Thus, if the driver were negligent while pursuing activities unrelated to employment during ordinary working hours, this would be considered **frolic and detour**, and the employer would not be vicariously liable. Under the more modern view, an employee whose deviation is slight in terms of distance and time is considered to be acting within the scope of employment.

Independent Contractors

An **independent contractor** is someone who has entered into a contract with another person to perform a specific task. The independent contractor controls how he or she accomplishes the job. The individual hiring the independent contractor simply agrees to pay him or her for doing the chore. Independent contractors are distinguishable from employees in that the employer does not control how an independent contractor does the job. In contrast, employers do control how their employees perform their tasks. While an employer must deduct Social Security and withholding taxes from an employee, this is not required for an independent contractor. (See Internal Revenue Ruling 87-41.) Adjunct college instructors are an example of independent contractors.

No Vicarious Liability for Independent Contractors

Persons hiring independent contractors are not vicariously liable for the independent contractors' negligence. The reasoning is that the independent contractor is engaging in his or her own work and should be responsible for his or her own negligence. The hirer is simply buying the independent contractor's finished service, and has nothing to do with how the independent contractor achieves the desired results.

For example, suppose Manuel hires a plumber to install a new shower in his house. Manuel has nothing to do with the actual job; in fact, he only lets the plumber in to go to work. The plumber negligently installs the water lines so that the hot faucet is connected to the cold water line and vice versa. After the shower is completed, Manuel's visiting friend is the first to use it and shockingly discovers the mistake, suffering severe burns. Is Manuel vicariously liable to his friend for the plumber's negligence? No. The plumber was an independent contractor. Manuel had no say in how the plumber completed the job. Manuel merely paid the final price

frolic and detour rule†
Conduct of an employee that falls outside of the scope of employment that is purely for the benefit of said employee. An employer is not responsible for the negligence of an employee on a "frolic of his/her own."

independent contractor A person who contracts with an "employer" to do a particular piece of work by his or her own methods and under his or her own control.

after the plumber did the work. Thus, Manuel cannot be vicariously liable for the plumber's negligence. Instead of suing Manuel, his friend should sue the plumber.

Motor Vehicle Vicarious Liability

Since the first half of the twentieth century, courts have ruled that passengers in automobiles could be held vicariously liable for the driver's negligence. Using this analysis, if the automobile occupants were involved in a joint enterprise, such as a family traveling to a single destination, then the driver's negligence could be imputed to the passengers. This outcome may seem unfair, because a passenger has no actual control over how the driver operates the vehicle. Legal commentators have long criticized this type of vicarious liability. The better principle, long employed by the courts, holds the vehicle owner vicariously liable for the negligence of a driver other than the owner. For instance, suppose Britney's younger brother is driving her car negligently. He crashes into a motorcyclist, injuring her. Under vicarious liability, Britney would be accountable for her brother's negligence, because he was carelessly using her vehicle and injured another person as a result.

Many state legislatures have enacted statutes imposing vicarious liability on owners for the negligence of others who drive their vehicles. These are sometimes called *motor vehicle consent statutes.* An example of this is California's Vehicle Code § 17150 *et seq.*

Table 3-2 outlines vicarious liability.

TABLE 3-2
Vicarious liability summary

Vicarious Liability	Liability of principal for negligent actions of agent serving on principal's behalf. Commonly involves employer/employee relationships.
Respondeat Superior	"Let the master answer." Doctrine through which employers may be held vicariously liable for employees' negligent actions committed within the scope of employment.
Scope of Employment	Range of conduct that employer expects of employee during performance of assigned employment responsibilities.
Coming and Going Rule	Employers are not vicariously liable for employees' negligence while employees are coming to and going from work, unless employer has specifically requested employee to carry out a specific work-related task during such times.

TABLE 3-2
(*continued*)

Frolic and Detour Rule	Employers are not vicariously liable for employees' negligence when employees deviate from assigned tasks within scope of employment, unless the deviation is minor. Usually this involves employees going off on their own to pursue personal needs.
Independent Contractors	Employers are not liable for independent contractors' negligence, because independent contractors act independently and are responsible for their own conduct.
Motor Vehicle Vicarious Liability	Motor vehicle owners may be held vicariously liable for the driver's negligence. Liability may also be established in motor vehicle consent statutes.

─ HYPOTHETICALS ──────────

Sarah is a physician. Her nurse's aide, Gladys, draws blood from patients as part of her responsibilities on the job. One day, Gladys used a contaminated needle and thus infected a patient when she drew blood for testing. Would Sarah be vicariously liable for Gladys's negligence?

Gladys was performing a specific job assignment on Sarah's behalf. Drawing blood falls within Gladys's scope of employment. Under respondeat superior, Sarah would be accountable for Gladys's negligent act of using a contaminated needle and infecting a patient.

Suppose Gladys worked for a blood bank that routinely did blood draws and tests for area physicians. Under this scenario, Sarah would not have control over how Gladys acted. Gladys's employer is the blood bank, which would be an independent contractor in relation to Sarah. Accordingly, Sarah would not be accountable for Gladys's negligence.

* * *

Fargo is a fast-food restaurant manager. Mitchell is one of his employees. Fargo asked Mitchell to drive across town to a soft drink supplier and pick up additional carbonated water. While on this errand, Mitchell stopped by the post office to check his mail. As he was leaving the post office parking lot, he failed to look both ways and collided with another vehicle. Would Fargo be vicariously liable for Mitchell's negligent driving?

Although Mitchell was running a business-related errand on Fargo's behalf, stopping by the post office to check personal mail falls outside

> Mitchell's scope of employment. However, as this is only a slight deviation, frolic and detour would not apply here. Thus Fargo would be responsible for Mitchell's negligent conduct.
>
> Suppose Fargo had been a passenger in Mitchell's car during this incident. Fargo (as the boss) could have controlled his employee, Mitchell, and instructed him not to stop at the post office. By permitting Mitchell to check his mail, Fargo implicitly consented to Mitchell's detour. This would place the detour within the scope of Mitchell's employment. Assuming that no statutes stated differently, Fargo would be vicariously liable. ∎

§ 3.4 Negligent Infliction of Emotional Distress

emotional distress
Mental anguish. Non-physical harm that may be compensated for by damages in some types of lawsuits. *Mental anguish* may be as limited as the immediate mental feelings during an injury or as broad as prolonged grief, shame, humiliation, despair, etc.

negligent infliction of emotional distress†
Outrageous conduct by the tortfeasor that the tortfeasor reasonably should have anticipated would produce significant and reasonably foreseeable emotional injury to the victim.

Emotional distress consists of mental anguish caused by a tortfeasor. This condition includes fright, anxiety, shock, grief, mental suffering, shame, embarrassment, and emotional disturbance. The tort exists when the tortfeasor inflicts psychological injury on the victim. **Negligent infliction of emotional distress** consists of: (1) Conduct by the tortfeasor, which (2) the tortfeasor reasonably should have anticipated would produce (3) significant and reasonably foreseeable emotional injury to the victim; when (4) the tortfeasor breached his or her duty of reasonable care to avoid causing such emotional harm to the victim; and (5) the victim was a reasonably foreseeable plaintiff.

Extra Elements in the Common Law

These generalized elements of negligent infliction of emotional distress are synthesized from those of many jurisdictions. Different courts apply various special requirements to negligent infliction cases, and it is always wise to check the rules and cases of the particular jurisdiction in which your case lies.

Impact Rule

impact rule The rule (used today in very few states) that damages for emotional distress cannot be had in a negligence lawsuit unless there is some physical contact or impact.

A minority of courts insist that some physical impact accompany the emotional injury. Thus, the tortfeasor must negligently do something that physically touches the victim if the victim is to recover damages for negligent infliction of emotional distress. This is often called the **impact rule**, and it has been severely criticized in the legal literature and judicial decisions.

The purpose of the impact requirement is to protect against false claims of emotional distress. Because mental anguish is largely invisible, courts at the turn of the century felt that the defendant had to make contact with the plaintiff to justify compensating something as easy to fake as mental harm. Modern courts utilizing the impact rule have seen impact in almost any physical touching. Something as casual as putting one's hand on a classmate's shoulder would be considered sufficient contact to satisfy the impact rule. Hence, it would seem that, as a safeguard against faked claims of emotional distress, the physical impact requirement does little or nothing to ensure honesty and sincerity for allegations of mental hurt.

Physical Manifestations Rule

physical manifestations rule†
Doctrine applied in negligent infliction of emotional distress cases. Under this rule, the plaintiff may recover damages if physical symptoms accompanied his or her mental anguish.

The majority of courts have abandoned the impact rule in favor of the **physical manifestations rule**. This requires that, in addition to mental suffering, the plaintiff must experience physical symptoms as a result of the emotional distress. This rule is also thought to protect against bogus claims of emotional injury. After all, if a victim experiences some physical malady associated with an emotional harm, such as an ulcer, hives, sleeplessness, weight loss, or bowel dysfunction, then the probability is that the emotional harm is genuine.

Zone of Danger Rule

What happens when the negligent action occurs to someone else, and the plaintiff is a bystander who witnesses a negligent injury to another person? Could the tortfeasor be liable to the bystander for negligent infliction of emotional distress? Consider an example. Suppose parents witnessed their child being struck by a negligent driver. Would the parents have a cause of action against the driver for negligent infliction of emotional distress?

No impact occurred to the parents, although they may suffer physical manifestations as a result of witnessing their child's injury. The proper question, however, may be phrased in ordinary negligence terms: Did the driver owe (and breach) a duty of reasonable care to the parents by injuring their child? Did the driver's actions cause the parents' emotional suffering? Does proximate cause exist? Were the parents injured?

zone of danger rule
The rule in some states that a plaintiff must be in danger of physical harm, and frightened by the danger, to collect damages for the negligent infliction of emotional distress that results from seeing another person injured by the plaintiff.

Certainly, the driver could not reasonably anticipate that any bystander would suffer emotional distress as a result of the driver's negligent act of hitting a pedestrian. There must be some way to limit the scope of duty (and, hence, the range of foreseeable plaintiffs). Courts have attempted to establish such limits by creating the **zone of danger rule**. Under this rule, only bystanders who fall within the zone of danger can recover for negligent infliction of emotional distress. In other words, these individuals must have been threatened by the original negligent action (e.g., negligent driving of a vehicle) and have reasonably feared for their own safety, or have certain family relationships, as discussed next.

<◆>

The Case of the Return of the Living Dead

In *Decker v. Princeton Packet, Inc.,* the New Jersey Supreme Court held that a false obituary was not defamatory per se, when published without malicious intent or additional defamatory information. The opinion also discussed intentional and negligent infliction of emotional distress.

DECKER
v.
PRINCETON PACKET, INC.
Supreme Court of New Jersey
[116 N.J. 418, 561 A.2d 1122 (1989)
[August 8, 1989

* * *

Finally, the [trial] court concluded that plaintiffs were not entitled to any recovery based on any claims for negligent or intentional infliction of emotional distress. It rejected plaintiffs' negligent infliction of emotional distress claim because New Jersey case law does not allow recovery for the negligent infliction of emotional distress outside the zone-of-risk and family-observation theories.

Plaintiffs appealed to the Appellate Division, which upheld the trial court's ruling ... .

... [P]laintiff alleged that the publication of the false obituary based on an unsigned death notice left at defendant's office without any attempt to ascertain its truth or falsity constituted negligence that caused her emotional distress. These injuries included the loss of her job in part due to the obituary ... and the aggravation of emotional distress.

The tort involving the negligent infliction of emotional distress can be understood as negligent conduct that is the proximate cause of emotional distress in a person to whom the actor owes a legal duty to exercise reasonable care. Thus, to establish liability for such a tort, a plaintiff must prove that defendant's conduct was negligent and proximately caused plaintiff's injuries. The negligence of defendant, however, depends on whether defendant owes a duty of care to the plaintiff, which is analyzed in terms of foreseeability. "[L]iability should depend on the defendant's foreseeing fright

or shock severe enough to cause substantial injury in a person normally constituted."

While the foreseeability of injurious consequences is a constituent element in a tort action, foreseeability of injury is particularly important in the tort of negligent infliction of emotional harm. This reflects the concern over the genuineness of an injury consisting of emotional distress without consequent physical injury. In these situations, there must be "an especial likelihood of genuine and serious mental distress, arising from special circumstances, which serves as a guarantee that the claim is not spurious." In emotional distress cases, there has been "a constant concern about the genuineness of the claim."

The progression has been from denying recovery unless the emotional distress is accompanied by physical impact, to permitting recovery if the emotional distress results in physical injury. More recently, we have found a sufficient guarantee of genuineness, even in the absence of physical injury, if the plaintiff perceives an injury to another at the scene of the accident, the plaintiff and the victim are members of the same family, and the emotional distress is severe. Thus, recovery for negligent infliction of emotional harm requires that it must be reasonably foreseeable that the tortious conduct will cause genuine and substantial emotional distress or mental harm to average persons.

Unless a plaintiff's alleged distress is truly genuine and substantial, the tort of negligent infliction should not be broadened to permit recovery of damages. ... Thus, in the *Buckley* case, the Court observed that plaintiff's emotional distress "complaints amount to nothing more than aggravation, embarrassment, an unspecified number of headaches, and loss of sleep," and, as a matter of law, could not constitute severe mental distress sufficient to impose liability.

* * *

In this case, the emotional distress alleged by Marcy Decker resulting from the false report of her death, and, derivatively, the emotional distress assertedly experienced by Ms. Decker's son and mother, are not materially different from that described in cases like *Buckley*, in which the injury is not sufficiently palpable, severe, or enduring to justify the imposition of liability and the award of compensatory damages. Rather the alleged emotional distress approximates the subjective reactions of ordinary persons who feel victimized by the false report of death, namely, annoyance, embarrassment, and irritation. ... [T]here is no suggestion in the record that any serious or substantial distress on the part of Ms. Decker and her family would be particularly foreseeable. These considerations dictate rejection of the claim for the negligent infliction of emotional distress under these circumstances as a matter of law.

Case Questions

1. Do you agree with the court that the plaintiff and family's emotional distress was not reasonably foreseeable? How would a newspaper reasonably expect a person and family to react to reading an erroneous obituary for which no attempt at verification was made?

2. How does the court's discussion of the elements of negligent infliction of emotional distress compare with this chapter's presentation?

family relationships rule† Doctrine used in negligent infliction of emotional distress cases. Under this rule, a bystander may recover damages if he or she witnesses the tortfeasor injuring one or more of the bystander's relatives.

sensory perception rule† Doctrine used in negligent infliction of emotional distress cases. Under this rule, a bystander may recover damages if he or she witnesses a tortfeasor injuring another person, so long as the bystander perceives the event directly through his or her own senses.

Family Relationships Rule

Other courts have restricted recovery in negligent infliction cases to bystander plaintiffs who are related to the victim whom they witnessed being injured. This may be called the **family relationships rule.**

Sensory Perception Rule

Still other courts have insisted that the bystander perceive the traumatic, negligent event directly through the senses (e.g., seeing the collision; hearing the child's screams; feeling the heat of the car exploding; smelling the burning clothing). This may be labeled the **sensory perception rule**.

California Approach

The California courts were first to produce a further evolutionary development in negligent infliction law. In *Dillon v. Legg*, 68 Cal. 2d 728, 441 P.2d 912, 69 Cal. Rptr. 72 (1968), the California Supreme Court jettisoned the zone of danger rule and focused upon pure foreseeability. The straightforward question was, simply: Was the emotional injury reasonably foreseeable, given the tortfeasor's actions? This analysis neatly handled bystanders as well as immediate victims of negligent conduct. The court produced the following guidelines to decide the foreseeability issue:

1. The bystander's closeness to the emotionally disturbing incident (*physical proximity*)
2. The bystander's relationship to the injured party (*family relationships rule*)
3. The bystander's personal perception of the emotionally distressing occurrence (*sensory perception rule*)
4. Physical manifestations arising from the emotional distress.

The *Dillon* approach has been both praised and debunked by other courts and legal scholars. It presents another twist in negligent infliction cases, in a continuing attempt to clarify the circumstances in which a plaintiff may hold a defendant liable for this type of negligent tort.

The diversity of negligent infliction of emotional distress formulas used in different jurisdictions makes analysis dependent upon a specific state's version. The following hypothetical considers the varieties discussed in this section.

─ HYPOTHETICAL ─

Heddison owns an apartment building. Skyler and Melville are brothers who share an apartment. One day, while barbecuing on their apartment balcony, Skyler stepped upon rotten floorboards, which collapsed. Heddison had known about this dangerous condition for months but did not correct it. Skyler fell through the balcony floor and hung upside down by one leg 30 feet above the ground. Meanwhile, Melville, who was waxing his car in the parking lot below, became very upset upon seeing this situation develop. As he ran upstairs to assist his brother, Skyler fell and suffered debilitating injuries. Subsequently, Melville began having horrible nightmares involving endless falling. He would awaken nightly in cold sweats. He lost weight, had little appetite, and developed a phobia about heights. This phobia made it extremely difficult for Melville to continue his occupation as a roofing installer. Heddison's liability to Skyler is an issue of land owner liability, which we discussed at the beginning of this chapter. Would Heddison be liable to Melville for negligent infliction of emotional distress?

Clearly, Melville suffered no physical impact as a result of Heddison's negligence. Melville did not come into contact with the rotten balcony when it gave way. In states following the impact rule, Melville could not recover damages against Heddison for negligent infliction.

In states following the zone of danger rule, Melville was not sufficiently close to the dangerous balcony to be threatened by its condition. He was not even below the point at which Skyler fell, which would have placed him at risk. Under the zone of danger test, Melville could not recover.

In jurisdictions following California's approach, it was reasonably foreseeable that Melville would be emotionally harmed by witnessing Skyler's life-threatening situation, which Skyler became involved in because of Heddison's negligent maintenance of the balcony. Melville is Skyler's brother, so the family relationship test is met. Melville saw Skyler dangling from the balcony and knew that he could fall and be killed. This satisfies the sensory perception rule. Melville was standing close to the accident site, and thus met the physical proximity standard. He also displayed physical symptoms resulting from his mental anguish. All of the *Dillon* criteria have been satisfied. Accordingly, Heddison would be liable to Melville for negligent infliction of emotional distress, under the California theory. ■

Table 3-3 illustrates the various analytical approaches to negligent infliction of emotional distress.

TABLE 3-3
Elements of negligent infliction of emotional distress

Common Elements (applying standard negligence theory to emotionally distressing conduct)	(1) conduct by tortfeasor, when (2) tortfeasor reasonably should have anticipated that behavior would produce (3) significant and reasonably foreseeable injury in plaintiff, (4) tortfeasor breached duty of reasonable care, and (5) victim was foreseeable plaintiff.
Impact Rule	Plaintiff must experience physical impact from defendant's actions to recover for negligent infliction of emotional distress.
Physical Manifestations Rule	No physical impact is required, but plaintiff must experience physical symptoms associated with mental anguish that defendant caused.
Zone of Danger Rule	Bystander witnessing negligent injury to third party must have been immediately threatened by the negligent activity.
Family Relationships Rule	Bystander must be a family relative of the person injured by the tortfeasor's negligent act.
Sensory Perception Rule	Bystander must perceive with his or her senses (sight, hearing, smell, touch, taste) the injury to another person as a result of the tortfeasor's negligent act.

§ 3.5 Negligence Per Se

negligence per se†
Negligence that cannot be debated due to a law that establishes a duty of care that the defendant has violated, thus causing injury to another.

Negligence per se is negligence that is beyond debate because the law, usually a statute or ordinance, has established a duty or standard of care that the defendant has violated, thus causing injury to the plaintiff. When a statute defines certain conduct as negligent, and a tortfeasor violates the statute by engaging in that activity, then the tortfeasor is presumed to have been negligent by violating the statute. To meet the burden of proof, a plaintiff need only show that the defendant's actions violated the negligence statute. The defendant is then presumed negligent. This shifts the proof burden to the defendant, who must then present effective negligence defenses to avoid liability. A per se negligent defendant might also avoid liability by showing that he or she was not the proximate cause of the plaintiff's injuries. In other words, the defendant would have to prove that his or her violation of the statute did not proximately cause the plaintiff's harm.

Defenses to Negligence Per Se

The negligence defenses of contributory negligence, comparative negligence, and assumption of risk also apply to negligence per se cases.

◆◆◆

The Case of the Statutory Hangover

In *Ohio Casualty*, partially reprinted in Chapter 2, the reader faced an intriguing negligence issue: Did a tavern owner violate a duty of care by serving alcohol to an intoxicated customer who subsequently injured himself? The Oklahoma Supreme Court said no. Review the earlier reprint for the relevant facts. In the portion of its opinion reprinted here, the court rules on the negligence per se issue. After the court's decision, the inebriated driver must have felt a severe case of statutory hangover.

OHIO CASUALTY INSURANCE CO.
v.
TODD
Supreme Court of Oklahoma
813 P.2d 508 (Okla. 1991)
June 11, 1991
Summers, Justice

... Section 537(A)(2) [Oklahoma Statutes] states in relevant part that no person shall "[s]ell, deliver or knowingly furnish alcoholic beverages to an intoxicated person."

A. NEGLIGENCE PER SE

Robertson [the intoxicated driver/customer] urges that Todd [the tavern owner] violated Section 537(A)(2) and that the violation amounted to negligence per se. In *Hampton v. Hammons,* we explained the elements which must be found before the violation of a statute is negligence per se. ... [W]e pointed out that (1) the injury must have been caused by the violation, (2) the injury must be of a type intended to be prevented by the ordinance, and

(3) the injured party must be one of the class intended to be protected by the statute.

Because we find the third element to be missing, we do not address the first two. In *Brigance*, we stated that the purpose behind Section 537(A)(2) was to protect innocent third parties who were injured by intoxicated persons. In *Cuevas v. Royal D'Iberville Hotel*, the Mississippi Supreme Court construed a statute similar to Section 537(A)(2), and found that the intoxicated person was excluded from the class of persons meant to be protected by the statute. In making this determination, the court pointed out the class to be protected was the general public, and that this class, while broad in range, could not be said to include "an adult individual ... who voluntarily consumes intoxicants and then, by reason of his inebriated condition, injures himself." We agree.

We find nothing in Section 537(A)(2), or in any of the statutes regulating the sale of alcohol, which indicate[s] that the legislature intended to protect the intoxicated adult who, by his own actions, causes injury to himself. Instead, it appears that the legislature intended to protect the "unsuspecting public"—in effect all of the populace except the willing imbiber. Thus, a violation of Section 537(A)(2) does not amount to negligence per se under the facts of this case.

Case Questions

1. What if a passenger riding in Robertson's vehicle had been injured? Would the passenger then have a cause of action against the tavern owner for violating § 537(A)(2), under negligence per se theory? Explain.

2. Do you agree with the court that Robertson does not fall within the scope of the class protected by § 537(A)(2)? Explain.

Plaintiff Within Class of Persons Protected by Statute

Not every statutory violation constitutes negligence per se. To recover under negligence per se theory, the plaintiff must be within the class of persons protected by the statute or ordinance and the statute must be designed to protect the class of persons from the type of harm that occurred. For example, suppose a restaurant serves maggot-infested meat to its customers. This violates several state and local health statutes. Suppose Kent ate at the restaurant and became ill. He would fall within the class of persons protected by the health statutes that require restaurants to serve wholesome food to patrons. The restaurant's violation of the statutes would be considered negligence per se, and Kent would have an excellent cause of action against the establishment.

Absolute Liability Mislabeled as Negligence Per Se

Courts occasionally equate negligence per se with strict, or absolute, liability. However, the two tort theories are distinct. Negligence per se simply presumes negligence because of the tortfeasor's violation of a statute. Negligence is based upon the tortfeasor's failure to exercise reasonable care. Absolute liability holds the tortfeasor accountable, regardless of fault, for doing an abnormally dangerous activity. No degree of care is sufficient to avoid strict liability.

This confusion between absolute liability and negligence per se occurs because of the outcomes in each type of case. If the defendant violates a negligence statute, he or she automatically is presumed negligent. Liability is almost as certain as in strict liability cases. Thus, the two concepts are often equated, although they are substantially different.

Toxic Torts as Negligence Per Se

Statutes sometimes declare that violations of regulations regarding the transportation, disposal, or management of hazardous or toxic substances create a presumption of negligence as a matter of law. These statutory provisions boost plaintiffs' causes of action against tortfeasors who carelessly control abnormally dangerous materials.

Not every statutory violation is negligence per se. All elements must be satisfied for the doctrine to apply. The following hypotheticals further demonstrate this principle.

⎯ HYPOTHETICALS ⎯

Woodrow Smelter was driving his automobile at night along the Old River Road. Although it was pitch black, he did not have his headlights on. This violated a local county ordinance and state statute requiring headlight use at all times beginning an hour before sundown and ending an hour after sunrise. Woodrow collided with Bertha Godfrey, a pedestrian walking along the side of the road. Bertha sues Woodrow for negligence per se. Was he?

By driving without headlights, Woodrow violated an ordinance and statute that required motor vehicles to use lights at night. This was intended to protect other drivers and pedestrians from "invisible" vehicles hitting them in the dark. Bertha falls within the classification of persons protected by the statute and ordinance. Therefore, she could successfully sue Woodrow for negligence per se.

* * *

Consider another hypothetical. Barfly Beer Company sells "Brewster's Choice," a "light" beer low in calories. One of its distributors, the Barley Brothers Emporium, sells the product in town. A state health statute requires any manufacturer or seller of items for human consumption to distribute them in containers free from foreign substances. Barley collected empty bottles to send back to Barfly to be cleaned and reused. Sometimes, drinkers would put cigarette butts into the bottles.

Neither Barley nor Barfly checked the bottles for foreign substances; they were simply sent back to the Barfly plant, refilled, and redistributed. Leigh Ann drank one of the beers from a bottle with a cigarette butt floating in the bottom. As one might imagine, Leigh Ann became physically ill as a result. Aside from the clear products liability issue, has Barfly or Barley been negligent per se?

The health statute was intended to protect consumers like Leigh Ann from injuries caused by foreign objects floating inside beverage bottles. Barfly and Barley each violated the statute. Their negligence may be presumed. ∎

Table 3-4 summarizes negligence per se.

TABLE 3-4
Elements of
negligence
per se

Defendant's actions are automatically considered negligent because they violated a negligence statute or ordinance
Plaintiff must fall within class of persons protected by statute
Defendant's actions must fall within the area for which the statute was created
Defendant's statutory violation must proximately cause plaintiff's injuries
Negligence defenses apply to negligence per se

Summary

In premises liability, owners and occupiers of land owe special duties of reasonable care to individuals who are injured while visiting the premises. Traditionally, courts have defined these duties differently, depending upon the injured party's status on the realty. There are three such distinctions: trespasser, licensee, and invitee. Land owners owe no duty of reasonable care to trespassers; they must simply refrain from intentionally injuring trespassers. Special rules, called attractive nuisance theory, apply to trespassing children. Licensees are persons that the owners permit to come onto their real estate. To licensees, land owners owe a duty to correct known dangers on the premises. Land owners owe a duty to discover and correct unknown risks on the premises for invitees, who have come onto the premises at the owners' expressed or implied invitation. The owner may limit the places on the land to which such invitation extends. Many courts have abandoned this three-tier analysis in favor of regular negligence theory.

Vicarious liability is the liability of one person (principal) for the negligent actions of another (agent). Many vicarious liability situations involve employer/employee relationships. Under the doctrine of respondeat superior, the employer must answer to the injured party for the employee's negligence when the employee has acted within the scope of his or her employment. This normally involves assigned tasks during normal working hours. Special rules apply for employees coming to and going from work, and for employees who frolic and detour from assigned tasks to pursue personal pleasures. A person hiring independent contractors is not vicariously liable for their negligence. Many states have motor vehicle consent statutes holding a vehicle owner liable for another driver's negligence.

Negligent infliction of emotional distress occurs when the tortfeasor engages in conduct that produces a reasonably foreseeable mental injury in a reasonably foreseeable victim. Many states have different rules to decide negligent infliction cases. A few courts require that the tortfeasor cause some physical impact to the emotionally distressed victim. Many courts hold that mental anguish is recoverable when accompanied by physical manifestations or symptoms. Others allow bystanders to recover when they witness negligent injuries to other people when the bystanders fall within the zone of danger. Courts that follow California's reasoning base liability upon foreseeability, using physical manifestations, physical proximity, family connection, and whether the bystander witnessed the injury to determine the outcome of negligent infliction litigation.

Negligence per se is any activity that violates a negligence statute. It is considered automatic negligence simply because the defendant's conduct violated the statutory provisions. To recover damages, the plaintiff must fall within the class of persons that the statute was intended to protect. The same defenses apply to negligence per se that apply to ordinary negligence cases. Furthermore, the defendant's statutory violation must have proximately caused the plaintiff's injuries.

Key Terms

attractive nuisance	impact rule	occupier
attractive nuisance doctrine	independent contractor	physical manifestations rule
(attraction theory)	invitee	respondeat superior
coming and going rule	licensee	scope of employment
emotional distress	negligence per se	sensory perception rule
family relationships rule	negligent infliction of	vicarious liability
frolic and detour rule	emotional distress	zone of danger rule

Problems

In the following hypotheticals, determine which type of special negligence action applies, if any. For sake of convenience, use the three-tier analysis for landowner/occupier liability.

1. "Softy" Clydesdale rents an apartment from Whisperwood Property Management, Inc. His next-door neighbor, Leslie Steymore, frequently visits to watch basketball on Softy's big-screen television. Softy had a can of aerosol cleaner in his utility closet. He set the can too close to the gas furnace, and the can slowly became overheated. One evening while watching the game, Leslie dropped and broke a glass. She opened the utility closet to fetch a broom to clean up the mess. Unfortunately, the cleaner can exploded just as she opened the closet door, injuring her severely.

2. Emily Waters owns a pasture outside of town upon which she has her cattle and horses graze. Ted Virtue sometimes crosses the pasture as a shortcut to work. All around the property are posted signs stating in clear, red-and-black letters, "NO TRESPASSING! YES, *YOU!*" One day Emily saw Ted cutting across her land and warned him not to continue doing so in the future. Ted ignored the warning. Weeks later, Ted fell into a mud bog (which he could not see, because it was covered by fallen leaves). He sank to his chest and could not escape. He remained there for three days until a passing postal carrier stumbled upon his predicament. Ted suffered from severe malnutrition and exposure from the incident. As a result, he contracted pneumonia and was hospitalized for two weeks.

3. Davis Marlowe operates a beauty shop. Margaret Vestibule comes in regularly for perms and haircuts. One of Davis's employees, Flower Wilson, absentmindedly left her electric shears on the seat of one of the hair dryers. Davis did not notice the shears when he had Margaret sit in that chair to dry her newly permed hair. Unknown to everybody, the shears had an electrical short. When Davis turned on the hair dryer, the shears shorted out and electrocuted Margaret, who was unkowningly sitting against the shears.

4. Susan Rayfield hired Grass Goddess, a lawn care company, to fertilize and water her yard. One of the company's employees, Sylvester Pell, incorrectly mixed the fertilizer so that it contained 12 times the necessary amount of potassium. Pell applied this mixture to Susan's grass. Honey Kinfinch, Susan's neighbor, came to Susan's party that night and played volleyball in the backyard. She frequently fell and rolled on the grass while diving to return the ball over the net. The next day, Honey developed a painful rash all over her body. She usually noticed these symptoms, although less severely, when she ate bananas, which are high in potassium.

5. John Stokely is a sales executive for a local automobile dealership. He often drives to the manufacturing facility 150 miles from the dealership to check on new orders. John's employer reimburses him for gasoline, food, and lodging, and provides John with a dealer car to drive. While driving to the manufacturing plant, John decided to stop by his cousin's house for dinner. His boss accompanied him on the visit "to get a decent meal for a change." While on the way there, John collided with and injured a motorcyclist.

6. Tilford Matthews has a five-year-old son with whom he often plays catch in the front yard. Sometimes the wind catches their ball and blows it into the street. Tilford has warned his son never to chase the ball into the road, but one day, when the ball blew into the street, Tilford's son ran after it. A truck driver swerved and struck the boy with the edge of the vehicle's bumper. The child suffered only a few bruises and scrapes. Tilford, however, developed a nervous twitch, ulcers, and an extreme sensitivity to sudden movements. He lost weight and experienced terrible nightmares about the incident.

Review Questions

1. Define the three classes of plaintiffs to whom land owners and occupiers owe duties of reasonable care.

2. Describe the land owner/occupier's duty of reasonable care to trespassers. Does the rule apply to all trespassers?

3. What is attractive nuisance? To which type of plaintiffs would the doctrine apply? Why is the land owner/occupier's duty of reasonable care different for these plaintiffs?

4. Using common-law principles, discuss the land owner/occupier's duty of reasonable care to licensees. How do licensees differ from trespassers? From invitees?

5. Using common-law principles, what duty of reasonable care does the land owner/occupier owe to invitees? Why and how are invitees distinguishable from licensees and trespassers?

6. Explain how you might use traditional negligence theory to determine land owners'/occupiers' liability to persons injured on the real estate. Do you find this approach easier than the three-tier analysis discussed in problem 1? Why or why not?

7. Define vicarious liability. What types of relationships involve this theory? What is respondeat superior? Explain scope of employment, the coming and going rule, and the frolic and detour rule. Why are these important to your analysis? How does vicarious liability relate to independent contractors? To motor vehicle owners or passengers?

8. Explain negligent infliction of emotional distress. What are its elements? In what types of factual situations would the tort apply? Describe the different analytical approaches to this tort. Define the impact rule, the physical manifestations rule, the zone of danger rule, the family relationships rule, and the sensory perception rule. How have the California courts combined these concepts in negligent infliction cases?

9. What is negligence per se? How does negligence per se differ from negligence?

Projects

1. Which special negligence actions discussed in this chapter are included in your state's common law? Are any controlled by statute? Has your state legislature enacted a motor vehicle consent statute?

2. Suppose a partner in your firm asks you to interview a potential client about an alleged negligent infliction of emotional distress claim. What issues will you need to cover to have sufficient information to state a cause of action for negligent infliction of emotional distress in your jurisdiction?

Internet Resources

This chapter focuses on special negligence actions. To learn more about special negligence actions, the following sites can be accessed:

General Information
http://www.findlaw.com
http://www.law.emory.edu/LAW/refdesk/subject/tort.html
http://www.lawguru.com/search/lawsearch.html
http://www.prairielaw.com/
http://www.courttv.com/legaldocs/

For additional resources, visit our Web site at
www.paralegal.delmar.cengage.com

CHAPTER 4

DEFENSES TO NEGLIGENCE

CHAPTER OUTLINE

§ 4.1 Introduction
§ 4.2 How Negligence Defenses Are Used
§ 4.3 Contributory Negligence and Last Clear Chance
§ 4.4 Comparative Negligence
§ 4.5 Assumption of Risk
§ 4.6 Statutes of Limitations

EQUAL JUSTICE UNDER LAW

—⟨ ◆ ⟩—

The business of the law is to make sense of the
confusion of what we call human life—to reduce
it to order but at the same time to give it
possibility, scope, even dignity.
ARCHIBALD MACLEISH

§ 4.1 Introduction

Tort defenses are an important protection for defendants. They provide legal justification for the defendants' actions.

Defendants' defenses excuse negligent behavior. In effect, defenses provide defendants with a blame-shifting weapon. Negligence defenses examine any plaintiff misconduct that was involved in causing the plaintiff's injuries. Even though the tortfeasor was negligent toward the victim, the tortfeasor's mischief may be forgiven (totally or partially) because of the victim's participation in producing his or her injuries.

This chapter discusses:

♦ How negligence defenses are used

♦ Contributory negligence

♦ Last clear chance

♦ Comparative negligence

♦ Assumption of risk

♦ Statutes of limitations.

§ 4.2 How Negligence Defenses Are Used

Once the plaintiff has alleged a cause of action for negligence in the complaint, it is assumed that the defendant has no defense unless he or she pleads one (or more) in his or her answer. Always remember these basic analytical rules:

1. *Negligence defenses are used only by the defendant against the plaintiff.*

   Put more generally, these defenses are responses to negligence allegations. The party alleged to have been negligent can use defenses against the party alleging negligence. In cases involving counterclaims, in which the defendant counter-sues the plaintiff, remember that the defendant becomes a counter-plaintiff against the original plaintiff, who becomes a counter-defendant, at least as far as the counterclaim is concerned. The same holds true for third-party complaints and answers.

2. *Negligence defenses are applied only in response to the plaintiff's allegations that the defendant acted negligently or with willful and wanton negligence, not to claims of intentional action.*

   Again, in counterclaims and third-party claims, remember who is the alleging party and who is the alleged wrongdoer. In a counterclaim, the defendant might allege that the plaintiff acted negligently toward the defendant. Retitle the parties to reflect their new roles toward each other with respect to the counterclaim. The counter-defendant (i.e., the plaintiff) would be entitled to use negligence defenses against the counter-plaintiff (i.e., the defendant).

   The same is true for third-party claims. Recall that defendants may become third-party plaintiffs, bringing third-party defendants who were not a part of the lawsuit into the litigation through **impleader**. The scenario is this: A plaintiff sues a defendant, alleging that a tort has been committed. The defendant impleads a third-party defendant for that third party's participation in committing the tort. Negligence defenses are available to the third-party defendant against the third-party plaintiff's negligence claims.

3. *Ask who is alleging negligence and who is alleged to have been negligent.*

   The alleged tortfeasor, usually the defendant, is the person who may utilize defenses.

implead Bring into a lawsuit. For example, if A sues B and B sues C in the same lawsuit, B *impleads* C, and the process is *impleader*.

§ 4.3 Contributory Negligence and Last Clear Chance

With this fundamental approach in mind, it is time to examine contributory negligence, used by a minority of jurisdictions. The majority use comparative negligence as a primary defense, which is described later in this chapter.

Contributory Negligence Defined

Contributory negligence is the plaintiff's own negligence that contributed to his or her injuries. The elements of contributory negligence include duty, breach, causation, and injury.

Duty of Care to Oneself

Suppose that Zelda is speeding while driving to school. Suppose that another driver runs a stop sign and the vehicles collide with one another. By

contributory negligence
Negligent (careless) conduct by a person who was harmed by another person's negligence; a plaintiff's failure to be careful that is a part of the cause of his or her injury when the defendant's failure to be careful is also part of the cause.

failing to stop at the sign, the other driver breached the duty of reasonable care to other vehicle users such as Zelda. The other driver's negligence proximately caused injuries to Zelda and her vehicle. However, because Zelda was speeding, she contributed to her own injuries.

Common Law Rule

At common law, contributory negligence barred the plaintiff from recovering any damages from the defendant. Even if the defendant were negligent in causing 99 percent of the plaintiff's harm, and the plaintiff were only 1 percent contributorily negligent, the courts ruled that the plaintiff could collect nothing against the defendant. There are very few states that still use contributory negligence as a defense. Because of the harshness of the rule, courts have sought ways to avoid it.

Last Clear Chance

last clear chance doctrine The legal principle that a person injured in (or having property harmed by) an accident may win damages even when negligent if the person causing the damage, while also negligent, could have avoided the accident after discovering the danger and if the person injured could not have. This rule is not accepted in every state and, where accepted, has many different forms (and names).

When a defendant uses the contributory negligence defense against a plaintiff, the plaintiff has a responsive weapon to defeat this defense. This is called **last clear chance** and is a rebuttal to a contributory negligence defense. Last clear chance theory states that, although the plaintiff was contributorily negligent in causing his or her own injuries, the defendant had the last opportunity to avert harm and failed to do so; therefore, the plaintiff can still recover.

In other words, the defendant cannot escape liability for his or her negligence (by invoking the contributory negligence defense) if the defendant had the last clear chance to avoid the injury.

Table 4-1 summarizes the elements of contributory negligence and last clear chance.

TABLE 4-1
Contributory negligence and last clear chance

Contributory Negligence	Last Clear Chance
Plaintiff's duty of reasonable care to himself or herself	Although plaintiff was contributorily negligent, defendant had the last reasonable opportunity to avoid harming plaintiff (as a consequence of defendant's negligence)
Plaintiff breaches duty	Nullifies contributory negligence defense
Plaintiff acts, or fails to act, which contributes to his or her injuries (causation and proximate cause)	Plaintiff uses last clear chance to respond to defendant's use of contributory negligence defense
Plaintiff is injured	

§ 4.4 Comparative Negligence

comparative negligence A legal rule, used in many states, by which the amount of "fault" on each side of an accident is measured and the side with less fault is given damages according to the difference between the magnitude of each side's fault.

The comparative negligence defense has replaced contributory negligence in most states' common law or statutes. Since the 1960s, courts and legislatures increasingly have adopted the defense as an alternative to the rigid, unfair results that contributory negligence often produced. The defense of comparative negligence enables the defendant's liability to be adjusted according to the extent of the plaintiff's contribution to his or her own injuries. **Comparative negligence** may be defined as a measurement and comparison of the plaintiff's and the defendant's negligence in causing the plaintiff's injuries.

Elements

The comparative negligence defense has three elements:

1. The plaintiff was negligent in contributing to his or her own injuries.
2. Calculation of the percentage of the plaintiff's negligence that contributed to his or her injuries.
3. Calculation of the percentage of the defendant's negligence that produced the plaintiff's injuries.

In some jurisdictions, a fourth element is included: the defendant must have been more negligent than the plaintiff.

The Balancing Act

culpability factoring (liability apportionment)† A defense to negligence. When the plaintiff's negligence contributed to his or her injuries, comparative negligence calculates the percentage of the defendant's and the plaintiff's negligence and adjusts the plaintiff's damages according to the numbers. The trier-of-fact decides the percentages.

Comparative negligence balances the degrees of each party's negligence that produced the plaintiff's harm. In effect, the plaintiff's and defendant's negligence are compared to see which was more responsible for causing injury. This comparative negligence balancing is typically measured in percentages of negligence. This is sometimes called **culpability factoring** (**liability apportionment**).

For instance, consider the speeding/stop sign example discussed earlier in this chapter. The defendant ran a stop sign. This is more negligent than merely speeding, as the plaintiff's speeding alone would not have produced the accident. It took the greater negligence of the defendant (i.e., failing to stop at the sign) to cause the damage. The defendant was more negligent than the plaintiff in that example. But what percentages of negligence would be assigned to the plaintiff (for contributing to the injuries) and the defendant (for negligently causing the harm)? Well, the defendant was more than half responsible, so the defendant's percentage must be higher than 50 percent. What percentages would be used? Defendant 75 percent, plaintiff 25 percent? 60/40? 90/10?

Readers may find this approach frustrating. What are the correct percentages? There is no exact formula. It depends upon the facts of each case. Whatever percentages are selected, readers and triers-of-fact probably rely on intuition and gut feeling as much as anything.

Who Decides the Percentages

The trier-of-fact decides the percentages in comparative negligence. Thus, the jury (or judge, in a bench trial) must closely examine the facts and assign negligence percentages to the plaintiff and the defendant.

Why Calculate Percentages

Comparative negligence is used to calculate the amount of the defendant's liability to the plaintiff. Assume that the following percentages were selected for the speeding/stop sign problem: defendant 75 percent negligent, plaintiff 25 percent negligent. What would be the outcome of the case? The defendant would be liable to the plaintiff for 75 percent of the amount plaintiff received in damages. If the plaintiff recovered judgment against the defendant, receiving a $100,000 damages award, under this percentage the defendant would be liable for $75,000, with $25,000 having been subtracted out for the plaintiff's comparative negligence.

The advantages of comparative negligence are immediately apparent. Instead of completely barring the plaintiff's recovery (as common-law contributory negligence would have done), culpability factoring enables the plaintiff to recover damages for the defendant's share of responsibility in causing the injuries. Liability apportionment also protects the defendant from paying for the plaintiff's share in harming himself or herself. The result is a just and equitable outcome to the litigation. It allows a plaintiff to bring an action even though he or she is somewhat at fault.

Criticism of Comparative Negligence

Comparative negligence has been criticized for its arbitrary and capricious approach to assigning percentages of negligence. Critics complain that liability apportionment is imprecise and based entirely upon the emotional attitudes of the jury or judge. Think back to the speeding/stop sign illustration. If one disapproved of running stop signs more than speeding, would one not be more likely to raise the defendant's percentage of liability? Of course, juries are composed of several people, a fact that is intended to balance out such personal biases. Still, disapproval of comparative negligence continues in legal literature and court opinions.

Table 4-2 on page 99 lists the elements of comparative negligence.

The Case of the Un-Easy Rider

Negligence is contagious. Those around a careless person sometimes find themselves infected by carefree, irresponsible attitudes. As a result, it is occasionally difficult to determine the degree to which each party is at fault.

The old contributory negligence defense made no effort to apportion fault. It simply and arbitrarily torpedoed the plaintiff's action if he or she were the least bit at fault for his or her injuries. As § 4.4 discusses, comparative negligence attempts to resolve this unfairness. The following case discusses last clear chance and contributory and comparative negligence, as modified by Arizona statute.

DYKEMAN
v.
ENGLEBRECHT

Court of Appeals of Arizona
166 Ariz. 398, 803 P.2d 119 (1990)
August 16, 1990
Voss, Presiding Judge

Appellant/Plaintiff Heidi Leigh Dykeman appeals from a jury verdict finding her 60 percent at fault and apportioning damages accordingly. She raises the following issue on appeal:

Did the trial court err by refusing to instruct the jury on the last clear chance doctrine?

* * *

Plaintiff, a passenger on a motorcycle driven by defendant, was injured when the motorcycle hit a curb during a turn. Defendant contended that plaintiff jerked and improperly shifted her weight during the turn, causing the accident. Both plaintiff and defendant had been drinking alcoholic beverages. It is undisputed that plaintiff was very intoxicated at the time of the accident, and that defendant had a blood alcohol content of .128 two hours after the accident.

* * *

Plaintiff contends that the trial court erred by refusing to give the jury an instruction regarding the last clear chance doctrine. She argues that defendant had the last clear chance to avoid the accident when he allowed her to get on the motorcycle in an inebriated condition. Defendant asserts that last clear

chance is not applicable, and, in any event the doctrine was effectively abolished by the enactment of [Ariz. Rev. Stat.] § 12-2505, the comparative negligence statute in Arizona.

Prior to the enactment of Arizona's comparative negligence statute, a contributory negligence defense could preclude a plaintiff, whose own negligence contributed in any degree to his injury, from recovering from a negligent defendant. The last clear chance doctrine was judicially created to alleviate the harshness of the contributory negligence rule. Arizona recognized this doctrine. The doctrine provides that a contributorily negligent plaintiff may recover from a negligent defendant if:

1. The plaintiff could not have avoided the injury after he negligently subjected himself to risk of harm;
2. The defendant knew or should have known of the plaintiff's perilous situation; and,
3. The defendant had the last clear chance to avoid the harm by the exercise of reasonable care and failed to do so.

The doctrine has been criticized because of the confusion it creates in the law of torts.

In 1984 our state legislature enacted the Uniform Contribution Among Tortfeasors Act. This legislation established comparative negligence in Arizona. The statute provides:

[Ariz. Rev. Stat.] § 12-2505
  The defense of contributory negligence or of assumption of risk is in all cases a question of fact and shall at all times be left to the jury If the jury applies either defense, the

claimant's action is not barred, but the full damages shall be reduced in proportion to the relative degree of the claimant's fault which is a proximate cause of the injury or death, if any.

Under this statute a negligent plaintiff is not prohibited from recovering from a negligent defendant; instead his award is reduced by the percentage of his own fault.

Plaintiff asserts that last clear chance remains a viable doctrine despite Arizona's adoption of comparative negligence. We disagree and agree with the jurisdictions that have found that the last clear chance doctrine is superfluous in a comparative negligence system.

The last clear chance doctrine was specifically created to enable a negligent plaintiff to recover from a negligent defendant in a contributory negligence system. However, its application in a comparative negligence system would directly contravene the intent of the statute because [last clear chance] provides complete recovery to a negligent plaintiff rather than apportioning recovery based upon degrees of fault. An instruction on the doctrine, then, would misstate the law and confuse the jury. ...

Additionally, the doctrine is unnecessary in a comparative negligence system. By definition, comparative negligence avoids the harshness inherent in an all-or-nothing contributory negligence system because it "distribute[s] responsibility, in proportion to the degree of fault attributable to the parties who have negligently caused an injury." A comparative negligence system, then, accomplishes the same result as the last clear chance doctrine as it enables a negligent plaintiff to recover from a negligent defendant. The trial court correctly refused the instruction.

* * *

Affirmed.

Case Questions

1. Which do you consider the more just doctrines: (a) contributory negligence and last clear chance, or (b) comparative negligence? Do you agree with this court's opinion? Explain.
2. Has your state adopted a statute similar to the Arizona statute discussed here?

— HYPOTHETICAL

Ikeda Osaka manages and owns a hotel. Frances Borgioni is a guest. The smoke detector in Frances's room has a dead battery and does not function. None of Ikeda's employees has checked the detector recently, despite a management protocol instructing maintenance to check batteries every month. The customer staying in the room next to Frances's smoked in bed and started a fire. Smoke poured under the door adjoining the two rooms, but the malfunctioning detector did not awaken Frances before the room became filled with smoke. Frances awoke, coughing, and stumbled to the hallway door. He could not get the door open, however, because he had placed his own safety lock on the door, and that lock jammed as he was trying to escape. Frances passed out from smoke inhalation and suffered severe burns. Fortunately, the fire department rescued him.

Frances sued Ikeda for negligently failing to maintain an operative smoke detector in the room. Ikeda responded that Frances had contributed to his own injuries by placing his own lock on the door, so that he could not escape. May Ikeda invoke the defense of comparative negligence?

Was Ikeda negligent in failing to maintain a functioning smoke detector in Frances's room? Analyze the facts and apply the elements of negligence. If one decides that Ikeda was negligent (which is arguably the correct answer), then the comparative negligence defense should next be considered. Apply its elements. Was Frances negligent in contributing to his own injuries? Frances breached his duty of reasonable care to himself by placing a defective lock on the door, which prevented his escape during the fire. But for this act, Frances could have escaped before passing out from the smoke. Frances was negligent in harming himself. Next, decide if Ikeda's negligence exceeded Frances's. Would Frances have been endangered by the smoke at all if the smoke detector had activated? This would have given Frances more time to escape the room before the smoke thickened and knocked him unconscious. Ikeda's negligence exceeded Frances's. Now use liability apportionment. What percentages would be assigned? Ikeda's must be at least 51 percent. 60/40? 70/30? 80/20? There is no single correct answer here. A juror must use his or her best judgment based upon the facts.■

TABLE 4-2
Comparative
negligence

Elements of Comparative Negligence
Plaintiff was negligent in contributing to his or her own injuries (defendant was also negligent in causing plaintiff's injuries)
Culpability factoring (liability apportionment): Calculate each party's percentage of negligence [How much did plaintiff contribute to his or her own injuries?] [How much was defendant responsible for plaintiff's harm?]
In some jurisdictions, defendant's percentage of negligence must be greater than plaintiff's percentage of negligence

§ 4.5 Assumption of Risk

assumption of risk
Knowingly and
willingly exposing
yourself (or your
property) to the
possibility of harm.

Assumption of risk is another defense to negligence. **Assumption of risk** means that the plaintiff assumed the risk of doing (or not doing) something that resulted in his or her injuries. Assumption of risk involves (1) the plaintiff's voluntary assumption of a known risk (2) with a full appreciation of the dangers involved in facing that risk. It is important to note that not all risks are assumed; just those that are reasonable.

Voluntary Assumption of Known Risk

For the assumption-of-risk defense to insulate the defendant from negligence liability, the plaintiff must have voluntarily decided to engage in an activity that the plaintiff knew (or reasonably should have known) was dangerous. In other words, the plaintiff must willfully face a known risk.

For instance, suppose Gilda's employer orders her to carry stacked boxes down a long flight of stairs. Her employer specifically instructs her to carry all the boxes in a single trip. To do this, however, Gilda must hold the boxes in front of her, blocking her forward vision. She knows that it is dangerous to descend stairs when she cannot see where she is going. Gilda slips and falls because her right foot misses a step. She sues her employer for negligence. The employer alleges that Gilda assumed the risk. Did she? No. Gilda did not voluntarily assume the dangerous activity. In fact, she was coerced into carrying all the boxes in one trip. She would not have done so but for her employer's command. Thus, Gilda did not voluntarily assume the risk of falling down the stairway.

Suppose that Brian slipped on some liquid somebody had spilled on the stairway. Brian thought the stairs were clean and dry, because he had walked up them just a few minutes earlier. He was unaware of the new danger that had appeared to threaten his safety. Brian did not assume a known risk.

Suppose that Gilda was carrying the boxes into a storeroom instead of down a stairway. The room was pitch black, and she knew that the ceiling lightbulb was burned out. Nevertheless, she carried the boxes into the room in which she could not clearly see. Gilda stumbled over a mop and broom on the floor, and the boxes fell upon and injured her. Again, she sues her employer for negligence in failing to replace the burned-out bulb. Her employer replies that Gilda voluntarily assumed a known risk—she knew the bulb was burned out. Further, she knew that the room was so dark that it would take her eyes several minutes to adjust. Still, she entered the room despite the obvious danger that she could fall over invisible objects. Gilda assumed the risk in this version of the facts.

Full Appreciation of Danger

The plaintiff must fully understand the dangerous nature of the activity that he or she voluntarily undertakes. Suppose that Brett visits a friend's woods. He comes across a cavern and decides to explore it. He has no way of knowing that higher above him, on a nearby hill, a highway construction crew is preparing to detonate dynamite. They explode a powerful charge, which sends a shock wave through the ground and causes part of the cavern walls to collapse, trapping Brett inside the cave. He sues the highway company for negligence in detonating excessively powerful explosives. Run through the negligence formula to determine if the company was negligent toward Brett, closely examining foreseeability of the injury and foreseeable plaintiffs theory. Presuming that the company acted negligently, it responds with the defense of assumption of risk.

Did Brett voluntarily assume a known risk with a full appreciation of the dangers involved? He willfully entered the cave. He knew (or reasonably should have known) that cavern walls sometimes fall in. That risk was known, but he had no way to anticipate the additional danger created by a forceful explosion. He did not fully appreciate this aspect of the risk in entering the cave. Arguably, the dynamite was also an unknown risk to him. Thus, the company's defense would fail.

Proof of Assumption of Risk

There are two categories of assumption of risk. In *express assumption-of-risk* cases, a plaintiff voluntarily assumes a known risk by an express agreement. An example of this would be a plaintiff being given an agreement with a release clause to sign, thus acknowledging a particular danger associated with an activity and agreeing not to hold the other party liable; for example, a boxing match. This express assumption is valid so long as it does not violate public policy, such as a situation in which there is unequal bargaining power between the parties.

In *implied assumption of risk*, a plaintiff accepts a risk knowingly and voluntarily by reason of the plaintiff's knowledge. In implied assumption, while there is no express agreement, the assumption is implied based upon a party's conduct; for example, a plaintiff entering a barricaded structure despite seeing a large no-entry sign at the entrance. Just as with express assumption cases, the implied assumption cannot violate public policy.

The Complete Defense

Assumption of risk is a complete defense to negligence in some jurisdictions. Like common-law contributory negligence, it totally bars the plaintiff's recovery. If the plaintiff assumed the risk, the defendant cannot be liable for negligence.

Assumption of the risk is commonly raised in spectator sport situations. There is a known risk that if you attend a baseball game, you might get hit by a ball hit into the stands. Likewise, observers of speed car races or demolition derbies might get hit by a car or piece of equipment hurled into the air. A spectator assumes these risks with full appreciation of the dangers and thus is barred from bringing suit as a result of any injuries sustained. Conversely, consider a situation in which bleachers collapse at a football stadium. Seats caving in is not a known or foreseeable risk, nor could the dangers be appreciated; thus, in this case assumption of the risk would not apply and suit would be allowed.

Assumption of risk is somewhat more difficult to establish than contributory or comparative negligence. The following example demonstrates how the elements must be carefully considered.

⟨◆⟩

The Case of the Speedway Release

When plaintiffs and defendants share a negligent experience, it is inevitable that the defendants will argue assumption of risk. Because the plaintiff volunteered to share the dangers, he or she should not recover, says the defendant.

Notice: This opinion has not been released for publication in the permanent law reports. Until released, it is subject to revision or withdrawal.

DEAN & a.
v.
MacDONALD

Supreme Court of New Hampshire
147 N.H. 263, 786 A.2d 834
December 10, 2001

Mr. Dean became involved in automobile racing in 1968. In August 1998, while attending a race at the Lee USA Speedway (the Speedway), he sought entrance to the pit area to work on a race car. Before entering the pit area, he was required to sign a "Release and Waiver of Liability and Indemnity Agreement" (Release) that purported to release the defendants from liability for negligence claims. On the approximately six other occasions on which Mr. Dean entered the pit area at the Speedway, he was required to sign a similar form. He has also signed a form each time he entered the pit area of any race track in the five years preceding the accident.

* * *

The bottom portion of the Release stated that the signer "acknowledges and agrees that the activities of the event are very dangerous and involve the risk of serious injury and/or death and that the signer has read and signed the Release voluntarily. The signature lines also stated, "THIS IS A RELEASE OF LIABILITY" and "I HAVE READ THIS RELEASE."

Mr. Dean signed the Release before entering the infield pit area. At some point, he left the infield pit area to measure tires. Before crossing the track to return to the infield, he waited for a race official to indicate that it was safe to cross. Once the official so indicated, Mr.

Dean began to cross the track and was struck by a race car doing practice laps.

Mr. Dean brought a negligence claim and his wife brought a loss of consortium claim. The defendants moved for summary judgment upon the negligence claim, arguing that it was barred by the Release. ...

On appeal, Mr. Dean argues that the Release is unenforceable because: (1) he did not contemplate the risk that he would be injured while crossing the track at a race official's direction; (2) he was not given an opportunity to read the release; and (3) the Release failed to identify the defendants by name.

* * *

Although New Hampshire law generally prohibits exculpatory contracts, we will enforce them if: (1) they do not violate public policy; (2) the plaintiff understood the import of the agreement or a reasonable person in his position would have understood the import of the agreement; and (3) the plaintiff's claims were within the contemplation of the parties when they executed the contract. ...

"As long as the language of the release clearly and specifically indicates the intent to release the defendant from liability for personal injury caused by the defendant's negligence, the agreement will be upheld."

Mr. Dean urges us to determine the scope of the Release according to his subjective intent, arguing that it was not intended to cover the risk that he would be injured while crossing the race track at an official's direction because neither he nor the defendants had ever known anyone to be injured in this way. We "judge the intent of the parties by objective criteria rather than the unmanifested states of mind of the parties," however.

* * *

This language "clearly and specifically" indicates the intent to release the defendants from liability for the consequences of their own negligence and is sufficient "to cover a broad range of accidents" occurring at automobile races. Moreover, Mr. Dean's claim fits within this broad scope. He sustained injuries while in or upon a restricted area (the racing surface) due to the alleged negligence of one of the Releasees (a race official).

* * *

The parties may not have contemplated the precise occurrence which resulted in plaintiff's accident, but this does not render the exculpatory clause inoperable. In adopting the broad language employed in the agreement, it seems reasonable to conclude that the parties contemplated the similarly broad range of accidents which occur in auto racing.

Although we hold that the Release was intended to apply to a broad range of accidents occurring in automobile racing, we observe that this range is not without limitation.

* * *

The risk of being hit by an automobile while on the racing surface of a race track is an ordinary risk inherent in the sport of automobile racing. "Driving competition vehicles on a racing surface during a race is inherently dangerous; attempting to walk on the surface during a race is flirting with a high risk of being seriously injured. Absent impaired mental faculties, one need not be an experienced spectator or competitor to recognize the potential for injury." ...

Affirmed and remanded

Case Questions

1. What risk did Mr. Dean assume?
2. What affect does signing a release have on assumption of the risk?

— HYPOTHETICAL

Erving Tanford owns East of Tansmania, a tanning salon. Elizabeth Bundy is one of Tanford's customers. She has been visiting the salon twice a week for ten years. She always uses the same tanning bed. Because of faulty equipment, Elizabeth was exposed during each session to five times more ultraviolet radiation than is normally emitted by tanning equipment. Elizabeth was diagnosed with skin cancer. She sues Tanford for subjecting her to excessively intense ultraviolet light, which is a powerful carcinogen. Tanford was negligent in exposing Elizabeth to such extremely high doses of ultraviolet radiation. Can he offer assumption of risk as a defense?

Did Elizabeth voluntarily assume a known risk with a full appreciation of the dangerous consequences? Clearly, she willfully visited the salon twice weekly for ten years. She chose to use the same bed each time. She knew (or reasonably should have known) that ultraviolet radiation is carcinogenic. But did she fully understand the danger? Did she realize that the equipment emitted five times more radiation than normal? Could she have known about this aspect of the threat? Not likely. Accordingly, she did not assume the risk, and the defense would not protect Tanford from liability.

Suppose a warning were posted above the tanning bed that Elizabeth used, declaring, "DANGER! EMITS EXCESSIVE ULTRAVIOLET LIGHT. USE AT YOUR OWN RISK." Now Elizabeth would have been alerted to the threatening condition. She would have a full appreciation of the dangers involved in using the equipment. Under this version of the facts, Elizabeth would have assumed the risk, and Tanford would not be liable for negligence. ■

Table 4-3 outlines the elements of assumption of risk.

TABLE 4-3
Assumption of risk

Elements of Assumption of Risk
Plaintiff voluntarily assumes a known risk
Plaintiff fully appreciates the dangers involved in facing the risk

§ 4.6 Statutes of Limitations

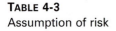

statutes of limitations Laws that set a maximum amount of time after something happens for it to be taken to court, such as a "three-year statute" for lawsuits based on a contract, or a "six-year statute" for a criminal prosecution.

Statutes of limitations are statutes restricting the time within which a plaintiff may file a lawsuit for particular causes of action against a defendant. (In some jurisdictions, these statutes are called *limitations of actions*.) There are also such statutes for negligence actions. Many of these statutes specify that various negligence lawsuits must be filed within two years of the negligent acts giving rise to the plaintiff's claims.

States' statutes of limitations vary in numbers of years and among the different types of negligence. The period for medical malpractice claims, for instance, may be two years in one state and three years in another. Similarly, lawsuits involving premises liability may have one-year statutes of limitations in one state and three-year statutes in another. One should become familiar with the specific statutes of limitations in one's own state for the various types of negligence causes of action.

Note that the statute of limitations is one of the few areas in the practice of law for which there is no remedy if one misses the deadline. Generally, there are provisions throughout the various civil practice acts that allow attorneys to amend, change, supplement pleadings, and remedy oversights in their handling of a case. Should a statute of limitations run out, though—no matter what the reason—judges are powerless to help you. Consequently, this is one of the areas in the practice of law in which malpractice claims most frequently arise.

Practical Application

To obtain malpractice insurance, attorneys must assure the malpractice insurance carrier that they have a reliable calendaring system. In fact, backup systems for recording important dates and deadlines are often required as well. Frequently, a paralegal is called upon to maintain a diary system and keep members of the firm alerted to approaching deadlines and dates. In addition, some firms automatically have all files pulled for review every three months, six months, and yearly to ensure that the cases are not being neglected.

The Case of Continuous Representation

The outcome of this lawsuit rests on the calculation of the applicable statute of limitations. In this case, the running of the statute of limitations for malpractice was found to be tolled or stopped, giving the plaintiff additional time in which to bring his action. Notice the ten-year lapse between the time the plaintiff initially sought legal counsel for his injuries and the time of this appeal.

POLLICINO
v.
ROEMER AND FEATHERSTONHAUGH P.C.

Supreme Court, Appellate Division, Third Department, New York
260 A.D.2d 52, 699 N.Y.S.2d 238
December 2, 1999

This appeal requires us to decide a question of first impression, namely, whether in a legal malpractice action a law firm's continuous representation of a client should be imputed to a former associate for purposes of tolling the Statute of Limitations against the associate. On the particular facts presented herein, we hold that it should be and reverse the contrary determination of Supreme Court.

On April 11, 1989, plaintiff retained the law firm of defendant Roemer and Featherstonhaugh P.C. (hereinafter the law firm) to represent him in connection with a July 1, 1988 accident wherein he lost sight in his right eye. His injury is alleged to have occurred when a New York City Transit Authority bus ran over a glass bottle, the bottle exploded and a shard of glass struck plaintiff in the eye. In September 1989, the law firm moved for leave to serve a late notice of claim against the Transit Authority. Attached to its moving papers was a proposed notice of claim reflecting the accident date of July 1, 1988. After the motion was granted, however, a notice of claim incorrectly listing the accident date as June 30, 1988 was served. ...

It was not until December 1, 1992 that the law firm moved on behalf of plaintiff for leave to serve an amended notice of claim to set forth the correct date of plaintiff's accident. ...

While a cause of action for legal malpractice accrues on the date on which the claimed malpractice occurred, under the rule of continuous representation the Statute of Limitations is tolled while representation on the same matter in which the malpractice is alleged is ongoing. A twofold rationale underlies this rule, which is derived from the "continuous treatment" doctrine earlier crafted in medical malpractice actions. First, having sought professional assistance, the client "'has a right to repose confidence in the professional's ability and good faith, and realistically cannot be expected to question and assess the techniques employed or the manner in which the services are rendered' ...

* * *

Here, it is uncontroverted that without application of the continuous representation rule, plaintiff's suit against defendant is time barred. The gravamen of plaintiff's malpractice claim is the erroneous accident date listed on the notice of claim, which led to dismissal of plaintiff's suit against the Transit Authority in 1994. His cause of action thus accrued when defendant allegedly committed the original error in November 1989 (or when he failed to correct it when a similar error in the summons and complaint was discovered and corrected in December 1989). Supreme Court held that since defendant's professional relationship with plaintiff ended when he left the law firm in September 1990, the rule of continuous representation did not apply. ... Supreme Court's decision, however, failed to squarely address the question presented: whether the law firm's continuous representation of plaintiff should be imputed to defendant so as to toll the Statute of Limitations against him.

We conclude that under the circumstances of this case, the principles underpinning the continuous representation rule militate in favor of its application to defendant. As a starting point, we observe that without application of this rule, the Statute of Limitations against defendant would have expired *before* plaintiff's

action against the Transit Authority was dismissed based on the faulty notice of claim. We also note that beginning in December 1992 and continuing through May 1997, the law firm undertook efforts to rectify the 1989 error which, if successful, would have rendered plaintiff's malpractice claim moot.

Critical to our resolution of the question, however, is the fact that in retaining the law firm to represent him, plaintiff forged his professional relationship with the firm, not with any individual attorney. Defendant, as well as several other associates, worked on plaintiff's case as employees or agents of the law firm, whose representation of plaintiff was continuous and uninterrupted until May 1997. ... Given the law firm's legal responsibility for the actions of defendant, its employee, commencing an action against defendant would have required plaintiff to sever his relationship with the law firm. Prevention of such a disruption in the professional relationship, together with any ongoing efforts, is a paramount value underlying the doctrine of continuous representation.

* * *

... "The Statute of Limitations was enacted to afford protection to defendants against defending stale claims after a reasonable period of time had elapsed during which a person of ordinary diligence would bring an action." Largely based on the same principles informing the continuous representation rule and rendering its application appropriate here, we do not believe it can be fairly said that plaintiff lacked diligence or failed to bring his action within a reasonable period of time.

Case Questions

1. Explain why the statute of limitations was tolled and what effect this had on the case.
2. How can you explain the ten-year passage of time between when legal counsel was originally retained and this appeal?
3. What lesson concerning the drafting of pleadings can a paralegal learn from this case?

Table 4-4 shows two typical statutes of limitations for negligence actions. Table 4-5 shows sample statutes of limitations for negligence by state.

TABLE 4-4 Sample negligence statutes of limitations

Two-Year Statute of Limitations (with three-year absolute limit for injuries not discovered within two years)	Three-Year Statute of Limitations
Connecticut General Statutes Annotated § 52-584 (West): No action to recover damages for injury to the person, or to real or personal property, caused by negligence, or by reckless or wanton misconduct, or by malpractice of a physician, surgeon, dentist, podiatrist, chiropractor, hospital or sanatorium, shall be brought but within two years from the date when the injury is first sustained or discovered or in the exercise of reasonable care should have been discovered, and except that no such action may be brought more than three years from the date of the act or omission complained of, except [for counterclaims].	New York Civil Practice Law & Rules § 214 (McKinney): The following actions must be commenced within three years: * * * 5. an action to recover damages for a personal injury except as provided in sections 214-b, 214-c and 215; . . . [providing special rules concerning specific torts and time injury was detected]

TABLE 4-5 Sample statutes of limitations for negligence actions by state

State	Negligence	Medical Malpractice
Alabama	2 years	2 years
California	1 year	3 years
Florida	4 years	2 years
Massachusetts	3 years	3 years
New York	3 years	2 years
Texas	2 years	2 years
Washington	3 years	3 years
Wyoming	4 years	2 years

Summary

Negligence defenses are used only by the defendant against the plaintiff. The defenses are applied only in response to the plaintiff's allegations that the defendant acted negligently. To determine which party uses negligence defenses, one should ask who is alleging negligence and who is alleged to have been negligent.

Contributory negligence is the plaintiff's negligence that contributed to his or her own injuries. The plaintiff was negligent toward himself or herself and caused (in whole or in part) the harm. This defense exonerates the defendant whose negligence harmed the plaintiff. At common law, any amount of contributory negligence by the plaintiff, however small, would bar the plaintiff's recovery against the negligent defendant. Critics have argued that this defense is unreasonably harsh. Last clear chance is the plaintiff's response to the contributory negligence defense. Last clear chance means that, although the plaintiff was contributorily negligent, the defendant still had the last opportunity to avoid harming the plaintiff. Last clear chance nullifies the contributory negligence defense.

Comparative negligence is an alternative defense that has largely replaced contributory negligence in both the common law and statute. Comparative negligence measures and compares the negligence of both the plaintiff and the defendant. This allows the trier-of-fact to adjust the plaintiff's recovery to reflect more accurately each party's degree of negligence in causing the harm. The calculation is often in percentages of negligence. This is sometimes called culpability factoring or liability apportionment. These percentages are based entirely upon the trier-of-fact's subjective opinion regarding the specific facts of each case. Critics have criticized the defense for this uncertainty.

Assumption of risk is another negligence defense. It states that the plaintiff voluntarily assumed a known risk with full appreciation of the dangers involved. Like contributory negligence, assumption of risk is a complete defense to negligence. In other words, it totally excuses the defendant's negligence and erases the defendant's liability to the plaintiff.

Most state statutes of limitations restrict the time period within which a plaintiff may file a negligence cause of action against a defendant. In most states, these are two-year statutes, meaning that a plaintiff has two years from the date that the negligent act was committed within which to file a lawsuit against the tortfeasor. It is vital to research the specific statutes of limitations for each particular tort.

Key Terms

assumption of risk
comparative negligence
contributory negligence
culpability factoring
(liability apportionment)
implead
last clear chance doctrine
statutes of limitations

Problems

In the following hypotheticals, determine which negligence defense applies, if any.

1. The Tàpàjós Inn, owned by Guillermo Estaben, has a swimming pool with no lifeguards on duty. The pool is surrounded by a high-wire fence, and access to the pool is restricted to guests, who must use their room keys to reach the facility. Signs posted in several places on the fencing read, in bold, black lettering: "NO LIFEGUARD ON DUTY. SWIM AT YOUR OWN RISK! NO DIVING, RUNNING, OR HORSE PLAY. ADULTS MUST SUPERVISE CHILDREN. BE CAREFUL!" Tony Harmon,

a 16-year-old, and his family are staying at the Inn. Tony and his 17-year-old girlfriend, Tanya Martin, went swimming in the pool after midnight. There were no signs indicating times when the pool was opened or closed. At 1:45 A.M., hotel maintenance activated the automatic pumps to drain the pool for cleaning. None of the Inn staff checked to see if the pool was being used. While swimming underwater, Tanya got her left foot caught in a pool drain as a result of the powerful suction of the pumps. She would have drowned had Tony not rescued her. She suffered torn tendons in her foot and ankle, and she developed an extreme phobia of water. She experienced nightmares and acute nervousness after the incident. There were no signs indicating that the pool could be drained remotely nor that the drains were dangerous when the pumps were running.

2. Farabee St. Claire owns an ice-skating rink. Charles and Martha Samuelson visited the rink on their 10th wedding anniversary. Charles had not skated since high school (15 years earlier), but Martha often went skating at the rink. Because of a broken thermostat, one corner of the ice thawed and a small puddle formed. As Charles skated through the water, he slipped and fell to the ice, breaking his right arm. Martha, who was skating close behind, collided with Charles and also fell to the ice, suffering a concussion. Martha was a talented skater and could have avoided Charles by leaping over his body, but she did not think to do so in her surprise and confusion.

3. The Happy Hollow Mental Hospital houses many emotionally disturbed individuals. One patient, Marjorie Magpie, a convicted arsonist, escaped from her maximum-security room. No guards were on duty in that part of the hospital, and an attendant had left Marjorie's door unlocked. As Marjorie wandered out of a wooded area onto a highway, she hitchhiked a ride from Pamela Sweetbird, who was driving back to the university at which she worked. Pamela noticed that Marjorie was dressed in a hospital gown and blue jeans, but Marjorie explained that she was a medical student at the university and often wore these gowns because they were comfortable. Pamela dropped Marjorie off at a bus stop located only a few hundred yards from Pamela's home. Marjorie saw Pamela stop at the house and then drive away again. Later that day, Pamela's house burned down. Police arrested Marjorie for having set the fire.

4. Beth Sageveil is an accountant. Pavel Rubenstein is one of her clients. Beth completed Pavel's federal and state tax returns for 1991. Beth made a critical addition error, however, and as a result, Pavel underpaid his taxes. Both the Internal Revenue Service and the State Department of Revenue assessed hefty penalties against Pavel for the underpayment. Pavel had signed the returns without reading them, although the instructions on each return clearly advised the taxpayer to read carefully through the returns to verify their accuracy, even if a professional tax preparer had been used.

5. Malt Finchley owns a sporting-goods store. Abraham Waite came in to buy a new shotgun. One of Malt's employees, Saul Demure, handed Abraham a shotgun that, unbeknownst to Saul or Abraham, was loaded. Neither Saul nor Abraham checked the gun to see if it was loaded. The trigger, however, had a keyed lock that prevented it from being pulled. Abraham asked that the lock be removed so that he could feel the trigger's sensitivity. Saul opened the lock and Abraham tested the trigger. The gun discharged, shooting another customer, Toby Benchsmith, in the stomach. Toby saw Abraham aim the gun in his general direction. Instead of stepping aside, Toby jokingly shouted, "Hey, don't shoot me, I'm on your side!"

Review Questions

1. How are negligence defenses used? Which party uses them? Against whom are the defenses used? What is the purpose of negligence defenses?

2. Define *contributory negligence*. What are its elements? What is the common-law rule? Why was contributory negligence a particularly effective defense? How would it arise today?

3. Explain last clear chance. How is it used? Who uses it against whom? What is its importance to contributory negligence?

4. Why is the contributory negligence defense unfair? What changes have courts and legislatures made to create a more equitable defense? What is this defense called?

5. Define *comparative negligence*. What are its elements? What is culpability factoring? Liability apportionment? Why are percentages used? Who decides these percentages? Is this defense more fair than contributory negligence? Why or why not?

6. What is assumption of risk? List its elements. Who uses the defense against whom? Must the risk be voluntarily assumed? What is "full appreciation of danger" and why is it significant? How effective is this defense in avoiding the defendant's liability? What level of risk does a person assume?

7. What are statutes of limitations? What time period is most commonly allowed for negligence causes of action? How can limitations statutes be used as a defense to negligence?

Projects

1. Does your state have one (or more) comparative negligence statutes? Have the courts in your state modified the common-law contributory negligence or assumption of risk defenses?

2. In class or study groups, create your own hypotheticals using the negligence defenses discussed in this chapter. Then change the facts to alter the outcomes of the problems.

3. An elevator does not level properly and stops five inches above the floor of a building. A man hurriedly enters the elevator without looking and trips on the threshold. What percentage of liability do you think the jury might apportion between the owner of the elevator and the man who tripped? Explain.

4. What is the statute of limitations for bringing a negligence action in your state?

5. Does the same statute of limitations apply for medical, dental, and legal malpractice actions in your state?

Internet Resources

This chapter focuses on defenses to negligence actions. To learn more about defenses to negligence actions, the following sites can be accessed:

General Information
http://www.uscourts.gov
http://www.courts.net
http://www.firstgov.gov/Government/State_Local.shtml
http://www.findlaw.com/01topics/22tort/database.html

For additional resources, visit our Web site at
www.paralegal.delmar.cengage.com

CHAPTER 5

INTENTIONAL TORTS: INJURIES TO PERSONS

CHAPTER OUTLINE

§ 5.1   Intentional Torts in General
§ 5.2   Assault and Battery
§ 5.3   False Imprisonment
§ 5.4   Infliction of Emotional Distress
§ 5.5   Fraud and Misrepresentation
§ 5.6   Malicious Prosecution and Abuse of Process
§ 5.7   Invasion of Privacy
§ 5.8   Defamation: Libel and Slander

———————————— ‹ ◆ › ————————————

When you have the facts on your side,
argue the facts.
When you have the law on yor side,
argue the law.
When you have neither, holler.
ALBERT GORE, JR.

§ 5.1 Intentional Torts in General

Generally, a person has a right to be free of threats and actual contact that injures or offends him or her. Therefore, one has a duty not to intentionally injure, offensively touch, or threaten other people.

Intentional torts consist of conduct that is fashioned to harm another person or his or her property. The mischief is directed with the purpose of inflicting injury. All intentional torts include three elements: act, intent, and injurious behavior. **Intent** can be broadly defined as the desire to achieve a particular result. Specifically, the tortfeasor must intend to accomplish the harmful consequences of his or her actions. This does not require malice or ill will; the tortfeasor simply must intend to cause the consequences that give rise to the tort or the tortfeasor must know with substantial certainty that certain consequences would result from that act. Commonly, though, those consequences include some type of harm. These acts also must actually conclude in the injury that was intended.

For certain peculiar intentional torts, intent, strictly speaking, is not required. For example, for reckless infliction of emotional distress, intent is not essential. The tortfeasor need only know (or reasonably should know) that his or her outlandish or outrageous actions will produce emotional injury. This knowledge element acts as a substitute for intent.

Intentional torts involve intentional acts, and as such carry a high degree of risk of injury, and usually a low degree of social benefit. The risk generally greatly outweighs the benefit received. Therefore, the duty not to intentionally injure someone or something is great.

Intent and Action Together

Intent reflects the tortfeasor's state of mind and must occur simultaneously with the misconduct. For example, assume that David and Steven are carpenters. Steven tosses a piece of wood across a room into a pile, but before it lands the wood strikes David in the throat. Steven would not be

intentional injury (tort)† An injury *designed* to injure a person or that person's property as opposed to an injury caused by negligence or resulting from an accident.

intent The resolve or purpose to use a particular means to reach a particular result. *Intent* usually explains *how* a person wants to do something and *what* that person wants to get done, while *motive* usually explains *why*.

liable for battery because, although the board struck David, Steven did not intend this to happen. Suppose David thought about throwing the board back at Steven, but did nothing and walked away. David would not be liable for assault because no action accompanied his desire.

Intentional torts present a relatively black-and-white image of the law, in which it is fairly easy to distinguish the "good" person from the "bad." The victim seems truly exploited, and the tortfeasor is clearly responsible and to blame (from a moral or ethical point of view) for having purposefully injured the victim. Our sense of fair play is rewarded when intentional tortfeasors are held accountable for their mischief.

Crimes versus Torts

It is important to note that a single act can be the basis for both a tort and a criminal action. Both crimes and torts involve wrongs. A *crime* is considered a wrong against the state or society as a whole, in addition to the actual victim. Therefore, the state brings actions against alleged criminals. With tort actions, one person brings suit against another individual; the action is brought by a private attorney on behalf of the injured party. Thus, a tort is considered a civil action.

Suppose that a person is walking down the street at night. Another person comes up, aims a gun, and then shoots the pedestrian. In this situation both an assault and a battery have occurred. The pedestrian was first put in fear of harm and then actually harmed. As a result of the same act, the attacker may face both criminal and civil prosecution. The state may seek criminal damages against the attacker. In addition, the injured party may proceed with a civil action to be reimbursed for injuries caused as a result of the attack. Table 5-1 compares torts versus crimes.

TABLE 5-1
Comparison of torts versus crimes

	Tort	**Crime**
Goal	Compensation	Punishment and deterrence
Burden of Proof	Preponderance of Evidence	Beyond Reasonable Doubt
Victim Harmed	Individual	Society
Rules of Evidence	Civil Rules	Criminal Rules

§ 5.2 Assault and Battery

The preceding example of the careless carpenters depicts two of the most common intentional torts: assault and battery. Of all torts, these are perhaps the most straightforward.

Assault Defined

assault An intentional threat, show of force, or movement that could reasonably make a person feel in danger of physical attack or harmful physical contact.

Assault is an attempt by one person to make harmful or offensive contact with another individual without consent. Actual physical contact is not necessary; in fact, contact converts an assault to a battery. Assault is distinguishable from battery in that no touching is required.

Freedom from Apprehension

apprehension Fear.

The rights being protected by recognition of this tort involve each person's right to control what touches his or her person. The tort of assault is also intended to protect individuals from the fear or apprehension that unconsented contact will take place. **Apprehension** means that a person reasonably fears for his or her physical safety in anticipation of being struck by the unconsented harmful or distasteful contact. This apprehension must be *reasonable,* meaning that the anxiety must be rational given the perceived threat of contact. For example, if a four-year-old warns that she is going to punch her father's head off, her father probably would not be overly concerned, as it would be unreasonable for an adult to fear a child's threatened battery under such circumstances. Threats at a distance do not present sufficient reason for alarm because it is physically impossible for the threatening party to fulfill the threat. This states the next legal requirement for assault: immediate threat of contact.

Imminent Threat of Contact

Assault involves the imminent or immediate threat that unconsented contact is about to occur. The fear arises from the likelihood that someone or something unwanted is about to strike. For instance, Michelle's threat to hit George while talking to him on the telephone does not present an immediate risk, as the task cannot be completed at the time the threat was made. Therefore, no assault has taken place.

Examples should illustrate these elements. Although assault is a fairly straightforward tort, its elements can best be explored hypothetically.

‹♦›

The Case of the Crazy Trucker

Assault involves more than just an errant punch or kick. The imminent threat of battery can occur through an object that the tortfeasor directs at the victim. An example is a thrown rock that misses the victim. An assault occurred if the victim was placed in reasonable apprehension of being struck by the approaching stone.

In the following case, note how the "insane" truck driver commits assault against the plaintiffs through his reckless driving.

ROSENBERG
v.
PACKERLAND PACKING CO.

Appellate Court of Illinois
55 Ill. App. 3d 959, 370 N.E.2d 1235 (1977)
December 13, 1977
Pusateri, Justice

In this consolidated appeal, we are concerned with whether each count of plaintiffs' ... complaint states a cause of action. ... [P]laintiffs-appellants appeal from the dismissal of Counts I and III of their complaint for failure to state a cause of action. ... [P]laintiffs ... alleged that an agent, servant, or lessee of defendant Packerland Packing Co. controlled its tractor and trailer, which defendant owned and operated as an interstate common carrier, in such a manner as to come within two feet of plaintiffs' vehicle at speeds of seventy to eighty miles per hour, and even after signalling by the plaintiffs that said truck should pass them, the unknown operator of defendant's truck continued to make feints at the rear of plaintiffs' vehicle as if he were going to strike the plaintiffs' vehicle, all of this occurring over a "long span of time." It was alleged that the date of the occurrence was March 9, 1975, that the place of occurrence was I-94 in Lake County, Illinois, and that both vehicles were proceeding in a southerly direction. ... [Plaintiffs alleged that the truck driver] was probably insane.

Count II alleged that the truck driver's conduct constituted the intentional infliction of emotional distress and an intentional assault, and that defendant Packerland was liable ... .

[W]e believe the conduct alleged in Count II may constitute the intentional tort of assault. An assault is a reasonable apprehension of an imminent battery.

* * *

We affirm the trial court's ruling that Count II of the complaint states a valid cause of action and reverse the dismissal of Count III. The cause is remanded for further proceedings.

Affirmed in part, reversed in part, and remanded.

Case Questions

1. What specific actions did the defendant's truck driver engage in that constituted assault?
2. What if the driver's truck had touched the plaintiffs' vehicle? What additional intentional tort would then have occurred?
3. The court's discussion of the intentional infliction of emotional distress claim was omitted here. You may wish to look up the full opinion and compare the Illinois common law elements with those discussed in § 5.4.

─ HYPOTHETICALS ─────

Palmer and Davis begin arguing in a bar. Palmer balls up his fists and pulls his arm backward as if to swing at Davis. Davis ducks in anticipation of a punch. Has Palmer committed assault?

Applying the legal elements of assault, as previously discussed (which are (1) the tortfeasor's attempt to make unconsented harmful or offensive contact, which (2) makes the victim apprehensive for his or her physical safety, and (3) the threat of contact is imminent), it is clear that Palmer has assaulted Davis. Palmer attempted to touch Davis in a harmful or offensive manner when he drew his arm back to swing. Davis did not consent to this action and feared for his safety, as is obvious because he ducked, expecting to be pelted with Palmer's fist. The danger of contact was immediate, as Palmer could complete his swing and punch within a matter of seconds.

* * *

Consider another example. Morrison and Fleetly are playing basketball in a gymnasium. Fleetly yells that Morrison stepped out of bounds as he dribbled the ball upcourt. Morrison smiles and fakes a forceful pass to Fleetly's head, causing Fleetly to flinch in anticipation that the ball will hit him in the face. Has Morrison committed assault?

Consent is the key to this hypothetical. Morrison and Fleetly had agreed to play basketball together. It is well known that sports activities such as this involve a certain degree of incidental contact to which participants consent. This could involve being struck by the ball as it is deliberately passed from one player to another. Because Fleetly implicitly agreed in advance to such types of contact while playing the game, Morrison did not assault him.

All elements must exist for assault to occur. If any one feature is absent, then there is no assault. For instance, suppose in the first illustration that Davis had not reacted at all to Palmer's arm gesture. Perhaps Palmer and Davis often indulged in horseplay, such as by pantomiming fist fights, and so Davis assumed that it was just another joking episode. That would remove the apprehension element and thus there would be no assault. Suppose in the second example that Morrison simply threw the ball down and shouted at Fleetly, "Next time you call me a liar, I'll plant this right upside your head!" In that case, the threatened contact would not be imminent, as Morrison warned only of behavior at some unspecified future time, which might in fact never take place. Accordingly, no assault would have happened. ■

Battery Defined

battery An intentional, unconsented to, physical contact by one person (or an object controlled by that person) with another person.

A completed assault is called a battery. Strictly defined, a **battery** is the intentional, unconsented touching of another person in an offensive or injurious manner. There are three basic elements to this tort:

1. Unconsented physical contact
2. Offensive or harmful contact
3. The tortfeasor's intent to touch another person in an offensive or injurious manner.

Physical Contact Required

Actual touching is necessary for a battery to occur. However, contact need not be made with a person's body. It is sufficient for the tortfeasor to touch the victim's clothing, or an object that the victim is carrying, such as a purse, or an object in which the victim is sitting, such as a chair or automobile. These items are said to become *extensions* of the person which, if touched, translates into touching the person himself or herself.

Lack of Consent

Battery occurs only if the victim did not consent to the physical contact. Consent can be *expressed* or *implied*. Expressed consent is relatively easy to identify. For example, participants in sporting events readily consent to physical contact routinely associated with the activity. Implied consent arises out of particular situations in which individuals, by being involved, implicitly agree to some types of minor contact. For instance, people walking in crowds implicitly consent to incidental contact as they accidentally bump into passersby. It is reasonable and normal to expect that this will occur in crowded places, and those involved are (or should be) willing to tolerate some minor jostles.

Harmful or Offensive Contact

Battery requires touching that is harmful or offensive. Although harmful contact should be relatively simple to perceive, offensive touching may present some surprises. Often, offensive contact may be intended as positive or complimentary, such as a pat on the back or kiss on the cheek from a co-worker. The recipient, however, may find these actions distasteful. This addresses the consent issue. People do not usually consent to touching that repulses them.

Whether or not the physical contact is offensive is judged by a **reasonable person standard**. Would a reasonable person have been insulted by the contact, given the same or similar circumstances? Reasonableness is often based upon the victim's actions in conjunction with the tortfeasor's. For example, if two co-workers are accustomed to "goofing around" by jokingly touching one another (pats on the back, fake punches, tickling, etc.), then such behavior would not be reasonably offensive. In effect, the participants consented to the activity. In contrast, a male supervisor touching a female employee in a sexually explicit fashion could reasonably be perceived as degrading and offensive.

reasonable person test (standard)† A means of determining negligence based on what a reasonable person would have done in the same or similar circumstances. Basically, it is a measurement of the failure to do that which a person of ordinary intelligence and judgment would have done in the same circumstances.

Intent

Like all intentional torts, battery includes an element of intent. The tortfeasor must have intended to make contact with another individual in a harmful or offensive manner. Thus, accidentally bumping into someone in an elevator as it jerked into motion would not be a battery, because the contact was unintentional. But pinching that person while leaving the elevator would be battery, as the act was purposefully designed to make offensive contact.

Transferred Intent

transferred intent In tort law, the principle that if a person intended to hit another but hits a third person instead, he or she legally *intended* to hit the third person. This "legal fiction" sometimes allows the third person to sue the hitter for an intentional tort.

Sometimes the tortfeasor tries to strike someone but ends up hitting someone else or intends one wrongful act and another occurs. For instance, if Robert threw a stone at Stuart but struck Mark instead, then Robert has committed battery against Mark. Although Robert intended to strike Stuart, his intent is said to be carried along by the object he set into motion—the stone—and his intent is thus transferred with the stone onto whomever it reaches—in this case, Mark. Note, too, that Robert has assaulted Stuart by throwing the stone and missing, provided that Stuart was placed in reasonable apprehension, and so on.

Transferred intent is an effective tool for protecting persons from misdirected physical contacts. It holds the tortfeasor accountable for the consequences of his or her actions even though, strictly speaking, he or she did not desire to hit the third person involved.

‹♦›

The Case of the "Nuked" Plaintiff

Transferred intent is not restricted to objects one can hold in one's hand. Battery can occur if the tortfeasor contacts the victim with any offensive or harmful substance, such as liquids (acids) or toxic gases.

The following case demonstrates how radioactive gases caused a battery. The facts are supplied in great detail so that the reader may fully appreciate the horror of the defendant's alleged behavior and the apparent subsequent cover-up. In this case, the alleged conduct was deliberate, which makes the facts even more chilling.

FIELD

v.

PHILADELPHIA ELECTRIC CO.

Superior Court of Pennsylvania

388 Pa. Super. 400, 565 A.2d 1170 (1989)

September 12, 1989

Hester, Judge

This is an appeal from an April 29, 1988 order which granted appellees' demurrer to five counts of appellants' eight-count complaint. George and Dawn Field (appellants) instituted this action against Philadelphia Electric Co., Bartlett Nuclear, Inc., ... (appellees) to recover for injuries resulting from an alleged intentional exposure to high levels of radiation .... [T]he trial court dismissed the counts of appellants' complaint which sought damages for intentional exposure to radiation ... and intentional infliction of emotional distress ....

The trial court determined that: ... there was no common law cause of action for intentional exposure to radiation .... We reverse and remand for proceedings consistent with this opinion.

Initially, we examine the facts upon which we base this adjudication. ...

Accordingly, for purposes of this appeal, we accept as true the following allegations, which are contained in appellants' complaint. George Field was employed by Bartlett Nuclear, Inc. ("Bartlett") and hired as an independent contractor by the Philadelphia Electric Co. ("PECO") to work at its Peach Bottom Nuclear Plant as a health physics technician. Bartlett is a corporation which provides personnel to manage operational problems at utilities which own and operate nuclear power plants. ...

On February 6, 1985, as a result of a plant shutdown, George Field was directed by PECO personnel to enter an off-gas pipe tunnel in unit three of Peach Bottom. He observed standing water on the floor of the tunnel and radioed to PECO personnel that he thought it unsafe to remain in the water. In response, he was ordered to test for radiation, which he did. After performing the tests, he returned from the tunnel and advised PECO personnel that the standing-water problem should not be resolved while the plant was being operated since it would be dangerous to work in the tunnel while the plant was operational.

Despite these warnings from Field, who was trained and hired in the area of safety control and cleanup, on March 1, 1985, while Peach Bottom was operating, PECO ordered Field and other personnel into the tunnel to resolve the standing-water situation. While Field was in the tunnel, PECO personnel deliberately vented radioactive gases into the tunnel where they knew Field was working. This action was taken in order to keep the reactor operating. The highly radioactive steam triggered a survey meter, a device in Field's possession that measures radiation levels. Field's survey meter went off-scale in the tunnel. As this indicates levels of radiation in excess of that permitted by the Nuclear Regulatory Commission ("NRC"), ... Field immediately directed all personnel to leave the tunnel. He was not aware why the radiation level increased at that

time. Two radiation detectors, one located at the tunnel entrance and another located at the control point to the tunnel, both alarmed when Field passed through them. This also indicated radiation exposure in excess of that permitted by NRC regulations. Field then analyzed air samples at the tunnel entrance with his survey meter, and the meter once again indicated radiation levels in excess of levels permitted by NRC regulations.

Field posted warning signs to the entrances to the contaminated areas, but PECO ordered the signs removed. Later that day, Field asked that his internal exposure to radiation be determined by equipment that was unavailable to him, but PECO refused the request and refused to answer his questions regarding the incident. ...

On March 4, 1985, Field discovered that the reactor operators on March 1, 1985, had deliberately ordered the radioactive steam to be bypassed from the regular system and vented into the tunnel where the operators knew Field was working. This action was taken solely to keep the reactor operational. Field asked three other PECO personnel about the level of his exposure; he was assured that the matter was being investigated, and he was ordered not to discuss the incident with anyone. ... In late July, Field was told by his supervisor that the investigation was complete and documentation regarding the event had been discarded. Field then told his supervisor that he was going to report the incident to the NRC. ...

At one point during Field's inquiries about the incident, PECO personnel made two false statements to Field. They told Field that his field badge indicated that he had not been exposed to radiation on March 1, 1985. They also told him that on March 1, 1985, his survey meter had given an incorrect reading regarding the level of radiation due to moisture in the instrument.

On August 8, 1985, Field again was ordered into the off-gas tunnel at unit three to perform work. He performed tests on the standing water which established that it contained such high levels of radiation that Field believed that he had been misinformed by PECO about the level of his exposure to radiation on March 1st. Later that day, Field demanded that water be retrieved from the tunnel for analysis.

In the meantime, on August 6 and 7, 1985, the NRC conducted an unannounced investigation. ... On September 25, 1985, Field was terminated for alleged absenteeism. A subsequent NRC investigation of Field's termination led it to conclude that Field had been terminated because he had reported his overexposure to radiation to the NRC. ...

The next issue before us is whether count one of appellants' complaint, entitled tort of intentional exposure to radiation, states a cognizable cause of action. We conclude that it does. In the count, appellants allege that PECO deliberately exposed Field to radiation by operating the reactor knowing that Field would be exposed to dangerous levels of radiation and by deliberately venting radioactive steam on Field knowing his location. We believe this states a cause of action in battery. See Restatement (Second) of Torts § 18 comment c (intent to contact someone with offensive foreign substance constitutes contact for purposes of battery).

Barber v. Pittsburgh Corning Corp., 365 Pa. Super. 247, 529 A.2d 491 (1987), *rev'd on other grounds*, 521 Pa. 29, 555 A.2d 766 (1989), provides a dispositive analysis on whether an "intent" to cause harmful contact is present based on the allegations in appellants' complaint. ... We noted that intent in the context of tort litigation is defined to include the desire to bring about the likely consequences of an intentional act. ...

Instantly, the intent to contact is established by the deliberate venting of steam on Field, with knowledge of his whereabouts. Under *Barber*, the fact that PECO did not intend to harm Field is immaterial. If there is intentional contact, the consequences substantially certain to follow from such contact are within the scope of the tort. ... Accordingly, we conclude that count one states a cause of action in battery under Pennsylvania law.

* * *

In accordance with the foregoing, the order is reversed and the case is remanded for proceedings consistent with this opinion.

Case Questions

1. Although the court did not discuss the point, how does transferred intent apply in *Field*?
2. Did the court determine the defendant's intent to commit battery by exposing Field to radioactive steam? What was the court's rationale?
3. The court's discussion of the plaintiffs' intentional infliction of emotional distress claims was omitted here. You may wish to read the full opinion to compare Pennsylvania common law with the elements discussed in § 5.4.

Battery lends itself to a variety of boisterous hypotheticals. Consider the examples on the next page.

Table 5-2 on page 122 summarizes the elements of assault and battery.

Other intentional torts are less straightforward than assault and battery. False imprisonment poses particular wrinkles and is discussed in the next section.

─ HYPOTHETICALS ─────────────────────────────

Helen is a production analyst for a local investment firm. She is one of only three women in the operation. Another analyst, Calvin, regularly flirts with her. Helen responds politely but coolly to these episodes. One day Calvin, while standing behind Helen, takes hold of her upper arms and leans over her shoulder as if to inspect the file she has before her on her desk. Calvin wisecracks about the "nice view," to which Helen responds by grimacing. Has Calvin committed battery against Helen?

The three basic elements of battery have been satisfied. Helen did not consent to Calvin's touching. Her previous encounters with Calvin did not establish a playful relationship in which she might have encouraged such actions; in fact, she expressly discouraged Calvin's flirting. A reasonable person would have found Calvin's behavior offensive. Helen was insulted by the contact, as evidenced by her expression. Calvin intended to touch Helen in the way she found distasteful. Accordingly, Calvin is liable to Helen for battery. If Calvin's behavior continues to be a problem, it might also be actionable as sexual harassment, which is discussed later in this chapter.

* * *

Consider another illustration. Shelley is a clerk at a hotdog stand in a football stadium. Phillip, a customer, purchased lunch from another clerk. Shelley thought Phillip unusually rude, so, as Phillip turned to walk away, Shelley threw Phillip a plastic catsup bottle, shouting that he had forgotten his condiments. The bottle brushed Phillip's jacket sleeve and caused him to spill his beverage onto his pants. The bottle then struck Iris in the head, covering her with catsup. Has Shelley committed battery against Phillip and Iris?

Again, the elements unfold clearly. Phillip did not consent to being touched. Shelley's intent to make contact transferred to the catsup bottle that struck Phillip's clothing, which was an extension of his person. Shelley's contact was harmful because it caused Phillip to spill his drink onto himself. Shelley purposefully touched Phillip in a fashion that injured him. Furthermore, Shelley's intent to strike Phillip was transferred with the bottle, so that in hitting Iris, transferred intent applied. Shelley is liable to both Phillip and Iris for battery.

What if Shelley had been merely another spectator at the football game and, instead of throwing anything, had simply jostled Phillip, causing the spillage onto both Phillip and Iris, as they all were walking down the stairway to their seats? This would be considered incidental contact to which Shelley, Iris, and Phillip impliedly consented. Thus, no battery would have happened. ∎

TABLE 5-2
Elements of assault
and battery

Assault	Battery
Attempt to make harmful or offensive contact with another person without consent	Unconsented physical contact
Placing the victim in reasonable apprehension for physical safety	Offensive or harmful contact
Threat of imminent contact	Intent to touch another person in offensive or injurious manner

§ 5.3 False Imprisonment

false imprisonment
An unlawful restraint or deprivation of a person's liberty, usually by a public official.

False imprisonment occurs when the tortfeasor intentionally confines someone without that person's consent. This tort is meant to protect each individual's right to control his or her own freedom of movement. Essentially, there are four elements to false imprisonment:

1. Confinement without captive's consent
2. Tortfeasor's intent to confine victim
3. Confinement for an appreciable length of time
4. No reasonable means of escape.

Confinement

All methods of confinement include (1) a restriction of the victim's freedom of movement, (2) the captive's awareness or fear of the restriction, and (3) the victim's nonconsent to the restriction. The second element prevents the victim from escaping, either because no routes of escape are available, or because the victim is afraid to attempt escape for fear of the tortfeasor's reprisals.

There are several ways in which the tortfeasor may confine his or her captive. These include physical barriers and express or implied threats of force. Table 5-3 illustrates the elements of false imprisonment.

TABLE 5-3
Elements of false
imprisonment

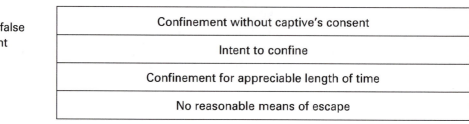

Confinement without captive's consent
Intent to confine
Confinement for appreciable length of time
No reasonable means of escape

‹♦›

The Case of the Minor Imprisonment

In this case a minor claims false imprisonment and battery following a shoplifting investigation. The minor was allegedly seen placing a pack of gum in her purse while her mother was grocery shopping. This case illustrates how a different rule applies for claiming damages in an intentional tort case versus a negligence action.

JOHNSON
v.
VALU FOOD, INC.
Court of Special Appeals of Maryland
132 Md. App. 118, 751 A.2d 19
May 2, 2000

This appeal stems from a dismissal of appellant Lakesha Johnson's amended complaint for failure to state a claim upon which relief could be granted.

* * *

Appellant timely noted this appeal and presents for our review the following question:

Did the trial court err by dismissing appellant's amended complaint, which contained general pleas of damages resulting from the torts of false imprisonment and battery?

For the reasons set forth herein, we answer appellant's question in the affirmative and reverse the judgment of the trial court.

On May 5, 1996, appellant was a business invitee on the retail premises of appellee located at 2655 Old Annapolis Road, Hanover, Maryland. Appellant accompanied her mother, who had gone to appellee's store, Valu Food, in order to purchase groceries for dinner. While in the supermarket, according to Dawn Lohman, one of the appellee's employees, she saw appellant take gun from the candy stand and place it in her purse. Suspicious that she had observed appellant shoplifting, Lohman approached to question her about the gum; Lohman then proceeded to detain her against her will. Specifically, appellant alleges that Lohman put her arm around her and led her down the aisle toward the back of the store. As a result of Lohman's actions, appellant filed a complaint in the Circuit Court of Baltimore City against appellee. Count I of appellant's complaint alleges that being detained against her will constituted the tort of false imprisonment; Count II alleges the tort of battery as a result of her physical contact and restraint by Lohman.

* * *

Appellant contends that the trial court erred by dismissing her complaint for failure properly to plead damages in accordance with Maryland law. In support of her claim, she argues that the intentional torts of false imprisonment and battery do not require a separately pleaded element of damages. Rather, appellant asserts that a general plea of damages is sufficient to sustain claims involving intentional torts. ...

We begin our discussion by briefly examining the elements of the intentional torts of false imprisonment and battery. In order to establish a claim for false imprisonment, "'the plaintiff must prove that the defendant deprived him or her of his or her liberty without consent and without legal justification.'" Punitive damages are recoverable in an action for false imprisonment, as long as the plaintiff can show actual malice. Alternatively, the elements of the tort of battery consist of the unpermitted application of trauma by one person upon any part of the body of another person. Further, "any claim for relief based upon an alleged tort, intentional or non-intentional, must allege facts, if proven true, sufficient to support each and every element of the asserted claim."

* * *

Well, the way I look at it, I'm inclined to agree with [appellee] in this case that there's no specific damage to the [appellant] alleged. There's no nature and extent of any harm that's resulted. As a result of what's being alleged, there's nothing stated about any physical injury or any embarrassment or any anxiety or any emotional damage or anything else. I mean, just simply to say that they were falsely imprisoned and there was a battery with no resulting damages seems to me lacks—is lacking in its complaint.

Appellant contends that her general plea of damages in her complaint is sufficient. ...

Appellant's amended complaint, however, alleges a prima facie case in intentional tort and sufficiently sets forth a plea for damages. Her complaint states in relevant part:

COUNT 1—FALSE IMPRISONMENT

1. On or about May 5, 1996, [appellant], [sic] was an invitee on the retail premises of the [appellee] at its store located at 2655 Old Annapolis Road, Hanover, Maryland 21076.
2. While on said premises, [appellant] was detained against her will by an agent, servant and[/]or employee of [appellee], without probable cause, and accused of theft. The agent, servant, and[/]or employee put her arm around [appellant] and escorted her down an aisle in the store and interrogated [appellant] concerning the theft of merchandise from [appellee]. WHEREFORE, this suit is brought and [appellant], [sic] claims the sum of Twenty-five Thousand

Dollars ($25,000.00) compensatory damages and One Hundred Thousand Dollars ($100,000.00) punitive damages against [appellee].

COUNT 2—BATTERY

* * *

5. The allegation contained in paragraphs 1 through 3, are adopted by reference with the same effect as if herein fully set forth.
6. Such actions by the agent, servant, and[/]or employee constituted an offensive, intentional touching of [appellant] and was without the consent of [appellant].

WHEREFORE, this suit is brought and [appellant], [sic] claims the sum of Twenty-five Thousand Dollars ($25,000.00) compensatory damages and One Hundred Thousand Dollars ($100,000.00) punitive damages against [appellee].

While it is necessary to prove actual damages to obtain recovery in negligence actions, the same rule does not apply to international torts. For example, a plaintiff who proves a prima facie case for an international tort, but fails to prove damages, will always be allowed to obtain at least a nominal recovery. ...

We hold, therefore, that the trial court erred by dismissing appellant's claim and we remand the case for trial.

Case Questions

1. Why was the appellant's general plea of damages in her complaint deemed sufficient?
2. After reviewing the appellant's complaint, do you feel she sustained any damages? Explain.

Physical Barriers Restricting Movement

Physical barriers are the most common method of falsely imprisoning someone. Placing the captive in a locked room or a moving automobile (while refusing to stop) are common examples. However, the physical barriers need not be so small as a single room or vehicle. A captive may be restricted to the grounds of a series of adjacent buildings. It is even possible for the victim to be penned in by such unexpected blockades as an automobile blocking the victim's access from a driveway to a street. The physical barrier need only restrict the captive's freedom of movement. This essentially traps the victim, either by some actual physical obstruction, such as a locked door, fence, or wall, or by an object which the tortfeasor is using to restrain the captive, such as the automobile blocking the driveway or even the tortfeasor's own body obstructing a doorway.

Express or Implied Threats of Force

Sometimes no locked door or wall is necessary to confine a person. Threats of physical or emotional violence can be quite effective, as are threats against the victim's family or property. In this way, confinement is achieved by expressed intimidation. The victim is afraid to escape for fear of physical or emotional injury. For example, when the tortfeasor warns, "If you leave this room, I will break your legs," the captive is likely to remain as instructed. Similarly, the tortfeasor could threaten, "If you leave this house, I will tell Joe that you wrecked his new car." In this situation, the victim is restrained by the threat of emotional injury, if certain information is revealed that would incriminate the captive.

These types of threats need not be explicit, however. Implied threats also work effectively. For instance, if a store manager tells a shoplifting suspect to wait in a room for questioning "so that nobody has to telephone the police," the threat of arrest and criminal prosecution is clearly implied, and the suspect will probably comply out of fear.

Captive's Consent to Confinement

consent Voluntary and active agreement.

The intentional tort of false imprisonment cannot occur if the victim consents to the captivity. **Consent** includes awareness and acceptance of the confinement. Thus, if a shoplifting suspect agrees to remain in a room pending questioning by store security, this would constitute consent, because the patron knows and accepts the restriction to the room.

Intent to Confine

The tortfeasor must intend to confine the victim for false imprisonment to happen. Consider the example of an accidental lock-in at a department store, where a customer is inadvertently locked inside the store after closing hours. There would be no false imprisonment, because the store management had no desire to confine the patron.

Intent may be expressed or implied by conduct. The tortfeasor who states his or her intention to confine another person is easiest to identify. Often, however, intent is indicated by conduct. Again, the shoplifting illustration presents a good example. A shoplifting suspect is stopped by store security and is asked to accompany the guard. Without any word of explanation, the guard takes the suspect to a back room, has the suspect enter, closes the door, and departs. There have been no explicit indications of confinement—the door was not locked—but implicitly it is understood, based on the behavior of the guard, that the suspect is to remain in the room. Accordingly, the intent to restrain may be implied.

Confinement for Appreciable Time Period

Although no definite time period is required, false imprisonment occurs only if the confinement has existed for an appreciable length of time. This depends upon the specific facts of each case. Usually, *appreciable confinement* is defined as unreasonable under the circumstances. That could be a matter of seconds, if someone is restrained in an extremely hazardous situation, such as in a burning building; or it could be a question of an hour or two, such as during a shoplifting investigation.

No Reasonable Means of Escape

False imprisonment cannot happen if the captive has a reasonable avenue of escape. In other words, the confinement must be complete. If the victim could simply walk away from the situation, then no false imprisonment transpired. Reasonable means of escape depends upon the facts of each case, but usually includes any route that a reasonable person would use to flee given the circumstances. For example, if Roger makes improper advances upon Betty in his automobile, and Betty has only to open the door to leave, then she has a reasonable avenue of escape, and no false imprisonment has happened. However, if Roger made the same advances on Betty in a fourth-floor apartment, in which the only exits were one door (which Roger blocked) and the windows, then false imprisonment would have occurred. Betty could hardly be expected to escape by leaping from a fourth-story window.

Many false imprisonment cases involve shoplifting or alleged shoplifting. The difficulty in these cases stems from the conflicting interests involved: the patron's freedom to move about freely versus the business's right to protect its property from theft. Notice that there are competing tort interests here. The customer seeks protection from false imprisonment, while the store owner wishes to prevent conversion and trespass to chattel.

The Case of the Overzealous Store Security Officer

Many false imprisonment cases involve shoplifting. All too often, store employees, anxious to curb theft of merchandise, become overzealous in their efforts. Suspected shoplifters, on the flimsiest circumstantial evidence, are occasionally subjected to unreasonable searches, confinements, interrogations, and the accompanying stresses and embarrassment. When the evidence against such suspects is extremely speculative, as in the case reprinted here, the result is often tort litigation. The suspect becomes the plaintiff. The store, as the defendant, suddenly finds itself attempting to justify its employees' outrageous conduct. Depending upon the facts, possible causes of action may include false imprisonment, infliction of emotional distress, assault, battery, invasion of privacy, or defamation. In the following case, false imprisonment and intentional infliction of emotional distress were successfully claimed, although only the issue of punitive damages was being considered on appeal.

ROGERS

v.

T.J.X. COS.

Supreme Court of North Carolina
329 N.C. 226, 404 S.E.2d 664 (1991)
June 12, 1991
Martin, Justice

This action was filed on 12 August 1988 by the plaintiff for compensatory and punitive damages for false imprisonment and intentional infliction of emotional distress. Summary judgment for defendants was granted. The Court of Appeals reversed the trial court on all claims except the punitive damages issue. ... The only issue before this Court is whether there is a genuine issue of material fact on the plaintiff's claim for punitive damages. We hold that the trial court erred in granting summary judgment for the defendants on that issue and therefore reverse the Court of Appeals.

The action arose out of events occurring on 17 July 1988 at the T.J. Maxx department store in Cary, North Carolina, owned by defendant T.J.X. Companies, Inc. Taken in the light most favorable to the plaintiff, as we must for summary judgment purposes, the evidence tends to show the following. Plaintiff entered T.J. Maxx, hereinafter "the store," about 4:30 P.M. shopping for linens. She wore bermuda shorts and a T-shirt and carried a pocketbook, approximately twelve inches by twelve inches. The purse contained two cosmetic bags, a wallet, two pens, a glasses' case, and a ziploc bag containing material and wallpaper samples. Plaintiff went first to the cosmetics area and then to the linens department. After leaving the linens department, she walked around a counter containing dishes and crystal and then

left the store without making a purchase. Plaintiff never entered the lingerie department and never examined any items of lingerie.

As plaintiff exited the store, Michael Nourse stopped her, identified himself as a store security officer, and asked her to return to the store because he wished to talk with her about some merchandise. Nourse carried a badge of his own design and an identification card issued by the company; he showed these items to plaintiff. Plaintiff told him that he was making a mistake, but complied with his request and accompanied Nourse to his office at the back of the store. Plaintiff testified that she did not feel that she had a choice about accompanying Nourse because "he was the law of the store" and she had to obey him. On the way to the office, Nourse asked another store employee, Sheri Steffens, to join them and act as a witness.

Once inside the small office, plaintiff immediately dumped the contents of her purse onto the desk. Nourse told plaintiff to take a seat, but she refused, saying that this would not take long because she was a good customer and had not stolen anything. Nourse responded, "Good customers will steal," and again directed her to have a seat. Telling her he would soon return, he then left the office for five to fifteen minutes. Plaintiff testified that she believed that he might have gone to call the police, and she stepped out of the office to look for them. Seeing no one, she gathered up her belongings, but did not feel free to leave because Nourse had told her he would return. Steffens paged Nourse, who returned momentarily. He said to plaintiff, "Ma'am, all we want is our merchandise. What did you do with it? You were in our lingerie department." Plaintiff denied wrongdoing, again dumped her purse on the desk, and told him that he must have seen her putting the packet of material samples into her purse. As she reached to gather her belongings, Nourse instructed her not to touch anything.

Nourse pulled down a clipboard hanging on the wall and showed her a card which said that the store employees had the right to detain her if they had reason to believe she had been shoplifting. Nourse repeatedly questioned plaintiff about the location of the missing merchandise as she tried to read the card. Plaintiff told him to "shut up" so that she could concentrate. Nourse remarked to Steffens, "Usually the dog that barks the loudest is guilty." Nourse then told plaintiff that he could call the police if she wanted them to settle it; that he could handcuff her to a chair; and that he would call the police and have them put her in jail. Plaintiff continued to deny the allegations and asked if he wanted her to take her clothes off to prove that she had not done anything, even though she was a very modest person. Steffens testified that plaintiff was very upset throughout the incident and that Nourse's attitude and demeanor toward plaintiff was sarcastic.

Nourse instructed plaintiff to sign two forms, one of which was a waiver of Miranda rights. The other form released T.J. Maxx from liability for any claims arising out of the incident. Neither of the papers had been filled out when plaintiff signed. Plaintiff testified that she signed the release form only because she believed that she would not be allowed to leave the store and go home if she did not sign it. Nourse refused to give plaintiff copies of the forms, because it was not company policy. After signing the papers, plaintiff left the store and drove home. She had been in the security office approximately 35 minutes. About one-half hour after plaintiff left the store, Nourse announced to Steffens that he had found the missing merchandise, a beige brassiere.

Plaintiff's evidence showed that she became sick, nervous and upset as a result of the incident. She had difficulty sleeping and took sleeping pills for two weeks as prescribed by her doctor. In addition, she testified that she no longer went shopping, because she felt as if someone was always looking over her shoulder.

False imprisonment is the illegal restraint of the person of any one against his or her will. The tort may be committed by words or acts; therefore, actual force is not required. Restraint of the person is essential, whether by threats, express or implied, or by conduct. The Court of Appeals held that plaintiff had established facts sufficient to support her claim for false imprisonment ... .

[The Court's discussion of punitive damages and intentional infliction of emotional distress is omitted.]

Taken in the light most favorable to the plaintiff, the evidence tends to show that (1) defendant Nourse impersonated a police officer by using a badge of his own design; (2) plaintiff was restrained against her will in the store security office for approximately one-half hour; (3) plaintiff was badgered, insulted and pressured to confess by defendant Nourse despite her efforts to prove her innocence; (4) plaintiff was frightened and upset and asked if she could leave; (5) defendant unlawfully detained plaintiff after [a] determination that no offense had been committed; (6) plaintiff was made to give up personal information including her driver's license number, telephone number, and social security number; and (7) plaintiff was forced to sign a release of liability as a condition to her release from Nourse's custody. ...

We hold that there was sufficient evidence of outrageous conduct, in addition to that conduct constituting the false imprisonment, to survive defendants' motion for summary judgment.

... Accordingly, we reverse in part the decision of the Court of Appeals and remand the case to them for further proceedings not inconsistent with this opinion.

REVERSED IN PART AND REMANDED.

Case Questions

1. Given the facts in *Rogers,* did the plaintiff establish the elements (as discussed in this chapter) for assault, battery, and intentional infliction of emotional distress?

2. You might want to read the complete *Rogers* opinion to compare North Carolina's common law regarding intentional infliction of emotional distress with the elements discussed in § 5.4, as well as in some of the other cases partially reprinted in this chapter.

— HYPOTHETICALS

Consider Sophie's predicament. A cashier thought he spotted Sophie taking some merchandise and placing it in her purse without paying for it. As Sophie walked out the exit, store security grabbed her. She violently protested, but the guards, without explanation, bodily forced her into a small, unlit room in the rear of the store. They then locked the door, and Sophie sat for three hours until the store manager, who had been on a delivery errand, returned to question her. She was, in fact, innocent of any wrongdoing. Was there false imprisonment?

The confinement was without Sophie's consent, as evidenced by Sophie's protests of the guards' physical handling of her. The restraint was obvious because the door was locked. The store security guards intended to confine Sophie by locking her in the room. She was restrained there for three hours, which would probably be considered unreasonable, particularly because the room was small and unlit. She had no reasonable means of escape, again because the only door to the room was locked. Therefore, the store would be liable to Sophie for false imprisonment.

* * *

Consider also the case of Murphy. Murphy drove his automobile into a restricted area of a manufacturing plant. Plant security instructed him to remain parked in his vehicle pending the arrival of the supervisor. Murphy said he had no reason to hang around, as he had done nothing wrong. The security officers then left. There were no barriers preventing Murphy from simply driving off the premises, through an open gate, to the highway. Was there false imprisonment?

The critical element in this hypothetical is the reasonable route of escape. Murphy could easily have slipped away, and the guards made no implied or expressed threats (such as arrest and criminal prosecution if he attempted to leave). Accordingly, no false imprisonment took place. ■

§ 5.4 Infliction of Emotional Distress

We have all encountered episodes in our lives in which other persons have intentionally caused us emotional upset. Anyone with a sibling can relate to misconduct designed to annoy and distress. In the law of intentional torts, infliction of emotional distress has developed as a separate cause of action to protect injured parties from other people's efforts to cause shock, fright, or other psychological trauma. One owes a duty to others not to intentionally inflict emotional distress. The breach of that duty is called intentional infliction of emotional distress.

emotional distress
Mental anguish. Non-physical harm that may be compensated for by damages in some types of lawsuits. *Mental anguish* may be as limited as the immediate mental feelings during an injury or as broad as prolonged grief, shame, humiliation, despair, etc.

Emotional distress can be broadly defined as mental anguish caused by a tortfeasor. Synonyms such as fright, anxiety, shock, grief, mental suffering, or emotional disturbance are commonly used by the courts to describe this tort. The condition can include shame or embarrassment as well.

The critical aspect of infliction of emotional distress is that the victim suffers from mental anguish rather than from some physical injury caused by the tortfeasor. It is the psychological harm that this tort intends to remedy.

Not just any insult or offensive behavior will result in this tort, however. The misdeed must be so outrageous that a reasonable person would suffer severe emotional injury as a consequence. This is the key element to all infliction of emotional distress cases. Minor annoyances or indignities are part of everyday life, and these are not included in this tort. If it were otherwise, the courts would overflow with lawsuits, based upon the irritations we all encounter from other people almost daily. Obviously, the law cannot reshape the world into the loving, peaceful utopia we might prefer, but it can discourage flagrant actions tailored to cause mental suffering.

In the field of intentional torts, there are two varieties of infliction of emotional distress: intentional and reckless. A third version, negligent infliction, is discussed in Chapter 3.

Intentional Infliction

intentional infliction of emotional distress†
An intentional tort that occurs when the tortfeasor's outrageous conduct, which is intended to cause severe emotional anguish in the victim, actually causes the victim such emotional suffering as a result of the tortfeasor's actions.

Intentional infliction of emotional distress contains three elements:

1. Outrageous conduct by the tortfeasor
2. Conduct intended to cause severe mental anguish in the victim
3. The victim's suffering severe mental anguish as a consequence of the tortfeasor's behavior.

Outrageous Conduct

As noted earlier, the tortfeasor's behavior must be sufficiently outrageous. The common test for outrageous conduct is one of reasonableness. Would a reasonable person suffer substantial emotional distress as a result of the tortfeasor's actions? Were these activities so outlandish as to *shock the conscience* of a reasonable person? Or, put another way, would a person of *ordinary sensibilities* suffer mental pain as a consequence? This generally excludes all but the most extreme types of egregious conduct.

Examples of outrageous conduct abound in legal literature. Tasteless practical jokes often provide fodder for emotional distress litigation. Consider the person who places a dead mouse inside a soda-pop bottle from which someone is drinking and then tells the drinker about the mouse. Or the heartless prankster who tells a parent that his or her child has just been struck and killed by an automobile when, in fact, this never occurred, as the joker knew perfectly well. Or the person who places revealing photographs of a nude sunbather all around the sunbather's place of employment for fellow workers to see. Or the individual who repeatedly telephones another at all hours of the day and night over several weeks. These are clear instances of outrageous conduct that most people would agree are highly offensive and would cause intense emotional dismay to the victims.

Intentional Acts

Obviously, intentional infliction cases must include the element of intent. The tortfeasor must purposefully behave so as to create mental anguish in the victim; the tortfeasor desires to cause anguish. This separates intentional infliction from reckless infliction, which does not require that the tortfeasor tailor his or her acts to cause mental suffering, as is discussed later in this section.

Actual Emotional Distress

Naturally, the victim must actually suffer emotionally as a result of the tortfeasor's antics. Again, the test for anguish revolves around the way a reasonable person of ordinary sensibilities would react to the tortfeasor's actions. Courts have often complained that determining genuine emotional suffering from faked distress is extremely difficult, because anyone can pretend to be upset by something. However, physical symptoms usually accompany mental distress, such as loss of sleep, weight, appetite, or vigor; illnesses brought on after the mental shock; or other signs of effect, such as tremors, twitches, or sensitivity to loud or sudden noises. It is important to note, though, that modern courts do *not* require physical manifestations in intentional infliction cases. Mental suffering alone, unaccompanied by physical effects, is sufficient, provided that the trier-of-fact is convinced of the authenticity of the distress.

The Case of the Bashful Bad Boy

In this case a couple's intimate moments are shared with the reader because the defendant failed to disclose his sexual history to his girlfriend. The defendant is accused of negligent infliction of a sexually transmitted disease. The Court found the defendant breached his duty by failing either to warn of his condition or to abstain from relations.

DEUSCHLE
v.
JOBE

Missouri Court of Appeals, Western District
30 S.W.3d 215
October 31, 2000

Ms. Deuschle contends that Missouri recognizes a cause of action for reckless infection of a sexually transmitted disease. She alleges that her sexual partner, Mr. Jobe, infected her with herpes and genital warts. Ms. Deuschle claims Mr. Jobe knew he was infected with the diseases at the time he had sexual relations with her, and he failed to disclose his condition.

Three is no statutory basis for this cause of action. But since 1986, Missouri common law has recognized a cause of action for negligently transmitting herpes.

* * *

In our case, the parties are unmarried. However, we find no justification for excluding an unmarried individual from bringing suit against her sexual partner for transmitting herpes under general tort law. ...

Here, Ms. Deuschle alleged both intentional and negligent transmission of the disease. In Missouri, it has long been established that the elements of a negligence action are "(1) [a] legal duty on the part of the defendant to conform to a certain standard of conduct to protect others against unreasonable risks; (2) a breach of that duty; (3) a proximate cause between the conduct and the resulting injury; and (4) actual damages to the claimant's person or property."

... Missouri courts have long recognized the importance of preserving public health and welfare by creating legal duties, which help prevent the spread of dangerous, communicable diseases.

In furtherance of this objective, we hold that one has a legal duty to exercise reasonable care by disclosing a contagious venereal disease before entering into sexual relations with another. Several other jurisdictions that recognize this cause of action support this proposition. In an action for negligent transmission of a venereal disease, a person is liable if he knew or should have known that he was infected with a disease and failed to disclose or warn his sexual partner about this unreasonable risk of harm before engaging in a sexual relationship.

In order to establish whether or not this duty has been breached, we must determine if the foreseeability of actual harm exists. ... The standard for foreseeability is measured by "whether or not a reasonably prudent person would have anticipated danger and provided against it."

When a disease such as herpes is almost exclusively spread through sexual contact, it is foreseeable that one's sexual partner is susceptible to the contagion if the infected partner is aware he has the disease or suffers from symptoms of the disease. ...

Ms. Deuschle also alleges in the petition that Mr. Jobe's actions were the direct and proximate cause of her medical conditions. ... As with any incurable sexually transmitted disease, once infected we infer that actual harm exists. Hence, a negligence action has been sufficiently pled by Ms. Deuschle in the petition.

As noted previously, the petition in some respects sounds like an intentional tort claim in alleging that Mr. Jobe knowingly failed to tell her of his disease, and knowing she was likely to become infected, that he intended injury, and that his conduct was outrageous. It is unclear exactly what intentional tort she is attempting to plead. ... We direct the trial court to allow her to amend the petition to allege a specific intentional tort.

Case Questions

1. What is the difference between negligent infliction of a disease and intentional infliction of a disease?

2. Is there an intentional tort in Missouri that would have been applicable to Ms. Deuschle's claim?

The Case of the Humiliated Newspaper Lady

In this case, the court debated what it was "worth" to ninety-six-year-old Nellie Mitchell to suffer the humiliation, embarrassment, damage to reputation, and mental suffering of having her picture inserted in a supermarket tabloid. This case focused on the tort of intentional infliction of emotional distress.

MITCHELL

v.

GLOBE INTERNATIONAL PUBLISHING, INC.

United States District Court, W.D. Arkansas, Harrison Division
817 F. Supp. 72 (W.D. Ark. 1993)
March 15, 1993
Waters, Chief Judge

In the October 2, 1990, edition of *The Sun*, a supermarket tabloid published by defendant, Globe International Publishing, Inc., a photograph of Nellie Mitchell, a 96-year-old resident of Mountain Home, Arkansas, was used to illustrate a story about "Paper Gal, Audrey Wiles" in Sterling, Australia, who had become pregnant by one of her customers, a "reclusive millionaire" she met on her newspaper route. In fact, Mrs. Mitchell made her living running a newspaper stand and delivering newspapers in Mountain Home.

She sued Globe for defamation, invasion of privacy, and intentional infliction of emotional distress, and the case was tried to a jury in Harrison, Arkansas, beginning on December 2, 1991. The jury found that the defendant's conduct had invaded Mrs. Mitchell's privacy by placing her in a false light and had amounted to an intentional infliction of emotional distress. She was awarded compensatory damages in the amount of $650,000 and punitive damages of $850,000.

* * *

[I]t is the court's duty, as directed by the Court of Appeals, to reduce the compensatory damage award by some unspecified amount with the only guideline received from the Court of Appeals being that it should be "substantial."

The Court of Appeals said:

> Though we are convinced that sufficient evidence exists to sustain a compensatory award for damage to Mitchell's reputation and her mental suffering, we also conclude the amount of the award is shocking and exaggerated.

Thus, it appears that it is this court's duty to determine, in whatever manner, what it is "worth" to Mrs. Mitchell to suffer the humiliation, embarrassment, mental suffering, and damage to her reputation caused by the egregious conduct by defendant in placing her picture and her very existence in the middle of an odious supermarket tabloid which, among other things, had a "road kill cannibal" describing his preference for human flesh from adults over that of children ... . This court still believes that the Harrison, Arkansas, jury, chosen from all walks of life, was better situated to make that decision than this court is, but, as indicated, that is beside the point, because this court has been directed to do it.

This is an especially difficult task where the damages to be awarded are based upon intangibles such as damage to reputation and mental suffering. ...

Of course, because of the nature of the damages in this case, there are no identifiable amounts that can be deducted, so any remittitur will, by its very nature, have to be somewhat arbitrary and speculative ... .

In short, this court has been directed to order a "substantial remittitur" so it must do so. For reasons stated in the earlier opinion, this court is convinced that Mrs. Mitchell suffered substantial damages to her reputation and was caused mental suffering by being a part, against her will, of a detestable publication issued and sold across the country by the defendant.

Vada Sheid, a friend of Mrs. Mitchell described the humiliation that she suffered beginning at page 156 of Vol. I of the trial transcript as follows:

> And I called Nellie and told her that I had the paper, and she came to the store to see this paper, and she said, where did you get this and how did this get into your store? ... And she says, well, that's me, but you know that I'm not pregnant. And I said, of course not. ... [S]he became so disturbed and so humiliated, and she said, but what will my kids think about this? Do you think they'll believe this, and how will I ever explain it to the people in town? And then she said, I'm going to buy up all the papers there is in this town so people in Mountain Home won't know about this.
>
> * * *
>
> [S]he went home, and she did not stir out for a few days. ... [S]he was very depressed and humiliated, and she just didn't deliver her papers even for the following week.
>
> * * *
>
> Nellie was hurt. She said, I don't know why they're doing this to me; why it was done to me. She said, I've tried not to hurt anyone ... why did they do it? ... But she was hurt, and after that, she said that people would come in and, they'd—She said they look down at my belly, and they'll say, well, Nellie, haven't you had that baby yet? Nellie, when are you going to have that baby? Nellie, you should have had that baby by now.
> And she said that it bothered her.

What is all that "worth"? A Harrison, Arkansas, jury believed that it was worth $650,000, but this court has been directed to reduce that award by ordering a "substantial remittitur." ...

This court recognizes, and recognized from the very first, that Mrs. Mitchell did not show at the trial a great deal of outward evidence of the humiliation, anger, and disgust that many would express under the same circumstances, but the court attributed a great deal of that to her advanced age. ... Admittedly, the court cannot take the evidence and point to any "specials" as lawyers call them, or any other identifiable dollar figures which can, with any certainty, justify an award of damages satisfactory to those who believe that these matters should be determined by some kind of formula. However, under all of the circumstances, the court is convinced that it is "worth" a minimum of $150,000 for Mrs. Mitchell to have been forced to endure what defendant heaped upon her, and the court, therefore, determines that a "substantial remittitur" in this case, as directed by the Court of Appeals, is $500,000. A reduction of a half million dollars is certainly "substantial", and the court believes that an award of at least $150,000 in compensatory damages is justified by the evidence.

This court will deny the motion for a new trial filed herein in behalf of the defendant on the express condition that plaintiff has, within 14 days of the date of this opinion, accepted a remittitur in the amount of $500,000. If, within such period, plaintiff has not notified the court of acceptance of a remittitur in such amount, the motion for a new trial will be granted, and a new trial ordered.

Case Questions

1. Why was the United States District Court so reluctant to reduce or change the award originally made by the jury?

2. Do you feel the original jury verdict was excessive? Explain.

Reckless Infliction

reckless infliction of emotional distress†
An intentional tort that occurs when the tortfeasor's outrageous conduct causes the victim to suffer severe mental anguish. Intent to produce the emotional suffering is not necessary. Instead, it is sufficient that the tortfeasor knew, or reasonably should have known, that his or her misbehavior would produce emotional distress. Often with this tort, the tortfeasor's conduct is wanton, with no apparent regard for the victim's suffering.

In general, recklessness is often a substitute for intent in tort law. Many **reckless infliction of emotional distress** cases include the mishandling of the remains of deceased persons. Consider a common fact pattern: A funeral home cremates the deceased instead of following the family's clear and explicit instructions regarding burial. Even though the funeral home did not intend this error, the conduct could be construed as so reckless as to fall within this tort.

Another type of fact situation involves the unanticipated effect of a practical joke. Consider the pranksters who vandalized someone's automobile by smearing it with manure, knowing that the vehicle owner took enormous pride in the car's appearance. The jokers knew that the owner had a weak heart, but were only expecting to shake up the owner. When the owner saw his prize automobile, he collapsed from a heart attack. This illustrates wanton misconduct. Although the pranksters did not intend the victim to suffer heart failure as a consequence of their deed, the tortfeasors' behavior revealed utter disregard for the health and well-being of the victim, and accordingly they would be liable for reckless infliction of emotional distress.

Claims of reckless infliction of emotional distress are sometimes made regarding unwanted, insulting, and demeaning sexual advances from a supervisor or co-worker at a place of employment. These claims are also known as sexual harassment suits.

Sexual Harassment

Title VII of the Civil Rights Act of 1964 makes it unlawful for an employer to discriminate against an individual because of that individual's race, color, religion, sex, or national origin. 42 U.S.C. § 2000-2(a)(1). In addition to tort actions, sexual harassment claims can be brought under the provisions of Title VII. A claimant must show that the workplace is permeated with discriminatory intimidation, ridicule, and insult that alters the conditions of the victim's employment, thereby creating an abusive and hostile work environment. Tangible psychiatric injuries need not be proven.

It should not be very difficult to imagine other emotional damage infliction scenarios like those previously mentioned. However, there are many instances in which the behavior is more subtle.

The Case of Presidential Passion

In one of the most infamous cases of sexual harassment, a former state employee brought a suit against the president of the United States. The case involves alleged sexual advances made while the president was serving as governor of Arkansas.

JONES

v.

CLINTON

United States District Court, E.D. Arkansas, Western Division

990 F.Supp. 657

April 1, 1998

The plaintiff in this lawsuit, Paula Corbin Jones, seeks civil damages from William Jefferson Clinton, President of the United States, and Danny Ferguson, a former Arkansas State Police Officer, for alleged actions beginning with an incident in a hotel suite in Little Rock, Arkansas.

* * *

This lawsuit is based on an incident that is said to have taken place on the afternoon of May 8, 1991, in a suite at the Excelsior Hotel in Little Rock, Arkansas. President Clinton was Governor of the State of Arkansas at the time, and plaintiff was a State employee with the Arkansas Industrial Development Commission

("AIDC"), having begun her State employment on March 11, 1991. Ferguson was an Arkansas State Police officer assigned to the Governor's security detail. ...

Plaintiff states that she and another AIDC employee, Pamela Blackard, were working at a registration desk for the AIDC when a man approached the desk and informed her and Blackard that he was Trooper Danny Ferguson, the Governor's bodyguard. ... The conversation between plaintiff, Blackard, and Ferguson lasted approximately five minutes and consisted of light, friendly banter; there was nothing intimidating, threatening, or coercive about it.

* * *

Plaintiff states that Ferguson later reappeared at the registration desk, delivered a piece of paper to her with a four-digit number written on it, and said that the Governor would like to meet with her in this suite number. She states that she, Blackard, and Ferguson talked about what the Governor could want and that

Ferguson stated, among other things, "We do this all the time." ...

Plaintiff states that upon arriving at the suite and announcing herself, the Governor shook her hand, invited her in, and closed the door.

[S]mall talk ensued, which included the Governor asking her about her job and him mentioning that Dave Harrington, plaintiff's ultimate superior within the AIDC and a Clinton appointee, was his "good friend."

[T]he Governor then "unexpectedly reached over to [her], took her hand, and pulled her toward him, so that their bodies were close to each other." She states she removed her hand from his and retreated several feet, but that the Governor approached her again and, while saying, "I love the way your hair flows down your back" and "I love your curves," put his hand on her leg, started sliding it toward her pelvic area, and bent down to attempt to kiss her on the neck, all without her consent. Plaintiff states that she exclaimed, "What are you doing?," told the Governor that she was "not that kind of girl," ... [she] told the Governor that she had to go, saying something to the effect that she had to get back to the registration desk. Plaintiff states that the Governor, "while fondling his penis," said, "Well, I don't want to make you do anything you don't want to do," and then pulled up his pants.

She states that as she left the room ...[he] "looked sternly" at her, and said, "You are smart. Let's keep this between ourselves."

* * *

Plaintiff states that the Governor's advances to her were unwelcome, that she never said or did anything to suggest to the Governor that she was willing to have sex with him.

* * *

Plaintiff continued to work at AIDC following the alleged incident in the hotel suite. One of her duties was to deliver documents to and from the Office of the Governor, as well as other offices ... She states that in June 1991, while performing these duties ... that the Governor wanted her phone number and wanted

to see her. Plaintiff states she refused to provide her phone number to Ferguson. She states that Ferguson also asked her how her fiance, Steve, was doing, even though she had never told Ferguson or the Governor his name, and that this "frightened" her.

* * *

Plaintiff states that she continued to work at AIDC "even though she was in constant fear that [the Governor] would retaliate against her because she had refused to have sex with him." She states this fear prevented her from enjoying her job. Plaintiff states that she was treated "very rudely" by certain superiors in AIDC, including her direct supervisor, Clydine Pennington, and that this "rude treatment" had not happened prior to her encounter with the Governor. She states that after her maternity leave, she was transferred to a position which had much less responsibility and that much of the time she had nothing to do.

* * *

To make a *prima facie* case of *quid pro quo* sexual harassment, this plaintiff must show among other things that her refusal to submit to unwelcome sexual advances or requests for sexual favors resulted in a tangible job detriment.

* * *

It is plaintiff's burden to come forward with "specific facts" showing that there is a genuine issue for trial, and the Court finds that her testimony on this point, being of a most general and non-specific nature (and in some cases contradictory to the record), simply does not suffice to create a genuine issue of fact regarding any tangible job detriment as a result of her having allegedly been discouraged from seeking more attractive jobs and reclassification.

* * *

The Court now turns to plaintiff's hostile work environment claim. Unlike *quid pro quo* sexual harassment, hostile work environment harassment arises when "sexual conduct has the purpose or effect of unreasonably interfering with an individual's work performance or creating an intimidating, hostile, or offensive working environment."

* * *

Plaintiff certainly has not shown under the totality of the circumstances that the alleged incident in the hotel and her additional encounters with Ferguson and the Governor were so severe or pervasive that it created an abusive working environment.

* * *

Accordingly, the President is entitled to summary judgment on plaintiff's claim of hostile work environment sexual harassment.

* * *

Finally, the Court addresses plaintiff's state law claim of intentional infliction of emotional distress or outrage. ...

To establish a claim of intentional infliction of emotional distress, a plaintiff must prove that: (1) the defendant intended to inflict emotional distress or knew or should have known that emotional distress was the likely result of his conduct; (2) the conduct was extreme and outrageous and utterly intolerable in a civilized community; (3) the defendant's conduct was the cause of the plaintiff's distress; and (4) the plaintiff's emotional distress was so severe in nature that no reasonable person could be expected to endure it. ...

The President argues that the alleged conduct of which plaintiff complains was brief and isolated; did not result in any physical harm or objective symptoms of the requisite severe distress; did not result in distress so severe that no reasonable person could be expected to endure it; and he had no knowledge of any special condition of plaintiff that would render her particularly susceptible to distress. ...

One is subject to liability for the tort of outrage or intentional infliction of emotional distress if he or she willfully or wantonly causes severe emotional distress to another by extreme and outrageous conduct. ... Whether conduct is "extreme and outrageous" is determined by looking at "the conduct at issue; the period of time over which the conduct took place; the relation between plaintiff and defendant; and defendant's knowledge that plaintiff is particularly susceptible to emotional distress by reason of some physical or mental peculiarity." ...

While the Court will certainly agree that plaintiff's allegations describe offensive conduct, the Court, as previously noted, has found that the Governor's alleged conduct does not constitute sexual assault. Rather, the conduct as alleged by plaintiff describes a mere sexual proposition or encounter, albeit an odious one, that was relatively brief in duration, did not involve any coercion or threats of reprisal, and was abandoned as soon as plaintiff made clear that the advance was not welcome. The Court is not aware of any authority holding that such a sexual encounter or proposition of the type alleged in this case, without more, gives rise to a claim of outrage.

* * *

In sum, plaintiff's allegations fall far short of the rigorous standards for establishing a claim of outrage under Arkansas law and the Court therefore grants the President's motion for summary judgment on this claim.

Case Questions

1. What facts would have had to be different to succeed on the quid pro quo claim?
2. Why did the Court decide that Ms. Jones had not sustained intentional infliction of emotional distress?

— HYPOTHETICALS —

Phyllis could offer an example. She owed money on a charge account at a local appliance store. Unfortunately, she missed several payments because of financial difficulties. Susan, the store sales manager, began repeatedly telephoning Phyllis at work and late in the evenings at home, demanding that Phyllis pay the balance due. The calls continued over several weeks. Phyllis's supervisor became angry that Phyllis was wasting company time taking these phone calls. The calls at night woke Phyllis several times and agitated her enough to keep her awake. As a result, Phyllis's job performance slumped. Phyllis lost weight and became irritable because of lack of sleep. Has Susan intentionally inflicted emotional distress upon Phyllis?

Susan's actions were designed to upset Phyllis greatly to coerce Phyllis to pay the overdue debt. Susan acted in an outrageous manner—reasonable persons would find repeated telephone calls late at night and on the job to be highly offensive. Phyllis suffered substantial mental anguish (with physical manifestations) as a result of Susan's conduct. Accordingly, Susan would be liable to Phyllis for intentional infliction of emotional distress.

* * *

Consider another illustration. Baker and Mortimer are accountants with the same firm. Baker planted a fake letter of termination on Mortimer's desk, in which the office manager accused Mortimer of misappropriation of client funds. Upon reading the letter, Mortimer became distraught, shaking and sweating violently and feeling nauseous. Mortimer burst into the manager's office to deny the allegations, at which time Baker disclosed his gag. Has Baker inflicted emotional distress upon Mortimer?

All the elements are present in this hypothetical, including intent to cause mental anguish. Baker should tally his own personal accounts, because he will be liable to Mortimer for intentional infliction of emotional distress. ∎

Table 5-4 summarizes the elements of infliction of emotional distress.

TABLE 5-4
Elements of infliction of emotional distress

Intentional Infliction	Reckless Infliction
Outrageous conduct	Outrageous conduct
Conduct intended to cause severe mental anguish	Conduct known (or reasonably should be known) to cause severe mental anguish
Victim suffers severe mental anguish as result	Victim suffers severe mental anguish as result

§ 5.5 Fraud and Misrepresentation

fraud (deceit) Any kind of trickery used to cheat another of money or property.

misrepresentation
1. *Innocent misrepresentation* is a false statement that is not known to be false.
2. *Negligent misrepresentation* is a false statement made when you should have known better.
3. *Fraudulent misrepresentation* is a false statement known to be false and meant to be misleading.

Fraud, or **deceit** as some states call it, occurs when a tortfeasor makes false statements to entice the victim to give up something of value to the tortfeasor. **Misrepresentation** exists when the tortfeasor knowingly makes false statements or purposefully behaves in such a way as to deceive the victim. The two torts are quite similar. Both involve false statements or actions. Both include deception as the tortfeasor's objective. Yet fraud features the element of underhanded economic gain: the victim surrenders something valuable to the tortfeasor as a result of the spurious comments. As a practical matter, however, a tortfeasor who commits fraud also commits misrepresentation, although they technically are not the same tort. Still, many courts view them as synonymous.

Definitions and Distinctions

Fraud

For fraud, the following must exist:

1. The defrauder must intend to deceive by making a false representation of material fact
2. The defrauder must know that the statements made are false
3. The purpose of the false statements must be to entice the victim into giving the tortfeasor something of value
4. The innocent party must justifiably rely on the misrepresentation
5. The innocent party must be injured.

Misrepresentation

For misrepresentation, the first two elements of fraud must occur. Some courts, however, also add the other elements to misrepresentation, making it identical to fraud. In such jurisdictions, the two concepts are thus redundant. Table 5-5 outlines the elements of fraud and misrepresentation.

TABLE 5-5
Elements of fraud and misrepresentation

Fraud	Misrepresentation
False statements intended to deceive	False statements intended to deceive
Knowledge of falsity of statements	Knowledge of falsity of statements
Statements designed to entice victim into surrendering something of value	Innocent party suffers damages
The innocent party is injured	

False Statements Intended to Deceive

A tortfeasor commits fraud or misrepresentation by making material false statements designed to delude the victim. For example, if Aaron tells Stephanie that he can repair her broken dishwasher for $100, when Aaron knows that he lacks the requisite skill and knowledge to do so, then Aaron has made false statements intended to mislead Stephanie into paying him the money for work he cannot perform.

Knowledge of Falsity of Information

The tortfeasor must know that the information given to the victim is false for fraud or misrepresentation to happen. For instance, if Henry sells Michelle a new computer with a defective floppy disk drive of which Henry is totally unaware, then Henry has not engaged in either fraud or misrepresentation, because he did not know about the product defect when he made the sale.

Tortfeasor's Profit from Deception

For fraud, the defrauder must make false statements tailored to encourage the victim to surrender something of value to the tortfeasor. In the preceding example, Aaron duped Stephanie in order to receive her money. This constitutes fraud.

Innocent Party's Injury

Like all torts, the innocent party must prove actual injury as a consequence of the false statements or misrepresentation.

The Case of the Faked Financing

Fraud and misrepresentation often involve money matters. For a variety of reasons, funds may be promised but not delivered. Sometimes, deceit is the root of the evil. In the following case, a lending institution fails in its loan obligation and commits misrepresentation into the bargain. In Arkansas, this tort is called *deceit*.

FIDELITY MORTGAGE CO.
v.
COOK
Supreme Court of Arkansas
307 Ark. 496, 821 S.W.2d 39 (1991)
December 23, 1991
Brown, Justice

The appellant, Fidelity Mortgage Company of Texas, appeals from a judgment for deceit in favor of the appellee, James Martin Cook, d/b/a Cook Construction Company, in the amount of $35,538.29. The salient issue on appeal is whether the circuit judge, who tried the case without a jury, clearly erred in finding that the elements of deceit existed in this case.

We hold that the circuit judge did not err in his findings, and we affirm his decision.

The facts involve the building of a hunting lodge instigated by two men who had formed a partnership—James Cunningham and John Staggers. The partners had agreed between themselves that Cunningham would put up the land for the lodge and Staggers would arrange the financing for the construction. The original contractor for the job quit, apparently due to a problem in getting paid. Staggers then approached a second contractor, James Cook. Cook was agreeable to doing the job for $250,000 but only if he could receive assurances that he would be paid.

Staggers had had a previous business relationship with W.R. Parker, a principal with Fidelity Mortgage Company. They discussed the need for financing to build a hunting lodge, and Parker put Staggers in touch with James Trimble, a vice-president of Fidelity. Trimble faxed Staggers a letter on September 23, 1988, which stated that Fidelity "hereby agrees … to loan up to $250,000 (new loan) at a rate of 12% per annum." A commitment fee of $2,500 was required from Staggers. There was no statement in the letter that Fidelity would act as a broker for the loan or seek participation from other financial institutions. Staggers in turn faxed a copy of the letter to Cook's attorney that same day.

On the following day, September 24, 1988, Cook entered into a construction contract with Staggers and Cunningham to build the hunting lodge. Under that contract, Staggers and Cunningham were to pay Cook $150,000 after a certain part of the project had been completed. Cook began construction on September 26, 1988. During the first week of construction, Cook's attorney called Fidelity and talked to Trimble and was assured that Fidelity would pay the money to Cook in accordance with the construction contract. Trimble also testified that during the last week in September Staggers asked him to write a letter stating that the Fidelity loan was to be used to build a hunting

lodge and that payments would be made to Cook pursuant to the construction contract.

On October 11, 1988, Cook submitted a bill for $150,000 to Staggers after completing the requisite part of the project. Payment was not made on that date, and Cook's attorney advised him to stop work. Due to assurances from Trimble that payment would be forthcoming, Cook continued work on the project.

Three days later, on October 14, Trimble, on behalf of Fidelity, wrote the letter that Staggers had requested in which he specifically stated that the loan was for the hunting lodge property and that payments would be made to Cook in accordance with the construction contract. By letter dated October 18, Trimble wrote Staggers that payment would be delayed because one of the trustees (later identified as W.R. Parker) was needed to approve the check, and he was out of the country.

At some point between October 17 and October 21, 1988, Cook stopped work on the project. The amount of work performed by Cook and the fact that Cook was not paid are not in dispute. Fidelity, through Trimble, finally severed its business relationship with Staggers in November or December. At that time Trimble advised Cook's attorney that Staggers had never paid the $2,500 loan commitment fee.

Cook first sued Staggers and Cunningham for $150,000. He obtained judgment and foreclosed his lien against the hunting lodge property, thereby realizing $50,000. …

Cook next sued Fidelity for deceit on the basis that Fidelity misrepresented its capacity to make the loan and to pay him and further that it intentionally induced him to rely on these false representations. After the bench trial, the circuit judge found for Cook and assessed damages against Fidelity in the amount of $35,538.29, which represented Cook's out-of-pocket expenses for the job, less the amounts received by garnishment and foreclosure.

Fidelity urges on appeal that the elements of deceit were not proven in this case and that the circuit judge clearly erred in finding that they were. We have had occasion recently to discuss the five elements of deceit, which are:

1. The defendant makes a false representation—ordinarily, one of fact;
2. The defendant knows that the representation is false or he does not have a sufficient basis of information to make it; that is, scienter;
3. The defendant intends to induce the plaintiff to act or to refrain from acting in reliance upon the misrepresentation;
4. The plaintiff justifiably relies upon the representation;
5. The plaintiff suffers damage as a result of the reliance.

Each element must be proven by a preponderance of the evidence in order to prove deceit.

A. FALSE REPRESENTATION

We have no trouble in sustaining the circuit judge's finding of misrepresentation. Simply stated, Fidelity agreed to loan $250,000 to Staggers when its net worth totalled less than $50,000. Had there been any hint that Fidelity would act as the broker for the loan or would ask for institutions to participate in the loan, our conclusion would be different. But there was no such intimation in the loan commitment letter signed by Trimble on behalf of Fidelity on September 23. There, he stated clearly and unequivocally under a heading entitled "Commitment:"

Fidelity Mortgage Company of Texas hereby agrees to loan up to $250,000 (new loan) at a rate of 12% per annum.

This Fidelity simply did not have the capability to do.

We have noted recently that many courts now construe false representation to include "(1) Concealment of material information and (2) Nondisclosure of certain pertinent information." If Fidelity did not have sufficient assets of its own as of September 23 to make

the loan, Trimble should have arranged for independent financing from other institutions before writing the loan commitment letter. But he did not do this. Rather, he obligated Fidelity to make the loan while concealing insufficient net worth and knowing full well that Fidelity did not have the capability to make good on its promise.

Fidelity argues that it was not obligated to make payments because it never received the $2,500 loan fee from Staggers. In the numerous conversations and letters between Fidelity and Cook during September and October 1988, there was no mention that the fee had not been paid. Yet all during this period Trimble made verbal and written assurances on behalf of Fidelity that Cook would be paid for his work. The trial judge correctly found that this conduct constituted a false representation.

B. SCIENTER

Nor do we agree that Fidelity lacked the intent to misrepresent. Trimble and Parker did not reveal the net worth of Fidelity to Cook or his attorney during the critical period of construction. Nor did they indicate that the loan fee had not been paid. On the contrary, the statements of Trimble were in the nature of assurances that all was well and that the delay in payment was only due to Parker's temporary unavailability. Only much later did the true circumstances concerning Fidelity and its relationship to Staggers come to light.

* * *

D. JUSTIFIABLE RELIANCE

There is no question that Cook relied on the loan commitment. Equally as clear is the fact that Fidelity, through Trimble, knew about the construction contract and gave assurances to Cook and his lawyer that it would be paid. Neither Cook nor his attorney were alerted to the fact that anything was amiss. The trial judge's finding of justifiable reliance is not in error.

* * *

The decision of the trial judge is affirmed.

Case Questions

1. What is *scienter*? What is its importance to misrepresentation?
2. Why did the court say that its decision would have been different if Fidelity had arranged independent financing from other institutions? Would this have negated the first two elements of deceit?

Classic illustrations of fraud or misrepresentation seem to utilize used car sales situations, which have become the brunt of many jokes. Still, the examples profile the elements quite well.

─ HYPOTHETICALS ─

Ask Mayfield, for instance, who purchased an automobile from Honest Eddy's Used Car Palace. Honest Eddy himself assured Mayfield that the chosen vehicle had been driven only 5,000 miles by a driving instructor from Ontario, that the brakes had just been replaced, and that the engine had been re-tuned. Honest Eddy knew that none of this was true and merely wanted to make the sale at all costs. Mayfield bought the car and drove away. Much to Mayfield's horror and embarrassment, within a week the automobile began to emit huge plumes of blue smoke from its exhaust. It also shook violently upon acceleration and made grinding noises. Has Honest Eddy committed fraud and misrepresentation against Mayfield?

The elements piece together. Honest Eddy knew that the automobile was defective, but lied about its condition to induce Mayfield to buy it. Mayfield surrendered to Honest Eddy something of value (namely, money—the car's purchase price). Because there was deception, misrepresentation exists. Honest Eddy is liable to Mayfield for fraud and misrepresentation.

* * *

Richard supplies another good illustration. He purchased a home from Quality Construction Company (QCC). QCC's sales director assured Richard that the house had been treated for termites when, in fact, it had not. QCC had paid an exterminator to inspect the house, and the exterminator's report advised of the need for termite treatment. After living in the house for a few months, Richard discovered a serious termite infestation. Did QCC engage in fraud or misrepresentation?

The critical elements here are intent and knowledge. Did QCC's sales director know that no termite treatment had been done? QCC had received the exterminator's report recommending treatment. Thus, the sales director should have known that treatment was necessary and should have known that QCC had not performed this task. Thus, knowledge may be *imputed* under the circumstances. Intent, however, is more difficult to ascertain. Did the sales director purposefully mislead Richard? Since the director should have known that no treatment had been applied, his contrary statement to Richard demonstrated his desire to delude Richard. This equals intentional deception. Thus, misrepresentation can be proven. Also, because QCC's objective was to entice Richard to buy the house, the third element of fraud exists. ■

§ 5.6 Malicious Prosecution and Abuse of Process

Usually the common law distinguishes malicious prosecution from abuse of process in this way: Malicious prosecution occurs in criminal prosecutions, whereas abuse of process happens in civil litigation. They are similar intentional torts.

Malicious Prosecution

malicious prosecution
A tort committed by bringing charges against someone in order to harm that person and with no legal justification for doing it.

Malicious prosecution arises when a private citizen files with the prosecutor a groundless criminal complaint against another person (who is named as the defendant in the subsequent criminal proceeding). This tort is comprised of the following elements:

1. Groundless criminal prosecution against the accused without probable cause
2. The complainant's malice in filing the spurious charges
3. The accused's acquittal from, or dismissal of, the criminal charges
4. Injury to the accused as a result of the prosecution.

Groundless Criminal Prosecution

complainant 1. A person who makes an official complaint. 2. A person who starts a lawsuit.

probable cause† A reasonable belief that the accused is guilty of the alleged crime.

malice 1. Ill will. 2. Intentionally harming someone; having no moral or legal justification for harming someone. 3. In defamation law, with knowledge of falsity or with reckless disregard for whether or not something is false.

The individual registering a criminal complaint with the police or prosecutor is sometimes called the **complainant**. The complainant's actions are considered bogus if he or she preferred criminal charges without probable cause that the accused was guilty of the crime. **Probable cause** is routinely defined as the reasonable belief that the accused is guilty of the alleged crime. This belief need exist only at the time the criminal charges are initiated for probable cause to exist. However, if it later becomes obvious through investigation that the accused did not commit the alleged crime, then the complainant's insistence on the government's continuing prosecution would be malicious prosecution.

Malice

Malice in filing spurious criminal charges may be inferred from the circumstances surrounding the case. If the complainant knew (or reasonably should have known) that the accused did not commit the alleged crime, then malice is implied. Also, if the complainant is using the criminal prosecution to obtain some improper objective, such as intimidating the accused into settling a disputed civil claim or to extort money from the accused, then this likewise implies malice.

Accused's Acquittal from, or Dismissal of, the Criminal Charges

To recover successfully for malicious prosecution, the accused must have been acquitted of the groundless criminal charges initiated by the complainant, or the prosecution must have been otherwise disposed of in the accused's favor (dismissal of charges, for instance).

Injury to the Accused

Like all torts, the accused must prove actual injury as a consequence of the wrongful prosecution. This is most often accomplished by showing damage to the accused's reputation in the community or financial standing, mental anguish, or legal expenses associated with defending the criminal charges.

Abuse of Process

abuse of process
Using the legal system unfairly; for example, prosecuting a person for writing a "bad check" simply to put on pressure to pay.

Abuse of process is the civil equivalent of malicious prosecution. It occurs when the tortfeasor misuses a legal proceeding against another person to achieve an unlawful objective. The elements of abuse of process are

1. Misuse of a legal proceeding, or threat of such misuse
2. Misuse to achieve unlawful objectives
3. Injury to the victim as a result of the misuse.

Misuse of Legal Proceedings to Achieve Unlawful Goals

The tortfeasor must intentionally misuse (or threaten to misuse) a legal proceeding against another person to accomplish an objective to which the process abuser is not legally entitled. The tortfeasor normally threatens frivolous civil litigation in an attempt to frighten the victim into paying a disputed claim. For example, the process abuser might file a groundless lawsuit against an innocent defendant in an attempt to "scare up some quick money." This occasionally occurs in personal injury litigation when fault is difficult to assign and prove; the personal injury plaintiff abuses process by suing a convenient (but innocent) defendant (who usually has assets or insurance but seems unlikely to defend a frivolous lawsuit).

Litigation is not the only legal process that may be misapplied, however. Creditors filing improper mechanic's liens against debtors to collect on disputed debts, or a wife accusing her spouse of sexually abusing their children to gain an advantage in a custody hearing, when there are no grounds for the claim and she knows the claim is false, would also be guilty of abuse of process.

The pivotal aspect of abuse of process is the tortfeasor's misuse of a legal proceeding to gain some indirect benefit to which he or she is not legally entitled. The tortfeasor has an ulterior motive for manipulating the legal proceeding. The following hypotheticals illustrate how legal process may be exploited in this way.

When tortfeasors engage in malicious prosecution and abuse of process, their victims are often left with an unpleasant taste as a result of the experience. The victims develop a cynical bitterness toward the apparent ease with which the legal system was manipulated against them. But tort law strives to restore the balance (and the victims' faith in the system) by affording remedies against these intentional torts. The following examples demonstrate how the legal system bites back when misused in this fashion.

◄ ♦ ►

The Case of Bulldozing Legal Process

Anger causes people to act irrationally. Persons wishing to attack others may, out of exasperation, turn to the legal system to exact revenge, even though no legal rights have been violated. Many abuse of process and malicious prosecution cases arise in this fashion, as the following case illustrates.

POTE

v.

JARRELL

Supreme Court of West Virginia
412 S.E.2d 770 (W. Va. 1991)
December 17, 1991

PER CURIAM:

The appellants, Richard Jarrell and Hollis Jarrell, appeal from a jury verdict entered in the Circuit Court of Lewis County, awarding damages to the appellee, Kenneth Pote ... . Appellee Pote filed a civil action against the appellants primarily on the theories of malicious prosecution and abuse of process ... . The appellants' principal argument on appeal is that the trial court erred in denying their motions for a directed verdict on the grounds

that they relied on the advice of counsel in initiating criminal charges against appellee Pote and that they did not willfully or maliciously misuse lawfully issued process. This Court is of the opinion that there is no reversible error, and accordingly, the judgment of the circuit court is affirmed.

* * *

The incident ... occurred in October of 1987. Because of the nature of this case, it is necessary to recite the facts at some length.

Pote, in his capacity as manager of Interstate Drilling, Inc., arranged to have the appellants, Richard and Hollis Jarrell, who, were partners in an independent contracting business known as Rick's Dozer Service, provide a TD-15 bulldozer on Interstate Drilling's site to rework a road to a well location and to assist in moving pipe and equipment to the well site. The appellants provided Pote with a bulldozer and a bulldozer operator, Doyle James. Mr. James operated the bulldozer on the day of the incident for approximately three to four hours. Upon completing his work, Mr. James drove the bulldozer to the bottom of the hill near the well location ... and left for the day. Pote and some other workers, however, continued to work on the well in an effort to remove a "packer." At approximately 5:30 P.M., the well had a sudden release of pressure which caused oil and water to surge to the top of the well rig and spill onto the ground. Pote and the other workers attempted to control the flow with shovels. When their attempts to control the flow were unsuccessful, two of the workers ... suggested to Pote that they go to the bottom of the hill to get the bulldozer and use it to dig a ditch to contain the flow. ... Pote, who asserted he was faced with an emergency situation, authorized [the two workers] ... to use the bulldozer. With the use of the bulldozer, they were successful in digging a ditch to contain the flow and in keeping it from going over the hill onto the landowner's property.

* * *

Pote and Richard Jarrell eventually had a heated confrontation over Pote's use of the bulldozer without authorization. After their argument, however, Pote telephoned Richard Jarrell to apologize and assured him that Interstate Drilling would pay for any damage done to the bulldozer.

* * *

Richard Jarrell followed the recommendation of his attorney and went to the office of the magistrate to inquire about a warrant for Pote's arrest. Upon hearing the facts involved in the incident, the magistrate informed Richard Jarrell that he believed it was a civil matter. He did not issue a warrant. Richard Jarrell then went to the office of the prosecuting attorney [... and] filed a complaint for a warrant charging the appellee with the offense of feloniously and willfully injuring and tampering with a vehicle in violation of [state statutes for felonious or willful vehicular damage].

Pote received an invoice from appellants ... requesting payment in the sum of $3,560.21 for damages to the bulldozer and for lost time and income. ... Pote then met with Hollis Jarrell and advised him that he would only reimburse [Jarrell] for the actual damage to the bulldozer and not for the lost time and income. Pote gave Hollis Jarrell a check for [the bulldozer damage]. Hollis Jarrell advised Pote that if he did not pay the entire amount of the invoice, he would have him arrested. ... Pote [later] mailed the appellants a check covering the amount of lost income and time.

The magistrate sent Pote a summons to appear which was received by Pote the day after he mailed the check to the appellants. Pote did not appear and a warrant was then issued for his arrest. Pote was arrested, photographed and fingerprinted, and then released on his own recognizance.

... At trial, the circuit court directed a verdict of acquittal on the felony charge in favor of Pote and the case was submitted to the jury on the misdemeanor offense. Within minutes, the jury found that Pote was not guilty. ...

It is well established in West Virginia that a cause of action may lie for malicious prosecution or abuse of process. At the outset of our resolution of the issues before us, we shall distinguish between malicious prosecution and abuse of process.

... "In an action for malicious prosecution, plaintiff must show: (1) that the prosecution was set on foot and conducted to its termination, resulting in plaintiff's discharge; (2) that it was caused or procured by defendant; (3) that it was without probable cause; and (4) that it was malicious. If plaintiff fails to prove any of these, he cannot recover."

... "Generally, abuse of process consists of the willful or malicious misuse or misapplication of lawfully issued process to accomplish some purpose not intended or warranted by that process."

It appears from the record before us that Pote presented sufficient evidence from which a jury could find that he established all of the elements of his causes of action. The evidence presented to the jury showed that the appellants procured a felony warrant against Pote and caused him to be prosecuted ... . [T]he case against Pote was prosecuted to its termination, resulting in Pote's discharge. ... With respect to the issue of whether there was probable cause to instigate a criminal prosecution against Pote, there was no evidence presented to the jury indicating that Pote feloniously and willfully damaged the bulldozer. Furthermore, the jury heard testimony from the magistrate that the appellants were informed that this was a civil matter rather than a criminal matter. Moreover, the appellees introduced evidence to the jury attempting to show that the appellants misused the criminal process by initiating criminal proceedings against Pote for the sole purpose of obtaining payment for damages to the bulldozer. Thus, we find that Pote established the elements ... and presented sufficient evidence from which the jury could conclude that they proved those elements by a preponderance of the evidence.

* * *

Thus, for the reasons stated herein, we conclude that the judgment of the Circuit Court of Lewis County should be affirmed.

Affirmed.

Case Questions

1. Did the court find that the Jarrells had committed *both* malicious prosecution and abuse of process? Explain.
2. If the Jarrells had filed a civil action against Pote to recover the bulldozer damages, would that have been abuse of process? Why or why not?

— HYPOTHETICALS

Martin was offended when a bookstore that sold provocative literature opened in his neighborhood. He registered with the prosecutor a criminal complaint for pornography against the bookstore in the hope that it would shut down or move away. Nothing that the bookstore sold violated the city's pornography ordinance, as the prosecutor informed Martin. Nonetheless, Martin exerted pressure on the prosecutor (through a contact in the mayor's office) to proceed, and subsequently the court dismissed the charges upon the bookstore's attorney's motion. The bookstore lost substantial business as a result of adverse publicity in the newspapers surrounding the case. Has Martin maliciously prosecuted?

Martin's criminal complaint against the bookstore was frivolous, because its merchandise did not violate any criminal ordinance. The prosecutor had told Martin that the bookstore was not acting illegally, so Martin lacked probable cause to believe in the bookstore's guilt. Martin's malice could be inferred, because he knew of the bookstore's innocence but insisted on pressing the criminal prosecution to coerce the bookstore into closing or moving. The bookstore successfully dismissed the criminal charges. It also suffered financial injury as a result of Martin's actions. Accordingly, Martin is liable to the bookstore for malicious prosecution.

* * *

Felmore's Shipping Company delivered a shipment of desks to Northern Office Supply Corporation. One of Northern's employees, Tony, damaged several desks while moving them into storage with a fork loader truck. The desks were undamaged previously. Northern's president, Gertrude, filed suit against Felmore's, claiming that the desks had been damaged in shipment by Felmore's employees. Has Northern abused process against Felmore's?

Gertrude knew that Felmore's was not responsible for the marred desks, as she had observed Tony carelessly operate the fork loader and damage the desks. Thus, Northern's lawsuit against Felmore was groundless. Filing frivolous litigation constitutes misuse of legal process. It may be deduced that Gertrude's purpose in filing Northern's lawsuit was to intimidate Felmore's into settling the case out of court through its insurance carrier. Felmore's injury exists in that it must defend against this baseless legal action, incurring attorneys' fees, litigation expenses, and lost time for employees required to testify. The lawsuit could also damage Felmore's reputation if the business community became aware of the action, which could easily occur, as lawsuits are a matter of public record. Northern will therefore be liable to Felmore's for abuse of process. ■

Table 5-6 specifies the elements of malicious prosecution and abuse of process.

TABLE 5-6
Elements of malicious prosecution and abuse of process

Malicious Prosecution	Abuse of Process
Groundless criminal prosecution	Misuse of legal proceeding (or threat of misuse)
Complainant's malice	Misuse to achieve unlawful objectives
Accused's acquittal or dismissal of charges	
Accused's injury	Injury to victim

§ 5.7 Invasion of Privacy

Invasion of privacy is largely a twentieth-century concept. In 1888, Judge Cooley of the Michigan Supreme Court, in his famous torts treatise, analyzed a series of nineteenth-century court decisions on defamation, trespass upon a personal property right (such as lectures or publications), and breach of confidence under implied contract law. Cooley surmised that a broader right was being protected and defined the legal interest in the famous phrase *the right to be let alone* (Cooley, *Torts* 29 [2d ed. 1888]). In 1890, a famous *Harvard Law Review* article co-authored by (later United States Supreme Court Justice) Louis Brandeis substantially expanded Cooley's theory, coining the phrase *right to privacy* (Warren & Brandeis, "The Right to Privacy," 4 *Harv. L. Rev.* 193 [1890]). American courts and legislatures throughout the twentieth century have incorporated this tort into their common law and statutes. It may be fairly said that this cause of action arose primarily because of this seminal law-review article.

invasion of privacy
Publicizing someone's private affairs that are of no legitimate public concern; using a person for publicity without permission; eavesdropping; or violation of the right to be left alone.

Simply put, **invasion of privacy** exists when someone publicly exploits another person's private affairs in an unreasonably intrusive manner. In tort law, there are four separate types of invasion of privacy:

1. Appropriation
2. Unreasonable intrusion
3. Public disclosure of private facts
4. False light in the public eye.

The United States Supreme Court also recognizes a fifth type of invasion of privacy protected under the United States Constitution. This includes actions by governmental agencies that infringe upon a citizen's life, liberty, or property interests safeguarded by the Constitution. However, this type is not covered by tort law; it is a due-process issue.

Appropriation

appropriation
Taking something wrongfully.

Appropriation occurs when the tortfeasor uses a person's name or likeness without permission to gain some benefit. For example, if an advertising company used a person's photograph to sell a product without that person's consent, then the firm would be liable to the person for invasion of privacy by appropriation. Most cases involving this variety of invasion of privacy consist of the unauthorized use of photographs, artist's sketches, or quotations associated with names to sell someone else's goods or services.

Unreasonable Intrusion

unreasonable intrusion† One type of the intentional tort of invasion of privacy. Occurs when the tortfeasor engages in an excessive and highly offensive invasion upon another person's seclusion or solitude.

Unreasonable intrusion involves an excessive and highly offensive assault upon one's seclusion or solitude. Several illustrations should clarify. If store security personnel demand that a suspected shoplifter disrobe, or if they rifle through the suspect's personal belongings in an illegal search, this would be considered unreasonable intrusion. Intentional eavesdropping upon a private conversation is another example. Recall the Phyllis/Susan hypothetical discussed in connection with infliction of emotional distress. Susan's incessant telephone calls would also constitute unreasonable intrusion. Searching another's mail to discover private information or obtaining unauthorized access to someone's bank account or tax records are yet other instances. Courts have also found that illegal, compulsory blood tests equal unreasonable intrusion. Simple trespassing onto an individual's land to snoop would also violate this version of privacy.

The Case of the False Still

In this case, computer technology is used to alter famous still photography. Despite this false depiction, the actor is left powerless.

HOFFMAN

v.

CAPITAL CITIES/ABC, INCORPORATED

United States Court of Appeals, Ninth Circuit
255 F.3d 1180 (9th Cir. (Cal.))
Argued and Submitted Oct. 10, 2000
Filed July 6, 2001

In 1982, actor Dustin Hoffman starred in the movie "Tootsie," playing a male actor who dresses as a woman to get a part on a television soap opera. One memorable still photograph from the movie showed Hoffman in character in a red long-sleeved sequined evening dress and high heels, posing in front of an American flag. The still carried the text, "What do you get when you cross a hopelessly straight, starving actor with a dynamite red sequined dress? You get America's hottest new actress."

In March 1997, Los Angeles Magazine ("LAM") published the "Fabulous Hollywood Issue!" An article from this issue entitled "Grand Illusions" used computer technology to alter famous film stills to make it appear that the actors were wearing Springs 1997 fashions. The sixteen familiar scenes included

movies and actors such as "North by Northwest" (Cary Grant), "Saturday Night Fever" (John Travolta), ... "Gone with the Wind" (Vivian Leigh and Hattie McDaniel) ... The final shot was the "Tootsie" still. The American flag and Hoffman's head remained as they appeared in the original, but Hoffman's body and his long-sleeved red sequined dress were replaced by the body of a male model in the same pose, wearing a spaghetti-strapped, cream-colored, silk evening dress and high-heeled sandals. LAM omitted the original caption. The text on the page identified the still as from the movie "Tootsie," and read, "Dustin Hoffman isn't a drag in a butter-colored silk gown by Richard Tyler and Ralph Lauren heels."

LAM did not ask Hoffman for permission to publish the altered photograph. Nor did LAM secure permission from Columbia Pictures, the copyright holder. ...

California recognizes, in its common law and its statutes, "the right of a person whose identity has commercial value—most often a celebrity—to control the commercial use of that identity." Hoffman claims that LAM violated his state right of publicity by appropriating his name and likeness. He also claims that LAM violated his rights under the federal Lanham Act.

LAM replies that its challenged use of the "Tootsie" photo is protected under the First Amendment. We evaluate this defense aware of "the careful balance that courts have gradually constructed between the right of publicity and the First Amendment and federal intellectual property laws."

LAM argues that the "Grand Illusions" article and the altered "Tootsie" photograph contained therein are an expression of editorial opinion, entitled to protection under the First Amendment. Hoffman, a public figure, must therefore show that LAM, a media defendant, acted with "actual malice," that is, with knowledge that the photograph was false, or with reckless disregard for its falsity. Because Hoffman did not produce clear and convincing evidence that LAM acted with actual malice, LAM contends that all Hoffman's claims are barred by the First Amendment.

* * *

"Commercial speech" has special meaning in the First Amendment context. ... Such speech is entitled to a measure of First Amendment protection. ... Commercial messages, however, do not receive the same level of constitutional protection as other types of protected expression. ... [C]ommercial speech receives limited amount of protection compared to speech at core of First Amendment and may freely be regulated if it is misleading). When speech is properly classified as commercial, a public figure plaintiff does not have to show that the speaker acted with actual malice.

In many right of publicity cases, the question of actual malice does not arise, because the challenged use of the celebrity's identity occurs in an advertisement that "does no more than propose a commercial transaction" and is clearly commercial speech. ... In all these cases, the defendant used an aspect of the celebrity's identity entirely and directly for the purpose of selling a product. Such uses do not implicate the First Amendment's protection of expressions of editorial opinion.

Hoffman points out that the body double in the "Tootsie" photograph was identified as wearing Ralph Lauren shoes and that there was a Ralph Lauren advertisement (which did not feature shoes) elsewhere in the magazine. (Insofar as the record shows, Richard Tyler, the designer of the gown, had never advertised in LAM.) Hoffman also points to the "Shopper's Guide" in the back of the magazine, which provided stores and prices for the shoes and gown.

These facts are not enough to make the "Tootsie" photograph pure commercial speech. ... LAM did not use Hoffman's image in a traditional advertisement printed merely for the purpose of selling a particular product. ... "Grand Illusions" appears as a feature article on the cover of the magazine and in the table of contents. It is a complement to and a part of the issue's focus on Hollywood past and present. Viewed in context, the article as a whole is a combination of fashion photography, humor, and visual and verbal editorial comment on classic films and famous actors.

* * *

We conclude that LAM's publication of the altered "Tootsie" photograph was not commercial speech.

* * *

We have concluded that LAM is entitled to the full First Amendment protection accorded noncommercial speech. Because a public figure such as Hoffman can recover damages for noncommercial speech from a media organization such as LAM only by proving "actual malice," we now must determine whether the district court was correct in concluding that LAM acted with "reckless disregard for the truth" or a "high degree of awareness of probable falsity." ...

To show actual malice, Hoffman must demonstrate by clear and convincing evidence that LAM intended to create the false impression in the minds of its readers that when they saw the altered "Tootsie" photograph they were seeing Hoffman's body. It is not enough to show that LAM unknowingly misled readers into thinking Hoffman had actually posed for the altered photograph. Mere negligence is not enough to demonstrate actual malice. ... The evidence must clearly and convincingly demonstrate that LAM knew (or purposefully avoided knowing) that the photograph would mislead its readers into thinking that the body in the altered photograph was Hoffman's.

We do not believe that the totality of LAM's presentation of the article and the "Tootsie" photograph provides clear and convincing evidence that the editors intended to suggest falsely to the ordinary reader that he or she was seeing Hoffman's body in the altered "Tootsie" photograph. All but one of the references to the article in the magazine make it clear that digital techniques were used to substitute current fashions for the clothes worn in the original stills.

* * *

Because there is no clear and convincing evidence of actual malice, we must reverse the district court's judgment in Hoffman's favor and the court's award of attorney fees.

Case Questions

1. Explain why the altered "Tootsie" photograph was not considered commercial speech.
2. Explain why the Court concluded that there was no actual malice.

The Case of the Truthful Video Camera

Increasingly, our ability to protect our privacy is being eroded. Law enforcement units are now using video cameras to catch speeders in the act. Even employers have begun using video cameras with greater frequency to monitor employee and customer behavior. But what are the bounds? Can an employer turn the video camera on at all times and in all locations? In the following case, an employee who was caught on tape "lock-picking" claimed that such taping was an invasion of his privacy.

MARRS

v.

MARRIOTT CORP.

United States District Court for Maryland
830 F. Supp. 274 (D. Md. 1992)
December 21, 1992
Nickerson, District Judge

This case arises out of the termination of Plaintiff Timothy H. Marrs ["Marrs"] from his position as a security guard for Defendant Marriott Corporation ["Marriott"]. Marrs was hired by Marriott on January 15, 1982 and until the events that immediately led to his termination, consistently received positive evaluations of his job performance. Due to religious beliefs which prohibited his working on Saturdays, Marrs was generally assigned to work the night shift as an accommodation to his request to have Saturdays off.

On the morning of September 7, 1990, Defendant Timothy Spicer ["Spicer"], a security investigator for Marriott, noticed that some papers in the locked file drawer of his desk had been tampered with. After finding on September 10, 1990 that the drawer had again been opened and papers disturbed, Spicer requested and received permission to monitor the desk in question with a hidden video camera. On September 11, Spicer, along with Night Shift Supervisor Ed Capers, reviewed the video tape and observed Marrs picking the lock on the desk drawer with a paper clip and flipping through the files.

Marrs does not deny that he picked the lock on the desk. The essence of Marrs' explanation for his activities is that he was merely "practicing his lock picking skills." Because of Marrs' conduct, he was immediately placed on a three day suspension pending an investigation. After the investigation was completed, Marrs was informed that he would be terminated because of the incident. Plaintiff was given the option of resigning in lieu of termination, which he did.

On October 22, 1990 Marrs filed a charge of discrimination with the Montgomery County Human Relations Commission alleging that he was discriminated against on the basis of his religion. ... The Complaint [contained a count for] Invasion of Employee Privacy—Surveillance ... .

* * *

Summary Judgment is proper if the evidence before the court, consisting of the pleadings, depositions, answers to interrogatories, and admissions of record, establishes that there is no genuine issue as to any material fact and that the moving party is entitled to judgment as a matter of law.

* * *

Finally, in assessing such a motion, the Court must view the evidence and all justifiable inferences in the light most favorable to the party opposing the motion.

* * *

Marrs asserts in Count VI that Defendants' videotaping of his activities on the night in question constitutes an invasion of his privacy. Although Marrs has not specified which branch of the tort of invasion of privacy he is alleging, it is assumed that he is alleging an intrusion upon his seclusion. To prove such an invasion, Marrs is required to show that the employer intentionally intruded upon his solicitude, seclusion or private affairs in a manner that would be highly offensive to a reasonable person. The Court finds no support for the conclusion that Marrs had a reasonable expectation of privacy in an open office. In fact, Plaintiff admits that the area "was a common area that all of [the security guards] had access to." [T]his type of invasion of privacy [,i.e., surveillance,] generally is inapplicable to most areas of the workplace because there can be no liability for observing an employee at work since he is then not in seclusion.

* * *

For all the above stated reasons, Defendants' Motion for Summary Judgment will be granted for all counts with the exception of Count IV as that count relates to Defendant Spicer.

Case Questions

1. Does an employee have an expectation of privacy at work?
2. What would the employee have had to show for the court to have reached a different result?

Public Disclosure of Private Facts

public disclosure of private facts† One type of the intentional tort of invasion of privacy. Occurs when the tortfeasor communicates purely private information about a person to the public without permission, and a reasonable person would find this disclosure extremely objectionable.

When a tortfeasor communicates purely private information about a person to the public without permission, and a reasonable person would find this disclosure extremely objectionable, then invasion of privacy by **public disclosure of private facts** has taken place. Truth is *not* a defense against this tort, because it is the unauthorized and offensive public revelation of private facts that is being protected against.

The most common example of such disclosure involves communications by the mass media. For example, if a newspaper article mentions an ordinary citizen by name and discusses in detail his or her drug dependency problems, and the person did not consent, then public disclosure of private facts has occurred. Public figures, however, generally do not succeed in lawsuits against the media when such disclosures are made without malice.

The Case of the Viewing Room Covered by the Umbrella

In some cases, the statement "truth is stranger than fiction" really rings true. As a paralegal you will be privy to numerous stories—some of which, if you heard them outside the law office, would cause you to burst out laughing in disbelief. As a professional, you must learn to maintain your composure no matter what the client reveals to you. In this example, you get to see a case from an insurance company's perspective.

LINEBERRY
v.
STATE FARM FIRE & CASUALTY CO.

**United States District Court,
Middle District of Tennessee
885 F. Supp. 1095 (M.D. Tenn. 1995)
April 4, 1995
Echols, District Judge**

Plaintiffs, Dewey Lineberry and Bill Robinson, seek a declaratory judgment requiring State Farm Fire & Casualty Co. ["State Farm"] to defend and indemnify them against actions in state court pursuant to personal liability policies of insurance ... .

Plaintiffs are currently defending four separate actions brought in the Circuit Court of Wilson County, Tennessee by four women. The allegations of all four suits are essentially the same. Lineberry apparently had sexual relationships with the four women over the period of time stated in the lawsuits. In the course of building himself a new office building, Lineberry enlisted the help of Robinson to construct a "secret" viewing room adjoining the recreation room and the restroom of Lineberry's personal office. Two-way mirrors were constructed into the walls of the recreation room and restroom so that anyone in the viewing room could look through the mirrors and observe occupants of the recreation room and bathroom without the occupant's knowledge. The occupants of the recreation room and restroom could see only their own reflections in the mirrors. Lineberry and Robinson set up a video camera in the viewing room so that the persons and activities in the recreation room and restroom could secretly be filmed through the two-way mirrors.

On occasions Lineberry brought the unsuspecting females to his office where Robinson, who was hiding in the viewing room, secretly videotaped their sexual activities. Lineberry contends this scheme was approved or suggested by his attorney as a way to preserve proof of his sexual activities in the event one of his unsuspecting female guests falsely accused him of some impropriety. He maintains that this extraordinary precaution was taken only for his own protection, and that he had no intention of disclosing the video tapes of his sexual escapades to any other person. At some later time, Lineberry and his attorney had a dispute. Subsequently, Lineberry's attorney notified the Wilson County District Attorney of Lineberry's clandestine videotaping activities. After a search warrant was obtained, Lineberry's office was searched, and the tapes were seized by local law enforcement officials. The women depicted in the videotapes were then asked to come to the Sheriff's Department, identify themselves on the videotapes, and explain their actions. All four women deny they were aware they had been filmed.

Each of the four women filed a separate lawsuit in the Circuit Court of Wilson County. The suits charge Lineberry and Robinson with outrageous conduct, intentional infliction of emotional distress, fraud or constructive fraud, misrepresentation, appropriation, and invasion of their rights to privacy. Each of the women seek recovery for humiliation, mental distress, and emotional pain and suffering which resulted from the actions of Lineberry and Robinson.

Both Lineberry and Robinson possess personal liability umbrella insurance policies with State Farm. They contend that pursuant to the provisions of those policies, State Farm must defend and indemnify them against the claims for invasion of privacy in the four lawsuits filed in Wilson County, Tennessee.

* * *

The policies also contain a provision which excludes coverage for intentional acts or acts which are expected. ...

Plaintiffs contend that State Farm, having specifically insured them against losses caused by the invasion of the right to privacy, must both defend them against the claims presented in the four lawsuits and indemnify them for any damages awarded to the four women. State Farm contends it is not required to defend or indemnify against these claims because the losses were not the result of an "accident" and the claims fall within the policy's exclusion for intentional or expected acts.

Plaintiffs counter Defendant's arguments by pointing to the language in the policy which defines "personal injury" by specifically listing a number of intentional torts, including invasion of the right of privacy. In other words, the losses insured against are those resulting in personal injury, which under the policy's definition includes certain types of intentional torts. An intentional tort is a civil wrong or injury which occurs as a result of the intentional act of another person. For example, one cannot commit an act of assault and battery accidentally. ...

Defendant alleges that the insurance policy provisions are not contradictory and the coverage is not illusory, because an invasion of the right to privacy is not necessarily an intentional tort. If that were correct, the policy would not necessarily be ambiguous, as the policy would cover injuries resulting from unintentional invasions of the right of privacy and would exclude those which are intentional.

* * *

In the instant case, the umbrella policy expressly covered injuries resulting from invasion of the right of privacy, an inherently intentional tort, but excluded injuries which were intended or expected. Therefore, the Court finds the coverage is illusory, and the policy is ambiguous and must be interpreted against the insurer and in favor of the insured. Accordingly, State Farm must idemnify Plaintiffs for injuries (humiliation, mental distress, emotional pain and suffering) arising from Plaintiffs' alleged invasion of rights to privacy.

The Court will now turn to State Farm's duty to defend. ... The obligation to defend arises whenever the complaint against the insured alleges a claim upon any ground for which there might be a recovery within the terms of a policy. ... The purpose of such duty ... is for the insured to obtain protection against the expense of defending suits, whether meritorious or groundless, *within the area and scope of liability covered by the policy.*

Because this Court has found that the claims for injuries resulting from the alleged invasion of the right to privacy fall within the coverage of the policies, State Farm has a duty to defend against that portion of the complaints against Lineberry and Robinson.

For the foregoing reasons, Lineberry's Motion for Summary Judgment is GRANTED, Plaintiff Robinson's Motion for Summary Judgment is GRANTED, and Defendant State Farm's Motion for Summary Judgment is DENIED.

Case Questions

1. Why did the court find that the defendant insurance company had an obligation to defend the plaintiffs?
2. Do you think that insurance was designed to cover deliberate and intentional acts of insureds? Explain.

False Light in the Public Eye

false light in the public eye† One type of the intentional tort of invasion of privacy. Occurs when the tortfeasor publicly attributes to another individual spurious opinions, statements, or actions.

Invasion of privacy by placing a person in a **false light in the public eye** happens if the tortfeasor publicly attributes to that individual spurious opinions, statements, or actions. For instance, if a magazine uses someone's photograph and name without permission and in an embarrassing fashion, this would place the victim in a false light publicly. One fact pattern repeated in many court cases concerns a plaintiff's photograph and name appearing in a newspaper adjacent to a negative story appearing on the same page, when the story and photograph appear in such a way as to suggest a connection between the two. Another example would be the advertisement mentioned previously regarding appropriation.

Perhaps no other intentional tort excites the public indignation more than invasion of privacy. Almost everyone desires a sanctuary from the daily intrusions that dominate our urbanized, highly technological, and mobile society. However, the popular conception of the right to privacy does not always afford legal remedies. The following hypotheticals illustrate how the tort elements must first be satisfied.

─ HYPOTHETICALS ─────────────────────

Mel rents a house from Mickey. After Mel had lived there for six months, Mickey notified Mel to move out of the house within ten days, because Mickey needed the house for his bedridden mother. Mel refused, pointing out that the lease ran for a full year and that it could not be terminated by either party without thirty days' advance notice. After ten days, Mickey moved into the house with his mother and her two grandchildren. Mel refused to leave the house, and everyone lived in a state of considerable tension for two weeks before Mel could not stand it any longer and left. Did Mickey invade Mel's privacy by unreasonable intrusion?

Mickey's actions interfered with Mel's solitude in an excessive and highly offensive manner. Mel had complied with the lease agreement and had a legal right to occupy the premises. Mickey's invasion with his invalid mother and two grandchildren substantially disrupted Mel's domestic tranquility. The stress among the house occupants became so extreme that Mel was at last compelled to abandon his residence. Accordingly, Mickey would be liable to Mel for invasion of privacy by unreasonable intrusion.

* * *

Herman was aghast when he opened the day's newspaper to see an advertisement with his picture, in which he was holding a can of Bartell's Beenie-Weenies. Under the photograph was the caption, "Bartell's Makes the Best Beenie-Weenies!" Herman could not recall ever buying this brand and made no such endorsement to anyone associated with the product. He did not give his permission to use the photograph. Has Bartell's invaded Herman's privacy by appropriation?

Bartell's used Herman's likeness in its photograph without his consent. Bartell's hoped to profit from increased sales as a result of this "customer's" endorsement. Bartell's would thus be liable to Herman for invasion of privacy by appropriation.

Furthermore, Bartell's publicly attributed a spurious opinion to Herman in its photograph caption. This would place Herman in a false light in the public eye. Thus, Bartell's would also be liable to Herman for this type of invasion of privacy. ■

Table 5-7 on page 160 summarizes the elements of the four types of invasion of privacy.

Appropriation	Unreasonable Intrusion	Public Disclosure of Private Facts	False Light in the Public Eye
Unconsented use of person's name or likeness for profit	Excessive and highly offensive invasion of one's seclusion or solitude	Public communication of private information about person without permission	Publicly attributing spurious opinions, statements, or actions to a person
		Reasonable person finds disclosure extremely objectionable	

TABLE 5-7 Elements of invasion of privacy

§ 5.8 Defamation: Libel and Slander

defamation Transmission to others of false statements that harm the reputation, business, or property rights of a person. Spoken defamation is *slander* and written defamation is *libel*.

libel Written defamation. Publicly communicated, false written statements that injure a person's reputation, business, or property rights. ... [A] "reckless disregard" for whether the statement is true or false.

slander Oral defamation. The speaking of false words that injure another person's reputation, business, or property rights.

publication Making public. ... In the law of defamation, *publication* usually means communicating defamatory information to a person other than the person defamed.

Defamation consists of two varieties: libel and slander. **Libel** is a written false and disparaging statement about an individual that the tortfeasor communicates to a third party. **Slander** is an oral false and disparaging statement about a person that the tortfeasor communicates to a third party. Courts often refer to this communication element as **publication**. Publication of the defamatory information must injure the victim's reputation in the community. The elements can be outlined as follows:

1. Written (libel) or oral (slander) statement
2. False and defamatory statement about a person
3. Tortfeasor's communication of the statement to a third party
4. Harm to the victim's reputation in the community.

Although the first element is obvious, the others require some elaboration.

Nature of the Statement

For libel, the statement must generally be written in some fashion. This does not necessarily mean writing, such as handwriting, or printed words, such as those appearing on this page. There are many forms of written expression, including such unusual methods as billboards, skywriting with smoke or banners pulled by an airplane, or placing objects such as stones into the shapes of letters. The critical element of writing is whether the information is communicated visually through means of an alphabet.

For slander, the statement must be orally delivered. But it does not have to be words. Gestures, particularly obscene ones, also qualify, provided that the meaning of the gestures is sufficiently clear to onlookers to be defamatory.

Harm to Reputation in the Community

community
1. Neighborhood, locality, etc. A vague term that can include very large or very small areas. 2. A group with common interests. 3. Shared.

A statement is considered *defamatory* if it causes the fourth element—namely, injury to the victim's reputation in the community. For purposes of libel and slander, **community** is narrowly defined as a significant number of persons acquainted or familiar with the victim. Although some courts have held that "a community of one" is sufficient under certain circumstances, most courts maintain that larger numbers are required. Nevertheless, certain expressions, such as "a handful," "a closely associated group," and "associates in the neighborhood or workplace," suggest small numbers in most instances.

Many courts define the victim's injury in more emotional terms. For example, it has commonly been held that statements are libelous or slanderous if they ridicule, humiliate, or subject the victim to contempt or hatred from among his or her peers.

Publication

The tortfeasor must communicate the false and derogatory statement to a third party. That means that statements made by the tortfeasor directly to the victim are defamatory only if seen or heard by another or others.

Publication takes place through any means by which the false information is disseminated. This includes anything spoken, either in person or over amplification (megaphone or loudspeaker at a ballpark, for instance), radio, television, or telephone; or anything written, including letters, telegrams, scribbled messages, billboards, or printed and published works (such as a letter to the editor in the local newspaper, for instance).

Public Figures

Public figures, such as movie and television celebrities or public officers and employees who exercise substantial governmental power, are treated differently than private individuals. These people are used to being under the public eye and have greater access to the media to refute untrue charges than the ordinary person. Accordingly, not as much protection is afforded to public figures. To be successful in claiming defamation, a public figure must show that a statement was made with actual malice. Because this is very hard to prove, few public figures bring lawsuits to challenge statements about them even when they know the assertions to be totally false.

Slander Per Se

Per se is a term indicating that something is automatic or presumed. Some words in and of themselves are defamatory; therefore, injury and damage need not be proven when slander per se is shown. For example, words that imply criminal conduct, or words that are harmful to one's business, or words implying that one has a loathsome and communicable disease are all presumed to damage one's reputation, so the victim need not prove damages to be successful in a slander per se claim.

Truth and Privilege as Absolute Defenses

Truth is considered an absolute defense in defamation cases. If the information the tortfeasor communicates is true, then no libel or slander occurred. To successfully use this defense, the tortfeasor must prove the veracity of the statement.

What is true is often a matter of opinion. It always depends upon the nature of the derogatory comments. For example, to call a person born out of wedlock a "bastard" is technically accurate, but in today's society the term is rarely used as defined in the dictionary. Similarly, to refer to a sexually promiscuous individual as a "harlot" or "gigolo" could be deemed factual by reasonable persons, particularly those who are morally opposed to the conduct described. Courts have struggled with the elasticity of truth, and a variety of formulas for pinpointing truth have been posited in court opinions. The most common court opinion states that literal truth in every detail is unnecessary. If the statement is substantially true, so that a reasonable person would decide that the accusations were justified given the facts, then truth will operate as a defense to defamation actions.

Privilege is also considered an absolute defense in defamation cases. Statements made by attorneys and judges during trials are privileged and cannot be the grounds for a defamation charge. Likewise, legislators are immune from liability for false statements made during debate, even if the lawmakers deliberately make the untrue statements. Members of Congress have an absolute privilege while speaking on the floor of Congress. Privilege allows all these persons to do their best jobs without fear of repercussions should a statement they make later prove to be untrue.

Defamation is another intentional tort, like assault and battery, that virtually everyone has experienced, either as victim or tortfeasor (or both). One need only recall a recent imprudent remark to mentally invoke accusations of slander or libel. Nevertheless, the elements determine whether defamation has occurred, as the following illustrations show.

Table 5-8 on page 168 lists the elements of libel and slander.

‹♦›

The Case of the Living Dead

Imagine one's horror at opening the daily newspaper and, while glancing quickly at the obituaries, spotting oneself listed as recently deceased! Although this may be a shocking revelation, it is the type of mistake that newspapers easily and promptly correct. As the following case illustrates, an erroneous obituary does not always constitute defamation.

DECKER
v.
PRINCETON PACKET, INC.
Supreme Court of New Jersey
116 N.J. 418, 561 A.2d 1122 (1989)
August 8, 1989
Handler, J

This case involves a tort action brought against a newspaper seeking damages for defamation and emotional distress attributable to the publication of a false obituary. The Court is called on to address whether an obituary that reports a death, this being the only false statement, can possibly have a defamatory interpretation. ... The trial court and Appellate Division held that defamation and emotional-harm claims were without merit as a matter of law. Plaintiffs appeal these rulings arguing that defendant's publication of a false obituary without verifying its accuracy caused damage to reputation and emotional harm that should be compensated under our tort law.

On February 15, 1985, the defendant, a newspaper, The Princeton Packet, Inc. ("The Packet"), which publishes on Tuesday and Friday of each week, reported the following obituary for Marcy Goldberg Decker, the plaintiff:

> Marcy Goldberg Decker of Princeton died suddenly Feb. 11. She was 31.
> Ms. Goldberg was the fiance of Robert J. Feldman of Princeton.
> She was a lifelong resident of Princeton and is survived by a son, Jackson T.; her mother, Charlotte Goldberg of Trenton; and a brother, Ronald Goldberg of California.
> Funeral arrangements were incomplete at press time.

This obituary is incorrect because Marcy Decker was not dead.

All other information in the obituary—her age, residence, and family relationships—was accurate ... . Plaintiff notified defendant by a telephone call two days after the publication that she was in fact alive. The Packet printed the following retraction on February 19, 1985:

> The Packet erroneously reported in Friday's edition that Marcy Decker of Princeton died

Feb. 11. The obituary was false. The Packet regrets the error and any inconvenience this may have caused Ms. Decker or her family.

* * *

Plaintiffs deposed three employees of defendant to establish their claims that The Packet was unaware of who had submitted the obituary, [and] that it took no steps to determine the validity of the notice ... .

* * *

A defamatory statement is one that is false and is "'injurious to the reputation of another' or exposes another person to `hatred, contempt or ridicule' or subjects another person to `a loss of the good will and confidence' in which he or she is held by others." Thus, if the statement of Marcy Decker's death in the false obituary could be interpreted by a reasonable person to expose the plaintiff to "hatred, contempt, ridicule or disgrace or subject ... [her] to loss of the good will and confidence of the community," then her action for defamation could proceed to trial.

The principle generally endorsed by most authority throughout the country is that an obituary in which the only false statement concerns the death of the individual, published without malicious intent, is not defamatory *per se.* These cases suggest that publication of a notice of death is usually not defamatory because it does not injure one's reputation. As one court explained, "one is [not] demeaned or belittled by the report of his or her death."

The general rule, however, does have an exception where the false obituary contains additional false information that may be defamatory. ...

This Court finds that the general rule and its limited exception should govern this case and other similar cases. Here, the only false aspect of the obituary was the death of plaintiff Marcy Decker. Therefore, under the general rule, the obituary is not defamatory *per se* because the reported death of an individual when viewed from the perspective of a reasonable person of ordinary intelligence and experience does not impugn reputation. As the trial court observed, the publication of the death notice did not impute to the plaintiff any wrong and did not hold her up to ridicule. Death is a natural state and demeans no one.

... Moreover, the chance of an obituary being incorrect appears slight, and the newspaper can promptly publish a correction, which occurred in this case. Thus, the plaintiffs did have an adequate remedy to correct any false statement and the published correction should have prevented the false obituary from causing any continuing effects.

... Therefore, we hold that where a newspaper mistakenly prints an obituary for a person who is still alive and then retracts its mistake, there is no defamation *per se,* since announcing the death of someone is not by itself injurious to one's reputation.

* * *

Accordingly, the judgment below is affirmed.

Case Questions

1. Do you believe the facts in *Decker* satisfy an action for intentional or reckless infliction of emotional distress? For invasion of privacy? Explain.
2. If the plaintiff could discover who planted the false obituary at the newspaper's offices, could she recover for any intentional torts discussed in this chapter against this unknown person? Why or why not?

— HYPOTHETICALS

Arnold owns an automobile painting service. One of his customers, Ginger, was dissatisfied with Arnold's paint job on her automobile; several spots that had not been polished stood out against the rest of the finish. Rather than complain directly to Arnold, Ginger called in to a live local radio station and said that Arnold was a "con artist" and that he had swindled many other people with sloppy work. Has Ginger slandered Arnold?

Ginger communicated information about Arnold to third persons, and so publication occurred. The information was false, as Ginger's dissatisfaction with a single paint job hardly documented Arnold's dishonesty. The critical issue is whether Ginger's statements were defamatory. It is likely that Ginger's accusations about Arnold's honesty and integrity will substantially injure Arnold's business reputation in the community. This is particularly true because the allegations suggest criminal conduct by an innocent person. Thus, Ginger has slandered Arnold and is liable to him for damages.

* * *

Consider the hypothetical of Helga. She enjoyed writing letters to the editor and her missives regularly appeared in the newspaper. One day

Helga turned to the editorial page and read the following response to one of her letters:

Dear Editor:

In response to Helga Goldblatt's letter in last week's edition, I must say that this woman is mentally ill and needs psychiatric treatment. She suffers from delusions and cannot be trusted. How can she make those ridiculous statements about the city's snow removal policy? I happen to work for the city street department, and I know that we regularly clear side streets after handling the main streets. It usually only takes a few extra days to get to the side streets, not weeks as she said. Why doesn't she take her medicine and get a grip?

Jackson Winderson

Has Jackson libeled Helga? Jackson's written communication was published—literally—by appearing in the newspaper. Many people would have been exposed to the letter. Helga's reputation in the community undoubtedly will suffer from Jackson's accusations that she is "mentally ill." Although it may be true that Helga was uninformed about the city's snow removal policy, truth as to these matters is irrelevant— the defamatory remarks pertained to Helga's mental capacity. Jackson would be liable to Helga for libel. ■

The Case of the "Woodchipper Murderer"

In this case, a man's wife—a stewardess—disappeared. A news broadcaster suggested that the pilot-husband had murdered his wife like another pilot had in a similar case. Is mere inference enough, or must defamation be proved by explicit words?

BROWN
v.
HEARST CORP.
United States Court of Appeals, First Circuit
54 F.3d 21 (1st Cir. 1955)
May 11, 1995
Boudin, Circuit Judge

In March 1987, Regina Brown, the then-wife of appellant Willis Brown and mother of three children, disappeared. At the time Regina was employed as a flight attendant, and Willis as a pilot, for American Airlines; the couple had lived together in Newtown, Connecticut, but had been separated for four months and were living apart. The police investigated the disappearance and found Regina's car abandoned in New York but no trace of her. The investigation remains open. It is not known whether Regina is alive or dead.

Later in the same year the Browns were divorced in a Connecticut state court, the contested proceedings being completed in Regina's absence. The state court trial was prolonged and a detailed opinion was written by the trial judge pertaining to custody and support. ...

The trial was widely reported in the press, and publicity continued even after the decree. This was due partly to further litigation and the continuing police investigation, but also to a freakish coincidence. About six months before

Regina's disappearance, another woman who lived in Newtown, a Pan Am flight attendant married to an Eastern pilot, had disappeared. Fragments of her bone were found in a nearby river, and her pilot husband was convicted in the so-called woodchipper murder.

In November 1990, appellee Hearst Corporation d/b/a WCVB-TV Channel 5 in Boston ("Channel 5") broadcasted from Massachusetts a segment entitled "The Other Pilot's Wife" as a part of the station's regular "newsmagazine" program. It was prepared by Mary Richardson, a journalist with the station, who conducted a substantial amount of research and a number of interviews in preparing the broadcast.

The broadcast opens with the leitmotif—"Tonight the bizarre story of a small New England town where one stewardess is dead, another is missing"—and then offers a brief reprise of the 1986 murder of the Pan Am flight attendant. Next, turning to the Browns, the broadcast describes and depicts an apparent storybook marriage going sour, the divorce petition, and Regina's disappearance. "In the days following Regina's disappearance," says Richardson, "Willis showed no interest in what had happened to her."

* * *

There is other incriminating information about Willis recounted in the program, and the police are described as having suspected Willis and as believing still that "Mr. Brown knows more about the disappearance of his wife than he is letting on." No evidence even remotely exculpatory of Willis is described. On the other hand, Mary Richardson, the "voice over" throughout the program, never asserts that Willis is guilty or even says that she thinks he is guilty. Formally, the program describes the disappearance as a mystery or, at worst, a possible murder still unsolved.

In February 1993, Willis brought the present action against Channel 5 in state court in Texas. The case was removed to federal court and thereafter transferred to the federal district court in Massachusetts. As subsequently amended, Willis' complaint charged defamation, invasion of privacy under Mass. Gen.L. ch. 214 § 1B, "false light" invasion of privacy, and intentional infliction of emotional distress.

After discovery, Channel 5 moved for summary judgment. In a detailed opinion dated July 21, 1994, the district court granted the motion. As to the defamation claim, the court relied in different respects on lack of falsity, the limited protection available for statements of opinion, the "fair report" privilege, and lack of fault. The privacy and intentional infliction claims were dismissed on grounds described below. Willis has now appealed, asserting that all of his claims should have been submitted to a jury.

On appeal from a grant of summary judgment, we review the decision de novo, drawing inferences in favor of the party opposing the motion. …

Channel 5 does not appear to dispute that the broadcast charges Willis with murder or at least that a jury would be entitled to find this to be the import of the program. The broadcast never flatly expresses that accusation. Indeed, it says that the murder is unsolved and makes clear that the police have nothing much in the way of direct evidence against Willis. But defamation can occur by innuendo as well as by explicit assertion, and the suggestion here is a fairly strong one.

* * *

The broadcast makes clear that the police suspect Willis, and Regina's parents are filmed making even stronger statements of suspicion. Material from the divorce trial is used to establish or buttress doubts about Willis' character and history. The suggestion of murder runs through the program like a gold thread. The broadcast opens with the dramatic footage relating to the woodchipper murder and closes with Richardson's rhetorical question, could "someone" get away with murder?

A common defense to a charge of defamation is "truth." The Supreme Court tells us that in a suit like this one against the media the burden is upon the defamed plaintiff to show that the statements are not true. Neither side addresses this issue. Perhaps each assumes that to carry his burden of proof, Willis could testify at trial that he did not murder his wife and a jury might believe him. In all events, we take the case as one in which a jury might find that murder had been charged and that the charge was false.

Channel 5's primary response is that "[m]uch of the [b]roadcast, and the entirety of its allegedly defamatory sting, is in essence a `fair report' of the Brown's divorce trial in Connecticut" and thus falls under the Massachusetts privilege allowed for media coverage of an official proceeding. Such a privilege certainly exists in Massachusetts, and there is little doubt that much of the material in the broadcast is drawn from, and attributed to, the divorce proceeding.

For present purposes, we will assume that the privilege extends to non-contemporaneous reports and that the program—so far as it related to the divorce proceeding and the information developed there—conveyed a fair and accurate report of the proceeding. But only a portion of the broadcast purported to be drawn from the proceeding. And, while that portion may be privileged, we are skeptical of Channel 5's claim that the the entire "sting" of the broadcast is privileged material.

* * *

Where the evidence is thus enlarged and the charge cast in a more lurid light, it is not clear to us that the fair report privilege automatically shields the larger whole.

The problem for Willis, we think, is that the Supreme Court has instructed that a state libel-suit plaintiff must demonstrate fault on the part of the media; and this requirement applies even where the plaintiff is not a public official or public figure. In such cases Massachusetts has imposed a requirement that the newspaper or broadcaster be shown to be negligent or worse. Thus, even if a false charge of murder has been made, it remains to see whether

Willis provided evidence of negligence to justify submitting the case to a jury. ...

So far as the murder goes, Willis points to nothing to suggest that Channel 5 was negligent in its mustering of the available evidence. Some might think the broadcast gaudy journalism; certainly the interpolation of the woodchipper murder is largely gratuitous. ...

Willis' brief says tersely that the police admitted that they had no evidence against him; and he reasons that it was thus "negligent disregard for the truth" for Channel 5 to "insinuate" that "[he] murdered his wife and disposed of her body in the same fashion as did [the woodchipper murderer]." ...

A different problem is presented by Willis' suggestion that the broadcast charged him with disposing of his wife's body "in the same fashion" as the woodchipper murder. Patently, the broadcast did not so charge; no reasonable juror could draw such an inference. Willis offers no argument to support such an inference, and it is not surprising that elsewhere in his brief he retreats to a more cautious assertion: that the juxtaposition "conveys the message that Brown also murdered his wife and disposed of her body *in some insidious fashion*" (emphasis added).

* * *

Even if all of these doubts are resolved in Willis' favor, we think this narrow remaining claim is too thin to survive summary judgment. About the most one can get from the woodchipper episode is the suggestion that, if Willis killed his wife, he also took steps to assure that her body would not be found.

* * *

A writing or program is normally viewed as a whole; and that requirement has special force here because the woodchipper episode was assertedly about someone else, and its connection to Willis depended upon the rest of the program. We conclude as a matter of law that the broadcast, taken as a whole, cannot reasonably be taken to charge that Willis brutally disposed of his wife's body.

Willis' non-libel claims do not require much discussion. On appeal, Willis' has narrowed his privacy claim to the contention that the program places him in a false light by leaving the viewer with "a false impression," *i.e.*, that Brown killed Regina and disposed of her body in the same fashion as did the woodchipper murderer. The district court thought it sufficient that Massachusetts has never adopted the false light theory of privacy invasion.

* * *

Lastly, Willis charged Channel 5 with intentional infliction of emotional distress. This is a recognized tort under Massachusetts law requiring intended or foreseeable infliction of such distress, "extreme and outrageous conduct," and causation of distress so severe that no reasonable person could be expected to endure it. The district court said that Channel 5's conduct was not negligent and therefore could hardly be "extreme and outrageous."

In all events, many of the legitimate news stories that appear in the media involve foreseeable distress for the subject of the story, probably severe distress in some cases. Regina's disappearance and the divorce trial were news stories, and so was her continued absence and the failure of the police to solve the case. Willis provides no basis to think that generally accurate coverage in such a case is even remotely close to conduct "beyond all possible bounds of decency" and "utterly intolerable in a civilized community."

Affirmed.

Case Questions

1. Which of the parties is described as having a privilege?
2. What was the effect of the privilege?

TABLE 5-8
Elements of libel and slander

Libel	*Slander*
Written statement	Oral statement
False and defamatory statement	False and defamatory statement
Publication to third party	Publication to third party
Injury to victim's reputation in the community	Injury to victim's reputation in the community

Summary

Intentional torts include actions designed to injure another person or his or her property. All intentional torts embrace an act, intent, and injurious conduct. These elements must occur together. Intentional torts harming the individual include assault, battery, false imprisonment, infliction of emotional distress, fraud, misrepresentation, malicious prosecution, abuse of process, invasion of privacy, and defamation.

Assault is the tortfeasor's attempt to inflict harmful or offensive contact upon another person without consent. Assault places the victim in fear of his or her physical safety, even if the anticipated contact would produce only a distasteful reaction. The threat of contact must be imminent. Battery is a completed assault. It is the intentional, unconsented touching of another person in a harmful or offensive manner. Physical contact is required, although it may occur only with the victim's clothing or objects held. Transferred intent means that the contact directed at one person carries over to another individual who was inadvertently struck; battery would thus have occurred to the unintended victim.

False imprisonment is the confinement of someone without his or her consent. Confinement must exist for an appreciable length of time. The victim must have no reasonable means of escape. The tortfeasor must intend to confine the victim and act to accomplish confinement. Confinement may be achieved either by physical barriers or by threat of force which intimidates the victim into remaining in the restricted area.

Intentional infliction of emotional distress involves outrageous conduct designed to cause severe mental anguish in the victim. The victim must actually suffer emotional turmoil as a result of the tortfeasor's actions. Reckless infliction of emotional distress includes outrageous conduct that the tortfeasor knew, or reasonably should have known, would produce significant emotional injury to the victim. The conduct is considered outrageous if it shocks the conscience of a reasonable person with normal emotional sensibilities. Therefore, intent is not necessary.

Fraud consists of false statements made to entice the victim to surrender something of value to the defrauder. Misrepresentation includes false statements or behavior designed to deceive the victim. In many jurisdictions, the two intentional torts are considered virtually identical and interchangeable. The tortfeasor must know that the statements made are false and intend to deceive the victim.

Malicious prosecution happens when a private citizen files a groundless criminal complaint with the prosecutor against an innocent person who is named as the defendant in a criminal prosecution action. To sue the complainant, the innocent defendant must be either acquitted or otherwise victorious in the criminal lawsuit. The complainant must have filed the frivolous criminal charges out of malice for the innocent defendant, and malice may be implied from the circumstances surrounding the case. The innocent defendant must be injured as a consequence of the baseless prosecution. Abuse of process is the misuse (or threat of misuse) of a legal proceeding against another to obtain an unlawful objective. The victim must be harmed by the frivolous legal action. It is the civil equivalent of malicious prosecution.

Invasion of privacy consists of four independent varieties: appropriation, unreasonable intrusion, public disclosure of private facts, and false light in the public eye. Appropriation is the use of a person's name or likeness, without consent, for profit in some way. Unreasonable intrusion involves excessive and highly offensive interference with an individual's seclusion or solitude. Public disclosure of private facts happens when a tortfeasor publicly communicates purely private information about another person and such a disclosure would offend a reasonable person. False light in the public eye occurs when a tortfeasor publicly attributes to another spurious statements, opinions, or actions.

Defamation includes libel and slander. Libel is written communication of false and disparaging statements about an individual to third parties. Slander involves oral communication that does the same thing. Communication to third persons is called publication. The misinformation disseminated must injure the victim by harming his or her reputation in the community. Community can be narrowly defined as a small number of persons who know the victim. Even one third party is sufficient in some cases for publication to exist. Truth is an absolute defense in defamation actions. Public figures must prove actual malice to succeed in a defamation claim.

Key Terms

abuse of process	false light in the public eye	probable cause
apprehension	fraud (deceit)	publication
appropriation	intent	public disclosure of
assault	intentional infliction of	private facts
battery	emotional distress	reasonable person standard
community	intentional injury (tort)	reckless infliction of
complainant	invasion of privacy	emotional distress
consent	libel	slander
defamation	malice	transferred intent
emotional distress	malicious prosecution	unreasonable intrusion
false imprisonment	misrepresentation	

Problems

In the following hypotheticals, identify the intentional tort(s) committed, if any, and support your answer.

1. Alicia Teldare was waiting in line outside The Elegant Shop just before the store opened on the day of the shop's annual savings sale. Dozens of customers milled around the entrance in anticipation. Many patrons began to grow impatient. Suddenly, the doors were opened, and Alicia was knocked to the ground by Marie Harrington, another customer. Alicia covered her face with her arms in anticipation of being trampled. In her haste to enter, Marie stepped on Alicia's hand and broke Alicia's ring finger.

2. Malcolm Harberry is the manager of The Soft Touch, a ladies clothing store. Madge Strident, a customer, was looking at accessory jewelry next to the full-length mirrors. Malcolm glanced at the mirrors and thought he saw Madge place something in her purse. He thought it might be jewelry, but he did not actually see the object. As Madge began to exit the store, Malcolm asked her politely to stop. She did so, whereupon Malcolm identified himself and requested that she accompany him to the back room for questioning. She refused. Malcolm insisted, threatening to telephone the police if she attempted to leave the store. She then agreed and the two went to a small room at the rear of the store. Inside, Malcolm asked Madge to empty her pockets and purse, which she did. No jewelry was found. He asked her a few questions about the jewelry and what he had seen. She explained that she had put a handkerchief into her purse, and there was in fact a kerchief inside it. Malcolm apologized for any inconvenience and Madge then left. The interview in the room lasted five minutes.

3. Eugene Bagley III was an aspiring literature student at the state university. He had submitted several short stories and poems to *Rhapsody*, a college literary magazine. Irving Buchanan lived in Eugene's dormitory and had a reputation for playing pranks on fellow dorm residents. Irving wrote a fake letter of rejection on *Rhapsody* letterhead, which a friend had taken from the magazine's office supplies. The letter was a scathing indictment of Eugene's work as plagiarism and amateurish. The letter threatened to notify the English department and academic dean about the alleged plagiarism. Irving signed the editor of the magazine's name. When Eugene received the letter, he became physically ill and had to visit the university hospital for medication to sleep and concentrate.

4. Dudley Dooley was a salesperson at a local hardware store. Samuel Feeber was a customer looking to buy exterior paint for his storage shed. When Samuel told Dudley he needed paint that could be used on metal siding, Dudley indicated a wood paint. Samuel inquired about this, but Dudley said that it was not just for wood but for any surface. In fact, the paint would not adhere to any surface other than wood. Dudley had worked in the store for only a few days and knew nothing about any of the paint supplies. Samuel bought the paint and applied it. Within two weeks, the paint peeled off.

Review Questions

1. Define and discuss the specific intentional torts causing injuries to persons. Can you give examples of each? Do the intentional torts share any basic elements?

2. What is assault? What is battery? How are the two distinguishable? Similar? When is apprehension necessary? When is physical contact required? What types of contact are included? Must the threat of contact be imminent? Why are intent and consent important? What is transferred intent?

3. Define *false imprisonment*. What is confinement? How may it be accomplished? How are intent and consent relevant? Must confinement exist for any length of time? What role does escape play?

4. In the field of intentional torts, what is the intentional infliction of emotional distress? What is mental anguish? Outrageous conduct? When is intent necessary?

5. Define *fraud* and *misrepresentation*. How are they similar? Distinguishable? Is intent required? What objectives must the tortfeasor have in giving false information?

6. Describe malicious prosecution and abuse of process. Can you determine why they are separate intentional torts? What makes criminal prosecution groundless? What is malice? Must the victim win in criminal litigation? What injury is required? For abuse of process, how can legal proceedings be misused? To what purpose?

7. What are the four varieties of invasion of privacy in tort law? How is each defined? Do you see any similarities between invasion of privacy and any other intentional torts?

8. What are the two aspects of defamation? How are they comparable? What is publication? What makes a statement false and defamatory? What is the role of truth in defamation?

Projects

1. Which intentional torts discussed in this chapter are included in your state's common law? Are any defined by statute? Does your state have any additional intentional torts that deal with harm to persons?

2. Paralegal students often separate into small study groups to discuss cases and problems. You may wish to meet with several classmates to discuss the theories in this and other chapters of the book. You might wish to create your own hypothetical fact situations utilizing the intentional torts discussed in this chapter.

3. Read the case of *Cinel v. Connick* in Appendix C. Was the plaintiff Cinel successful in pursuing his right-to-privacy claim? Do you agree with the appellate court's reasoning in its decision? Explain.

4. Read the *Pepsico, Inc. v. Redmond* case in Appendix C. Do you think the Quaker Oats Company wanted to hire Redmond solely for the trade secrets and confidential information he had access

to, or could there have been any other reason for the job offer? Is it possible, when starting a new job, to totally disregard any information or secrets learned in a prior position?

5. Read the *Roach v. Stern* case in Appendix C. What elements were needed to successfully plead intentional infliction of emotional distress?

Internet Resources

This chapter deals with intentional torts and injuries to persons. To learn more about personal injury law, the following sites can be accessed:

General Information

http://www.personal-injury-law.com
http://www.lawnewsnetwork.com

Publications

http://www.lawofficecomputing.com
http://www.lawtechnews.com
http://www.nylj.com

Medical Information

http://www.nlm.nih.gov

Expert Witnesses and Consultants

http://www.nocall.org/experts.htm
http://www.claims.com
http://www.findlaw.com/13experts/index.html

For additional resources, visit our Web site at
www.paralegal.delmar.cengage.com

CHAPTER 6

INTENTIONAL TORTS: INJURIES TO PROPERTY

CHAPTER OUTLINE

§ 6.1 Introduction
§ 6.2 Trespass to Land
§ 6.3 Toxic Tort Actions
§ 6.4 Trespass to Chattel
§ 6.5 Conversion
§ 6.6 Slander of Title, Commercial Disparagement, and Defamation by Computer

EQUAL JUSTICE UNDER LAW

---◆---

Ownership does not always mean absolute dominion.
Justice Hugo Black

§ 6.1 Introduction

The previous chapter examined intentional torts involving injuries to persons. This chapter deals with injury to the rights of a property owner or possessor. (An owner's duty to others was discussed in Chapter 5.)

This chapter includes:

◆ Intentional torts dealing with injuries to property rights

◆ Trespass to land

◆ Toxic torts

◆ Trespass to chattel

◆ Conversion

◆ Slander of title

◆ Commercial disparagement

◆ Defamation by computer.

§ 6.2 Trespass to Land

Trespass is an ancient concept in tort law. In medieval English law, torts originated from trespass and trespass on the case. Under modern American law, trespass is recognized in two varieties: trespass to land and trespass to chattel.

Elements of Trespass to Land

trespass A wrongful entry onto another person's property.

Trespass to land occurs when a tortfeasor enters upon a land owner's real estate without consent. The tortfeasor trespasses when he or she intentionally acts in such a way as to violate the land owner's exclusive right to use the land. The elements of trespass to land are threefold:

1. Unauthorized entry upon another person's real estate

2. Tortfeasor's intent to enter without consent

3. Tortfeasor's actions interfering with the land owner's exclusive right to use the land (possession).

Entry Defined

entry The act of entering [as upon real property].

The tortfeasor must enter upon a land owner's real estate without permission. **Entry** occurs when the tortfeasor acts so as to interfere with the land owner's exclusive right to use the property. For example, walking across someone's front lawn constitutes entry, because the tortfeasor entered the land. Also, entry happens if a person throws trash in a neighbor's backyard, because the trash depositor placed an unwanted substance (trash) on the land. Both these examples include the interference element. The front-lawn owner cannot utilize his or her property exclusively if someone is walking across it. The neighbor's use of his or her backyard is severely hampered by the accumulation of another's trash. The tortfeasor's conduct in either case has disrupted the land owner's exclusive use of the real estate. This is the foundation of trespass to land.

Unauthorized Entry

The entry must be without consent. This essentially translates as a permission element. For instance, if a farmer allows a person to cross his fields to reach a lake in which to fish, then that person has not committed trespass—the entry was authorized. Similarly, homeowners may invite visitors onto their premises by extending an implied welcome, such as clearing sidewalks of snow up to a house door or placing doorbells outside the doors. This suggests that people may come upon the property to speak with the land owner. Consequently, door-to-door salespersons would not necessarily be trespassing if they had reason to believe that the homeowner welcomed their presence. However, if the yard were fenced in, with a "no soliciting" sign displayed, then the salespersons would know that they did not have permission to enter the property.

Sometimes persons have a lawful right to enter upon another's land. For example, if the land owner gives an easement to a utility company to install utility lines across his or her property, then the utility company has the legal right to enter the premises to install and maintain the lines. Accordingly, no trespass to land could happen. Also, a process server, such as the county sheriff, generally has the legal right to enter the defendant's land to deliver a plaintiff's complaint and summons. No trespass to land would occur in such an instance.

One's lawful right to be upon another's premises may be withdrawn, however. Consider the example of the patron of a store. Customers are invited to come upon the premises to spend money. Suppose one such individual becomes disruptive, annoying other shoppers and employees. The store manager could demand that the agitator leave immediately. At this point, the customer becomes a trespasser, because remaining means that he or she is present upon another's land without consent. Although the customer was originally invited into the store as a patron, once he or she is ordered to leave, trespass occurs.

No Actual Harm Required

It is important to note that, under trespass law, the unauthorized entry need not cause any damage to the real estate. It is sufficient that the transgression occurred. Trespass law presumes that injury has happened simply because the tortfeasor has interfered with the land owner's use of the realty. Thus, simply walking across someone's front lawn without permission is trespass to land, although no actual harm arises from the conduct. These types of trespasses to land are often called *technical trespasses*. Courts generally award only nominal damages in such cases. **Damages** are dollar amounts that the defendant must pay the plaintiff if the plaintiff wins judgment against the defendant. In technical trespass cases, courts usually award a paltry sum, such as one dollar in **nominal damages**, because no actual injury resulted from the trespass. The judgment award is ceremonial or symbolic of the technical invasion of the land owner's property rights.

As a practical matter, few lawsuits involve technical trespasses. It is simply too expensive to litigate a trespass action when no injury has resulted. Litigants frequently speak of suing "as a matter of principle," but plaintiffs are rarely sufficiently affluent to afford it.

Intentional Interference

The tortfeasor must have intended to enter the land owner's real estate without consent. Thus, if Twila is forced to cross a neighbor's front yard to escape a pursuing wild animal, she has not committed trespass to land. Twila did not intend to cross her neighbor's property without permission; rather, she was essentially forced across by the chasing animal. However, if she deliberately strolls across her neighbor's yard, the entry was intentional.

Possession: Land Owner's Exclusive Right to Use

To constitute trespass to land, the tortfeasor's unauthorized entry must interfere with the land owner's **exclusive right** to use his or her realty. This is sometimes called the **exclusive right of possession**, which entitles the land owner to use the property without anyone else's meddling. Recall the illustrations from the discussion of entry: the neighbor could not use his or her land exclusively if someone else's trash was being dumped on it. Nor could someone use his or her front lawn exclusively if another person walked across it.

This exclusivity requirement may at first appear overly harsh. One might well ask what wrong has been done just by crossing someone's land. Trespass intends to protect one's real estate in much the same way as

---

damages Money that a court orders paid to a person who has suffered damage (a loss or harm) by the person who caused the injury.

nominal damages† Small or symbolic damages awarded in situations in which no actual damages have occurred, or the right has not been proven even though a right has been violated in an intentional tort action.

exclusive right† A right granted to no one else.

exclusive right of possession† A land owner's right to use his or her property without interference from other persons.

assault and battery are intended to protect one's person. The objective is protection from undesired interferences. In this respect, trespass seeks merely to protect one's realty from other people encroaching upon it, just as assault and battery are meant to deter unwanted physical contact.

The Case of the Unholy Waters

Many invasions onto one's realty can result in trespass to land. Persons and manmade objects readily come to mind as examples. But what about natural substances, such as rainwater? This, too, can provide an injured land owner with a cause of action, should the water, as it often does, cause structural damage.

In the following case, displaced rainwater created a multitude of problems for the property owners. Although the church believes that rain is an act of God, there are times when even the most pious institutions fall victim to poor drainage and even poorer land-use planning.

BURT
v.
BEAUTIFUL SAVIOR LUTHERAN CHURCH
Colorado Court of Appeals
809 P.2d 1064 (Colo. Ct. App. 1990)
October 25, 1990
Davidson, Judge

Defendant, Beautiful Savior Lutheran Church of Broomfield, appeals a judgment entered on a jury verdict in favor of plaintiffs, Wayne Burt, Donna Draper, and Curtis Draper, for water damage to Burt's real property resulting from defendant's negligence and trespass. We affirm in part, reverse in part, and remand with directions.

Defendant and Burt are adjoining landowners. The Drapers are Burt's daughter and son-in-law, and are tenants in the Burt residence. Defendant's property, which is immediately west of Burt's, is markedly sloped downwards directly toward the Burt property. Both properties have been plagued with water drainage problems for many years.

In 1964, Burt's property was flooded by surface water from a heavy rain. At that time, he installed an underground drain from his backyard to his front yard which emptied into the street. Then, in 1979, defendant converted the area immediately west of Burt's property into a paved parking lot.

Approximately four years later, in August 1983, after another heavy rain caused flooding on his property, Burt dug a ditch, in part on defendant's property, to drain water into a storm drain on the street. At the same time, in response to flooding on its property, defendant constructed a 15-foot manhole with a sump pump at a corner of its foundation wall and installed a drainpipe underground from the sump pump to the street. This drainpipe extended along the boundary between defendant's and Burt's property, emptying into the street just west of the Burt property. According to defendant's evidence, at the time the drainpipe was installed, the church pastor asked Burt if he objected to the removal of certain trees which Burt had planted on defendant's property in 1961. The pastor testified that, although he told Burt there was a danger of roots clogging the new drainpipe, Burt replied he did not want the trees removed.

In 1984, approximately six months after defendant's drainpipe was installed, Burt noticed that water was coming into his basement through cracks in the foundation. Responding to Burt's complaint, defendant constructed a dirt berm on its property to deflect surface water flowing down towards Burt's property. Nevertheless, Burt's foundation continued to crack and deteriorate.

Evidence at trial indicated that defendant had installed a drainpipe which was inadequate in size and had unsealable joints that were virtually certain to leak. The evidence also showed that the drainpipe had been improperly installed and was clogged with tree roots. In June 1987, defendant replaced the drainpipe and the water flow into Burt's basement stopped.

Burt then brought this action seeking damages for the repair of his basement foundation, alleging theories of negligence and trespass. At the close of the evidence, the court instructed the jury, without objection, on both trespass and negligence. The trial court, however, refused defendant's request to instruct the jury on comparative negligence. In its ruling, the trial court reasoned that comparative negligence was not appropriate because "it's just for the jury to decide whether there is ground water that was there historically or whether it was created by the church's actions." The trial court also refused defendant's requested instruction of plaintiffs' failure to mitigate damages.

The jury returned a verdict for plaintiffs on both trespass and negligence, and defendant appeals, alleging the refusal to so instruct the jury, and other actions by the trial court, constituted reversible error. Plaintiffs cross-appeal on the issues of costs and interests. We affirm the judgment and reverse and remand on the issue of costs and interest.

[The court's discussion of comparative negligence issue is omitted. The court concluded that the doctrine was inapplicable to trespass actions.]

In early English law, the writ of "trespass" had a basic criminal character and provided a cause of action for all direct and immediate injuries to person or property. "Trespass on the case," a separate writ which developed later, originally allowed remedies for all indirect injuries. ...

In Colorado, liability for trespass requires only an intent to do the act that itself constitutes, or inevitably causes, the intrusion. Specifically, trespass is the physical intrusion upon property of another without the permission of the person lawfully entitled to the possession of the real estate. "One is subject to liability to another for trespass, irrespective of whether he thereby causes harm to any legally protected interest of the other, if he intentionally ... enters land in the possession of the other, or causes a thing or a third person to do so. ..."

Thus, a landowner who sets in motion a force which, in the usual course of events, will damage property of another, is guilty of trespass on such property. Here, defendant's act of constructing the drainpipe in such a way as to cause water leakage into Burt's property amounted to a trespass.

* * *

Here, defendant does not dispute that the evidence was sufficient to support the jury's verdict for plaintiffs on their trespass claim. Therefore, because the defense of comparative negligence is inapplicable to trespass, the failure of the court to instruct the jury thereon was not error.

[The Court's discussion of the mitigation of damages issue is omitted.]

Compensation for injury resulting from trespass can include (a) the diminution of market value or the costs of restoration, (b) the loss of use of the property, and (c) discomfort and annoyance to the occupant. Since the Drapers were in possession of the property and therefore are entitled to damages for trespass, defendant is liable to the Drapers for the damage to their possessory interests.

These damages include the loss of use of their basement and the discomfort and annoyance caused by the smell in their home.

[The Court's discussion on the remaining, tangential issues is omitted.]

Case Questions

1. How does the definition of trespass to land in *Burt* compare with the general description in this chapter?
2. When Burt dug his ditch partially upon the defendant's land in August 1983, was this trespass to land?

Trespass Above and Below Land: Is the Sky the Limit?

Trespass to land may occur not only upon the surface of the realty, but also above and below it. In property law, a Latin phrase summarizes the extent of one's ownership of land: *cujus est solum ejus est usque ad coelum* ("he who has the soil owns upward unto heaven and downward to perdition"). Thus, it is possible for trespass to occur in the air above one's land. For instance, if a utility company erects wires across one's land without consent, this would constitute trespass to land, because the land owner owns the air above the soil. This could present insurmountable difficulties for aircraft. Fortunately, modern common law implies an exception for aircraft to fly over private property.

Similarly, one owns the resources under the earth. Although this enters into the complex area of oil, gas, and mineral law (within which special legal theories have evolved), it may be said generally that one owns the mineral resources beneath one's real estate. Accordingly, if someone mines under a person's land without permission, trespass to land has occurred. Cave exploration cases provide an interesting aspect of this theory. In a famous Indiana court case, *Marengo Cave Co. v. Ross*, 212 Ind. 624, 10 N.E.2d 917 (1937), the Supreme Court of Indiana stated that it was a trespass for the cave company to charge admission for tourists to explore caves below the surface of a land owner's property.

The sanctity of land is an ancient aspect of the human psyche. For millennia, people have used physical force and, as civilization progressed, force of law to protect against such invasions. Today, trespass to land remains an active intentional tort, as these hypotheticals demonstrate.

— HYPOTHETICALS

Burrough Excavating Company was digging a basement for a new home. Burrough's backhoe operator dumped the dirt on a vacant lot next to the construction site. This lot was owned by Mark, who never gave Burrough permission to use his lot. Has Burrough trespassed to land against Mark?

The elements line up nicely. Mark did not consent to Burrough's dirt dumping, and so Burrough engaged in unauthorized entry upon another's realty. Burrough obviously intended this entry, as the backhoe operator dumped the dirt on Mark's lot. This dumping interfered with Mark's exclusive use of his property, because he will now have to contend with the dirt pile if he wishes to use his lot. Therefore, Burrough has committed trespass to land against Mark.

* * *

Consider another hypothetical. George owns a house next to Elizabeth. Elizabeth planted several oak trees on her property with branches that hang over a fence separating her property from George's. George thought the trees were unsightly and trimmed the limbs that hung over onto his yard. He did not ask Elizabeth for permission to remove the limbs. Has a trespass occurred?

Who has trespassed? By allowing her tree branches to cross over onto George's property, Elizabeth committed unauthorized entry onto another's land without consent. Her trees interfered with George's exclusive right of possession, because the branches obstructed George's use of this part of his property. Recall, too, that George owns to the top of the sky under the *ad coelum* doctrine discussed earlier. Anything encroaching upon his airspace constitutes entry. Intent may be implied, as Elizabeth knew the trees crossed the fence but did nothing to remove the overhanging limbs. Thus, Elizabeth has trespassed upon George's land.

Somewhat more problematic is the inverse inquiry: namely, did George trespass against Elizabeth by pruning the trees? Because the trees grew on Elizabeth's property, George's trimming (without permission) encroached upon Elizabeth's use of her trees. But does this constitute unauthorized entry onto another's land? The branches hung over onto George's property, so he did not actually enter upon Elizabeth's land to cut the limbs. He was simply "defending" his property from the encroaching branches. Accordingly, George did not commit trespass to land against Elizabeth. ∎

Recent trespass actions have involved one of the most complex and dynamic developing areas of tort law—namely, toxic tort litigation. Section 6.3 discusses this type of trespass.

§ 6.3 Toxic Tort Actions

toxic tort actions[†]
Actions involving toxic chemicals, pollution, hazardous waste disposal and transportation, and other environmentally sensitive issues. This litigation applies many tort theories, including trespass to land, negligence, absolute liability for ultrahazardous substances, products liability, and nuisance.

A significant percentage of modern tort litigation is devoted to actions involving toxic chemicals, pollution, hazardous waste disposal and transportation, and other environmentally sensitive issues. These are sometimes referred to as **toxic tort actions**. These lawsuits cover causes of action involving the following: trespass to land, negligence, absolute liability for ultrahazardous substances, products liability, and nuisance. This chapter focuses on the trespass to land aspects of toxic tort litigation.

Nature of the Problem

For much of this century, toxic waste disposal was considered simple. Manufacturers or chemical processors applied a centuries-old approach: "out of sight, out of mind." Hazardous waste was simply buried, dumped into waterways, or burned. Much toxic waste found its way into public and private landfills, rivers, and smoke belching incinerators. This did not eliminate the noxious nature of the waste products; it simply shifted the problem to another location. As the years passed, barrels buried at the underground sites rusted and leaked, sending lethal seepage through the soil, contaminating underground water supplies, and injuring people who drank contaminated well water. Toxic burial leakage also percolated from underground through springs, exposing innocent bystanders to carcinogenic or otherwise lethal substances in surface waters. Rivers and streams simply carried the sludge to haunt downstream land owners, who came into contact with the poisons through irrigation or otherwise working with the polluted waters. Residents near the incineration plants suffered a variety of lung ailments from poisonous air pollutants.

Traditionally, all these intrusions fell neatly within the intentional tort of trespass to land. Nuisance provided neighboring land owners another cause of action with which to litigate against the industrial toxic polluters. Absolute liability also applied under the ultrahazardous substances theory. Negligence lent further legal aid to plaintiffs seeking relief against injuries from the unwanted and toxic invaders.

The Case of the Toxic Tort: Who Pays for the Mess?

Two sisters brought this toxic tort action against Kerr-McGee Chemical Corporation, alleging that their parents contracted and died of cancer as a result of toxic wastes generated and deposited on the factory site of Kerr-McGee's predecessor company, Welsbach. Although Kerr-McGee acquired Welsbach's business, it did not acquire the land or factory in question. The sisters maintain that Kerr-McGee should still be held liable on a theory of strict liability even though the company did not cause or ever own the polluted land in contovery.

LEO v. KERR-MCGEE

United States Court of Appeals
Third Circuit
37 F.3d 96 (3d Cir. 1994)
September 19, 1994
Greenberg, Circuit Judge

This matter is before the court following entry of our order on November 30, 1993, granting defendant-appellant Kerr-McGee Chemical Corporation permission to appeal pursuant to 28 U.S.C. § 1292(b). We will reverse the order of the district court denying Kerr-McGee's motion for summary judgment entered on September 8, 1993, and we will remand the matter to the district court for entry of a summary judgment in its favor.

The facts are largely not in dispute, and, in any event, we accept the allegations of the plaintiffs-appellees Elaine Leo and Linda Yoder for purposes of this appeal. From prior to the turn of the 20th century continuing until 1940, the Welsbach Incandescent Light Company maintained and operated a factory in Gloucester City, New Jersey, for manufacturing incandescent gas mantles, a process involving extracting thorium from monazite ores. This process generated toxic wastes consisting of thorium by-products which Welsbach deposited on the factory site, thus contaminating the surrounding land. In 1940, Welsbach's Illinois-based competitor, Lindsay Light and Chemical Company, purchased Welsbach's gas mantle business. In the sale, Lindsay acquired Welsbach's outstanding orders, records, formulas, raw materials, inventory, customer lists, gas mantle production line, and the right to use the "Welsbach" name. However, Lindsay did not acquire the Gloucester City land and factory. Rather, it moved the gas mantle business to its own plant in Illinois.

Following a series of acquisitions, Kerr-McGee acquired Lindsay, and it thus concedes that in this litigation it stands in Lindsay's shoes. Accordingly, we will refer to Lindsay and Kerr-McGee simply as Kerr-McGee. ...

In 1961, Leo and Yoder, who are sisters, and their parents, Thomas and Catherine Bekes, moved to a home close to the former site of the Welsbach factory in Gloucester City, though Leo and Yoder now live elsewhere. On December 5, 1988, Thomas Bekes died from bladder cancer. In March 1991, the New Jersey Department of Environmental Protection notified Catherine Bekes of the high levels of gamma radiation and thorium on her property and on June 3, 1991, the New Jersey Spill Compensation Fund acquired her residence, forcing her to relocate. Soon thereafter she also died from bladder cancer. Leo and Yoder allege that their parents contracted their bladder cancer from exposure to thorium and other waste substances deposited on the Welsbach land.

On January 29, 1993, Leo and Yoder filed suit, individually, and on behalf of their parents' estates, in the Superior Court of New Jersey against Kerr-McGee and certain other defendants to recover for death, injuries, and the potential risk of cancer arising from their exposure to thorium and other waste substances generated in the Welsbach gas mantle operation and deposited on the Gloucester City property. As germane here, Leo and Yoder seek to impose liability on Kerr-McGee on a theory of strict liability. While Leo and Yoder do not claim that Kerr-McGee itself generated the waste which caused the deaths and injuries, they assert that it is liable by reason of its acquisition of Welsbach's gas mantle business. On March 4, 1993, one of the other defendants removed the case to the United States District Court for the District of New Jersey on the basis of diversity of citizenship.

Subsequently, Kerr-McGee filed a motion to dismiss under Fed.R.Civ.P. 12(b)(6) on the ground that the complaint did not state a claim on which relief may be granted inasmuch as Kerr-McGee never has owned the Gloucester City land and factory. ...

[T]he court denied Kerr-McGee's motion [which it treated as a summary judgment motion], by the order of September 8, 1993. Kerr-McGee then moved for an amendment of the order to allow an interlocutory appeal, and the district court granted the amendment by an order entered on November 1, 1993. We then granted Kerr-McGee leave to appeal.

... Thus, we undertake to predict how the Supreme Court of New Jersey would resolve the issues in this case.

We start, of course, with *Ramirez*, 431 A.2d 811, in which the Supreme Court of New Jersey held that:

> where one corporation acquires all or sub-stantially all the manufacturing assets of another corporation, even if exclusively for cash, and undertakes essentially the same manufacturing operation as the selling corpo-ration, the purchasing corporation is strictly liable for the injuries caused by defects in the units of the same product line, even if previously manufactured and distributed by the selling corporation or its predecessor.

431 A.2d at 825. As the district court acknowl-edged, *Ramirez* is distinguishable from this case. Unlike the injuries in *Ramirez*, the injuries of Leo, Yoder, and their parents were not caused by a unit in the product line man-ufactured first by Welsbach and then by Kerr-McGee. Instead the injuries in this case were caused by conditions created by Wels-bach's operations on land which Welsbach retained at the time of the sale of the gas mantle business to Kerr-McGee and on which Kerr-McGee never conducted any manufac-turing activities. ...

The *Ramirez* court predicated its conclusion that the successor corporation could be liable for injuries caused by its predecessor's defec-tive product on three rationales: (1) the sale of the enterprise virtually destroyed the injured party's remedy against the original manufac-turer; (2) the successor has the ability to assume the original manufacturer's risk-spreading role; and (3) it is fair to require the successor to assume a responsibility for defective products as that responsibility was a burden necessarily attached to the original

manufacturer's good will being enjoyed by the successor in the continued operation of the business. Clearly these rationales do not support the extension of successor liability to Kerr-McGee in this case.

The first factor, the destruction of the injured party's remedy is a *necessary* but not a *sufficient* basis on which to place liability on the successor. Accordingly, if the selling corporation remains a viable entity able to respond in damages to the injured party, a successor acquiring a product line will not be liable for injuries caused by the predecessor's product after the product's sale as in that circumstance there would be no reason to impose successor liability. This initial rationale for the product-line doctrine of successor liability merely focuses on the need for imposi-tion of successor liability rather than whether it is fair to impose it. ...

The second rationale on which the Supreme Court of New Jersey based its result in *Ramirez* was the successor's ability to assume the predecessor corporation's risk-spreading role. We think that the Supreme Court of New Jersey would recognize that Kerr-McGee does not have the capacity to assume Welsbach's risk-spreading role. ...

The impediment to commercial transac-tions from such a process is evident. Indeed, inasmuch as a manufacturer might build a product or its component parts at more than one facility, a purchaser of a product line might face daunting obstacles in attempting to assess its risks of successor toxic tort liability for conditions on property to be retained by the seller of the product line. Furthermore, a product-line purchaser not acquiring its prede-cessor's manufacturing facility probably would not be able to lessen the risks of toxic tort liability associated with the real estate. It is doubtful that such a product-line purchaser would be able to undertake cleanup operations on land it did not own. Moreover, the product-line purchaser might be unwilling to undertake such potentially costly projects. It seems clear, therefore, that if *Ramirez* applies here, a purchaser of a product line will be subject to liabilities for toxic torts of unpredictable scope for a indefinite period. ...

In contrast, a successor to a product line may be able to take steps to reduce its risk of liability for injuries caused by the predecessor's products through recall and educational programs which include those products. Furthermore, successor liability for injuries caused by units manufactured by the predecessor, at least when compared to potential toxic tort liability, is a discrete manageable matter. ...

This constant diminution of exposure to product liability is enhanced by the rule followed in New Jersey and elsewhere that a manufacturer cannot be strictly liable unless there was a defect in the product when it left the manufacturer's control. It seems apparent that, except perhaps in design defect cases, a defect in a product when the manufacturer distributed the product is likely to manifest itself and cause injury within a reasonable time after the product is manufactured. Accordingly, as a practical matter, successor liability under *Ramirez* is likely to be imposed in most cases, if at all, for a limited period. ...

On the other hand toxic tort liability can be imposed for activities in the distant past. This tail on potential toxic tort liability following the disposal of chemical wastes is attributable to the fact that the toxic wastes may remain in the ground for long periods, thus exposing persons and property to injury long after manufacturing has ended. ...

The third *Ramirez* rationale, that it is fair to require a successor to assume a responsibility for defective products as that responsibility is a burden necessarily attached to the successor's acquisition of the predecessor's good will, has no application in this case. The good will that Kerr-McGee acquired from Welsbach was attached to the product line it acquired, gas mantles, rather than to the site at which Welsbach manufactured the product.

* * *

We could allow liability to be imposed in this case on Kerr-McGee only if we stretched *Ramirez* far beyond its original scope ... . [W]e will not do that. While the district court believed that this case could come within the *Ramirez* holding, in large part it reached that conclusion because of what it thought was "the traditional New Jersey view that if you are injured somebody ought to be liable for it." But we reject that approach.

* * *

CONCLUSION

We will reverse the order of September 8, 1993, and will remand the matter to the district court for entry of a summary judgment in favor of Kerr-McGee.

Case Questions

1. Why did the appellate court find that Kerr-McGee should not be held liable for the toxic waste caused by the predecessor corporation?
2. The United States Court of Appeals rejected "the traditional New Jersey view that if you are injured somebody ought to be liable for it." What was the end result of this case to the plaintiffs?

Toxic Trespass

Trespass to land occurs when toxic substances enter upon another's property. The trespass elements remain the same:

1. Unauthorized entry upon another person's real estate
2. Tortfeasor's intent to enter without consent
3. Tortfeasor's actions interfering with the land owner's exclusive right to use the land (possession).

In the case of toxic substances, the unauthorized entry is seepage or accumulation of the hazardous material on the victim's land. Few owners consent to having toxins placed over, upon, or under their realty. Most people want such materials to be taken as far away from them as possible.

The tortfeasor's intent to enter without permission may be implied from the disposal method used. For instance, toxic waste buried in metal barrels will, over time, rust through and seep into the underground soil, unless the material is contained in an isolated fashion, such as an underground concrete crypt. If the tortfeasor failed to take sufficient precautions to prevent subterranean seepage, then the intent to trespass may be implied. Another example of implied intent is dumping toxic fluids into waterways. The tortfeasor desired the river or stream to carry the dangerous substances downstream, which would plainly deposit the toxins on the shores of other people's property.

The tortfeasor's interference with the plaintiff's exclusive possession of his or her land is equally clear. The toxic residues are a highly offensive and potent invasion, making some real estate uninhabitable. A more significant illustration of trespass would be difficult to imagine.

When land owners' underground water supplies are contaminated with buried toxic waste seepage, trespass to land occurs. A quick review of the elements shows that they are readily satisfied. Many cases in the court reports tell sad tales of families irreparably harmed through long-term consumption of chemically contaminated well water, poisoned as a result of improper underground waste disposal.

―――――――――――――――――――⟨♦⟩―――――――――――――――――――

The Case of the Nuisance Lake

The owner of property near an artificial lake brought this action for nuisance and trespass against both the owner of the lake and the operator of a textile mill. The plaintiff claims that the mill discharged wastewater, which polluted the lake. Plaintiff further alleges that the owners of the lake allowed this to occur, thereby harming plaintiff's neighboring property. Even though plaintiff's expert testified concerning the contaminants in the lake, the court was not willing to make the inference that plaintiff's land was actually contaminated.

RUSSELL CORPORATION
v.
SULLIVAN et al. AVONDALE MILLS, INC.
Supreme Court of Alabama
2001 WL 29264
January 12, 2001

Russell and Avondale Mills operate textile plants in Alexander City. As part of their operations, they discharge directly into the Sugar Creek Plant large volumes of wastewater containing dyes used in processing textiles. After the wastewater is treated at the Sugar Creek Plant, it is discharged into Sugar Creek at a rate of five to six million gallons a day. This output flows through Sugar Creek, runs into Elkahatchee Creek, and, eventually, into Lake Martin. The plaintiffs are all residents of the Raintree subdivision located on Lake Martin. [APCo owns Lake Martin, a manmade lake APCo uses to generate power.]

The wastwater from Russell and Avondale constitutes 70–80% of the water treated daily at the Sugar Creek Plant. This wastewater contains dyes, salts, acid surfactants, and heavy metals, making the water difficult to treat. At least one type of dye treated at the Sugar Creek Plant, azo dye, has been shown to have carcinogenic properties. The plaintiffs presented evidence indicating that the dyes, which are resistant to fading, are also difficult to remove from the wastewater during treatment. As a result of problems in removing color from the treated water, the City of Alexander City installed a chlorination/dechlorination facility at the Sugar Creek Plant.

The Sugar Creek Plant uses an activated-sludge process to treat the wastewater. In that process, the waste is combined with oxygen and bacteria; it then forms a sludge that is removed from the water. The remaining water is decontaminated and is then discharged into Sugar Creek. ...

Testimony at trial indicated that the plaintiffs noticed the [floating sediment] flocs floating in the lake water near their property. At times, they claim, the water was so stained by the dyes that it would color T-shirts. ... No evidence was presented to indicate that the dyes or any of the components released by Russell and Avondale in their wastewater were actually found on any of the plaintiffs' properties. The plaintiffs relied on the testimony that waves and high waters could wash the materials ashore. The plaintiffs testified that because the water in Lake Martin is contaminated, their property is not as valuable as it could have been.

... The plaintiffs' action against APCo rests on the theory that APCo has a duty to keep Lake Martin clean, and that it breached that duty by allowing Russell and Avondale to discharge contaminants into Lake Martin.

Trespass requires an intentional act by the defendant. ... [T]hat in order for one to be liable to another for trespass, the person must intentionally enter upon land in the possession of another or the person must intentionally cause some 'substance' or 'thing' to enter upon another's land.

The plaintiffs argue that APCo committed trespass by allowing Russell and Avondale to discharge contaminants into Lake Martin and then by allowing those contaminants to remain on the bottom of the lake. ... In this case, there is no agency relationship between APCo, on the one hand, and Russell and Avondale, on the other. No evidence was presented to indicate that APCo directed Russell and Avondale to discharge their waste in any manner or to indicate that APCo aided or participated in the discharge. Therefore, there was no intentional act by APCo to support a claim of trespass.

* * *

APCo operates Lake Martin pursuant to a license issued by the Federal Energy Regulatory Commission ("FERC"). During the trial, the plaintiffs, over APCo's objection, placed that license in evidence.

"In the construction, maintenance, or operation of the project, *the Licensee shall be responsible for, and shall take reasonable measures to prevent*, soil erosion on lands adjacent to streams or other waters, stream sedimentation, and *any form of water or air pollution. ...*"

* * *

Where a plant discharges effluent into a stream that ultimately runs into a reservoir created by a dam, the owner of the reservoir cannot be liable for maintaining a nuisance, absent evidence indicating that it authorized or participated in the deposit of pollutants or that it had control over the deposits. The only prong of this test that arguably might apply to APCo is the "control-over-the-deposits" prong. However, as previously noted, that control cannot be grounded upon the FERC license charging APCo with a duty to take reasonable measures to prevent water pollution. The record is devoid of any other basis for concluding that APCo had any control over the activities of Russell and Avondale.

We therefore reverse the trial court's judgment as to APCo and render judgment for APCo on both the trespass claim and the nuisance claim.

* * *

In this case, whether water actually splashed onto the plaintiffs' property is sharply contested. ...

In summary, several conclusions urged by the plaintiffs are unsupported by evidence: ... The ultimate conclusion that any chemicals were deposited onto the plaintiffs' properties is, at best, speculative. ...

The lack of scientific evidence indicating the presence of any chemicals causing "actual substantial damage" to the plaintiffs' properties or to support any of Dr. Gould's opinions is fatal to the plaintiffs' trespass claims. ...

"A 'nuisance' is anything that works hurt, inconvenience or damage to another. The fact that the act done may otherwise be lawful does not keep it from being a nuisance. The inconvenience complained of must not be fanciful or such as would affect only one of fastidious taste, but it should be such as would affect an ordinary reasonable man." Therefore, although Russell and Avondale argue that their actions were in accordance with state and federal regulations and that they were permissible under various permits, the plaintiffs may still maintain an action against Russell and Avondale if they can prove the elements of nuisance.

In Alabama, a nuisance can be either private or public. "A public nuisance is one which damages all persons who come within the sphere of its operation, though it may vary in its effects on individuals. A private nuisance is one limited in its injurious effects to one or a few individuals."

The distinction between a private and a public nuisance is an important one. "A private nuisance gives a right of action to the person injured" while "a public nuisance gives no right of action to any individual, but must be abated by a process instituted in the name of the state." ... In order to support an individual's cause of action for a public nuisance, the nuisance must cause a "special damage" that is different in "kind and degree from [the damage] suffered by the public in general." Therefore, if the nuisance allegedly created by the discharge of wastewater into Sugar Creek, and ultimately into Lake Martin, is a public one, the plaintiffs in this case must show that the discharge has caused them special damage, i.e., damage that is different than that suffered by others. ...

The plaintiffs in the present case, however, have presented no evidence indicating such special damage. The plaintiffs alleged that Russell's and Avondale's actions resulted in the loss of the use and enjoyment of Lake Martin.

The plaintiffs claim that the nuisance they suffered was a private nuisance. ...

Russell and Avondale correctly argue that the nuisance, if any, is a public nuisance, because, they say, the alleged nuisance is in the water of Lake Martin, a public waterway whose bed is owned solely by APCo. The discharge of contaminants into a public body of water constitutes a public nuisance. Russell and Avondale argue that the plaintiffs never proved that the alleged nuisance prevented them from using or enjoying their "own" property. While the plaintiffs offered evidence that they were unable to use and enjoy the lake, the use and enjoyment of a public area is a public right. ... Any nuisance caused by the discharge of contaminated wastewater into Lake Martin is a public, not a private, nuisance.

Because the plaintiffs expressly waived any claim to recovery under a public-nuisance theory, thereby avoiding the necessity of proving that they suffered special damage not suffered by members of the general public, it is unnecessary to address whether the record contains substantial evidence of such damage.

The trial court erred in denying Russell, Avondale, and APCo's motion for a judgment as a matter of law. Therefore, its judgment is reversed and a judgment is rendered in favor of Russell, Avondale, and APCo.

Case Questions

1. Explain the difference between a public and a private nuisance.
2. Why was no trespass found?

Importance of Environmental Statutes

Aside from trespass, nuisance, absolute liability, and negligence, there are a variety of federal, state, and local statutes regulating environmental toxins. One important federal statute is the Toxic Substances Control Act. This act regulates the manufacture, distribution, processing, use, and disposal of hazardous materials. Detailed recordkeeping regarding the hazardous materials must be maintained, 15 U.S.C. § 2601 *et seq.* (1992). The Hazardous Materials Transportation Act establishes strict requirements for transporters of hazardous waste. Detailed recordkeeping is required to ensure compliance with the act, 49 U.S.C. §§ 1801–1812 (1992). Another federal statute, the Comprehensive Environmental Response, Compensation and Liability Act (CERCLA), addresses any "imminently hazardous chemical substance or mixture" and allows the federal Environmental Protection Agency (EPA) to file civil lawsuits when the use of such a material will pose imminent risk to health or the environment and the EPA has not issued a final rule to protect against such risk.

Trespass to land is merely one type of trespass action. Trespass to chattel is the other.

§ 6.4 Trespass to Chattel

A tortfeasor commits **trespass to chattel** when he or she possesses someone's personal property without consent. A **chattel** is personal property, as opposed to real property, which is land. An automobile, a textbook, a pet

trespass to chattel[†]
Occurs when the tortfeasor intentionally deprives or interferes with the chattel owner's possession or exclusive use of personal property. The tortfeasor's possession or interference must be unauthorized, which means that the owner cannot have consented.

chattel Item of personal property. Any property other than land.

dispossession[†]
Wrongfully taking away a person's property by force, trick, or misuse of the law.

dog or cat, and a desk are examples of chattels. Trespass to chattel has elements similar to those of trespass to land:

1. Unauthorized possession of, or interference with the use of, another individual's personal property

2. Intent to deprive (or interfere with) the owner's possession or exclusive use of his or her chattel.

Unauthorized Possession of Another's Chattel

Suppose Nadene takes a neighbor's textbook during class. Unless Nadene obtained the neighbor's consent before seizing the text, Nadene has engaged in unauthorized possession of another's personal property. The book's owner did not give Nadene permission to possess the chattel. When a tortfeasor takes possession of another's personal property without consent, this is sometimes described as the act of **dispossession**.

Consent may be implied under certain circumstances. For instance, if Alfred gives his car keys to a friend, the implication is that the friend may use Alfred's motor vehicle. Similarly, hotel guests may presume that the management intended them to use the electricity, water, soap, and tissues supplied to the rooms. However, if a patron takes the hotel's pillows, sheets, and towels, this would be unauthorized possession, as staying in a hotel does not implicitly entitle guests to keep such items.

Unauthorized Interference with Use

It is possible to trespass to chattel without actually wrenching possession of the personal property from its rightful owner. Interference with the chattel owner's use of the property is sufficient. For instance, if a tortfeasor purposely fed Reggie's prize hogs a contaminated food, so that the hogs became ill and lost weight, then the tortfeasor engaged in unconsented interference with Reggie's use of the animals. If Cherrie's landlord shuts off the electricity to her apartment without permission, then this would also constitute unauthorized interference with the use of her personal property (provided, of course, that Cherrie had paid her electric bill).

The Case of the Personal-Property Pet

Frequently, legal decisions must define exactly how property is characterized under the law. In this case, man's best friend is defined as personal property, nothing more. A dog's owner has sued the treating veterinarian, and seeks emotional damages as a result of alleged malpractice.

KOESTER
v.
VCA ANIMAL HOSPITAL
Court of Appeals of Michigan
244 Mich.App. 173, 624 N.W.2d 209
December 26, 2000

Plaintiff left his dog at defendant VCA's kennel for a weekend. Plaintiff left explicit instructions not to use a collar on the dog because of a salivary gland problem for which VCA had previously treated the pet. Upon returning for the dog, plaintiff noticed that the dog's neck area was swollen. Within a few days, when the dog continued to exhibit swelling in the neck area, plaintiff returned to defendant VCA. Defendant Field, a veterinarian, treated the dog by draining its enlarged gland and bandaging its neck and head. When plaintiff returned to pick up his dog after the procedure, he noticed that the dog appeared to have trouble breathing and asked defendant Field whether the bandages were too tight. Field responded that the dog would be fine once it calmed down. Later that same day, plaintiff left the dog alone for ten to fifteen minutes to run an errand. When plaintiff returned home, he discovered the dog laying motionless on the floor, having apparently choked to death. An autopsy determined that the dog suffocated to death because the bandages were wrapped too tightly.

Plaintiff brought the instant negligence action pleading damages that included plaintiff's pain and suffering, extreme fright, shock, mortification, and the loss of the society and companionship of his dog. Defendants moved for summary disposition pursuant to MCR 2.116(C)(8), for failure to state a claim upon which relief could be granted, arguing that plaintiff was not entitled to the damages pleaded as a matter of law. The trial court agreed, holding that emotional damages for the loss of a dog did not exist.

* * *

On appeal, plaintiff alleges that the trial court erred in summarily disposing of his negligence claim. Plaintiff primarily argues that companion animals should not be considered merely personal property. In support of his argument, plaintiff offers the alleged practice of other jurisdictions which have acknowledged the value of companion animals by awarding damages for emotional distress associated with the loss of a pet. Although we recognize that domesticated pets have value and sentimentality associated with them which may not compare with that of other personal property, we cannot agree with plaintiff.

... In this matter, plaintiff pleaded damages of emotional distress and loss of society and companionship of his dog. Pets have long been considered personal property in Michigan jurisprudence (see *Ten Hopen v. Walker*, 96 Mich 236, 239; 55 NW 657 (1893)). Consequently, the issue before this Court is whether plaintiff can properly plead and recover for emotional injuries he allegedly suffered as a consequence of his property being damaged by defendants' negligence. There is no Michigan precedent which permits the recovery of damages for emotional injuries allegedly suffered as a consequence of property damage. Plaintiff requests that we allow such recovery when a pet is the property that is damaged, arguing that pets have evolved in our modern society to a status which is not consistent with their characterization as a "chattel." ... Although this Court is very sympathetic to plaintiff's position, we defer to the Legislature to create such a remedy.

There are several factors that must be considered before expanding or creating tort liability including, but not limited to, legislative and judicial policies. In this case, there is no statutory, judicial, or other persuasive authority that compels or permits this Court to take the drastic action proposed by plaintiff. Case law on this issue from sister states is not consistent, persuasive, or sufficient precedent. We refuse to create a remedy where there is no legal structure in which to give it support. ...

We decline to allow the recovery of emotional distress damages arising from negligence committed against plaintiff's pet; therefore, plaintiff's complaint failed to plead legally cognizable damages and was properly dismissed by the trial court.

Affirmed.

Case Questions

1. Why couldn't the dog owner recover for emotional distress?
2. Do you think tort liability should be expanded to cover emotional injuries for damages to property?

Intent to Deprive or Interfere

To commit trespass to chattel, the tortfeasor must intend to interfere with or deprive the chattel owner of possession or the exclusive use of his or her personal property. Intent may be expressed, as it was when Nadene took her neighbor's book. It may also be implied under the circumstances. For example, assume that Cherrie's landlord changed the locks on her apartment door in order to lock her out, although she had paid her rent and had done nothing to violate her rental agreement. This would imply the landlord's intent to deprive Cherrie of possession of her personal property inside the apartment. Her use of the chattels would definitely be hindered.

Similarly, lack of intent may be implied. For example, assume Bud found his neighbor's cow grazing along a public highway and took the animal to his barn for safekeeping until he could telephone the neighbor. Although Bud took possession of the cow without his neighbor's consent, Bud did not intend to interfere with the neighbor's use of the cow. Nor did he wish to deprive his neighbor of possession. Bud simply wished to protect the animal from harm. This is emphasized by his efforts to contact his neighbor to come claim the cow. Thus, Bud lacked intent to trespass to chattel.

Table 6-1 on page 194 summarizes the elements of trespass to land and trespass to chattel.

A Case of Not-So-Gut-Wrenching Conflict

Not every invasion of one's personal property constitutes trespass to chattel. Actual dispossession must occur. A trifling interference, fleeting and momentary, will be tolerated under the law. As the following case demonstrates, the invasion of this plaintiff's chattel was insufficient to give rise to this cause of action.

KOEPNICK
v.
SEARS, ROEBUCK & CO.
Court of Appeals of Arizona
158 Ariz. 322, 762 P.2d 609 (1988)
June 16, 1988
Froeb, Presiding Judge

... The issues presented on appeal are: ... whether the trial court erred in granting Sears' motion for judgment notwithstanding the verdict (judgment n.o.v.) on Koepnick's trespass to chattel claim. ...

FACTS

Koepnick was stopped in the Fiesta Mall parking lot by Sears security guards Lessard and Pollack on December 6, 1982, at approximately 6:15 P.M. Lessard and Pollack suspected Koepnick of shoplifting a wrench and therefore detained him for approximately 15 minutes until the Mesa police arrived. Upon arrival of the police, Koepnick and a police officer became involved in an altercation in which Koepnick was injured. The police officer handcuffed Koepnick, placed a call for a backup, and began investigating the shop-lifting allegations. Upon investigation it was discovered that Koepnick had receipts for the wrench and for all the Sears merchandise he had been carrying. Additionally, the store clerk who sold the wrench to Koepnick was located. He verified the sale and informed Lessard that he had put the wrench in a small bag, stapled it shut, and then placed that bag into a large bag containing Koepnick's other purchases. The small bag was not among the items in Koepnick's possession in the security room. To determine whether a second wrench was involved, the police and Lessard searched Koepnick's truck which was in the mall parking lot. No stolen items were found. Having completed their investigation, the police cited Koepnick for disorderly conduct and released him. The entire detention lasted approximately 45 minutes.

Koepnick sued Sears for false arrest, assault, trespass to chattel, invasion of privacy and malicious prosecution. The trial court directed a verdict in favor of Sears on all charges except false arrest and trespass to chattel. After a trial on these claims, a jury awarded Koepnick ... $100 compensatory damages and $25,000 punitive damages for trespass to chattel. Sears timely moved for judgment n.o.v. and alternatively for a new trial. The trial court ... granted Sears' motion for judgment n.o.v. on the trespass to chattel charge. ...

Koepnick appeals, challenging the trial court's order granting Sears ... judgment n.o.v. on his trespass to chattel claim. ...

We find no reversible error and therefore affirm the trial court's order granting ... judgment n.o.v. on the trespass to chattel claim.

* * *

TRESPASS TO CHATTEL

Arizona courts follow the Restatement (Second) of Torts absent authority to the contrary. The Restatement provides that the tort of trespass to a chattel may be committed by intentionally dispossessing another of the chattel or using or intermeddling with a chattel in the possession of another. Restatement (Second) of Torts § 217 (1965).

The Restatement (Second) of Torts § 221 (1965) defines dispossession as follows:

A dispossession may be committed by intentionally
  (a) taking a chattel from the possession of another without the other's consent, or

  ...

  (c) barring the possessor's access to a chattel ... .

Comment b to § 221 provides that dispossession may occur when someone intentionally assumes physical control over the chattel and deals with the chattel in a way which will be destructive of the possessory interest of the other person. Comment b further provides that "on the other hand, an intermeddling with the chattel is not a dispossession unless the actor intends to exercise a dominion and control over it inconsistent with a possession in any other person other than himself."

The Restatement (Second) of Torts § 218 (1965) provides:

> One who commits a trespass to a chattel is subject to liability to the possessor of the chattel if, but only if,
>
> (a) he dispossesses the other of the chattel, or
>
> (b) the chattel is impaired as to its condition, quality, or value, or
>
> (c) the possessor is deprived of the use of the chattel for a substantial time, or
>
> (d) bodily harm is caused to the possessor, or harm is caused to some person or thing in which the possessor has a legally protected interest.

Koepnick argued at trial that Lessard's participation in searching his truck constituted an actionable trespass to the truck. He was awarded $100 damages by the jury which he characterizes as damages for a dispossession pursuant to subsection (a) or deprivation of use pursuant to subsection (c) of § 218.

* * *

Sears' actions with respect to the trespass consisted of Steve Lessard accompanying a Mesa police officer out to the parking lot and looking in the truck. There is no evidence in the record of an intent on the part of Sears' employee to claim a possessory interest in the truck contrary to Koepnick's interest. No lien or ownership interest claim of any kind was made. Further, there is no evidence that Sears intentionally denied Koepnick access to his truck.

Koepnick was in the City of Mesa's custody at the time of the search and Sears had no control over how the police department conducted its investigation ... .

... In order that an actor who interferes with another's chattel may be liable, his conduct must affect some other and more important interest of the possessor [than for harmless intermeddlings]. Therefore, one who intentionally intermeddles with another's chattel is subject to liability only if his intermeddling is harmful to the possessor's materially valuable interest in the physical condition, quality, or value of the chattel, or if the possessor is deprived of the use of the chattel for a substantial time ... . Sufficient legal protection of the possessor's interest in the mere inviolability of his chattel is afforded by his privilege to use reasonable force to protect his possession against even harmless interference.

Sidebar: The *Koepnick* court stated that an owner could protect his or her chattel from harmless interference through the defense of property defense, discussed in Chapter 7. The court felt this was sufficient legal protection of the chattel owner's interests. But how could Koepnick proect his truck from intrusion by the police officer and Sears' security guard, as the defense would lawfully premit, when he was handcuffed and held elsewhere?

The search in question took approximately two minutes. Neither the truck nor its contents were damaged in any manner by the police or Sears' employee. As a matter of law, Sears' action did not constitute an actionable trespass under § 218(c).

... For a deprivation of use caused by a trespass to chattel to be actionable, the time must be so substantial that it is possible to estimate the loss that is caused. The record in the present case lacks any evidence to permit a jury to estimate any loss caused to Koepnick [as a result of the police officer and Lessard's search of his truck].

* * *

We conclude that there was no dispossession of the vehicle as contemplated under § 218 of the Restatement nor was Koepnick deprived of its use for a substantial period of time. ...

The judgment of the trial court is affirmed ... .

Case Questions

1. Why do you suppose the jury awarded Koepnick such a large damages award, which prompted the trial court to grant judgment notwithstanding the verdict (judgment n.o.v.)? Do you think the jurors would agree that Koepnick suffered no harm as a result of the defendants' actions? Do you?

2. Do you believe that Koepnick satisfied the elements for assault, invasion of privacy, and malicious prosecution?

TABLE 6-1
Elements of trespass to land and trespass to chattel

Trespass to Land	Trespass to Chattel
Unauthorized entry upon another person's real estate	Unauthorized possession of another individual's personal property *or* unauthorized interference with another's use of his or her chattel
Intent to enter without consent (no harm to land required)	Intent to dispossess or interfere with owner's use of his or her personal property
Interference with land owner's exclusive right to use land (possession)	Similar to conversion, which also requires tortfeasor to put dispossessed chattel to his or her own use

§ 6.5 Conversion

In the early history of tort law, trespass to chattel was frequently subject to litigation, often in cases involving domestic livestock. Court opinions from the nineteenth century abound. More recent cases, however, have tended to focus upon conversion, which is a similar but separate tort.

History

conversion Any act that deprives an owner of property without that owner's permission and without just cause.

Conversion occurs when a tortfeasor, without consent, deprives an owner of possession of the owner's chattel and puts or *converts* the property to the tortfeasor's own use. It is essentially a broader version of trespass to chattel, but both torts developed separately.

Conversion evolved from the common law action of *trover*, which appeared in England during the fifteenth century as a specific type of trespass on the case action. In trover lawsuits, the court determined that the plaintiff, the chattel owner, had a legal right to possess the personal property (namely, because of ownership), and that the defendant, the tortfeasor, had taken possession of the chattel for his or her own use. Gradually, this element (taking for one's own use) was described in the English court opinions as "converting the property for one's own use." Thus, the term *conversion* began to replace *trover*, and the modern tort of conversion emerged.

Elements of Conversion

Under modern tort law, conversion consists of three elements:

1. Depriving the owner of possession of a chattel
2. Intent to deprive possession and convert the property to one's own use
3. The owner's nonconsent to the tortfeasor's possession and use of the chattel.

Depriving of Possession

Under conversion, the tortfeasor must actually deprive the owner of possession of personal property. The common law usually employs the phrase *exercising dominion and control over the chattel which is inconsistent with the owner's right to exclusive use*. This means that the tortfeasor controls another's personal property so as to prevent the owner from using it. For example, suppose Nadene took her neighbor's textbook and refused to return it. Nadene's "dominion and control" over the book prevents the neighbor from using his or her chattel.

Extent of Deprivation

Normally, conversion is differentiated from trespass to chattel based upon the scope of the deprivation. With trespass to chattel, many courts have held that the deprivation need only be minor or temporary. With conversion, several courts have ruled that the deprivation must be so extensive as to suggest a desire to deprive the owner of possession permanently. There is considerable disagreement among different jurisdictions as to this issue, however. The majority of courts maintain that conversion has occurred simply because the tortfeasor deprived the owner of dominion and control over the chattel, regardless of length of time or permanent intent.

Methods of Depriving

Deprivation of possession may occur in a variety of ways. *Physical possession* of the chattel is most common, although deprivation may happen through *damage or destruction* of the personal property. For instance, if someone plows under Kathy's garden to plant grass seed, this amounts to deprivation of possession, because Kathy can no longer use her vegetables. Similarly, if someone opens a window during a thunderstorm, and rain floods Sig's stereo, the injury has deprived Sig of the use of his chattel.

Deprivation may also take place simply through use. Some forms of personal property cannot be picked up and carried away. For instance, electricity, free-flowing liquids, and other intangible items are commonly defined as chattels under state commercial codes. One possesses such things by using them. If Morgan, Colleen's neighbor, plugs his garage heater into her electric outlet without permission, and Colleen's electric bill suddenly soars, Morgan has deprived her of dominion and control over her electricity. This translates as deprivation of possession.

Intent to Deprive and Convert to Own Use

First of all, conversion requires that the tortfeasor intend to deprive the owner of possession of his or her chattel. This is comparable to trespass to chattel. However, unlike trespass to chattel, conversion also requires that the tortfeasor convert the personal property to his or her own use. For example, assume Joey and Lisa are acquaintances at school. Then suppose that Joey found Lisa's earrings on a bench at the mall. Joey might keep the earrings until he saw Lisa at school later in the week. Because Joey did not intend to use the earrings himself, he is not guilty of conversion. However, if Joey wore the earrings to the school dance, he would have converted them to his own use.

It is important to note that the tortfeasor does not have to injure the chattel to convert it. Conversion occurs simply because the owner has been deprived of the use of the personal property without having given permission. Injury occurs to the owner's right to exclusively use the chattel.

Lack of Consent

Naturally, the owner cannot have granted permission to someone to use or possess the chattel. If Victoria allows a classmate to borrow her text overnight to study, then the classmate has not converted the book. Consent may be expressed, as in the book-borrowing situation, or it may be implied. For example, suppose that when Bob leaves his automobile at a mechanic's for an oil replacement the mechanic also repairs a broken valve and pipe. The mechanic did not convert Bob's property, because Bob impliedly gave the mechanic permission to possess the vehicle for repair purposes. Of course, Bob did not authorize the additional work, but that is a breach-of-contract question. However, if the mechanic went joyriding in Bob's car after changing the oil, this would be conversion, because Bob did not implicitly consent to that use of his car.

Even though the chattel owner may have consented to a tortfeasor's possession, this permission may be revoked. This could result in a conversion. For example, Bob complains that he did not authorize the additional work done on his automobile, but he is willing to pay for the oil change, which he did request. The mechanic insists that Bob also pay for the unauthorized repairs and refuses to return Bob's car until he pays the extra amount. Because Bob did not agree to these additional charges, he insists that his vehicle be returned immediately. Thus, Bob has revoked the permission he originally gave the mechanic to possess the chattel. If the mechanic does not comply with Bob's demand, the mechanic will be liable for conversion.

The Case of the Purloined Purse

Money is a cherished chattel. It is never in sufficient abundance for most people. Occasionally, some individuals decide to supplement their cash supplies through somewhat unorthodox and illegal means. The following case appears to fit within this category. Although, as the Alabama Supreme Court notes, money is not usually subject to conversion claims, currency from identifiable sources, if converted, will allow the victim a cause of action against the converter.

GREENE COUNTY BOARD OF EDUCATION
v.
BAILEY

Supreme Court of Alabama
586 So. 2d 893 (Ala. 1991)
August 23, 1991
Houston, Justice

The plaintiff, Greene County Board of Education, appeals from the dismissal of its complaint alleging conversion on the part of the defendants, Roland S. Bailey [and] Sarah N. Bailey ... . We reverse and remand.

* * *

[According to the Plaintiff's complaint, between 1972–84, Paramount High School participated in the U.S.D.A.'s National School Breakfast and Lunch Programs. The school filed monthly claims with the State Department of Education for reimbursement for subsidized meals. Roland S. Bailey, sales manager of Alabama Institutional Foods, Inc. (AIF), was directly involved in food sales to Paramount High School. Between 1972–80, Bailey purchased 84 money orders and cashier's checks drawn on the Paramount lunchroom account.

Of these, Bailey negotiated 42 checks through AIF's account at a bank at which his wife, Sarah Bailey, worked as a teller. Sarah processed these checks. The 84 checks were valued at $407,883.50, and only $263,425.65 went toward payment of Paramount's food purchases. $144,457.85 was never credited to Paramount's account nor used in the feeding programs. Bailey allegedly submitted false invoices to Paramount.]

The defendants moved to dismiss the complaint under Rule 12(b)(6) ... . Specifically, the defendants argued that the plaintiff had failed to allege that specific money capable of identification had been converted. The trial court granted the defendants' motion, stating, in pertinent part, as follows:

"The plaintiff contends that the defendants converted money; however, the money was not any specific money and [the complaint states] a general claim for relief. The plaintiff's theory is that the defendants wrongfully obtained money from the account of the plaintiff through a scheme of false invoices. No particular identifiable earmarked money is alleged to have been taken. Under these circumstances, this Court is of the opinion that a count for conversion is not appropriate."

We disagree.

* * *

To constitute conversion, there must be a wrongful taking or wrongful detention or interference, or an illegal assumption of ownership, or an illegal use or misuse of another's property. The gist of the action is the wrongful exercise of dominion over property to the exclusion or in defiance of a plaintiff's rights, where the plaintiff has a general or specific title to the property or the immediate right to possession.

Generally, an action will not lie for the conversion of money. However, if the money at issue is capable of identification, then a claim of conversion may be appropriate. In *Lewis v. Fowler,* this Court discussed at length the circumstances under which an action for conversion will lie to recover a sum of money:

"[T]rover lies for the conversion of 'earmarked' money or specific money capable of identification ... .

"Money in any form is generally regarded and treated as property, and it is well settled that an action will lie for the conversion thereof, where there is an obligation to keep intact and deliver the specific money in question, and where such money can be identified.

* * *

"Now, in conversion cases, the courts are not confronted so much with a particular piece of money, i.e., a coin or a bill, but with identified or segregated from which money has come or types of accounts into which money has been deposited.

... [M]oney directly traceable to a special account is sufficiently identifiable to support an action for conversion.["] ...

Applying the applicable standard of review to the present case, we are not persuaded that the plaintiff has failed to state a claim for conversion. The allegations of the complaint suggest that the plaintiff may be able to prove that the defendants, through an intricate scheme involving bogus invoices and checks and money orders, converted to their own use funds that had been specifically deposited in the "[Paramount High School] lunchroom account" to pay for the high school's breakfast and lunch programs. ...

Based on the foregoing, we hold that the plaintiff has stated a claim for conversion and, therefore, that the trial court's order dismissing the plaintiff's complaint is due to be reversed and the case remanded for further proceedings.

REVERSED AND REMANDED.

Case Questions

1. Based on the facts, did the plaintiff also state a claim for trespass to chattel? Explain.
2. Should the defendants in this case have also been subjected to criminal prosecution for conversion, under the applicable Alabama statutes? Why or why not?

Conversion as a Crime

Many state statutes define conversion as a criminal offense. Some statutes use the term *theft* instead of *conversion*. Simultaneously, conversion is considered an intentional tort under the common law. This means that the chattel owner may sue in a civil action under the tort theory of conversion and may also contact the county prosecutor (or other local law-enforcement authority) to file a criminal complaint for conversion.

These separate legal actions are commonly pursued simultaneously in most jurisdictions.

Conversion, like trespass to chattel, is a mobile tort, as it is easy in most instances to grab and carry away someone else's personal property. If the personal property can be carried away, it may be converted. Hence, there are an infinite variety of fact situations involving conversion. Both torts fire the victim's blood: While reading the following examples, imagine that your own chattels have been converted; your emotional response may make clear why so many such cases are brought.

Table 6-2 outlines the elements of conversion.

─ HYPOTHETICALS

Buford is painting his wooden fence in his backyard. His neighbor, Starling, needs some paint for his garage door. He notices that Buford has more than enough paint to finish the fence, and so Starling "borrows" two gallons to paint his door. Has Starling converted Buford's paint?

Starling deprived Buford of possession of the paint. Starling clearly intended to deprive possession and convert the paint to his own use, as he applied the paint to his garage door. Buford did not consent to Starling's use of the paint. Starling has committed conversion.

* * *

Consider Beatrice, who works at an advertising agency. One of her duties is to telephone clients to discuss accounts. Frequently, however, Beatrice telephones long-distance to relatives to discuss family matters. The company has strict regulations prohibiting use of company phones for personal calls. Has Beatrice engaged in conversion?

Deprivation of possession becomes a perplexing query in this hypothetical. Did Beatrice deprive her employer of possession of the telephone? The actual property right being taken here is the use (and cost) of the telephone for placing long-distance calls. Most courts would agree that this satisfies the deprivation requirement. Beatrice intended to use the company's phones for personal use. The company expressly forbade such activities, and so consent was lacking. Accordingly, Beatrice has converted her employer's rights in the telephone system. ■

TABLE 6-2
Elements of
conversion

Depriving owner of possession of his or her personal property (dispossession)
Intent to dispossess and convert chattel to tortfeasor's own use
Chattel owner did not consent to tortfeasor's possession and use of personal property

§ 6.6 Slander of Title, Commercial Disparagement, and Defamation by Computer

The intentional torts of slander of title, commercial disparagement, and defamation by computer involve defamed property interests. The trio has a common ancestry. All arose from the intentional tort of defamation, which concerns personal impugnation.

Slander of Title

slander of title[†]
Occurs when a tortfeasor makes false statements about an individual's ownership of property.

Slander of title results when a tortfeasor makes false statements about an individual's ownership of property. The false statements are not designed to defame the owner personally; rather, the purpose of the aspersions is to injure the owner's ability to use the property. Slander of title contains three basic elements:

1. False statements regarding a person's ownership of property
2. Intent to hinder or damage the owner's use of the property
3. Communication (publication) of the falsehoods to third parties.

False Statements Regarding Ownership

A tortfeasor commits slander of title by making false statements about a person's ownership of property. This usually occurs when the tortfeasor falsely impugns the title to another's property. Normally, cases involving this tort include real estate and the filing of spurious liens. Often, businesses that provide services to customers who do not pay will file liens against the customers' real estate. The lien attaches to the title of the land so that the property cannot be leased or sold without the lien. Suppose a business threatens to file a lien against a customer who does not owe the business any money. If the lienholder wrongfully files a lien, then the lien has defamed the integrity of the land owner's title. The improper lien falsely suggests to the world that the land owner has not properly paid his or her debts to the lienholder. Anyone thinking of buying or leasing the property will think twice, because lien property may be sold under certain circumstances to satisfy the debt. Few buyers or tenants would want to become entangled with property that is encumbered by a lien. Thus, a spurious lien could injure the land owner's ability to use the property, even though in actuality the lienholder has no legal right to file the lien against the land owner. This improper lien filing constitutes making false statements about someone's ownership of property.

Intent to Hinder or Damage Owner's Use of Property

By making the false statements about ownership, the tortfeasor must intend to hamper or injure the owner's use of his or her property. This is visibly demonstrated in the preceding lien example. The lienholder filed the lien to prevent the land owner from selling or using his or her realty without first paying the debt supposedly owed to the lienholder. But, in fact, no money was due, so the lien was falsely filed.

Communication (Publication) to Third Parties

The false statements about another's property ownership must be transmitted to third parties in slander of title actions. The slander in the preceding lien example is communicated to the public when the lien is recorded at the county recorder's office. It then becomes a matter of public record for the world to take notice.

Commercial Disparagement

commercial disparagement[†] An intentional tort that occurs when a tortfeasor communicates false statements to third parties about a person's goods, services, or business enterprise. The tortfeasor must intend to harm the victim's ability to use goods, furnish services, or conduct business. There are three categories: disparagement of goods, disparagement of services, and disparagement of business.

Another type of slander focuses directly upon the chattel itself: commercial disparagement. **Commercial disparagement** may be defined as false statements communicated (published) to third parties about a person's goods, services, or business enterprise. The intentional tort of commercial disparagement includes three varieties: disparagement of goods, disparagement of services, and disparagement of business. Like slander of title, *disparagement of goods* impedes the chattel owner's ability to use his or her personal property. *Disparagement of services* interferes with a service provider's ability to engage in provision of services. *Disparagement of business* occurs when the tortfeasor impugns the integrity of another's business venture. Commercial disparagement can be divided into three elements:

1. False statements about an individual's goods, services, or business
2. Intent to injure the victim's ability to use goods, furnish services, or conduct business
3. Communication (publication) to third parties.

False Statements about Goods, Services, or Business

The tortfeasor must express false statements about another's personal property, services, or business reputation (sometimes called *goodwill*). For example, if someone carries a sign in front of a grocery store declaring, "This store sells spoiled fruit!," when in fact the store carries fresh and wholesome fruit, then the sign carrier has made disparaging remarks about the quality of the grocery's foodstuffs. This impugns the integrity of both the goods themselves and the store's reputation. Similarly, if someone tells his or her friends that a particular dentist uses inferior materials to fill cavities when, in reality, the dentist uses professionally acceptable materials, then the dentist's services and reputation have been wrongfully impaired.

The Case of the Errant Lot Line

Slander of title is usually limited to cases involving improperly filed liens. However, the intentional tort surfaces in other lawsuits, such as the one excerpted here. In *Hossler* the dispute involved an uncertain property line. In addition to slander of title, the case demonstrates why it is vital to obtain correct surveys before purchasing or selling real estate.

HOSSLER
v.
HAMMEL

Court of Appeals of Indiana
587 N.E.2d 133 (Ind. Ct. App. 1992)
February 24, 1992
Hoffman, Judge

This appeal arises from a property dispute between Roger and Sandra Hossler (plaintiffs) and Michael Hammel (defendant), owners of adjoining lots in Austin's Addition to the original plat of the town of Etna, Indiana.

The facts relevant to the appeal disclose that the Kecks and the Wheelers, the original owners of the lots, had surveys made in 1953, after which they agreed upon a common boundary line. When plaintiffs purchased their lot in 1970, they agreed to the established boundary line without a survey, and when defendant purchased his lot in 1977, he, too, agreed to the established boundary line without a survey. Plaintiffs rented their lot for several years and had a survey made in 1988 in order to sell the lot. The survey indicated the Addition was 9 feet longer east to west than shown in the original plat, and the surveyor allocated the extra footage equally among 6 lots. When defendant became aware of the survey, he insisted that the entire 9 feet be allocated to his lot due to his previous purchase of property in the original plat. After numerous threats from defendant to demolish 8 feet of their garage, plaintiffs filed an action to quiet title in the disputed strip of land. Following a bench trial, the court entered findings of fact and conclusions of law establishing the property line as that which the parties had originally agreed upon but denying damages to plaintiffs for slander of title.

The sole issue for our review is whether plaintiffs failed to meet their burden of proving the elements necessary to prevail on their slander of title claim.

To prevail in a slander of title action, the plaintiff must prove that the defendant made false statements regarding the plaintiff's ownership of the land in question, that the defendant made the statements with malice, and that the statements caused the plaintiff pecuniary loss. As plaintiffs note [in] their brief, "[t]he bone of contention in this case is whether the Defendant uttered statements with malice." Malicious statements are those made with knowledge of their falsity or with reckless disregard for whether or not they were false.

In *Freiburger v. Fry,* this Court found malice where, despite the description in his deed, the Defendant had actual knowledge of an existing fence separating the property and that the owner of the other side refused to move it. The instant case is similar to *Freiburger* in that, while defendant may have been relying on the results of plaintiffs' survey in making his statements, he had actual knowledge of the boundary line from the realtor who sold him the lot as well as from the survey. Moreover, the evidence was undisputed that the boundary line had been agreed upon for over 30 years, and once a person possesses property for 10 years in a continuous, adverse, notorious and exclusive manner, title vests in that person by operation of law.

As the party with the burden of proof on the slander of title issue, plaintiffs are appealing from a negative judgment. Therefore, to be successful they must establish that the judgment is contrary to law. As both parties note, defendant did not testify at trial, and neither of his two witnesses testified as to any statements he made regarding the boundary line. Plaintiffs, on the other hand, presented evidence that defendant threatened to bulldoze their garage, cut holes in their garage with a chainsaw, and keep livestock in their garage. Because this evidence and the evidence of defendant's actual knowledge of the agreed-upon boundary line was without conflict and led to a conclusion opposite that reached by the trial court, the judgment of the trial court is contrary to law and reversed.

Reversed and remanded for determination of damages.

Case Questions

1. Would the defendant's actions, rather than statements, have been sufficient to constitute slander of title? Assume that the defendant did not communicate with the plaintiffs. What if the defendant had parked a bulldozer next to the plaintiffs' garage? What if the defendant had placed livestock on his property adjoining the plaintiffs'? Would these actions satisfy the Indiana common law elements? Would they satisfy the elements discussed in this chapter?

2. Assuming the hypothetical facts from question one, what additional tort(s) would the defendant have committed through his actions?

Intent to Harm Victim's Ability to Use Goods, Supply Services, or Conduct Business

Disparagement of goods requires that the tortfeasor intend to injure the victim's capability to use chattels, provide services, or engage in business. Normally, cases involving goods relate to sales. In the preceding illustrations, the sign carrier obviously desired to discourage other shoppers from buying fruit at that particular grocery. The person criticizing the dentist wished to dissuade friends from seeking the dentist's services. The clear underlying objective in both examples is to hamper the ability of these enterprises to conduct business.

Communication (Publication) to Third Parties

Like slander of title, commercial disparagement requires that the false statements be communicated to third parties. In the examples, the sign carrier transmitted the false complaints to anyone reading the sign. The friends of the disgruntled patient heard the falsehoods about the dentist. Like the intentional torts of slander and libel (defamation) discussed in Chapter 5, publication may occur through oral or written means. The preceding examples illustrate both media.

Defamation by Computer

Defamation by computer is a relatively recent intentional tort. Because of the proliferation of computerized databases that can store virtually any information about anyone, the likelihood of mistakes has increased. Further, as access to computerized material expands, the dissemination of inaccurate information can become enormously damaging to the victim.

Computerized Credit Reporting

Customers who are the subjects of credit reports are protected by the stringent guidelines of the Fair Credit Reporting Act (FCRA), 15 U.S.C. § 1681 *et seq.* Defamation by computer most frequently involves cases concerning erroneous credit information entered into a readily accessible computer database. A credit company reports to a national credit reporting agency that a particular individual has become delinquent in account payments. This bad credit rating can have alarmingly negative effects upon the person being reported. If the information reported is false, the injury is especially annoying, as future credit may hang in the balance of good credit reports.

defamation by computer† An intentional tort that occurs when the tortfeasor includes false information about a person's credit or credit rating in a computer database. This false information must be communicated to third parties, and must injure the victim's ability to obtain credit.

Defamation by computer can be defined as the inclusion of false information about a consumer's credit rating in a computer record-keeping system that harms the consumer's ability to secure credit. The tort includes four elements:

1. False information about a person's credit rating
2. Entering such erroneous data into a computerized recordkeeping system
3. Communication (publication) of the incorrect information to third parties
4. Injuring the victim's ability to obtain credit as a result of the false computerized data.

The Case of the Infringing Song

Many new computer torts are developing as a result of increased use of computers and access to the Internet by the public. In this case on appeal, record companies and music publishers have brought suit to enjoin Napster, Inc. from facilitating the transmission of digital audio files to the public. At the heart of the suit is whether Napster is responsible for copyright infringement of protected works. On August 10, 2000, the District Court issued a preliminary injunction against Napster, and required the successful plaintiffs to post bond in the sum of $5 million. For the later appeal concerning the injunction issue, see 284 F.3d 1091 (2002.)

A&M RECORDS, INC.
v.
NAPSTER, INC.
United States Court of Appeals
Ninth Circuit
239 F.3d 1004
2001

Plaintiffs are engaged in the commercial recording, distribution and sale of copyrighted musical compositions and sound recordings. The complaint alleges that Napster, Inc. ("Napster") is a contributory and vicarious copyright infringer. ... The district court preliminarily enjoined Napster "from engaging in, or facilitating others in copying, downloading, uploading, transmitting, or distributing plaintiff's copyrighted musical compositions and sound recordings, protected by either federal or state law, without express permission of the rights owner." ...

* * *

Napster facilitates the transmission of MP3 files between and among its users. Through a process commonly called "peer-to-peer" file sharing, Napster allows its users to: (1) make MP3 music files stored on individual computer hard drives available for copying by other Napster users; (2) search for MP3 music files stored on other users' computers; and (3) transfer exact copies of the contents of other users' MP3 files from one computer to another via the Internet. These functions are made possible by Napster's MusicShare software, available free of charge from Napster's Internet site, and Napster's network servers and server-side software. Napster provides technical support for the indexing and searching of MP3 files, as well as for its other functions, including a "chat room," ... and a directory where participating artists can provide information about their music.

* * *

Plaintiffs must satisfy two requirements to present a prima facie case of direct infringement: (1) they must show ownership of the allegedly infringed material and (2) they must demonstrate that the alleged infringers violate at least one exclusive right granted to copyright holders under 17 U.S.C. § 106. See 17 U.S.C. § 501(a). ... Plaintiffs have sufficiently demonstrated ownership. The record supports the district court's determination that "as much as eighty-seven percent of the files available on Napster may be copyrighted and more than seventy percent may be owned or administered by plaintiffs."

... We agree that plaintiffs have shown that Napster users infringe at least two of the copyright holders' exclusive rights: the rights of reproduction, § 106(1); and distribution, § 106(3). Napster users who upload file names to the search index for others to copy violate plaintiffs' distribution rights. Napster users who download files containing copyrighted music violate plaintiffs' reproduction rights.

Napster contends that its users do not directly infringe plaintiffs' copyrights because the users are engaged in fair use of the material. Napster identifies three specific alleged fair uses: sampling, where users make temporary copies of a work before purchasing; space-shifting, where users access a sound recording through the Napster system that they already own in audio CD format; and permissive distribution of recordings by both new and established artists.

The district court considered factors listed in 17 U.S.C. § 107, which guide a court's fair use determination. These factors are: (1) the purpose and character of the use; (2) the nature of the copyrighted work; (3) the "amount and substantiality of the portion used" in relation to the work as a whole; and (4) the effect of the use upon the potential market for the work or the value of the work. ... The district court concluded that Napster users are not fair users. We agree.

[Purpose and character of use] focuses on whether the new work merely replaces the object of the original creation or instead adds a further purpose or different character. In other words, this factor asks "whether and to what extent the new work is 'transformative.'"

The district court first concluded that downloading MP3 files does not transform the copyrighted work. This conclusion is supportable. ...

A commercial use weighs against a finding of fair use but is not conclusive on the issue. The district court determined that Napster users engage in commercial use of the copyrighted materials largely because (1) "a host user sending a file cannot be said to engage in a personal use when distributing that file to an anonymous requester" and (2) "Napster users get for free something they would normally have to buy." The district court's findings are not clearly erroneous.

Direct economic benefit is not required to demonstrate a commercial use. Rather, repeated and exploitative copying of copyrighted works, even if the copies are not offered for sale, may constitute a commercial use.

* * *

The district court determined that plaintiffs' "copyrighted musical compositions and sound recordings are creative in nature ... which cuts against a finding of fair use under the second factor." We find no error in the district court's conclusion.

The district court determined that Napster users engage in "wholesale copying" of copyrighted work because file transfer necessarily "involves copying the entirety of the copyrighted work." ...

"Fair use, when properly applied, is limited to copying by others which does not materially impair the marketability of the work which is copied." ...

Addressing this factor, the district court concluded that Napster harms the market in "at least" two ways: it reduces audio CD sales among college students and it "raises barriers to plaintiffs' entry into the market for the digital downloading of music."

* * *

We, therefore, conclude that the district court made sound findings related to Napster's deleterious effect on the present and future digital download market. Moreover, lack of harm to an established market cannot deprive the copyright holder of the right to develop alternative markets for the works. ... Having digital downloads available for free on the Napster system necessarily harms the copyright holders' attempts to charge for the same downloads.

Napster maintains that its identified uses of sampling and space-shifting were wrongly excluded as fair uses by the district court.

Napster contends that its users download MP3 files to "sample" the music in order to decide whether to purchase the recording. ...

The district court determined that sampling remains a commercial use even if some users eventually purchase the music. ...

Plaintiffs have established that they are likely to succeed in proving that even authorized temporary downloading of individual songs for sampling purposes is commercial in nature. ... Napster users download a full, free and permanent copy of recording. The determination by the district court as to the commercial purpose and character of sampling is not clearly erroneous.

The district court further found that both the market for audio CDs and market for online distribution are adversely affected by Napster's service. As stated in our discussion of the district court's general fair use analysis: the court did not abuse its discretion when it found that, overall, Napster has an adverse impact on audio CD and digital download markets. ... The record supports the district court's preliminary determinations that: (1) the more music that sampling users download, the less likely they are to eventually purchase the recordings on audio CD; and (2) even if the audio CD market is not harmed, Napster has adverse effects on the developing digital download market.

* * *

Napster also maintains that space-shifting is a fair use. Space-shifting occurs when a Napster user downloads MP3 music files in order to listen to music he already owns on audio CD.

... [I]t is obvious that once a user lists a copy of music he already owns on the Napster system in order to access the music from another location, the song becomes "available to millions of other individuals," not just the original CD owner.

Permissive reproduction by either independent or established artists is the final fair use claim made by Napster. The district court noted that plaintiffs did not seek to enjoin this and any other noninfringing use of the Napster system, including: chat rooms, message boards and Napster's New Artist Program. Plaintiffs do not challenge these uses on appeal.

We find no error in the district court's determination that plaintiffs will likely succeed in establishing that Napster users do not have a fair use defense. ...

We first address plaintiffs' claim that Napster is liable for contributory copyright infringement. ... [L]iability exists if the defendant engages in "personal conduct that encourages or assists the infringement."

The district court determined that plaintiffs in all likelihood would establish Napster's liability as a contributory infringer. ...

Contributory liability requires that the secondary infringer "know or have reason to know" of direct infringement.

* * *

The record supports the district court's finding that Napster has actual knowledge that specific infringing material is available using its system, that it could block access to the system by suppliers of the infringing material, and that it failed to remove the material.

Under the facts as found by district court, Napster materially contributes to the infringing activity. [T]he district court concluded that "[w]ithout the support services defendant provides, Napster users could not find and download the music they want with the ease of which defendant boasts." We agree that Napster provides "the site and facilities" for direct infringement.

We affirm the district court's conclusion that plaintiffs have demonstrated a likelihood of success on the merits of the contributory copyright infringement claim.

* * *

The preliminary injunction which we stayed is overboard because it places on Napster the entire burden of ensuring that no "copying, downloading, uploading, transmitting, or distributing" of plaintiffs' works occur on the system. As stated, we place the burden on plaintiffs to provide notice to Napster of copyrighted works and files containing such works available on the Napster system before Napster has the duty to disable access to the offending content. Napster, however, also bears the burden of policing the system within the limits of the system. ...

Even though the preliminary injunction requires modification, appellees have substantially and primarily prevailed on appeal.

AFFIRMED IN PART, REVERSED IN PART AND REMANDED.

Case Questions

1. Explain why "fair use" was not found.
2. List two ways Napster was found to harm the market.

The Case of the Rejected Check

Imagine your frustration if, when shopping, you got all the way up to the cashier and realized you had forgotten to bring your checkbook. In this case, a man was shopping with his secretary. Upon discovering that he did not have his checkbook, the man returned to his office with his secretary and then sent the secretary back with a check to pay for the merchandise. Can the store request a consumer report before accepting a check for a transaction, or is this an invasion of privacy?

ESTIVERNE
v.
SAK'S FIFTH AVENUE

**United States Court of Appeals
Fifth Circuit
9 F.3d 1171 (5th Cir. 1993)
December 28, 1993
Davis, Jones, and Duhé, Circuit Judges**

Appellant, Nicolas Estiverne, appeals from the district court's grant of summary judgment for the Defendants, Sak's Fifth Avenue and JBS, Inc., and the imposition of Rule 11 sanctions. Estiverne sued Defendants for discrimination under 42 U.S.C. § 2000a and invasion of privacy when Sak's declined to honor a check written by Estiverne. ...

On November 26, 1991, Nicolas Estiverne and his secretary went to Sak's Fifth Avenue in New Orleans to purchase a watch. After selecting a watch, Estiverne realized that he had left his checkbook at his office. After returning to his office, Estiverne gave his secretary a signed check, together with a credit card and his driver's license, to return to the store to pay for the watch. After receiving the check, the Sak's salesclerk, in accordance with standard policy, submitted it to JBS for approval. Sak's declined to honor the check after JBS refused to approve it. Estiverne sued both JBS and Sak's alleging that his check was not accepted because he is black. He also alleged that Sak's and JBS's inquiry into his credit information was an invasion of privacy. The district court granted summary judgment for Defendants and imposed Rule 11 sanctions

against Estiverne totaling more than $15,000. Estiverne appeals. ...

There is no genuine issue of material fact in dispute in this case. The only issue as to summary judgment Estiverne raises on appeal is whether the district court correctly applied the Fair Credit Reporting Act ("FCRA"), 15 U.S.C. §§ 1681 1681t, specifically §§ 1681a(d) and 1681b(3)(E). The district court held that JBS's reports were consumer reports under § 1681a(d) and that Sak's had a "legitimate business need" under 15 U.S.C. § 1681b(3)(E) for the reports for the purpose of deciding whether to accept or reject Estiverne's check. Estiverne argues that paying by check is not a business transaction that authorizes Sak's to obtain a credit history report under the FCRA because he made no application for credit.

This is an issue of first impression for this Court. Section 161a(d) provides that a consumer report is:

> any written, oral, or other communication of any information by a consumer reporting agency bearing on a consumer's credit worthiness, credit standing, credit capacity, character, general reputation, personal characteristics, or mode of living which is used or expected to be used or collected in whole or in part for the purpose of serving as a factor in establishing the consumer's eligibility for ... (3) other purposes authorized under § 1681b of this title.

Section 1681b(3)(E) states that one of the authorized purposes for disclosure of consumer information is "a legitimate business need for the information in connection with a business transaction involving the consumer."

* * *

The FTC has interpreted the definition of consumer report to include lists devised to inform merchants about consumers who have had checks previously dishonored. The FTC stated in its commentary:

> *Bad check lists.* A report indicating that an individual has issued bad checks, provided by printed list or otherwise, to a business for use in determining whether to accept consumers' checks tendered in transactions primarily for personal, family or household purposes, is a consumer report. The information furnished bears on consumers' character, general reputation and personal characteristics, and it is used or expected to be used in connection with business transactions involving consumers. ...

We defer to the FTC's interpretation of the statute and hold that JBS's reports fall squarely within the definition of a consumer report and that Sak's obtaining of this report for the purpose of deciding whether to accept or reject a check in payment is a "legitimate business need." This holding is also in accord with results reached by other courts that have addressed this issue. Accordingly, the district court did not err in granting summary judgment for JBS and Sak's.

Estiverne does not contest the imposition of Rule 11 sanctions; rather, he contends that sanctions totaling more than $15,000 are unreasonable. We review a district court's calculation of sanctions for an abuse of discretion.

The district court has broad discretion in imposing sanctions reasonably tailored to further the objectives of Rule 11. ...

The district court adopted the amounts found by the magistrate judge as the proper sanctions in line with the objectives of Rule 11. It represented less than the attorneys fees and expenses incurred by Defendants. Estiverne failed to produce any evidence to support his allegations that his check was refused because of his race. The facts alleged in his complaint were misleading and factually incorrect. ... [W]e find no abuse of discretion in the amount of sanctions imposed against Estiverne.

Invoking Federal Rule of Appellate Procedure 38, Sak's seeks sanctions against Estiverne for filing a frivolous appeal. ... Because the issue regarding the FCRA was novel to this Court, we decline to impose sanctions on appeal.

For the foregoing reasons, the district court's grant of summary judgment for Defendants and imposition of Rule 11 sanctions against Estiverne is AFFIRMED.

Case Questions

1. Why do you think Sak's Fifth Avenue's employee requested a consumer report before accepting Mr. Estiverne's check?

2. Is it an invasion of privacy for a store to request a consumer credit report before deciding whether to accept a customer's check?

3. What kind of facts would Mr. Estiverne have needed to include in his complaint for the court to have considered his claims of racial discrimination?

Creation of a New Tort

Legal commentators occasionally spur the development of tort law through their law review articles and treatises. Perhaps the best example is law professor William L. Prosser's writings, which have had significant and immeasurable influence over courts for decades. Prosser's tort handbook is the bible for legal students and remains the best available dissertation on the subject.

Other commentators have entered onto the tort scene with exciting new ideas that spurred courts and legislatures to change the course of the law. The article excerpted here, first published in 1977, blazed the trail for establishment of the intentional tort of defamation by computer. From G. Stevens & H. Hoffman, "Tort Liability for Defamation by Computer," 6 *Rutgers Journal of Computers & the Law* 91 (1977) (footnotes omitted):

> Protection of the individual from the misuse of computerized personal information has received considerable scholarly attention, but little has been written on the tort liability of the information processor. Eventually, courts will be faced with questions concerning the processor's legal responsibilities for defamation and invasion of privacy. Actions to recover damages for such injuries are possible not only against recipients of computerized reports who make the information public, but also against information processors and suppliers. ...

> ### Defamation

> Under common law, a prima facie case for defamation is established if the plaintiff successfully pleads that he was identified in a defamatory matter through a "publication" of the charge by the defendant. The message need only be communicated to one person other than the defamed to be actionable, and any means through which a third party receives it can be considered a publication. While an oral statement may be classified as slander and a written statement as libel, a defamatory message designed for visual perception will be considered libelous. ... Liability could be extended to a key punch operator or a programmer under the theory that without their neglect of duty a defamatory statement might not have appeared.

* * *

> The States should enact uniform guidelines for those in the computer information processing chain. ...

― HYPOTHETICALS

Heather moved from her apartment in the city of Shelbydale to a house in the town of Wellington. Heather had a charge account with The Prime Account, a national credit card company. Heather wrote all of her credit card companies to report her address change. The Prime Account failed to change Heather's address in its computer billing system and continued to send its monthly invoices to Heather's

Shelbydale address. After 90 days, The Prime Account reported Heather's account as delinquent to a national credit rating service. The service indicated Heather's delinquency in its computerized records, which were included in various credit reports to banks. When Heather applied at the Wellington State Bank for a mortgage loan, the bank refused her request, based upon the bad credit information. Is The Prime Account liable to Heather for defamation by computer?

The Prime Account reported that Heather's account was delinquent, and this was accurate. However, the delinquency was due to Heather's failure to receive her monthly statements. The mailing mistake was The Prime Account's fault. However, this error does not negate the truth of Heather's delinquency. The information reported in the computerized credit systems was correct, and thus defamation by computer has not occurred.

* * *

Sylvia owns a bowling alley. Marshall is a professional bowler who frequents one of Sylvia's competitors but occasionally bowls at Sylvia's establishment. Marshall's scores were repeatedly lower at Sylvia's than at any other bowling alley in town. One day, after a particularly frustrating series, Marshall lay down to "sight" the levelness of the alleys. To his eyes, the lanes looked uneven. Marshall telephoned the American Bowling Federation (ABF) to report that Sylvia's alleys did not comply with their standards. If such a criticism were true, the ABF could revoke its certification of Sylvia's facility. This could result in lost business if bowling leagues relocated to other alleys. In fact, the alleys complied with ABF standards. Has Marshall disparaged Sylvia's business enterprise?

Marshall's comments about Sylvia's alleys were false. The defamed article was the quality of Sylvia's bowling alleys, which would include the integrity of the business itself. Marshall communicated these falsehoods to a third party by telephoning the ABF. Marshall's intent may be implied by his conduct. What purpose could he have furthered by telephoning the ABF? The reasonable response would be that he hoped that the ABF would remove its certification from Sylvia's and thus discourage patronage. This translates as intent to injure another's ability to conduct business. The damage to Sylvia's goodwill would be substantial if the ABF revoked its certification. Therefore, Marshall has committed commercial disparagement. ■

Table 6-3 on page 212 illustrates the requirements for slander of title, commercial disparagement, and defamation by computer.

TABLE 6-3
Elements of slander of title, commercial disparagement, and defamation by computer

Slander of Title	Commercial Disparagement	Defamation by Computer
False statements regarding person's property ownership	False statements about person's goods, services, or business	False information about a person's credit rating
Intent to impede or injure owner's use of property	Intent to harm victim's ability to use goods, furnish services, or conduct business	Inputting false information into computerized database
Communication (publication) of falsehoods to third parties	Communication (publication) of falsehoods to third parties	Communication (publication) of falsehoods to third parties
Usually involves filing of spurious liens against real estate	Includes disparagement of goods, disparagement of services, and disparagement of business	Injury to victim's ability to secure credit, as a result of erroneous credit data

The Case of the Intentional Cyber Squatter

In the ever-expanding law of computer torts, this court explores the rights associated with the owner of a domain name, versus the rights of a cyber squatter with a confusingly similar domain name.

SHIELDS
v.
ZUCCARINI

**United States Court of Appeals, Third Circuit
2001 WL 671607 (3rd Cir.(Pa.))
June 15, 2001**

John Zuccarini appeals from the district court's grant of summary judgment and award of statutory damages and attorneys' fees in favor of Joseph Shields under the new Anticybersquatting Consumer Protection Act ("ACPA" or "Act"). In this case of first impression

in this court interpreting the ACPA, we must decide whether the district court erred in determining that registering domain names that are intentional misspellings of distinctive or famous names constitutes unlawful conduct under the Act. ...

Shields, a graphic artist from Alto, Michigan, creates, exhibits and markets cartoons under the names "Joe Cartoon" and "The Joe Cartoon Co." His creations include the popular "Frog Blender," "Micro-Gerbil" and "Live and Let Dive" animations. Shields licenses his cartoons to others for display on

T-shirts, coffee mugs and other items, many of which are sold at gift stores across the country. He has marketed his cartoons under the "Joe Cartoon" label for the past fifteen years.

On June 12, 1997, Shields registered the domain name joecartoon.com, and he has operated it as a web site ever since. Visitors to the site can download his animations and purchase Joe Cartoon merchandise. Since April 1998, when it won "shock site of the day" from Macromedia, Joe Cartoon's web traffic has increased exponentially, now averaging over 700,000 visits per month.

In November 1999, Zuccarini, an Andalusia, Pennsylvania "wholesaler" of Internet domain names, registered five world wide web variations on Shields's site: joescartoon.com, joecarton.com, joescartons.com, joescartoons.com and cartoonjoe.com. Zuccarini's sites featured advertisements for other sites and for credit card companies. Visitors were trapped or "mousetrapped" in the sites, which, in the jargon of the computer world, means that they were unable to exit without clicking on a succession of advertisements. ...

In December 1999, Shields sent "cease and desist" letters to Zuccarini regarding the infringing domain names. Zuccarini did not respond to the letters. Immediately after Shields filed this suit, Zuccarini changed the five sites to "political protest" pages and posted the following message on them:

> This is a page of POLITICAL PROTEST
>
> —Against the web site joecartoon.com—
>
> joecartoon.com is a web site that depicts the mutilation and killing of animals in a shock-wave based cartoon format—many children are inticed [sic] to the web site, not knowing what is really there and then encouraged to join in the mutilation and killing through the use of the shockwave cartoon presented to them.

* * *

On November 29, 1999, the ACPA became law, making it illegal for a person to register or to use with the "bad faith" intent to profit from an Internet domain name that is "identical or confusingly similar" to the distinctive or famous trademark or Internet domain name of another person or company (see 15 U.S.C. § 1125(d) (Supp. 2000)). The Act was intended to prevent "cybersquatting," an expression that has come to mean the bad faith, abusive registration and use of the distinctive trademarks of others as Internet domain names, with the intent to profit from the goodwill associated with those trademarks.

* * *

To succeed on his ACPA claim, Shields was required to prove that (1) "Joe Cartoon" is a distinctive or famous mark entitled to protection; (2) Zuccarini's domain names are "identical or confusingly similar to" Shields's mark; and (3) Zuccarini registered the domain names with the bad faith intent to profit from them.

Under § 1125(d)(1)(A)(ii)(I) and (II), the district court first had to determine if "Joe Cartoon" is a "distinctive" or "famous" mark and, therefore, is entitled to protection under the Act. ...

Shields runs the only "Joe Cartoon" operation in the nation and has done so for the past fifteen years. This suggests both the inherent and acquired distinctiveness of the "Joe Cartoon" name. In addition to using the "Joe Cartoon" name for fifteen years, Shields has used the domain name joecartoon.com as a web site since June 1997 to display his animations and sell products featuring his drawings. ...

Joe Cartoon T-shirts have been sold across the country since at least the early 1990s, and its products appear on the web site of at least one nationally known retail chain, Spencer Gifts. ... Shields's cartoons and merchandise are marketed on the Internet, in gift shops and at tourist venues. The Joe Cartoon mark has won a huge following because of the work of Shields. In light of the above, we conclude that "Joe Cartoon" is distinctive, and, with 700,000 hits a month, the web site "joecartoon.com" qualifies as being famous. Therefore, the trademark and domain name are protected under the ACPA.

Under the Act, the next inquiry is whether Zuccarini's domain names are "identical or confusingly similar" to Shields's mark. The domain names—joescartoon.com, joecarton.com, joescartons.com, joescartoons.com and cartoonjoe.com—closely resemble "joecartoon.com," with a few additional or deleted letters, or, in the last domain name, by rearranging the order of the words. To divert Internet traffic to his sites, Zuccarini admits that he registers domain names, including the five at issue here, because they are likely misspellings of famous marks or personal names. The strong similarity between these domain names and joecartoon.com persuades us that they are "confusingly similar." ...

The statute covers the registration of domain names that are "identical" to distinctive or famous marks, but it also covers domain names that are "confusingly similar" to distinctive or famous marks. ...

[C]ybersquatters often register well-known marks to prey on consumer confusion by misusing the domain name to divert customers from the mark owner's site to the cybersquatter's own site, many of which are pornography sites that derive advertising revenue based on the number of visits, or "hits," the site receives. ...

We conclude that Zuccarini's conduct here is a classic example of a specific practice the ACPA was designed to prohibit. The district court properly found that the domain names he registered were "confusingly similar."

* * *

Case Questions

1. What is the definition of cybersquatting?
2. For what purpose did Zuccarini deliberately use a confusingly similar domain name to "joecartoon.com"?

Summary

Trespass to land occurs when a tortfeasor enters upon another's real estate without permission. The tortfeasor must intend to invade the premises without consent. Also, the tortfeasor's entry must interfere with the land owner's exclusive right to use the land, which is called possession.

Toxic tort actions involve toxic chemicals, pollution, hazardous waste disposal and transportation, and other environmentally sensitive issues. This litigation applies many tort theories, including trespass to land, negligence, absolute liability for ultrahazardous substances, products liability, and nuisance. The same formula for trespass to land applies in cases involving toxic substances that invade an innocent land owner's property through underwater seepage or surface or air contamination.

Trespass to chattel occurs when the tortfeasor possesses or interferes with the use of another's personal property without permission. The tortfeasor must intend to dispossess the owner of his or her chattel, or to interfere with the owner's exclusive use of the chattel.

Conversion deprives a chattel owner of possession of personal property, which the tortfeasor converts to his or her own use. The tortfeasor must intend to dispossess the owner of the chattel and then use it without consent. Conversion occurs whenever the tortfeasor deprives the owner of dominion and control over the personal property. In many jurisdictions, statutes define conversion as a crime, in addition to the common law intentional tort.

Slander of title occurs when false statements are made about an individual's ownership of property. The tortfeasor's intentions are to handicap or harm the owner's use of the property. Commercial disparagement includes disparagement of goods, of services, and of business. Commercial disparagement involves false statements about a person's goods, services, or business intended to injure the victim's ability to use the property, supply the services, or conduct business. Defamation by computer concerns false information about a person's credit rating that is entered into a computer database. Communication, or publication, of the false information to third parties is required of all three of these intentional torts.

Key Terms

chattel	dispossession	slander of title
commercial disparagement	entry	toxic tort actions
conversion	exclusive right	trespass
damages	exclusive right of possession	trespass to chattel
defamation by computer	nominal damages	

Problems

In the following hypotheticals, identify the intentional tort(s) committed, if any, and support your answers.

1. Pestro Chemical Corporation manufactures *Dredroxiphine*, a poison used in insect sprays. A railway line delivers tanker cars full of the chemical to be unloaded into the plant. On breezy days, the fumes from the unloading stations drift across the highway onto Elmer Parsley's farm. The odors are pungent and are especially irritating to the sinuses. When Elmer and his family work outside on windy days, they are constantly besieged by the poison's smells. Their eyes water excessively, their noses run, and they are gripped by sneezing fits. Other farmers in the area have complained of similar symptoms. Visits to the family physician have revealed that Elmer has absorbed minute amounts of the chemical in his lungs and through his skin. Medical studies link exposure to the chemical with several forms of cancer. Elmer has farmed on his property since 1999. Pestro constructed its plant in 2001.

2. Ben Stalwart left the Pick-Em-Up saloon after an evening of heavy drinking. Intoxicated, he stumbled across the street to the Tao, an oriental restaurant, and ordered a hamburger. The waitress, an exchange student at the local high school, did not understand English well, and because Ben's speech was slurred, she misunderstood him. When she returned with an oriental dish, Ben jumped from his chair and shouted loudly, "I didn't order this stinking slop! Get it outta my face!" Several customers stared at Ben as he yelled at the waitress, "I'll get the health department to shut this dump down, before somebody else gets poisoned!" The manager ran out from the kitchen and demanded that Ben leave the premises immediately. Ben refused to leave.

3. Paula Johannsen operates a day-care center for children. Crawford Lawley, a nine-year-old, attended the center after school while his parents worked. Paula discovered Crawford's parents were delinquent in paying their fees by three months. One day Crawford brought in his father's portable computer for show-and-tell. Paula asked Crawford if he would like her to keep the computer locked up for safekeeping. Crawford agreed. At the end of the day, Crawford asked Paula to return the computer, but she refused, stating that she would keep the computer until Crawford's parents paid their bill.

4. Theresa Ishmarz rented an apartment from Whisperwood Apartments. Under the lease, she was responsible for paying for electricity and gas heat. When she moved into the apartment, she noticed that the electricity and gas were already on; the apartment owners paid for the utilities while apartments were vacant. She did not contact the utility companies to have the accounts transferred into her name, and she did not notify the apartment manager about the situation. Theresa lived in the apartment for three months before the error was discovered. She never paid any money for utilities, although utility bills for the apartment totaled $250 for this time period.

5. Harlow Barley is a mason. He installed a concrete patio at the home of James and Zella Grey. Zella stopped by Barley's house one day and paid his wife (in cash) for the work. Zella did not get a receipt. Barley's wife, however, never told Barley about the money. Barley sent several invoices to the Greys, but they ignored them. Thinking the bill remained unpaid, Barley filed a mechanic's lien against the Grey's real estate. Once the Greys discovered the lien, they angrily telephoned Barley and explained about the cash payment. Barley's wife admitted to receiving the money, so Barley considered the matter settled. However, Barley did not release the lien at the county recorder's office.

6. Homer Diemtry owed his dentist for oral surgery. Homer faithfully made monthly payments to the dentist. The dentist's accountant reported to a local credit rating service that Homer had defaulted on the bill. The service included this information in its computerized credit files. Homer applied for a credit card at a local department store, but was denied as a result of the bad credit rating. The department store was a client of the credit-rating service and received monthly credit-rating summaries.

Review Questions

1. What are the intentional torts that involve injuries to property rights? How are these distinguishable from intentional torts in which the harm is focused on persons?

2. Define *trespass to land* and *trespass to chattel*. How do the two intentional torts differ? How are they similar? What is entry? What is exclusive use? What is possession? Can trespass occur above or below land? What role does consent play in trespass? Is harm to the property required? Must the trespass be intentional? Why or why not? Must trespass to chattel involve dispossession?

3. What are toxic torts? What causes of action are available for injured persons? What federal statutes exist to regulate hazardous or toxic substances? What are the provisions of these statutes?

4. What is conversion? How is it different from trespass to chattel? How is it similar? To what extent must the chattel owner be deprived of possession? How might such deprivation occur? Must the tortfeasor do more than simply dispossess the chattel owner? What are dominion and control, and why are they important? What are the roles of intent and consent in conversion? Can conversion also be a crime? Why?

5. Explain slander of title. How might false statements be made about one's ownership of property? Provide an example of this intentional tort. What intent is involved? What is publication and why is it necessary?

6. List the different types of commercial disparagement. What are the elements of this category of intentional tort? What intent is involved? Why is communication important?

7. What is defamation by computer? Under what circumstances is this intentional tort most likely to arise? Why is communication significant?

Projects

1. Which intentional torts discussed in this chapter are included in your state's common law? Are any defined by statute? Is conversion considered both an intentional tort and a crime in your state? If so, how are the two types of conversion similar and different?

2. Separate into study groups with several classmates to discuss the theories of intentional torts to property. You might wish to create your own hypothetical fact situations utilizing the intentional torts outlined in this chapter. Use the analytical methods discussed in Chapter 1 to answer your group's questions.

3. Slander of title often involves the filing of frivolous or unlawful mechanic's liens. How are mechanic's liens filed in your state? Examine your state's statutes pertaining to mechanic's liens. You might also wish to contact your county recorder's office to discover the procedures used for filing mechanic's liens.

4. Read the *Napster* case in Appendix C. What issues besides copyright infringement were addressed by the court?

Internet Resources

This chapter deals with intentional torts to property. To learn more about intentional torts to property, the following sites can be accessed:

Governmental Agencies
http://www.statelocal.gov
http://www.findlaw.com/01topics/22tort/database.html

Legal Discussion Groups
http://www.lib.uchicago.edu/e/law/lists.html

Attorneys
http://www.martindale.com
http://www.lawoffice.com

Law List Servs and News Groups
http://barratry.law.cornell.edu:5123/notify/buzz.html

State Law and Codes
http://www.washlaw.edu/uslaw/statelaw.html
http://www.law.cornell.edu/statutes.html

For additional resources, visit our Web site at
www.paralegal.delmar.cengage.com

CHAPTER 7

DEFENSES TO INTENTIONAL TORTS

CHAPTER OUTLINE

§ 7.1 Introduction
§ 7.2 Self-Defense
§ 7.3 Defense of Persons or Property
§ 7.4 Rightful Repossession
§ 7.5 Consent
§ 7.6 Mistake
§ 7.7 Privilege
§ 7.8 Necessity
§ 7.9 Public Officer's Immunity for Legal Process Enforcement
§ 7.10 Warrantless Arrest by Law Enforcement Officials or Citizens
§ 7.11 Statutes of Limitations
§ 7.12 Workers' Compensation

EQUAL JUSTICE UNDER LAW

---

*Laws are felt only when the individual
comes into conflict with them.*
SUZANNE LAFOLLETTE

§ 7.1 Introduction

defense 1. The sum
of the facts, law, and
arguments presented
by the side against
whom legal action
is brought. 2. Any
counter-argument
or counter-force.

Sometimes intentional torts are legally justified; thus, the person engaging in the intentional tort is not liable to the victim. These are collectively called **defenses** to intentional torts. For instance, conduct that normally would constitute an intentional tort, such as battery, could be excused under the theory of self-defense. Defenses are commonly used by the defendant in a civil lawsuit to exonerate the defendant from liability to the plaintiff.

A legal defense arises only when one party responds to another party's allegations in a lawsuit. Usually, the defendant answers the plaintiff's complaint with defenses. However, if the defendant counterclaimed against the plaintiff, it would be the plaintiff who replied with defenses. If third parties were involved in the litigation through cross-complaints, these third parties would answer with defenses. This presumes, of course, that defenses are available with which to respond.

This chapter focuses on *justification of intentional tortious conduct through defenses.* The following questions may be helpful:

1. May the tortfeasor use a defense to excuse his or her misconduct?

2. Which defenses apply to which intentional torts?

Intentional torts involve intentional acts. Thus, they carry a high degree of risk of injury to others, and usually there is a low degree of social benefit from the act involved. The risk of injury outweighs the benefits received from the act. Therefore, the duty not to intentionally injure someone or something is great.

There are several types of legal defenses to intentional torts. This chapter describes:

♦ Self-defense (defense against assault, battery, or false imprisonment)

♦ Defense of persons or property (defense against assault, battery, or false imprisonment)

♦ Rightful repossession (defense against trespass to land, trespass to chattel, conversion, assault, and battery)

- Consent (defense to all intentional torts)
- Mistake (defense to most intentional torts)
- Privilege (broad category of defense against intentional torts)
- Necessity (defense to various intentional torts)
- Public officer's immunity for legal process enforcement, and law enforcement and private citizen's defense for warrantless arrest
- Statutes of limitations (defense to all intentional torts)
- Workers' compensation.

Due to the fact that intentional torts are rarely covered by insurance, intentional torts and their defenses are far less common in legal practice than negligence actions.

§ 7.2 Self-Defense

self-defense
Physical force used against a person who is threatening physical force or using physical force. This is a right if your own family, property, or body is in danger, but sometimes only if the danger was not provoked. Also, deadly force may (usually) only be used against deadly force.

Of the legal defenses, self-defense is probably the most familiar to the average person. It is most commonly applied to the intentional torts of assault and battery, but it may also be used in cases involving false imprisonment. **Self-defense** is the exercise of reasonable force to repel an attack upon one's person or to avoid confinement. The nature of the action is simple: the victim of an assault or battery may use that degree of force necessary to prevent bodily injury (or offensive contact) from the attacker. Similarly, the victim of false imprisonment may use the force needed to prevent or escape confinement.

Consider this likely scenario. Walter is angry at Milo and throws a punch at Milo's face. Milo responds by blocking Walter's fist, grabbing his wrist, and twisting his arm behind his back until he agrees to calm down. This illustrates assault and self-defense: by throwing the punch, Walter placed Milo in reasonable apprehension of an unconsented contact that endangered his physical safety. Under self-defense, Milo was entitled to use whatever force was necessary to repel the attack.

The issue of self-defense would only arise if Walter (as plaintiff) sued Milo (as defendant) for battery. Walter would allege that Milo committed battery by grabbing his wrist and twisting his arm. Milo would reply with the legal defense of self-defense, which justified his actions. Remember that the defendant uses legal defenses to avoid liability to the plaintiff. In our hypothetical, Milo's self-defense argument would defeat Walter's complaint for battery. Bear in mind that Milo would have his own cause of action against Walter for assault, and Walter would not be able to use self-defense as a defense because he initiated the attack upon Milo.

The elements of self-defense are (1) use of reasonable force (2) to counter an attacking or offensive force that is (3) necessary to prevent bodily injury, offensive contact, or confinement.

Reasonable Force

The neutralizing force a person uses in self-defense is limited. The force cannot be greater than what is reasonably necessary to dispel the attacking force. This is called **reasonable force**. In the preceding example, Milo applied only as much force as needed to prevent Walter from striking Milo. Had Milo broken Walter's arm in retaliation, this would clearly have been excessive force, because breaking Walter's arm was unnecessary to stop the assault. Thus, Milo could not use self-defense as a legal justification. Instead, Milo would have become the aggressor and have engaged in battery against Walter. Common law maintains that the victim of an assault or battery may not turn aggressive once the assailant is incapacitated. Thus, if Walter collapsed after Milo twisted his arm, Milo could not kick Walter into unconsciousness and then claim self-defense.

What constitutes reasonable force varies depending upon the circumstances of each case. If Walter attacked Milo with an axe, then deadly force would be involved. Milo would therefore be warranted in responding with deadly force to repulse the onslaught. If Walter threw rocks at Milo, his force would threaten severe bodily harm. Thus, Milo could react with similarly powerful force, such as knocking Walter down with a pole.

The reasonableness issue is difficult to reduce to clearly defined, black-and-white terms. Much depends upon the options available to the victim. Many courts hold that, in the face of deadly force, if a victim might reasonably escape from the attack, then this choice must first be selected before deadly force may be used in self-defense. Several courts apply the same rule to situations involving threats of serious bodily injury. However, the majority of jurisdictions maintain that a person is not required to flee his or her home if threatened by an intruder. This is sometimes called the **castle doctrine**, in which a dweller is considered "king" or "queen" and may use any amount of force, including deadly force, to resist an intruder, such as a burglar.

Countering an Attacking or Offensive Force

The party exercising self-defense must be opposing an attacking or offensive force. Walter's fist is obviously an attacking force. But suppose Walter spit at Milo. This would be an example of an offensive force, as it is contact by which Milo would probably be offended.

Force Necessary to Prevent Injury, Offensive Contact, or Confinement

The force used in self-defense must be necessary to prevent bodily injury, offensive contact, or to avoid confinement. **Necessary force** is that which is reasonably perceived as required to rebuff an attack or confinement.

When Milo grabbed Walter's wrist and twisted his arm, Milo felt this action was required to prevent Walter from continuing his assault. The question again becomes one of reasonableness: Did Milo respond with reasonable force necessary to allay Walter's attack? Or was Milo's force unnecessary (and thus excessive) given Walter's actions? Suppose Walter had only tapped Milo on the shoulder with his finger. Milo's wrist-and-arm twist in response would then be considered unreasonable, unneeded, and extreme. Thus, Milo could not avail himself of a self-defense argument against Walter's battery claim.

Say that Walter was attempting to lock Milo in a room against Milo's will. In self-defense, Milo could reply with as much force as required to avoid being confined. This means that Milo could use that degree of force necessary to escape Walter.

Self-defense is perhaps the easiest legal justification to illustrate. Almost any child who has engaged in a playground shoving match can explain the fundamental concept. However, the legal elements require a more discerning eye, as shown in the following example.

— HYPOTHETICAL

Toby Nesmith sat alone at a table in a local tavern. He was waiting to meet a friend from work when two men standing nearby got into a shoving match. One of the men, John, pushed the other man, Bruce, into Toby. Toby shoved Bruce back into John, knocking them both to the floor.

John committed battery against Bruce by pushing him. Under the doctrine of transferred intent, when Bruce bumped into Toby, John transferred his battery onto Toby. By pushing Bruce away, Toby used reasonable force to repel an attacking force to prevent injury to himself. Accordingly, Toby could claim self-defense against John.

There remains a puzzling question, however. Could Toby claim self-defense against Bruce, or did Toby commit battery against Bruce? Bruce was essentially the instrumentality that John put into motion to strike Toby, albeit accidentally. Bruce did not intend to contact Toby. Therefore, Bruce did not commit battery or assault against Toby.

Toby could still claim self-defense against Bruce, however. Toby responded to protect himself against injury from both participants in the shoving match. Thus, self-defense would apply. Further, because Bruce was a voluntary participant in the struggle with John, Bruce consented to physical contact associated with a shoving match. This would include inadvertently bumping into an innocent bystander like Toby. Accordingly, Toby did not commit battery against Bruce, because Bruce impliedly consented to the incidental contact involved, which would include Toby's return shove. ∎

The elements of self-defense are summarized in Table 7-1.

Assault and battery may be justifiable in the defense of others or of property, as discussed in § 7.3.

TABLE 7-1
Elements of
self-defense

Use of reasonable force
Countering an attacking or offensive force
Actions necessary to prevent bodily injury, offensive contact, or confinement

§ 7.3 Defense of Persons or Property

As a legal justification for assault or battery, defense of other persons or defense of injury to property is similar to self-defense. A person who would otherwise have committed assault or battery may be excused if the action was taken to protect another individual or property from harm. This would include freeing someone subject to false imprisonment.

Defense of Persons: Elements

defense of persons†
A defense to the intentional torts of assault, battery, and false imprisonment. Its elements include the use of reasonable force to defend or protect a third party from injury when the third party is threatened by an attacking force.

Defense of persons as a legal justification for assault or battery has the following elements: (1) use of reasonable force (2) to defend or protect a third party from injury (3) when the third party is threatened by an attacking force. For example, if Marie were about to throw a vase at Marjorie, Simon could use reasonable force to subdue Marie before she could complete the throw. Simon would not have committed battery, because he grabbed Marie to prevent her from harming Marjorie. Simon would be entitled to the legal defense of defense of another person to avoid liability for battery.

The same principles used in self-defense to define reasonable force also apply to defense of persons. Thus, Simon could not use excessive force to repel Marie's attack against Marjorie. For instance, if Simon struck Marie sharply in the head with a two-by-four, this would be unnecessarily brutal force to subdue the vase attack.

Also, like self-defense, the repelling force must be used to counter an attacking force. If Marjorie telephoned Simon to complain that Marie had just thrown a vase at her, Simon could not run over and strike Marie and then claim defense of another as an excuse.

Defense of Property: Elements

defense of property†
A defense to the intentional torts of assault and battery. Its elements include the use of reasonable force to protect property from damage or dispossession when another person, called the *invader*, attempts to injure or wrongfully take possession of the property.

Conduct that otherwise might be assault or battery may be vindicated if the action is taken to defend property from damage or dispossession. A property owner has the right to possess and safeguard his or her property from others. The elements of **defense of property** are (1) use of reasonable force (2) to protect property from damage or dispossession (3) when another person, the *invader*, attempts to injure or wrongfully take possession of the property.

The reasonable force contemplated here is essentially identical to that discussed in regard to self-defense. Many courts, however, restrict the defensive force to the least amount necessary to protect the property from harm or dispossession. This is a narrower definition of *reasonableness*, suggesting that human well-being is more important than the safety of property. Under this theory, most courts would not allow deadly force or extreme force likely to cause serious bodily injury to be used to defend property under any circumstances.

The property owner or possessor uses reasonable force to repulse an attacking force that is attempting to harm or possess the property. For example, if Frederick is in the process of committing conversion or trespass to chattel, then Helen, who owns the personal property in danger, may use reasonable force to dispel Frederick's efforts at dispossession.

ejectment The name for an old type of lawsuit to get back land taken away wrongfully.

The use of reasonable force to expel a trespasser to land is called **ejectment**. Defense of real property cases frequently involve land owners who have placed dangerous traps for trespassers. The trespassers are often seeking to steal personal property and usually violate various criminal statutes involving theft or burglary. Nevertheless, land owners may not set up deadly traps to inflict serious bodily injuries upon such criminals. Spring-loaded guns have been the most common snares litigated. A land owner places a shotgun inside a barn or outbuilding that is triggered by a trip-wire placed across a window or doorway. The thief steps upon the wire while trying to enter and is shot. Courts universally condemn this use of deadly force to defend property.

It should be relatively easy to imagine situations in which reasonable force is used to defend another person from attack. Defense of property, however, may be more difficult to conjure.

The Case of the Defiant Trucker

In 1966 the Bobby Fuller Four recorded a popular rock song in which the refrain declared, "I fought the law, and the law won." As this case demonstrates, this is usually the result. However, note the dissent's approach to defense of property against an arguably unlawful seizure by law enforcement officers. Although this case involved criminal law, the court's discussion of defense of property is relevant to tort law.

JURCO
v.
STATE

Court of Appeals of Alaska
825 P.2d 909 (Alaska Ct. App. 1992)
February 14, 1992
Mannheimer, Judge

David Jurco was convicted, following a jury trial in district court, of disorderly conduct and resisting arrest. These offenses resulted from a confrontation between Jurco and members of the State Troopers who had come to Jurco's residence to serve a court order directing them to take possession of Jurco's truck; the Kenai District Court had ordered forfeiture of the vehicle because Jurco had used it in furtherance of a violation of the fish and game laws.

Unbeknown to the troopers, Jurco had recently filed for bankruptcy. The federal bankruptcy court had directed Jurco not to sell or transfer any of his property or allow creditors to take any of his property without court order. Jurco believed that the bankruptcy court's directive obliged him to resist the troopers' attempt to seize his truck. At first, Jurco argued with the troopers. Finding he could not dissuade them, Jurco got into the truck and started it. With Trooper Eugene Kallus trying to hang on to the side of the truck, Jurco drove the truck away to a different location on his property. Jurco then got out of the truck, removed the battery from the vehicle, and began to let the air out of the truck's tires.

At this point, Trooper Kallus informed Jurco that he was placing him under arrest for disorderly conduct. …

But even if we assume for purposes of argument that Jurco's interpretation of bankruptcy law is correct, the question remains whether Jurco was entitled to forcibly resist the troopers when they came to execute the Kenai District Court's warrant. We conclude that Jurco was not entitled to forcibly resist the troopers even if he reasonably believed that the seizure of his truck was illegal.

* * *

[At common law] a property owner was entitled to use force to resist an unlawful taking of his property. "One whose lawful possession of property is threatened by the unlawful conduct of another, and who has no time to resort to the law for its protection, may take reasonable steps, including the use of force, to prevent or terminate such interference with the property." This … common-law rule has also been codified in Alaska; AS [Alaska Statutes] 11.81.350-(a) provides:

> Justification: Use of force in defense of property and premises.
> (a) A person may use nondeadly force upon another when and to the extent the person reasonably believes it is necessary to terminate what the person reasonably believes to be the commission or attempted commission by the other of an unlawful taking or damaging of property or services.

For purposes of deciding this appeal, we assume that Jurco reasonably believed that the Kenai District Court's order to seize his truck ran afoul of the federal bankruptcy court's order to keep his property together. [Another Alaska statute, Alaska Stat. § 11.81.420, authorized law enforcement officers to use reasonable force, including deadly force, to enforce a court order to seize property, even if the court decree is later determined to have been unlawful.] In such a situation, the joint operation of Alaska Stat. §§ 11.81.420 and 11.81.350(a) would seemingly allow Jurco to use force against the troopers to resist the taking of his truck while at the same time authorizing the troopers to respond with force of their own against Jurco—creating an escalating confrontation that would end only when the troopers resorted to deadly force against Jurco. …

Sidebar: Is the Alaska Court of Appeals being just a bit melodramatic when characterizing the "escalating confrontation" between Jurco and the troopers as ending only when the police ultimately kill Jurco? The court concludes that the state legislature could not have intended two conflicting statutes—one governing defense of property and the other concerning law officers' enforcement of court orders—to permit members of the public to wrestle with police over chattel possession. Was the court simply exaggerating to justify its rationale?

This could not have been the legislature's intention. With emotions running high on both sides, a property owner who sees that non-deadly force is not enough to make law enforcement officials back down might well begin (unlawfully) to use deadly force on the officers. Or, in the heat of the moment, the officers might mistakenly conclude that the property owner has begun to use deadly force upon them and respond in kind. Both possibilities could easily lead to the infliction of serious injury or death.

Thus, the question presented by Jurco's case is: which of these two statutes did the legislature intend to take precedence when law enforcement officers attempt to execute a court order calling for a seizure of property?

Sidebar: As the Alaska Court of Appeals has framed the issue, which statute will prevail? Are you surprised by this outcome? Or was it predictable from the outset?

We conclude that a person is not entitled to use force to resist the taking of property by law enforcement officers pursuant to a court order.

* * *

It follows that Jurco was not entitled to forcibly resist the State Troopers' efforts to seize his truck under the order issued by the Kenai District Court.

* * *

The judgment of the district court is AFFIRMED.

BRYNER, Chief Judge, dissenting.

I disagree with the court's decision … . In my view, Jurco was entitled to [a jury instruction] on his theory of defense … that he was seeking to protect his property from what he reasonably believed to be an unlawful taking.

* * *

The majority of this court effectively amends the defense of property statute by engrafting to it an exception that the legislature evidently chose not to include. The court does so in reliance on its own notions of desirable social policy. It is not this court's prerogative, however, to substitute its political views for those expressed by the legislature in the clear and unrestricted language of [Alaska Stat. §] 11.81.350(a).

Case Questions

1. Do you agree with the majority that the legislature intended the law officer enforcement-of-court-orders statute to override the defense-of-property statute? Explain.

2. Do you agree with the dissent that the majority rewrites the two statutes to suit its own vision of preferred social policy?

─ HYPOTHETICAL ─────────────────────────

Consider the case of Isaac, who discovered two teenage hoodlums throwing bricks and stones at his house windows. Isaac crept up behind the duo and leapt from behind some bushes. The delinquents were taken by surprise, and Isaac knocked one to the ground and kicked him in the stomach and tackled the other. Although both hoodlums suffered minor abrasions and bruises, neither was injured severely. The two hoodlums claim that Isaac has committed battery against them. Does Isaac have a defense?

Isaac used force against the rowdies to prevent damage to his property. The hoodlums were attempting to injure Isaac's house. The primary question is whether Isaac used reasonable force to prevent the property damage. Because neither of the two teenagers suffered severe harm as a result of Isaac's actions, the force should be deemed reasonable to neutralize the teenagers. Accordingly, Isaac could successfully apply defense of property against the allegation of battery. ◼

The elements of defense of persons or property are listed in Table 7-2.

Defense of property is often used in situations in which sellers repossess property from defaulting buyers.

TABLE 7-2
Elements of defense of persons or property

Defense of Persons	*Defense of Property*
Use of reasonable force	Use of reasonable force
To defend or protect a third party from harm	To protect property from damage or dispossession
Third person is threatened by attacking force	Someone attempts to harm or wrongfully possess property

§ 7.4 Rightful Repossession

rightful repossession[†]
A defense to trespass to land, trespass to chattel, conversion, assault, and battery. Its elements include the use of reasonable force to retake possession of personal property of which the owner has been wrongfully disposed, or to which the owner has been wrongfully denied possession.

An owner of personal property generally has the right to repossess, by force if necessary, a chattel that has been wrongfully taken or withheld. This is the defense of **rightful repossession**. The defense is generally applied to allegations of trespass to land, assault, battery, and sometimes conversion and trespass to chattel. However, the amount of force that may be used is extremely limited. Generally, the elements of rightful repossession include the following: (1) use of reasonable force (2) to retake possession of personal property (3) of which the owner has been wrongfully dispossessed (or to which the owner is denied possession), (4) provided the efforts to retake the chattel are made promptly after the original dispossession or denial of possession occurs. For this defense, reasonable force is defined along the same lines as defense of property.

Retaking Possession of Personal Property

The chattel owner seeks to repossess personal property to which he or she is entitled. This is the crux of the defense. If someone has wrongfully dispossessed an owner of his or her chattel, then the owner is entitled to enter upon the dispossessor's land to recover the chattel. This provides a defense to trespass to land. Reasonable force may be applied to recover possession of the personal property.

To illustrate, suppose Raymond took Carl's motorcycle without asking permission and drove the cycle back to his own garage. Carl would be entitled to enter Raymond's garage to recover the cycle. If Raymond attempted to prevent Carl from entering, Carl could use reasonable force to vanquish Raymond and recover the cycle. Carl would not be liable for either trespass to land or battery, because he would have the defense of rightful repossession.

Prompt Repossession Efforts

hot (fresh) pursuit
The right of a person who has had property taken to use reasonable force to get it back after a chase that takes place immediately after it was taken.

Older common law cases held that a chattel owner's efforts to repossess personal property must occur soon after the chattel had been wrongfully taken away. However, just how promptly this had to occur was not clearly defined. Many nineteenth-century opinions ruled that hot pursuit was necessary. Hot pursuit is usually defined for purposes of criminal law, but its meaning is the same for this tort defense. **Hot (fresh) pursuit**, in this context, may be described as a rapid chase as soon as possible after the owner has discovered that his or her chattel is missing. This presumes, of course, that the personal property owner knows who took the chattel.

Wrongful Denial of Possession

The chattel owner need not be dispossessed of the personal property for this defense to apply. Consider the example of someone who originally took possession of the chattel with the owner's consent, but later wrongfully refuses to return it. If the owner then attempted to retake possession and was accused of trespass to land, assault, or battery, the owner could apply rightful repossession as a defense.

Most cases involving denial of possession deal with bailments, in which the owner has delivered possession of the chattel to someone else for a specific purpose, with the explicit understanding that the chattel is to be returned at a certain time or upon demand. When an automobile is taken to a mechanic for repair, for instance, there is a bailment. The mechanic would have lawful possession of the vehicle, because the owner left it for repairs. Suppose, however, that the mechanic made unauthorized repairs and sought to charge the owner. If the owner demanded return of the car and the mechanic refused, then this refusal would constitute wrongful denial of possession. The owner could use reasonable force to enter the mechanic's premises to retake the chattel. The owner would not be liable to the mechanic for trespass to land because of the rightful repossession defense.

Note that this result would be different if there had been a dispute over authorized repairs. Most state statutes provide mechanics with possessory liens, which empower repair persons to keep possession of vehicles until repair charges have been paid. However, some statutes provide that the amounts due must be undisputed.

Wrongful Dispossession

For the defense of rightful repossession to apply, the owner's chattel must have been unlawfully dispossessed, or its return have been unlawfully denied. This means that the dispossessor or retainer must not have a legal right to possess (or deny return of) the chattel.

In the preceding bailment example, the mechanic did not possess the automobile unlawfully because the owner had left it for repairs. However, when the mechanic performed unauthorized work and sought payment, and the owner demanded the car's return, then the mechanic wrongfully possessed the vehicle—specifically, the repair person committed trespass to chattel and possibly conversion. Thus, the owner would be entitled to repossess with reasonable force and could use that defense against the mechanic's lawsuit for trespass to land, assault, or battery.

Rightful repossession seems a noble defense, albeit more difficult to conceptualize than self-defense or defense of others and property. One might express the emotional essence of the doctrine as, "It's mine and I'm taking it back now!" The defense appeals to a sense of entitlement. As you read the following hypothetical, with whom do your sympathies lie?

The Case of the Free-Roaming Feline

The following case illustrates an unusual application of rightful repossession. Any pet owner, however, will immediately sympathize with the Blanchards. The court discusses self-defense and defense of property, but the case is a classic rightful repossession scenario.

SHEHYN
v.
UNITED STATES

District of Columbia Court of Appeals
256 A.2d 404 (D.C. 1969)
August 7, 1969
Fickling, J.

Appellant was convicted by a jury of assault, D.C. Code § 22-504. After the court charged the jury on assault and self-defense, the instruction [on defense of property] ... was given and objected to on the ground that it did not correctly state the law on the defense of one's property. The objection was well taken. However, we hold it was harmless error in the context of the case as a whole.

Mr. Blanchard, the complainant, and his wife, who were next door neighbors of appellant, went upon appellant's parking lot to retrieve their pet cat which had escaped from their house and had hidden in appellant's air shaft. Appellant ordered the Blanchards off his property. After they refused, he went inside his house and got a wooden camera tripod about four feet in length and again ordered them to leave. When they refused to leave until they recovered their cat, appellant pushed Mrs. Blanchard aside and struck Mr. Blanchard with the tripod causing injury to his hand, requiring five stitches, and lacerations to his chest. The testimony is conflicting as to why appellant struck Mr. Blanchard. Appellant testified he went into the house to get the tripod because Mr. Blanchard picked up a brick. Blanchard testified he picked up a brick after appellant came out of his house with the tripod, and then he dropped the brick as appellant was advancing upon him because he did not want to strike appellant, who is an elderly man.

It is well settled that a person may use as much force as is reasonably necessary to eject a trespasser from his property, and that if he used more force than is necessary, he is guilty of assault. This is true regardless of any actual or threatened injury to the property by the trespasser, although this would be a factor in determining the reasonableness of the force used. However, in the instant case, Blanchard was not a trespasser. He had a privilege to go peaceably upon appellant's property to retrieve his cat. In *Carter v. Thurston*, 59 N.H. 104 (1877), where logs went upon a riparian owner's property because of a flood, the court stated:

> This right of pursuit and reclamation [of logs] rests upon the same natural right as that which permits the owner of cattle to pursue into an adjoining field and recover his beasts straying from the highway; but in the pursuit and recovery of his cattle or his logs, the owner must do no unnecessary damage, and is responsible for any excess or abuse of his right.

In an assault case where the complainant was injured while recovering his carpenter's plane, the court stated in *Stuyvesant v. Wilcox*, 92 Mich. 233, 52 N.W. 465, 467 (1892):

> But it is a rule well settled that one has such a right in personal property that he may recapture it and take it into his own possession whenever and wherever he may peaceably do so.

This principle was also followed in *Pierce v. Finerty*, 76 N.H. 38, 76 A. 194, 196 (1910), which involved reclamation of trees upon the land of another:

> There is a right of recaption or reclamation of personal property upon another's land without fault of the owner. In such cases, under certain circumstances, the owner of personal property has a right to enter to retake his property, and is not a trespasser if he does so. ... But the right does not extend to cases where the situation is created by the fault or wrong of such owner.

The applicable rule, which we adopt, is stated in *Restatement (Second) of Torts* § 198 (1965):

> (1) One is privileged to enter land in the possession of another, at a reasonable time and in a reasonable manner, for the purpose of removing a chattel to the immediate possession of which the actor is entitled, and which has come upon the land otherwise than with the actor's consent or by his tortious conduct or contributory negligence.
>
> (2) The actor is subject to liability for any harm done in the exercise of the privilege stated in Subsection (1) to any legally protected interest of the possessor in the land or connected with it, except where the chattel is on the land through the tortious conduct or contributory negligence of the possessor.

In this case there is no evidence in the record which would indicate that the Blanchards acted in an unreasonable manner or at an unreasonable time when they went upon the parking lot to get their cat. The [jury] instruction, even though erroneous, was actually beneficial to appellant since he had no right to eject the Blanchards while they were exercising a privilege given to them by law, and appellant was not entitled to any defense of property instruction.

Affirmed.

Case Questions

1. Although Shehyn, the appellant, was prosecuted under a criminal statute for assault, the defenses used in the case would be identical to those pleaded in a civil lawsuit involving the tort of assault or battery. Did you notice that the Blanchards were alleged to have committed trespass to land? What were their defenses as discussed in *Shehyn*? What portions of the court's opinion alerted you to these defenses?

2. Although the court in *Shehyn* quoted several persuasive precedents from other jurisdictions, it chose to adopt the rule stated in the *Restatement (Second) of Torts* § 198. Why did the *Shehyn* court quote these other state court opinions? Why do you think it adopted the *Restatement* rule, which is considered secondary legal authority, as opposed to the quoted court cases, which are primary authority?

3. Are there any other intentional tort defenses that were not discussed in *Shehyn* but that would apply? What are these? Why do you think they would succeed or fail?

4. Would the decision in *Shehyn* have been different if the Blanchards' cat had entered the appellant's land as a result of the Blanchards' actions? Suppose Mr. Blanchard threw a cat toy too high into the air, causing it to land on top of the appellant's roof, thereby enticing the cat to climb up onto the roof and become trapped there? Would the Blanchards have been legally justified in entering the appellant's real estate under these circumstances?

― HYPOTHETICAL ―

Ann was buying an automobile from Victor. Ann wrote a check to Victor for the final payment and this check bounced (i.e., the bank did not pay it because there were insufficient funds in Ann's account). Victor angrily went over to Ann's house and drove away in the car. As soon as Ann discovered the check problem, she telephoned Victor's apartment and left a message on his answering machine that she would be over directly to pay cash.

The first issue is whether Victor had the right to repossess the automobile once Ann's check bounced. This would depend upon the terms of their agreement or, if the agreement did not address the problem, then upon creditors' rights statutes. For the sake of example, assume that no statutes address the question and that the parties' contract was silent as well. Although it is true that Ann breached her contract by bouncing her payment check to Victor, she also swiftly corrected the error. Most courts would hold that Victor could not use self-help remedies such as repossession without first contacting Ann to see if she could make good on the check. By repossessing the car without first talking with Ann, and because Ann has paid nearly the entire purchase price (and thus has a substantial equity, meaning property interest, in the vehicle), Victor has committed trespass to chattel. Thus, Ann has been wrongfully dispossessed of her chattel. She could then enter

Victor's real estate to recover her automobile without being liable to Victor for trespass to land. Ann would be entitled to the defense of rightful repossession.

It should also be noted that Victor would not be able to claim rightful repossession as a defense to trespass to chattel. Because Victor did not first communicate with Ann regarding the bad check and alternative means of payment, most courts would say that Victor could not defend his retaking of the car on the grounds of rightful repossession. However, if Victor had telephoned Ann about the check, and she had replied that she could or would not make the final payment, then Victor would be legally entitled to repossess the vehicle. Under this set of circumstances, Victor could use rightful repossession as a defense to trespass to chattel. ■

A synopsis of rightful repossession appears in Table 7-3.

TABLE 7-3
Elements of rightful repossession

Use of reasonable force
To repossess personal property
Owner has been wrongfully dispossessed of the chattel or has been improperly denied possession
Owner's efforts to repossess chattel occur promptly after original dispossession or denial of possession

§ 7.5 Consent

consent Voluntary and active agreement.

Consent is a broad defense applicable to every intentional tort. **Consent** occurs when the victim of an intentional tort voluntarily agrees to the tortfeasor's actions, provided that the victim understands (or reasonably should understand) the consequences of the tortfeasor's deeds. This knowledge factor is sometimes called **informed consent**.

informed consent
A person's agreement to allow something to happen (such as surgery) that is based on a full disclosure or full knowledge of the facts needed to make the decision intelligently.

The consent defense contains the following elements: (1) Voluntary acceptance of an intentionally tortious act (2) with full knowledge or understanding of the consequences. Actually, consent is not a legal defense at all. As shown in the previous two chapters, it is a deliberately missing element of intentional torts. If consent existed, then the intentional tort could not have occurred. The ancient common law applied the Latin maxim, *volenti non fit injuria*, which translates as, "No wrong may occur to one who is willing." As a practical matter, courts over the centuries have treated consent as a defense to intentional torts.

Informed Consent: Voluntary Acceptance

Consent will be a successful defense to an intentional tort action only if the victim willingly and knowingly agreed to the tortfeasor's conduct. Accordingly, a victim who is coerced into tolerating an intentional tort cannot consent to it, because the victim was compelled to undergo the tort. Further, the victim must comprehend the implications of the tortfeasor's actions to consent to them.

For instance, suppose Randy agrees to wrestle Ralph. Assume that both Randy and Ralph understand the repercussions of wrestling, including possible inadvertent injury. Randy and Ralph will have mutually consented to battery, and so neither could sue the other for this intentional tort if harm did happen. However, assume Randy did not want to wrestle Ralph, but Ralph ridiculed Randy in front of friends, in effect coercing Randy to wrestle. Randy would not have consented because of duress.

Part of the voluntary, or *volition*, factor of consent is the victim's mental capacity to agree. Some persons simply lack sufficient mental abilities to understand the consequences of a tortfeasor's actions. Severely retarded or mentally incapacitated individuals, for example, might not grasp the implications of a tortfeasor's misbehavior. Intoxicated individuals may also have insufficient mental faculties to comprehend the results of an intentional tort. Children, particularly when very young, may lack cognitive development adequate to grasp the ramifications of intentional torts. For such persons, consent could become virtually impossible.

Implied Consent

Consent may be expressed, either orally or in writing, or it may be implied by conduct or circumstances. For instance, public officials or famous persons are assumed to consent to adverse publicity merely by placing themselves in the public limelight. Consent to publicity is therefore implied, and public officials or celebrities cannot recover for libel or slander, unless malice is proven.

The most common example of implied consent involves emergency medical treatment. If a patient is unconscious and is taken to a hospital emergency room, the medical personnel may presume that the patient consents to treatment, at least to the extent of the emergency condition. Thus, if someone is found unconscious on the pavement, suffering from gastrointestinal bleeding, and an ambulance takes her to the hospital, the patient is presumed to agree to treatment of the emergency condition, in this case a "G.I. bleed," which is often life-threatening. Later, if the patient regains consciousness and protests against the treatment (perhaps upon religious grounds), the patient cannot sue for battery for the unauthorized emergency care. However, once conscious and clear-minded, the patient could insist that further treatment be forgone. Failure to stop treatment would then constitute battery. Suppose, instead, that the medical personnel treated beyond the emergency condition, such as removing a portion of diseased skin while treating the intestinal bleeding. Implied consent does not apply to nonemergency treatment, and thus battery would have occurred.

Consent is sometimes characterized as the "you asked for it" defense. However, as the following hypothetical demonstrates, there can be doubt as to what the "it" was to which the victim consented.

The Case of the More-Than-Touch Football Game

Almost everyone has played contact games. Children delight in games such as "tag," "keep-away," and "hide-and-seek," which usually involve some physical contact. Older children and adults engage in rougher sports in which implied consent accepts incidental contact. Sometimes, however, a player forgets that there are limits to the reasonable force to which participants consent. In the following case, it becomes clear that the plaintiff felt that the defendant went well beyond these acceptable lines. The California Court of Appeal, however, was unimpressed. Perhaps none of the judges had ever played a rough game of touch football.

KNIGHT v. JEWETT

California Court of Appeal
232 Cal. App. 3d 1142,
275 Cal. Rptr. 292 (1990)
November 27, 1990
Review granted, 278 Cal. Rptr. 203,
804 P.2d 1300 (Cal. 1991)
Todd, Acting Presiding Justice

Kendra Knight appeals a summary judgment granted in favor of Michael Jewett in her lawsuit against Jewett for negligence and assault and battery stemming from a touch football game in which she was injured. Knight contends ... it was error to apply the doctrine of assumption of risk to defeat the assault and battery cause of action and ... there were triable issues of fact that should have precluded the granting of summary judgment.

FACTS

On January 25, 1987, Knight and several other individuals, including Jewett, gathered at the Vista home of Ed McDaniels to observe the Super Bowl football game. Knight and Jewett were among those who decided to play a game of co-ed touch football during half-time using a "pee-wee" football often used by children. Apparently, no explicit rules were written down or discussed before the game, other than the requirement that to stop advancement of the player with the ball it was necessary to touch that player above the waist with two hands. Knight and Jewett were on different teams.

Previously, Knight had played touch football and frequently watched football on television. Knight voluntarily participated in the Super Bowl half-time game. It was her understanding that this game would not involve forceful pushing, hard hitting or hard shoving during the game. She had never observed anyone being injured in a touch football game before this incident.

About five to ten minutes after the game started, Jewett ran into Knight during a play and afterward Knight asked Jewett not to play so rough. Otherwise, she told him, she would stop playing.

On the next play, Knight suffered her injuries, when she was knocked down by Jewett and he stepped on the little finger of her right hand. Kendra had three surgeries on the finger, but they proved unsuccessful. The finger was amputated during a fourth surgery.

According to Jewett, he had jumped up to intercept a pass and as he came down he knocked Knight over. When he landed, he stepped back and onto Knight's hand.

According to Knight's version, her teammate, Andrea Starr had caught the ball and was proceeding up the field. Knight was headed in the same direction, when Jewett, in pursuit of Starr, came from behind Knight and knocked her down. Knight put her arms out to break the fall and Jewett ran over her, stepping on her hand. Jewett continued to pursue Starr for another 10 to 15 feet before catching up with her and tagging her. Starr said the tag was rough enough to cause her to lose her balance and fall and twist her ankle.

Jewett did not intend to step on Knight's hand and did not intend to hurt her.

* * *

Knight contends her cause of action for assault and battery is viable and she should be allowed to proceed to trial on it.

… Jewett argued it must fail because Knight consented to the physical contact.

Consent is a viable defense to the tort of assault and battery. "A person may, by participating in a game, or by other conduct, consent to an act which might otherwise constitute a battery." Here, however, we need not dwell on whether Jewett can successfully interpose a defense of consent to Knight's assault and battery cause of action.

Inasmuch as this case reaches us on appeal from a summary judgment in favor of Jewett, it is only necessary for us to determine whether there is any possibility Knight may be able to establish her case.

A requisite element of assault and battery is intent. Here, however, there is no evidence that Jewett intended to injure Knight or commit a battery on her. Moreover, the record affirmatively shows Knight does not believe Jewett had the intent to step on her hand or injure her. Without the requisite intent, Knight cannot state a cause of action for assault and battery.

A motion for summary judgment is addressed to the sound discretion of the trial court and, absent a clear showing of abuse, the judgment will not be disturbed on appeal. On this record, we discern no abuse of discretion; the granting of summary judgment was proper. … Affirmed.

Case Questions

1. *Knight* demonstrates how the defense of consent cannot be reached unless the elements of intentional torts (in this case, assault and battery), are satisfied. Although the evidence suggested that the defendant lacked the necessary intent to cause injury, could you imply such intent from Jewett's rough conduct during the game?

2. Presume that Knight had proven Jewett's intent to harm her, thus making a prima facie case for assault and battery (the other elements being satisfied under the facts of the case as given in the opinion). Would Jewett's consent defense prevail? Did Knight consent to the harsh play that Jewett was engaging in? If so, did Knight withdraw her consent when she told Jewett to stop playing so roughly?

3. Are there any other intentional tort defenses that were not discussed in *Knight* but that would apply? What are they? Why do you think they would succeed or fail?

— HYPOTHETICAL ——————————————————————

Colleen attended a company banquet in her honor as "sales director of the year." The dinner was a "roast" at which co-workers made humorous remarks about the guest of honor. Several of these comments were loaded with sarcasm and a few were in questionable taste. However, none of the comments was taken seriously by the audience, which understood that it was all in good fun. Under other circumstances, however, some members of the audience might have been offended. Colleen, however, took offense at the more colorful character references. Could she sue her co-employees for slander?

Colleen voluntarily agreed to attend the banquet with a complete understanding that co-workers would use the forum to tease and joke about her. She should have known that some of her fellow employees would push the limits of propriety with a few harsh remarks. Because the audience was not offended (given the "roast" atmosphere), and because Colleen knowingly accepted the potentially slanderous conduct, consent would be a defense to Colleen's slander claim. ■

The components of consent are listed in Table 7-4.

Consent is clearly the most pervasive defense to intentional torts. Mistake is also quite extensive, as discussed in the next section.

TABLE 7-4
Elements of
consent

Voluntary acceptance of an intentionally tortious act
Full knowledge or understanding of the consequences

§ 7.6 Mistake

Sometimes people act based upon inaccurate information or incorrect interpretations of events. The actor intended the result of his or her conduct but behaved under false beliefs. Often, had a person known the true state of affairs, he or she would have behaved differently. Tort law recognizes this tendency toward error, in which everyone has engaged at one time or another. The defense of mistake provides individuals with an escape route from intentional tort liability. As a legal defense, **mistake** is the good-faith belief, based upon incorrect information, that one is justified in committing an intentional tort under the circumstances. The elements may be detailed as follows: (1) Good-faith conviction that one's actions are justified (2) with the belief based upon faulty information; and (3) the conduct would otherwise be considered tortious but for the erroneous belief.

mistake
An unintentional
error or act.

Good-Faith Conviction

The actor must reasonably believe that, under the incorrect facts the actor thinks are true, the actor's conduct will be legally excused. For instance, if Sandra thought Martina was converting Sandra's jacket when, in actuality, Martina was merely picking it up off the floor, then Sandra would be justified in using reasonable force to recapture her chattel (as she reasonably believed that Martina was attempting to keep it). Naturally, the question revolves around the reasonableness of Sandra's perception of events. Was it obvious that Martina was simply picking up the jacket? Did it look as if Martina might have been rifling through the pockets looking for valuables? The good faith conviction, like all elements of mistake, depends heavily upon the specific facts of each case.

Belief Based upon Inaccurate Information

To use mistake as a defense to intentional torts, the actor must base his or her conviction upon erroneous details which, if they had been true, would have justified the conduct. Had Martina actually been trying to take Sandra's jacket (or valuables in its pockets), then Sandra would have been entitled to use reasonable force under the defense of rightful repossession. Assume that Sandra saw Martina looking through the jacket's pockets. Suppose that Martina was simply looking to see if anything had fallen out, but to Sandra it appeared that Martina was searching for valuables. This mistaken perception would be reasonable and would excuse Sandra's repossession efforts (such as grabbing Martina's arm and pulling the jacket out of her hands). Sandra would not be liable to Martina for battery, because of the mistake defense.

Otherwise Tortious Acts

It may seem apparent that the defense of mistake applies only if the actor has engaged in behavior which, except for the defense, would be considered tortious. For example, Sandra would have had to commit an intentional tort against Martina (such as battery) in order to claim the defense of mistake or rightful repossession. Otherwise, Sandra would not need to argue any defenses, because she would not need to justify her actions. This factor is present in all intentional tort defenses.

The *Restatement (Second) of Torts*

For decades, the American Law Institute has assembled Restatements of the Law, which summarize the legal principles discussed in common law decisions. These include the *Restatement of Torts* and its successor, the *Restatement (Second) of Torts.*

In the *Restatement (Second)*'s chapter 45, justification and excuse to tort liability are discussed. The following is an excerpt applicable to the mistake defense.

Restatement (Second) of Torts § 890
Comments a & f
American Law Institute (1979)

In some cases the law creates a privilege ... . [A] privilege is given although it adversely affects the legally protected interests of another. This is ordinarily true when the actor is protected although mistaken (see Comment *f*), as when one acts in self-defense against another whom he reasonably but erroneously believes to be an aggressor. ...

f. Mistake. ...

When the privilege is conditional, a person is sometimes protected by his reasonable belief in the existence of facts that would give rise to a privilege, even though the facts do not exist. Thus one is not liable for using reasonable force in the protection of himself or another against what he reasonably believes to be an aggression of another ... ; a policeman is not liable for mistakenly arresting one whom he believes to have committed a felony ... and a private person is similarly protected if a felony has been committed ... ; a parent or teacher is not liable for mistakenly but reasonably disciplining a student.

─ HYPOTHETICAL ─

Diedra was shopping at a local convenience store. The manager thought she saw Diedra put a pack of chewing gum into her purse. When Diedra left the store without stopping at the cashier, the manager asked her to step back inside the store to see the contents of her purse. The manager explained that she thought she had seen her take merchandise without paying. Diedra emptied her purse, but no store items were included. If Diedra claimed that the manager had committed false imprisonment, defamation, or infliction of emotional distress, could the manager use mistake as a defense?

Assume that the manager's acts arguably constituted any one of these intentional torts. Nevertheless, courts would readily rule that, under these circumstances, the manager was justified in detaining Diedra for questioning. So long as the interrogation was conducted reasonably (such as in private for a short time period), then the courts would consider the manager's behavior to be acceptable. The manager had a good-faith belief that Diedra had shoplifted (although, in fact, she had not). The manager acted based upon this erroneous conviction, expecting that her conduct would be legally excused under the circumstances. ■

Mistake is summarized in Table 7-5.

TABLE 7-5
Elements of
mistake

Good faith conviction that actor's conduct is justified
Belief based upon erroneous information
Behavior would be tortious except for incorrect belief

§ 7.7 Privilege

privilege†
As a defense against
an intentional tort,
privilege is a legal
justification to engage
in otherwise tortious
conduct in order
to accomplish a
compelling social goal.

As an intentional torts defense, **privilege** is a legal justification to engage in otherwise tortious conduct in order to accomplish a compelling social goal. This defense is based upon the right of a person to do what most people are not permitted to do. It is a right conferred on a person by society. For example, as a land owner, one may eject a person from one's own property, but other people may not do this. Only the land owner is thus privileged.

Privilege is most commonly a defense to trespass to land, trespass to chattel, conversion, assault, battery, and false imprisonment, although it may be applied against other intentional torts as well. Privilege includes the following considerations:

1. Do the actor's motives for engaging in an intentional tort outweigh the injury to the victim or his or her property?

2. Was the actor justified in committing the intentional tort to accomplish his or her socially desirable purposes, or could a less damaging action have been taken instead?

This formula shows how courts balance values between the socially acceptable motives of the tortfeasor (actor) and the tort victim's compensation for injury. Privilege presumes that the intentional tort is legally justified because of the higher purposes to be achieved.

motive The reason
why a person does
something.

intent The resolve
or purpose to use a
particular means to
reach a particular
result. *Intent* usually
explains *how* a person
wants to do some-
thing and *what* that
person wants to get
done, while *motive*
usually explains *why.*

Motives and Socially Desirable Goals

Motive describes the goal that a participant wishes to accomplish by taking a particular action. Motive may be discovered by probing the mental state of the actor. This mind-reading occurs in many areas of law. For example, in criminal law, *mens rea* loosely translates from the Latin as "evil thoughts" and suggests a psychological component to criminal conduct. In tort law, motive is synonymous with **intent**, which is broadly defined as the desire to attain a certain result. For purposes of the privilege defense, motive must be socially advantageous to a point that excuses intentional harm to another person or his or her property. The example of trespassing to save a drowning child's life sharply illustrates the clearly superior social objective that would give rise to the defense against the land owner's trespass-to-land lawsuit.

Less Injurious Alternatives

With privilege defenses, courts frequently ask whether the tortfeasor's objectives could have been reached through behavior that would have been less harmful to the victim. Suppose Karen discovers an automobile on fire next to a natural gas storage facility. Given the likelihood that the burning car will ignite the gas tanks, which would explode along with a sizeable portion of the surrounding neighborhood, Karen sprays the flaming vehicle with water, irreparably damaging the engine. The car owner would complain against Karen's conversion or trespass to chattel. Karen would defend by arguing privilege. The court would query: Could Karen have saved the storage facility (and surrounding area) through a less damaging act?

The answer to this question depends upon the extent of the fire. If only a small portion of the automobile were burning, such as something in the trunk, Karen could have isolated the danger by concentrating water only into the trunk compartment. If the interior were also ablaze, Karen would be forced to expose more car to the water to put out the fire. Still, she might have spared the engine compartment. However, if the inferno had engulfed the entire vehicle, she would have no choice other than to inundate it with water.

Similarity Between Privilege and Other Defenses

Several distinct intentional tort defenses, such as rightful repossession, self-defense, or defense of others or property, are simply particular types of privilege. Each has a social benefits component that justifies otherwise tortious misconduct. Necessity is another form of privilege that has also become a separate defense in its own right. The same is true of public officer's immunity for legal process enforcement, warrantless arrest, and reasonable discipline. These defenses to intentional torts are discussed in the remaining sections of this chapter.

The *Restatement (Second)* Position

Restatement (Second) of Torts § 890 focuses on privileges, noting that the term is broadly defined to include many of the specific defenses discussed throughout this chapter. The illustrations in the Comments are particularly helpful in understanding the scope of privilege.

Restatement (Second) of Torts § 890 & Comments
American Law Institute (1979)

§ 890. Privileges

One who otherwise would be liable for a tort is not liable if he acts in pursuance of and within the limits of a privilege of his own or of a privilege of another that was properly delegated to him.

Comment:

a. As stated in § 10, the word "privilege" is used throughout this Restatement to denote the fact that conduct that under ordinary circumstances would subject the actor to liability, under particular circumstances does not subject him to the liability.

* * *

In some cases the law creates a privilege ... as when the owner of land is given a privilege to eject a trespasser upon his land or to enter the land of another to abate a private nuisance, or when a citizen is given the privilege of arresting a felon ... .

c. Purpose of privilege—Conditional privileges created by rule of law. Most of the privileges that are not based on consent are conditioned upon their being performed for the purpose of protecting the interest for which the privilege was given. This is illustrated in cases in which force is used against another; in self-defense or in defense of a third person ... ; in the defense of the possession of land ... ; in the recapture of land or chattels ... ; in an arrest by a private person or a peace officer ... ; in the prevention of crime ... ; in the disciplining of children .... .

d. Purpose of privilege—Absolute privileges. In certain cases in which the interests of the public are overwhelming, the purpose of the actor is immaterial. Thus for some or all statements, complete immunity from civil liability exists as to defamatory statements made during the course of judicial proceedings ... , as well as to statements by legislators and certain administrative officers while acting in the performance of their functions.

— HYPOTHETICAL —

Livingston owns a grocery in town. One of his customers notified him that several cans of Buddy Boy's Baked Beans were bulging, which is a symptom of contamination. Livingston opened these cans and discovered that the food had spoiled. He placed an advertisement in the local newspaper warning his customers to return any can of Buddy Boy's, whether bulging or not, because of spoilage. In fact, only four cans of

the product were defective. Buddy Boy's manufacturer, E. I. Wilcott &
Company, sued Livingston for disparagement of goods. Livingston
claimed privilege, arguing that his motive was to protect the public
from food poisoning. Would the defense carry the day?

Truth is an absolute defense in any type of defamation action,
including commercial disparagement. In our hypothetical, however, the
truth was exaggerated. Only a few cans were tainted. Nonetheless,
there was no way of determining this without recalling as many cans
as possible from Livingston's customers. A court would rule that
Livingston was justified in advertising the warning to his customers,
and so Livingston would not be liable to E. I. Wilcott & Company for
disparagement of goods. ■

The elements of privilege are abstracted in Table 7-6.

TABLE 7-6
Elements of
privilege

Actor's motives in committing intentional tort outweigh injury to victim or property
Actor was justified in engaging in intentional tort to accomplish socially desirable goals
No less-damaging alternative action could have been taken
Exception: Absolute privilege of judges, legislators, etc. These actors' motives are immaterial.

§ 7.8 Necessity

necessity Anything
from an irresistible
force or compulsion
to an important, but
not required action.
Necessity often refers
to a situation that re-
quires an action that
would otherwise be il-
legal or expose a per-
son to tort liability.

Necessity is another variety of privilege that excuses otherwise tortious
misconduct. Under this defense, the tortfeasor is justified in engaging
in an intentional tort to prevent more serious injury from an external
force. **Necessity** contains three elements: (1) Committing an intentional
tort (2) to avert more serious injury (3) caused by a force other than
the tortfeasor (4) and the tortfeasor's actions were reasonably necessary to
avert the greater harm. This defense is based on the theory that the benefit—prevention of a greater harm—outweighs the risk of the intentional
injury.

Thwarting a More Substantial Harm

In a necessity situation, the tortfeasor is usually faced with having to
choose between the lesser of two evils. On the one hand, the tortfeasor

must inflict injury upon a victim or the victim's property. On the other hand, the tortfeasor could do nothing and watch a greater havoc occur. For example, suppose Antonio is aboard a ship that suddenly begins to sink. There are several passengers aboard, including Antonio, as well as valuable cargo. If the cargo were thrown overboard, the boat could stay afloat long enough for help to arrive. So Antonio elects to jettison the cargo and save the passengers' lives. The cargo owner could sue Antonio for trespass to chattel, but the defense of necessity would insulate Antonio from liability. Although Antonio committed an intentional tort, he sought only to prevent greater harm caused by a force beyond his control (namely, the ship's sinking).

External Forces

For necessity to operate as a defense to an intentional tort, the more significant danger being averted must originate from a source other than the tortfeasor. For instance, in the previous illustration, the boat began to sink through no fault of Antonio's. However, suppose he had caused an explosion in the engine room by improper fuel mixing, and thus blew a hole in the hull of the craft. Because Antonio created the greater hazard, he could not claim necessity in throwing the cargo overboard. Had it not been for his misconduct in the engine room, the extreme peril would never have happened. The necessity defense cannot protect a tortfeasor who creates the catastrophic condition and then must engage in an intentional tort to resolve the crisis.

Reasonably Necessary Action

As is generally true with privilege, necessity requires that the tortfeasor's conduct be reasonably necessary to prevent the more substantial danger. Thus, the tortfeasor must use only that degree of force required to avert the greater risk. Using the sinking ship example, suppose that the leak in the ship's hull occurred not because of Antonio's misbehavior but because of faulty sealing techniques. If Antonio could plug the leak rather than abandon ship, it would not be necessary for him to jettison the cargo to save the passengers.

Fires further illustrate this aspect of reasonably required action; many necessity cases involve burning buildings. Several nineteenth-century court opinions discussed "row" structures, which were many discrete buildings attached in long rows down a street. If one were to catch fire, it was likely that the entire block would burn to the ground. To avoid this calamity, the flaming building was often destroyed. There simply was no less-damaging alternative when the building was fully ablaze. If the building owner sued for trespass to land, the courts routinely applied the necessity defense to protect the tortfeasor from liability to the building owner.

The *Restatement (Second)* Position

The *Restatement (Second)* addresses necessity as a defense in emergency situations in which the tortfeasor is compelled to immediate action by a crisis. In such cases, the defense operates to protect the defendant from liability. Note how the *Restatement*'s elements are distinguishable from those previously discussed in the text.

Restatement (Second) of Torts §§ 890, 892D & Comments
American Law Institute (1979)

[§ 890, Comment a.] [The emergency defense exists] when the protection of the public is of overriding importance, as when one is privileged to destroy buildings to avert a public disaster. ...

§ 892D. Emergency Action Without Consent
Conduct that injures another does not make the actor liable to the other, even though the other has not consented to it if

(a) **an emergency makes it necessary or apparently necessary, in order to prevent harm to the other, to act before there is opportunity to obtain consent from the other or one empowered to consent for him, and**

(b) **the actor has no reason to believe that the other, if he had the opportunity to consent, would decline.**

Comment:
a. The rule stated in this Section covers a group of exceptional situations in which the actor is privileged to proceed without the consent of another and without any manifested or apparent consent, on the assumption that if the other had the opportunity to decide he would certainly consent. This privilege must necessarily be a limited one and can arise only in situations of emergency, when there is no time to consult the other or one empowered to consent for him, or for reasons such as the unconsciousness of the other his consent cannot be obtained. The mere possibility that the other might consent if he were able to do so is not enough; and the conduct must be so clearly and manifestly to the other's advantage that there is no reason to believe that the consent would not be given. If the actor knows or has reason to know, because of past refusals or other circumstances, that the consent would not be given, he is not privileged to act. ...

Necessity can be a puzzling defense. Its elements compel courts to balance competing interests, employing somewhat more value judgment than usual. This hypothetical illustrates.

─ HYPOTHETICAL ───────────────────────────

Kenneth owns an exotic pet store, in which he sells, among other wild animals, several species of snake. One day a customer accidentally knocked a cage containing a python onto the floor, causing the door to spring open. The snake slithered out into the aisles searching for food. An infant was strapped in an automobile safety seat that her mother used as a carrier while shopping. The youngster's mother was several feet away looking at some unusual fish. The snake approached the infant and clearly intended to consume the child. Quickly, another patron, Jeffrey, impaled the python with a hunting knife (which was on display on a nearby shelf). Kenneth sued Jeffrey for trespass to chattel. Could necessity excuse Jeffrey's actions?

Reasonably necessary action is the critical element in this hypothetical. Did Jeffrey have to kill the snake to prevent it from attacking the baby? Could Jeffrey have taken other action to protect the child? Jeffrey could have grabbed the infant seat and carried the child to safety. Then Jeffrey could have summoned Kenneth or another store employee to capture the python. Accordingly, necessity would not be a successful defense, and Jeffrey would be liable to Kenneth for trespass to chattel. ■

A short review of the elements of necessity is provided in Table 7-7.

TABLE 7-7
Elements of
necessity

Committing intentional tort
Purpose to avert more harmful injury
Harm threatened by force other than tortfeasor
Tortfeasor's actions were reasonably necessary to prevent danger of greater harm

§ 7.9 Public Officer's Immunity for Legal Process Enforcement

Public officials often engage in activity that normally would be considered intentionally tortious. However, because such persons are authorized by law to engage in such conduct, they are protected from liability. Several types of governmental action fall within this protected class. The most common include: (1) process serving; (2) execution sales; (3) attachment or replevin; (4) arrest by warrant; (5) prosecutors acting in official capacity; and (6) judges acting in official capacity.

Service of Process

process A court's ordering a defendant to show up in court or risk losing a lawsuit; a summons.

process serving† The method by which a defendant in a lawsuit is notified that the plaintiff has filed suit against the defendant. Also called *service of process.* Governmental officials engaged in process serving are generally immune from intentional tort liability.

service of process The delivery (or its legal equivalent, such as publication in a newspaper in some cases) of a legal paper, such as a writ, by an authorized person in a way that meets certain formal requirements.

execution sale† A public sale held by a sheriff or other public official of property seized under a writ of execution.

sheriff's sale A sale [of property] held by a sheriff to pay a court judgment against the owner of the property.

attachment Formally seizing property (or a person) in order to bring it under control of the court. This is usually done by getting a court order to have a law enforcement officer take control of the property.

Process, process serving, or **service of process** are the methods by which a defendant in a lawsuit is notified that a plaintiff has filed suit against the defendant. Service of process is the means used to notify the defendant. Most commonly, the court clerk either mails a copy of the summons and the plaintiff's complaint to the defendant (usually by certified or registered mail), or the sheriff delivers the summons and complaint directly to the defendant, or a private process server does so. It is the latter cases of actual physical delivery that give rise to litigation. The defendant might sue the sheriff for trespass to land when the sheriff arrived on the defendant's real estate to deliver the summons. However, the sheriff has the power, either by statute or common law, to enter another person's land to serve process. The land owner's lawsuit against the sheriff would fail as a result of this defense.

Execution Sales

When a plaintiff wins judgment against the defendant in a civil action, the defendant usually has a certain period of time, often thirty days, within which to pay the judgment. If the defendant fails to pay, the plaintiff may return to court and file a *writ of execution* requesting the court to order the defendant's property sold to satisfy the judgment. These forced sales are often referred to as **execution sales** or **sheriff's sales**, because the sheriff is frequently the public official responsible for seizing and selling the defendant's property. The defendant might sue the sheriff for trespass to land, trespass to chattel, and conversion after the sheriff comes and gets the defendant's property. However, once again the sheriff is legally protected. Statutes and common law empower law enforcement officials to seize and sell property to satisfy judgments. Therefore, the sheriff would be immune from liability.

Attachment or Replevin

Attachment is a court-ordered remedy in a lawsuit. When a plaintiff is entitled to a remedy against the defendant in a lawsuit, and the defendant is likely to dispose of his or her property to avoid losing it in a subsequent execution action, the plaintiff may ask the court to attach the property on the plaintiff's behalf. The court then orders a law enforcement officer, such as the sheriff, to seize the defendant's property subject to attachment. The defendant might think to sue the sheriff for conversion or trespass to chattel, but the defendant should think again. The sheriff is authorized by statute or common law to take the defendant's property into custody under attachment, and the defendant's cause of action against the sheriff would fail.

replevin A legal action to get back property wrongfully held by another person.

Replevin is another court-ordered remedy. A plaintiff sues a defendant who wrongfully possesses the plaintiff's chattel and refuses to return it. The plaintiff asks the court for replevin, which means that the court would order the defendant to return the personal property to the plaintiff. If the defendant still refuses to comply, the court could instruct the sheriff to seize the chattel. The defendant's lawsuit for conversion or trespass to chattel against the sheriff would again be defeated by the law enforcer's defense of legal authority to act.

Arrest by Warrant

Police officers often arrest suspected criminals under the authority of a court-issued warrant for arrest. Suppose the suspect were innocent of any crimes. Could the suspect sue the police department for false imprisonment, assault, battery, and infliction of emotional distress for having been arrested? If the law enforcement personnel were acting pursuant to an arrest warrant properly ordered by a judge, and if they acted in good faith to apprehend the suspect named in the warrant, then they would not be liable for any intentional torts as a consequence of taking the suspect into custody.

Prosecutors and Judges

prosecutor
1. A public official who represents the government's case against a person accused of a crime and who asks the court to convict that person. 2. The private individual who accuses a person of a crime is sometimes called the *private prosecutor*.

judge
The person who runs a courtroom, decides all legal questions, and sometimes decides entire cases by also deciding factual questions.

Prosecutors and **judges** acting in the scope of their positions are privileged and immune from liability for their actions. If this were not so, no one would accept such a position. It is inherent in these positions to occasionally intentionally injure someone mentally, emotionally, and by reputation. Prosecutors are charged with the responsibility of proving bad things about bad people. Liability for their mistakes would have a chilling effect on their performance; that is, they would be too afraid of making a mistake and thus err against social benefit. Judges must make decisions that intentionally injure persons and property. Again, without privilege and/or immunity, there would be a chilling effect that would render judges afraid to make a decision for fear of being wrong. Therefore, public policy has always been to allow these persons immunity from liability in the honest performance of their positions and the privilege to act accordingly.

As a practical matter, the public officer immunity defense is not commonly litigated. The power of its protection precludes intentional tort recovery in most cases.

Nevertheless, there are exceptions to the privilege and immunity doctrines. 42 U.S.C. § 1983 permits liability of public officers (usually other than prosecutors and judges) if the performance of their duties involves activities that deprive persons of their civil rights. Such an action is called a civil rights action or a "1983" action (*1983* is the section number of the law permitting this action, not the year it was passed). If a police officer arrests someone without a warrant and without probable cause, it is a violation of civil rights and the officer may be liable. If excessive force is used in an arrest, it is a violation of civil rights and the officer may be liable. If any action under color or authority of the government—whether local, state, or federal—violates civil rights, the actor(s) may be liable regardless of immunity.

The Case of the Defiant Trucker (Part II)

In *Jurco v. State*, partially reprinted in § 7.3, the Alaska Court of Appeals addressed conflicting defenses: namely, defense of property versus law enforcement officers' immunity for legal process enforcement. Reread the case as it applies to this latter defense and as a refresher for the facts. The court also discussed warrantless arrests, which are discussed in a further analysis of this case in § 7.10.

JURCO v. STATE

Court of Appeals of Alaska
825 P.2d 909 (Alaska Ct. App. 1992)
February 14, 1992
Mannheimer, Judge

At common law, a public officer was authorized to use reasonable force against other persons when executing a court order requiring or authorizing the officer to seize another person's property. This common-law rule has been codified in Alaska; [Alaska Statutes §] 11.81.420 provides:

> Justification: Performance of public duty.
> (a) Unless inconsistent with AS 11.81.320—11.81.410, conduct which would otherwise constitute an offense is justified when it is required or authorized by law or by a judicial decree, judgment, or order.

(b) The justification afforded by this section also applies when ... the person reasonably believes the conduct to be required or authorized by a decree, judgment, or order of a court of competent jurisdiction or in the lawful execution of legal process, notwithstanding lack of jurisdiction of the court or defect in the legal process[.]

Under this statute, law enforcement officers are empowered to use force to execute court decrees, even if it is later shown that the court had no authority to issue the decree. Thus, in Jurco's case, the State Troopers were authorized to use all reasonable force to execute the Alaska District Court's order to seize Jurco's vehicle, even if Jurco was correct in claiming that the pendency of his bankruptcy petition deprived the state district court of the judicial authority to issue orders affecting his property.

— HYPOTHETICAL

Dawn sued Debra. The sheriff delivered a copy of the summons and Dawn's complaint to Debra's house. Debra did not appear at trial, and Dawn won a default judgment against Debra. After thirty days, Debra had failed to pay the judgment. Dawn filed a writ of execution with the court, which ordered the sheriff to seize Debra's property. The sheriff again returned to Debra's house to garner the chattels that could be sold at an execution sale. The proceeds from the sale went to satisfy

Dawn's judgment. Debra sued the sheriff for trespass to land, trespass to chattel, and conversion. The sheriff applied the defense of legal process enforcement.

This hypothetical is probably the easiest to answer of any in the text. The sheriff was acting under court order to enforce legal processes, and so the defense would succeed. Debra's lawsuit would be promptly dismissed. ■

The elements of the legal process enforcement defense are listed in Table 7-8.

TABLE 7-8 Types of legal process enforcement defenses and elements of warrantless arrest defenses

Legal Process Enforcement	Warrantless Arrest
Process serving	Law enforcement officers' power to arrest pursuant to court- ordered arrest warrant
Execution sales	Citizen's arrest (felonies or breaches of peace)
Attachment or replevin	
Arrest by warrant	

§ 7.10 Warrantless Arrest by Law Enforcement Officials or Citizens

Police officers, and sometimes even ordinary citizens, engage in *warrantless arrests*. Could they be liable for false imprisonment, battery, assault, trespass to land, and infliction of emotional distress?

Statutes and common law authorize law enforcement personnel to arrest criminal suspects, even without court-issued warrants, under certain circumstances. For example, when a police officer witnesses a felony, he or she may arrest the suspect immediately. This proper enforcement of a legal process would be a defense against the suspect's intentional torts lawsuit.

Private citizens, too, may take suspected criminals into custody under the theory of *citizen's arrest*. Under the common law, a private citizen may take a suspect into custody if the citizen has witnessed the suspect commit a felony or breach of the peace. This would include situations in which the citizen reasonably thinks that the suspect has committed a felony. Historically, this defense was often used to protect store owners who detained suspected shoplifters from liability for false imprisonment actions.

Normally, modern warrantless arrest does not involve private citizen participation to the extent the pre-twentieth-century cases did. However, private police, such as company security, are often involved in today's cases.

─ HYPOTHETICAL ───────────────────────

Carter is a night watchman at a local factory. He noticed someone suspicious lurking in the shadows near a restricted-access building containing company records and other valuables. He turned his flashlight on the suspect, whom he did not recognize. He demanded identification and the reason the stranger was present on factory grounds. The stranger said nothing and attempted to flee. Carter tackled the individual, forcibly returned him to the security office, and telephoned the police. The stranger turned out to be an employee of a competitor to Carter's employer. The stranger sued Carter for battery, false imprisonment, and infliction of emotional distress. Would Carter be entitled to a defense under citizen's arrest theory?

Carter witnessed a simple trespass to land, which is not a felony under either statutory or common law. The stranger had merely trespassed onto the factory's property. Further, the stranger had not breached the peace. However, Carter reasonably believed that the suspect was about to engage in a felony (namely, burglary or theft). In his experience as a security guard, Carter had seen many felons behave just as the stranger had acted. Thus, Carter's reasonable belief that the suspect was about to commit a felony was sufficient to justify his behavior. Carter would not be liable to the stranger for any of the intentional torts. ■

‹◆›

The Case of the Defiant Trucker (Part III)

Jurco v. State, discussed earlier in §§ 7.3 and 7.9, also involved warrantless arrest. As it had done with Jurco's previous issues on appeal, the Alaska Court of Appeals, with "arresting" analysis, ruled against the appellant. Although the court's discussion did not involve tort liability as a result of a warrantless arrest, it is clear that there could be no such liability, because the arrest was lawful.

JURCO

v.

STATE

Court of Appeals of Alaska
825 P.2d 909 (Alaska Ct. App. 1992)
February 14, 1992
Mannheimer, Judge

Jurco also argues that his arrest was illegal because the troopers did not have an arrest warrant. Jurco acknowledges that [Alaska Stat. §] 12.25.030 authorizes police officers to arrest without a warrant when a misdemeanor is committed in their presence ... .

Finally, even if some additional justification were needed for the troopers' decision to make an arrest instead of issue a citation, that justification was present. It was clear that Jurco was intent on thwarting the troopers' performance of their duty under the court order directing seizure of Jurco's truck; the troopers could reasonably conclude that Jurco would continue to impede their efforts unless he were physically taken into custody.

The warrantless arrest defense, together with the defense of legal process enforcement, are both summarized in Table 7-8 on page 250.

§ 7.11 Statutes of Limitations

Statutes of limitations are statutes restricting the time within which a plaintiff may file his or her lawsuit for particular causes of action against a defendant. All states have statutes of limitations for almost all tort actions, including intentional torts. (Sometimes they are called *limitation of actions*.) The most common tort statutes of limitations are two years. This means that the plaintiff has two years from the date that an intentional tort occurred to file his or her lawsuit against the defendant. If the plaintiff fails to file within this statutory time period, then his or her cause of action against the defendant is barred forever.

Although two years is a common statute of limitations period for many torts, the exact time period varies among states and different types of torts. One should always research the specific statute of limitations for each cause of action, whether in tort or in other areas of law. This is a vital piece of information for both the plaintiff and the defendant. If the statute of limitations has expired, the defendant may respond with this defense and have the plaintiff's case dismissed or otherwise disposed of (usually by summary judgment). The plaintiff's attorney must be aware of the statute of limitations and file the lawsuit in a timely manner, or risk a malpractice suit.

‹♦›

The Case of the Applicable Statute

This case involves several different issues: vehicular negligence, medical malpractice, and the applicable statute of limitations. Note the pivotal role the statute of limitations issue plays in resolving this case. Depending on whether a motorist's claims against a hospital are defined as medical malpractice or general negligence, a two year or five year statute of limitations is applicable.

ROBINSON
v.
HEALTH MIDWEST DEVELOPMENT GROUP
Supreme Court of Missouri, En Banc
58 S.W.3d 519
October 23, 2001

On November 17, 1993, Rosemary Schmidt presented to LRHC [dba Health Midwest Development Group] complaining of a headache. After her initial assessment she was treated with an intravenous dose of five milligrams of Compazine, a non-narcotic medication commonly used to treat nausea.

After receiving the medication and without alerting the staff, Schmidt spontaneously left the hospital's emergency department. Consequently, she failed to receive the appropriate discharge assessment and warnings with regard to her symptoms and prescribed treatment. Compazine is known by medical personnel to cause drowsiness, dizziness, and hypotension.

After leaving the hospital, Schmidt's vehicle crossed the centerline of Highway 13 and struck Robinson's vehicle head-on resulting in the personal injuries that form the basis for this suit. Robinson' petition, filed February 14, 1997, alleged LRHC's medical staff negligently failed to warn Schmidt not to drive while under the influence of the Compazine and that the failure to warn was the direct and proximate cause of Robinson's injuries. LRHC's answer, filed April 17, 1997, denied all liability and raised the affirmative defense of the claim being barred by the applicable statute of limitations.

* * *

To succeed on her claim of negligence Robinson must plead and prove that the defendant had a duty to protect her from injury, that the defendant breached that duty, and that the defendant's failure directly and proximately caused her injury. Robinson contends the various theories of negligence pled do not restrict her claim to the areas of failure to warn or medical malpractice; that instead, a general negligence theory applies and the duty owed to her by LRHC's staff can be imposed by public policy considerations. Robinson further argues there is no need to establish the existence of a physician-patient relationship to prevail on her general negligence claim.

* * *

Section 516.105 provides in pertinent part:

> All actions against physicians, hospitals, ... for damages for malpractice, negligence, error or mistake related to health care shall be brought within two years from the date of occurrence of the act of neglect complained of.

All of Robinson's allegations relate to negligent medical treatment for failing to appropriately inform, assess, monitor, and supervise Ms. Schmidt in conjunction with the treatment she received and with her subsequent unannounced exodus from the hospital while in a medically created impaired state of mind. The clear and unambiguous language of section 516.105 indicates that actions based in negligence brought against the enumerated health care providers in relation to the provision of health care services must be brought within two years from the date of occurrence of the alleged negligent act. ...

Robinson argues that since her claim is based in general negligence that the five-year statue of limitations in section 516.120.4 applies. However, the rules of statutory construction are clear that in situations where the same subject matter is addressed in general terms in one statute and in specific terms in another, and there is a "necessary repugnancy" between statutes, the more specific statute controls over the more general. The two statutes of limitation in controversy are necessarily repugnant as each provides a different time limit for initiating a cause of action for negligence, and Missouri's legislature has identified a specific class of defendants and actions in section 516.105 to receive the shorter statute of limitations.

Robinson filed her claim on February 14, 1997, while the act serving as the basis of her claim occurred on November 17, 1993, some three years and three months after the alleged error related to Ms. Schmidt's health care. The trial court's decision granting LRHC summary judgment was correct even if based upon different reasoning and "a correct decision will not be disturbed because the trial court gave a wrong or insufficient reason therefore." On the basis of Robinson's claim being time-barred by the relevant statute of limitations, the judgment is affirmed.

Case Questions

1. Why did Robinson claim that her case against LRHC should be based on negligence and not malpractice?

2. Why would a plaintiff wait so long to bring a law suit?

§ 7.12 Workers' Compensation

Another defense to an intentional tort action might be that the action is prevented by a state's workers' compensation statute. These statutes cover workers who are injured or killed as a result of incidents occurring during the course and scope of their employment. Workers' compensation statutes bar tort actions against the employer and are considered a worker's sole remedy for on-the-job injuries and death, regardless of fault. Workers' compensation is also addressed in Chapter 11 in relation to tort immunities.

Workers' compensation is insurance that provides cash benefits and/or medical care for workers who are injured on the job or who become ill as a result of their job. Employers pay for this insurance. This is a form of strict liability, a no-fault system by state. In workers' compensation cases, no one party is found to be at fault. However, an employee's injury must "arise out of," and occur in the "course of employment." This means that an injury that occurs at work and is related to work will be covered. In contrast, if an employee is on the way to or from work and injuries are sustained, they will generally not be covered.

The amount a worker collects is not based upon, nor is it affected by, whether an employer is at fault. Unlike a traditional negligence claim, the employee does not have to worry that his or her claim will be defeated by the employer's assertion of defenses such as the employee's contributory negligence, assumption of the risk, or that the injury was actually caused by a fellow employee rather than the employer.

It is important to note that while workers' compensation statutes all but eliminate suits between injured employees and employers, an employee still retains the right to bring an action against a third party who may have also caused or contributed to the injuries. Workers' compensation only bars suits against the employer, not outside third parties. Accordingly, an employee might bring a workers' compensation claim and still sue a private entity such as a janitorial service that left a floor dangerously slippery with wax or a manufacturer that produced a defective product that was used at work.

However, if an employee intentionally tries to injure him or herself, or is injured as a result of drug or alcohol intoxication, then the employee cannot collect benefits. Workers' compensation statutes specify which type of employers and which employees are covered by the acts. Not all employees or all forms of employment are covered by workers' compensation.

Employees must report workplace injuries to their employer and fill out a claim form in order to apply for benefits. Generally, there is a waiting period before the employee can collect benefits. An employer cannot fire an employee solely because the employee has filed for benefits.

The injured employee's medical provider determines the extent of disability, if any. Cash benefits are based upon and determined according to disability classifications ranging from temporary partial disability to permanent total disability. In the event of the death of an employee as a result of a workplace injury, the surviving spouse and family may be entitled to a cash benefit. In the event an employee can no longer return to his or her previous type of work, vocational rehabilitation is offered to train the employee for a new career.

Summary

Self-defense is the exercise of reasonable force to repel an attack upon one's person or to avoid confinement. Self-defense counters an offensive force that threatens bodily injury, repugnant contact, or sequestration. The amount of force a person may use in self-defense is limited to that amount necessary to repel the attacking force. Any greater resistance is excessive and the defense would be ineffective. The defense is used against allegations of assault, battery, or false imprisonment.

Defense of persons or property is another legal justification for assault or battery. Defense of persons involves the use of reasonable force to defend or protect a third party from injury when the third person is threatened by an attacking force. Here, reasonable force is defined identically as for self-defense. Defense of property allows reasonable force to protect property from damage or dispossession when an invader attempts to injure or wrongfully take custody of the property. Reasonable force to protect property is usually defined as less force than would ordinarily be allowed to protect persons. Courts generally do not permit deadly force to be used to protect property, although one may apply deadly force in defense of one's home against intruders, under the castle rule.

Rightful repossession empowers a chattel owner to enter upon another's real estate to legally repossess personal property that has been wrongfully taken or withheld. The chattel owner would not be liable for trespass to land, trespass to chattel, or conversion, because he or she was justified in retaking control of the property. The defense also may protect against claims of assault or battery. Reasonable force may be used to repossess the chattel. Reasonable force is defined along the same lines as for defense of property. The efforts to regain possession must occur promptly after the property is first taken from the owner, or from the time the possessor wrongfully refuses to return the property to the owner. For the defense to succeed, the chattel owner must have been wrongfully dispossessed, or return of the property must have been improperly refused.

Consent may be a defense to all intentional torts. Consent occurs when a victim of an intentional tort voluntarily agrees to endure the tortious actions. Voluntary agreement involves the victim understanding the consequences of the tortfeasor's conduct. This is called informed consent. Consent may be expressed or implied based upon the behavior of the parties.

As a defense to intentional torts, mistake is a good-faith belief, based upon incorrect information, that a person is justified in committing an intentional tort under the circumstances. This belief must be reasonable, and reasonableness is determined on a case-by-case basis. This belief must be based on erroneous details which, if they had been true, would have excused the intentional torts committed.

Privilege is sometimes considered a broad category embracing all the other defenses discussed in this chapter. To use the defense, one must ask if the actor's motives for engaging in the intentional tort outweigh the injury to the victim or property. Further, one must ask if the actor was justified in committing the intentional tort to achieve socially desirable goals (which outweigh the injury factor). Could these goals have been accomplished without inflicting the harm to the victim?

The necessity defense allows a tortfeasor to commit an intentional tort to prevent more serious injury from an external force. The tortfeasor's actions must be reasonably necessary to avert the more substantial danger. Necessity is basically a choice between the lesser of two evils. The tortfeasor cannot cause the greater threat of harm if the necessity defense is to insulate him or her from liability.

Public officials are immune from intentional tort liability for the proper enforcement of legal processes, such as service of process, execution sales, attachment, replevin, or arrest by warrant. Both statutes and common law protect governmental employees involved in these activities, as legal process enforcement is necessary to implement the judicial system. Normally, law enforcement officers, such as sheriffs, participate in these processes.

Law enforcement officials are authorized by statutes and common law to make warrantless arrests, usually when a felony is committed or suspected in their presence. Under the defense of citizen's arrest, private persons may restrain suspected felons without liability for assault, battery, false imprisonment, infliction of emotional distress, trespass to land, or other intentional torts.

Most state statutes of limitations restrict the time period within which a plaintiff may file his or her intentional tort causes of action against a defendant. In most states, these are two-year statutes, meaning that a plaintiff has two years from the date that the intentional tort was committed within which to file his or her lawsuit against the tortfeasor. It is vital to research specific statutes of limitations for each particular tort.

State workers' compensation statutes bar tort actions against workers' employers regardless of fault.

Key Terms

attachment	informed consent	process serving
castle doctrine	intent	prosecutor
consent	judge	reasonable force
defense	mistake	replevin
defense of persons	motive	rightful repossession
defense of property	necessary force	self-defense
ejectment	necessity	service of process
execution sale	privilege	sheriff's sale
hot (fresh) pursuit	process	

Problems

In the following hypotheticals, identify the intentional torts and available defenses involved, if any, and support your answers.

1. Kimberly Bach drives a delivery truck for The Dough Boy, a local bakery. One day, while making a delivery, Kimberly saw an automobile parked along the side of the street begin to move. There was no one inside the car, and it appeared to have slipped out of gear. The car rolled with increasing speed down a hill toward a crowded sidewalk along which several businesses were having outdoor sales. None of the shoppers saw the runaway vehicle approaching. Kimberly rammed her truck into the rear right side of the car, causing it to spin sideways. This stopped it from rolling into the pedestrians. The auto owner sued Kimberly for damaging the car, and the owner of The Dough Boy also sued Kimberly for injuring the delivery truck.

2. Memphis Safeway, a student at the city college, visited the school bookstore to purchase some notebooks. Outside the bookstore were a series of locking boxes within which students placed their backpacks, briefcases, or other belongings that the bookstore forbade customers to bring into the store. Memphis placed his backpack into one of the lockers and entered the bookstore. However, he forgot to take the key from the box. Harper Ridgewell, another student, opened the box and thought the backpack was his, as he owned a pack almost identical to Memphis's. Harper had placed his own pack in one of the boxes but had also forgotten to take the key. Later, Memphis discovered the pack missing, and a bookstore cashier described Harper as the culprit. Harper had not examined the pack closely but had thrown it into his car trunk and forgotten about it. Memphis sued Harper.

3. Leroy McPhillen frequented a pub called Bottom's Up!. Late one Saturday night, an intoxicated man began shouting obscenities at a woman sitting at the table next to Leroy's. The woman ignored the man and continued to drink her beer. The man approached the lady, looking ominous. Leroy stood and asked the fellow over to the bar for a drink. The man grumbled that Leroy should mind his own business. The man reached out and grabbed the woman's wrist, and Leroy neatly twisted the man's other arm behind his back while restraining him with a neck hold. The man protested vehemently, but Leroy did not let go. Leroy placed the man firmly into a chair and told him not to move or else Leroy would have to punch him. The woman told Leroy that the man was her husband and asked him to leave them both alone. Leroy left the bar. The man sued Leroy.

4. Peter Delaney works as an assistant manager at a local clothing store. One evening, while emptying trash outside the back of the store, Peter saw someone toying with a lock on the back door of another store. He could not see who the person was. Peter telephoned the police from inside his store and returned to the alley. He yelled out to the mysterious person not to move, because he was armed, and the police were coming. In fact, Peter did not possess any weapons, but bluffed to scare the culprit. The suspicious character turned out to be a new employee at the neighboring store who was trying to determine which key opened the rear door lock. Peter did not know this individual. The person sued Peter.

5. Maybelle Startler was purchasing some merchandise on layaway at a local department store. She had made her final payment and had requested that the items be delivered to her house. After a few days, she telephoned the store manager to complain that the goods had not been delivered. The manager explained that she would first have to pay the entire purchase price before delivery would be possible. She protested that she had, in fact, paid in full. She went to the store and showed the layaway clerk her payment receipts. The clerk refused to produce the merchandise. Maybeele walked behind the counter, went up the stairs to the layaway storage area, and retrieved her items. The clerk notified store security, who took Maybelle into custody and locked her in an empty storeroom next to the restrooms. The room was unlit and not heated. The police arrived after an hour to question Maybelle, and after a few minutes she was released. Maybelle sued the store and the store counterclaimed against Maybelle.

Review Questions

1. What are defenses? How are they applied against intentional torts? In what type of situation would a defense most likely be raised?

2. Explain self-defense. Against which intentional torts might this defense be used? What is reasonable force? How is it defined? How is it similar to necessary force?

3. Discuss defense of persons or property. How is it similar to self-defense? Different? How is defense of persons different from defense of property? Similar? How is reasonable force defined for this defense?

4. What is rightful repossession? What type of property is involved? Against which intentional torts might this defense be applied? How is reasonable force defined? What is the role of wrongful dispossession or denial of possession? Must the property owner's efforts to repossess be taken within a certain time frame? What is this called?

5. Describe consent. Is the defense widely applicable to the intentional torts? What is informed consent? Implied consent?

6. Explain mistake. What is the role of the good-faith conviction? Why must the information believed be inaccurate? How broad is the defense?

7. Does privilege include all defenses to intentional torts? Why? Against which intentional torts would the defense be utilized? What are its characteristics? What is the role of motive? Of socially acceptable goals? Of less injurious alternatives?

8. What are the elements of necessity? How is it used as an intentional tort defense? What is the significance of external forces? Why must the action be reasonably necessary?

9. Discuss the various types of public official immunity for legal process enforcement. What intentional torts might apply to these cases? How does the defense operate in each such instance?

10. What is warrantless arrest? Citizen's arrest? How are these protected from intentional tort liability?

11. What are statutes of limitations? What is the time period most commonly used for tort causes of action? How can statutes of limitations be used as a defense to intentional torts?

12. What kinds of activities that result in injury at work would not be covered under workers' compensation?

Projects

1. Does the common law of your state recognize all the defenses discussed in this chapter? Is any of the terminology different? Are any defenses defined under statutes?

2. Read the case of *Jordan v. Town of Pratt* in Appendix C. What immunity defense was raided? Was it successful? Explain.

Internet Resources

This chapter focuses on defenses to intentional torts. To learn more about defenses to intentional torts, the following sites can be accessed:

General Information

http://www.uscourts.gov
http://vls.law.vill.edu/compass/
http://www.atra.org
http://www.law.indiana.edu/v-lib
http://www.dri.org

For additional resources, visit our Web site at
www.paralegal.delmar.cengage.com

CHAPTER 8

STRICT, OR ABSOLUTE, LIABILITY

CHAPTER OUTLINE

§ 8.1   Introduction
§ 8.2   An Overview of Strict Liability
§ 8.3   Abnormally Dangerous Activities
§ 8.4   Mass Torts
§ 8.5   Animal Owners' Liability
§ 8.6   Scope of Liability: Proximate Cause

―――――――――――〈◆〉―――――――――――

If there were no bad people
there would be no good lawyers.
CHARLES DICKENS

§ 8.1 Introduction

Intentional torts and negligence account for the bulk of torts. However, there remain several important torts to study. The remainder primarily consists of strict, or absolute, liability. Products liability is one form of strict liability. The terms *strict liability* and *absolute liability* are interchangeable. Strict liability differs from intentional torts and negligence in that fault is unnecessary to establish liability. From the defendant's standpoint, absolute liability can be serious trouble.

This chapter discusses the following:

◆ Absolute liability for abnormally dangerous activities

◆ Wild animal owner absolute liability

◆ Distinctions between wild and domestic animals

◆ Toxic tort strict liability

◆ Proximate cause in strict liability cases.

§ 8.2 An Overview of Strict Liability

Under intentional torts and negligence, tortfeasors are held accountable for their wrongful actions. Fault is an essential part of the reasoning. What was the defendant's misconduct that hurt the plaintiff? Was it intentional, willful, and wanton, or was it negligent action? Placing the blame is second nature in negligence or intentional torts analysis.

absolute (strict) liability The legal responsibility for damage or injury, even if you are not at fault or negligent.

Fault Is Irrelevant

Absolute (strict) liability holds the tortfeasor responsible for his or her behavior regardless of fault. In other words, the tortfeasor could have used every possible degree of care to protect against injuring the victim, but this would not prevent liability. Fault is irrelevant to absolute liability. The tortfeasor would be strictly liable just because he or she did something specific that hurt the plaintiff.

Limitations to Absolute Liability

One's sense of fair play may rebel against strict liability. One might think that it is unfair to hold a defendant accountable even if he or she did not intentionally or negligently misbehave. This fault concept extends throughout every area of law. This is why absolute liability is restricted to certain types of activities, such as abnormally dangerous tasks and defectively manufactured products, where the risk involved substantially outweighs the benefit.

Public Policy Objectives Behind Strict Liability

Under strict liability, society (through its courts and legislatures) has decided that the person engaged in certain ventures should bear the risk of liability to individuals innocently injured as a consequence of the dangerous or defective item or action. It is society's decision that persons owning wild animals, using fire or explosives, or manufacturing defective products are in the best economic position to pay for plaintiffs' injuries arising from these activities.

Insurance Analogy

Absolute liability resembles insurance. Defendants are insuring, or guaranteeing, the safety of plaintiffs who come into contact with what tort law calls **abnormally dangerous (ultrahazardous) instrumentalities**. These activities or objects are dangerous by their very nature. Even if all precautions are taken, an injury might still occur.

abnormally dangerous (ultrahazardous) instrumentalities†
Activities or objects that are, by their very nature, extremely hazardous to persons or property. These are relevant to strict (absolute) liability cases.

Historical Development

Ancient English common law held the owners of animals, slaves, or objects absolutely liable for causing the death of another person. For instance, suppose a boat broke its mooring and floated downstream, colliding with and drowning a swimmer. In medieval England, the boat would be considered a *deodand*, because it killed someone. The term originated from the Latin *Deo dandum*, which translates as "a thing to be given to God." The ecclesiastical courts insisted that the offending, sinful property be seized and placed into God's service. Deodands had to be forfeited to the church or the crown, or sometimes to the injured party's surviving family, to be used in pious pursuits. It was seen as a charitable redemption: the owner would pay for his or her sinful chattel by giving it up. It did not matter that the chattel killed accidentally. This was probably one of the earliest forms of strict liability.

§ 8.3 Abnormally Dangerous Activities

Abnormally dangerous activities are inherently perilous because of the actions and the devices involved. Common examples include the use of explosives, flammable substances, noxious gases, poisons, hazardous wastes (the so-called **toxic tort actions**), or (in some jurisdictions) electricity, natural gas, and water supplied through unprotected utility lines. Many early twentieth-century cases refer to *ultrahazardous activities*. This is the term used by the original *Restatement of Torts* § 520 (the oft-called *First Restatement*). Although some courts split hairs distinguishing ultrahazardous from abnormally dangerous, the expressions are essentially interchangeable.

toxic tort actions†
Actions involving toxic chemicals, pollution, hazardous waste disposal and transportation, and other environmentally sensitive issues. This litigation applies many tort theories, including trespass to land, negligence, absolute liability for ultrahazardous substances, products liability, and nuisance.

Restatement (Second) Rule

Restatement (Second) of Torts § 520 declares that persons engaged in abnormally dangerous activities shall be strictly liable for injuries caused by their actions. The *Restatement* lists several criteria for absolute liability:

1. The abnormally dangerous activity created a high risk of substantial injury to an individual or his or her property.
2. This risk could not be removed through the use of reasonable care.
3. The activity is not commonly undertaken (the common usage principle).
4. The activity was inappropriately undertaken in the place in which the victim was harmed.
5. The hazards that the activity creates outweigh the benefits that the activity brings to the community.

High Risk of Substantial Injury

To be abnormally dangerous, the defendant's activity must create a great threat of seriously injuring the plaintiff or the plaintiff's property. For instance, consider a highway construction company that uses dynamite to excavate rock and earth. Dynamite is dangerous stuff. It presents an enormous risk of injuring others nearby if it is not used properly. The threat of harm is significant, as people could be killed or their property destroyed if the dynamite is not used correctly.

Reasonable Care

If the tortfeasor could have eliminated the risk of harm through the use of reasonable care, then the activity is not abnormally dangerous, and absolute liability does not apply. For example, a utility company could exercise reasonable care and protect citizens from the great threat posed by electricity or natural gas simply by using insulated wires or double-sealed underground pipelines. Reasonable care could easily eliminate the risks of electrocution or explosion. If the utility company actually used these (or other) reasonable precautions, but a victim nonetheless was injured, then the activity (supplying electricity or natural gas) would not be ultrahazardous.

Note the hidden implication in this element, though. Failure to use reasonable care to safeguard others from the risks involved in the activity could make it abnormally dangerous. For instance, suppose a utility company ran electricity through uninsulated wires. Many courts have held that this would make the activity ultrahazardous, so the utility company would be strictly liable for injuries. However, not all courts interpret the *Second Restatement*'s reasonable care standard in this way.

Common Usage Principle

common use principle† Doctrine in strict liability cases that defines abnormally dangerous activities and substances as those not commonly undertaken or used in everyday life.

Abnormally dangerous activities and substances are those not commonly undertaken or used in everyday life. This is sometimes called the **common use principle**. For instance, consider explosives, toxic chemicals, or poisonous gases. How often does the average person use them? Does anyone in the reader's neighborhood? What about the manufacturing plant across town? In oter words, it could be said that the vast majority of the public does not use such substances. These, then, would be examples of abnormally dangerous substances, because they are not commonly used.

What about flammable substances? Many courts have included these as ultrahazardous items. But virtually everyone uses gasoline every day. Would gasoline not fall within common usage? Whether gasoline is abnormally dangerous depends upon how it is being used. Suppose SludgeCo Oil Company operates a gasoline refinery, with several massive fuel tanks storing hundreds of thousands of gallons. Few people in a community have such facilities in their backyards. Gasoline may be commonly used, but not in the way this storage facility uses it. The gas one keeps in his or her garage for the lawn mower would not be ultrahazardous; however, the huge storage tanks would be abnormally dangerous.

Inappropriate Use in Certain Place

To be ultrahazardous, the activity or substance must have been inappropriately performed or used in the place in which the victim was harmed. For example, suppose a chemical manufacturer opened a plant adjacent to a housing subdivision that uses well water. Suppose that the plant dumped toxic chemicals into holding ponds on its premises. Harmful chemicals could seep into the ground and contaminate the water supplies of nearby residents. Perhaps several of these homeowners became ill as a consequence. The activity (using toxic chemical retention ponds) is abnormally dangerous because it created a serious risk of substantial harm, was not of common usage, and was inappropriately undertaken at the location in which the plaintiffs were harmed (adjacent to residences).

Hazards Outweigh Benefits: Balancing Test

Courts often apply a balancing test to decide if an activity is abnormally dangerous. Such an analysis compares the dangers created by the activity with the benefits that the community derives from the activity. This is similar to the benefits analysis used in many nuisance cases.

For example, suppose a local builder is building a new road to improve access between hospitals and an isolated rural town. The construction crew uses dynamite to clear the area for the road. A nearby homeowner suffers structural damage to her house as a result of the blasting and sues the builder under strict liability theory. Courts following the *Second Restatement* would balance the benefits derived against the risks involved. The road would improve the community's access to hospital facilities. The dangers created by dynamite use, which in this case involved structural damage, are probably outweighed by these benefits.

Many courts have applied the *Second Restatement*'s approach throughout this century. Several jurisdictions, however, have rejected the rule, either in whole or in part. Still, the *Second Restatement* provides a comprehensive, general formula for analyzing abnormally dangerous activities and absolute liability.

The Case of the Ultrahazardous Activity

Land owners are becoming increasingly concerned with the safety of their groundwater. In this case, the plaintiffs claimed that the use of certain industrial solvents, which were used as degreasers in preparation for painting, was an ultrahazardous activity, and that defendants should be strictly liable.

CEREGHINO v. BOEING CO.

United States District Court for the District of Oregon
826 F.Supp. 1243 (D. Or. 1993)
May 10, 1993
Jelderks, United States Magistrate Judge

Plaintiffs Joseph A. Cereghino, on his own behalf and as personal representative of the estate of Angelo Cereghino, and Mario Cereghino (collectively Cereghinos) bring this action, based on the release of certain chemicals, against the Boeing Company (Boeing), International Controls Corporation (ICC), Datron Systems, Inc. (Datron), and Elecspec Corporation (Elecspec). ...

The Cereghinos own farmland in Multnomah County, Oregon, located on the north side of Northeast Sandy Boulevard near the intersection of Northeast 185th Avenue and Sandy Boulevard. Industrial activities giving rise to this action began in 1964 on the south side of Sandy Boulevard, opposite the Cereghinos' land. At that time, Electronic Specialty Company (ESC), which is not a party to this action, began to operate a manufacturing facility on the site.

* * *

In early 1986, Boeing discovered that groundwater on the industrial site contained hazardous industrial solvents. It reported this finding to the United States Environmental

Protection Agency, and to the Oregon Department of Environmental Quality. In July 1986, Boeing entered into a Consent Order and Compliance Agreement with those agencies. ...

In August 1986, the Cereghinos were notified that the groundwater in their land was contaminated with trichloroethylene (TCE). They subsequently learned that TCE and trichloroethane (TCA) had migrated into their groundwater from neighboring property. TCE and TCA are industrial solvents used as degreasers and in preparation for painting. These compounds are listed as hazardous wastes under the Federal Resource, Conservation and Recovery Act. 40 C.F.R. § 261.31. Boeing stopped using TCE in 1980. The levels of TCA detected in the groundwater on the Cereghinos' property do not exceed federal drinking water standards. TCE levels do exceed those standards.

Plaintiffs filed this action in January 1992. Their amended complaint, filed in January 1993, asserts that Boeing has owned the industrial site and has operated industrial facilities on that site "from about 1963 to the present, and at all material times thereto ... ." They also allege that, from 1968 to 1985, ICC, Datron, and Elecspec operated manufacturing facilities on the land owned by Boeing, and that these defendants "used, handled, stored and disposed of hazardous substances, including but not limited to [TCE] and [TCA], in the course of the operation of the manufacturing and/or industrial facilities located on Boeing's land."

* * *

[The court's discussion of issues other than the ultrahazardous activity claim have been omitted.]

Plaintiffs' ultrahazardous activity claim asserts that defendants' "use, handling, storage and disposal of hazardous substances" constituted an ultrahazardous activity. This claim adds that defendants knew, or in the exercise of reasonable care should have known, that releases resulting from these activities would substantially harm landholders such as themselves.

Strict liability may be imposed on those who engage in "ultrahazardous" activities. An activity is considered ultrahazardous if it is "extraordinary, exceptional, or unusual, considering the locality in which it is carried on; when there is a risk of grave harm from such abnormality; and when the risk cannot be eliminated by the exercise of reasonable care ... ." No Oregon court has decided whether the use of solvents such as TCE and TCA constitutes an ultrahazardous activity.

Boeing has submitted the uncontroverted affidavit of an expert who states that TCE and TCA are commonly-used degreasing agents, and opines that "it is entirely feasible to use both TCA and TCE in ways that would prevent any contamination of soil or groundwater." Boeing has also submitted uncontroverted evidence that use of degreasing solvents is common in the area around its property, and that plaintiffs themselves use solvents in maintenance of their farming equipment.

Boeing has shown the absence of material issues of fact as to whether use of the solvents in question here constituted an ultrahazardous activity. Use of solvents cannot be classified as ultrahazardous in this case and the motion for summary judgment on this claim should be granted.

Case Questions

1. Do you agree with the United States District Court's decision?
2. What could a home purchaser do to prevent being surprised about potentially toxic chemicals being found on land years after the purchase?

Defenses

Many state legislatures have enacted statutes protecting certain abnormally dangerous activities from strict liability. These statutes usually shield public utilities distributing electricity and natural gas, private contractors performing construction (particularly highway) work for the government, and municipal zoos or parks that maintain wild animals. Under these statutes, the protected entities cannot be held absolutely liable for injuries caused by wild animals or ultrahazardous activities. Instead, plaintiffs must prove that the protected defendants were negligent or committed intentional torts, unless the defendants have purchased liability insurance to cover injuries under these circumstances.

◇◆◇

The Case of Asbestos in the Air

John Maiorana, a 40-year-old man, died of cancer. Thirteen years prior to his death, Maiorana was exposed to asbestos on the job. How can his estate show a definite connection between the cancer and the asbestos? In toxic tort actions, plaintiff's counsel has the difficult task of proving causation, when the onset of disease may occur many years after exposure to a potentially harmful substance.

IN RE JOINT EASTERN & SOUTHERN DISTRICTS ASBESTOS LITIGATION

United States District Court of Appeals, Second Circuit
52 F.3d 1124 (2d Cir. 1995)
April 6, 1995
Cabranes, Circuit Judge

This case marks the convergence of epidemiological evidence, probabilistic causation in carcinogenic torts, and the important issue of the extent to which a trial court may assess the sufficiency of scientific evidence, in light of the Supreme Court's recent holding in *Daubert v. Merrell Dow Pharmaceuticals, Inc.*, _____ U.S. _____, 113 S.Ct. 2786, 125 L.Ed.2d 469 (1993). That decision enlarged district courts' "gate-keeping" roles in appraising the admissibility of scientific evidence. The central question before us is the standard governing federal judges' evaluation of the *sufficiency*—as opposed to admissibility—of scientific evidence already admitted.

In 1983, John Maiorana ("Maiorana") died of colon cancer. His widow, plaintiff/appellant Arlene M. Maiorana ("plaintiff"), claimed that her husband's illness was caused by exposure to Cafco D., an asbestos spray manufactured by defendant-appellee United States Mineral Products Co. ("USMP"). This spray was used for insulation on two construction sites—the World Trade Center in New York City and Meadowbrook Hospital in Nassau County, New York—where Maiorana was employed as a sheet metal worker.

The scientific community is divided on whether asbestos exposure significantly increases the risk of contracting colon cancer. At trial in the United States District Court for the Southern District of New York ... , both plaintiff and USMP brought expert witnesses and numerous epidemiological studies to bear on their likely causal factors. After considering this evidence, the jury on February 10, 1993, returned a verdict in favor of the plaintiff.

In an opinion dated July 23, 1993, the district court granted USMP's motion for judgment as a matter of law, setting aside the jury verdict. We believe that the district court ... inappropriately usurped the role of the jury. ...

Cafco D is a fireproof asbestos spray formerly used for insulating construction sites. In the fall of 1969 and spring of 1970, two major construction projects where Cafco D was used were the World Trade Center ("WTC") in Manhattan and the Meadowbrook Hospital ("Meadowbrook") in Nassau County, New York.

Maiorana was employed as a sheet metal worker for a small company which performed sheet metal work on both the WTC and Meadowbrook projects. Plaintiff contends that Maiorana and the other sheet metal workers—who worked in close proximity to the asbestos sprayers—were exposed to asbestos through contact with Cafco D.

In January 1983, Maiorana was diagnosed with colon cancer. Six months later, on June 16, 1983, Maiorana died from the disease. He was 40.

Plaintiff filed her original complaint on July 28, 1987, in connection with a case brought by sixteen plaintiffs on behalf of themselves and their deceased spouses against a number of manufacturers of asbestos-containing products. These manufacturers included USMP, the producer of Cafco D. By way of several third-party complaints and impleaders, a number of third-party defendants were added to the litigation ... .

In a series of rulings in 1991, the district court awarded summary judgment in favor of defendants, including USMP, on the grounds that the epidemiological and clinical evidence of causation were insufficient to meet the preponderance standard.

On appeal, we reversed the grant of summary judgment and remanded for further proceedings, concluding that the evidence was sufficient to survive summary judgment. We found that plaintiff had presented not only epidemiological studies in support of a causal connection between asbestos exposure and colon cancer, but also clinical evidence—in the form of Maiorana's own medical records and personal history, which plaintiff's experts used to exclude other possible causal factors. We found that the statements of the plaintiff's experts, viewed in the light most favorable to plaintiff, were the "equivalent of stating that asbestos exposure more probably than not caused the colon cancer."

From January 20 to February 10, 1993, the case was tried before a jury. By the time the jury was ready to deliver its verdict, all the original direct defendants but USMP had settled. The jury found in favor of plaintiff in the amount of $4,510,000. After allocating percentages of fault among USMP and third-party defendants, the jury found USMP 50% responsible for plaintiff's damages and found three of the third-party defendants approximately equally negligent (both Tishman and Castagna were assessed to be 14% responsible; subcontractor Mario & DiBono was assessed to be 15% responsible). In addition, the jury absolved the Port Authority of any liability.

On March 10, 1993, USMP moved for judgment as a matter of law ... .

In an extensive and thoughtful opinion dated July 23, 1993, the district court granted USMP's motion for judgment as a matter of law. The district court based its decision on its findings that (1) plaintiff's epidemiological evidence was insufficient to support a causal connection between asbestos exposure and colon cancer, and (2) plaintiff had failed to present affirmative clinical evidence to overcome the paucity of statistically significant epidemiological proof.

Epidemiology is the study of disease patterns in human populations. It "attempts to define a relationship between a disease and a factor suspected of causing it." As the district court observed, epidemiological evidence is indispensable in toxic and carcinogenic tort actions where direct proof of causation is lacking.

Epidemiologists speak in the statistical language of risks and probabilities. ...

In order for plaintiff to present a jury question on the issue of causation, the district court noted that she bore the burden of demonstrating that asbestos exposure was "more likely than not" the cause of Maiorana's colon cancer.

* * *

Plaintiff's expert witnesses—Dr. Steven Markowitz and Dr. Carl Shy—testified at trial that there was a causal relationship between asbestos exposure and colon cancer. The district court, however, conducted an independent and detailed analysis of many of the epidemiological studies and concluded that there was no basis for plaintiff's experts' conclusions. ... The district court criticized the methodologies employed in these studies, however, and found that when considered in the context of all the studies, plaintiff's evidence "establishe[d] only the conclusions that the association between exposure to asbestos and developing colon cancer is, at best, weak, and that the consistency of this purported association across the studies is, at best, poor."

* * *

Given plaintiff's failure to show that any asbestos fibers were found in Maiorana's cancerous tissues, the district court found that the sum total of plaintiff's evidence did not justify the jury's finding of causation, and that "the jury's finding could only have been the result of sheer surmise and conjecture."

* * *

In the present case, the sufficiency inquiry bears on the factual issue of causation—whether the body of plaintiff's evidence was sufficient to persuade a rational jury that Maiorana's exposure to asbestos more likely than not caused his colon cancer. Causation in toxic torts normally comprises two separate inquiries: whether the epidemiological or other scientific evidence establishes a causal link between *c* (asbestos exposure) and *d* (colon cancer), and whether plaintiff is within the class of persons to which inferences from the general causation evidence should be applied.

For the reasons stated below, we hold that the district court overstepped the boundaries set forth in *Daubert*. It impermissibly crossed the line from assessing evidentiary reliability to usurping the role of the jury. Accordingly, we reverse the district court's entry of judgment as a matter of law with respect to the jury verdict in favor of plaintiff.

* * *

The issue before the district court in this case, then, was whether the epidemiological and clinical data already in evidence was sufficient to justify the jury's verdict finding causation.

* * *

In rejecting plaintiff's experts' differential diagnosis, the district court gave little weight to Maiorana's relatively young age of death. While conceding it was "uncommon for a 40-year-old man to develop colon cancer," the court emphasized the absence of asbestos fibers in Maiorana's colon cancer tissues and the typical latency period of more than 20 years for colon cancer, compared to only 13 years for Maiorana. The district court's conclusions regarding latency periods, however, ignored Markowitz's testimony on the study by Seidman which indicated an increased incidence of gastrointestinal cancer among individuals exposed to asbestos 10 years previously. That a latency period of 13 years was too short appeared to constitute an independent medical conclusion by the district court.

For the above reasons, we hold that the district court erred in ruling that plaintiff presented insufficient epidemiological and clinical evidence to support the jury's verdict finding causation. In our view, the district court impermissibly made a number of independent scientific conclusions—without granting plaintiff the requisite favorable inferences—in a manner not authorized by *Daubert*.

* * *

By way of summary:

On the issue of causation, we reverse the district court's entry of judgment as a matter of law, and we reinstate the jury verdict in favor of plaintiff. The district court erred in failing to draw all reasonable inferences in favor of plaintiff ... .

In view of the conditional order for a remittitur, we remand to the district court to provide plaintiff with the requisite opportunity to decide whether to accept the reduced verdict or submit to a new trial.

Case Questions

1. Normally, the statute of limitations for tort actions is just a few years. Is it fair to hold a defendant liable for an incident that may have occurred ten, twenty, or more years ago? Explain.

2. What are some of the potential problems a defendant would face in defending a matter based on an occurrence that transpired many years ago?

Public Policy Objectives Behind Statutory Immunity

Legislatures often justify immunity statutes on the grounds that government (and the private companies that often work under governmental contracts) must be protected from the harshness of strict liability if certain essential activities are to be performed. How, the argument goes, can governments build roads, operate zoos or parks, supply utilities, or enable private industry to satisfy energy demands, if these activities carry the burden of strict liability whenever someone inadvertently gets hurt? This reasoning is similar to the benefits balancing act that courts often apply under the *Second Restatement* approach. Because legislatures enact statutes, and the public can change the legislature (through voting) and thus change the statutes, citizens who disagree with the immunity laws can elect new legislators to modify these provisions.

Cases involving toxic substances often revolve around absolute liability theory, applying the abnormally dangerous activity analysis. Of all the causes of action usually associated with toxic torts (including trespass to land, negligence, nuisance, and strict liability), absolute liability offers the best common law avenue for plaintiffs to recover.

The Case of the Saturday Night Special

Many Americans recall the 1981 assassination attempt on President Ronald Reagan. Several bystanders were seriously injured when John Hinckley fired his fateful shots. Searching for a deeper pocket than Hinckley's, one injured person sued the manufacturer of Hinckley's gun, commonly called a "Saturday Night Special," under ultrahazardous activity and products liability theories. The D.C. Court of Appeals shot down the appellants' attempt to hold the manufacturer absolutely liable.

DELAHANTY v. HINCKLEY
District of Columbia Court of Appeals
564 A.2d 758 (D.C. 1989)
October 11, 1989
Ferren, Associate Judge

Thomas and Jean Delahanty, appellants, filed suit in the United States District Court for the District of Columbia against John Hinckley for injuries Thomas suffered when Hinckley attempted to assassinate President Ronald Reagan. The Delahantys also sued the manufacturer of the gun, R.G. Industries, Inc., its foreign parent company, Roehm, and individual officers of Roehm.

Appellants advanced three legal theories for holding the gun manufacturers liable in these circumstances: negligence, strict products liability ... , and a "social utility" claim apparently based on strict liability for abnormally dangerous activities under *Restatement (Second) of Torts* §§ 519, 520 (1977) ... .

The District Court dismissed appellants' complaint against the gun manufacturers and their officers for failure to state a claim upon which relief could be granted. On appeal, the United States Court of Appeals for the District of Columbia Circuit *sua sponte* asked this court ... to decide whether, in the District of Columbia, "manufacturers and distributors of Saturday Night Specials may be strictly liable for injuries arising from these guns' criminal use." On consideration of this question, we conclude that traditional tort theories—negligence and strict liability under the *Restatement (Second) of Torts*—provide no basis for holding the gun manufacturer liable. ...

We reject each of the theories appellants have advanced in the federal courts and in this court. ...

Appellants also present what they call a "social utility claim," arguing that the manufacturer should be held strictly liable because the type of gun in this case is "inherently and abnormally dangerous with no social value." Appellants appear to base this claim ... on liability for abnormally dangerous activities, *Restatement (Second) of Torts* §§ 519, 520, a doctrine not yet explicitly adopted in the District of Columbia ... .

Like other courts that have considered the issue ... we reject application of the "abnormally dangerous activity" doctrine to gun manufacture and sale.

Appellants argue that the marketing of the guns is the abnormally dangerous activity for which the manufacturers should be held liable. We cannot agree. The cause of action under *Restatement* § 519 applies only to activities that are dangerous in themselves and to injuries that result directly from the dangerous activity. "The marketing of a handgun is not dangerous in and of itself, and when injury occurs, it is not the direct result of the sale itself, but rather the result of actions taken by a third party." Furthermore, handgun marketing cannot be classified as abnormally dangerous by applying the factors of *Restatement* § 520 ... . For example, any high degree of risk of harm, or any likelihood that such harm will be great, would result from the use, not the marketing as such, of handguns. ...

In sum, given appellants' proffered theories, we perceive no basis under the facts alleged for holding the gun manufacturers and their officers liable under the law of the District of Columbia for Hinckley's criminal use of the gun.

Case Questions

1. Apart from negligence or strict liability, is there another avenue by which manufacturers and sellers of "Saturday Night Specials" could be held absolutely liable for resulting injuries when the weapons are used in crimes? What governmental agency would have to be involved in this process?

2. What does *sua sponte* mean, as used in the court's opinion?

§ 8.4 Mass Torts

mass tort[†] When large groups of people are injured as a result of a single tortious act. A mass tort typically involves thousands of claimants, years of litigation, and millions of dollars in attorneys' fees and costs. Generally, a smaller number of defendants are involved.

class action
A lawsuit brought for yourself and other persons in the same situation. To bring a *class action* you must convince the court that there are too many persons in the class (group) to make them all individually a part of a lawsuit and that your interests are the same as theirs, so that you can adequately represent their needs.

A **mass tort** occurs when a large group of people are injured as a result of a single tortious act. As the world becomes more densely populated, the chances for mass injury to people resulting from a single incident, product, or exposure greatly increases.

The tragic events of September 11, 2001, when planes crashed into the World Trade towers in New York, are examples of a mass tort. Over a hundred thousand people in New York were affected by this attack through loss of life, injury, property, or lost jobs. Countless others have been displaced from their apartments and offices.

Recent cases brought against the tobacco companies, manufacturers of silicone breast implants, and security companies are just a few other examples of large numbers of people injured as a result of the same incident, accident, product, exposure, or misrepresentation. Very few law firms could handle the enormous time and money constraints posed by mass tort claims. Accordingly, some firms have joined together to act in representing those injured by mass torts.

A mass tort is distinguishable from a **class action**. A class action encompasses a smaller group of plaintiffs that are harmed. In a class action a lawsuit is brought by an individual for him or herself and other persons in the same situation. To bring a class action you must convince the court that there are too many persons in the class (group) to make them all individually a part of the lawsuit and that your interests are the same as theirs so that you can adequately represent their needs. See Figure 8-1 on page 274, a legal notice seeking claimants to join a class action.

─ HYPOTHETICAL ─

Suppose local businesses operated a Fourth of July fireworks celebration, which involved shooting the fireworks into the air high above town. Suppose excessive explosives were used in the fireworks. When they were detonated, flaming debris fell onto nearby houses, causing many fires. Could the homeowners succeed in a strict liability lawsuit against the companies responsible for the fireworks display?

Were the fireworks abnormally dangerous activities? Apply the *Second Restatement*'s criteria for absolute liability. Fireworks exploding in mid-air create a tremendous risk that flaming debris could fall onto buildings' roofs, setting fires. The threat and the harm are substantial. Could reasonable care have avoided the risk? Fireworks that explode in the air are going to fall somewhere, perhaps in flaming pieces. No degree of reasonable care could prevent the danger of resulting fires. Aerial fireworks of the types described in this example are not commonly used by the public. The fireworks were inappropriately used in the area in which the fires occurred, because the power used was

TO THOSE WHO PLAYED OR ATTEMPTED TO PLAY A MCDONALD'S GAME

NOTICE OF PROPOSED SETTLEMENT, CLASS CERTIFICATION, AND HEARING TO THE FOLLOWING CLASS: All persons who, from January 1, 1979, through December 31, 2001, participated in, or obtained or attempted to obtain an official game piece, stamp or card in any game of chance, or chance and skill, whereby prizes were to be distributed among participants through the use of game pieces, stamps, cards, random drawings or random selection sponsored by McDonald's or any McDonald's restaurants in the U.S., Canada, Puerto Rico, Guam, U.S. Virgin Islands, Aruba, Jamaica, Bahamas, Curacao, Saipan, St. Maarten, Suriname, and Trinidad ("Giveaway Territory") other than those who were employed by or agents of Simon Marketing of McDonald's.

Plaintiffs in a case pending in the Circuit Court of Cook County, Illinois, individually and on behalf of the Class, have sued Simon Marketing, Inc. and McDonald's Corporation ("Defendants") relating to the embezzlement of winning prizes from McDonald's games. The suit alleges unjust enrichment and violations of consumer fraud laws of all fifty states. McDonald's has agreed to a settlement. In doing so, McDonald's continues to vigorously deny that it violated any law. Your rights may be affected by the settlement. The Honorable Stephen A. Schiller ("Court") has preliminarily approved the settlement and scheduled a Final Fairness Hearing ("Hearing"). The Court has appointed plaintiffs in <u>Boland et al. v. Simon Marketing, Inc. and McDonald's</u>, case no. 01CH13803 as Class representatives and Ben Barnow, Aron D. Robinson, and Steve G. Schulman as Plaintiffs' Lead Counsel ("Class Counsel"). Plaintiffs and Class Counsel believe the settlement confers substantial benefits upon the Class and that it is fair, adequate, reasonable and in the best interest of the Class.

THE RELEASE TO BE GIVEN TO DEFENDANTS IN THE SETTLEMENT IS BROAD AND WILL RELEASE OTHER CLAIMS <u>UNDER FEDERAL AND STATE LAW</u> WHICH YOU MAY HAVE AGAINST DEFENDANTS. IF YOU BELIEVE YOU HAVE OTHER CLAIMS, YOU SHOULD CAREFULLY CONSIDER WHETHER YOU WISH TO REMAIN A MEMBER OF THE CLASS, OR WHETHER YOU SHOULD EXCLUDE YOURSELF FROM THE CLASS.

Under the terms of the settlement, McDonald's has agreed to: (1) run a prize giveaway in which fifteen $1 million prizes (twenty annual $50,000 payments) will be randomly awarded to persons in attendance at McDonald's restaurants in the Giveaway Territory with no purchase necessary. (2) expend not less than $2 million to publish notice of the settlement and administer the giveaway; (3) pay legal fees and expenses awarded by the Court; Class Counsel will seek no more than $3 million; and (4) permit Class Counsel to seek approval to pay incentive awards to Class representatives ($1,000) and certain named plaintiffs ($500).

If you agree with the settlement and wish to participate, you need do nothing. You have a right to exclude yourself from the Class, or object to the terms of the proposed settlement. Requests for exclusion and/or objections must be in writing and signed by you personally, or by your legal representative or counsel, in accordance with these procedures: **(A) If you choose to exclude yourself, your request for exclusion must state:** **(1)** your name and address, and **(2)** if you can, to the best of your recollection, the name(s) of the McDonald's game(s) you played and the approximate date(s) and city(ies) of your participation. Your request must be sent by mail to P.O. Box 3009, Oak Brook, IL 60522-3009 and postmarked no later than August 28, 2002; and **(B) If you choose to object, you must (1)** submit documentary proof or affidavit that you are a member of the Class; **(2)** state the basis for your objection(s); **(3)** if you choose to appear at the Hearing, file a written notice of your intention to appear with the Clerk of the Court, Circuit Court of Cook County, 8th Floor, Richard J. Daley Center, Chicago, Illinois 60602 by August 28, 2002; and **(4)** serve copies of the foregoing papers, by the same date to the following: Ben Barnow, Esq., Barnow and Associates, P.C., One N. LaSalle Street, Suite 4600, Chicago, IL 60602 and David J. Doyle, Esq., Winston & Strawn, 35 W. Wacker Drive, Chicago, IL 60601.

If you timely exclude yourself from the Class, you will not be bound by the settlement, nor will you be eligible to win any of the $1 million prizes in the giveaway. **If you remain a member of the Class and there is final approval of the Class settlement, you will be bound by its terms and you will have fully and finally released McDonald's Corporation, all McDonald's franchisees, Simon Marketing, Inc., Simon Worldwide, Inc.**, and each of their officers, employees, agents, related entitities and vendors from all claims based upon, related to or arising out of, during the period of 1/1/1979 to 12/31/01: (1) the theft, conversion, misappropriation, seeding, dissemination, redemption or non-redemption of a winning prize or winning game piece in any McDonald's game; (2) any advertisement, publication, representation, statement, assertion or omission directly pertaining to any McDonald's game; (3) the administration, execution or operation of any McDonald's game; and (4) the $10 million Instant Giveaway by McDonald's over Labor Day weekend of 2001. All persons who do not validly exclude themselves from this Class will be precluded from instituting or continuing to pursue other lawsuits against Defendants if this settlement is approved. For a copy of the notice containing more information regarding claims to be released, log on to www.gamessettlement.com or send a request with your address to P.O. Box 3009, Oak Brook, IL 60522-3009.

The Hearing has been scheduled for September 17, 2002 at 2:00 p.m., in the Circuit Court of Cook County, Richard J. Daley Center, Chicago, Illinois, Room 2402, before the Court to determine whether the proposed settlement should be finally approved as fair, reasonable, and adequate; to hear and rule upon objections, if any; and to determine whether and in what amount legal fees and expenses should be awarded. The terms of the settlement are set forth in detail in the parties' Settlement Agreement, which is available at www.gamessettlement.com or at the office of the Clerk of the Court, Circuit Court of Cook County, 8th Floor, Richard J. Daley Center, Chicago, Illinois 60602. **By order of the Honorable Stephen A. Schiller, Judge of the Circuit Court of Cook County, Illinois, County Department, Chancery Division.**

FIGURE 8-1 Class action notice

excessive and the fireworks detonated above the houses, subjecting them to the severe fire risk. The threat of harm outweighs the benefits to the community, as fireworks displays are conducted only once or twice per year and the benefits are purely aesthetic and momentary. The fireworks promoters will be strictly liable to the homeowners. (This conclusion assumes, of course, that there are no state statutes or local ordinances granting the fireworks promoters immunity from absolute liability.) ∎

Table 8-1 summarizes absolute liability for abnormally dangerous activities. All absolute liability cases, as discussed in this chapter, must satisfy the requirements of proximate cause, discussed in § 8.6.

TABLE 8-1
Absolute liability for abnormally dangerous activities and defenses

Definitions and Examples	Restatement (2d) of Torts § 520	Defenses
Abnormally dangerous = Ultrahazardous	Activity creates high risk of substantial harm	Statutory immunities for certain types of ultrahazardous activities
These activities are, by their very nature, perilous	Risk could not be eliminated through exercise of reasonable care	Most often include governmental activities involving uses of explosives, chemicals, or energy service
Examples: use of explosives, flammable substances, noxious gases, or poisons	Activity is not commonly undertaken (common usage principle)	Immunities reflect public policy objectives to balance necessary public services against individual right to compensation for injury
Some courts include unprotected use of utilities (electricity, natural gas, water)	Activity is inappropriate in place where injury happened	
	Hazards created outweigh community benefits from activity	

§ 8.5 Animal Owners' Liability

Modern absolute liability first arose in the common law involving private ownership of wild animals and the use of fire or explosives. This section discusses owners' liability for injuries inflicted by their wild animals.

Wild Animals Defined

ferae naturae (Latin) "Of wild nature." Naturally wild animals.

domitae naturae[†] (Latin) "Domesticated nature." Tame, domestic animals.

The ancient common law cases use the Latin term *ferae naturae*, meaning "wild nature," to refer to wild animals. These are animals that have naturally wild dispositions, as opposed to tame animals, which are called *domitae naturae*, meaning "domesticated nature." Examples of *ferae naturae* include deer, bison, elk, bear, snakes, bees, stream or ocean fish, coyotes, foxes, wild birds, lions, tigers, gophers, raccoons, opossums, or prairie dogs.

Ownership of Wildlife

dominion Legal ownership plus full actual control over something.

control[†] The power or authority to direct or oversee.

Under ancient English common law, the king owned all wildlife in the realm. This is why poachers were often hanged or beheaded for taking the crown's property during medieval times. As English law evolved, an average person could claim ownership of a wild animal—the trick was to catch the beast. Once someone had control over a wild animal, it was considered to be his or her property until it escaped to its natural, free state. The common law cases call this ownership the exercise of **dominion** and **control** over the wild animal. American common law holds that the state (or the federal government), under its police power, owns wildlife in trust for the benefit of all citizens. This is why one must obtain state or federal hunting or fishing licenses to take wildlife.

For example, suppose Kathleen has an apiary—in other words, she is a beekeeper. The bees are wildlife, *ferae naturae*. However, if Kathleen catches and places them in her apiary hives, they may stay and produce honey for her. Now Kathleen owns the bees. As long as she exercises dominion and control over the insects, they are hers. But once the bees fly away, they are *ferae naturae* again, and Kathleen does not own them (that is, unless she catches them again).

Importance of Wildlife Ownership

Wildlife ownership is important for purposes of absolute liability. If a wild animal injures someone, the victim cannot sue the beast (or, at the very least, cannot easily collect judgment). Instead, the plaintiff looks to the animal's owner for compensation. Owners are strictly liable for the injuries their wildlife inflicts. It does not matter that the owner exercised every precaution to safeguard others from being hurt by the wild animals. If the beast attacks and hurts someone, the owner must compensate the victim for the injuries. Because the common law presumes that wild animals are dangerous by nature, strict liability applies to any injuries they cause.

Suppose Ken's pet bear mauls a visitor to Ken's home. The victim will sue Ken under strict liability. One might argue that premises liability, using negligence theory, should apply instead, because Ken owns the land and the chattels that harmed the plaintiff, but this argument would lose. Because bears are wildlife, Ken is absolutely liable for his pet's mischief.

Comparison with Domesticated Animals

Domitae naturae are animals that the law presumes to be harmless. Examples of domestic animals include dogs, cats, pet birds, or livestock such as pigs, horses, cows, or sheep. When domesticated animals hurt someone, the common law states that the owner is liable if he or she was negligent in handling the animals. Liability would also arise if an owner intentionally used domestic animals to hurt someone. For example, suppose an attack dog's owner ordered the animal to attack a victim. This is a form of battery, as the animal would be considered an extension of the tortfeasor's body.

Practical Application

Check to find out if your local jurisdiction has an applicable leash law. Many municipalities have local laws requiring pet owners to keep their pets fenced in or on a leash. Should a victim be injured by a stray dog, you should inquire about local leash laws.

Vicious Propensity Rule

vicious propensity rule[†] Doctrine in absolute liability cases involving domestic animals. Normally owners are not strictly liable for injuries caused by their domestic animals. However, if the animals display vicious propensities and hurt someone or their property, then the owner is absolutely liable. Vicious propensities are proven by past episodes of the animal's nasty behavior.

Owners may be held absolutely liable for injuries caused by their domestic animals if the animals exhibit vicious tendencies. When a dog growls or snarls, when a bull paws the ground and snorts, or when a cat arches its back and hisses, these are all demonstrations of vicious propensities. When a domestic animal routinely displays these characteristics to the point that it gets a reputation for viciousness, it is said to have *vicious propensities*. An owner of such an animal will be held strictly liable for any injuries the beast inflicts, under the so-called **vicious propensity rule**. All states except Indiana have adopted this common law principle. Indiana has a hybrid vicious propensity rule, peculiar to its common law heritage, under which an owner's negligence in handling the animal must be proven, whether or not the animal displays a vicious propensity.

Defenses in Animal Absolute Liability Cases

Normally, negligence or intentional tort defenses are ineffective against strict liability. However, certain exceptions have arisen in the common law for particular types of absolute liability, such as cases involving animals. The following defenses can protect an animal owner from strict liability:

1. Assumption of risk
2. Contributory and comparative negligence
3. Consent
4. Self-defense and defense of others
5. Provocation.

Assumption of Risk

If the individual injured by a wild (or vicious-propensity domestic) animal voluntarily assumed a known risk, with full appreciation of the dangers involved, then the owner is not strictly liable for the inflicted injuries. Courts justify this defense on equitable grounds. It would be unfair to hold owners absolutely liable for harm their animals caused if the victims chose to subject themselves to the danger. This may colloquially be phrased as the "you got what you asked for" theory.

Contributory and Comparative Negligence

Courts often rule that the plaintiff's contributory or comparative negligence in an animal attack will prevent the owner's absolute liability. Some courts state that a plaintiff's contributory negligence bars strict liability altogether. This means that the plaintiff would have to prove that the defendant (owner) was negligent in keeping the animal that attacked and hurt the plaintiff. Other courts simply ignore absolute liability theory and reshape the case in a negligence mold, in which the plaintiff's and defendant's respective degrees of negligence are compared.

Consent

An injured plaintiff might have consented to exposure to a dangerous animal. Consent is usually based upon a person's employment responsibilities while working around animals. For example, suppose Gordon works for a police-dog training facility, where he serves as an attack victim. He knows from observation and experience that the dogs are dangerous. Even if Gordon was not wearing his protective padding, and he was bitten by one of the dogs, he has implicitly consented to this danger as part of his job. Basically, this is assumption of risk couched in consent terms. The same reasoning would apply for keepers, trainers, or feeders of wild animals for zoos or circuses.

Self-Defense and Defense of Others

When a wild or vicious domestic animal attacks a victim, but the owner used the animal as a means of self-defense or defense of other persons, then the owner would not be strictly liable for the inflicted injuries. For instance, suppose someone attacks Arthur while he is out walking his dog, which has a vicious reputation around the neighborhood. To repel the danger, Arthur commands his dog to attack. His assailant is knocked to the ground, chewed up a bit, and scared away. Arthur would not be absolutely liable for the injuries caused by his dog. The same scenario would arise if Arthur saw someone attacking a member of his family or a friend and he used the dog to protect that person. However, remember the limitations to these defenses; one may not become the aggressor and still use them to escape liability. Hence, if Arthur's dog had chased the fleeing attacker down the street, Arthur could not use these defenses to avoid liability.

Dog-Bite Statutes

Most jurisdictions have statutes that have changed the common law owner liability (and the available defenses) in dog-bite cases. These statutes can substantially affect a dog owner's liability and defenses.

Dog-bite hypotheticals present interesting applications of absolute liability. In the following example, consider the vicious propensity rule and its effects on the canine owner's liability.

See the case of *Knoller v. City and County of San Francisco* in Chapter 12, where the court addresses the issue of what to do with a dog that has been found to be "vicious and dangerous."

The Case of Bite-Worse-Than-Bark

Postal carriers have an endless series of anecdotes about nasty dogs. Fortunately, most such encounters end without serious harm to either person or pet. In this case, the plaintiff was faced with an extremely vicious canine breed, as the expert testimony established. But a dog is a dog, and dogs are presumed harmless, according to the traditional common law.

POWERS v. PALACIOS
Court of Appeals of Texas
794 S.W.2d 493 (Tex. Ct. App. 1990),
rev'd on other grounds,
813 S.W.2d 489 (Tex. 1991)
June 29, 1990
Seerden, Justice

Brenda Powers sued Paul Palacios, seeking damages for injuries, including loss of a finger, sustained when a pit bull dog kept at his residence attacked her while she was delivering mail. Following a jury trial, the trial court rendered a take-nothing judgment. ...

Appellant's point of error number four complains of the refusal of the trial court to submit her proposed Question 4 to the jury.

Appellant presented expert testimony that these dogs have a savage and vicious nature and are dangerous to humans.

Appellant's requested Special Issue 4 would have inquired of the jury:

Did Defendant Paul Palacios allow, either by express consent or implied consent, Jessie Palacios (the dog's owner) to have on Paul Palacios's premises a vicious animal on Feb. 23, 1987, the day of the attack?

Appellant correctly cites *Marshall v. Ranne,* [citation omitted] which is the leading Texas case relating to the law of wild and vicious animals. It holds that suits for damages caused by vicious animals should be governed by the law of strict liability. It also expressly adopts as the correct rule the *Restatement (Second) of Torts* §§ 507, 509 (1938).

These sections provide a distinction between the strict liability of a possessor of a "wild animal" (§ 507) and an "abnormally dangerous domestic animal" (§ 509) by providing that the possessor of the latter must have "reason to know" that the animal has dangerous propensities abnormal to its class, while the only condition for imposing liability on the possessor of a "wild animal" is that the damage result from a dangerous propensity characteristic of wild animals of its class.

Appellant's proposed Question 4, and her argument in support thereof, presupposes that the pit bull is a wild animal. The court refused to submit the request, but submitted Question 5, which inquired whether appellee had reason to know that the dog had dangerous propensities abnormal to its class. This question is consistent with the *Marshall* rule on abnormally dangerous domestic animals. The jury answered Question 5 "No."

We have been cited no cases differentiating between wild and domestic animals. *Black's Law Dictionary* contains these definitions:

> Domestic animals. Such as are habituated to live in or about the habitations of men, or such as contribute to the support of a family.
> Wild animals. Animals of an untamable disposition; animals in a state of nature.

We hold that the trial court was correct in refusing to submit to the jury the question based on appellant's theory that the dog in question was a wild animal. ...

The judgment of the trial court is affirmed.

Case Questions

1. The plaintiff's expert testimony established that the defendant's pit bull had "a savage and vicious nature" that is "dangerous to humans." Would this not satisfy the *Black's Law Dictionary* definition of *wild animal* as one with "an untamable disposition"? Explain.

2. Why do you think the jury did not apply the strict liability rule applicable in vicious propensity cases? How could the defendant not have reason to know of the pit bull's viciousness, given the plaintiff's expert testimony about their inherent malevolence?

— HYPOTHETICAL

Toby Jones owns a towing service. He uses Doberman pinscher dogs to guard the parking lot in which he keeps towed vehicles. The area is surrounded by large, barbed-wire fences with "no trespassing" signs attached every few feet. The guard dogs would bark, snarl, bite, and lunge at anyone who came near the fencing. Early one morning, Chet Paisley stopped by to claim an automobile that had been towed for illegal parking. After paying the storage fees, Chet walked back to the holding area. Toby had forgotten to chain the dogs from the night before, and they were running loose in the parking lot. When they saw Chet, they attacked and severely injured him.

The common law presumes that dogs are harmless, domestic creatures. However, there is considerable evidence that Toby's Dobermans displayed vicious propensities. Accordingly, the harmlessness presumption falls aside, and the dogs are viewed as potentially dangerous, like wild animals. Under absolute liability, Toby would be responsible for Chet's injuries. Toby's negligence or intent are irrelevant here. It only matters that the dogs were abnormally dangerous instrumentalities, because of their vicious propensities. Once strict liability applies, the result is easy: the animal owner must compensate the victim for his or her injuries.

Would the result have been different if Toby had posted signs stating, "WARNING! DANGEROUS ATTACK DOGS! DO NOT ENTER WITHOUT AUTHORIZED PERSONNEL TO ACCOMPANY YOU"? If Chet had seen such signs but entered regardless, he would have assumed the risk. Chet would have voluntarily assumed a known risk (the dangerous dogs) with full appreciation of the threat involved (being bitten or mauled). Chet would also have been contributorily negligent in entering the enclosed parking lot without Toby or another employee accompanying him. ∎

Table 8-2 summarizes animal owner strict liability and the available defenses.

TABLE 8-2
Animal owners' absolute liability and defenses

Wildlife (ferae naturae)	Domestic Animals (domitae naturae)	Defenses
Owner strictly liable for injuries caused by wild animals	Owner absolutely liable for injuries caused by domestic animals *only* if such animals display vicious propensities, or liability is imposed by statute or local ordinance	1. Assumption of risk 2. Contributory negligence 3. Comparative negligence 4. Consent 5. Self-defense 6. Defense of others 7. Provocation

§ 8.6 Scope of Liability: Proximate Cause

Proximate cause in absolute liability cases is defined similarly to proximate cause in negligence cases. Animals or abnormally dangerous activities must proximately cause the victim's injuries if the tortfeasor is to be held strictly liable. For absolute liability purposes, **proximate cause** has the following elements:

1. The plaintiff's injuries must have been a reasonably foreseeable consequence of the defendant's actions.

2. The victim must have been a foreseeable plaintiff (meaning that it must have been reasonably foreseeable that the plaintiff would be injured as a result of the defendant's activities).

These elements are defined the same as in negligence theory.

No Duty of Reasonable Care

Negligence is irrelevant to strict liability; therefore, the duty of reasonable care, as used in negligence, is also irrelevant.

In the hypotheticals discussed throughout this chapter, apply the proximate cause standard to each example. Did the tortfeasor's actions proximately cause the victim's injuries? A variety of answers are possible. As with negligence, proximate cause in absolute liability cases can be a puzzle.

Summary

Fault is irrelevant to strict liability. If the tortfeasor is found to be absolutely liable, his or her negligence or intent does not affect the liability. This may seem harsh and unfair, because a tortfeasor might exercise every degree of care to avoid injuring others and still be held responsible under absolute liability. Strict liability is limited to cases involving abnormally dangerous instrumentalities, such as wild animals, vicious domestic animals, ultrahazardous activities, and products liability. Through its courts and legislatures, the public has established absolute liability as an insurance measure to protect innocent victims from harm caused by particularly perilous pursuits.

Abnormally dangerous, or ultrahazardous, activities are inherently perilous. Use of explosives, flammable substances, noxious gases, poisons, hazardous wastes, and sometimes electricity, natural gas, or water utilities are examples. *Restatement (Second) of Torts* § 520 states that persons engaged in abnormally dangerous activities are strictly liable for injuries caused by these activities. The activity must create a high risk of substantial harm, which risk could not have been eliminated through the exercise of reasonable care; the activity or substance must not be commonly undertaken or used; the activity must have been inappropriately used in the place in which the injury happened; and the activity's hazards must outweigh the activity's benefits to the community. As a defense to strict liability, many legislatures have enacted statutes protecting certain activities from absolute liability. Some toxic torts have injured so many people that mass tort actions or class actions were needed for legal recourse.

The common law calls wild animals *ferae naturae* ("wild nature") and domestic animals *domitae naturae* ("domesticated nature"). At common law wild animals are presumed to be naturally dangerous, while domestic animals are assumed to be harmless and docile creatures. Wild animals may be owned by individuals who capture and restrain the beasts. This is called exercising dominion and control. Owners are absolutely liable for injuries their wild animals inflict. However, owners are strictly liable only for injuries caused by their domestic animals if these animals exhibited vicious propensities. The defenses of assumption of risk, contributory and comparative negligence, consent, and self-defense or defense of others apply to animal liability cases.

Absolute liability in animal and abnormally dangerous activity cases is limited by proximate cause. For strict liability to apply, the defendant's actions must have proximately caused the plaintiff's injuries. This means that the plaintiff's injuries must have been reasonably foreseeable as a consequence of the defendant's conduct, and it must have been foreseeable that the plaintiff could be injured as a result of the defendant's actions. This is called the foreseeable plaintiffs theory. There is no duty of reasonable care in strict liability cases, because the duty involves negligence theory, which is irrelevant to absolute liability.

Key Terms

absolute (strict) liability
abnormally dangerous
  (ultrahazardous)
  instrumentalities
class action

common use principle
control
dominion
domitae naturae
ferae naturae

mass tort
proximate cause
toxic tort actions
vicious propensity rule

Problems

In the following hypotheticals, determine if absolute liability applies and if the tortfeasor will be strictly liable to the injured party. Are any defenses relevant? If so, how would they be applied?

1. Heather Muffin works at the municipal zoo. She feeds and cleans the cages for the various species of monkey on exhibition. One day, Heather received a telephone call from "Spider" Tomey, exhibits supervisor, who instructed her to report to the exotic bird building to substitute for another employee who was ill. Heather had never worked with these birds before and was unfamiliar with their habits, although she received feeding and watering instructions from Spider. As she was cleaning one of the walk-in cages, a toucan landed on the back of her neck, scratching and biting at her ears. The scratches required stitches. There were no municipal ordinances discussing the zoo or its operation, apart from the enabling act that established the zoo and its supervision by the city's department of parks and recreation.

2. Miller Thurber owns a bulldog, which he kept chained in his backyard. The dog often barked and growled at anyone passing by the house on the sidewalk. One morning, Josie Taylor, an employee of the electric company, visited Thruber's house to read the meter, which was located in the backyard. Josie had read Thurber's meter before and knew about the dog. She peeked around the house but could not see the dog. She assumed it was inside the house, because the chain was lying on the ground. As she walked over to the meter, the dog leaped from the bushes, knocked Josie down, and chewed on her arms and hands. Josie was hospitalized as a result of these injuries.

3. Olaf Nurdoff owns a gas station. While a tanker truck was filling his underground fuel tanks, Olaf was using a welding torch inside his garage area to repair a customer's car. He inadvertently knocked over the torch, still lit, which fell into a puddle of gasoline from the tanker. The puddle ignited and burned across the ground to the tanker pipe connected to the underground tanks. Both the tanker truck and the fuel in the underground tanks then ignited and exploded. Several patrons were severely injured and their vehicles damaged.

4. The Belladonna Pharmaceutical Company manufactures medicines. It uses certain chemical solutions that turn bad and must be destroyed. These solutions are kept in steel barrels in the firm's back lot, awaiting pickup from a local waste disposal company. Bud Marvelle works for the trash company. He had never collected trash from Belladonna before, as he normally rode the residential trash routes. Bud's supervisor failed to instruct him to take a special sealed tank truck to get Belladonna's chemicals. Instead, Bud drove an open-top trash truck used to haul dry garbage. Bud tossed the barrels into the truck, and several of them ruptured and leaked. As Bud drove down the highway to the dump, chemical sludge spilled out the back of the truck onto an automobile driven by Madison Ventura. Madison stopped and touched the sludge caked across the front of his car. It made his hands burn. Frightened, Madison drove to a local hospital emergency room. His skin had absorbed much of the chemical waste, and he became severely ill and had to be hospitalized for several weeks.

Review Questions

1. How is strict, or absolute, liability different from negligence and intentional torts? What role does fault play in absolute liability? What are the limitations to strict liability? What are the public policy objectives behind absolute liability? How is strict liability like insurance?

2. What are abnormally dangerous activities? Ultrahazardous activities? How does the *Restatement (Second) of Torts* define the term? What elements are required for absolute liability to apply? What is the function of reasonable care? What is the common usage principle? What balancing test do courts apply in abnormally dangerous activity cases?

3. How does the common law define wild animals? Domestic animals? What does the common law presume about each type of animal? How can wildlife be owned? Why is this important to the question of liability? When does strict liability apply to injuries inflicted by wild animals? By domestic animals? What is the vicious propensity rule? What defenses apply to animal owner absolute liability cases?

4. How is proximate cause defined in strict liability cases? Why is it important?

5. What is a mass tort?

6. How is a class action different from a mass tort?

Projects

1. Does your state have any statutes concerning dog-bite liability? If so, what defenses are included in the statutes?

2. Does your state have any statutes that limit absolute liability for abnormally dangerous activities? Are there any state statutes pertaining to hazardous waste disposal or transportation?

3. Do your state courts follow the *Second Restatement* approach to strict liability in abnormally dangerous activities?

4. In class or study groups, create your own hypotheticals using the strict liability theories and defenses discussed in this chapter. Then change the facts to affect the outcomes of the problems.

5. Look up § 240 of New York's labor law. How does this law relate to absolute liability?

6. What is the difference between a mass tort action and a class action?

Internet Resources

This chapter focuses on Strict and Absolute Liability. To learn more about strict or absolute liability, the following sites can be accessed:

General Information

http://www.productslaw.com

http://www.rand.org/publications/RB/RB9021/RB9021.word.html

http://www.toxlaw.com

http://www.osha.gov

http://www.thefederation.org

http://www.access.gpo.gov/su_docs

For additional resources, visit our Web site at
www.paralegal.delmar.cengage.com

CHAPTER 9
PRODUCTS LIABILITY

CHAPTER OUTLINE

§ 9.1   Introduction
§ 9.2   Products Liability Theory and History
§ 9.3   Parties
§ 9.4   Elements
§ 9.5   Defenses
§ 9.6   Comparison to Contract Law Warranties
§ 9.7   Bad Faith

EQUAL JUSTICE UNDER LAW

*Law and order exist for the purpose of establishing
justice and ... when they fail in this purpose
they become dangerously structured dams
that block the flow of social progress.*
MARTIN LUTHER KING, JR.

§ 9.1 Introduction

product(s) liability
The responsibility
of manufacturers
(and sometimes sellers)
of goods to pay for
harm to purchasers
(and sometimes
other users and even
bystanders) caused by
a defective product.

Products liability is any form of liability arising out of the use of a defective product. A plaintiff has a choice of three different causes of action depending on the facts: strict tort liability, negligence, or breach of warranty. This chapter focuses on the cause of action for strict liability in tort. Generally, under products liability, the manufacturer or seller of a product is absolutely liable for any injuries caused by a defect in the product. Products liability occupies a prominent position in torts study, as it is involved in a sizeable portion of tort litigation. It is probably the most significant development in tort law since the courts accepted negligence theory as a separate tort.

This chapter includes:

- The parties in products liability cases
- The elements of products liability
- *Restatement (Second) of Torts* § 402A
- The defenses to products liability
- Comparison of products liability with contract law warranties.

§ 9.2 Products Liability Theory and History

Products liability was established as a distinct tort theory in the landmark case of *Greenman v. Yuba Power Products, Inc.*, 59 Cal. 2d 57, 377 P.2d 897, 27 Cal. Rptr. 697 (1962). In this case, the California Supreme Court completed over 100 years of legal evolution that culminated in strict products liability.

Public Policy Objectives Behind Products Liability

Products liability is society's decision, through its courts and legislatures, that businesses manufacturing and selling defective products are in the best economic position to bear the expenses incurred when a faulty product injures an innocent user. The theory may be simply put: Why should the hapless victim shoulder the burdens (medical costs, permanent injuries, etc.) produced by a defectively made product? Instead, should not the manufacturer or seller of that product be liable for the resulting harms? Does that not seem reasonable and ethical? If one has ever been hurt by a defective product, one might answer affirmatively. If one were a manufacturer or seller, however, he or she might feel differently.

Historical Development of Products Liability

In the early nineteenth century, English and American common law held that persons injured by defective products had to sue under contract law rather than tort law. These courts felt that the appropriate cause of action was breach of contract or, more precisely, breach of warranty. A **warranty** is a guarantee that a product or service meets certain quality standards. If a product fails to meet such standards, as is the case when a product is defective, then the warranty has been breached.

warranty
Any promise (or a presumed promise, called an *implied warranty*) that certain facts are true. ... In consumer law, ... any obligations imposed by law on a seller that benefit a buyer; for example, the warranty that goods are merchantable and the warranty that goods sold as fit for a particular purpose are fit for that purpose.

privity of contract†
A legal relationship that exists between parties to a contract. In some cases privity must exist in order for an individual to make a claim against another.

Under early nineteenth-century English and American common law, only persons who had made contracts with the manufacturer or seller of a defective product could recover damages for breach of warranty or breach of contract. This contractual relationship is called **privity of contract**. Privity exists when parties are directly engaged in an agreement between them. If Joseph enters into a contract with Harris, in which Joseph agrees to sell Harris a product for a certain price, then there is privity of contract between them. The landmark case that announced the privity rule was *Winterbottom v. Wright*, 10 Meeson & Welsby 109, 152 Eng. Rep. 402 (1842). In this case, the plaintiff drove a horse-drawn coach for the postmaster general. This coach was manufactured especially for the postmaster general by the defendant. The plaintiff was maimed when the vehicle's axle broke and threw him from the carriage seat. The plaintiff sued the defendant for failing to properly maintain the coach under a service contract. The court held that the plaintiff was not a party to either the service agreement or the manufacturing agreement. Thus, the plaintiff lacked privity of contract and therefore could not recover for the injuries caused by the defectively assembled coach. The only party that could sue under such circumstances would be the postmaster general, with whom the defendant contracted to make the carriage. But in this case the postmaster general was not harmed. The injured plaintiff was left without compensation.

Almost immediately, American courts began to carve out exceptions to the privity-of-contract rule. In *Thomas v. Winchester*, 6 N.Y. 397

(1852), the New York Court of Appeals ruled that a mislabeled medicine (which actually contained poison) was inherently dangerous, and accordingly the injured party did not have to have privity of contract with the manufacturer or seller to recover damages. In this case, the plaintiff's husband had purchased a bottle, labeled "dandelion extract," that in actuality contained belladonna, a deadly poison. The defendant manufacturer who mislabeled the product sold it to a druggist, who resold it to a physician, who prescribed it to the plaintiff. There was no privity of contract between the plaintiff and the defendant. Nonetheless, the court permitted the plaintiff to recover damages for injuries caused when she took the poison from the mislabeled bottle. The court reasoned that poisons are imminently dangerous by their very nature. Accordingly, remote users of a mislabeled drug could be seriously injured. Thus, privity of contract is unnecessary if the defective product (such as a mislabeled poison) is imminently dangerous. Later courts characterized this as the **imminent danger exception** to the privity-of-contract rule.

imminent danger exception[†]
A nineteenth- and early twentieth-century exception to the privity of contract requirement in defective product cases.

Throughout the nineteenth century, the New York Court of Appeals, and many courts following its lead, expanded the imminent danger rule to include spoiled food, explosives, improperly assembled scaffolding, an exploding coffee urn, and defectively made automobile wheels. Many courts found liability in contract warranty law, but this still required privity of contract. The landmark case in this century, which is often said to have sparked modern products liability law, is *MacPherson v. Buick Motor Co.*, 217 N.Y. 382, 111 N.E. 1050 (1916), reprinted in Appendix C. Writing for the majority, Justice Cardozo declared that privity of contract was obsolete. If a product, because of its defective manufacture, became unreasonably dangerous, then the manufacturer or seller would be liable for injuries caused by the defective product. Cardozo applied negligence theory to determine whether the defective product was unreasonably dangerous. The manufacturer had to be negligent in making the faulty product.

MacPherson ushered in a cascade of court opinions following and expanding its precedent. In *Escola v. Coca Cola Bottling Co.*, 24 Cal. 2d 453, 150 P.2d 436 (1944), Justice Traynor of the California Supreme Court, in his concurring opinion, opined that negligence was no longer necessary for defective product manufacturers to be liable. Instead, he proposed strict liability. It took eighteen years before the California Supreme Court adopted this view in *Greenman v. Yuba Power Products*, reprinted in Appendix C. Many other state courts quickly joined the new common law theory.

The American Law Institute followed *Greenman* with its famous *Restatement (Second) of Torts* § 402A, which virtually every American jurisdiction has adopted (in some form or another) as the definitive rule for strict products liability. The *Restatement*'s position is discussed in greater detail in § 9.4.

The Case of the Sleeping Driver

A car leaves the roadway, travels over the median, crashes over a retaining wall, and then is engulfed in fire. No other vehicles are involved in the accident. From the plaintiff's standpoint, there must be something terribly wrong with the car. From the defendant's perspective, the driver must not have been paying attention to the road. A jury must find the truth. The result of this case hinges on the elements needed to sustain a products liability cause of action.

BOUTTE
v.
NISSAN MOTOR CORP.

Court of Appeal of Louisiana, Third Circuit
663 So. 2d 154 (La. Ct. of App. 1995)
September 13, 1995
Cooks, Judge

Defendant in this products liability case appeals and seeks reversal of an adverse judgment. Plaintiff also appeals assigning as sole error that the jury's award is inadequate. For the following reasons, we amend and affirm as amended.

On July 23, 1989 John Boutte (plaintiff) was returning to his home in Grand Marais, near New Iberia, when involved in a one-car accident. Boutte was travelling on Highway 90 when his 1987 Nissan Maxima left the roadway, travelled through the median, crashed over the concrete retaining wall of a culvert in the median knocking out a large piece of the wall, and stopped approximately 210 feet from the point where it left the roadway. As the car drove over the wall, the underbody of the automobile was damaged. After Boutte escaped from the vehicle, it was engulfed by fire. Boutte's ankles were severely fractured during the accident.

The day before the accident, Boutte woke up at 5:00 A.M. and reported to work at 7:00 A.M. After working an eight-hour day, he returned home to eat, showered and dressed for a party. He drove to Lafayette to pick up his girlfriend. While at her home, Boutte consumed one straight drink of Crown Royal. Boutte and his girlfriend rode to New Iberia together for a Hawaiian luau where he consumed two more drinks of Crown Royal and coke. After the party, he dropped his girlfriend off at her home in Lafayette and began the return trip to Grand Marais. When his vehicle left the road at 2:10 A.M., Boutte had been awake for 21 hours.

Boutte filed suit against Nissan Motor Corporation (Nissan) alleging a defect in the brakes or steering of his automobile caused it to travel off the roadway. He later amended his petition alleging a defect existed in the passive restraint system of the automobile. Nissan argued there were no defects existing in Boutte's automobile. It asserted the automobile left the roadway because Boutte fell asleep while driving. Nissan further asserted Boutte's injuries were not caused by the restraint system.

* * *

Nissan argues Boutte failed to establish by competent expert testimony there was a defect in the 1987 Maxima because he did not: (1) Prove a defect existed by way of competent expert testimony; (2) prove he sustained enhanced injuries as a result of an alleged defect; and (3) prove any design alternative would have prevented or lessened his injuries. Nissan also asserts it should not have been assessed any fault for Boutte's injuries.

It is well-settled that an appellate court may not set aside a trial court's or a jury's finding of fact in the absence of "manifest error" or unless it is "clearly wrong."

* * *

Nissan acknowledges that the United States Supreme Court recently, in *Daubert v. Merrell*

Dow Pharmaceuticals, Inc., _____ U.S. _____, 113 S.Ct. 2786, 125 L.Ed.2d 469 (1993), rejected the rigid "general acceptance" test first memorialized, 72 years past, in *Frye v. United States*, 54 App.D.C. 46, 47, 293 F. 1013, 1014 (1923). The *Frye* test found life in "a short and citation-free 1923 decision concerning the admissibility of evidence derived from a systolic blood pressure deception test, a crude precursor to the polygraph machine." Ruling inadmissible expert testimony relating to blood pressure as a "truth" indicator on test results, the *Frye* court stated: "... *the thing from which the deduction is made must be sufficiently established to have gained general acceptance in the particular field in which it belongs.*"

We must presume that the trial judge performed his "gatekeeping function" in ruling admissible the expert testimony Nissan now complains should have been excluded. ...

Boutte presented the testimony of William H. Muzzy III, as an expert in mechanical engineering with expertise in injury mechanics, occupant motion and restraint systems. ... Muzzy's testimony concerned the relationship between Boutte's injuries and the restraint system. We find Muzzy's testimony had a reliable foundation; and, it was relevant.

Nissan presented the testimony of Dr. Charles Hatsell, a medical doctor who also obtained a Ph.D. in electrical engineering. ... Dr. Hatsell, however, acknowledged he never tested restraint systems.

Muzzy testified the lap belt anchor point of Nissan's restraint system did not meet the requirements of Motor Vehicle Safety Standard 209, which provides the lap belt must stay on the occupant's pelvis in all cases including crashes and rollovers. When Boutte fastened the lap belt, it was positioned over his thighs. In Muzzy's opinion Boutte's legs slid forward during the accident and became entrapped by the knee bolsters located on the lower portion of the dashboard because the lap belt was not properly positioned on his pelvis. ...

On the contrary, Nissan's expert concluded Boutte's injuries were not caused by his knees becoming entrapped in the knee bolsters. Hatsell postulated Boutte's right ankle broke because it was on the brakes when the accident occurred. ... In Dr. Hatsell's opinion Boutte would have sustained the same injuries to his ankles even if the restraint system suggested by his expert was installed. As a consequence, Nissan urges the alleged defective restraint system was not a *cause in fact* of Boutte's injury; and it should not have been assigned any fault in causing his injuries. ... We cannot say the trial judge manifestly erred in admitting Boutte's expert's testimony; and we are prevented from second-guessing the jury's findings based on this evidence.

* * *

The jury assessed Boutte with 84% fault. Boutte complains he should not have been assessed any fault. He argues his injuries would have been minor but for Nissan's defective lap belt.

* * *

It appears the jury accepted Nissan's evidence suggesting Boutte fell asleep while driving his vehicle after being awake for 21 hours, which caused him to travel off the road. On this record, we cannot say the jury manifestly erred in finding Boutte at fault for *causing the accident.* However, under our comparative fault system, Boutte's fault in *causing the accident* does not relieve Nissan of liability for the harm occasioned by the defect existing in the vehicle's restraint system.

When apportioning fault, the trier of fact shall consider the nature of the conduct of each party at fault and the extent of the causal relation between the conduct and the damages claimed. After considering the fault of the parties in causing Boutte's *harm,* we find Nissan has a greater degree of fault. ... When Boutte's vehicle left the roadway, he could not take any steps to prevent the risk of harm occasioned by the vehicle's impact with the concrete retaining wall and the ground below. Once the jury found the vehicle's restraint system was defective in design and this defect contributed to the injury Boutte sustained, Nissan's fault should have been assessed in relation to the *injury sustained* by Boutte rather than the *cause of the accident.* The record evidence convinces us that Nissan's fault was substantially greater than Boutte's in *causing injury* to his knee. Boutte's expert testified the injury he sustained would not have occurred or would have been reduced significantly if the vehicle's restraint system was not defective. The jury obviously found Boutte's expert's testimony on this issue more credible. Its factual findings, thus, compel that we reallocate fault in this case and assign Nissan 75% fault in causing Boutte's injury. Therefore, we amend the judgment to reduce Boutte's liability to 25% and increase Nissan's liability to 75%.

Boutte complains his lump sum award of $450,000 is inadequate to compensate him for the injuries he sustained. He argues after totalling the stipulated past medical expenses ($32,118.48), estimated possible future medical expenses ($15,000), estimated lost past earnings ($136,150), and estimated lost future earnings ($521,423), he has not been compensated for all of his estimated lost future earnings as well as pain and suffering.

* * *

Because we find the jury did not abuse its vast discretion in awarding damages, we are prevented from comparing the awards in the referenced cases with the present. Accordingly, we affirm the jury's lump sum damages award.

Case Questions

1. Apparently, the jury accepted Nissan's evidence that the plaintiff fell asleep at the wheel after twenty-one hours without sleep. Under these facts, because it was the plaintiff's negligence that set the accident in motion, is it fair to hold the defendant liable for any portion of the accident? Explain.

2. How did the court of appeal apportion fault? How would you have allocated fault if you were on the jury? Explain.

§ 9.3 Parties

product manufacturer†
The maker of a product that, if defective, gives rise to product liability.

seller† One who sells property, either their own or through contract with the actual owner.

wholesaler† One who sells goods wholesale, rather than retail.

Three classes of parties are involved in products liability cases: the product manufacturer, the seller, and the ultimate user.

Manufacturers and Sellers

The **product manufacturer** makes the defective product that gives rise to the entire products liability lawsuit. **Seller** includes anyone who is in the business of selling goods such as the one that is faulty. This includes the manufacturer as well as wholesalers and retailers. **Wholesalers** are businesses that buy and sell goods to **retailers**, which in turn sell the products to customers, usually individual persons.

The Ultimate User

When we buy a product, we are **purchasers**. In products liability law, however, the party injured by flawed merchandise need not be the original buyer. Instead, a member of the purchaser's family, or a friend of the buyer, could recover damages if hurt by a defective product. The key is whether it is reasonably foreseeable that the user would have utilized the product. This individual is called the **ultimate user**, because that person eventually used the product that caused an injury.

In products liability litigation, the ultimate user becomes the plaintiff who sues various defendants: the retailer, the wholesaler(s), and the manufacturer. The plaintiff uses a shotgun approach to products liability—namely, sue all the sellers. This may seem excessive, but the plaintiff has a logical explanation. The plaintiff sues all the sellers along the product distribution chain to ensure that one of them (probably the manufacturer) will have sufficient monies to pay a judgment. In tort law, this is called "going for the **deep pocket**." In other words, the plaintiff tries to sue defendants that have money and could satisfy a damages award. Figure 9-1 shows the product distribution chain between manufacturers, sellers, purchasers, and ultimate users. The deficient product passes through many hands before reaching its unfortunate victim.

Now that we have met the parties to products liability actions, it is time to investigate the elements of products liability.

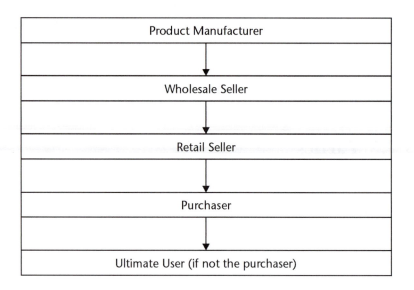

FIGURE 9-1 Product distribution chain

§ 9.4 Elements

Products liability is defined as strict, or absolute, liability for the seller or manufacturer of a defectively made product that injures a user of the item.

No Privity of Contract Requirement

Privity of contract is not required in products liability. The ultimate user need not have purchased the merchandise directly from the seller or manufacturer, although some states require that a sale of the product have occurred somewhere between the manufacturer and the ultimate user. However, it need not be a direct transaction between the two.

Negligence Is Irrelevant

Remember that the seller or manufacturer's negligence is irrelevant to strict liability. It does not matter how much care the seller or manufacturer used in making or maintaining the product. Every possible precaution could have been utilized, but that simply makes no difference. If the product was defective, and a user was harmed as a result, absolute liability applies—period.

A Typical Products Liability Formula

There are five elements of products liability, as defined by most state courts or statutes:

1. The defect must render the product unreasonably dangerous to use.
2. The seller or manufacturer must be in the business of selling products such as the flawed one(s).
3. The product cannot have been substantially changed between the time it left the seller or manufacturer's hands and the time it reached the ultimate user.
4. The defect must have proximately caused the ultimate user's injuries.
5. The ultimate user must have used the product properly, that is, in the way that the product was designed to be used.

In some jurisdictions, several additional elements are required:

6. The ultimate user must have been foreseeable (foreseeable plaintiffs theory).
7. The seller or manufacturer must have been responsible for the condition in which the product was maintained.
8. In a few states, a sale of the product must have occurred. This could be a sale between the manufacturer and a wholesaler, or a wholesaler to a retailer, or a retailer to a customer. Basically, someone at some point had to buy the defective item.

Restatement (Second) Rule

Section 402A of the *Restatement (Second) of Torts* contains fewer elements than those just discussed. It states:

(1) One who sells any product in a defective condition unreasonably dangerous to the user or consumer or to his property is subject to liability for physical harm thereby caused to the ultimate user or consumer, or to his property, if

    (a) the seller is engaged in the business of selling such a product, and

    (b) it is expected to and does reach the user or consumer without substantial change in the condition in which it is sold.

(2) The rule stated in Subsection (1) applies though

    (a) the seller has exercised all possible care in the preparation and sale of this product, and

    (b) the user or consumer has not bought the product from or entered into any contractual relation with the seller.

Subsection (2)(a) of § 402A indicates that the seller is liable regardless of the degree of care used to safeguard the public from injury by the defective product. Subsection (2)(b) states that privity of contract is unnecessary for strict liability to apply. Table 9-1 illustrates tort recovery, and Table 9-2 lists the elements required.

TABLE 9-1 Tort recovery

Negligence	Express Warranty	Implied Warranty	Strict Liability
Personal injuries	Personal injuries	Personal injuries	Personal injuries
Property damage	Property damage	Property damage	Property damage
Economic loss	Pure economic loss	Pure economic loss	Economic loss if there is also personal injury or property damage

Unreasonably Dangerous Products

The product must be unreasonably dangerous as a result of its defect. Courts look to see if the product has become unreasonably threatening because of its defect. There are four types of unreasonably dangerous defects: (1) fault in product design; (2) error in product manufacture or assembly; (3) improper product maintenance; and (4) manufacturer/seller's failure to warn.

TABLE 9-2
Elements required
for tort recovery

Negligence	Express Warranty	Implied Warranty	Strict Liability
Duty	Statement of fact that is false	Sale of goods by merchant	Seller
Breach	Made with the intent or expectation that the statement will reach plaintiff	The goods are not merchantable	Defective product that is unreasonably dangerous to people or property
Causation	The plaintiff relies on the statement	Causation	Causation
Damages	Damages	Damages	Damages

Faulty Product Design

Products can be unreasonably dangerous if they have a defective design. Courts look to see whether the product is inherently dangerous because of a poor design but for which (that is, if such a defect did not exist) the product would have been safe to use. For instance, suppose a manufacturer assembles a toy with small, removable parts that can be swallowed by an infant, and thereby cause serious injury or death. The toy would be inherently dangerous, because the removable-parts design would expose small children to the dangers of choking. This design defect makes the product unreasonably dangerous.

Courts decide faulty design (which make products unreasonably dangerous) in terms of three tests: the consumer contemplation test, the danger/utility test, and the state-of-the-art discoverability test.

Consumer Contemplation Test In its Comments, *Restatement* § 402A states that a product is unreasonably dangerous if the consumer ordinarily would not appreciate the threat inherent in its design. This assumes that the ultimate user, like most people, understands that some products have dangers built in to their uses. The defect becomes unreasonably hazardous because the reasonable person would not be expected to anticipate the danger created by the faulty design. Legal commentators and courts have labeled this the **consumer contemplation test**.

For example, suppose that Nicholas bought a top-loading washing machine. He had to lean across the control panel to load his clothing inside. In doing so, he might accidentally press the start button with his body. This might start the machine while his hands were inside the washing drum. Nicholas could get his fingers caught, which would probably produce some nasty injuries.

consumer contemplation test†
A theory in products liability concerning faulty product design that makes a product unreasonably dangerous. If a reasonable person would not have anticipated the danger created by the fault in the product, then the product is unreasonably dangerous.

Under the consumer contemplation test, would a reasonable person have anticipated this situation? Nicholas should have seen where the start button was located as he began loading his laundry into the machine. He knew that the machine could begin operating once this button was pushed. He should have known that his body could press against the switch and start the washer. In other words, he should have contemplated the risk inherent in the product's poor design. Thus, the product was not unreasonably dangerous under the consumer contemplation test.

Danger/Utility Test Many courts and legal scholars have formulated another test to determine if a product is unreasonably dangerous by its design. This is called the **danger/utility test**. Under this standard, a product is unreasonably hazardous if the danger created by its design outweighs the benefits derived from its use. Consider the previous washing-machine example. The danger created by the poorly located button arises only if Nicholas happens inadvertently to press it with his body while his arms are inside the machine. Normally, he derives tremendous benefits from the device—he gets clean clothes. If he is cautious about where he stands while loading, Nicholas should be able to avoid the accidental start risk. Using the danger/utility test, the washer is not unreasonably dangerous.

State-of-the-Art Discoverability Test If manufacturers could have discovered hazards created by defective product designs, using current, state-of-the-art technologies, then failure to do so makes a design-flawed product unreasonably dangerous. For example, suppose an automobile manufacturer installed ordinary glass in the small vent windows in a vehicle's doors. State-of-the-art crash testing would quickly indicate that this glass shatters into sharp, pointed fragments during a collision. This glass could seriously harm a driver or passenger. If the car maker did not discover this defect through modern testing procedures, then it would be strictly liable for any injuries caused by the fragile windows.

Error in Product Manufacture or Assembly

Safely designed products may become unreasonably dangerous as a result of improper assembly or manufacture. For instance, suppose a lawn-mower manufacturer failed to tighten the bolt holding the blade with sufficient torque. This could result in the blade flying off during use. Suppose this happened to a purchaser, who was severely cut by the blade. The lawn mower, although designed properly, became unreasonably dangerous because it was not suitably assembled. This is sometimes called an **assembly defect**.

Improper Product Maintenance

Sellers occasionally fail to maintain merchandise properly. When a buyer purchases the product, it might not function correctly because of a **maintenance defect**. For example, suppose a lawn and garden shop sells chain saws. The chain on such a saw must be oiled frequently to operate

---

danger/utility test[†]
A theory in products liability design that makes a product unreasonably dangerous. Under this test, a product is unreasonably dangerous if the danger created by its design outweighs the benefits derived from its use.

assembly defect[†]
A theory in products liability concerning whether a defective product is unreasonably dangerous. Errors in production, manufacture, or assembly may render a product unreasonably hazardous despite safe design.

maintenance defect[†]
A theory in products liability concerning whether a defective product is unreasonably dangerous. If a seller fails to maintain a product properly, and the product later causes injury to the ultimate user, then the product was unreasonably dangerous.

appropriately. Oil is stored inside the saw in a special reservoir. Suppose the seller forgot to keep oil in its chain saws. While displaying one model to a customer, one of the seller's employees started a saw. Without oil, the saw froze up and the chain snapped, sailing through the air into the face of the surprised customer. The product was unreasonably dangerous because the seller did not properly maintain it.

The seller was negligent in forgetting to keep oil in the saw. Using the negligence formula, the seller would also be liable under negligence theory, as well as products liability.

Seller or Manufacturer's Failure to Warn

Sometimes products are unreasonably dangerous by their very nature. Lawn mowers, chain saws, poisons, and chemicals can be lethal if not cautiously used. However, purchasers may not always spot the obvious dangers in a product. Accordingly, manufacturers and sellers have an obligation to warn the ultimate user about inherent product dangers. Failure to warn could result in strict liability. For instance, look at almost any household appliance. Each one warns not to place hands or feet here or there, because of rotating knives, extremely hot surfaces, or the presence of scalding liquids. If one uses rat poison or insect sprays, the containers warn not to ingest the contents or get them in one's eyes. These are common examples of warnings that manufacturers and sellers use to avoid absolute liability. If the user is warned, then the user knows the risks. To apply, the warning must be in an obvious and noticeable place.

Business Requirement

Section 402A of the *Restatement (Second) of Torts,* and most common law and statutory versions of products liability, insist that the manufacturer or seller be engaged in the business of selling products such as the defective item(s) that injured the ultimate user. This requirement is easily met in most cases involving manufacturers, wholesalers, or retailers. Its purpose is to exclude products liability for people who are not in the business of selling such goods. For example, suppose Laurie sold Micron a vacuum cleaner, which she had bought from a department store. Because of a design defect, it exploded and injured Micron. Products liability is not intended to hold Laurie liable for this mishap, because she neither manufactured nor was in the business of selling such merchandise. Laurie, like Micron, is essentially an innocent bystander. Under products liability theory, she would not be liable for the defective product. Instead, Micron would sue the department store and manufacturer.

Substantially Unchanged Condition Requirement

For products liability to apply, the product must reach the ultimate user without any substantial changes in its condition from the time it left the manufacturer or seller. This is a crucial requirement. If something happened along the product distribution chain to alter the product (perhaps creating the unreasonably dangerous condition), then it would be unfair to hold manufacturers or sellers accountable for something they did not cause.

For instance, suppose Rachel purchased milk at a nearby grocery. The milk was fresh when she bought it. However, during the drive home, Rachel gets caught in traffic because of an automobile accident. As a result, it takes her over an hour to arrive home. The temperature outside was 100 degrees, and her vehicle had no air conditioning. During this period, the milk spoiled. A visiting relative later drank the milk and suffered food poisoning. The relative wishes to sue the grocery. However, products liability would not apply, because the milk did not reach the ultimate user (Rachel's relative) in a substantially unchanged condition.

In some states, products liability common law or statutes require that, for strict liability to exist, the manufacturer or seller must be responsible for how the defective product was maintained. This seems logical. If the seller were not in any way responsible for how the product was assembled or stored (until it was sold or used), then that seller would have no control over the products it distributes. Products liability attempts to place the blame on the party responsible for the defect, so this requirement seems sensible to protect innocent sellers from absolute liability for product defects caused by someone else.

Proximate Cause

Recall the discussion of proximate cause in strict liability cases. That analysis also applies in products liability cases: the defective product must have been the proximate cause of the plaintiff's injury if liability is to attach.

Proper Use Requirement

The ultimate user must use the defective product properly in order for products liability to apply. In other words, the user must use the product for some function for which it was designed or intended to be used. For example, if Cliff wanted to climb onto his roof, he would probably use a ladder. If one of the ladder's rungs broke (because of the manufacturer's failure to use proper glues), and Cliff fell to the ground and broke various bones, he would be entitled to sue the manufacturer and seller under products liability. However, if he had used stacked vegetable crates to climb upon instead of a ladder, and these collapsed under his weight, Cliff could not sue under products liability. Vegetable crates are neither designed nor intended for people to climb on. They are supposed to be used to store produce.

◄◆►

The Case of the Not-So-Bright Light

This case demonstrates the risk versus utility analysis used in evaluating allegedly dangerous products. The court must decide whether, as a matter of social policy, the risk of loss should be placed on the manufacturer or supplier of a butane lighter that was not child proof.

SMITH
v.
SCRIPTO-TOKAI CORP.

United States District Court,
W.D. Pennsylvania
170 F.Supp.2d 533
November 2, 2001

This is a case for damages arising out of a residential fire started by plaintiffs' three-year-old child using a butane utility lighter manufactured by defendants. On June 15, 2000, we granted defendants' motion to dismiss all claims except negligence. As to the negligence claim, we explained that we were bound to follow the Court of Appeals' decision in *Griggs v. BIC Corp.*, 981 F.2d 1429 (3d Cir.1992), and chastised defendant's counsel for his lack of candor to the tribunal in failing to acknowledge that case.

* * *

As set forth in *Griggs*, 981 F.2d at 1434, plaintiff must establish the following elements of a negligence action: (1) defendants had a duty; (2) defendants failed to conform to the standard required; (3) there was a causal connection between defendants' conduct and the resulting injury; and (4) damages. The "duty" element has two components: foreseeability and unreasonableness. Although foreseeability is not part of a strict liability claim, foreseeability "is an integral part of a determination that a duty does exist in Pennsylvania negligence law." ...

In this case, the Aim 'n Flame lighter is a consumer product and there is "abundant empirical data demonstrating that Tokai could have foreseen the risk of an unsupervised child causing injury by using a lighter." Further, the

risk is unreasonable because the high social value placed on the safety of people and property threatened by childplay fires, the high gravity and considerable probability of the risk, and the likelihood of a reasonably available alternative (childproofing) outweigh defendants' interest in producing its lighters without childproofing features. Thus, as the Court of Appeals held in *Griggs*, "if a manufacturer of cigarette lighters may reasonably foresee that they will fall into the hands of children, who, albeit unintended users, can ignite them with a probability of serious injury to themselves and others, and if childproofing the lighters is economically feasible, the manufacturer would have a duty to guard against the unreasonable risk of harm by designing the lighter to be childproof." Accordingly, plaintiffs have established the "duty" element of their negligence claim. Plaintiffs have also established that defendants breached that duty. Indeed, defendants do not seriously contend that the Aim 'n Flame lighter at issue here had appropriate safety features.

There are material disputes of fact that prevent causation from being established as a matter of law. Plaintiffs point out that an Aim 'n Flame lighter was recovered from the wreckage of the home, underneath the point of origin of the fire. Defendants, not so subtly, seek to imply that this evidence was planted. If defendants wish to risk alienating the jury by pursuing this line of reasoning, they shall have that opportunity.

Finally, the existence of damages is undisputed. However, a jury will have to determine the amount of such damages.

... Plaintiffs have established, as a matter of law, that defendants had a duty to manufacture a childproof lighter and breached that duty. The case will proceed to trial on the issues of causation and damages.

A defendant may be liable for negligence if he (1) knows that the chattel is in a dangerous condition; (2) has no reason to believe that those for whose use the chattel is supplied will realize the dangerous condition; and (3) fails to warn those for whose use the chattel is supplied of the dangerous condition. A warning is sufficient if it adequately notifies the intended user of the unobvious dangers inherent in the product.

* * *

Pennsylvania adopted the Restatement (Second) of Torts Section 402A as the law of strict products liability. [T]he Pennsylvania Supreme Court announced a threshold question of law for the court to decide: whether, as a matter of social policy, the product's condition justifies placing the risk of loss on the manufacturer or supplier. A risk-utility analysis, using the Dean John Wade factors, is appropriate in performing this threshold social policy inquiry. If the claim survives this threshold determination, "the jury must determine whether, under the facts, the product, at the time it left the defendant's control, lacked any element necessary to make it safe for its intended use or contained any condition that made it unsafe for use."

* * *

We conclude that reinstatement of the products liability claim is appropriate. Developments of the law in the Pennsylvania intermediate courts and in the Court of Appeals have clearly indicated that the threshold products liability question should be based on the risk-utility analysis. The Superior Court has applied this analysis in a closely analogous case and we have no reason to believe that the Supreme Court would apply risk-utility factors any differently. ...

Case Questions

1. How would you apply a risk-utility analysis in this case?
2. Why would Scripto have produced a lighter that was not childproof?

Foreseeable Plaintiffs Theory

In some jurisdictions, it must have been reasonably foreseeable that the ultimate user would use the defective product. This is called the zone of danger (or foreseeable plaintiffs) theory in negligence. Some ultimate users are not reasonably foreseeable and no duty is owed to them. For example, it is highly improbable that a one-year-old infant would come into contact with industrial cleaners used in manufacturing processes. Such a person could not be a reasonably foreseeable ultimate user of such a product. However, members of a product purchaser's family, or the buyer's neighbors, could be foreseeable users of defective goods. How many times in one's family has more than one individual used an appliance or tool? Have you ever borrowed products from your neighbors?

Consider Diana, who borrowed a pen from a classmate with which to take notes during the lecture. The pen had a manufacturing defect that made the plastic casing unusually brittle. While writing, the pen shatters in Diana's hand, and she is cut by the many tiny fragments. Was Diana a reasonably foreseeable ultimate user? Yes. Classmates often share pens, pencils, notebooks, and many other products during classes. It was reasonably foreseeable that someone might borrow a pen to take notes in class. Diana could sue the pen manufacturer under products liability as a foreseeable plaintiff.

Having analyzed the various elements of products liability, we may now proceed to apply the theory to hypotheticals.

— HYPOTHETICALS

Burgess Primer Corporation manufactures paint. Eleanor bought Burgess's "Supreme Ease" paint at Painter Place, a local retailer that carried Burgess products. Eleanor selected various colors, which store employees mixed together. While applying the paint indoors, Eleanor noticed that the paint stung her skin as it splattered from her roller. Apparently, Eleanor was allergic to certain oils that had been mixed into the paint. When she showered later that day, she noticed that the paint had left her arms and face mottled with burn marks. Many of these became infected. Medical tests indicated that a significant percentage of the population suffered this allergic reaction to the paint mix.

Are Burgess Primer Corporation (as manufacturer) and Painter Place (as seller) strictly liable for an unreasonably dangerous product? Applying the generic formula, first ask if the defect made the product unreasonably dangerous. The fault here is product assembly (i.e., how the paint was mixed). Using the consumer contemplation test, would a reasonable person anticipate that he or she might be allergic to paint oils? This is not an obvious hazard that an ordinary person would detect from a can of paint. Thus, the product's dangerous condition rendered it unreasonably dangerous to the ultimate user, Eleanor. Under the danger/utility test, the hazard in using the product outweighed the benefits, as many people were allergic to the particular mix.

Both Burgess and Painter Place were engaged in the business of selling paint. The product reached the ultimate user, Eleanor, in the same condition as it left the retailer. Also, Eleanor used the paint properly, in a way in which paint is intended to be used. It was reasonably foreseeable that Eleanor would use the paint she bought at a retail store, so she is a foreseeable plaintiff. Both Burgess and the retailer were responsible for how the paint was maintained. Further, a sale occurred (for those jurisdictions requiring it). So far, even with the extra elements, it seems as though strict liability will favor Eleanor.

But who was the proximate cause of Eleanor's injuries? Burgess manufactured the paint base and the various colors. However, the paint did not become unreasonably dangerous until Painter Place's employees mixed it. Therefore, Burgess, as manufacturer, did not proximately cause Eleanor's injuries. Painter Place was clearly the proximate cause of the harm. Proximate cause is a crucial determination, because it absolves Burgess from strict products liability. Painter Place is absolutely liable for Eleanor's injuries under products liability theory.

* * *

Consider another hypothetical. Fairfield Seed Company sold sweet corn seeds to retail variety stores. Fairfield had erroneously treated the seeds with a toxic insecticide used for field corn seeds. As the corn grew, this chemical was absorbed into the ears of sweet corn. When the gardeners (who had bought the seed from the retailers) ate the corn, they became ill.

Would the retail variety stores and Fairfield be strictly liable for the gardeners' injuries from an unreasonably dangerous product? Apply either the consumer contemplation test or the danger/utility test. The reasonable gardener would not expect sweet corn seeds to be treated with a poison harmful to humans. The risks far outweigh the benefits. Both Fairfield and the retailers were in the business of selling garden seeds. Fairfield improperly prepared the seeds, which would be a manufacturing defect. The dangerous seeds reached the ultimate users in the same condition as when they left the manufacturer. Fairfield was responsible for the condition of the product. Fairfield's insecticide coating proximately caused the gardeners' injuries, because the ultimate users ate the contaminated ears of corn grown from the poisoned seed. The gardeners used the product as it was designed (i.e., to grow corn to eat) and were foreseeable plaintiffs. All the elements of products liability have been met; thus, Fairfield is strictly liable for the gardeners' injuries caused by the poison corn.

What about the retailers' liability, however? There are two critical queries here. First, did the retailers proximately cause the ultimate users' injuries? Second, were the retailers responsible for the condition in which the defective product was maintained?

The retailers did not contaminate the seeds. The seeds came in sealed packages, which the retailers simply stocked on shelves for customers to pick up and purchase. Thus, the retailers did nothing to proximately cause the gardeners' injuries. Furthermore, the retailers had no control over the manufacturing processes that contaminated the seeds. They were not responsible for how the seeds were prepared. The retailers maintained the condition of the seeds just as they were supposed to, namely, by stocking their shelves with sealed packages. Under this analysis, the retailers would not be strictly liable for the harm to the gardeners. ■

Table 9-3 on page 306 summarizes the elements of products liability, under both the generic, common law formula and the *Second Restatement* § 402A.

<♦>

The Case of the Saturday Night Special (The Sequel)

In the last discussion of this case, the D.C. Court of Appeals ruled that the sale of a "Saturday Night Special" handgun was not an ultrahazardous activity for purposes of absolute liability. The appellants also argued products liability theory, but as in the first round, the court once again guns down this proposition, exempting the manufacturer from strict liability. Reread the earlier excerpt in Chapter 8 for the facts and procedural history.

DELAHANTY
v.
HINCKLEY

District of Columbia Court of Appeals
564 A.2d 758 (D.C. 1989)
October 11, 1989
Ferren, Associate Judge

Appellants advanced three legal theories for holding the gun manufacturers liable in these circumstances: negligence, strict products liability under the *Restatement (Second) of Torts* § 402A (1965), and a "social utility" claim apparently based on strict liability for abnormally dangerous activities ... . Appellants alleged in their complaint that: Hinckley needed an easily concealable weapon for his assassination attempt; the gun manufactured by [the defendant] is an easily concealable, inexpensive handgun; the gun is poorly constructed, unreliable, and therefore not useful for legitimate purposes such as military use, target practice, or self-defense; as a result of the gun's low price, it is used for criminal

purposes; and the manufacturers knew of the gun's criminal uses.

* * *

Appellants first claim the manufacturers of the gun used by Hinckley are strictly liable for sale of a defective product. They rely on *Restatement (Second) of Torts* § 402A, which imposes liability for the sale of "any product in a defective condition unreasonably dangerous to the user or consumer ... ". We join the other courts which have rejected the application of this theory in circumstances such as these. Appellants point to no malfunction of the gun caused by improper design or manufacture that led to Thomas Delahanty's injuries. Instead, appellants argue that the manufacturers had a duty to warn of the dangers of criminal misuse of the gun. There is no duty to warn, however, "when the danger, or potentiality of danger, is generally known and recognized." *Restatement (Second) of Torts*, § 402A comment j. Because hazards of firearms are obvious, the manufacturer had no duty to warn.

Case Questions

1. Suppose that, when Hinckley fired at the president, the handgun had exploded because of a defective firing pin. Suppose also that Delahanty had been injured by the flying shrapnel. Would Delahanty's products liability claim against the manufacturer have succeeded under these facts? Would Delahanty have been the ultimate user under these facts? Explain.

2. What if the bullets that struck Delahanty had been defectively manufactured, so that they exploded upon impact. Would Delahanty then have had a products liability claim against the bullet manufacturer? Would Delahanty have been the ultimate user under these facts? Explain.

	Typical Common Law or Statutory Formula	Comparison with Restatement (2d) of Torts § 402A	Additional Elements (in Some States)
1.	Defect makes product unreasonably dangerous	Common law or statutory formula same as *Restatement*	Ultimate user must be reasonably foreseeable (foreseeable plaintiffs theory)
2.	Manufacturer or seller must be in business of selling products such as the defective one(s)	Common law or statutory formula same as *Restatement*	Manufacturer or seller must be responsible for condition in which defective product was maintained
3.	Defective product cannot have been substantially changed from time it left manufacturer or seller until it was used by ultimate user	Common law or statutory formula same as *Restatement*	A sale of the defective product must have occurred
4.	Defect must have proximately caused the ultimate user's injuries	Not included	
5.	Ultimate user must have used the product properly (in the way in which it was designed or intended to be used)	Not included	
6.		Degree of care that manufacturer or seller used in making or maintaining the defective product is immaterial; also, no contractual relationship or sale is required	Some states, by statute or common law, require a sale

TABLE 9-3 Elements of products liability

§ 9.5 Defenses

There are several defenses to absolute liability. Some of those defenses also apply to products liability.

Contributory or Comparative Negligence Not a Defense

Courts have generally held that contributory negligence is not a defense in products liability cases. This seems logical, because contributory negligence is a defense to negligence and negligence has no place in strict liability cases. Allowing the ultimate user's contributory negligence to bar absolute liability for a defective product would be the legal equivalent of mixing apples and oranges.

Ultimate User's Misuse of Product

Saying that contributory or comparative negligence is not a defense is not to say, however, that the plaintiff (the ultimate user) can use a defective product irresponsibly or wantonly. The ultimate user is expected to use the product properly, as it was intended to be used. This is an element of products liability, although some courts consider product misuse to be a defense. If the ultimate user misuses a defective product and is injured as a consequence, his or her products liability claim against the manufacturer or seller will be denied because the harm resulted from the plaintiff's misuse of the product. This defense is effective even though the misused product was defective.

Some product uses may be unusual, but are not actually misuses. For example, chairs are designed to be sat on. Yet how often have you used a chair as a stepping stool to reach something stored on a high shelf? Using a chair as a ladder is not a misuse of the product, because it is reasonably foreseeable that one might use a chair for such a purpose. In other words, reasonably foreseeable uses, even though the product may not originally have been intended or designed for such functions, are acceptable uses. A products liability claim would not be barred if the ultimate user used the product in a reasonably foreseeable fashion.

Removal of Safety Devices

Adult smokers commonly remove the "childproof" safety devices on butane lighters, increasing the risk of injury.

Employees who are under great pressure to produce a lot while working on an assembly line or in a factory may deliberately dismantle the very safety device that is there to protect them. If the safety device is removed, a machine might run faster than was intended, or it may become easier to get to the interior of the machine when it jams or needs cleaning. For these injured parties, a products liability cause of action will not be available, because the product was misused and altered.

Practical Application

Unfortunately, you will frequently see misuse of products by injured parties who will tell you that they removed the guard or safety device from a machine at work.

Assumption of Risk

Assumption of risk, however, is usually accepted as a defense. The ultimate user assumes the risk of being injured by a hazardous product in three ways: (1) by discovering the defect but disregarding it and using the product anyway; (2) by failing to properly maintain the product; and (3) by failing to follow instructions or heed warnings for safe product use.

Ignoring a Discovered Defect

assumption of risk
Knowingly and willingly exposing yourself (or your property) to the possibility of harm. In most states, a person who assumes a risk of harm cannot win a negligence lawsuit against the person responsible for the harm....

Recall the basic definition of assumption of risk. **Assumption of risk** is the plaintiff's voluntary assumption of a known risk with a full appreciation of the dangers involved in facing that risk. In products liability cases, the plaintiff is the ultimate user. The ultimate user assumes the risk by discovering a product defect and then ignoring the risks involved and using the product anyway. For example, suppose Steve discovers that his circular saw blade is bent. The warp would cause the blade to rub against the saw's protective sheathing when it rotated. This would create sparks, which could burn him. Steve decides that the risk is worth taking and he uses the saw. Sparks fly into his eyes (because he does not wear protective eyewear). Steve assumed a known risk with a full comprehension of the possible hazardous consequences.

Failure to Properly Maintain Product

Ultimate users cannot recover in products liability if they failed to properly maintain the product for safe uses. Courts often characterize this as an assumption-of-risk defense. The circular saw example illustrates this type of assumption of risk. Steve did not maintain the saw so that it could be safely used. The blade was bent. Before using it, he should have replaced the damaged blade with a new blade, or at least had the bad blade repaired. It is the ultimate user's responsibility to maintain the merchandise for safe uses.

Consider another illustration. Suppose Gil failed to put motor oil in his automobile. If he proceeded to drive for hundreds of miles, his motor would undoubtedly burn out. He failed to properly maintain the vehicle by putting in the suitable amount of lubrication. Gil could not recover under products liability from the manufacturer or seller. He assumed the risk of ruining his car by not properly maintaining it.

Failure to Follow Instructions or Heed Warnings

How often have you used a product without first reading the instructions? Surely everyone has done this. Most of the time the products we use are sufficiently simple that we can use them properly after a quick glance. With a complex product, however, following instructions could prevent injuries. Products liability plaintiffs often argue that defectively designed products are unreasonably dangerous. However, sometimes these plaintiffs did not follow the manufacturer's instructions for product use and as a consequence were hurt. Also, an ultimate user occasionally disregards manufacturer's warnings that specifically point out the dangers inherent in the product design. Both of these actions are types of assumption of risk.

Assume, in the saw example, that the manufacturer printed on the side of the saw, "WARNING! DO NOT USE IF BLADE IS BENT!" If Steve disregarded this warning and were hurt from the bent saw, he could not recover damages for a defectively designed product. Steve assumed the risk by ignoring the warning.

Suppose, instead of a bent blade, that the blade was merely loose. The instructions included directions for blade tightening. If Steve did not read or follow these directions, and he was hurt because the blade flew off while he was using the saw, he could not recover damages under products liability. Steve assumed the risk by failing to follow instructions to properly maintain the product.

⟨♦⟩

The Case of the Toxic Fire Paint

Product misuse does not always require an unusual use of an item. Sometimes the product may be applied to achieve the results for which it was intended, but the actual operation of the item is inappropriate and causes the user's injuries. As the following case illustrates, the paint was used as paint is ordinarily intended. However, the way in which the paint was applied was the misuse. Nor were the firefighters reasonably foreseeable plaintiffs. Although one cannot help but sympathize with the plaintiffs, the Fourth Circuit's analysis of products liability theory reaches the correct result.

HIGGINS

v.

E.I. DUPONT DE NEMOURS & CO.

U.S. Court of Appeals, Fourth Circuit
863 F.2d 1162 (4th Cir. 1988)
December 23, 1988
Murnaghan, Circuit Judge

Plaintiffs Higgins and Jones appeal from the district court's order granting summary judgment in favor of defendant, E.I. DuPont de Nemours & Co., Inc. ("DuPont"), regarding their survival actions. Plaintiffs also appeal the dismissal of their wrongful death actions ... .

Plaintiffs brought the actions to recover for the deaths of their children and fetuses who allegedly died from the teratogenic effect of chemicals contained in Imron paint. Each of the husbands had worked for the Baltimore City Fire Department in the same fire house, where they used Imron paint to "touch up" the fire engines. Plaintiffs claimed that the deaths were caused by glycol ether acetates and lead supplied by Dow and contained in Imron paint which was developed, manufactured and distributed by DuPont. DuPont advertised Imron paint for sale through distributors for use by industrial professionals, such as fleet truck and transit systems, body shops, marinas, car dealers and manufacturers of aircraft, fire engines, heavy duty construction equipment, and utility vans. Imron was sold and delivered by DuPont to C & R Paint Supply, Inc. ("C & R"), which in turn, sold and delivered the product to the Key Highway repair yard of the Baltimore City Fire Department, where fire apparatus was regularly painted and repainted. C & R never sold or delivered Imron paint directly to the City firehouses nor did it directly solicit business from the Fire Department through sales representatives. Furthermore, it is undisputed that C & R understood that the City's fire vehicles were repaired and painted only at the Key Highway repair shop. Nothing suggests that C & R even suspected that Imron paint was sent out to the individual fire houses until 1985 when it received an unusual request from the City Fire Department for some empty quart containers.

However, from 1979 to 1985, the City Fire Department's Key Highway facility redistributed quantities of Imron in both marked (i.e., with DuPont's labels affixed) and unmarked one-gallon paint cans, coffee cans, or glass jars to the plaintiffs for their use in touching up fire apparatus in the firehouse. The city did not provide the plaintiffs with separate instructions or warnings as to the use of Imron, or with protective clothes to wear while applying the Imron paint.

Each of the labels affixed to the Imron paint products which C & R sold to the City Fire Department stated in clear lettering on the front of the cans:

> FOR INDUSTRIAL USE ONLY by professional, trained personnel. Not for sale to or use by the general public.

This warning was accompanied by instruction on the back of the label which required the use of a supplied-air respirator, eye protection, gloves, protective clothing and adequate ventilation. Furthermore, C & R supplied Material Safety Data Sheets ("MSDS") to the City Fire Department which repeated the safety precautions … . However, none of the information constituting a warning specifically warned of the possible teratogenic effects of the product.

* * *

The district court found that the firefighters were not "professional, trained personnel" for the obvious use of Imron products, i.e., painting. That they were professional firefighters and not professional painters was evidence from the manner in which they mixed and applied the paint. The evidence shows that the firefighters painted in their fire department work uniforms, mixed the paint in cups and sometimes with their fingers and did not heed any of the label precautions which a professional painter would have taken seriously. We agree with the district court that the labels were adequate enough to warn plaintiffs that they were not sufficiently well-trained to use Imron paint. Therefore, DuPont did not distribute a product which was unreasonably dangerous when used for a purpose and in a manner that is reasonably foreseeable, i.e., for industrial use by trained painters. Imron paint was not defective.

Because plaintiffs did not fall into the class of foreseeable users of Imron paint which DuPont had specifically circumscribed to limit its potential liability, the district court held that had the City heeded the warning and not redistributed Imron paint in unlabeled cans to the firehouse, plaintiffs would not have been injured. Likewise, plaintiffs could not complain when they failed to observe the warnings on the Imron paint cans which the City redistributed to them in the original, labeled cans. The district court held that such a misuse of the product barred recovery as a matter of law. Although our sympathy rests with the plaintiffs who have suffered unspeakable losses, we must agree with the district court that plaintiffs' real complaint lies with the City Fire Department and not DuPont.

* * *

Misuse of a product may bar recovery against the manufacturer where the misuse is the sole proximate cause of damage, or where it is the intervening or superseding cause. Product misuse is defined as use of a product in a manner that could not reasonably be foreseen by the defendant. Reasonably foreseeable uses include "'the incidental and attendant consequences that accompany normal use.'" The district court found that the normal use of Imron paint was restricted to industrial purposes for which professional painters, who appreciated the attendant risks, were required. The district court held that DuPont could not reasonably foresee that either the City would redistribute Imron paint in either labeled or unlabeled containers or that plaintiffs, who were amateur painters, would use Imron paint after reading the various conspicuous warnings contained on the labeled cannisters [*sic*] which did reach them. ... [W]e still agree with the basic reasoning of the district court, ... that the firefighters were not professional, trained personnel. Plaintiffs failed to provide any contradictory evidence. DuPont had a right to rely on its warning to cut off the chain of causation and to insulate it from becoming a virtual insurer against all injuries arising from its product.

Affirmed.

Case Questions

1. Was it not reasonably foreseeable that Imron paint might be shifted into unmarked containers for easier use? Why or why not? What is the significance of DuPont's labeling for this issue?

2. Two of the multiple defendants in this case were the mayor and city council of Baltimore, Maryland. Do you believe the plaintiffs would succeed against them, under respondeat superior, for the torts of the Baltimore City Fire Department? Explain the tort theories that the plaintiffs could successfully apply.

Defenses are a defective product manufacturer's best friend. Even if every products liability element is satisfied, defenses can spare the seller from the wrath of strict liability, as the following hypotheticals illustrate.

— HYPOTHETICALS

Douglas owns a tire repair shop. He sells new tires from all the national brands and repairs old tires. Marjorie came into the shop one day with a punctured tire. Douglas agreed that it could be patched and repaired, but he instructed Marjorie to use the tire only as a spare for emergencies. He recommended that she purchase a reconditioned tire for regular use. Marjorie insisted that Douglas put her patched tire back onto her car. Douglas warned that the patch might not hold up over long-term, constant use. Nevertheless, he had the repaired tire re-mounted on her car. Later the following month, while Marjorie was driving to work, the patch failed and the tire blew out. Marjorie's car ran off the road, collided with a telephone pole, and injured her.

Marjorie's products liability claim against Douglas would fail. Marjorie assumed the risk of using the patched tire contrary to Douglas's specific instructions and warnings. She voluntarily assumed a known risk with a full appreciation of the hazards involved. The defense of assumption of risk would protect Douglas from strict products liability.

* * *

The Oasis Sprinkler Company manufactures underground lawn sprinkler systems. Oasis offers a do-it-yourself kit for handy customers. Josephine purchased one of these kits. The detailed assembly instructions directed her to attach the sprinkler heads to the underground pipe using a special copper clamp. "Be certain to crimp the clamp with pliers to ensure a snug connection," read the instructions. Josephine did not crimp the clamps, although she did put them in place. Later, while the sprinkler system was in use, one of the sprinkler heads flew into the air under the force of the water pressure. It struck Josephine's daughter, Janice, in the forehead, causing a wound that required several stitches.

Could Janice and Josephine win a products liability lawsuit against Oasis? Not if the assumption-of-risk defense can be successfully applied. Josephine disregarded the manufacturer's specific instructions for assembling the product. However, Oasis failed to warn about the possible dangers that could occur if the clamps were not crimped. So we have a manufacturer's failure-to-warn situation versus a user's failure-to-follow-instructions defense. Which wins? Is the manufacturer's failure to warn sufficient to hold Oasis liable for an unreasonably dangerous product? Or is Josephine's failure to obey instructions a complete defense under assumption of risk?

The key to this problem is whether a reasonable ultimate user (i.e., a reasonable person) would have anticipated that the sprinkler heads might fly off under high water pressure if the clamps were not crimped. Most people know that water carried through pipes is under great pressure, which makes the water a powerful, focused force. A loose connection could easily give way and send a sprinkler head flying in any direction. Reasonable persons know this from everyday experience with garden hoses or plumbing. Josephine should have anticipated this risk; therefore, it is considered a known risk that she voluntarily assumed, despite a full appreciation of the dangers involved. Assumption of risk will overpower the manufacturer's failure to warn of this particular hazard. Accordingly, the defense of assumption of risk will protect Oasis from strict products liability.

* * *

The Comfort King Corporation manufactures recliner chairs. When Herbert visited a friend, who owned such a recliner, Herbert noticed that a lightbulb was burned out in his friend's hallway. He used the recliner as a ladder to reach the light fixture. As he stood on the chair, it reclined, sending him sprawling across the hall where he smashed his head into a closet doorknob. Herbert thought the chair was unreasonably dangerous, so he sued Comfort King under products liability.

Comfort King, however, shrugged off the lawsuit. The product misuse defense was there to protect the company from strict liability. Recliner chairs are not designed or intended to be used as ladders or stoops. After all, recliners *recline*. They cannot be safely stood upon for that reason. Herbert should have reasonably anticipated the danger created by misusing the chair in this fashion. Herbert's misuse of the product is a solid products liability defense for Comfort King. ■

Table 9-4 lists the defenses to products liability.

TABLE 9-4
Defenses to products liability

Contributory Negligence	Assumption of Risk	Product Misuse by Ultimate User
Not considered a defense in products liability cases	Ultimate user's voluntary assumption of known risk with full appreciation of dangers involved	If ultimate user misuses the product, then he or she cannot recover under products liability
	Occurs when ultimate user ignores a discovered defect and uses the product while knowing of its dangerous condition	Reasonably foreseeable uses are *not* misuses of products
	Occurs when ultimate user fails to properly maintain product	
	Occurs when ultimate user fails to follow instructions or heed warnings for safe product use	

§ 9.6 Comparison to Contract Law Warranties

Products liability has roots in contract law warranties. A *warranty* is a guarantee that a product seller gives a buyer. The guarantee states that the product will perform to certain standards or will not break down over a period of time. This warranty is part of the contract between the buyer and the seller.

breach of warranty[†]
The violation of either an express or implied warranty.

If the product fails to comply with the guarantee, the warranty is *breached*. This **breach of warranty** is also a violation of the parties' agreement that the product shall remain in a particular condition while used.

The Uniform Commercial Code (UCC) is a model (suggested) statute concerning the sale of goods that has been adopted by all states. One of its provisions, § 2-314, concerns implied warranties that all sellers of goods provide with their goods as to the goods being "merchantable," which means that all goods must be of fair average quality and fit for their ordinary purpose. This warranty protects the buyer against defective goods.

Another provision of the UCC, § 2-315, provides that if the seller knows of a particular purpose for which the buyer is buying, then the goods must be fit for that purpose.

These two provisions have allowed liability for injuries sustained as a result of defects in products. Because the UCC has been adopted by all states, decisions on these points tend to be congruent nationwide.

§ 9.7 Bad Faith

A tort is society's method of addressing the injuries that occur to people and property. As evidenced by all the new tort actions in this chapter, the tort field has greatly developed in response to modern problems; legal theories that allow an injured party to prevail can be flexible to fit the times. An example of this is the tort of **bad faith**, which has developed from California legal cases.

bad faith Dishonesty or other failure to deal fairly with another person.

When an insurance company unreasonably denies a claim or fails to pay it in a timely fashion within the policy limits, this is called the *tort of bad faith*, or *bad faith liability*. Obviously, where liability is not clear-cut or certain, this tort will not apply. Insurance companies are expected to negotiate in good faith on behalf of an insured person and promptly settle claims for which liability is reasonably clear.

An example of bad faith would be when a plaintiff is willing to settle a lawsuit within the defendant's insurance policy limits, the defendant is clearly responsible for the plaintiff's injuries, and the defendant's insurance company refuses to settle the claim or even make a settlement offer. The plaintiff might then proceed to trial, and the jury may end up awarding a verdict greatly in excess of the amount of the defendant's insurance coverage. In this instance, the defendant ends up owing money to the claimant out of pocket, when this did not need to occur. If an insurance company refuses to bargain in good faith when there was available coverage for an incident, this defeats the purpose of insurance and subjects an insured to unnecessary liability.

The tort of bad faith demonstrates how tort law and contract law can intersect. When an insurance company fails to settle a tort case, the company may be liable to their insured on the basis of contract law as set forth in the terms of the insurance policy.

Summary

Products liability became a distinct tort theory in the early 1960s. For more than 100 years, American and English courts combined contract law and negligence to hold manufacturers and sellers liable for injuries caused by defective products. Finally, in 1962, strict liability was applied to such cases. As a matter of public policy, products liability places the risk of harm created by unreasonably dangerous products upon those who make and sell them. The law presumes that the innocent user should not be forced to bear the costs associated with harmful products.

The parties in products liability cases include the manufacturer, other sellers (such as retailers or wholesalers), and the consumers, or ultimate users, of the product. Often the ultimate user is a member of the product buyer's family or a neighbor or friend. By looking at a product's distribution chain, it becomes clear how the product leaves the manufacturer and reaches the ultimate user.

Products liability is strict, or absolute, liability. No privity of contract is required between the manufacturer or seller and the ultimate user. The manufacturer or seller's negligence is irrelevant. The product must contain a defect rendering it unreasonably dangerous to use. This fault may arise in a design defect, by improper product maintenance, or by the manufacturer or seller's failure to warn the buyer of hazards inherent in using the product. The manufacturer or seller must be engaged in the business of selling products like the defective one. The product cannot be substantially changed from the time it left the manufacturer or seller and reached the ultimate user. The defect must proximately cause the ultimate user's injuries. The ultimate user must use the product in the way in which it was designed or intended.

Contributory negligence is not a defense to products liability. Product misuse is a defense, although it is often included as an element in the products liability formula. If the ultimate user misuses the product, even though the product is defective, the manufacturer and seller will not be strictly liable for the harm. Assumption of risk is another defense to products liability. If the ultimate user ignores a discovered defect and, by using the product, is hurt, the user has assumed the risk, and the manufacturer or seller would not be strictly liable. The same is true if the ultimate user fails to properly maintain a product, follow instructions, or heed warnings for safe use.

Products liability is similar to contract law warranties. First, both involve absolute liability. Second, both involve defective or unreasonably dangerous products. Third, under many warranty statutes and common law, the ultimate user is protected even if he or she was not the original product purchaser.

The tort of bad faith occurs when an insurance company fails to reasonably or timely settle a case that could have been settled within the policy limits.

Key Terms

assembly defect	deep pocket	purchaser
assumption of risk	imminent danger exception	retailer
bad faith	maintenance defect	seller
breach of warranty	privity of contract	ultimate user
consumer contemplation test	product manufacturer	warranty
danger/utility test	products liability	wholesaler

Problems

1. WedgeCorp manufactures golf clubs. The clubs have rubberized grips that golfers hold onto to swing them. Waldo Maillor bought his wife a set of clubs for her birthday. Cindy Maillor is an avid golfer and uses the clubs three times a week at the local country club. When WedgeCorp manufactured the clubs, they used an improperly mixed glue that did not tightly bond the grips to the end of the clubs. While Cindy was swinging a five iron, the grip came loose and the club sailed through the air, striking Cindy's golfing partner, Betty Payless, in the forehead.

2. Better Bovine, Inc. (BB) sells dairy cattle to farmers. These livestock are raised on one of the BB's pasturing farms outside of town. To control weeds, BB's employees sprayed pasture land with herbicides. The cattle ate this grass and absorbed the chemicals into their systems. These chemicals reduced the cows' milk production. Several farmers who purchased BB cows suffered substantial economic losses when the animals' milk productivity plummeted.

3. Whopper Toys Corporation manufactures "Mr. Killjoy," a combat doll. Mr. Killjoy comes equipped with sharp plastic swords that you can fit into his hands for mock battles. Whopper indicated on its packaging that this toy was not suitable for children under the age of six years. This was the only warning printed on the package. Franco Delgado bought a Mr. Killjoy figure for his four-year-old son, Francisco. While playing with Charlotte, a three-year-old neighbor girl, Francisco had the doll "attack" her. Its sword stabbed Charlotte through her nose, leaving a permanent scar.

4. Omar Muhammad is an accountant who lives in an apartment next to Joyce Madison. Omar sold his electric stove to Joyce for $200. Omar had never kept the electric heating elements on top of the stove particularly clean. In fact, they were caked with grease and dirt. The first time Joyce turned on the stove, the heating elements caught fire and set Joyce's long hair ablaze.

5. The Steak Out restaurant has a reputation for excellent steaks. One day it received a meat shipment from the Midwestern Meat Packing Company, a national meat distributor. When the shipment left Midwestern, it was shipped in a refrigerated truck. However, en route to The Steak Out, the truck's refrigeration system broke down, but the driver never noticed. The meat spoiled. When the Steak Out's employees unloaded the truck, they did not notice that the meat smelled bad. In fact, the meat did not smell much, if at all. Nevertheless, customers served from this shipment of beef became seriously ill from food poisoning.

6. Peter Breezeway bought a large screwdriver, made by the Hand Tool Manufacturing Company, from his local hardware store. Unknown to anyone, the screwdriver had a microscopic crack in its shaft. If excessive pressure were exerted on the screwdriver, it would snap. Peter used the screwdriver to pry open sealed crates that he received at work. One day, while prying open a crate, the screwdriver broke, severely cutting the tendons in Peter's left hand.

7. Bartholomew Benton works for the United States Department of Defense. One day he noticed that his paper-shredding machine made a loud grinding noise during operation. He opened the maintenance door, but could see nothing wrong with the parts inside. Bart continued using the machine, despite the horrible noise. Several co-workers complained to him about it. The grinding occurred because the machine was out of lubricating oil, which according to the machine's instruction manual, should have been checked at least monthly. No one had checked the oil level since the machine was purchased over a year ago. While Bart was using the machine, its gears froze up, and broke loose the paper-shredding blades. These lodged in Bart's thighs, cutting him deeply.

Review Questions

1. What are the public policy objectives behind products liability? How are they similar to the public policy objectives mentioned in Chapter 9 for "regular" strict liability?

2. How did modern products liability evolve? What were some of the landmark cases during the nineteenth and early twentieth centuries that led to these developments? What was the imminent danger exception? It was an exception to what rule?

3. How is negligence relevant to products liability? Is privity of contract required? Who are the parties in products liability cases? Who is the ultimate user?

4. Discuss the elements of a typical products liability formula. How are these different from the elements in *Restatement (Second) of Torts* § 402A? How are they similar?

5. How would you define an unreasonably dangerous product? What is faulty product design? Explain the consumer contemplation test, the danger/utility test, and the state-of-the-art discoverability test. Why are these tests important?

6. Explain how errors in product manufacture or assembly make a product unreasonably dangerous for products liability purposes.

7. In products liability, what role does improper product maintenance play? Manufacturer or seller's failure to warn of product hazards?

8. Define (a) the business requirement, (b) the substantially unchanged condition requirement, and (c) the proper use requirement. Why are they relevant to products liability? Does proximate cause play any role?

9. Is contributory negligence a defense to products liability? Why or why not? What about product misuse?

10. Explain how assumption of risk operates as a defense to products liability. Identify the three ways in which the ultimate user assumes the risk of using a defective product.

11. How does the tort of bad faith intersect with contract law?

Projects

1. Which version of products liability does your state courts follow? Is it different from, or identical to, the *Second Restatement*'s § 402A?

2. Has your state legislature enacted any products liability statutes? If so, how are they similar to the elements discussed in this chapter? How are they different?

3. How does a products liability case differ from a negligence case?

4. Read the complete case of *Greenman v. Yuba Power Products* in Appendix C. How did this landmark case change tort law?

5. Bring to class the warranty and the warning from a product you have recently purchased. Is the language similar? Can they be read together?

Internet Resources

This chapter focuses on Products Liability. To learn more about products liability, the following sites can be accessed:

General Information
http://www.personal-injury-law.com
http://www.hg.org/torts.html

OSHA
http://www.osha.gov

Products Liability
http://www.productslaw.com

Toxic Torts
http://www.tox.law.com

United States Product Safety Commission
http://www.cpsc.gov

Directory of Experts
http://www.expertpages.com

Internet Drug Index
http://www.rxlist.com

Mayo Clinic
http://www.mayoclinic.com

For additional resources, visit our Web site at
www.paralegal.delmar.cengage.com

CHAPTER 10

SPECIAL TORT ACTIONS

CHAPTER OUTLINE

§ 10.1 Introduction
§ 10.2 Nuisances
§ 10.3 Public Nuisances
§ 10.4 Remedies for Nuisances
§ 10.5 Survival Statutes and Wrongful Death Statutes
§ 10.6 Wrongful Birth

EQUAL·JUSTICE·UNDER·LAW

————————————— ‹ ◆ › —————————————

All that makes existence valuable to any one
depends on the enforcement of restraints
upon the actions of other people.
JOHN STUART MILL

§ 10.1 Introduction

You have now reached an area of torts that is often overlooked in paralegal education. These forgotten torts are just as important as the major torts of negligence and strict liability.

Special tort actions include nuisance, which involves issues of both tort and property law, and negligence per se, which is often a statutory tort. Tort litigation also often includes wrongful death actions, which are usually associated with negligence claims. Within the past thirty years a new, related tort, *wrongful life*, has emerged in the appellate courts. Another rapidly developing area of modern tort law is so-called toxic torts, which involve hazardous substances, toxic waste disposal, and other environmental issues.

This chapter investigates these special tort actions. Much of our discussion will incorporate negligence and absolute liability theories. Specifically, the following torts and issues are discussed:

- Private nuisances
- "Coming to the nuisance" defense
- Public nuisances
- Nuisances per se
- Nuisance remedies: abatement, damages, and injunctions
- Wrongful death and survival statutes
- Wrongful birth actions.

§ 10.2 Nuisances

A **nuisance** is an unreasonable or unlawful use of one's real property that injures another person or interferes with another person's use of his or her real property. Nuisances are defined by common law and by statute. There are two types of nuisances: private and public. Occasionally, the same

nuisance
1. Anything that annoys or disturbs unreasonably, hurts a person's use of his or her property, or violates the public health, safety, or decency. 2. Use of land that does anything in definition 1.

private nuisance
A tort that requires a showing of special harm to you or your property and allows the recovery of damages for the harm as well as an injunction.

activity constitutes both a private and a public nuisance. These are sometimes called *mixed nuisances.*

Private Nuisance Defined

A **private nuisance** occurs when someone (1) uses his or her land in such a way as to (2) unreasonably and substantially interfere with (3) another person's use and enjoyment of his or her land. The tortfeasor (defendant) is the land user whose activities offend his or her neighbors. The neighboring land user(s) (plaintiff[s]) sue the tortfeasor for engaging in a private nuisance. The second element in commission of a private nuisance, unreasonable and substantial interference, is the most susceptible of interpretation.

Unreasonable and Substantial Defined

Whether the tortfeasor's use of real estate is unreasonable and substantially interferes with another's land use is usually defined in terms of offensiveness. The critical question is: How offensive is the tortfeasor's land use? Offensiveness is determined by applying the reasonable person standard. Would a reasonable person with ordinary sensitivities find the tortfeasor's land use unreasonably offensive? If so, then the tortfeasor has unreasonably and substantially interfered with the plaintiff's use and enjoyment of his or her land. Therefore, the tortfeasor has committed a private nuisance.

Community Standard

The reasonable person standard is normally a community standard. In other words, it asks how people living in the community in which the alleged nuisance is taking place would react to the activity. This *reasonable community* reaction supposedly evaluates whether the tortfeasor's land use is unreasonable and a substantial interference with neighboring land uses. The finder of fact, usually a jury, makes this determination.

Use and Enjoyment

Use and enjoyment is a term of art in nuisance law. The two are always used together. The term *use* would be sufficient, but *enjoyment* imparts an emotional aspect to nuisance law. The alleged nuisance activity ruins the pleasure neighbors gain through the ways in which they use their real estate. This seems to make the tortfeasor's activities more blameworthy.

Classic Examples

There are many common examples of private nuisances to which to apply the elements just explained. These situations can be classified in broad categories: (1) physical effects on land; (2) health hazards or offending sensibilities; and (3) unwanted associations with neighboring uses.

Physical Effects on Land

Neighboring land users often complain if a tortfeasor's use of realty creates constant vibrations, pollution of water or soil, destruction of crops, flooding, excessive clutter, or unwanted excavations.

Ground Vibrations For example, suppose a manufacturing plant next door to Jenny's house operates twenty-four hours a day. This plant uses heavy machinery that produces powerful vibrations. These vibrations can be felt for hundreds of feet in all directions. The ground actually shakes slightly from the effect. Over several years, this phenomenon has caused Jenny's house foundation to crack. She would argue that these constant vibrations were an unreasonable and substantial interference with her use and enjoyment of her home. In short, the manufacturing plant would be creating a private nuisance.

Pollution of Water or Soil Consider another example. Suppose a chemical processing plant dumped its waste waters onto vacant land behind its buildings. These wastes seeped into the soil and polluted underground water supplies. The chemicals also spread across the soil surface onto neighboring lands, making them sterile. These are unreasonable and substantial interferences with the neighboring land owners' use and enjoyment of their realty. The chemical plant has produced a private nuisance.

Crop Destruction Take another hypothetical. The Blackout Power Company burns coal to produce electricity. Thick, black smoke belches from its tall smokestacks. As the wind disperses the smoke, coal dust settles on the neighbors' land, upon which grow corn and soybeans. The neighbors' crops grow poorly because of the coal dust on their leaves. Blackout's activity is an unreasonable and substantial interference with the neighboring farmers' use and enjoyment of their land. A private nuisance exists.

Flooding Flooding can also be a private nuisance. Suppose Deatra lives along a small creek. Several miles downstream, another land owner erects a dam to create a small lake for fishermen. However, the lake extends beyond the downstream user's land and floods Deatra's property, including her home. Although this case could involve issues of *riparian* (water) law, in terms of nuisance law, the downstream land owner has unreasonably and substantially interfered with Deatra's use and enjoyment of her real estate by flooding her out.

Excessive Clutter Few individuals would ever want to live adjacent to a junkyard or trash dump. Most people find such land uses to be offensive to many senses, one of which is sight. Having to look at junk or trash piled high next door can be aesthetically depressing. Many courts have found such uses to be private nuisances for this reason; although, more commonly, neighbors are also offended by refuse odors.

Unwanted Excavations Excavation companies sometimes purchase soil from vacant lot owners to haul away and use in construction projects. These excavations leave deep and, for some people, unsightly holes in the vacant lots. Suppose Andy's house is next to several vacant lots that have been excavated in this fashion. A quick search of the case law reveals that several courts would find this to be a private nuisance.

Health Hazards or Offending Sensibilities

sensibilities† In nuisance law, ways in which people's physical and emotional sense are affected.

People's **sensibilities** are ways in which their physical senses (sight, hearing, smell, taste, and touch) and their emotional senses (what they find disgusting, repulsive, threatening, and so forth) are affected. Private nuisances offend a person's sensibilities. They can also create health hazards.

Noxious Odors Land uses that produce harmful, obnoxious odors are frequent candidates as private nuisances, as in the previous trash-dump example. Suppose Nicki lives next to a livestock farm, a chemical processing plant, or a paper mill. These may not create any bad smells at all, but sometimes they emit a powerful and dreadful stench. Much nuisance litigation has involved offensive odors produced by activities such as these.

Smoke and Dust Smoke and dust emissions can produce serious health hazards for neighbors. Consider the Blackout Power Company example. Neighbors who breathe the coal-dust-laden air could suffer severe respiratory injury. If this happened, the courts would probably rule that Blackout was involved in creating a private nuisance.

Excessive Noise and Temperatures Land uses that produce excessive noise can harm neighbors' health. In nuisance litigation, many plaintiffs have complained of sleeploss, nervousness, and associated physical and emotional symptoms because of a neighbor's excessive noise. Imagine how Eric might be affected if he lived next to a motor-vehicle race track that ran late-night races on weeknights.

Factories producing extreme heat might also pose health problems for neighbors. Persons living adjacent to steel mills have sued for nuisance because of the high temperatures produced by the blast furnaces. The heat from these operations can raise air temperatures to uncomfortable levels. When the heat becomes unreasonable, the courts may find private nuisances.

Toxic Tort Nuisances The disposal and transportation of hazardous wastes or toxic chemicals are frequently grounds for private nuisance actions. Underground or surface water supplies that are contaminated by leaking toxic-chemical dumps, or air that is filled with poisonous dusts (such as uranium dust vented from a nuclear power plant) are excellent examples of private nuisances. Much of the toxic tort litigation brought today involves nuisance actions.

Incessant Telephone Calls Creditors occasionally use intimidation tactics to coerce customers to pay delinquent accounts. A favorite technique is the late-night telephone call. The creditor might telephone a delinquent customer several times late at night, every day for weeks or even months, to try to persuade the patron to pay the overdue amounts. Customers subjected to such harassment often suffer emotional distress and related physical manifestations.

Courts routinely determine that such activity constitutes a private nuisance. It is an unreasonable interference with the customer's use and enjoyment of the privacy of his or her home life. In fact, plaintiffs besieged with incessant phone calls often sue the culprit under several causes of action—namely, the intentional torts of invasion of privacy or intentional infliction of emotional distress—along with nuisance.

Unwanted Associations with Neighboring Uses

For decades, land owners have rushed to the courthouse to file private nuisance actions against the owners of houses of ill repute, X-rated movie theaters, adult bookstores, and liquor or gambling establishments. These cases illustrate clearly the personal nature of offensiveness. Some persons simply cannot abide living in the vicinity of these types of activities. They do not wish to be associated with these land uses. These persons typically become plaintiffs in nuisance lawsuits in an attempt to drive out activities that they find repugnant.

In cases such as these, courts often struggle with community standards to decide if the activities are private nuisances. Are the plaintiffs overreacting, or are their objections reasonable? Would reasonable persons agree that having to live adjacent to establishments engaged in these pursuits is an unreasonable and substantial interference with the use and enjoyment of the realty? This is not an easy question to answer, as can be seen by reading some of the hundreds of appellate court opinions discussing the subject.

⟨♦⟩

The Case of the Country Club Nuisance

The success of a pro se litigant's action against a country club hinges on the applicable statute of limitations. While living on lands adjoining a country club is often considered desirable, these litigants would beg to differ.

SILVESTER
v.
SPRING VALLEY COUNTRY CLUB

Court of Appeals of South Carolina
344 S.C. 280, 543 S.E.2d 563
February 12, 2001

In 1983, the Silvesters purchased a residence in Spring Valley subdivision. The rear of their lot adjoins a portion of the Club's golf course. Water from the Club's land channels onto the Silvesters' lot, allegedly causing erosion, the deposit of trash, and a potentially hazardous condition due to standing water. ... The problem manifested itself shortly after the Silvesters occupied the house in 1984.

The Silvesters brought this action in April 1996. They alleged for a first cause of action a trespass occurring in 1992 when the Club constructed a french drainage system to collect and concentrate surface water, thereby exacerbating the Silvesters' drainage problem. ... For their second cause of action, the Silvesters allege the Club's actions constitute a continuing nuisance affecting the enjoyment of their land.

The action was called to trial on June 17, 1998, with the Silvesters proceeding *pro se.* Prior to selecting a jury, the court heard the Club's motion to dismiss. During argument on the motion, Mr. Silvester admitted they realized the severity of the water problem by 1991. ...

Mrs. Silvester argued the action should not be dismissed based on the statute of limitations because it was an ongoing nuisance. ...

The trial court granted the motion to dismiss based on the statute of limitations. The Silvesters appeal.

* * *

The Silvesters pled trespass as the first cause of action in their complaint. However, at the hearing before the trial court, the continuing nuisance claim was the only issue clearly addressed. ... We therefore find the grant of summary judgment to the Club on the trespass cause of action is not presented to this court as an issue appropriate for appellate review. ...

The Silvesters contend the trial court erred in granting the Club summary judgment on their continuing nuisance cause of action. We agree.

South Carolina follows the common enemy rule which allows a landowner to treat surface water as a common enemy and dispose of it as he sees fit. However, an exception to this rule prohibits a landowner from using his land in such a manner as to create a nuisance.

The traditional concept of a nuisance requires a landowner to demonstrate that the defendant unreasonably interfered with his ownership or possession of the land. The distinction between trespass and nuisance is that trespass is any intentional invasion of the plaintiff's interest in the exclusive possession of his property, whereas nuisance is a substantial and unreasonable interference with the plaintiff's use and enjoyment of his property.

A nuisance may be classified as permanent or continuing in nature. A continuing nuisance is defined as a nuisance that is intermittent or periodical and is described as one which occurs so often that it is said to be continuing although it is not necessarily constant or unceasing. A permanent nuisance may be expected to continue but is presumed to continue permanently, with no possibility of abatement. As to a permanent nuisance, such as a building or a railroad encroaching on a party's land, the injury is fixed and goes to the whole value of the land.

When the statute of limitations begins to run hinges on whether a nuisance is classified as permanent or continuing. When the nuisance is permanent in nature and only one cause of action may be brought for damages, the applicable statute of limitations bars the action if not brought within the statutory period after the first actionable injury. When the nuisance is continuing and the injury is abatable, the statute of limitations does not run merely from the original intrusion on the property and cannot be a complete bar. Rather, a new statute of limitations begins to run after each separate invasion of the property.

In discussing the limitations period applicable in a continuing nuisance action, our supreme court has stated:

> Since every continuance of a nuisance is a new nuisance, authorizing a fresh action, an action may be brought, for the recovery of all damages, resulting from the continuance of a nuisance, within the statutory period of the statute of limitations, for which no previous recovery has been had, even though the original cause of action is barred, unless the nuisance has been so long continued, as to raise the presumption of a grant, or in case of injury to real property, unless the plaintiff's right of entry is barred. ...

Furthermore, although the statute of limitations may bar a nuisance action for damages, it "is not a defense in an action based upon nuisance for injunctive relief since such statutes do not bar the equitable relief of injunction."

The Silvesters argue water channels from a man-made ditch dug by the Club onto their property. The Club maintains water channeling through a naturally occurring stream passes over a portion of the Silvesters' lot and only "occasionally" overflows their yard. However, Mr. Silvester testified at the hearing "there was an enormous amount of water coming through the property," and Mrs. Silvester stated "our property daily is being damaged." After reviewing the record, we find there exist genuine issues of material fact making summary judgment inappropriate in this case.

The Silvesters alleged a continuing nuisance and requested damages and injunctive relief. The trial court summarily applied the three year statute of limitations to the continuing nuisance cause of action without considering the possibility of abatement, the Club's alleged negligence, or the Silvesters' request for injunctive relief. Viewing the evidence in the light most favorable to the Silvesters, we agree the trial court erred in applying the statute of limitations to their continuing nuisance claim and accordingly reverse the grant of summary judgment on this issue.

... We find no evidence in the record the trial judge's ruling was based on or influenced by any bias against either the Silvesters or *pro se* litigants as a class.

Based on the foregoing, the order on appeal is affirmed as to the dismissal of the trespass cause of action and reversed and remanded as to the nuisance cause of action.

Case Questions

1. Do you think this case would have had a different outcome if the Silvesters had not appeared *pro se*? Explain.
2. What affect does classifying a nuisance as permanent or continuing have on the statute of limitations?

"Coming to the Nuisance" Defense

Often, a person will move into a neighborhood in which one of the activities previously described is already situated. In many cases, the manufacturer, trash dump, junkyard, or adult bookstore has been doing business in the same location for years. The plaintiff came to the area after the alleged nuisance was already there. When this happens, and the plaintiff

coming to the nuisance defense†
A defense to private nuisance lawsuits that may be used successfully when a plaintiff owns or uses land at a location in which the alleged nuisance activity was previously occurring. The plaintiff is said to have "come to the nuisance" and thus cannot recover against the defendant.

then sues for private nuisance, the defendant may plead the "coming to the nuisance" defense. The **coming to the nuisance** defense involves the plaintiff who owns or uses land at a location in which the alleged nuisance activity was already occurring. If the plaintiff came to the nuisance, then he or she cannot recover against the defendant. The defense is similar to the defense of assumption of risk, in that the plaintiff knew (or reasonably should have known) that the preexisting activity would offend him or her. Consequently, a reasonable person would not have chosen to buy or use land adjacent to a known, present, and distasteful land use next door. In essence, the plaintiff assumes the risk of obnoxiousness from the nuisance activity by coming to the place while knowing that the nuisance is already there, waiting to offend the plaintiff.

Private nuisance hypotheticals provide the reader with some of the earthiest factual situations in tort law. Students can easily relate to intrusions upon their senses or values. However, one must guard against identifying too strongly with the offended individual over the business allegedly creating the nuisance. As the following examples illustrate, each party in the nuisance story has its side to tell.

The Case of Intrusion on Hog Heaven

Incompatible land uses often make unhappy neighbors. Unfortunately, it is not always apparent that such incompatibilities will exist until after the activities have cohabited for some time. Then one of the land owners usually is harmed by the other, and a nuisance action enters the picture. As the case here illustrates, a business can create a nuisance through its own actions or those of its customers.

SHERK

v.

INDIANA WASTE SYSTEMS, INC.

Court of Appeals of Indiana
495 N.E.2d 815 (Ind. Ct. App. 1986)
July 31, 1986
Conover, Judge

Plaintiff-Appellant Dale J. Sherk (Sherk) appeals a negative judgment in his nuisance action against Defendants-Appellees Indiana Waste Systems, Inc. (IWS) and Prairie View Farms, Inc.

We reverse.

ISSUES

Sherk presents three issues for review. Because we reverse we consider only two issues. Restated, they are

1. whether the trial court erred in finding IWS and Prairie View were not responsible for noise generated by others, and
2. whether the trial court erred in finding IWS's use of the land was reasonable and thus a good defense to this action.

FACTS

Sherk raises hogs. IWS operates a landfill on land adjacent to Sherk's former hog breeding facility. IWS leases its land from Prairie View. Sherk's hogs suffered a 50% reduction in conception rates from the time IWS started its operation there. Eventually, Sherk had to close down his hog breeding facility at that location because of such losses.

Sherk, attributing that reduction to noise from the landfill operation, sued IWS and

Prairie View Farms, Inc. (hereinafter collectively IWS). Sherk alleged IWS operated its landfill in such a noisy manner it constituted a nuisance and damaged him.

The case was tried by the court. ...

The trial court found *inter alia* (1) noise generated by IWS's operation of its landfill did not cause Sherk's problem, (2) truck traffic increased as a result of the opening of the landfill, (3) noise emanating from the increased truck traffic caused the reduction in conception rates, and (4) IWS's operation of the landfill was reasonable. The trial court entered judgment against Sherk. He appeals.

* * *

Sherk contends the trial court erred when it concluded IWS was not responsible for the noise and vibration generated by the trash hauling trucks entering and leaving its landfill. Sherk also contends the trial court erred when it decided reasonableness of use is a defense to an action for a nuisance and IWS's use of its land is reasonable. ...

When deciding whether one's use of his property is a nuisance to his neighbors it is necessary to balance the competing interests of the landowners. In so doing we use a common sense approach. Mere annoyance or inconvenience will not support an action for a nuisance because the damages resulting therefrom are deemed *damnum absque injuria* in recognition of the fact life is not perfect. Thus, "reasonable use" of one's property may be a defense to a nuisance action where the use merely causes *incidental* injury to another. Where, however, one uses his property for his profit so as to practically confiscate or destroy his neighbor's property he should be compelled to respond in damages, for it can hardly be said such use is reasonable. Whether one's use of property is reasonable is determined by the effect such use has on neighboring property. Liability is imposed in those cases where the harm or risk thereto is greater than the owner of such property should be required to bear under the circumstances.

Sherk argues but for the landfill operation there would have been no noise obstructing the free use of his property as a hog breeding facility. Thus, he opines, IWS should be liable for the noise generated by the trash hauling trucks. IWS in turn argues because the trial court found its use of its property was reasonable IWS is absolved of any responsibility for its customers' noisy trucks.

... [A] business may be liable for the acts of its customers or others if acts by them upon the business property or in going to or leaving it obstruct a neighbor's use of his property.

The facts found by the trial court here show (1) the conception rate of Sherk's pigs ranged between 70% and 90% before the landfill began its operations; (2) the rate was reduced to 30% following the opening of the landfill; (3) the reduction in rate of conception was due to the noise generated by the trash hauling trucks traveling to and from the landfill.

It is apparent but for the landfill there substantially would have been no noisy truck traffic in the vicinity of Sherk's pigs, and they would have continued breeding successfully in the peace and tranquility which they apparently require. The interference here is more than a mere annoyance or incidental harm. The use of IWS's property has destroyed the usefulness of Sherk's property as a hog breeding facility. The evidence and all reasonable inferences from it leads inescapably to the conclusion IWS's use of its property was unreasonable in relation to Sherk's use of his property as a hog breeding facility.

Because the trial court found no liability, it made no findings as to damages. While a proper remedy for nuisance may consist of damages or injunction or some combination of the two ... , Sherk seeks no injunction, only damages.

Reversed, and remanded for hearing and determination as to Sherk's damages only.

Case Questions

1. Do you agree with the court that IWS's use of its property was unreasonable? Why or why not?

2. Suppose that IWS had begun operating its landfill before Sherk established his hog breeding facility. Would the outcome of the case be different? Explain.

— HYPOTHETICALS —

Harvey Foreman bought a house in a residential subdivision in 1989. His real estate is adjacent to seventy acres of pasture land. In 1990, the pasture was sold to the Waste Away Company, which erected a trash processing plant and landfill in 1991. This plant began compacting trash for landfill use as well as incinerating trash. Early in 1992 Harvey began smelling unpleasant odors and smoke from the trash piles and smoke-stacks. In warm weather, the smell was extremely nasty. Fumes seemed to hover all around the neighborhood. Does Harvey have a cause of action for private nuisance?

When Harvey bought his home in 1989, he assumed that he would be living next door to pasture land, which is free from odors and has a clear, natural view. He probably anticipated that wildlife or livestock would graze the realty next door. This rustic expectation was shattered in 1990 when Waste Away transformed the land into a trash processing facility and landfill.

Using the private nuisance formula, first ask whether Waste Away's use of its real estate unreasonably and substantially interfered with Harvey's use and enjoyment of his property. Every day, odors and smoke floated across Harvey's land from the trash facility. The neigh-borhood became inundated with the foul smell of piled or burning trash. Reasonable persons with ordinary sensibilities (or, as it is some-times called, sensitivities) would find such odors and smoke to be offensive. Most subdivision residents in Harvey's community could reasonably be expected to react adversely to the invading stench. Waste Away has created a private nuisance.

* * *

The Sanctified Brethren Church purchased a building site for a new cathedral in July 1991. Across the street, one block away, were several taverns, an X-rated movie theatre, and an adult bookstore. Once con-struction began, members of the church filed suit against the owners of these businesses, claiming private nuisance. Would the church's lawsuit be successful?

No. Assuming that the church could first prove that these businesses constituted a private nuisance, the businesses could avail themselves of the coming to the nuisance defense. The church knew that these businesses were already located in the neighborhood when it purchased its building site. The church voluntarily decided to situate its cathedral within close proximity of activities that church members found offensive. Therefore, the church would fail in its lawsuit. ■

There are literally thousands of different factual patterns involving private nuisance to be found in the court reporters. This tort can be quite interesting to study, given the variety and peculiarity of the fact scenarios that allegedly produce nuisances. One might wish to consult the index to the *American Law Reports* series, published by The Lawyers' Cooperative Publishing Company. (These are abbreviated as ALR, ALR2d, ALR3d, ALR4th, ALR5th, and ALR Fed.) Each series contains many annotations involving different examples of nuisances. These are often entertaining as well as enlightening—one reason that nuisance is frequently regarded as a "fun" tort subject in law study. Table 10-1 lists the elements to private nuisance.

TABLE 10-1
Elements of private nuisance

Elements	Examples	Defense
Activity that unreasonably and substantially interferes with use and enjoyment of another's land	Physical effects on land (vibrations, pollution, crop destruction, flooding, junk clutter, or excavations)	Coming to the nuisance
Unreasonable and *substantial* defined by community standard (reasonable person standard) regarding offensiveness of activity	Health hazards and offending sensibilities (noxious odors, smoke, dust, extreme noise or temperature, incessant telephone calling)	Plaintiff arrives to use land after nuisance activity already exists
Defendant's activity must proximately cause plaintiff's injuries	Unwanted associations with neighboring uses (prostitution houses, distributors of explicit sexual material, gambling institutions)	

§ 10.3 Public Nuisances

public nuisance†
Activity by the tortfeasor that unreasonably and substantially interferes with the public's use and enjoyment of legal rights common to the public.

In addition to private nuisances, there are also public nuisances. A **public nuisance** is a land use that injures the public at large rather than just a single individual. A public nuisance unreasonably interferes with the public's enjoyment of legal rights common to the public. The elements of public nuisance may be broken down as: (1) The tortfeasor's activity that (2) unreasonably and substantially interferes with (3) the public's use and enjoyment of legal rights common to the public.

Unlike private nuisances, which can adversely affect a single person, a public nuisance must harm the general public. More than one person *must* be affected (or, at least, potentially affected) by the alleged nuisance activity. This does not require a multitude of angry citizens. Residents of a single neighborhood would suffice.

The standard of unreasonable and substantial interference is identical to that used in private nuisances, except that the interference must be to the public rather than a sole plaintiff.

Use and Enjoyment of Common Legal Rights

The use and enjoyment element in public nuisance is significantly different from the one discussed in private nuisances. With public nuisances, the tortfeasor's obnoxious land use interferes with the public's common legal rights, such as the right to peaceably assemble in public places, the right to use public streets and sidewalks without being subjected to offensive activities, or the right to safe and healthy conditions in one's neighborhood.

Governments as Plaintiffs

police power The government's right and power to set up and enforce laws to provide for the safety, health, and general welfare of the people.

Although citizens often file public nuisance complaints with their local governmental agencies, it is the government, through its municipal governing bodies (e.g., city council, county commissioners) or its prosecuting attorneys, that sues defendants alleged to be committing public nuisances. This is because the government represents the public at large and must enforce its citizens' legal rights against tortfeasors. At common law, or by statute or, in some states, by state constitutional provision, state and local governments have the authority to protect their citizens from public nuisances. The source of this power is the states' **police powers**, which give governments authority to file lawsuits or enact legislation to protect the public's health, welfare, safety, or morals. These are usually very broad powers that give governments considerable flexibility to forbid certain offensive activities.

Types of Public Nuisances

Almost all public nuisances are defined by statute or ordinance. Many such laws focus on land uses *that legislators believe* a majority of the population would find offensive, unhealthy, or immoral. The reader may know from personal experience that this belief may be unfounded or exaggerated. That, of course, depends upon whether one agrees or disagrees with what the government has labeled a public nuisance. Common targets of public nuisance laws include institutions devoted to (1) gambling, (2) prostitution, (3) distribution of sexually explicit materials, (4) sale of alcohol, or (5) toxic waste management. Other typical public nuisances include (1) allowing certain weeds or poisonous plants to grow on one's land; (2) failing to comply with health code provisions by keeping one's residence clean and vermin-free; and (3) keeping unrestrained wild or vicious animals on one's property. However, public nuisances may also include many of the same activities discussed in the private nuisances section.

Mixed Nuisances

mixed nuisance A nuisance that is both public and private.

Often, the same activity can constitute both a private and a public nuisance. These are sometimes called **mixed nuisances**. Apply this rule of thumb in such cases: The greater the number of persons adversely affected by an allegedly offensive land use, the more likely it will be considered a public, as well as a private, nuisance.

Nuisances Per Se

nuisance per se†
That which is considered a nuisance at all times and no matter the circumstances, regardless of location or surroundings.

Courts often consider activities violating public nuisance statutes to be **nuisances per se**. *Per se* is Latin meaning "by itself." In tort law, it usually means that some behavior has violated a statute, and therefore the defendant is automatically liable. Sometimes courts, in the common law, decree that certain conduct is per se tortious. Negligence per se is an example. Per se nuisances have also been established by common law court decisions.

A public nuisance per se is an activity that violates the statute and is automatically considered a public nuisance. The tortfeasor thus loses from the start of litigation, simply by violating the statute. Statutes (and, rarely, common law) may also declare certain private nuisances to be per se nuisances.

"Coming to the Nuisance" Not a Defense

Generally, courts do not recognize the coming to the nuisance defense in public nuisance cases. This defense focuses on the individual plaintiff who purchases or uses land next to a preexisting, private nuisance activity. Public nuisances, by definition, affect the public at large, and the very existence or continuation of the public nuisance activity is considered harmful, whether it was preexisting or not.

As *Jacobs* demonstrates, what constitutes a public nuisance or a nuisance per se is generally a question of common law interpretation and statutory construction. But underlying questions of substance and form are the value judgments implicit in all nuisance per se or public nuisance cases. The following examples present such choices. Despite the temptation to become caught up in "good" versus "bad," one must concentrate on the legal elements and their application to the facts. However, the remedy of ordering an injunction may involve a balancing of interests.

‹ ◆ ›

The Case of the Door-to-Door Solicitation

Many people commonly think of door-to-door salespersons as nuisances, but the law does not automatically define them as such. As the following case suggests, not all forms of solicitation are included in public nuisance ordinances.

JACOBS v. CITY OF JACKSONVILLE

U.S. District Court, Middle District of Florida
762 F. Supp. 327 (M.D. Fla. 1991)
April 8, 1991

Moore, II, District Judge

This cause was tried before the Court on March 11, 1990. ... [T]he Court now issues the following findings of fact and conclusions of law.

* * *

Plaintiff, Jerry L. Jacobs, does business under the fictitious name of Youth Opportunities Unlimited (hereinafter "Y.O.U."), and is a person who, personally and through his employees, sells or offers for sale merchandise by traveling from door-to-door, while carrying such merchandise. Y.O.U. is a for-profit organization which derives income through the sale of cookies, candy, and other items. These sales are conducted primarily by teenagers who are Y.O.U. members. Plaintiff holds a city permit to operate as a peddler of merchandise.

* * *

Plaintiff and the Y.O.U. salespersons conduct the door-to-door activities in various neighborhoods in Jacksonville on a rotating basis; as a result, sales in any particular neighborhood are made no more than a few times per year. Each individual Y.O.U. product item is sold to the consumer for $4.00. ... No evidence was introduced to show that a large number of the residences solicited found Y.O.U.'s sales activities to be annoying or injurious, although the evidence did show that Y.O.U. salespersons are occasionally unwelcome at a few residences.

* * *

The City of Jacksonville, through Officer J.P. Baptist of the Jacksonville Sheriff's Office, has threatened Plaintiff with arrest under [Jacksonville ordinance] § 250.303, for engaging in residential door-to-door peddling activities without invitation. ...

In most instances, Plaintiff has not been expressly "requested or invited" by the owner or occupant of the private residence before engaging in door-to-door sales activity. Plaintiff does not solicit at any private residence where a "No Solicitation" sign is visible.

... The Court finds that Plaintiff is a "peddler" as defined in the Code, ... subject to the prohibition on door-to-door peddling set forth in J.O.C. § 250.303.

* * *

Under Florida law, unless a homeowner manifests externally in some manner his or her wish to remain unmolested by the visits of solicitors or peddlers, a solicitor or peddler may take ... an implied invitation to call upon residences ... . (*Prior v. White*, 132 Fla. 1, 180 So. 347, 355 (1938)). In *Prior*, the Florida Supreme

Court invalidated an anti-peddling ordinance of New Smyrna Beach, Florida, as applied to the door-to-door sales activities of a Fuller Brush Company salesman. The New Smyrna ordinance was virtually identical to the Jacksonville ordinance now at issue. The court held that peddling and soliciting in New Smyrna was not a public nuisance because custom and usage established an implied invitation to solicit sales at private residences, and therefore could not be punished as a crime or misdemeanor. The court further held that a municipality cannot, through an attempted exercise of its police powers, declare by ordinance or otherwise that an activity is a public nuisance, when in fact such activity is not proved to be a public nuisance.

Prior v. White is still good law in Florida, never having been overruled by the Florida Supreme Court. Recent cases also have held that a municipality may not declare an activity to be a public nuisance unless that activity does in fact constitute a public nuisance. In addition, Florida courts continue to recognize the implied invitation theory. Since the principles set forth in *Prior* remain part of the law of Florida, *Prior* is binding upon this Court in its interpretation of Florida law. ... Thus, the facts of each case must be examined carefully to determine whether the type of door-to-door peddling engaged in by the parties in that case constitutes a public nuisance.

A public nuisance is defined as an activity that "violates public rights, subverts public order, decency or morals, or causes inconvenience or damage to the public generally." It is not completely clear under *Prior* which party bears the burden of proving that peddling is or is not a public nuisance. ...

In this case, door-to-door peddling in Jacksonville, Florida has not been proved to be a public nuisance. The Defendants have introduced virtually no evidence that proves peddling in Jacksonville by Y.O.U. or by others is a public nuisance, and have made little attempt to make such a showing. ...

Even assuming the Plaintiff bears the burden of proving that door-to-door peddling ... is not a public nuisance, the Court finds that Plaintiff has met this burden. The evidence introduced at trial showed that Y.O.U. sold 90,000 items in Jacksonville in 1990, an average of roughly one item per residence solicited. The evidence showed that a sizeable number, approximately one-half, of the residences solicited made a purchase from Y.O.U. Thus, thousands of customers in Jacksonville evidently did not find Plaintiff's organization materially annoying to them personally, which demonstrates that Y.O.U.'s activities do not materially inconvenience the public at large or subvert public order. ... Thus, Plaintiff has affirmatively proved, in the absence of any effective rebuttal evidence by the Defendants, that Y.O.U.'s activities do not inconvenience the public in a manner that amounts to a public nuisance. Accordingly, under the authority of *Prior v. White,* the ordinance is unreasonable and an invalid exercise of the police power as applied to the Plaintiff and the Y.O.U. organization.

* * *

ORDERED AND ADJUDGED:

... Defendants are permanently enjoined from arresting or prosecuting Plaintiff or any members of Youth Opportunities Unlimited under color of Jacksonville Ordinance Code § 250.303.

Case Questions

1. How does the court's definition of a public nuisance differ from that discussed in this chapter?
2. Do you agree with the court that the plaintiff's activities did not violate the ordinance? Explain.

— HYPOTHETICALS

Armstrong McCarter has an apiary in his backyard. He lives in a suburban neighborhood. Several hundred honeybees congregate in Armstrong's hives. The bees produce honey that Armstrong sells at local groceries. Frequently, children in the area have been stung by honeybees. Parents complained to Armstrong, but he simply shrugged off each incident, stating that there was no proof that his bees were responsible. However, there were no other honeybee colonies in the neighborhood. A town ordinance prohibits the keeping of wildlife within the city limits. Has Armstrong committed a public nuisance, a private nuisance, or a nuisance per se?

Armstrong's use of his land (maintaining an apiary) substantially and unreasonably interfered with his neighbors' use and enjoyment of the public streets and sidewalks in the area, as well as their own realty. Children were often stung by honeybees, and the only large honeybee colony in the neighborhood was Armstrong's. A trier-of-fact could reasonably infer that Armstrong's bees were responsible for the attacks. This would be a private nuisance. A local governmental agency could sue Armstrong for public nuisance. Reasonable persons would find these bee encounters to be offensive and dangerous. The public at large was threatened by Armstrong's *ferae naturae.* The bees unreasonably and substantially interfered with citizens' use of public streets and sidewalks. Under its police power, the local government would have authority to sue Armstrong for public nuisance.

Armstrong also violated the local ordinance prohibiting the keeping of wildlife within the city limits. This constitutes a nuisance per se, giving the town government another cause of action against Armstrong.

* * *

Darling Davis operates a massage parlor across from the local public high school. Although there is no evidence of prostitution at the establishment, Davis offers nude massages, during which both customers and masseurs disrobe. From across the street, high-school students can see clearly through the windows of Davis's building. Is Davis engaged in a public nuisance?

Davis's use of her land could adversely affect the students. The erotic views could disrupt school activities as children (and adults) cluster around windows to catch the revealing sights next door. Arguably, this is an unreasonable and substantial interference with a public right—namely, the right to use the public school for educational pursuits. Under its police powers, the municipal government could sue Davis for public nuisance. ∎

Admittedly, cases such as Davis's involve value judgments and presume a threat to the public morals. One may agree or disagree with the alleged public threat produced by a massage parlor next to a school. However, many cases have involved exactly these fact situations, and courts promptly conclude that public nuisances have occurred.

Table 10-2 lists the elements of public nuisances, mixed nuisances, and nuisances per se.

Elements	Examples	Defense
Activity that unreasonably and substantially interferes with public's use and enjoyment of legal rights common to public at large	Prostitution establishments Pornography distributors	Coming to the nuisance *not* a defense to public nuisances
Plaintiff is governmental agency responsible for protecting public interest harmed by public nuisance activity	Historically, gambling and alcohol establishments were often considered public nuisances, although not normally at the present time	
State and local governments have authority to litigate public nuisances under general police powers to protect public health, safety, morals, and welfare	Allowing noxious weeds to grow on one's land Failing to comply with public health statutes Keeping unrestrained wild animals on one's land	
Mixed nuisances include public and private nuisances		Coming to the nuisance defense effective against private nuisance portion of mixed nuisance actions
Nuisances per se are nuisance activities that violate statutes or ordinances		Coming to the nuisance defense not usually effective against nuisance per se actions

TABLE 10-2 Elements of public nuisances, mixed nuisances, and nuisances per se

§ 10.4 Remedies for Nuisances

When one has identified a private or public nuisance, what does one do about it? In other words, what remedies are available to plaintiffs against defendants? **Remedies** are the relief that plaintiffs receive against

remedy The means by which a right is enforced or satisfaction is gained for a harm done. The means by which a violation of rights is prevented, redressed, or compensated.

damages Money that a court orders paid to a person who has suffered damage (a loss or harm) by the person who caused the injury.

equitable relief (remedy)† A remedy available in equity; generally non-monetary relief.

injunction A judge's order to a person to do or to refrain from doing a particular thing.

mandamus (Latin) "We command." A *writ of mandamus* is a court order that directs a public official or government department to do something. It may be sent to the executive branch, the legislative branch, or a lower court.

abatement Reduction or decrease ... [or] complete elimination.

defendants in lawsuits. The most common remedy in tort actions is *money damages*, in which the defendant must pay the plaintiff a sum of money to satisfy the judgment. The trier-of-fact sets the amount owed after a trial has been held.

Other, nonmonetary remedies are also available for torts such as nuisance. These are called equitable remedies. **Equitable remedies** do not involve money damages; instead, the court orders the defendant to do (or, more commonly, *not* to do) something. When the court orders a defendant to do or not to do something, it is called an **injunction**. When a court orders a governmental official to perform a non-discretionary act, this is called a **mandamus** order.

For centuries, money damages were considered inappropriate in nuisance cases. Courts would apply only equitable remedies. In nuisance law, the most common equitable remedies include (1) abatement and (2) injunction, although now money damages are occasionally permitted in nuisance cases.

Abatement

In nuisance cases, abatement is the most common remedy plaintiffs seek. With **abatement**, the defendant is ordered to cease, or *abate*, the nuisance activity. Abatement is often permanent. The defendant must desist from conducting the nuisance activity after a judgment for abatement is entered. This provides complete relief for the plaintiff, because the nuisance activity will be discontinued. Abatement can create harsh economic consequences for defendants, but the public policy behind abatement is clear: Nuisance tortfeasors have injured someone (or, if the public, many people). As long as the nuisance continues, the plaintiff(s) will continue to be hurt. The only certain solution is to stop the nuisance altogether.

Money Damages

When abatement could impose an unreasonably severe economic burden upon the nuisance tortfeasor, courts have broken with the ancient common law tradition and awarded plaintiffs money damages instead of abatement. This way, the plaintiffs can be compensated for their injuries produced by the nuisance activities, and the defendant can survive (economically) by staying in business, even though the nuisance also continues. Courts using this alternative are usually attempting to balance interests between conflicting land uses.

Injunctions

Courts enforce abatement through injunctive relief. *Injunctions* are court orders to defendants to cease and desist from engaging in nuisance activities. There are two types of injunctions: (1) temporary injunctions, including temporary restraining orders (TROs); and (2) permanent injunctions.

Temporary Injunctions

temporary restraining order (TRO)
A judge's order to a person to not take a certain action during the period prior to a full hearing on the rightness of the action.

Temporary injunctions are often used from the time a plaintiff files suit until the first court hearing. The plaintiff, in his or her complaint, asks the court to issue a **temporary restraining order (TRO)**, forbidding the defendant from conducting an alleged nuisance activity until a court hearing can be held to determine if the activity constitutes a nuisance. Under most rules of civil procedure, TROs may be issued for up to ten days, while the court convenes a hearing to decide if a nuisance has occurred. After the hearing, if the evidence convinces the judge that a nuisance is happening, the court may order further temporary injunctive relief, banning the defendant's nuisance activity until a trial on the merits may be held.

The purpose of temporary injunctions is to protect the plaintiff from further harm if a nuisance is in fact occurring. Plaintiffs often must post bonds to compensate the defendant if the court or jury later decides that the defendant did not engage in a nuisance. This is to protect the defendant from economic losses suffered while the injunctions were in effect and the defendant was not permitted to conduct the nuisance activity (which could mean lost profits or extra expenses). The court must balance the hardship to the defendant against the interference suffered by the plaintiff.

permanent injunction†
Abatement orders instructing the defendant to permanently stop doing the nuisance activity. Usually issued after a full hearing.

contempt
1. An act that obstructs a court's work or lessens the dignity of the court.…
2. A willful disobeying of a judge's command or official court order.

Permanent Injunctions

Permanent injunctions are abatement orders instructing the defendant to permanently stop doing the nuisance activity. They are usually issued after a trial on the merits, once the trier-of-fact has concluded that a nuisance exists. If the defendant fails to obey a permanent injunction by continuing the nuisance, the court can punish the defendant by holding him or her in **contempt**. This punishment may involve monetary fines or even imprisonment.

The Case of the Polluting Toll Booth

Federal and state statutes often provide private citizens and public agencies with authority to litigate against public agencies concerning public or private nuisances. Private citizens may enforce nuisance actions under the Clean Air Act, Clean Water Act, and a variety of other environmental-protection statutes. However, there are certain precise statutory requirements to follow in order to proceed with these actions. This case clearly demonstrates the difficulties a pro se litigant can encounter in handling complex legal matters.

UNITED STATES ENVIRONMENTAL PROTECTION AGENCY

v.

THE PORT AUTHORITY OF NEW YORK AND NEW JERSEY, et al.

United States District Court, S.D. New York
162 F.Supp.2d 173
March 30, 2001

Plaintiffs Kevin McKeown ("McKeown") and his organization No More Tolls (collectively "plaintiffs") commenced this *pro se* citizen's suit against defendants, state authorities and officials responsible for operating toll roads, bridges and tunnels in New York, New Jersey, Delaware and Maryland, alleging that they operate and maintain toll booth facilities in violation of the Clean Air Act, ("CAA"), the Clean Water Act ("CWA"), the Resource Conservation and Recovery Act ("RCRA"), Occupational Safety and Health Administration ("OSHA") regulations, Federal Highway Administration regulations, nuisance law, and civil rights law.

* * *

Plaintiff No More Tolls is a public interest organization in Washington D.C. It is "dedicated to the protection and enhancement of the environment of the United States. ... [I]t supports effective enforcement of Federal and State CAA, CWA, RCRA, and other Federal and State laws." Plaintiff McKeown is the Executive Director of No More Tolls.

Defendants are state authorities and their directors who are responsible for the administration of public transportation including the operation of toll booths in New York (the "New York defendants"), New Jersey (the "New Jersey defendants"), (the "Delaware defendants") and Maryland (the "Maryland defendants").

On November 29, 1999, plaintiffs sent defendants a Notice of Intent to Sue. The Notice of Intent to Sue states that plaintiffs believe defendants are violating the CAA, CWA and RCRA by operating toll booths.

On February 3, 2000, plaintiffs filed this action by order to show cause, requesting a temporary restraining order and a preliminary injunction.

* * *

The CAA, CWA and RCRA all permit a citizen to bring a civil action to enforce those statutes on their own behalf. ... Moreover, McKeown and No More Tolls have not offered any reason why the EPA and Browner are necessary parties. ("The [CAA] citizen suit provision contemplates actions against the Administrator where he fails to perform a non-discretionary act. Alternatively, the citizen, after giving sixty days notice to the Administrator, can proceed directly against the violator. When the plaintiff elects this later course, the Administrator has the right to intervene in the suit, but he is not required to be a participant in such litigation and his absence does not render the action infirm.")

Accordingly, defendants' motions to strike the EPA and Browner from the amended complaint are granted. ...

Defendants argue that the complaint should be dismissed for lack of standing because plaintiffs have not alleged an injury in-fact, or alternatively, that any alleged injury is not redressable by this action.

An organization such as No More Tolls may have standing to "seek judicial relief from injury to itself and to vindicate whatever rights and immunities the association itself may enjoy. ... No More Tolls, however, has not asserted injury to itself.

... The only known member of No More Tolls is McKeown. ...

The only personalized injuries alleged in the amended complaint are that McKeown "has sustained damages as a result of the operation of toll booths" and that "[d]efendant[s'] operation of toll booths damage the business, property and health of the [p]laintiff" in violation of antitrust laws. Neither of those allegations is concrete or particularized, nor do they constitute a "distinct and palpable injury."

* * *

Further, even if plaintiffs could establish that they have standing to sue, they failed to comply with the mandatory notice requirement with respect to the Maryland and New Jersey defendants.

* * *

Accordingly, the New Jersey defendants' motion to dismiss plaintiffs' CAA, CWA and RCRA claims for failure to comply with the mandatory notice provisions pursuant to those statutes is granted.

Even if plaintiffs had complied with the notice requirements, venue is improper as to the Maryland, New Jersey and Delaware defendants. Moreover, plaintiffs have failed to state a claim upon which relief can be granted.

* * *

The CAA was implemented to prevent and control air pollution by providing "[f]ederal financial assistance and leadership ... for the development of cooperative Federal, State, regional, and local programs to prevent and control air pollution."

* * *

Plaintiffs claim that defendants have violated the CAA by slowing "vehicular movement which unnecessarily increases toxic tailpipe emissions." However, the complaint does not identify any violations of specific emissions standards, or limitations under the CAA or legally enforceable strategies or commitments that the defendants made under a current SIP.

Plaintiffs also claim that toll booths are major sources of hazardous air pollutants under 42 U.S.C. The CAA defines a "major source" as a "stationary source" that emits or has the potential to emit considering controls, in the aggregate 10 tons per year or more of any hazardous air pollutant or 25 tons per year or more of any combination of hazardous air pollutants ..." (42 U.S.C. § 7412(a)(1)). A stationary source is defined as "any building, structure, facility, or installation which emits or may emit any air pollutant," (42 U.S.C. § 7411(a)(3)).

Plaintiffs do not allege that toll booths emit or have the potential to emit air pollutants. They claim that motor vehicles emit the air pollutants. Motor vehicles, however, are specifically excluded from the definition of stationary source.

* * *

Accordingly, defendants' motions to dismiss plaintiffs' CAA claims for failure to state a claim are granted.

Citizen suits under the CWA are permitted only to enforce "an effluent standard or limitation" or "an order issued by the [EPA] Administrator or a State with respect to such a standard or limitation" (33 U.S.C. § 1365(a)). Effluent standards and limitations are administratively established regulations of particular types of dischargers on the amounts of pollutants that may be discharged.

Plaintiffs assert that "[t]oll booth operators violate 'an effluent standard or limitation' under ... 33 U.S.C. [§] 1365(a)(1)(A) because of illegal and unpermitted discharges of leachate from toll booth locations," that "[d]efendants violate CWA Section 311 by continuing to cause the dimunition of water quality of the surface and subterranean waters by release of pollutants into the surface waters and ground waters under and adjacent to toll booth areas," ...

Plaintiffs' sweeping allegations do no charge defendants with violating any effluent standards or limitations.

* * *

Moreover, the "leachate" that plaintiffs claim is released from toll booths, including carbon monoxide, nitrogen oxide and sulfur, are air emissions and not water pollutants, covered by CWA.

* * *

For all of the above stated reasons, defendants' motions to dismiss plaintiffs' CWA claims are granted.

Case Questions

1. What were the fatal flaws in the plaintiff's claim?
2. Do the precise requirements of the environmental statutes interfere with their intent?

Review of Hypotheticals

Review the hypotheticals from the previous sections of this chapter. Consider which remedies are suitable. In class or study groups, one may wish to discuss whether money damages is an appropriate alternative to abatement. Table 10-3 restates the remedies available in nuisance lawsuits.

TABLE 10-3
Remedies for nuisances

Equitable Remedies	Money Damages
Abatement (permanent prohibition against nuisance activity)	Money damages may be awarded if abatement would put unreasonable economic burdens on the defendant
Temporary injunctions (forbidding nuisance activity during litigation process)	
Permanent injunctions (used for abatement)	

The Case of the Statutory Hangover

In this case, the reader is faced with an interesting question. Did a tavern owner violate a duty of care when it served four alcoholic beverages in an hour to a patron, who later was injured when his motorcycle fell over? The New York Supreme Court said, "No."

CSIZMADIA
v.
TOWN OF WEBB
Supreme Court, Appellate Division, Third Department, New York
735 N.Y.S.2d 222
December 20, 2001

After consuming a number of alcoholic beverages at defendant Daiker's Restaurant and Tavern owned by defendant Margaret Daiker (hereinafter collectively referred to as Daikers), plaintiff George Csizmadia (hereinafter plaintiff) rode his motorcycle in a northerly direction on State Route 28.

Defendant Michael Gaffney, a police officer for defendant Town of Webb in Herkimer County, was traveling south on Route 28 and encountered plaintiff traveling in the middle of the south bound lane. Gaffney avoided a head-on collision by pulling to the side of the road where he made a U-turn to follow plaintiff. He activated his emergency lights. When plaintiff failed to stop, Gaffney radioed to defendant Russel Brombacher, a police officer for defendant Town of Inlet in Hamilton County, for assistance. Gaffney then pursued plaintiff with both his emergency lights and siren activated. In response to Gaffney's call, Brombacher parked his police vehicle on a level stretch of Route 28, "crosswise" in the northbound lane, and activated the emergency lights on the vehicle. ... When plaintiff (who was riding on the sidewalk) was approximately 10 to 15 feet from Brombacher's vehicle, he swerved left, collided with the vehicle, and then struck the guardrail.

As relevant to this appeal, the fifth cause of action, by plaintiff Ilona Csizmadia (hereinafter Csizmadia) only, asserts a violation of General Obligations Law § 11-101(1) and Alcoholic Beverage Control Law § 65(2) (the Dram Shop Act) against Daikers in that Daikers served plaintiff when he was visibly intoxicated. Plaintiff and Csizmadia, derivatively, assert a cause of action against the Town of Inlet, Town of Inlet Police Department and Brombacher (hereinafter collectively referred to as defendants) claiming that they improperly, and with reckless disregard for the safety of plaintiff, blocked plaintiff's lane of travel causing him physical injuries and economic loss and resulting in loss of consortium to his wife.

We first affirm dismissal of Csizmadia's cause of action, based on the Dram Shop Act, against Daikers. To establish liability, Csizmadia must prove that Daikers furnished alcoholic beverages to her husband while he was visibly intoxicated. The deposition testimony of Daikers' manager and bartender concerning the condition of plaintiff was sufficient to shift the burden to Csizmadia to submit evidence in admissable form demonstrating a material issue of fact as to his visible intoxication. In the absence of direct evidence that plaintiff demonstrated signs of intoxication while at Daikers, Csizmadia asserts that sufficient circumstantial evidence exists. Her reliance on the bartender's affidavit that four drinks in an hour—the amount of alcohol served to plaintiff at Daikers—would be "overserving" is misplaced since "it is well known that the effects of alcohol consumption 'may differ greatly from person to person' ... and that tolerance for alcohol is subject to wide individual variation." Further, we find that unpersuasive Csizmadia's reliance on the fact that plaintiff's motorcycle fell over as he attempted to mount it to leave the parking lot to demonstrate circumstantially that he was visibly intoxicated when served. Not only was the motorcycle parked on a slope, but plaintiff admitted that (1) this had happened to him before, (2) he told the manager that he was "all right" following this incident and refused a ride home, (3) he had no difficulty operating his motorcycle after he left Daikers, and (4) he never stated to anyone that he was intoxicated at that time. ...

We next turn to the denial of defendant's motion for summary judgment. The liability of these defendants is not judged in accordance with ordinary negligence principles because Vehicle and Traffic Law § 1104 qualifiedly exempts authorized emergency vehicles from certain traffic laws when they are "involved in an emergency operation." If the conduct is otherwise privileged, liability can be invoked only if the conduct rises to the level of recklessness. ... It requires evidence that "the actor has intentionally done an act of an unreasonable character in disregard of a known or obvious risk that was so great as to make it highly probable that harm would follow" and has done so with conscious indifference to the outcome. In evaluating police conduct, an officer's "split-second weighing of choices" should not be second-guessed, and liability should not be imposed for conduct which amounts to "a mere failure of judgment." Given that Brombacher, in establishing the roadblock, followed the police guidelines in effect (except for contacting a superior), and provided an escape route for plaintiff should he have decided not to stop, we hold that the evidence proffered by plaintiffs is insufficient as a matter of law to predicate a finding of recklessness sufficient to impose liability. ...

Case Questions

1. What would the plaintiff Ilona Csizmadia have needed to establish to succeed on her cause of action under the Dram Shop Act?
2. How might the use of expert testimony have aided the plaintiff's case?

§ 10.5 Survival Statutes and Wrongful Death Statutes

survival statutes A state law that allows a lawsuit to be brought by a relative for a person who has just died. The lawsuit is based on the cause of action the dead person would have had.

wrongful death statutes [Statutes that allow] a lawsuit [to be] brought by the dependants of a dead person against the person who caused the death. Damages will be given to compensate the dependants for their loss if the killing was negligent or willful.

Under common law, when a plaintiff died his or her tort action also died, and the spouse and children would lose all right to recovery. To avoid this harsh result, all states have passed survival statutes.

Survival statutes allow recovery to families of persons killed by tortious actions. In this way the injured party's claim survives his or her death. If successful, damages are awarded to the decedent's estate. This is contrasted with **wrongful death statutes**, which give the surviving family members of a deceased tort victim a cause of action against the tortfeasor whose negligence or intentional torts resulted in the victim's death.

Typical Facts in Wrongful Death Cases

The factual pattern in wrongful death actions may be summarized as follows: (1) a tortfeasor commits a tort against the victim; (2) the victim dies as a result of the tortfeasor's actions; (3) the victim's spouse, children, estate, or person who relied on the deceased person for economic support, or all of them, sue the tortfeasor for wrongfully causing the victim's death.

Plaintiffs in Wrongful Death Actions

Under wrongful death statutes, the surviving family members, usually the victim's spouse or children, become the plaintiffs. However, some statutes allow the victim's parents or siblings to become plaintiffs. The victim's estate may also be permitted to sue the defendant for wrongful death damages under some statutes.

Damages

Wrongful death statutes usually define the types of damages that plaintiffs may recover against defendants. These damages include lost lifetime earnings potential and loss of **consortium**.

consortium†
The rights and duties of both husband and wife, resulting from marriage. They include companionship, love, affection, assistance, cooperation, and sexual relations.

Practical Application

Be sure to check the precise wording of the wrongful death statute in your jurisdiction. In some states, such as California, the statute of limitations for wrongful death runs from the date of death, not the date of the accident.

Lost Lifetime Earnings Potential

A tort victim's surviving family members may recover damages for the lost income that the victim would likely have earned had he or she not been killed by the tortfeasor. Wrongful death statutes usually define these damages in terms of the decedent's lost earnings potential based upon income at the time of death. This income base is projected over time. The future time period used is normally the victim's life expectancy, which is calculated from insurance actuarial tables. The projected earnings potential is usually adjusted for the victim's projected living expenses, had he or she survived. An economist is usually hired as an expert witness to introduce this evidence at trial.

Loss of Consortium

Wrongful death statutes often permit a tort victim's surviving family to recover damages for the lost love and companionship of the decedent. This is similar to pain and suffering damages. However, many statutes do not allow recovery of such damages. Wrongful death statutes (or courts interpreting them) often label this type of damages **loss of consortium**. Many statutes define *consortium* as both economic and intangible benefits lost to a victim's surviving family because of the victim's death. The intangible element could include lost love, companionship, and even the survivors' mental anguish upon losing a loved one.

loss of consortium†
The loss of one of a spouse's duties. If such loss results from a tort, damages are sometimes given to one spouse to compensate for this loss of consortium.

Defenses

In wrongful death actions, the tortfeasor may use any defense applicable to the specific tort that produced the victim's injury. For example, suppose the victim had been contributorily or comparatively negligent, or assumed the risk of the defendant's actions that killed the victim. Suppose the tortfeasor killed the victim while acting in self-defense or defense of others. The tortfeasor may escape liability for wrongfully causing the victim's death if any of the suitable tort defenses apply in the case. Defenses are available in a wrongful death action just as if the victim were still alive and, as plaintiff, were suing the defendant.

A Case of "Death-Before-Litigation"

Some issues that come before appellate courts seem to have obvious answers. Some are so obvious, in fact, that one wonders why an appeal was necessary to answer them. The Montana Supreme Court may have been thinking this very question as it wrote the following straightfaced opinion, in response to a perfectly serious Ninth Circuit Court of Appeals query. Note Justice Gray's remarkable judicial restraint in avoiding humorous gibes that a lesser jurist might have felt compelled to include in the opinion. (Case questions are omitted following the case, as there is nothing left to ask.)

CARROLL v. W.R. GRACE & CO.

Supreme Court of Montana

830 P.2d 1253 (Mont. 1992)
January 14, 1992
Gray, Justice

This case is before us on certified questions from the Ninth Circuit Court of Appeals concerning the point at which a Montana wrongful death action accrues. ...

Appellant (and defendant), W.R. Grace and Company, claims that the action accrues at the date of injury. Respondent (and plaintiff), Edith Carroll, claims that a wrongful death action accrues at the death of the injured person. We conclude that a wrongful death action does not accrue until the death of the injured person.

Charles Carroll (decedent) was employed by W.R. Grace and Company (Grace) at its vermiculite mine located in Libby, Montana, from 1958 until 1976; he underwent yearly chest x-rays provided by Grace from 1967 until 1976. Decedent retired in 1976, but continued to seek medical help regarding shortness of breath and a heart condition.

Mr. Carroll died in 1989, thirteen years after retirement. His autopsy report listed the cause of death as "severe interstitial fibrosis with pulmonary failure, apparently due to 'asbestosis.'" Decedent's medical records show that he had been diagnosed as suffering from asbestosis as early as 1972.

Edith Carroll, wife of decedent, filed a survival claim and a wrongful death claim against Grace, her husband's former employer, assert-

ing that her husband's asbestosis was related to his employment at Grace's mine. She contends that she did not know his death was related to his employment until she read the autopsy report. She filed her suit as a diversity action in the United States District Court within two months of her husband's death.

Grace moved for summary judgment based on the running of the statutes of limitations for both survival and wrongful death claims. The U.S. District Court granted summary judgment, holding that the statute of limitations had run on both claims. Edith Carroll appealed to the United States Court of Appeals for the Ninth Circuit. The Ninth Circuit affirmed the District Court's holding that the survival claim was barred by the applicable three-year statute of limitations, but stated that Montana law was not definitive on the issue of when a wrongful death action accrues. ...

Wrongful death claims are creatures of statute in Montana. As such, the question of when a wrongful death claim accrues requires an analysis of the general accrual statute and the wrongful death statute itself.

The general accrual statute for all actions in Montana provides:

[A] claim or cause of action accrues when all elements of the claim or cause exist or have occurred, [and] the right to maintain an action on the claim or cause is complete ... .

The wrongful death statute reads:

Action for wrongful death. When injuries to and the death of one person are caused by the wrongful act or neglect of another, the personal representative of the decedent's estate may maintain an action for damages against the person causing the death ... .

The language of Montana's general accrual statute is plain and straightforward: "all elements" of a claim must exist before the claim can accrue. The meaning is equally clear and not susceptible to differing interpretations: only when all elements exist is a claim complete. [The general accrual statute] applies, by its terms, to all claims and causes of action. Thus, a wrongful death claim, like any other cause of action, accrues only when all elements of the claim have occurred; the claim simply does not exist until that time. The question, then, is whether death is an element of a wrongful death claim.

The wrongful death statute references "... injuries to *and the death* of one person ... ". (Emphasis added.) When these occurrences are caused by the "wrongful act or neglect of another," a wrongful death action may be maintained against the person who caused the death of the injured person. It is clear from the legislature's use of the conjunctive "and" that the death of the injured person is an element of a wrongful death claim.

The wrongful death statute contains additional language mandating the conclusion that death is an element of the claim. "[T]he personal representative of the decedent's estate ..." files a wrongful death action. A "decedent" is indisputably a person who has died and a personal representative of an estate cannot be appointed until there is a decedent. Thus, the death itself is a critical element in a wrongful death action.

To summarize, no claim exists until all elements of a cause of action occur pursuant to [the general accrual statute], and death is an element of a wrongful death claim under ... Montana's wrongful death statute. Therefore, we hold that a wrongful death action in Montana accrues at the time of decedent's death.

The following example illustrates how a wrongful death action might arise under a hypothetical statute.

— HYPOTHETICAL

Jordan Vic Orthmell owns a cement manufacturing plant. One of his employees, Toby Noogle, drives a cement truck. One of Jordan's customers is Sally Sinchim, who was installing a swimming pool at her home. Toby came to pour cement for the pool. Sally's husband, Abraham, stood beneath the truck inside the excavated pool area. Without first checking to see if anyone was in the way, Toby dumped the entire truckload of cement on top of Abraham, who suffocated and died. Assume that this jurisdiction's wrongful death statute permits family survivors to sue tortfeasors for "negligently, wantonly, or intentionally" causing a victim's death. What is the likely result?

Sally could sue Toby (and, by respondeat superior, Toby's employer, Jordan) for causing the wrongful death of her husband, Abraham. Toby was negligent in pouring the cement without first seeing if anyone was inside the dangerous dumping area. Because Abraham died, Sally has a cause of action for wrongful death. ■

The family survivors' specific legal rights are entirely dependent upon the language of each wrongful death statute. It is important to become familiar with the wrongful death statutes in one's state, if one intends to work with plaintiffs for this special tort action. Table 10-4 summarizes the standard ingredients of wrongful death statutes.

TABLE 10-4
Elements of
wrongful death
statutes

Tortfeasor commits tort against victim, causing victim's death
Victim's surviving spouse and children (or victim's estate) may sue tortfeasor to recover damages under wrongful death statute
Most statutes or courts allow damages for victim's lost lifetime earnings potential and for loss of consortium
Same tort defenses apply in wrongful death actions, depending upon the specific tort tortfeasor committed against deceased victim

§ 10.6 Wrongful Birth

wrongful birth† The birth of a child having serious defects that results from a doctor's failure to provide proper information (to advise, diagnose, or test properly). Can be the basis for a wrongful birth action.

Wrongful birth actions are lawsuits for the wrongful birth of a child. The plaintiffs are usually the surprised parents, and the defendant is normally the genetic counselor who missed or failed to reveal a genetic problem. Wrongful life, then, can be considered another form of medical malpractice, which is negligence.

Typical Fact Pattern: Genetic Counseling Gone Awry

The typical situation involving unwanted pregnancy is as follows: A couple visit a physician and rely on the physician's expertise in making their decisions to conceive a child or continue with a pregnancy.

The plaintiffs (parents) then sue the physician for the unwanted birth of a child born with birth defects or other congenital problems. The parents would seek to be reimbursed for the added expenses of raising a severely disabled child. This may occur when a doctor assures a couple that an unborn child will not be harmed by a disease the mother contracted during pregnancy, but when born, the child does in fact have substantial birth defects caused by the mother's infection. Another such situation involves a child who is born with genetic defects that a doctor assured the parents were not present or inheritable.

Damages

The parents sue to recover for emotional distress, the cost of prenatal care and delivery, and expenses associated with the child's impairment.

Wrongful Life: The New Tort

Wrongful life actions are a recent tort invention, having arisen within the last twenty-five to thirty years. This is typically an action by or on behalf of an unwanted child who is impaired. The child is seeking damages. This new tort has received mixed reviews from appellate courts across the United States. Some jurisdictions reject the tort altogether; others permit it in circumstances involving birth deformities; and still others allow the action even for healthy but unwanted children when sterilization has failed. Wrongful life litigation demonstrates the ingenuity of attorneys and legal scholars searching for new sources of recovery for harmed plaintiffs.

Damages

The child seeks (and sometimes recovers) damages from the responsible physician(s) for the difference in value of an impaired life versus an unimpaired life. Clearly, this is very difficult to calculate and is only allowed in a minority of states.

Wrongful life and birth cases often carry powerful emotional implications, but the temptation to become lost in value judgments must be resisted. Once again, focusing upon the legal elements carries the reader to the appropriate conclusions, as the following example demonstrates.

‹ ♦ ›

The Case of the Wrongful Life and Birth Pregnancy

In this case, the distinction between an action for wrongful birth and wrongful life are detailed. The child, the child's parents, and brothers and sisters have all brought an action against the doctor that delivered the child and the hospital where the child was born. Note that John, Jr. was born in 1982 and this case was decided in 2001. How can you account for the late date of this decision?

MOSCATELLO

v.

UNVERSITY OF MEDICINE AND DENTISTRY OF NEW JERSEY

Superior Court of New Jersey,
Appellate Division
342 N.J.Super. 351, 776 A.2d 874
Argued May 16, 2001
Decided June 21, 2001

In November 1978, Lucy Moscatello was referred to defendant, Dr. Lee, at the University of Medicine and Dentistry of New Jersey ("UMDNJ") for chromosomal and genetic testing. The referral was made because she had suffered three consecutive spontaneous miscarriages in 1977 and 1978. Lee, who at the time was an Associate Professor of Pediatrics at UMDNJ and Chief of its Division of Medical Genetics, performed an internal examination and a number of blood tests. These tests were analyzed by defendant Sciorra. Thereafter, Lee informed Lucy that she was genetically normal.

Following the genetic testing, Lucy became pregnant. On March 25, 1980, she gave birth to plaintiff Christina, a normal baby girl. Thereafter, she became pregnant again. On April 4, 1982, she gave birth to plaintiff John Jr., who was born with various physical deformities associated with chromosomal abnormalities.

As a result, in the spring of 1982, genetic testing was performed at Babies Hospital, a part of the Columbia-Presbyterian Medical Center in New York, which revealed that John Jr. was born with a partial trisomy of chromosome 14 and a partial deletion of chromosome 18. This is a rare disorder. In fact, in 1984 there were only six documented cases in the medical literature. Unfortunately, one of the six cases was Lucy's cousin.

… John Jr. is virtually unable to care for himself. … In sum, John Jr. functions on the level of someone approximately two years old.

Genetic testing revealed that Lucy has a balanced rearrangement between chromosome 14 and 18. The doctor's report explained that the condition was no threat to her health "because the rearrangement is balanced—no chromosomal material is missing or extra—only rearranged." However, because of her genetic deformities, the Columbia-Presbyterian doctors recommended that any future pregnancies be monitored by amniocentesis.

* * *

On November 27, 1984, the parties settled their dispute and placed the settlement on the court record. Mr. Gelzer stated that the plaintiffs were settling the claim for their "emotional losses" as a result of John Jr.'s birth, and "for the cost of extraordinary medical expenses incurred or to be incurred on behalf of John Moscatello [Jr.] to be borne by the parents." The settlement was for "the aggregate sum of $375,000." …

Nearly fourteen years later, on November 5, 1997, plaintiffs' current attorney filed the subject complaint in the Law Division.

* * *

First, we address John Jr.'s claim for wrongful life damages. The Supreme Court has explained that "[t]he terms 'wrongful birth' and 'wrongful life' are but shorthand phrases that describe the causes of action of parents and children when negligent medical treatment deprives parents of the option to terminate a pregnancy to avoid the birth of a defective child." The wrongful birth claim belongs to the parent, whereas the wrongful life claim belongs to the child him or herself.

The New Jersey Supreme Court first recognized the validity of the child's wrongful life claim in *Procanik* where a child born with congenital rubella syndrome was permitted to recover the cost of his extraordinary medical expenses. The ruling in the case is unambiguous: "we hold that a child or his parents may recover special damages for extraordinary medical expenses incurred during infancy, and that the infant may recover those expenses during his majority." It is unmistakable that the Court intended to create a separate claim to be brought by the disabled child. The Court remarked that "Peter's, [the child's], right to recover the costs of his health care is separate from his parent's claim[.]" It is important to note that wrongful birth and wrongful life claims for extraordinary medical expenses overlap. Both the parents and the child may recover for these expenses during the child's infancy, but only the child may recover for them during majority.

* * *

In the instant case, John Jr. has alleged that the UMDNJ defendants' negligently performed genetic testing on his mother, thereby mistakenly telling her that she was not at a risk to bear genetically disabled children. Lucy relied on this diagnosis, causing her to bring John Jr. to term despite his genetic deficiencies. As a result, John Jr. has and will continue to incur extraordinary medical expenses beyond his majority. Thus, he has established a factual basis for a wrongful life claim.

Importantly, *Procanik* was decided three months before the Moscatellos settled the first complaint. Therefore, at the time of the settlement, John Jr. had been given a right that was "separate" from his parents' claim for extraordinary medical expenses. The parties were charged with knowledge of all relevant law applicable to the matter in dispute, which, of course included knowledge of John Jr.'s separate right.

A child's separate claim for tort damages cannot be prosecuted except by a *guardian ad litem*, who is most often a natural parent. There was, however, no attempt to amend the 1983 complaint to assert a claim on John Jr.'s behalf through a *guardian ad litem*. Therefore, it cannot be said that John Jr. was a party bound by the proceedings.

* * *

The importance of such a proceeding is that once "the judge approves the amount and allocation of the settlement figure, the fully represented infant is bound by the settlement just as if he or she was an adult." "The purpose of the rule is not only to guard a minor against an improvident compromise but also to secure the minor against dissipation of the proceeds."

* * *

In conclusion, John Jr.'s claim for wrongful life, to the extent that it seeks damages for extraordinary medical care, is reinstated and the matter is remanded for further proceedings.

In addition to the reinstatement of his claim for extraordinary medical expenses, John Jr. also seeks to recover for "loss of enjoyment of life[,] including his diminished childhood." ...

A claim for loss of enjoyment of life, although different from a claim for pain and suffering, is indistinguishable from a diminished childhood claim. ... The Supreme Court in *Procanik*, however, stated that: "the infant's

claim for pain and suffering and for a diminished childhood presents insurmountable problems." Observing that the infant plaintiff in that case "never had a chance of being born as a normal, healthy child," and "[t]ragically, his only choice was a life burdened with his handicaps or no life at all," the court, nonetheless, rejected his claim for diminished life damages. Accordingly, the child's wrongful life claim was limited to the recovery of extraordinary medical expenses.

Therefore, we conclude that only the Supreme Court can expand the damages recoverable in a wrongful life cause of action. We affirm the Law Division's order to the extent that it dismissed John Jr.'s claim for loss of enjoyment of life and diminished childhood damages.

Plaintiffs next argue that the Law Division erred in dismissing Christina's and Carl's wrongful birth claims. Although acknowledging that a cause of action brought by siblings premised on the wrongful birth of a disabled sibling has not been recognized in this jurisdiction, plaintiffs contend "[i]t is now time to breathe life into the legal principles espoused in *Berman, Schroeder*, and *Procanik*." We disagree and affirm.

* * *

Attempts to extend wrongful birth claims beyond those brought by parents of the disabled child overlook the basic principle that undergirds the cause of action. ... Stated simply, the duty is owed to the parents and the birth disabled child within the limitations defined by case law, and to no others.

Case Questions

1. Why do you suppose the parents waited fifteen years after John, Jr.'s birth to bring this second claim?
2. What effect did the failure to appoint a guardian ad litem in the parent's first claim have on their bringing the instant claim?

— HYPOTHETICAL ——————————————————————

Paul and Vicky Jonson visited Dr. Fritz Halpner, M.D., to see if Paul could get a vasectomy. Paul was concerned that he could transmit a genetic disease to his unborn child. Several members of Paul's family had been afflicted with the congenital disease. Dr. Halpner performed the sterilization surgery. A few months later, Vicky discovered that she was pregnant. Paul's operation did not "take." The Jonsons refused abortion on religious grounds. The Jonsons' baby daughter was born deformed as a result of the genetic disease transmitted from Paul. The Jonsons sued Dr. Halpner for medical malpractice, specifically alleging wrongful life.

Dr. Halpner's vasectomy operation did not prevent Vicky from becoming pregnant. Worse yet, the Jonson child was afflicted with congenital deformities because of Paul's genetically defective sperm. This child would not have been born in this unfortunate condition but for the doctor's negligence in performing the faulty operation. The Jonsons would appear to have a valid claim against Dr. Halpner for the tort of wrongful life. ■

Table 10-5 lists the elements of wrongful life.

TABLE 10-5
Elements of wrongful birth actions

Usually a form of medical malpractice in which physician has negligently counseled parents concerning genetic issues
May include cases involving children born with birth defects
Damages include parents' medical expenses for unwanted birth and, in some jurisdictions, the costs of raising the child

Summary

A private nuisance is an unreasonable and substantial interference with another person's use and enjoyment of his or her land. Whether a nuisance activity is unreasonable and substantial depends upon its degree of offensiveness. The reasonable person standard is applied to test offensiveness and is based upon the community standard for persons living in the vicinity of the nuisance activity. Private nuisances often involve physical effects on the land, such as vibrations, pollution, and flooding. Private nuisance may also produce health hazards, such as poison gases, hazardous wastes, smoke, or dust, or effects offending the plaintiffs' sensibilities, such as odors or even incessant telephone calling. Private nuisances also include unwanted associations with neighboring uses, such as prostitution houses or gambling emporiums. "Coming to the nuisance" is the primary defense in private nuisance actions.

Public nuisances are activities that harm the public at large rather than a single individual. These nuisances unreasonably and substantially interfere with the public's use and enjoyment of legal rights common to the public. Governmental agencies litigate against public nuisance tortfeasors to enforce the general public's legal rights. State and local governments have the authority to litigate public nuisances under the police powers of the states. Public nuisances often involve so-called immoral activities, such as gambling, prostitution, distribution of sexually explicit materials, or the sale of alcohol. Others include permitting noxious weeds to grow on one's property, carelessly disposing of toxic substances, or violating public health laws. Often, nuisances may be both private and public. These are called mixed nuisances. Nuisances per se are activities that violate statutes or ordinances. Public nuisances are often per se nuisances. "Coming to the nuisance" is usually not a defense in public nuisance cases.

Equitable remedies are usually awarded in nuisance litigation instead of money damages. Money damages are sometimes given when equitable remedies would be excessively harsh to the defendant. The relief most often granted involves injunctions. In injunctions, the court orders the defendant to act or to cease and desist the nuisance activity. Permanent injunctions forbid the activity forever. Temporary injunctions, such as temporary restraining orders (TROs), merely halt the defendant's nuisance activity until the court can conduct hearings or a trial on the merits. Defendants who disregard injunctions may find themselves in contempt of court, for which they can be fined or imprisoned.

Survival statutes allow an injured party's claim to survive his or her death. The victim's estate pursues this action. Wrongful death statutes provide surviving family members of a deceased tort victim with the right to sue the tortfeasor for wrongfully causing the victim's death. The tortfeasor's wrong may include negligence or intentional torts. Wrongful death damages usually consist of the victim's lost lifetime earnings potential and loss of consortium. Consortium includes the lost love and companionship between the dead victim and his or her family. The tortfeasor may use any defenses applicable for the alleged tort that caused the wrongful death. If the tortfeasor were accused of negligently causing the victim's death, then negligence defenses would apply. If the tortfeasor's intentional tort killed the victim, then intentional tort defenses would apply.

Wrongful birth actions are lawsuits for the wrongful birth of a child. Usually, parents sue a physician for malpractice for negligently counseling them about genetic issues and concerns. Wrongful life cases often involve children born with birth defects. The tort has developed within the past quarter-century. Court reactions to the tort have been mixed. Some jurisdictions reject the tort altogether, while others embrace it in whole or in part.

Key Terms

abatement	mandamus	remedy
coming to the nuisance defense	mixed nuisance	sensibilities
consortium	nuisance	survival statutes
contempt	nuisance per se	temporary restraining order
damages	permanent injunction	(TRO)
equitable relief (remedy)	police power	wrongful birth
injunction	private nuisance	wrongful death statute
loss of consortium	public nuisance	

Problems

In the following hypotheticals, identify the relevant cause(s) of action, suitable defense(s) (if any), and appropriate remedies.

1. Pestro Chemical Corporation manufactures *Dredroxiphine*, a poison used in insect sprays. A railway line delivers tanker cars full of the chemical to be unloaded into the plant. On breezy days, the fumes from the unloading stations drift across the highway onto Elmer Parsely's farm.

The odors are pungent and are especially irritating to the sinuses. When Elmer and his family work outside on windy days, they are constantly besieged by the poison's smell. Their eyes water excessively, their noses run, and they are gripped by sneezing fits. Other farmers in the area have complained of similar symptoms. Visits to the family physician revealed that Elmer has absorbed minute amounts of the chemical in his lungs and through his skin. Medical studies link exposure to the chemical with several forms of cancer. Elmer has farmed on his property since 1947. Pestro constructed its plant in 1972.

2. Wowser's Video Palace rents X-rated videotaped movies. A local ordinance restricts rental of such materials to persons over the age of 18 years. Wowser's employees never check customer identifications, however, and often rent X-rated movies to underage individuals. Citizens Rallying Against Pornography, a local citizen's group, has asked the county prosecutor to take action against Wowser's. The prosecutor has asked you to summarize the appropriate cause(s) of action in a short paragraph.

3. Quintin and Ursella Xenopher were driving along Interstate 928 on the beltway around the city. Terri May Nordmeier was driving while intoxicated. Her blood alcohol level was .214, and a state criminal statute provides that .10 is legally drunk. A related state civil statute provides injured parties with a tort cause of action against a tortfeasor who causes injuries while violating criminal statutes. Terri's automobile collided with the Xenopher's vehicle, killing Quintin. Ursella suffered permanent disability in her left leg.

4. Dr. Sarah Davis Strongfelt, M.D., performed a tubal ligation upon Jennifer Colfield to prevent impregnation. Jennifer was a single, 24-year-old woman who had a sexual relationship with her boyfriend, Miles Vieman. Six months after her operation, Jennifer discovered that she was pregnant. She could not afford the costs of raising a child, but she did not want to get an abortion. Miles refused to subsidize Jennifer's medical expenses or contribute to the child's upbringing. The local adoption agencies (managed by rigid-thinking administrators) refused to speak with Jennifer, because she had a history of narcotic abuse. She did not consult with out-of-town adoption agencies, which would have been happy to assist her in placing the child in a foster home.

Review Questions

1. Define private nuisance. Who are the parties to this litigation? What is unreasonable and substantial interference? How is it determined? What is the role of the community standard? What is use and enjoyment?

2. Name the common types of private nuisance. Can you provide hypotheticals to illustrate each? What is "coming to the nuisance"?

3. What is a public nuisance? How is it distinguishable from a private nuisance? Who is affected by a public nuisance? Who acts as plaintiff? What are some common examples of public nuisance? Does "coming to the nuisance" apply? What are common legal rights? What are mixed nuisances? What is a nuisance per se?

4. What remedies are used in nuisance cases? What about money damages? What is abatement? What are injunctions? Explain the difference between temporary and permanent injunctions. When is a TRO used? What is contempt?

5. What are wrongful death statutes? Who are the plaintiffs in wrongful death litigation? What types of torts can be involved? What damages are awarded? What defenses apply?

6. What is wrongful birth? What are the usual fact situations involving this special tort? What damages may be awarded?

Projects

1. Read the case of *Fishman v. Beach* in Appendix C. What is the purpose of dram shop acts? Why did the Supreme Court limit liability to just a certain area?

2. Read the case of *Girdley v. Coats* in Appendix C. Should this case be treated as any other malpractice case should be treated? Explain.

3. How does your state define a wrongful birth action?

Internet Resources

This chapter focuses on Special Tort Actions. To learn more about special tort actions, the following sites can be accessed:

General Legal Sites
http://www.law.vill.edu
http://www.findlaw.com
http://www.law.cornell.edu
http://www.law.indiana.edu/v-lib/vlib.asp

Administrative Office of the United States Courts
http://www.uscourts.gov

Legal Dictionary
http://www.lectlaw.com/def.htm

Law Libraries
http://www.washlaw.edu/lawcat

For additional resources, visit our Web site at
www.paralegal.delmar.cengage.com

CHAPTER 11

TORT IMMUNITIES

CHAPTER OUTLINE

§ 11.1 Introduction
§ 11.2 Governmental, or Sovereign, Immunity
§ 11.3 Public Officers
§ 11.4 Children of Tender Years
§ 11.5 Family/Spousal Immunity
§ 11.6 Workers' Compensation

EQUAL JUSTICE UNDER LAW

———————————⟨◆⟩———————————

We may not all break the Ten Commandments,
but we are certainly all capable of it. Within us
lurks the breaker of laws, ready to spring out
at the first opportunity.
ISADORA DUNCAN

§ 11.1 Introduction

immunity
An exemption from a legally imposed duty, freedom from a duty, or freedom from a penalty.

privilege
1. An advantage; a right to preferential treatment. 2. An exemption from a duty others like you must perform. ... 5. A special advantage, as opposed to a right; an advantage that can be taken away. ...

Up to now, something has been missing from the torts analysis. That something is **tort immunities**—absolute defenses against a plaintiff's tort claims. If the defendant successfully invokes an immunity defense, he or she cannot be held liable for any torts committed. It is the reverse of absolute liability. Tort immunities absolutely protect the defendant from tort liability. There are many types of tort immunity, but the most common include sovereign (governmental) immunity and legal infirmities such as infancy or insanity. Tort immunities are similar to **privileges** and the terms are often used interchangeably.

This chapter includes a discussion of

◆ Sovereign (governmental) immunity

◆ Public officials' immunity

◆ Young children's immunity

◆ Family immunity

◆ Workers' compensation.

§ 11.2 Governmental, or Sovereign, Immunity

sovereign (governmental) immunity
The government's freedom from being sued. In many cases, the United States government has waived immunity by a statute such as the Federal Tort Claims Act.

Sovereign (governmental) immunity has a long and storied history throughout the annals of tort law. To understand modern applications of this doctrine, one must trace its roots and development.

History

In the history of tort law, governments have held an enviable position. Until the twentieth century, governments were immune from liability for torts committed by their employees. This immunity was called **sovereign immunity** or, in modern times, **governmental immunity**. It stemmed from the ancient English (and Western European) legal tradition that a king could not be sued by his subjects unless he consented. Official tortfeasors thus enjoyed an enviable immunity from liability unless they agreed to be sued, which consent one would naturally not give if one had committed any torts.

Courts applied the legal maxim *The king can do no wrong*. This maxim traces its origins to pre-Roman times when the emperor was considered divine and, thus, incapable of errors that the law could remedy.

Modern Applications

For centuries, sovereign immunity protected the Crown and all its subordinates. Later, English and American common law spoke of governmental bodies (and their employees) as enjoying sovereign immunity. The term *king* was replaced with *government* in the American system, because our sovereigns are elected officials serving as presidents, governors, mayors, legislators, or (at the state and local level) judges.

Beginning in the early twentieth century, American courts began to whittle away at the governmental immunity doctrine. Many state courts have abolished sovereign immunity as an absolute defense to governmental liability. Legislatures have enacted statutes, such as the Federal Tort Claims Act, that specifically authorize lawsuits against torts committed by governmental employees (for which governmental agencies could be responsible under respondeat superior).

Early Twentieth-Century Cases

Many courts found the absolute defense of sovereign immunity to be unreasonably harsh on the plaintiffs. To avoid the full force of the immunity, early in the twentieth century American courts began distinguishing the different types of governmental activities that were or were not exempt from tort liability. The result was two categories: governmental and proprietary. This is sometimes called the *governmental/proprietary distinction*.

Governmental Actions

When governmental bodies perform certain public protection activities, such as providing fire, police, or ambulance services, they are considered to be undertaking **governmental functions**. Persons performing governmental functions are immune from tort liability, under the early twentieth-century court decisions. Even if the fire, police, or ambulance departments committed torts against a citizen while performing their duties, the old case law would define these as governmental actions immune from liability.

Proprietary Actions

Governmental bodies also perform certain business-like activities (usually associated with the private sector). These are defined as **proprietary actions** and do not carry immunity from tort liability. For example, a municipality

governmental function(s) An action performed for the general public good by a governmental agency ... or by a private organization closely tied to the government. ... These functions are state actions subject to the due process of law and equal protection clauses of the Constitution. If performed by a government agency, they are usually free from tort lawsuits unless the suits involve constitutional issues or are otherwise authorized by statute.

proprietary actions† Certain business-like activities performed by governmental bodies (usually local government) that are usually associated with the private sector. These can be performed at the discretion of the governmental body and are not given immunity from tort liability.

may provide utility services to its residents, such as water, sewer, electric, or natural gas, but this activity more closely resembles a private business enterprise than a public, governmental function. If the governmental agency providing such services committed torts, the government would be liable, and the immunity defense would not prevent liability.

Difficulty with the Governmental/Proprietary Distinction

Courts have struggled with the governmental/proprietary distinction for decades. What about cities that provide garbage collection? What about public parks? Are these governmental or proprietary functions? Courts often decide based upon whether a fee is assessed to users of these services. If a fee is charged, then the activity is considered proprietary. If not, then it is governmental. This may be called the **fee standard**.

Similar to the fee standard is the *pecuniary benefit test*. When governments provide services for profit, then the activities are proprietary. If governments offer services for the common public good, without economic benefit to the governmental units themselves, then the activities are governmental.

fee standard†
A test courts use in applying the governmental/proprietary distinction. If a governmental agency assesses a fee for an activity, the activity is considered proprietary; if not, it is considered governmental.

Modern Steps to Eliminate the Distinction

Within the past twenty years, many state courts have abolished the governmental/proprietary distinction and with it the defense of sovereign immunity. These courts now focus upon whether the governments committed any torts—just as courts would handle any other tort lawsuit. Many state legislatures and Congress have enacted statutes eliminating or restricting sovereign immunity to particular types of services, such as public parks or utilities.

Suits Against States

Even though many courts have abolished sovereign immunity and allow tort suits, not all states permit all kinds of tort suits to be brought against them. The individual state can decide just what suits it will or will not allow. In fact, in some states there is a special court just for tort claims against the state. In New York, it is called the Court of Claims, and a notice of claim is required to bring the action.

Practical Application

The paralegal must be careful when preparing a tort claim against a state to see if there are any special rules. Your jurisdiction might require special procedures for bringing tort claims against the state. The pleadings might be different and have different or shorter time limits than usual. Because suits against the state were not always allowed, there may not be a provision for jury trial when the state is sued.

§ 11.3 Public Officers

Somewhat different from sovereign immunity is the individual tort immunity granted to certain public employees engaged in their official capacities. Certain governmental officials are immune from personal liability for any torts committed while they were performing their public duties.

Exceptions

There are exceptions to the privilege and immunity doctrines. 42 U.S.C. § 1983 permits liability of public officers (usually other than prosecutors and judges) if the performance of their duties involves activities that deprive persons of their civil rights. Such an action is called a civil rights action or a "1983" action; 1983 is the section number of the law permitting this action, not the year it was passed. If a police officer arrests someone without a warrant and without probable cause, the arrest is in violation of the detainee's civil rights and the officer may be liable. If excessive force is used in an arrest, it is a violation of civil rights and the officer may be liable (*Tennessee v. Garner*, 105 S.Ct. 1694). If any action under color or authority of the government—whether local, state, or federal—violates civil rights, the actor(s) may be liable regardless of immunity.

Who Is Protected

Legislators and judges enjoy an absolute immunity from tort liability for acts in their official governmental capacities. In performing legislative or judicial functions, it is possible that these public officials might commit torts against individual citizens. The common law protects judges and legislators from any liability whatsoever for having committed such torts. Executive branch officials, however, do not receive this blanket immunity, although administrative officers serving judicial or legislative functions do receive absolute immunity. For example, an agency adjudication officer, prosecutor, or county council legislator would be protected completely from tort liability.

Rationale for Immunity

Governmental official immunity is intended to ensure that legislators and judges may pursue their public duties without the chilling effect that fear of tort liability might create. Imagine how cautious legislators or judges would have to be in decision making if, with each sensitive topic, they had to worry about tort liability. These officials might become paralyzed by second-guessing, and the liability spectre could influence their public-policy decisions. This rationale for such immunity is often repeated in the common law. To encourage maximum public benefit from the services of the public's judges and legislators, the law must totally protect these officials from tort liability.

The Case of the Unhappy Probationer

This case concerns a man whose probation has been revoked after he received his second operating-while-intoxicated (OWI) conviction. The probationer brings suit for money damages against the Trial Judge, the State, the Chief Justice of the Supreme Court, and the Governor without success. This case illustrates how the defense of immunity is used to protect public employees from legal action while performing their services.

MARTIN
v.
HEFFELFINGER

Court of Appeals of Indiana
744 N.E.2d 555
March 15, 2001

Kirk R. Martin (Martin) appeals the trial court's dismissal of his complaint under 42 U.S.C. § 1983 and Indiana tort law against Judge Jeffrey R. Heffelfinger of Huntington County Superior Court, Chief Justice Randall T. Shepard of the Indiana Supreme Court, Governor Frank O'Bannon, and the State of Indiana for failure to state a claim. We find that, after accepting Martin's allegations in his complaint as true, Martin fails to state a claim. Therefore, we affirm.

In September of 1997, Martin pleaded guilty to two charges of Operating While Intoxicated (OWI), class A misdemeanors. Martin was sentenced to 365 days in jail, with all but 180 days suspended. Martin was also placed on probation for one year. Judge Heffelfinger of the Huntington County Superior Court presided over this matter. On January 26, 1998, Martin was arrested on a new OWI charge. On June 11, 1998, after a bench trial conducted by Judge Heffelfinger, Martin was convicted of this new charge.

* * *

Martin contends that the trial court erred in dismissing his complaint.

* * *

Martin first argues that the trial court erred in holding that Judge Heffelfinger was immune from suit under § 1983. "Section 1983 of Title 42 provides a civil remedy against any person who, under the color of state law, subjects a citizen of the United States to the deprivation of any rights, privileges, or immunities secured by the federal Constitution or federal laws."

It is well settled that a judicial defendant is immune from a suit seeking monetary damages for actions completed in the judge's official capacity. "The underlying purpose of the immunity is to preserve judicial independence in the decision-making process." ... Judges of courts of general jurisdiction are subject to civil liability under § 1983 only if they have acted in a clear absence of all jurisdiction. Further, judicial immunity is granted even when judges act maliciously or corruptly.

* * *

Martin cites *Pulliam v. Allen*, 466 U.S. 522, 104 S.Ct. 1970, 80 L.Ed.2d 565 (1984) to support his proposition. *Pulliam* held that judicial immunity does not bar prospective injunctive relief against a state judicial officer. However, Martin must prove that his remedies at law are inadequate before he can state a claim for equitable relief. ...

Here, Martin has failed to prove why the remedies available to him at law are inadequate. ...

Still, Martin insists that "Indiana State law for obtaining the removal of a judge from presiding over a case is fundamentally and U.S. Constitutionally flawed. ... Martin fails to cite any authority supporting this proposition, and he merely points to the fact that judges accused of bias decide whether to rescue themselves in a proceeding. Indiana law provides standards by which judges decide whether to grant a motion for a change of judge, and we see no reason why these standards are inadequate. Therefore, the trial court did not err when it held that Judge Heffelfinger was immune from suit and that it lacked jurisdiction to hear Martin's claims for equitable relief.

Next, Martin contends that the trial court erred in dismissing his claims against Chief Justice Shepard, Governor O'Bannon, and the State of Indiana. Martin contends that Judge Heffelfinger is clearly a state employee, and his supervisors, Chief Justice Shepard, Governor O'Bannon, and the State had a duty to train him. Martin's claims against these defendants must be brought under the Indiana Tort Claims Act (ITCA). The ITCA established procedures for tort claims filed against governmental entities. The policy underlying the statute is to protect public officials in the performance of their duties by preventing harassment with threats of civil litigation over decisions they make within the scope of their positions.

The ITCA list several situations where governmental entities are immune from suit. In particular, Ind. Code § 34-13-3-3(5) reads that "[a] governmental entity or an employee acting within the scope of the employee's employment is not liable if a loss results from: ... (5) the initiation of a judicial or administrative proceeding...." Most cases discussing this section of the ITCA involve malicious prosecution claims. Although Martin's claims against the named defendants do not involve malicious prosecution, his alleged loss certainly occurred as a result of the State's initiation of the judicial proceeding against him culminating in a conviction and the revocation of his probation. Further, Martin's complaint appears to sue Chief Justice Shepard and Governor O'Bannon only in their official capacities. Hence, they are immune as employees of the State acting within the scope of their positions.

Additionally, Governor O'Bannon and the State of Indiana have no supervisory power over Judge Heffelfinger's decisions made in judicial proceedings due to the independent nature of the judiciary. Also, to the extent that Chief Justice Shepard has supervisory power over Judge Heffelfinger due to his role as the leader of the state judicial system, he is also protected from suit by common law judicial immunity. Thus, the trial court did not error in granting the State's motion to dismiss for failure to state a claim. The facts underlying Martin's claims, even if true, do not support grounds for relief.

Case Questions

1. What is the purpose of judicial immunity?
2. Did judicial immunity adequately protect the Judge, the Chief Justice, and the Governor? Explain.

§ 11.4 Children of Tender Years

For centuries, the common law has held that young children, often referred to as "children of tender years" in the court opinions, may be immune, or are subject only to limited tort liability.

Definition

tender years†
Minors; usually those under the age of seven.

minor A person who is under the age of full legal rights and duties.

Children of **tender years** are usually defined as young children under the age of seven years. Under traditional common law, any person under the age of twenty-one (and in the past twenty-five or so years, eighteen) is classed as a **minor**. However, only very young children normally enjoy the tender-years immunity. Although many opinions, particularly older cases, have granted immunity to teenagers, most cases limit tender years to below age seven. A significant number of cases, however, include the eight-to-twelve age group within the immunity.

Absolute Immunity for Intentional Torts

Most states still follow the ancient common law rule that children of tender years are incapable of committing intentional torts; thus, they are immune from intentional tort liability. This immunity is based upon the concept that young children are mentally and emotionally incapable of having the proper intent to commit an intentional tort. Because they are so young, they lack the experience and development to appreciate fully the significance of their actions, which sometimes are tortious in nature.

For instance, suppose a four-year-old child tosses a sharpened pencil to get another child's attention. This pencil strikes the other child in the eye, causing injury. Had adults been involved, this would be a clear case of battery. However, most states would rule that the pencil-thrower was immune from liability for this intentional tort. Children of tender years are presumed to be incapable of the intent element in intentional torts.

Immunity from Negligence

Most courts do not grant absolute negligence immunity to young children. Instead, the child tortfeasor's age is merely one factor to be considered in determining the standard of reasonable care that the reasonable child of tender years would have used in a particular case. A minority of states have held that children below a certain age (usually seven years) cannot commit negligence and are therefore immune from liability. Most states, however, would agree that only extremely young children, often less than three or four years of age, are incapable of negligence and should be immune.

Children's immunity is never easy to determine. For example, suppose a five-year-old child swings a golf club backwards, planning to reverse the stroke and hit a golf ball. While doing the backswing, the club accidentally hits another child in the forehead, opening a nasty gash. Was the golfer negligent? Most states would apply a reasonable five-year-old child standard to gauge negligence. Some others follow the under-seven absolute immunity rule. This immunity varies widely among, or even within, jurisdictions.

The Case of Parental Control

As the two-wage-earner family becomes more and more common, a question frequently asked is "Who is minding the children?" When a minor kills another minor, can the killer's mother and grandparents be sued for negligent failure to control a minor? This case presents a threat to all grandparents who take on the role of babysitter to their grandchildren.

WELLS v. HICKMAN
Court of Appeals of Indiana
657 N.E.2d 172 (Ind. Ct. App. 1995)
November 8, 1995
Najam, Judge

Cheryl Wells ("Wells") filed a complaint for the wrongful death of her son, D.E., at the hands of L.H., the son of Gloria Hickman ("Hickman") and the grandson of Albert and Geneva Hickman (the "Grandparents"). L.H. beat D.E. to death while the two boys were in the woods behind the Grandparents' home. Wells alleged that Hickman and the Grandparents failed to control L.H. when they were aware or should have been aware that injury to D.E. was possible and that their negligence resulted in D.E.'s death.

* * *

Several issues are presented on appeal which we restate as follows:

1. Whether Indiana Code § 34-4-31-1 precludes the recovery of damages in a common law action for parental negligence by limiting parental liability for the wrongful acts of the parent's child.

2. Whether Hickman had a parental duty to exercise reasonable care to control L.H. for the safety of D.E.

3. Whether the Grandparents had a duty to protect D.E. from harm.

D.E. and his mother, Cheryl Wells, were neighbors to L.H. and his mother, Gloria Hickman. L.H. and Hickman lived in a trailer located on land owned by L.H.'s grandparents, Albert and Geneva Hickman. The trailer was parked within 100 feet of the Grandparents' house and L.H. was often at their home. Hickman worked the night shift and usually left for work at 10:00 P.M. The Grandparents cared for L.H. while Hickman was at work, and L.H. often ate his meals and snacks at the Grandparents' home. Either Hickman or the Grandparents always knew L.H.'s whereabouts.

Between the Fall of 1990 and October 15, 1991, L.H. killed a pet dog by beating it to death, and he killed a pet hamster. L.H. had also expressed his desire to commit suicide. L.H. often exhibited anger and, on one occasion, he came home from school with a black eye, cuts and bruises. ...

On October 15, 1991, D.E. was celebrating his twelfth birthday. After school, fifteen year old L.H. invited D.E. over to play video games. Wells, D.E.'s mother, agreed. The boys did not play video games and neither Hickman nor the Grandparents were aware that D.E. and L.H. were together. Around 6:30 P.M., L.H. returned home and appeared to be very nervous. Later, L.H. told his mother that he thought he had killed D.E. After a search, D.E.'s body was found lying beside a fallen tree on the Grandparents' property.

* * *

A negligence action is rarely an appropriate case for summary judgment. ... To be liable the parent must know that her child "had a habit of engaging in the particular act or course of conduct which led to the plaintiff's injury." The duty to control one's child is described in the Restatement (Second) of Torts as follows:

> A parent is under a duty to exercise reasonable care to control his minor child as to prevent it from intentionally harming others or from so conducting itself as to create an unreasonable risk of bodily harm to them, if the parent
>
> (a) knows or has reason to know that he has the ability to control his child, and
>
> (b) knows or should know of the necessity and opportunity for exercising such control.

* * *

The critical issue in this case is foreseeability and we must determine whether Hickman knew or with due care should have known that L.H. would injure D.E. ...

The record indicates Hickman knew that L.H. was a troubled child and she could anticipate the same type of conduct that he had exhibited in the past. Upon the advice of a school principal and from her personal observations, Hickman was aware that L.H. needed professional help. Nevertheless, we cannot conclude, based upon L.H.'s cruelty to animals and his comment about committing suicide, that it was reasonably foreseeable he would

kill a neighborhood friend. ... Neither the type of harm inflicted nor the victim in this case was foreseeable and, thus, cannot support the imposition of a duty upon Hickman.

Public policy supports the imposition of a duty to control on a parent under the proper circumstances, but it does not in this case. Parents are in a unique position in society because they have a special power to observe and control the conduct of their minor children. ... Parents have a duty to exercise this power reasonably, especially when they have notice of a child's dangerous tendencies. ...

We hold that a cause of action for parental negligence in the failure to control may be maintained in Indiana, but we decline to find a duty in this case. A duty may be imposed upon a parent for her failure to control her child when the parent knows or should know that the child has engaged in a particular act or course of conduct and it is reasonably foreseeable that this conduct would lead to the plaintiff's injuries. We conclude, as a matter of law, that Hickman had no duty to exercise control over L.H. because the harm and the victim were not reasonably foreseeable. ...

Wells next contends that the failure to control exception may be extended to the Grandparents in this case because they assumed a parental role over L.H., their grandson. We cannot agree.

As we have already stated, imposition of a duty under this exception requires that the parent knew or should have known that injury to another was reasonably foreseeable. ... [W]e concluded that Hickman could not have reasonably foreseen that L.H. would kill or even harm D.E. and, likewise, we conclude that the Grandparents could not have foreseen this occurrence. ...

Wells also asserts that the Grandparents are liable based on a negligent entrustment theory and claims that because L.H. was entrusted to their care, they are responsible for the death of D.E. Again, we must disagree.

There is a well recognized duty in tort law that persons entrusted with children have a duty to supervise their charges. ... The duty exists whether or not the supervising party has agreed to watch over the child for some form of compensation.

* * *

[T]he Grandparents were unaware of D.E.'s presence on their property. There was no relationship between the Grandparents and D.E. that would give rise to a duty under a negligent entrustment theory.

* * *

Case Questions

1. Based on the facts presented, do you feel that the death of D.E. was foreseeable? Explain.
2. What kind of facts would have had to be present for the court to have sustained an action for negligent failure to control?

§ 11.5 Spousal/Family Immunity

Spousal and family immunity defenses protect certain family members from law suits.

Spousal Immunity

Originally, common law dictated that spouses were immune from suit by each other. A husband and wife were considered to act as one unit. Additionally, there was a concern that if family members could sue each other, there was more apt to be fraud or collusion. This tort immunity for spouses has now been abolished to some degree by the majority of states. Some states have only abolished the immunity from suit for specific kinds of tort actions.

Family Immunity (parent/child)

At common law, suits between parents and children were also prevented, in the interest of maintaining family harmony and avoiding fraud. In some states this family immunity has now been abolished. This is particularly true where automobile accidents are concerned. Since most car accidents are typically covered by a policy of insurance, it is thought that there is less chance for causing family disharmony, as the suit would no longer be directly against a family member. It is important to note that the family immunity doctrine only covers parent and child, and not suits between brothers and sisters or other relatives.

§ 11.6 Workers' Compensation

Workers who are injured or killed as a result of incidents occurring during the course and scope of their employment are covered for their injuries by state workers' compensation statutes. An employee is covered regardless of the employer's fault. Recovery is limited to the amount set forth in statutory tables. This is generally much less than would be awarded for similar injuries in a common law tort claim. As a result of these workers' compensation statutes, employers are immune from employee suits. Workers' compensation is considered the employee's sole remedy. Note also that there are some federal workers' compensation statutes, which apply to certain employees of the United States government.

Workers' compensation is also discussed in Chapter 8 regarding strict liability in tort.

‹♦›

The Case of the Exclusive Workers' Compensation

Workers' compensation acts are generally considered an employee's exclusive remedy for on-the-job injuries. In this case, an employee alleges both negligent infliction of emotional distress and intentional infliction of emotional distress against her supervisor and employer. Are these the kinds of acts that workers' compensation statutes were designed to cover?

VORVIS
v.
SOUTHERN NEW ENGLAND TELEPHONE CO.

United States District Court for the District of Connecticut
821 F. Supp. 851 (D. Conn. 1993)
May 25, 1993
Edginton, Senior District Judge

Plaintiff, Joyce Vorvis, was employed by defendant, Southern New England Telephone Company ("SNET"), from July 13, 1981 to June 2, 1989, under the terms and conditions of an employment contract. Frank Kulaga was her direct supervisor beginning September 1, 1988. From this time until the end of her employment, plaintiff alleges that she was subjected to extreme and outrageous harassment by Kulaga. She claims he continually subjected her to verbal abuse and caused her

to work extra hours without compensation. She alleges that Kulaga made at least one false verbal statement about her job performance, which, along with the harassment, damaged her reputation. She alleges that Kulaga unfairly disciplined her for certain incompleted work assignments. As a result, she claims she suffered physical and emotional harm and was forced to leave her job on June 2, 1989. Defendants benefited from her departure, she contends, because SNET was in the process of reducing its workforce.

* * *

In Counts I and II, plaintiff alleges intentional infliction of emotional distress against Kulaga and SNET. She claims that from September 1, 1988 through June 2, 1989, SNET intentionally directed Kulaga to treat her in such a way as to cause severe emotional distress which would lead to her departure from SNET. This treatment began after she returned from foot surgery and while she was coping with the illness and death of her sister. The treatment allegedly took place almost every day for a period of over one year, and included chastising, criticism, humiliation in front of coworkers, threats to fire her, extra work assignments for the purpose of causing anxiety, uncompensated work on weekends and evenings, unwarranted vulgar remarks, and disciplinary actions for matters beyond her control. ...

The exclusivity provision of the Connecticut Worker's Compensation Act provides that:

> An employer shall not be liable to any action for damages on account of personal injury sustained by a employee arising out of and in the course of his employment or on account of death resulting from personal injury so sustained, but an employer shall secure compensation for his employees as follows, except that compensation shall not be paid when the personal injury has been caused by the wilful and serious misconduct between employer and employees ...

Conn.Gen.Stat. § 31-284(a). Under the Workers' Compensation Act, an employee surrenders his or her right to bring common-law action against employer. Intentional tort claims are not barred if the actor is acting with the knowing authorization of the employer. Thus, a claim will not be barred by the Workers' Compensation Act where the tort is intentional and where the defendant employer directed the supervisor to commit the tort.

Here, the exception for "personal injury ... caused by the wilful and serious misconduct between employer and employees" applies as to plaintiff's claims of intentional infliction of emotional distress. Plaintiff alleges an intentional tort that was knowingly authorized by the actor's employer. Thus, the Worker's Compensation Act does not bar this cause of action.

The next step is to determine whether plaintiff has made a claim for intentional infliction of emotional distress. Viewing the allegations in the complaint in the light most favorable to the plaintiff, the court finds that she does. Plaintiff has alleged in the complaint that: (1) defendant intended or knew that emotional distress would likely result from defendant's conduct; (2) defendant's conduct was extreme or outrageous; (3) defendant's conduct caused plaintiff's distress; and (4) plaintiff's emotional distress was severe.

Accordingly, the motion to dismiss must be denied as to Counts I and II.

Plaintiff alleges negligent infliction of emotional distress against Kulaga in Count III, and against SNET in Counts IV and V.

* * *

Under Connecticut law, the issue of compensability under the Workers' Compensation Act is determined by whether or not the worker's injury is one "arising out of and in the course of employment." ...

In the instant case, plaintiff's claim for negligent infliction of emotional distress is barred by the Connecticut Workers' Compensation Act because her alleged injuries arose out of and in the course of her employment, and because the exception for intentional torts does not apply.

Therefore, the motion to dismiss Counts III, IV, and V alleging negligent infliction of emotional distress must be granted.

Case Question

1. The plaintiff's claims of negligent infliction of emotional distress and intentional infliction of emotional distress were treated differently by the United States District Court. Explain which of the claims, if any, were covered under worker's compensation, and which were permitted as separate claims.

Summary

Tort immunities are absolute defenses against a plaintiff's tort claims. Sovereign, or governmental, immunity is an ancient common law defense that protected governments from tort liability. The doctrine was based on the presumption that "the king could do no wrong," which, in America, translated that the government could not be sued without its consent. American courts drastically reduced or eliminated sovereign immunity during the twentieth century. In the early decades of the century, courts avoided the immunity by distinguishing between governmental and proprietary actions in which government agencies were engaged. Many states have abolished sovereign immunity altogether as an absolute defense.

Public officers, such as judges or legislators, are immune from personal liability for any torts committed while they are performing their official duties. This ensures that governmental officials may act independently and freely to perform their civil responsibilities, without fear of constant tort liability for their every public action that might tortiously affect individual citizens in some way.

"Children of tender years" are very young children, often under the age of seven years, although many courts have defined the term as including children to age twelve or even through the teenage years. Children of tender years are immune from intentional tort liability in most jurisdictions. Often, a specific age boundary is used. Many courts state that children under seven years are absolutely immune. Others do not rigidly follow any age barrier. For negligence, most courts apply a reasonable child-of-tender-years standard to decide whether negligence has occurred. A minority of states use definite age limits, such as the seven-year-old rule, for negligence cases.

At common law, various family members were immune from suit. Spouses could not sue spouses, and children and parents could not bring actions against each other. These immunities have been abolished in varying degrees depending on jurisdiction.

State workers' compensation statutes prevent suits by injured employees against employers.

Key Terms

fee standard	minor	sovereign (governmental)
governmental function(s)	privilege	immunity
immunity	proprietary actions	tender years

Problems

1. Superior Court Judge Emily Doud McKinnley granted summary judgment to the defendant in a negligence lawsuit. The plaintiff had sued the defendant for negligently causing personal injuries. The plaintiff suffered extensive injuries and was unable to work for the remainder of his life. Upon appeal, the state court of appeals reversed Judge McKinnley's summary judgment order. The appellate court admonished the trial judge for refusing to accept certain key evidence that the plaintiff offered at hearing. The appellate court stated that there was no legal basis for granting summary judgment in the case. The trial transcript clearly indicated that the judge had become angry at the plaintiff's counsel's attempts to admit the evidence despite warnings to desist. After the appeal, the plaintiff wished to sue Judge McKinnley for judicial malpractice.

2. Shelby Sarville drives a garbage truck for the City of New Ventura. The city charges its customers a monthly trash-hauling fee, which is based upon the size of the trash container used. Citizens may use the city's service, although many people hire private trash companies instead. One day, while backing up to empty a trash dumpster, Shelby failed to look in his rearview mirrors. A five-year-old girl tried to squeeze between the truck and the dumpster on her bicycle. She mistimed the squeeze, and the truck crushed her against the dumpster, causing severe internal injuries. (Be sure to address the contributory negligence issue in this case.)

3. Daphne Torque is an eight-year-old girl who often plays with her neighborhood friends. While hiking through the woods on Saturday afternoon, two of Daphne's neighbors, Paul (age seven) and Anne (age ten) Heifer, decided to "ditch" Daphne, that is, the duo would abandon Daphne in the woods and flee the scene. The sun had just gone down, and it was becoming quite dark when Paul and Anne ditched Daphne. Once Daphne realized she was alone in the forest, she became frightened and ran toward home. She twisted her ankle and fell, striking her head against a tree root. She was knocked unconscious. Several hours later, a police search party located her. She suffered a concussion and dehydration.

Review Questions

1. What are tort immunities? What is their function in tort litigation? Who do they protect?

2. Define sovereign, or governmental, immunity. What is the historical rationale behind the defense? How have modern American courts applied the doctrine?

3. What is the governmental/proprietary distinction? How it is used? How are governmental actions defined? Proprietary actions? What is the significance of these distinctions?

4. How has the sovereign immunity defense changed during this century?

5. What are public officers' immunities? Who do they protect? Why are these governmental officials granted immunity?

6. Define *children of tender years*. Who is protected by this defense? How does the immunity differ for intentional torts and negligence?

7. What are the two family immunities?

8. What is the purpose of workers' compensation?

Project

Read the *Doe v. Cutter Biological* case in Appendix C. The plaintiff seeks to hold two defendants liable, although the plaintiff admits it is not possible to prove which defendant caused the plaintiff's injuries. Is the joint and several liability doctrine fair? Explain. Which particular immunity was involved in this case? What is the enterprise theory? Define the concert-of-action theory.

2. Define sovereign, or governmental, immunity. What is the historical rationale behind the defense? How have modern American courts applied the doctrine?

3. What is the governmental/proprietary distinction? How it is used? How are governmental actions defined? Proprietary actions? What is the significance of these distinctions?

4. How has the sovereign immunity defense changed during this century?

5. What are public officers' immunities? Who do they protect? Why are these governmental officials granted immunity?

6. Define *children of tender years*. Who is protected by this defense? How does the immunity differ for intentional torts and negligence?

7. What are the two family immunities?

8. What is the purpose of workers' compensation?

Project

Read the *Doe v. Cutter Biological* case in Appendix C. The plaintiff seeks to hold two defendants liable, although the plaintiff admits it is not possible to prove which defendant caused the plaintiff's injuries. Is the joint and several liability doctrine fair? Explain. Which particular immunity was involved in this case? What is the enterprise theory? Define the concert-of-action theory.

Internet Resources

This chapter focuses on tort immunity. To learn more about tort immunity, the following sites can be accessed:

For additional resources, visit our Web site at
www.paralegal.delmar.cengage.com

CHAPTER 12

PARALEGAL ETHICS

CHAPTER OUTLINE

§ 12.1 Introduction
§ 12.2 NALA Ethics Code and Guidelines
§ 12.3 NFPA Code and Model Rules
§ 12.4 ABA Code and Model Rules
§ 12.5 Hypothetical Problems
§ 12.6 Further Ethics Information

EQUAL JUSTICE UNDER LAW

━━━━━━━━━━━━━━━━━━━━━ ⟨ ◆ ⟩ ━━━━━━━━━━━━━━━━━━━━━

It is not unprofessional to give free legal advice,
but advertising that the first visit will be free is a bit
like a fox telling chickens he will not bite them
until they cross the threshold of the hen house.
WARREN E. BURGER

§ 12.1 Introduction

Ethical and unethical behavior exists in every profession. The role of legal ethics is to identify and remove inappropriate conduct from the legal profession. Honest legal practitioners strive to avoid ethical dilemmas. Unscrupulous persons are culled and expelled through disciplinary sanction from state supreme courts or disciplinary agencies.

This chapter discusses this extremely important aspect of paralegal work; namely, the real-world ethical concerns one encounters daily as a legal assistant. It is no exaggeration to say that legal ethics may be the most important area of study in the paralegal field. This chapter includes:

◆ NALA's ethics Code and guidelines applicable to paralegals
◆ NFPA's Code and Model Rules applicable to paralegals
◆ ABA's ethics Code and Model Rules applicable to paralegals.

§ 12.2 NALA Ethics Code and Guidelines

The National Association of Legal Assistants, Inc. (NALA) promulgated an ethics code designed specifically for paralegals. The Code of Ethics was issued in 1977. NALA updated and improved this code in 1984 with its Model Standards and Guidelines for Utilization of Legal Assistants, which was revised in 1991 and 1997. The NALA guidelines can be seen in Figure 12-1.

Restricted Duties

Paralegals shall not perform any duties that only lawyers may fulfill, nor shall paralegals perform activities that attorneys are prohibited from doing. For instance, paralegals may not engage in the unauthorized practice of law. Only attorneys licensed and in good standing with a state's bar

NALA Model Standards and Guidelines for Utilization of Legal Assistants

Guideline 1

Legal assistants should:

1. Disclose their status as legal assistants at the outset of any professional relationship with a client, other attorneys, a court or administrative agency or personnel thereof, or members of the general public;

2. Preserve the confidences and secrets of all clients; and

3. Understand the attorney's Rules of Professional Responsibility and these Guidelines in order to avoid any action which would involve the attorney in a violation of the Rules, or give the appearance of professional impropriety.

Guideline 2

Legal assistants should not:

1. Establish attorney-client relationships; set legal fees; give legal opinions or advice; or represent a client before a court, unless authorized to do so by said court; nor

2. Engage in, encourage, or contribute to any act which could constitute the unauthorized practice of law.

Guideline 3

Legal assistants may perform services for an attorney in the representation of a client, provided:

1. The services performed by the legal assistant do not require the exercise of independent professional legal judgment;

2. The attorney maintains a direct relationship with the client and maintains control of all client matters;

3. The attorney supervises the legal assistant;

4. The attorney remains professionally responsible for all work on behalf of the client, including any actions taken or not taken by the legal assistant in connection therewith; and

5. The services performed supplement, merge with and become the attorney's work product.

Guideline 4

In the supervision of a legal assistant, consideration should be given to:

1. Designating work assignments that correspond to the legal assistant's abilities, knowledge, training and experience;

2. Educating and training the legal assistant with respect to professional responsibility, local rules and practices, and firm policies;

FIGURE 12-1 NALA Guidelines

3. Monitoring the work and professional conduct of the legal assistant to ensure that the work is substantively correct and timely performed;

4. Providing continuing education for the legal assistant in substantive matters through courses, institutes, workshops, seminars and in-house training; and

5. Encouraging and supporting membership and active participation in professional organizations.

Guideline 5

Except as otherwise provided by statute, court rule or decision, administrative rule or regulation, or the attorney's rules of professional responsibility, and within the preceding parameters and proscriptions, a legal assistant may perform any function delegated by an attorney, including, but not limited to the following:

1. Conduct client interviews and maintain general contact with the client after the establishment of the attorney-client relationship, so long as the client is aware of the status and function of the legal assistant, and the client contact is under the supervision of the attorney.

2. Locate and interview witnesses, so long as the witnesses are aware of the status and function of the legal assistant.

3. Conduct investigations and statistical and documentary research for review by the attorney.

4. Conduct legal research for review by the attorney.

5. Draft legal documents for review by the attorney.

6. Draft correspondence and pleadings for review by and signature of the attorney.

7. Summarize depositions, interrogatories and testimony for review by the attorney.

8. Attend executions of wills, real estate closings, depositions, court or administrative hearings and trials with the attorney.

9. Author and sign letters providing the legal assistant's status is clearly indicated and the correspondence does not contain independent legal opinions or legal advice.

FIGURE 12-1 NALA Guidelines (*continued*)

licensing authority (usually the state bar or the state supreme court) may practice law. As explained in the Model Standards, this includes providing legal advice to clients, representing clients in court proceedings, contacting adverse parties on a client's behalf, establishing legal fees, accepting clients' cases on behalf of attorneys or the law firm, and preparing legal documents without attorney supervision.

Paralegal Representation Before Administrative Agencies

Many state and federal administrative agencies permit nonlawyers, including paralegals, to represent parties appearing before the agencies in adjudicatory or rulemaking hearings. Such representation is not the unauthorized practice of law, because it is expressly permitted by administrative rules and regulations.

Some state courts refuse to recognize such administrative authorization, and there are common law decisions declaring nonlawyer client representation before administrative agencies to constitute unauthorized legal practice. These courts argue that only the judicial branch has authority to regulate the practice of law. State constitutions or, more often, state statutes vest this regulatory power most frequently in the state supreme court, which might delegate supervisory authority to a state bar agency. In the case of legislative declarations, the state legislature may simply amend its statutes, excluding administrative agency party representation regulations from the courts' authority. However, when a state constitution plainly roots regulatory power over law practice in the courts, the legislature must pursue constitutional amendment procedures. This is a cumbersome process.

In most instances, however, the courts simply look the other way, allowing nonattorneys to represent clients before administrative agencies that have expressed a willingness to accept such circumstances.

Lay Representation in Justice or Small Claims Courts

Many state statutes permit nonlawyers to represent litigants before justices of the peace (commonly called justice courts) or small claims courts. The common law in most states narrowly construes such statutes, indicating that such lay representation is intended for (1) "one-time" appearances, (2) family or business employee representation, or (3) civil cases only. Thus, paralegals who attempt to carve a niche by representing clients in justice or small claims courts on a regular basis would, under these courts' interpretations, engage in unauthorized law practice.

Supervised Duties

Paralegals may perform any delegated tasks supervised by a licensed attorney. The supervising lawyer must remain directly responsible to the client, maintaining or establishing the attorney-client relationship and assuming full accountability for the legal services supplied. This provision permits paralegals to conduct initial consultations with clients, in which they gather factual information from the client. It also allows paralegals to complete legal research and writing tasks, investigate cases, compile evidence, arrange (but not conduct) discovery, and prepare materials for trial. However, at each phase, the attorney must guide and direct the paralegal's efforts.

A paralegal should disclose his or her status as a paralegal (rather than a lawyer) at the outset of any professional relationship with clients, or when dealing with other attorneys, courts, administrative agencies, or the general public. The Model Standards also emphasize the supervising attorneys' duty to monitor and train paralegals.

No Independent Legal Judgment

A paralegal may perform services for a lawyer, provided that they do not require the exercise of independent legal judgment, and provided that the attorney supervises the paralegal's efforts. Paralegals should act prudently so that they can determine the extent to which they may assist a client without an attorney's presence. This is especially important during fact-gathering client consultations or when discussing details with clients on the telephone.

Protecting Client Confidences

Paralegals must protect client confidences. It is unethical for a paralegal to violate any statute controlling privileged communications. Examples of privileged communications include discussions between attorney and client, physician and patient, husband and wife, clergy and parishioner, and counselor and patient.

Clearly, when clients speak with attorneys and their staff, there is an expectation that confidences and disclosures shall remain inside the office. The rule of thumb for paralegals, like all law-office staff, is simply not to discuss sensitive client information with anyone. One should always consult with the supervising attorney to see if particular client information is privileged.

Avoiding the Appearance of Impropriety

Paralegals should avoid conduct that would be considered, or even simply appear to be, unethical. An example of this would be if a paralegal working for a government agency accepted a free lunch from an employer she was investigating.

Integrity and Competency

Paralegals shall maintain their integrity and a high degree of competency. This may require paralegals to complete continuing legal education, as most states now require of attorneys. Paralegals should "strive for perfection through education" to better assist the legal profession and the public.

Lawyer Ethics Rule Application

The Model Standards includes paralegals within the coverage of the American Bar Association's ethics codes. The current version of the ABA regulations is the Model Rules of Professional Conduct, which replaced the Code of Professional Responsibility. All states have their own versions of these attorney ethics provisions, many of which are modeled directly upon the ABA versions. This is addressed in § 12.4.

Model Standards' List of Permissible Activities

NALA's Model Standards list permissible activities for paralegals to perform, provided that such items do not conflict with or contradict statutes, court rules, administrative rules and regulations, or the attorneys' ethics codes. Guideline five details the particular functions a paralegal may perform under an attorney's supervision.

Legal Effect of NALA Rules

It is important for the reader to note that NALA's ethics provisions have no force of law in and of themselves. NALA is a private organization, and accordingly its promulgations are advisory. However, courts are likely to give considerable credence to NALA's rules, as historically courts have accepted the ABA's ethics codes as definitive statements of the law.

The Case of the Not-So-Bright Light Revisited

This case is also referenced in Chapter 9, "Products Liability." As regards this chapter, the key issue raised in the case concerns an attorney's ethical obligation to disclose certain negative information to the court. Ideally, an attorney seeks to present evidence and court cases to persuade the court to find in his or her client's favor. Here, the attorney's obligation to advise of all relevant judicial determinations, even if negative, is discussed.

SMITH

v.

SCRIPTO-TOKAI CORP.

**United States District Court,
W.D. Pennsylvania
170 F.Supp.2d 533
November 2, 2001**

* * *

Duty to Disclose Adverse Legal Authority to the Tribunal

Defendant's motion for summary judgment has been pending since April 13, 2001. On September 21, 2001, the United States District Court for the Middle District of Pennsylvania issued a thorough opinion in *Hittle v. Scripto-Tokai Corp.*, 2001 WL 1116556 (M.D.Pa.2001). That case is strikingly similar to this one. ... The *Hittle* court analyzed the same Court of Appeals decisions, predicting the same unsettled areas of Pennsylvania law. The *Hittle* court's decision was clearly adverse to Scripto-Tokai's position on the negligent design claim. Counsel did not bring this case to the court's attention.

Pennsylvania Rule of Professional Conduct 3.3, Candor Toward the Tribunal, states:

> (a) A lawyer shall not knowingly:
>
> ...
>
> (3) fail to disclose to the tribunal legal authority in the controlling jurisdiction known to the lawyer to be directly adverse to the position of the client and not disclosed by opposing counsel
>
> ...

This Rule is identical to the ABA's Model Rule of Professional Conduct. The Rule serves two purposes. First, courts must rely on counsel to supply the correct legal arguments to prevent erroneous decisions in litigated cases. Second, revealing adverse precedent does not damage the lawyer-client relationship because the law does not "belong" to a client, as privileged factual information does.

Although there is not much case law interpreting this aspect of the Rule, the ABA issued a formal opinion, *Formal Opinion 280*, dated June 18, 1949. The Formal Opinion addressed the question: "Is it the duty of a lawyer appearing in a pending case to advise the court of decisions adverse to his client's contentions that are known to him and unknown to his adversary?" The ABA opined as follows:

> An attorney should advise the court of decisions adverse to his case which opposing counsel has not raised if the decision is one which the court should clearly consider in deciding the case, if the judge might consider himself misled by the attorney's silence, or if a reasonable judge would consider an attorney who advanced a proposition contrary to the undisclosed opinion lacking in candor and fairness to him.

The ABA explained that this Opinion was not confined to authorities that were decisive of the pending case (i.e., binding precedent), but also applied to any "decision directly adverse to any proposition of law on which the lawyer expressly relies, which would reasonably be considered important by the judge sitting on the case." We note that the Pennsylvania Bar Association's *Pennsylvania Ethics Handbook* § 7.3h1 (April 2000 ed.), opines that for a case to be "controlling," the opinion must be written by a court superior to the court hearing the matter, although it otherwise adopts the test set forth in the ABA Formal Opinion.

Because both the Pennsylvania and ABA standards are premised upon what "would reasonably be considered important by the judge," we briefly explain why we prefer the ABA's interpretation. The reason for disclosing binding precedent is obvious: we are required to apply the law as interpreted by higher courts. Although counsel might legitimately argue that he was not required to disclose persuasive precedent such as *Hittle* under Pennsylvania's interpretation of Rule 3.3, informing the court of case law that is directly on-point is also highly desirable. The court considers *Hittle* to be important, because it involved the same facts, issues and law. Knowledge of such opinions may save considerable time and effort in the court's own analysis. ...

One additional reason to disclose contrary authority is to preserve counsel's credibility. The same standard should apply to disclosure of negative authority as to counsel's supplementation of the record with a favorable case. We think it likely that defense counsel would have brought *Hittle* to the court's attention, and rightly so, had the result of that case been different. In this case, the argument in favor of disclosure was heightened by counsel's unique position to be aware of the adverse authority.

In sum, the court is aware of the limitation on the duty of disclosure as interpreted by the Pennsylvania Bar Association. However, at least as applied to cases such as the one before the court, it would seem that the ABA position is by far the better reasoned one. Certainly, ABA Formal Opinion 280 comports more closely with this judge's expectation of candor to the tribunal.

In accordance with the foregoing, defendants' Motion for Summary Judgment, Doc. No. 50, is DENIED. ... The parties are directed to submit a revised case management order within twenty (20) days of the date of this Order. Defendants' Motion to Strike Plaintiff's Supplemental Pretrial Statement. Doc. No. 67, is DENIED.

ATTACHMENT 1
American Bar Association

AN ATTORNEY SHOULD ADVISE THE COURT OF DECISIONS ADVERSE TO HIS CASE WHICH OPPOSING COUNSEL HAS NOT RAISED IF THE DECISION IS ONE WHICH THE COURT SHOULD CLEARLY CONSIDER IN DECIDING THE CASE, IF THE JUDGE MIGHT CONSIDER HIMSELF MISLED BY THE ATTORNEY'S SILENCE, OR IF A REASONABLE JUDGE WOULD CONSIDER AN ATTORNEY WHO ADVANCED A PROPOSITION CONTRARY TO THE UNDISCLOSED OPINION LACKING IN CANDOR AND FAIRNESS TO HIM.

June 18, 1949

Copyright (c) 1967 by the American Bar Association CANONS INTERPRETED: PROFESSIONAL ETHICS 5, 15, 22

Case Questions

1. What is the distinction between the ABA's position and that of the Pennsylvania Bar Association's interpretation as to what is required by counsel?

2. What are two reasons provided for counsel to disclose contrary authority to the court's attention?

§ 12.3 NFPA Code and Model Rules

The National Federation of Paralegal Associations (NFPA) has also established ethical rules for appropriate paralegal conduct. These rules alone have no legal effect upon paralegals. There are procedures in place for NFPA to sanction paralegals for misconduct. However, courts and bar authorities may incorporate them in their decisions, thus incorporating them into the common law or administrative law. NFPA adopted its Model Code of Ethics and Professional Responsibility (Model Code) in 1993.

In 1997, the NFPA adopted the Model Disciplinary Rules (Model Rules) to facilitate the enforcement of the NFPA Model Code. The Model Rules are similar in content to the NALA's Model Standards and Guidelines for Utilization of Legal Assistants. See Figure 12-2 on page 380.

For each of the rules, NFPA has also drafted ethical considerations that provide a set of standards relating to each of the rules. These ethical considerations set forth enforceable obligations for paralegals.

NFPA Model Rules

1.1 A paralegal shall achieve and maintain a high level of competence.

1.2 A paralegal shall maintain a high level of personal and professional integrity.

1.3 A paralegal shall maintain a high standard of professional conduct.

1.4 A paralegal shall serve the public interest by contributing to the improvement of the legal system and delivery of quality legal services, including pro bono publico services.

1.5 A paralegal shall preserve all confidential information provided by the client or acquired from other sources before, during, and after the course of the professional relationship.

1.6 A paralegal shall avoid conflicts of interest and shall disclose any possible conflict to the employer or client, as well as to the prospective employers or clients.

1.7 A paralegal's title shall be fully disclosed.

1.8 A paralegal shall not engage in the unauthorized practice of law.

FIGURE 12-2 NFPA Model Rules

The ABA's ethics rules also apply to paralegals. These standards are discussed in § 12.4.

§ 12.4 ABA Code and Model Rules

The American Bar Association (ABA) has promulgated its own set of ethical regulations for attorneys. Currently it follows the Model Rules of Professional Conduct (Model Rules), which replaced its older Code of Professional Responsibility (CPR). Many state bars and courts have adopted the ABA's Model Rules and/or Code as legally binding and enforceable regulations against attorneys and their employees. Courts have ruled that the ABA's standards apply to paralegals. Thus, paralegals should become familiar with the provisions of the ABA Model Rules and the CPR.

The ABA Model Rules cover the following topics: the lawyer-client relationship, the lawyer as a counselor and advocate, transactions with persons other than clients, law firms and associations, public service, information about legal services, and maintaining the integrity of the legal profession.

ABA Code of Professional Responsibility

The CPR is divided into nine Canons, all of which broadly prescribe ethical conduct for lawyers. Figure 12-3 summarizes the Canons. Within the Canons are Disciplinary Rules (DRs) and Ethical Considerations (ECs), which provide more-detailed guidance on ethical issues. The DRs and ECs carefully discuss permissible attorney conduct in advertising; soliciting clients; contacting clients, adverse parties, or the public; protecting client confidences; establishing and sharing legal fees; withdrawing from representation; undertaking unauthorized practice of law; maintaining prohibited interactions with client's interests; providing competent and zealous representation; and other ethical questions. The ABA Model Rules, although they use different phraseology, address similar concerns.

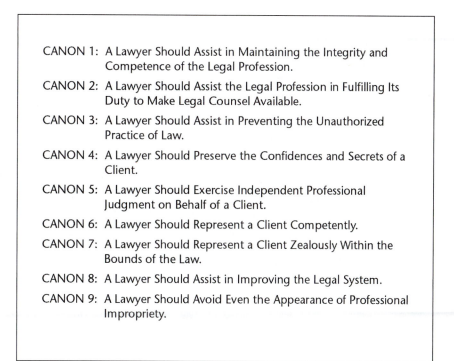

CANON 1: A Lawyer Should Assist in Maintaining the Integrity and Competence of the Legal Profession.

CANON 2: A Lawyer Should Assist the Legal Profession in Fulfilling Its Duty to Make Legal Counsel Available.

CANON 3: A Lawyer Should Assist in Preventing the Unauthorized Practice of Law.

CANON 4: A Lawyer Should Preserve the Confidences and Secrets of a Client.

CANON 5: A Lawyer Should Exercise Independent Professional Judgment on Behalf of a Client.

CANON 6: A Lawyer Should Represent a Client Competently.

CANON 7: A Lawyer Should Represent a Client Zealously Within the Bounds of the Law.

CANON 8: A Lawyer Should Assist in Improving the Legal System.

CANON 9: A Lawyer Should Avoid Even the Appearance of Professional Impropriety.

FIGURE 12-3 ABA Code of Professional Responsibility Canons

Ethics codes tend to be cut-and-dry when presented abstractly. It is more helpful to explore their application in real-world settings.

A Case of Unauthorized Practice

Several states have statutes permitting nonattorneys to represent clients in certain specialized courts (e.g., justice-of-the-peace, small claims, city, traffic). These statutes are often written plainly and clearly. The legislature's intentions should be sufficiently obvious, even to the courts. But as the following case illustrates, courts may be unwilling to permit uninitiated "outsiders" into the client representation arena. After reading the Montana Supreme Court's opinion, one might wonder if this is just another boost to the lawyers' practice monopoly.

SPARKS
v.
JOHNSON

Supreme Court of Montana
826 P.2d 928 (Mont. 1992)
February 6, 1992
Per curiam

This is an original proceeding arising out of a criminal theft prosecution in the City Court of Whitefish, Montana. Petitioners Karen Sparks, the defendant in that proceeding, and Jerry O'Neil, seek declaratory and injunctive relief, including a writ of mandamus. They request this Court's declaration that O'Neil and other non-attorneys similarly situated have the right, pursuant to §§ 25-31-601 and 37-61-210, MCA [Montana Code Annotated], to act as attorneys in Montana courts of limited jurisdiction on a regular and recurring basis. The Office of the Attorney General responded, as did Whitefish City Judge Brad Johnson.

The petition before us raises the question of lay representation in Montana's courts of limited jurisdiction. While it is clear that Article VII, § 2(3) of the 1972 Montana Constitution vests exclusive jurisdiction in this Court to make rules governing practice in all Montana courts, we have not heretofore comprehensively addressed this issue which now is arising with increasing frequency. Because of the statewide importance and implications of the issue, we accept original jurisdiction of this petition ... in order to provide guidance on the question of lay representation to the courts of limited jurisdiction throughout the state.

The underlying facts upon which this proceeding is based are not in dispute. The Whitefish City Attorney filed a complaint against Karen Sparks in Whitefish City Court for misdemeanor theft pursuant to § 45-6-301, MCA. At her initial appearance on September 18, 1991, Sparks appeared and acknowledged that she possessed a copy of the complaint and that she was aware an arrest warrant had been issued. Sparks was informed of her right to counsel and her right to a continuance so she could obtain counsel. Sparks pled not guilty and requested a court-appointed attorney. The court explained that it was not seeking confinement for Sparks and, therefore, would not provide her with a court-appointed attorney. Sparks persisted, prompting the court to provide defendant with an Affidavit/Request for Court Appointed Counsel form.

After Sparks' repeated attempts to secure court-appointed counsel, the court issued a Memorandum on Oct. 17, 1991, concluding again that she was not entitled to court-appointed counsel but could obtain private counsel. On or about Oct. 21, 1991, Jerry O'Neil filed a notice of appearance in the Whitefish City Court indicating that he would appear on behalf of defendant Sparks. The court subsequently denied O'Neil the right to represent Sparks in City Court and a jury trial was set for Nov. 7, 1991.

The present petition was filed with this Court on Nov. 8, 1991, seeking a stay of pending proceedings in the Whitefish City Court, a declaratory judgment that O'Neil has the right under §§ 25-31-601, MCA, and 37-61-210, MCA, to act as an attorney in the justice and city courts of Montana, and related injunctive and mandamus relief. This Court stayed the underlying proceedings. ...

Standing is a threshold issue. Thus, we must determine at the outset whether Jerry O'Neil has standing in the action before us. We conclude that he does not.

Although included as a "petitioner" in the caption of the petition to this Court, O'Neil essentially seeks to come before us as a legal representative of Sparks. O'Neil, an acknowledged lay person and not an attorney of record, possesses no legally recognized relationship to Sparks; therefore, he will not be recognized by this Court in the conduct or disposition of the case. We construe this action to be a pro se action by Karen Sparks seeking representation by the person of her choice in the city court criminal proceeding in which she is a defendant.

Sparks contends that § 25-31-601, MCA, authorizes lay representation in criminal cases in Montana justices' courts. She argues further that § 37-61-210, MCA, extends that right to lay representation in criminal cases to city courts. We disagree.

Section 25-31-601, MCA, provides that "[p]arties in justice's court may appear and act in person or by attorney; and any person, except the constable by whom the summons or jury process was served, may act as attorney." The statute is found in Title 25 of the Montana Code Annotated, entitled "Civil Procedure." Chapter 31 of that Title is "Procedure in Justices' Courts."

Section 25-31-601, MCA, is limited, by its plain language and placement in the Montana codes, to civil litigation in justices' courts. It does not apply to criminal proceedings in those courts or in other courts of limited jurisdiction. The criminal procedure statutes applicable to courts of limited jurisdiction, set forth in title 46, Chapter 17, parts 1 through 4, do not contain language permitting representation by "any person."

Sparks' further contention that lay representation in criminal proceedings is extended to city courts by virtue of § 37-61-210, MCA, is also incorrect, even aside from our conclusion above that Montana law does not authorize lay representation in criminal proceedings in justices' courts.

Section 37-61-210, MCA, is entitled "penalty for practicing without license" and provides that "[i]f any person practices law in any court, except a justice's court or a city court, without having received a license as attorney and counselor, he is guilty of a contempt of court." Sparks' reliance on § 37-61-210, MCA, as authority for legal representation by "any person" in a criminal proceeding in city court, is erroneous. Both the plain language and the placement of § 37-61-210, MCA, in the Licensing part of Title 37 (entitled "Professions and Occupations"), Chapter 61 (entitled "Attorneys at Law") of the Montana Code Annotated make it clear that it is a licensing and penalty statute. It does not, by its terms, authorize practice in either justices' or city courts; it merely alludes to, and exempts from penalty, such practice as may be authorized by other statutes. Therefore, we conclude that only such practice before courts of limited jurisdiction as is specifically authorized by existing statute or Court rule can be undertaken by lay people.

Sparks' reliance on a past Order of this Court in a case to which she was not a party is also to no avail. Orders without accompanying opinions have no precedential value from case to case, but pertain only to the circumstances of the action involved.

Sparks' final contention is that § 25-31-601, MCA, authorizes lay representation of parties in courts of limited jurisdiction on a regular and recurring basis. While this is a case of first impression in Montana, statutes similar to § 25-31-601, MCA, have been addressed in other states and held applicable only to a "one time" representation of a party in a justice or magistrate court.

State ex rel. Freison v. Isner (W. Va. 1981), 285 S.E.2d 641, involved a collection agency appearing in magistrate court on behalf of petitioner's creditors through its nonlawyer manager. The court found that the statute authorizing appearances by lay persons in civil litigation did not permit the unauthorized practice of law, but anticipated the representation of a party by a nonlawyer on a "casual, nonrecurring, non-pay basis as a means of assisting the party pro se." The *Freison* court concluded that the West Virginia law, similar to Montana's, provides only for "an isolated or casual appearance by a non-lawyer friend or relative of a party to proceedings in magistrate court … ."

Similarly, the Supreme Court of Iowa held that a bill collector who attempted to bring suit in justice court as an assignee of his various clients was prohibited from doing so. *Bump v. Barnett* (Iowa 1944), 16 N.W.2d 579. The Iowa court, in referring to a statute much like § 25-31-601, MCA, stated that:

> "The salutary purpose of the statute may not thus be perverted to encourage the growth of a class of 'justice court lawyers,' unfettered by the rules that bind licensed attorneys and without training in law and ethics."

The Iowa court concluded that the bill collector was engaged in the illegal practice of law by his repeated representations in justice court.

We agree with the reasoning of the West Virginia and Iowa courts. Section 25-31-601, MCA, was not intended to permit the unauthorized practice of law; the intent is to enable a friend or relative to assist and speak on behalf of a party at one proceeding. We hold that the statute is a "one-time only" grant of a privilege in justices' court civil proceedings. Further, we extend this specific privilege to civil proceedings in city courts pursuant to our constitutional authority to make rules governing practice for all Montana courts.

Finally, even if the underlying proceeding in Whitefish City Court were a civil one, it is clear that O'Neil's representation of Sparks would not be permissible. We take judicial notice that O'Neil attempted to represent at least one other person in a criminal action in a court of limited jurisdiction. We also note that petitioner's brief herein provides a list of O'Neil's "clients." Neither O'Neil nor any other lay person has authority to represent "clients" on a recurring basis in courts of limited jurisdiction. Such recurring representation constitutes the unauthorized practice of law.

Nothing herein impacts on the "student practice rule" at the University of Montana School of Law. Under this rule, students who have completed two years of law school are supervised by a licensed attorney and perform legal activities in Montana courts.

IT IS THEREFORE ORDERED that the Petition herein, and all relief requested therein, is denied and dismissed.

IT IS FURTHER ORDERED that the stay of further proceedings in *City of Whitefish v. Karen Sparks* is hereby lifted.

DATED this 6th day of February, 1992.

Chief Justice Turnage and Justices Harrison, Gray, Trieweiler, McDonough, Hunt, and Weber concur.

Case Questions

1. Under the Montana statute, "any person" other than the constable who delivered service of process is permitted to act as attorney for a litigant in justice court. How did the Montana Supreme Court discover, in this plain, unambiguous language, that the rule only applies to a litigant's "friend or relative to assist and speak on behalf of a party at one proceeding" on a "one-time only" basis? Do you agree with the court's interpretation?

2. Paralegals would be considered lay persons under *Sparks.* Thus, despite the Montana legislature's broad statutory authorization, paralegals would be engaging in the unauthorized practice of law by appearing in justice court to represent a litigant in more than a single case. Do you believe that this is simply the court's attempt to protect the state bar from nonattorney competition? Or do you believe the court was primarily motivated to protect the public from inexperienced lay legal representation? Explain.

3. The *Sparks* court notes that the Montana Constitution vests it with exclusive authority to regulate law practice before the state's courts. Why, then, did the court not rule Mont. Code Ann. §§ 25-31-601 and 37-61-210 unconstitutional, as an impermissible legislative encroachment upon judicial functions?

§ 12.5 Hypothetical Problems

Consider the following hypotheticals, which illustrate the various ethical precepts discussed in the first section. For convenience, assume that the courts would accept the NALA provisions as part of the common law pertaining to unethical conduct by legal professionals. Although these problems are hypothetical, they are captioned according to the format used in attorney disciplinary complaints or court contempt proceedings.

─ HYPOTHETICALS ─

1. *In re* Piper

Leslie Piper is a paralegal in the law firm of Hawker, Hillary, Iscoff, & Prill. The firm represents Carl "Bump" Ostrem in a matter involving fraud and misrepresentation. Ulysses Masterdam had sold Ostrem a hot tub, indicating that it was brand new when, in fact, it had been previously used and repossessed. Piper telephoned Masterdam, requesting a complete refund of Ostrem's payment as well as "damages" for misrepresentation. When Masterdam became angry and offensive, Piper threatened criminal prosecution against Masterdam under the criminal fraud statute. Under the ABA's Model Rules and CPR, it is impermissible for lawyers to coerce payment of civil obligations by threatening criminal action.

Has Piper acted unethically? Yes. Piper engaged in behavior prohibited by the ABA, CPR, and Model Rules by threatening criminal prosecution to settle Ostrem's civil claims. An attorney could not have ethically made such statements; neither could Piper.

* * *

2. *In re* Nover

Bradley Nover is a paralegal working for the mortgage department of First National City State Bank. One of Nover's duties is to file liens and mortgages at the county recorder's office. The department employs one attorney who is supposed to supervise its six paralegals, including Nover. However, because of the heavy workload, Nover often finds himself working solo. Nover left a draft of a mortgage release on the lawyer's desk for review. It was returned the next day with no changes. Nover notified Lester Arnold, against whose land the mortgage had been filed. Arnold had just paid the full balance due on the mortgage. Nover told Arnold that the mortgage release would be mailed within the next few days. However, Nover failed to follow through, and the release was never filed. Several months later, when Arnold attempted to sell his realty, he discovered Nover's error. Arnold sued the bank for slander of title.

Has Nover acted unethically? Yes. Nover should have filed the mortgage release after consulting with his supervising attorney and communicating with Arnold. Nover's failure to do so resulted in tortious injury to Arnold. This demonstrates incompetent and improper professional conduct.

* * *

3. *In re* Quentlen

Sandra Quentlen is a paralegal employed at the law firm of Bingham, Dingham, & Clingham. She works for three personal injury (P.I.) attorneys in the firm. During the first few months of her training, Quentlen spent much time discussing procedural and substantive legal questions with her supervising attorneys, particularly when she had questions concerning the appropriate discovery forms to use in different circumstances. After six months, however, Quentlen became sufficiently adept at handling discovery that the attorneys simply turned over the client files to her after the initial consultation. Quentlen then proceeded to handle each P.I. file herself, with the attorneys simply signing the appropriate documents. Quentlen met with clients and witnesses; she drafted and filed all interrogatories and motions for discovery; and she handled all witness interviews.

Has Quentlen acted unethically? Yes. Without her lawyers' active supervision, Quentlen has engaged in the unauthorized practice of law by single-handedly coordinating discovery. She has exercised independent legal judgment in preparing and filing discovery documents. She may also have used independent legal judgment in advising clients or discussing legal questions with witnesses. She met with litigants without disclosing her status as a legal assistant.

* * *

4. *In re* Madisson

Oscar Madisson is a paralegal in the insurance department of Indemni-corp, a large insurance corporation. His duties consist of researching recent developments in tort law pertaining to insurance. He has been employed by Indemnicorp for five years performing these tasks. However, he has not enrolled in any paralegal courses at the local university (which has a legal administration program) since he graduated from the institution six years ago. Unbeknownst to Madisson, the state legislature enacted new legislation substantially revising tort liability for municipal employees. Madisson advised one of the corporation's officers to settle an insurance claim, based upon the old municipal tort liability statute. As a consequence, the insured sued the company for negligence.

Has Madisson committed an ethical faux pas? Clearly. Madisson failed to remain abreast of current developments in the law. His carelessness would also render Indemnicorp liable, under respondeat superior, for his negligence.

* * *

5. *In re* Walkinski

Donna Walkinski is a paralegal working at the law firm of Cedar, Pine, Maple & Elm. One of her tasks is to handle initial client consultations. Walkinski met with John and Beverly Parker, both of whom wished to file an action against Michael Denton for cutting down several trees on the Parkers' land without permission. The following conversation excerpts transpired between Walkinski and the Parkers:

> WALKINSKI: "Hello, my name is Donna Walkinski. I'll be meeting with you today to discuss that lawsuit you want to file against Denton."
>
> [Walkinski then took the Parkers to the conference room.]
>
> WALKINSKI: "Now let me explain what we'll be doing today. I need to obtain some factual information to use when I prepare your court complaint."
>
> [Walkinski then proceeds to ask various factual questions.]
>
> J. PARKER: "After we complained to Denton about cutting down the trees, he offered to give us the wood for our fireplace. We took it. Does that affect our legal rights?"
>
> WALKINSKI: "No. Denton committed trespass to land by cutting the trees. You can still recover damages for the value of the trees."
>
> B. PARKER: "We sold the cut wood. Would we have to deduct that from what we ask for in court?"
>
> WALKINSKI: "No. Getting the wood doesn't matter at all, as a matter of law."
>
> [At the end of the meeting, Walkinski mentioned the following.]
>
> WALKINSKI: "Now it will take me several days to prepare these pleadings. I will give you a call when they're ready, so you can come back and we will review them and sign them."
>
> PARKERS: "Thank you. We'll make an appointment for next week as we leave."

Walkinski engaged in the unauthorized practice of law. She made no mention of her status as a paralegal to the Parkers. In fact, the Parkers may easily have believed Walkinski to be a licensed attorney, given her conduct during the consultation. Furthermore, Walkinski provided the clients with independent legal advice, which incidentally, was incorrect.

* * *

6. *In re* Larken

Edith Larken is a paralegal employed at the law firm of Tried, True, Tested & Tempered. One day she telephoned Simms O'Connor, a dishwasher employed at The Living End, a restaurant against which one of Tried's clients, Amanda Marcia, had several tort claims, including negligence, negligent infliction of emotional distress, and battery. Marcia had contracted food poisoning after eating at the restaurant. Larken telephoned O'Connor to see if he would be willing to make a statement in the case. The following conversation ensued:

LARKEN: "Do you remember anything about the food they were serving that night?"

O'CONNOR: "Yeah, well, the boss wouldn't like me saying this, but there was an awful stench back there [in the kitchen] when they were cooking something."

LARKEN: "Was it the pork? Did anyone say anything to the manager or the cook about it?"

O'CONNOR: "I don't rightly know if it was pork or not. I don't remember anyone talking about it. But the smell was pretty bad. Everybody back there must have noticed it."

LARKEN: "The doctors weren't sure whether the pork made our client sick or something else, so it's important that we know for sure whether the smell came from spoiled pork."

O'CONNOR: "I really don't know for sure. I'm the dishwasher, so I don't work much with the food before it's cooked and eaten. After some folks get done with a meal, it's hard to tell what was on the plate."

LARKEN: "Thanks for your help. I'll be in touch if I need any more information."

O'CONNOR: "Sure, glad to help out."

Larken disclosed client confidences when she told O'Connor about the physicians' uncertainty as to the cause of Marcia's ailment. This admission could be fatal to Marcia's case, in the event O'Connor related the statement to the restaurant management.

* * *

7. *In re* Dennison

Paul Dennison is a paralegal employed by Bartram J. Hollingsworth III, attorney at law. One of Hollingsworth's clients is Aslo, Simon & Conley, an investment firm. Hollingsworth instructed Dennison to telephone Doubleday Savings Bank to discuss a computer inaccuracy on one of Aslo's commercial investment accounts. Hollingsworth feared that Aslo might possibly be liable for defamation by computer. Dennison spoke with Ernest Duley, commercial investment coordinator, who himself was a paralegal, with whom Dennison attended college. Dennison mentioned the error to Duley. Duley inquired about the high frequency of withdrawals and deposits in the account. Dennison replied that Aslo had to cover "unexpected exigencies." Duley asked Dennison to elaborate. Dennison mentioned that Aslo had been the primary financing partner in the recent Southside Mall fiasco, in which both Aslo and several of their investment clients "lost a bundle." Dennison told Duley that, as a result, funds from Aslo's client investment accounts had had to be temporarily diverted. Duley warned that this "revenue dunking" was illegal comingling of client and nonclient funds. Dennison laughed, saying, "I guess we can't slip things past you, can we?" Later, Duley recommended to the bank's executive vice president to report Aslo's conduct to the attorney general's office.

Dennison acted unethically. Like Larken in the previous hypothetical, Dennison disclosed confidential client information (i.e., the Southside Mall losses, the comingling of funds). Furthermore, Dennison's involvement in illegal comingling violated the NALA and ABA rules precluding legal professionals from engaging in unlawful or inappropriate activities. ∎

§ 12.6 Further Ethics Information

The American Bar Association, as well as some state bars, issues ethics opinions to attorneys advising them of appropriate or inappropriate conduct under certain factual circumstances. State courts also report opinions involving attorney discipline that discuss ethical considerations. Although these cases involve attorneys, many also address legal ethics involving paralegals or legal secretaries. NALA and NFPA have also collected ethics opinions and court cases directly involving paralegal ethics problems. State paralegal associations may also have researched such cases. One is encouraged to contact these sources for additional ethics information pertinent to one's jurisdiction.

The following cases may be of particular interest to paralegals:

Taylor v. Chubb, 874 P.2d 806 (Okla. 1994)

Missouri v. Jenkins, 491 U.S. 274, 109 S.Ct. 2463, 105 L.Ed.2d 229 (1989), 11 U.S.C.A. § 330

Akron Bar Assn. v. Green, 673 N.E.2d 1307 (Ohio 1997)

Lousiana State Bar Assn. v. Edwins, 540 So.2d 294 (La. 1989)

The Case for Recusal

Not only are attorneys and paralegals bound by a code of ethics, but there are codes of judicial ethics that apply to judges as well. This case resulted from the headline tragedy where two dogs attacked and killed a woman. In addition to the criminal case brought against the owners of the dogs, there was an administrative hearing to determine the fate of Hera, one of the dogs. This appeal focuses on whether a police officer, whose department conducted the criminal investigation against the dog owners, could serve as an impartial hearing officer in the administrative hearing concerning the dog. *Note*: A *recusation*, or *recusal*, is the process by which a judge is disqualified (or disqualifies himself or herself) from hearing a lawsuit because of prejudice or because the judge is interested.

KNOLLER
v.
CITY AND COUNTY OF SAN FRANCISCO

Court of Appeal, First District,
Division 2, California
October 25, 2001
2001 WL 1295407

In this appeal, appellants contend they were denied a fair hearing before an impartial hearing officer. Specifically, they argue that because the hearing officer was a sergeant in the San Francisco Police Department—the very police department which instituted criminal charges against appellants stemming from a fatal dog attack involving Hera—the entire hearing process was irreparably tainted with bias and unfairness. ...

On January 26, 2001, two dogs, Bane and Hera, were involved in a vicious attack that resulted in the death of Diane Whipple, a fellow tenant in appellants' apartment building. Appellant Knoller, who was present during the attack, immediately signed documents giving ownership of Bane to San Francisco's Animal Care and Control (ACC), but refused to do so for Hera. Officers from the ACC [held an] administrative hearing to determine whether the dog was "vicious and dangerous" within the meaning of Health Code section 42.3.

The administrative hearing took place on February 13, 2001. The hearing officer was San Francisco Police Sergeant William Herndon, who had conducted vicious and dangerous dog hearings for more than eight years. Before the hearing commenced, appellants filed a challenge to Sergeant Herndon acting as the hearing officer, claiming he could not judge the evidence impartially. However, he refused to disqualify himself from the proceedings.

* * *

David Moser, a former tenant in appellants' apartment building testified that in June 2000, Hera bit him on the buttocks as he exited an elevator. ... One of the ACC officers described her as "crazed." The other ACC officer described her as "extremely aggressive."

* * *

Based on the evidence presented at the hearing, Sergeant Herndon concluded that Hera was a vicious and dangerous dog and that she must be destroyed to protect the health, safety and welfare of the community. Additionally, appellants were prohibited from "owning, possessing, controlling or having custody of any dog" for a three-year period.

* * *

Appellants' primary contention is that they were denied a fair hearing before an impartial hearing officer. It is uncontested that the hearing officer who presided over the administrative hearing, Sergeant Herndon, was employed by and subject to the supervision and control of the San Francisco Police Department. It is further uncontested that during the administrative proceedings, the San Francisco Police Department was conducting the investigation that led to the filing of criminal charges against appellants stemming from the dog attack that killed Diane Whipple. Appellants contend that, because there was an ongoing criminal investigation at the time the hearing was conducted and the investigating body employed the decision maker, they were deprived of a neutral hearing officer as required by the due process clause of the state and federal constitutions. ...

Appellants are correct that if there is to be a fair hearing, it must be presided over by an impartial trier of fact. However, contrary to appellants' argument, the standard of impartiality required in administrative hearings is different from that required of judicial bench officers, and has been met here.

The standards of impartiality affecting the ability of judicial officers to preside over adjudicative proceedings appear in both the Code of Civil Procedure and the California Code of Judicial Ethics (the Ethics Code). As potentially applicable here, Code of Civil Procedure section 170.1, subdivision (a)(6)(C) requires disqualification whenever "a person aware of the facts might reasonably entertain a doubt that the judge would be able to be impartial. Bias or prejudice toward a lawyer in the proceedings may be grounds for disqualification." It has been held that a trial judge may not sit in a matter in which the judge formerly participated in the investigation or charging of the incident in question. However, by its own terms, the disqualification statutes (Code Civ. Proc., § 170 et seq.) apply only to "judges of the municipal and superior courts, and court commissioners and referees."

Similarly, Canon 3E of the Ethics Code requires voluntary disqualification "in any proceeding in which disqualification is required by law." Yet once again, those affected by the canons are limited to "officer[s] of the state judicial system and who performs judicial functions. ..." Clearly, administrative hearing officers are not bound by the Ethics Code.

In the administrative context, a decision maker's familiarity with the facts of a case gained in the participation of the investigation that led to the action in question does not disqualify that person in the absence of a strong showing that he or she is incapable of judging the particular controversy fairly on the basis of its facts.

Thus, rather than requiring disqualification solely because "a person aware of the facts might reasonably entertain a doubt that the judge would be able to be impartial" (Code Civ. Proc., § 170.1, subd. (a)(6)(C)), to establish bias or prejudice of an administrative hearing officer, appellants must "set forth legally sufficient facts to demonstrate the bias of the judicial officer," and must further show that "such bias will render it probable that a fair trial cannot be held before that judge."

On this record, we conclude appellants have wholly failed to meet the higher standard necessary to establish bias or prejudice on the part of the hearing officer who presided over the administrative proceedings to determine Hera's fate. ...

Appellants' showing on this issue is entirely conjectural, and simply inadequate to overcome the presumption Sergeant Herndon was capable of deciding the matter conscientiously, fairly, and with honesty and integrity. This presumption of impartiality is bolstered by a declaration Sergeant Herndon filed in the trial court indicating he had "not participated in, or had any involvement with, the San Francisco Police Department's investigation" of possible criminal liability for the death of Diane Whipple. ...

When all is said and done, appellants have simply proposed a per se prohibition against police officers serving as hearing officers in vicious and dangerous dog hearings when there is a criminal investigation pending involving the dog. However, courts have consistently rejected the notion that strict separation of functions must be observed in order for an administrative adjudication to comport with due process guarantees.

... Therefore, it was not error for Sergeant   * * *
Herndon to refuse to disqualify himself.

Case Questions

1. Give an example of the facts that would have been needed to have required Sergeant Herndon to recuse himself from the case.
2. Does your state have codes of ethics for attorneys, paralegals, and judges? If so, give a brief description of the applicable provisions of the codes that address bias and impartiality.

Summary

NALA has issued an ethics code and guidelines applicable to paralegals. These rules broadly summarize the activities in which paralegals may ethically engage. NALA's Code and Model Guidelines declare that paralegals may not engage in the unauthorized practice of law, shall disclose their status, shall perform delegated duties under attorneys' supervision, shall not apply independent legal judgment, shall protect client confidences, shall maintain professional integrity and educational competence, and shall comply with the various rules and statutes regulating attorneys' conduct.

The NFPA, another national paralegal organization, has also issued a code of ethics and guidelines applying to paralegals. They emphasize the paralegal's role in working to provide legal services to the highest standards of ethics and professional integrity.

The ABA's Code of Professional Responsibility and Model Rules of Professional Conduct apply to paralegals. These rules provide both broad and particular guidance to attorneys and their staff regarding unethical behavior.

Hypothetical problems provide the best illustrations of unethical versus ethical conduct among paralegals. One should consult the state bar, the ABA, and paralegal associations, as well as NALA and NFPA for further information concerning paralegal ethics practices.

Problems

1. You just started working as a paralegal in a new law firm specializing in complex negligence cases. The attorneys are interested in using every kind of advertising that is permissible in your state. They would like giant billboards, television advertisements with paid actors, and colorful advertisements splashed across the outside of the city buses. The attorneys pride themselves on their expertise, and in addition to the information that is found on their letterhead, they would like each advertisement to say, "TOP GUNS, you tried the rest, but we are the best." Which of the nine Canons of the ABA Code of Professional Responsibility would most directly affect your research of this issue? Why?

2. A movie celebrity comes to your firm for legal representation concerning a drinking and driving automobile accident. You can't wait to get home so you can call your best friend and tell your significant other about who just walked into your office and all about the accident. Then you

start to think about the NFPA and the Model Disciplinary Rules. What rule should you consider before talking about your work with friends and family? What possible harm could result from violating a Disciplinary Rule?

3. After five years as a paralegal, you have earned the complete respect and admiration of the senior partner in your firm. She tells you that from now on you will each handle half of the cases in the office from start to finish. The partner tells you that she does not do trial work, if a case needs to be tried, she will make a referral to a colleague at the appropriate time. Which NALA Model Guideline would assist you in deciding if this suggested work arrangement is ethical for a paralegal? Explain your answer.

4. You are hired by a law firm specializing in products liability cases to perform legal research and draft documents. Based on the NALA Model Guidelines, are there any limits or conditions to your performing these tasks? What would be the harm if you did not adhere to the applicable NALA Guideline?

5. As a paralegal working for a single practitioner, you are responsible for answering all incoming calls. The attorney generally takes a fee of one-third of whatever is collected for negligence actions. A potential client calls explaining that he was just in an extremely serious multicar collision, and wants to know how much the attorney charges. The attorney is on the telephone, has two clients waiting in the waiting area, one call on hold, and a client sitting in the conference room. The caller tells you that he does not have all day, and can't wait for the attorney to call him back. You are afraid that the attorney might lose this new case if you do not provide an answer to the caller. You know for certain that the attorney had taken a fee of one-third of the recovery from his last ten negligence cases. In order to be helpful, you tell the client the fee will be one-third of whatever the attorney collects. Have you done anything wrong based upon the NALA Model Guidelines? Explain.

Review Questions

1. Which two organizations have designed ethics provisions specifically addressing paralegals?
2. In such ethics codes, what activities are specifically authorized? Under which ethics code are these listed?
3. What is the unauthorized practice of law? What types of actions can it include?
4. Under what circumstances are paralegals permitted to represent clients? What are some courts' reactions?
5. When can paralegals perform legal tasks? What restrictions apply under the ethics codes?
6. What must paralegals recall when dealing with clients, adverse parties, witnesses, or the general public?
7. What would you do if you observed a partner in your law firm engaging in an unethical act?

Projects

1. How is "unauthorized practice of law" defined in your state statutes? What are the penalties for violations?
2. Does your state have a statute that permits lay representation of clients in certain courts? If so, how does it compare to the Montana statute discussed in the *Sparks* case on page 382?

Internet Resources

This chapter focuses on paralegal ethics. To learn more about paralegal ehtcs, the following sites can be accessed:

NALA, NFPA, and ABA
http://www.nala.org
http://www.paralegals.org
http://www.abanet.org

Ethics
http://www.legalethics.com
http://www.findlaw.com/01topics/14ethics/bars.html

Law Schools
http://www.hg.org/schools.html

Law Firms
http://www.findlaw.com/14firms/index.html
http://www.martindale.com

Continuing Legal Education
http://www.ALI-ABA.org

Discussion Groups
http://www.lib.uchicago.edu/~llou/lawlists/info.html

Yahoo's Law Guide
http://www.yahoo.com/Government/Law

New York State Law Journal
http://www.nylj.com

CNN Interactive
http://www.cnn.com/

Legal Forms
http://www.lectlaw.com/forma.html

For additional resources, visit our Web site at
www.paralegal.delmar.cengage.com

CHAPTER 13

TORT INVESTIGATION

CHAPTER OUTLINE

§ 13.1   Tort Investigation
§ 13.2   Introduction to Investigation
§ 13.3   The Importance of Tort Case Investigation
§ 13.4   Witness Interview Techniques and Questions
§ 13.5   Determining and Locating Defendants
§ 13.6   Documenting the Scene
§ 13.7   Public and Private Sector Resources
§ 13.8   Additional Areas to Investigate
§ 13.9   Investigating Different Types of Tort Cases

It is difficult to make our material condition
better by the best of law, but it is easy
enough to ruin it by bad laws.
THEODORE ROOSEVELT

§ 13.1 Tort Investigation

Approximately 10 percent of the paralegals in the United States specialize in personal injury litigation. Many more paralegals work on personal injury cases from time to time as it is one of the many areas of law routinely handled by general-practice firms.

Some of the many tasks a personal injury paralegal performs are:

- Interviewing clients to elicit the particular facts of their cases
- Obtaining witness statements
- Investigating the accident, condition, or occurrence
- Assisting in the preparation of legal documents, such as the summons, complaint, answer, or reply
- Preparing settlement summaries
- Preparing discovery requests, tracking and monitoring responses to discovery requests, and summarizing deposition transcripts
- Researching legal issues and assisting in preparing motions
- Scheduling witnesses and experts for trial
- Preparing exhibits for trial
- Organizing evidence for trial
- Preparing cases for arbitration
- Preparing subpoenas for trial and arranging for service of process
- Aiding in preparing clients for testifying at trial
- Being present at trial to assist the attorney
- Assisting in the preparation and research of appellate briefs
- Researching different legal theories.

§ 13.2 Introduction to Investigation

Investigating the facts and circumstances surrounding tortious injury or death offers many challenges. Every tort case presents the following fundamental questions, which journalists use every day in a reporting context: *Who? What? Where? When? Why? How?* In tort cases, the paralegal queries: Who injured the victim (plaintiff)? What injuries happened? How did the victim (plaintiff) get hurt? Where and when did the injuries occur? Why did the victim (plaintiff) incur injuries (that is, did the defendant(s) cause the victim's/plaintiff's injuries)? How did the injuries occur?

This chapter examines the procedures paralegals use to investigate tort cases. These techniques are then illustrated in the context of specific types of tort cases.

§ 13.3 The Importance of Tort Case Investigation

investigation†
A systematic examination, especially an official inquiry.

Key facts must be ascertained if a law firm is to properly handle a personal injury or property damage lawsuit. This entails an **investigation**.

Paralegals and Investigators

Each attorney or law firm has its own specialized methods for conducting investigations. Some have in-house investigators; others hire outside investigators or investigation services. Some attorneys hire specialists for specific aspects of a tort case. Some rely on law clerks, paralegals, or other staff members to perform certain aspects of investigations.

Even if the paralegal is not required to conduct investigations, it is essential that he or she know what is needed for each type of case in order to supervise or monitor the investigation. Paralegals need to know when a particular piece of information may lead to something else and therefore merits additional investigation. Conversely, paralegals should develop a sense of what items of information are not useful or relevant. One must be able to review the investigation, make sure it has been done properly and completely, and ascertain whether further research is needed.

Many paralegals handle particular aspects of investigation, either in the stages of case evaluation and development or in the course of case management. This is especially true when the trial team is determining potential defendants and ascertaining the basic facts of what happened and why. At times, a knowledgeable paralegal will spot legal issues early on that have a significant bearing on the case investigation. For example, the paralegal might learn of the existence of photographs taken by a rescue squad that show details about the condition of an accident scene.

Customizing the Investigation

The tort trial team will want to adapt the investigation to fit the case. Investigations can be quite simple or highly complex and technical. Factors such as the severity of the injury involved and resources available often control the scope of the investigation. "Resources available" are such factors as the client's ability to pay, the attorney's ability to advance the costs of investigation, the financial condition of prospective defendants, and the existence of insurance, all of which must be considered.

Details, Details, Details!

In litigation, details are very important. An overlooked detail could make a real difference in the outcome of the case. Investigations must be customized, with more than a little creativity. For example, suppose that you are investigating an automobile accident. You cannot understand why the driver of the vehicle did not stop for the pedestrian in the crosswalk. A witness tells you that she noticed the driver was wearing glasses, but this should *not* be enough proof for you to automatically conclude that the driver could see properly. It is possible that the driver was only wearing reading glasses when distance glasses were needed. It is also possible that the driver was wearing an old pair of glasses and never bothered to get a new prescription. Little details like these can make or break a case.

Goals of Tort Case Investigation

Factual investigation is designed to shed light on liability and damages. Information is gathered in terms of what happened to the injured party, who may or may not have been responsible for the injuries, and any act or omission by the injured party that contributed to the accident.

If all else fails, it may be necessary to turn over the investigation, or portions of it, to a professional investigator who has access to automated databases and other resources. However, this is not practical in a small case or in a case where the firm's client has limited financial resources.

§ 13.4 Witness Interview Techniques and Questions

Witnesses will explain their account of the circumstances before and after the accident, how the accident occurred, and the damages or injuries received by the people involved. Some firms prefer that such interviews be electronically recorded, or written and signed by the witness for future reference or use. Witnesses sometimes forget or change their testimony. It is important to interview witnesses as soon as possible; they will be easier to locate, and their recollections will be clearer. Figure 13-1 shows a sample witness statement.

WITNESS STATEMENT

<u>14 Fern Dr.</u>　　　<u>Albany</u>　　　<u>N.Y.</u>　　　<u>5/03/03</u>
LOCATION　　　　　CITY　　　　STATE　　　　DATE

1. My name is Kris J. McGrail. I reside at 14 Fern Drive,
2. Albany, NY. I am employed by the Albany Police
3. Department. My date of birth is 10/10/59. On 4/28/03 I
4. witnessed an accident on Sand Creek Road east of Wolf
5. Road. I was sitting on my motorcycle at the Hess
6. Station on Sand Creek and Wolf Road. I was just
7. finished getting gas and was getting ready to leave when
8. I witnessed an accident. I was just about to leave the
9. gas station when I noticed a motorcycle heading across
10. Wolf Road going eastbound. This motorcycle had a green
11. light as it crossed Wolf Road on Sand Creek Road. I
12. noticed the motorcycle because the driver was wearing a
13. T-shirt and I thought he was brave because although it
14. was nice out it wasn't that warm. There was a gold-
15. toned vehicle behind me at the pumps at the Hess
16. Station facing north. This vehicle, which I later learned
17. was driven by Deborah Lawrence, pulled around me at
18. the pump and began to exit from the Hess Station. Ms.
19. Lawrence used the exit of the Hess Station going onto
20. Sand Creek Road. Ms. Lawrence came to a gliding stop
21. and exited the driveway going westbound. Ms. Lawrence
22. never brought her car to a full stop as she exited the
23. driveway. Ms. Lawrence did not have the directional
24.
25.
26.
27. Wit: Cathy Okrent　　　　　　　　　　Kris McGrail

DO NOT WRITE BELOW THIS LINE

FIGURE 13-1 Sample witness statement

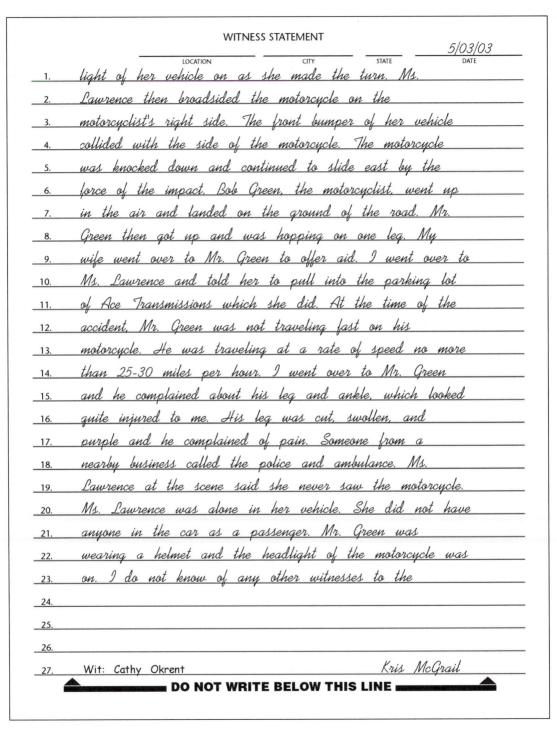

WITNESS STATEMENT

5/03/03

LOCATION   CITY   STATE   DATE

1. light of her vehicle on as she made the turn. Ms.
2. Lawrence then broadsided the motorcycle on the
3. motorcyclist's right side. The front bumper of her vehicle
4. collided with the side of the motorcycle. The motorcycle
5. was knocked down and continued to slide east by the
6. force of the impact. Bob Green, the motorcyclist, went up
7. in the air and landed on the ground of the road. Mr.
8. Green then got up and was hopping on one leg. My
9. wife went over to Mr. Green to offer aid. I went over to
10. Ms. Lawrence and told her to pull into the parking lot
11. of Ace Transmissions which she did. At the time of the
12. accident, Mr. Green was not traveling fast on his
13. motorcycle. He was traveling at a rate of speed no more
14. than 25-30 miles per hour. I went over to Mr. Green
15. and he complained about his leg and ankle, which looked
16. quite injured to me. His leg was cut, swollen, and
17. purple and he complained of pain. Someone from a
18. nearby business called the police and ambulance. Ms.
19. Lawrence at the scene said she never saw the motorcycle.
20. Ms. Lawrence was alone in her vehicle. She did not have
21. anyone in the car as a passenger. Mr. Green was
22. wearing a helmet and the headlight of the motorcycle was
23. on. I do not know of any other witnesses to the
24.
25.
26.
27.   Wit: Cathy Okrent   Kris McGrail

DO NOT WRITE BELOW THIS LINE

FIGURE 13-1 Sample witness statement (*continued*)

WITNESS STATEMENT

			5/03/03
LOCATION	CITY	STATE	DATE

1. *accident. I believe this accident was caused by Ms.*
2. *Lawrence's inattention and failure to yield the right of*
3. *way to Mr. Green, the motorcyclist.*
4.
5. *I have read the above statement and it is true to the*
6. *best of my knowledge.*
7.
8.
9.   *Kris McGrail*
10.
11.
12.
13.
14.
15.
16.
17.
18.
19.
20.
21.
22.
23.   Cathy Okrent
24.   Notary Public State of New York
                                Qualified in Schenectady County
25.   Commission Expires July 31, 2004
26.
27.

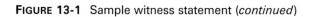
DO NOT WRITE BELOW THIS LINE

FIGURE 13-1 Sample witness statement (*continued*)

Client Interview Techniques

Personal injury paralegals are often involved in interviewing clients and witnesses. Some firms will have the client fill out an initial information questionnaire that is specifically geared to garner the information needed to handle a personal injury case. (See the client information questionnaire in Appendix A.) Other firms might desire a more informal initial contact with clients, and prefer that a paralegal or attorney greet the clients and interview them.

It is always important to put the client at ease. Be sure the client is comfortable with you and the law-office surroundings before getting down to details. Small talk of a general nature helps. When the client sees that you care about him or her as a person, rather than as the next slip-and-fall case, he or she will be more apt to confide in you and provide you with the information needed for the best possible representation.

It is important to remember that, for many clients, this injury claim represents the first time that they have been to an attorney's office. For some clients, an appointment with an attorney is a very intimidating experience, particularly when the attorney hastily greets them and then must excuse himself or herself to go to court at the last minute. The clients are left feeling that the attorney was too busy to see them. The paralegal then becomes an invaluable bridge between the attorney and the client. Eventually, the client will see that the paralegal often has more time to speak with the client and is more readily accessible by telephone or for office conferences than the trial attorney. Some clients prefer to speak with the paralegal working on their case for this very reason. You might even notice that clients will tell you things that they are reluctant to tell the attorney. Some clients are hesitant to take up the attorney's time, or feel that the attorney will think less of them, or will not want to represent them if they tell the attorney all the details of the case.

This is one reason why the role of the paralegal is so important. A paralegal who encourages the client to talk and thoroughly interviews the client about the accident provides a wealth of information for the attorney and other members of the litigation team who might later work on the file.

Depending on your jurisdiction, it could take anywhere from months to four or five years for a personal injury case to reach the trial date. At the time of trial, your client's only recollection of the accident may be that which previously was told to you and recorded in the file. The same is true of witnesses. The importance of a thorough interview, and possible followup interviews, at the outset of a case cannot be emphasized enough. In time, each paralegal develops his or her own method of interviewing. Some think of an interview like a tree. You proceed up the main trunk, but at any time, your client might say something that causes you to branch off to focus on specific facts or issues. Then it is up to you to determine if you need to return to your main series of questions, or if perhaps the new information obtained should be pursued first.

§ 13.5 Determining and Locating Defendants

Besides the client, the most critical participants in any tort litigation are any potential defendants. If a plaintiff's attorney cannot find someone to sue successfully, then the client's tort case comes to a halt. A paralegal may be asked to locate all prospective defendants. In most tort cases, determining defendants to sue is done through in-house investigation, although occasionally it will be necessary for an investigator with more extensive resources to locate a defendant or research information (for example, regarding the principals of a defunct partnership or corporation).

It is sometimes difficult to identify and locate defendants. This is particularly true if a business operating under a trade name has been dissolved or has otherwise "vanished" since the tort was committed. Even individuals can "disappear," as debt collectors and skip-tracers become acutely aware when searching for fleeing debtors. Some tortfeasors lie low to avoid service of process and liability. Some businesses create dummy corporations or partnerships to "front" for shareholders, who may be individuals, other corporations, or partnerships that hope to remain hidden from potential tort plaintiffs.In some instances, the client may simply be unaware of the defendant's correct corporate name.

Using Discovery to Locate Defendants

discovery
1. The formal and informal exchange of information between sides in a lawsuit. ...
2. Finding out something previously unknown. ...

Discovery is the phase in a lawsuit when information is exchanged between the parties and the issues for trial are narrowed. Occasionally, discovery will be served upon known defendants to uncover information about unknown defendants or ones that cannot be located. The paralegal should check the rules of civil procedure and discovery in his or her jurisdiction to see if prelitigation discovery is allowed, and if a court order is needed. If not, discovery will have to be conducted after the lawsuit commences. An example of this is California Civil Code § 2025, which puts a hold on discovery for ten days after the summons and complaint are served.

Study Documents Carefully

Every piece of paper a paralegal obtains regarding a client's tort case is a prospective source of information regarding potential defendants. Police accident reports (see Figure 13-2) are an obvious example in personal injury cases, but there are many others. Letters, invoices, leases, articles in newspapers, ambulance reports, witnesses' statements, and other documents often contain vital leads to find defendants. Any document connected to the parties and the circumstances involved in the tort might contain information a paralegal could use to locate defendants. Frequently one finds a clue about the accident through which one may determine a defendant's name, address, or parent company name—perhaps from the fine print in the document.

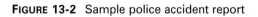

FIGURE 13-2 Sample police accident report

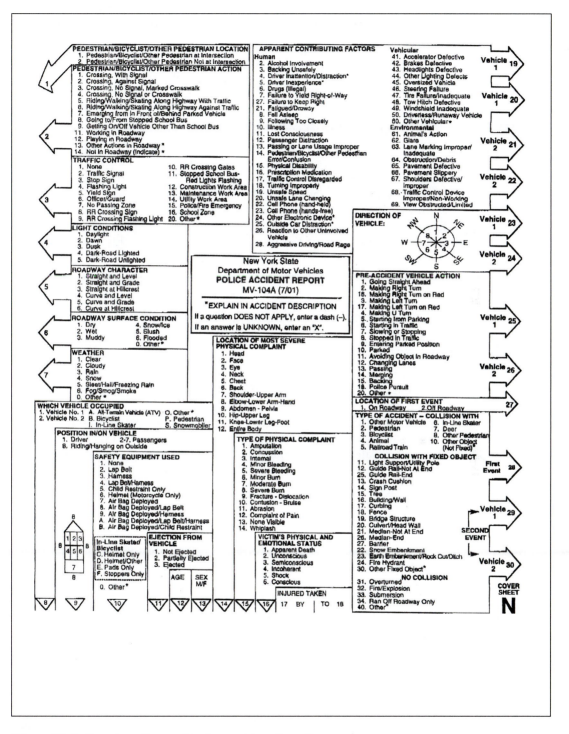

FIGURE 13-2 Sample police accident report (*continued*)

Use Caution When Naming Defendants

Paralegals must be certain to have the correct defendants before a tort lawsuit is filed. If one files notice, sues the wrong defendant, or fails to name a proper defendant, serious problems may arise. For instance, the attorney or law firm may be subject to legal action and/or disciplinary proceedings for filing a frivolous lawsuit against the innocent defendant. Additionally, the statute of limitations or a notice requirement may run on a client's lawsuit without the correct defendant(s) having been notified or sued. Mistakes in this area may even result in a claim of malpractice by the client against the attorney.

The paralegal should check all available resources to ensure that the correct individual or business entity is being identified as the defendant. Investigatory novices might be satisfied by pulling a company or individual's name out of the telephone directory, but this practice can be disastrous if the purported defendant turns out to be an innocent "same-name" person or business.

Using the Telephone as a Research Tool

Modern telecommunication has made pounding the pavement an obsolete method of obtaining some case information. Telephone calls are usually faster in uncovering details concerning defendants, particularly when the person called is cooperative and talkative. If a shopping center, apartment complex, or similar business or building is involved, chances are that someone at the office will tell a paralegal over the phone who the owners are or will reveal the name of the management company. Oral communication skills are at a premium here. A good investigative paralegal, like a good journalist, knows how to get information without giving away any secrets or motives. In general, information should flow *to* the paralegal from nonclient witnesses; the paralegal should be wary of giving out information.

With facsimile machines, an avalanche of documents can be secured without ever leaving one's law office, if one knows the correct contact person. With governmental agencies, however, one usually must still visit the appropriate offices to obtain documents, as there are usually photocopying fees associated with any governmental record, and governmental clerks are instructed not to release documents to someone making a nameless, faceless fax inquiry.

Internet Resources

A large part of tort investigation can now be completed using the Internet. There are a wide array of telephone, professional, and other directories that can now be accessed on the Web. You can research companies, get proper corporate names and addresses, and other information needed for suit directly from a company's Web site. Most government offices and agencies have Web sites where you can obtain information and even forms and brochures detailing the proper method for bringing a claim before the particular agency. A variety of the procedures described in this chapter for investigating a tort claim can also be conducted via the Internet.

Obtaining Information About Corporations

Most jurisdictions require corporations to be registered with the state in which they were incorporated, created, or are doing business.

Secretaries of State Offices

To locate a corporation, a paralegal should first contact the state agency that is responsible for keeping business organizational records. This is usually the secretary of state's corporate division for each state. Through a series of telephone calls, a paralegal may determine the correct names, addresses, officers, directors, and contact persons for service of process upon a corporation operating in a particular state. One may also discover the name of a parent corporation by searching the secretary of state's records. Figure 13-3 on page 408 shows a sample request to a secretary of state's office.

For a minimal fee, in most states the secretary of state's office will furnish other written documentation, such as a corporation's articles of incorporation, that has been filed with the governmental agency.

Business Directories

business directory†
A listing of corporations and other business organizations by name, geographic location, product or service, brand name, advertising, and other subject headings.

Business directories are another excellent source of information about business defendants. **Business directories** list corporations and other business organizations according to name, geographic location, product or service, brand name, advertising, and other subject headings. Most public or university libraries have these reference texts on reserve. Various private services, such as Dun & Bradstreet, Inc., also provide this information, in print or on-line.

Public Business Records

Other potential sources of information about business defendants include:

♦ Company annual reports

♦ The state attorney general's office

♦ The state or federal Departments of Commerce

♦ The Securities and Exchange Commission (SEC)

♦ Online services.

VAN & LIAL, P.C.
10 Church Street, New York, N.Y. 10007
Telephone (212) 732-9000

August 12, 2003

Department of State
Corporation Division
Albany, New York

Re: Koche v. Patrick

Gentlemen:

Kindly advise whether you have any filing for the following corporation: D. B. Associates, Inc., doing business out of Albany, New York.

Please indicate whether the above corporation is a New York corporation, and if so, when it was incorporated, where its principal office is, and whether the above designation is correct.

If it is not a New York corporation, kindly advise us in what state it was incorporated and if it is authorized to do business in the State of New York.

Thank you for a prompt reply to the undersigned.

Very truly yours,

VAN & LIAL, P.C.

By: _____
Donald Bronte, paralegal

DB/kn

FIGURE 13-3 Sample request to a secretary of state's office

SEC reports are surprisingly fertile sources of corporate information. The reports that companies are required to file with the SEC typically contain much more detailed information than is found in annual reports to stockholders. Also, SEC reports have the advantage of being more accessible than shareholder reports, which companies often consider rather confidential.

Obtaining Information About Partnerships

Partnerships can be more elusive than corporations. Investors sometimes form partnerships for specific projects, such as shopping centers or housing developments, and then disband them after the project is complete. Some jurisdictions require that partnerships be registered, in which case they can be located through the partnership section of the secretary of state's offices. However, there are fewer requirements for partnership registration than for corporations in some states. Most jurisdictions allow service of process upon any partner as notice to the partnership. **Process service** is the delivery of the summons to the defendant as a means of notifying the defendant of a pending action and compelling the defendant to appear in court.

service of process (process service)
The delivery (or its legal equivalent, such as publication in a newspaper in some cases) of a legal paper, such as a writ, by an authorized person in a way that meets certain formal requirements.

Obtaining the Names of Sole Proprietors and Partners

fictitious name†
A trade or assumed name used by corporations for the purpose of conducting business.

Many jurisdictions require that partnerships and individuals doing business under a trade name or assumed, **fictitious name** file a *doing business as (d/b/a)* certificate or affidavit with an appropriate governmental agency. Many local governments require sole proprietors and partnerships doing business in the county or city to file d/b/a certificates and affidavits with the local recorder's office.

Ambulance Services and Fire Departments as Defendants

Even the people called upon for assistance can end up being defendants in a lawsuit. If the fire department or ambulance service is called, and there is an unusual delay in their arrival, or if they do not have standard and appropriate equipment, the department may be liable. If equipment is not working properly, personnel are not properly trained to use it, or personnel are not supervised adequately, they may be potential defendants.

Usually the agency for which the offending individuals, firefighters, or ambulance service persons are working is added to the lawsuit for failure to supervise, failure to adequately train, or failure to provide appropriate and functional equipment. Of course, the theories of liability would depend upon the circumstances.

sunshine law
A law requiring open meetings of government agencies or allowing (or assisting) public access to government records.

A fire department or ambulance service is often owned or supervised by a governmental agency, such as the city, county, or town. However, there may be a volunteer organization in a small town or a rural or unincorporated area. If so, its contract with the cities or counties in the service area should be reviewed, if possible. **Sunshine laws** in each state usually provide for the disclosure of such information from governmental entities. Figure 13-4 on page 410 shows a typical request for information. Some local governments contract out ambulance services to private companies. Ambulances may also be owned and operated by hospitals and funeral homes.

Paralegals should carefully follow statutes or procedural rules for special notice requirements when suing governmental agencies. Some municipalities and governmental entities require prior notice of a condition or defect before a suit is permitted.

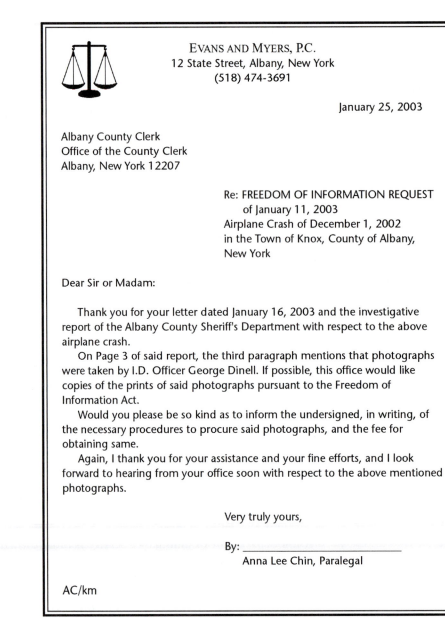

EVANS AND MYERS, P.C.
12 State Street, Albany, New York
(518) 474-3691

January 25, 2003

Albany County Clerk
Office of the County Clerk
Albany, New York 12207

Re: FREEDOM OF INFORMATION REQUEST
of January 11, 2003
Airplane Crash of December 1, 2002
in the Town of Knox, County of Albany,
New York

Dear Sir or Madam:

Thank you for your letter dated January 16, 2003 and the investigative report of the Albany County Sheriff's Department with respect to the above airplane crash.

On Page 3 of said report, the third paragraph mentions that photographs were taken by I.D. Officer George Dinell. If possible, this office would like copies of the prints of said photographs pursuant to the Freedom of Information Act.

Would you please be so kind as to inform the undersigned, in writing, of the necessary procedures to procure said photographs, and the fee for obtaining same.

Again, I thank you for your assistance and your fine efforts, and I look forward to hearing from your office soon with respect to the above mentioned photographs.

Very truly yours,

By: _____
Anna Lee Chin, Paralegal

AC/km

FIGURE 13-4 Sample request for information to government agency

Practical Application

When handling reports about situations in which negligence may be a factor, a paralegal should study the documents not only to determine the *facts* of what happened, but also to identify *who* was responsible.

Investigating Licensed or Regulated Businesses

Most states have a central department or agency that oversees licensed and regulated businesses. For example, in Texas this agency is the Texas Department of Licensing and Regulation. To uncover additional information about a licensed or regulated business, a paralegal should consult the state governmental listings in the telephone directory in the state in which the business is located.

Agencies can also provide listings of all state licensing requirements. By checking with the state agency, one may discover whether a potential business defendant's license, certification, or insurance has lapsed or is not in good standing. Also, information might be available about the defendant's proper name, address, and telephone number.

Typically, one must complete a request form to gain access to the information on file for a particular business at the state licensing agency. These documents will range from the business's initial application for the license to a copy of its insurance certificate. Many agencies have this information available on the Internet.

Practical Application

If the defendant is local, the paralegal should check the display advertisements in the telephone directory. Many businesses include their business license number in the advertisement or post it for inspection at the place of business. Having this information available may speed up one's request for information.

Sample Defendant Search

Consider the following hypothetical defendant search. The accident report lists Axtco Construction as the owner of a truck that struck the client's vehicle. The accident report will also have Axtco's address.

If Axtco is listed in the local telephone directory, the paralegal could first call to obtain the name of the president, owner, or chief executive officer. If the address on the accident report is an out-of-town address, obtain the number from directory assistance for that area code.

The paralegal should be prepared to reach an uncooperative Axtco employee who will not divulge any of this information without first knowing the reason. One should be extremely cautious regarding how much information to disclose during such direct telephone contact with a potential business defendant. Also recall that there are ethical considerations involved in such direct contact. The paralegal should consult with his or her supervising attorney to decide how much to tell the company personnel to obtain the names and addresses of the company chief executive officer, president, or other officer who can be sent a notice or demand letter and, subsequently, service of process. Usually, it is best to reveal as little as possible and to truthfully downplay any legal implications for which the information is being requested. Also, business directories (often found in reference sections of libraries) can be consulted for information about a business, as can online resources.

Assuming that the direct-contact approach yields little or no useful information regarding Axtco, the paralegal could next consult the secretary of state's corporate or partnership divisions to see if Axtco is a corporation or partnership authorized to conduct business in the state. If not, the paralegal could next contact the city or county governmental agency in which assumed or trade names are registered (e.g., the county recorder's office). The agency to consult will be located in the city or county in which Axtco's business offices are found. Then the paralegal could look up Axtco's trade or assumed name certificate or affidavit on file with the agency. Also, online resources might contain the needed information.

In case the accident report is unavailable or contains incomplete information about Axtco, the paralegal should look at any photographs of the vehicle from the accident scene. Do the company's name and address appear on the truck's doors or body? If not, the information may be available from the state's Department of Motor Vehicles.

Knowing who and where the defendants are is an important initial stage in every tort investigation. Another critical investigatory aspect involves the circumstances surrounding the victim/plaintiff's injuries. Section 13.6 considers how paralegals document tort accident scenes.

§ 13.6 Documenting the Scene

Although legal staff are almost never on the scene when a tort actually occurs, it is critical to document the scene of a tort injury as soon as possible.

Obtaining Visual Documentation, Measurements, and Other Details

Paralegals may take photographs or videotape recordings of accident scenes. Also, paralegals take measurements and describe physical conditions at the location itself. Documenting the scene should be done as soon as possible, because valuable evidence is often lost as conditions change over time. Accident scenes can alter naturally due to environmental changes; or, more frequently, people might deliberately modify conditions to prevent others from being harmed or to conceal possible liability.

Paralegals should be exceedingly thorough when documenting the scene of an accident or other tort. What seems insignificant at the time may be found to be important after more is known about the accident itself. For example, the distance between steps on a stairway, and whether the stairs were tiled or carpeted, could be vitally important in a slip-and-fall case. Also, it is meaningful when reconstructing an accident to have as much information about the actual scene at the time of the accident as possible. Figures 13-5 and 13-6 show sample accident reports. You might want to consider bringing a portable cassette tape recorder with you to supplement your investigatory notes.

Practical Application

> The scene of an accident should be documented as soon as possible. The paralegal should keep in mind that places and situations change, sometimes rapidly. Weather conditions can change streets and roads, construction projects may start or end, streetlights may be installed, or lighting that was on at the time of an accident may go out. A place of business may put up warnings or fences. A pool may be covered or drained. One may safely presume that potential defendants, if they are aware of their possible liabilities, will act quickly to have the cause of an accident repaired to prevent others from being injured.

Knowing the Evidentiary Rules for One's Jurisdiction

Every state has rules of evidence that regulate the admissibility of evidence. Not all evidence will automatically be admitted into evidence at the time of the trial. Sometimes the evidence must be in a specific form. You may have to obtain original records rather than photocopies. These rules can generally be obtained on-line.

As the tort investigation is conducted, the paralegal should put each item to be used at trial in admissible form. Rules of evidence from your jurisdiction should be consulted. Even evidence that will be used only for in-house purposes, or for settlement brochures or mediation packages, should be maintained in a form that could be admitted at trial if necessary. Documents that the trial team plans to use for evidence at trial *must* be suitable to present at trial. Otherwise, a paralegal may find himself or herself tracking down these documents at the last minute, having to put them into admissible form (such as certified copies, which also usually requires another fee), and generally wasting time that could have been better spent on other aspects of trial preparation. Sometimes opposing counsel will cooperate in stipulating to the admissibility of certain documents; sometimes not.

Using Proper Evidentiary Form

Looking ahead to trial, paralegals should consult the relevant state, local, or federal procedural and evidentiary rules to determine the form in which evidence must be submitted into the trial record and what type of documentation is required. For instance:

♦ Does the court require supporting affidavits for admission of medical records and bills into evidence?

♦ Is there a certain form or language for business records? If not, how are they proved in court? Are original records necessary, or will copies suffice?

STATE OF CALIFORNIA
DMV
DEPARTMENT OF MOTOR VEHICLES
A Public Service Agency

REPORT OF TRAFFIC ACCIDENT OCCURRING IN CALIFORNIA

DMV USE ONLY

READ IMPORTANT INFORMATION ON BACK

AS APPROPRIATE, PLEASE TYPE OR PRINT IN BOXES

\# OF VEHICLES | DATE OF ACCIDENT M M D D Y Y | CALIFORNIA COUNTY OF ACCIDENT | CALIFORNIA CITY WHERE ACCIDENT OCCURRED

REPORTING PARTY'S INFORMATION

TIME OF ACCIDENT
Hour ________ ☐ AM ☐ PM ☐ In Traffic ☐ Parked ☐ Pedestrian ☐ Bicyclist ☐ Other *(EXPLAIN, E.G., ROLLAWAY)*
DRIVING FOR EMPLOYER ☐ Yes ☐ No

DRIVER'S NAME (FIRST AND MIDDLE) | LAST NAME | DRIVER LICENSE NUMBER | STATE

DRIVER'S ADDRESS *(NUMBER)* | STREET | DATE OF BIRTH M M D D Y Y | DAMAGE AMOUNT .00

CITY | STATE | ZIP CODE | TELEPHONE NUMBERS Wk (   ) Hm (   )

VEHICLE OWNER—PERSON OR COMPANY | DATE OF BIRTH M M D D Y Y | VEHICLE LICENSE PLATE | STATE

ADDRESS | CITY | STATE | ZIP CODE

VEHICLE IDENTIFICATION NUMBER | INSURANCE COMPANY NAME *(NOT AGENT, UNDERWRITER, OR BROKER)* | COMPANY NAIC NUMBER

INSURANCE POLICY NUMBER COVERING THE VEHICLE ACCIDENT *(NOT CLAIM OR FILE NUMBER)* | POLICY PERIOD From ____________ To ____________

POLICY HOLDER'S NAME *(IF DIFFERENT)* | STREET ADDRESS | CITY | STATE | ZIP CODE

OTHER PARTY'S INFORMATION

☐ In Traffic ☐ Parked ☐ Pedestrian ☐ Bicyclist ☐ Other *(EXPLAIN, E.G., ROLLAWAY)*
DRIVING FOR EMPLOYER ☐ Yes ☐ No

DRIVER'S NAME (FIRST AND MIDDLE) | LAST NAME | DRIVER LICENSE NUMBER | STATE

DRIVER'S ADDRESS *(NUMBER)* | STREET | DATE OF BIRTH M M D D Y Y | DAMAGE AMOUNT .00

CITY | STATE | ZIP CODE | TELEPHONE NUMBERS Wk (   ) Hm (   )

VEHICLE OWNER—PERSON OR COMPANY | DATE OF BIRTH M M D D Y Y | VEHICLE LICENSE PLATE | STATE

ADDRESS | CITY | STATE | ZIP CODE

VEHICLE IDENTIFICATION NUMBER | INSURANCE COMPANY NAME *(NOT AGENT, UNDERWRITER, OR BROKER)* | COMPANY NAIC NUMBER

INSURANCE POLICY NUMBER COVERING THE VEHICLE ACCIDENT *(NOT CLAIM OR FILE NUMBER)* | POLICY PERIOD From ____________ To ____________

POLICY HOLDER'S NAME *(IF DIFFERENT)* | STREET ADDRESS | CITY | STATE | ZIP CODE

INJURY/DEATH PROPERTY DAMAGE

NAME AND ADDRESS OF INDIVIDUAL INJURED OR DECEASED
☐ Injured ☐ Deceased | ☐ Driver ☐ Passenger ☐ Bicyclist ☐ Pedestrian

NAME AND ADDRESS OF INDIVIDUAL INJURED OR DECEASED
☐ Injured ☐ Deceased | ☐ Driver ☐ Passenger ☐ Bicyclist ☐ Pedestrian

OTHER PROPERTY DAMAGED *(TELEPHONE POLES, FENCE, LIVESTOCK, ETC.)* | DAMAGE AMOUNT .00

PROPERTY OWNER'S NAME AND ADDRESS

I certify under penalty of perjury under the laws of the State of California that the information entered on this document is true and correct.

DATE | PRINTED NAME | SIGNATURE X

☐ ADDITIONAL INFORMATION ATTACHED

SR 1 (REV. 11/2002) **WWW**

FIGURE 13-5 Sample accident report

Section 399.125, Florida Statutes. Reporting of elevator accidents or incidents; penalties.--Within 5 working days after any accident or incident occurring in or upon any elevator, the certificate of operation holder shall report the accident or incident to the division on a form prescribed by the division. Failure to timely file this report is a violation of this chapter and will subject the certificate of operation holder to an administrative fine, to be imposed by the division, in an amount not to exceed $1,000.

SECTION 1 - ELEVATOR LOCATION		
Serial Number	Number of Landings	Date (MM/DD/YYYY)
Date of Accident (MM/DD/YYYY)	Time of Accident Hour Minute ☐ AM ☐ PM	
D/B/A Name (enter Business Name or Doing Business As Name of the building)		
Main Address (enter building address)		
City	County	State Zip Code
Primary Name (enter name of the building owner)		Phone Number

SECTION 2 - SERVICE MAINTENANCE	
Is the elevator or escalator under a service maintenance contract? ☐ Yes ☐ No	
Name of Elevator Maintenance Company	
Was the elevator service maintenance company notified? ☐ Yes ☐ No	If yes, indicate date (MM/DD/YYYY)
Most recent required test performed ☐ 6 months ☐ 1 year ☐ 3 years ☐ 5 years	Test Date (MM/DD/YYYY)

SECTION 3 - SIGNATURE	
Report Submitted by (print name)	Title
Signature	Phone Number

FIGURE 13-6 Sample elevator accident report

♦ Can documents or pleadings—the formal statements of the parties, such as the complaint and the answer—from other cases be used as evidence in one's case? If so, must they be certified by a court clerk or someone else?

Hearsay Problems

hearsay A statement about what someone else said (or wrote or otherwise communicated.)

Hearsay is an out-of-court statement offered as evidence to prove the fact contained in the statement. Statements may be verbal, written, or even gestural.

Some documents may not be admissible because they are considered hearsay. At times, only portions of documents may be admissible. For example, all or part of a police or ambulance report may be considered hearsay because the police officer and/or ambulance attendant who wrote the report did not actually see the accident. This person's report will contain information from someone else, such as the injured party or a witness. Hearsay is not admissible, but there are numerous exceptions to this rule.

The trial team will want to review the documents and the evidence rules. They may want to offer the reports into evidence simply as business records (an exception to the hearsay rule), or use them to refresh the memory of a testifying police officer or paramedic, without offering them as evidence.

Video and Computer Technologies

The use of video and computer animation technologies is a fast-growing practice in tort law. Videotape and computer animation are routinely used in accident reconstruction, "day-in-the-life" documentaries, and settlement brochures. Even video news footage is being utilized in the courtroom. Paralegals should know how to document the authenticity of this type of evidence so that it can be used during trial.

§ 13.7 Public and Private Sector Resources

Governmental agencies and private entities are sources of a variety of information that may be germane to the paralegal's tort case investigation. Online computer networks may be the information superhighway, but there are many more information side streets available to the paralegal in charge of investigating a tort case. Much of this information is stored the old-fashioned way—on paper, microfilm, microfiche, or other archival media—and paralegals need only know where to look to uncover this treasure-trove of material.

Local Governmental Agencies

Governmental agencies are literal stockpiles of information that the paralegal will find invaluable in tort case investigation. Sunshine laws provide for governmental disclosure of most contracts. Archives contain vital statistics, marriage licenses, civil suit records, and probate and estate records. One can obtain information from automobile license tag records, such as the name and current address of the owner of a vehicle involved in an accident. Also, information can be obtained from driver's license records, deeds, and liens. The tax assessor's office can provide property-ownership information by name or address of the property.

Newspapers

Newspapers and newspaper personnel can be good sources of information. For instance, an article about the tort incident might quote a witness about whom the paralegal did not know. There could also be helpful information about how the accident happened or who was involved. The paralegal should find out if a newspaper reporter took any photographs of the scene, even if none were printed in the newspaper.

There may be information about one's client, or a potential defendant, in the archives of the newspaper. The paralegal should look beyond articles about the tort incident for photographs or profiles of people involved. There may be information to document a client's activities before an accident or to aid in service on an individual or business. Many newspapers are now on-line, allowing for easy access to prior publications.

Television and Radio News Reports

If the accident that is the basis of the tort lawsuit was reported on the news, one may want to get an audiotape, videotape, or transcript of what was reported to the public. It may be useful if a jury trial is anticipated, because prior publicity may affect jurors and even the venue of the case.

Additionally, if video news footage was taken, the paralegal should obtain a copy. It may have scene footage that is not obtainable from any other source. This footage may also have been taken closer in time to the actual incident than later documentary efforts by the law firm. The trial team may be glad to have this footage when preparing a video settlement brochure or video recreation of the accident for trial. If the television station will not cooperate, consult your rules of discovery; it may be possible to subpoena the footage.

Paralegals should also give some thought to any local conditions that might have contributed to the accident. If a fire or storm occurred at the time, and was significant, it is possible that it was reported on the local news. For example, a client's case might involve a storm-damaged building that was not repaired. The client was later injured at that business when a portion of the roof caved in. In this case, it would be a good idea to check local television stations for any news footage that might have been taken of the storm or wind shears on the day the building was believed to have been originally damaged. If found, this footage would dramatically help document not only when the building was damaged, but also that the owner or manager of the building knew, or reasonably should have known, that the building needed repair, well in advance of the injury occurring. Official weather statistics are frequently obtained from the National Oceanic and Atmospheric Administration (NOAA), which is part of the United States Commerce Department. These statistics can be found at major airports. For local information, the department of meteorology at a local university or television station will have weather statistics. Such statistics are frequently used in arbitration and litigation.

Computerized Databases

There are many types of computerized databases and networks, each holding a wealth of information. Different jurisdictions have rules and requirements about how much information is accessible to the public or admissible at trial. Even with these restrictions, it is surprising what can be learned. Databases can be used to uncover:

◆ Driving records

◆ Driver's information (see Figure 13-7)

◆ Driver's licenses, which provide a history of residences

◆ Vehicle registration

◆ Credit reports

◆ Criminal history

◆ Public record filings, such as deeds and liens

◆ Business filings, such as assumed names, corporate filings, partnership filings, bankruptcy, and company officers and incorporators

◆ Civil lawsuits, including divorces

◆ Asset and other financial information.

Additional Information Regarding Criminal Acts

If the incident that is the basis of the tort lawsuit also involves a criminal act, such as a shooting or other type of assault or battery, there will be a criminal investigation, and additional information resources may be available to the trial team. The paralegal will want to review and possibly obtain copies of the following:

◆ Police report

◆ Criminal record of the perpetrator

◆ Trial transcript of any criminal trial, conviction, or judgment

◆ Exhibits used at criminal trial

◆ 911 or other emergency telephone call audiotapes and/or transcripts

◆ Floor plans or diagrams of the incident location

◆ Map of the area

◆ Crime statistics of the specific law enforcement jurisdiction.

Most tort cases involve damages, insurance coverage, and other elements that must be researched. Section 13.8 investigates these considerations.

DL-503 (5-02)

REQUEST FOR
DRIVER INFORMATION

PRINT OR TYPE ALL INFORMATION LEGIBLY

DO NOT SEND CASH

SEE REVERSE FOR INSTRUCTIONS / INFORMATION

CHECK (✔) ONE ONLY:

- [ ] BASIC INFORMATION: $5.00 FEE *(Driver history is not included)*
- [ ] 3 YEAR DRIVER RECORD: $5.00 FEE
- [ ] 10 YEAR DRIVER RECORD: $5.00 FEE *(Employment Purposes Only)*

- [ ] CERTIFIED DRIVER RECORD: $10.00 FEE
- [ ] COPY OF DOCUMENT FROM FILE (MICROFILM): $5.00 FEE
- [ ] CERTIFIED COPY OF DOCUMENT FROM FILE: $10.00 FEE

A | REQUESTER INFORMATION

NAME/COMPANY

ADDRESS *P.O. Box number may be used in addition to the actual address, but cannot be used as the only address.*

CITY | STATE | ZIP CODE

DAYTIME TELEPHONE NUMBER *(REQUIRED)*

RELATIONSHIP TO DRIVER *(REQUIRED)*

SIGNATURE X

NOTARIZATION **NOT** REQUIRED WHEN REQUESTING YOUR OWN RECORD

C | DRIVER INFORMATION

NAME: LAST | FIRST | INITIAL

ADDRESS

CITY

STATE | ZIP CODE

PHONE NUMBER

DRIVER NUMBER

| DATE OF BIRTH | | | SOCIAL SECURITY NUMBER |
| MONTH | DAY | YEAR | |

E | DRIVER RELEASE

I _____ hereby request
NAME OF DRIVER

the Department of Transportation to furnish a copy of my PA Driver's
Record to _____
NAME OF PERSON/COMPANY

X _____
SIGNATURE OF DRIVER | DATE

F | MICROFILM

TYPE OF DOCUMENT | DATE OF VIOLATION

(see list of available documents below)

Documents Available:
- Citations
- Court Certifications
- Applications
- License Renewals
- Judgments

- Suspension Credit Affidavits
- Suspension/Revocation Letters
- Restoration Letters
- Rescind Letters
- Department Hearing or Exam Notice

MESSENGER NO.

www.state.pa.us

B | END USER OF INFORMATION BEING REQUESTED

NAME/COMPANY

ADDRESS *(PO Box not acceptable), need to provide physical location of business/residence*

CITY | STATE | ZIP CODE

DAYTIME TELEPHONE NUMBER *(REQUIRED)*

RELATIONSHIP TO DRIVER *(REQUIRED)*

D | AFFIDAVIT OF INTENDED USE

Intended Use of the Information Requested: **CHECK ONLY ONE**

- [ ] **B = Driver Release** *(Driver has given written authorization to obtain his/her record.)*
- [ ] **C = Credit** *(In connection with a credit transaction involving the driver.)*
- [ ] **E = Employment** *(To support the hiring or the continuation of employment. Employer must have driver's signed release on file.)*
- [ ] **R = Insurance Company** requesting record of person it intends to insure, now insures, or has rejected for insurance.
- [ ] **K = Court Order** must be attached. *(A subpoena issued in compliance with Pa. R.C.P. 4009.21 will be accepted in lieu of a court order.)*
- [ ] **L = Attorney** representing driver identified in Section C *(Driver has given written authorization to obtain his/her record.)*

I hereby Certify that _____
PRINTED NAME OF REQUESTER

will use the driver record abstract(s) required pursuant to Section 6114 of the Pennsylvania Vehicle Code, for the purpose checked above only and no other reason. This affidavit is filed in compliance with Section 607 of the Fair Credit Reporting Act. I/We have read and signed this form after its completion, and I/We swear or affirm that the statements made herein are true and correct, and that any statement made on or pursuant to this form is subject to the penalties of 18 PA C.S. Section 4903(a)(2) (relating to false swearing), which shall include punishment of a fine not exceeding $5,000, or to a term of imprisonment of not more than two years, or both.

X _____
SIGNATURE OF REQUESTER

Title _____

SUBSCRIBED AND SWORN
TO BEFORE ME: | MONTH | DAY | YEAR

X _____
SIGNATURE OF PERSON ADMINISTERING OATH

NOTARIZATION

S E A L

SIGN IN PRESENCE OF NOTARY

FIGURE 13-7 Request for driver information

§ 13.8 Additional Areas to Investigate

Tort damages present a variety of details to investigate. These items include degree and permanence of the injury, employment and lost wages, injury expenses, insurance coverage, prior tort claims, preexisting injuries, past criminal records, and driving history, to name but a few.

Employment and Lost Wages

The plaintiff's damages may be based in part on the dollar amount of wages lost due to injuries. Another factor that is often considered is impairment of future earning capacity. The paralegal needs this earnings information for in-house evaluation, but the defendants will also be entitled to obtain certain information regarding wages. See Figure 13-8, a workers' compensation form notice to employer.

The plaintiff's income must be documented. It is not sufficient for a client to simply testify, "I could have made $175,000 this year if it weren't for this injury." Income and income potential must be substantiated by independent evidence.

Tax returns and affidavits from the client's employer are commonly used to document lost wages and the client's wage-earning capacity. The paralegal will also want to gather information from the client's W-2 forms, pay stubs for hourly or salaried workers, and, in some instances, documentation of employment contracts or fringe benefits.

The trial team may plan to have an economist, actuary, or accountant prepare an evaluation of economic damages. Most economic experts will request tax returns for at least three years preceding the date of injury, to make a determination as to future economic loss, when there has been impairment of future earning capacity.

Expenses Related to the Injury

The client should provide documentation of all expenses paid in relation to the injury and medical treatment. This includes receipts for equipment and supplies, such as:

◆ Canes, braces, and crutches

◆ Heating pads or ice packs

◆ Hospital bills

◆ Doctor bills

◆ Physical therapy bills

◆ Bandages

◆ Prescription medicines

◆ Over-the-counter medicines

ALASKA DEPARTMENT OF LABOR
Alaska Workers' Compensation Board
P.O. Box 25512
Juneau, Alaska 99802-5512 | Location Code | **090**

AWCB Case Number

6098

DO NOT
WRITE
IN THIS
COLUMN

NOTICE TO EMPLOYER	EMPLOYEE PLEASE ANSWER ALL QUESTIONS	

1. Name (Last, First, Middle Initial)
Scott, Mary B.

2. Telephone | 3. Date of Birth **02/11/70** | 4. Sex ☐ M ☒ F | 5. Soc. Sec. Number

Nature of Injury

6. Street and Number (Permanent Address)
24TH AVE

7. Street and Number (Current Mailing Address If Different)
24TH AVE

Part of Body

City **ANCHORAGE** State **AK** Zip Code **99517**

City **ANCHORAGE** State **AK** Zip Code **99517**

Source

8. Place of Injury or Exposure (City, Town, Village)
ANCHORAGE

9. Date & Hour of Injury or Exposure to Disease
Date **01** / **15** / **2003** Time **03:25** ☒ AM ☐ PM

10. On Employer's Premises? ☒ Yes ☐ No

Type

11. Full Name and Address of Attending Physician
PROVIDENCE
PO BOX 196

12. Hospitalized as In-Patient? ☒ Yes ☐ No

13. Name and Address of Hospital
N/A

City **ANCHORAGE** State **AK** Zip Code **99519**

City State Zip Code

14. Nature of Injury or Diagnosis and Part of Body Affected
BI-LATERAL PAIN & SWELLING, WRIST
☐ Left ☐ Right

842 - SPRAINS AND STRAINS OF WRIST AND HAND

15. Describe How the Injury or Illness Occurred (What Happened)
STATES HER HANDS SLIPPED WHILE

TRYING TO MOVE A FILE CABINET

Carrier Claim #:

16. Employee's Signature (If not Available, Explain)
SIGNATURE ON FILE

17. Date Signed
1 / **15** / **2003**

REPORT OF INJURY OR ILLNESS	EMPLOYER: PLEASE ANSWER ALL QUESTIONS	

18. Employer's Name
SECURITY SERVICES

19. Employer's Alaska Address (If Different From Mailing)
2909 ARCTIC BLVD
ANCHORAGE **AK** **99503**

20. Employer's Mailing Address (Street and Number)
ARCTIC BLVD.,

21. Name of Insurer
IS Portland WC Office

City **ANCHORAGE** State **AK** Zip Code **99503** Telephone

22. Full Name and Address of Adjusting Company
IS Portland WC Office

23. Date Employer First Knew Injury Is Work-Related **01/15/2003** Date /

24. Time Employee Left Work Hour **04:00** ☒ AM ☐ PM

Mailing Address (Street and Number)
68TH PKWY

25. Will Injury Result in Lost Time Beyond Date of Accident? ☐ Yes ☒ No

26. Date Returned to Work **01/15/2003**

27. Fatality (Death) ☐ Yes ☐ No Date / /

City **Portland** State Zip Code **OR 97223** Telephone

28. Place Where Injury or Exposure Occurred if Different from Employer's Mailing Address
ARCTIC BLVD.,

29. Employee's Occupation
DISPATCHER

30. Department in Which Employee Regularly Employed
DISPATCH

31. Date Hired with Present Employer **05** / **19** / **1999**

32. Wage (Incl. Board, Room, Gratuities) **$ 9.00** ☒ Hr. ☐ Day ☐ Wk. ☐ Mo.

33. Days Employee Works Per Week ☐ 3 or Less ☐ 4 ☒ 5 ☐ 6 ☐ 7

34. Name Scheduled Days Off **TH/FRI**

35. Workday Began **12:00** ☐ AM ☒ PM

36. Was Employee Paid for Day of Injury? ☒ Yes ☐ No

37. Alaska Unemployment Insurance Account Number (U.I. Acct No.)
N/A

38. How Did the Accident Occur? (Give Details)
EMPLOYEE TRIED TO LIFT A FILE CABINET WHEN HE

R HAND SLIPPED, CAUSING PAIN & SWELLING TO BOTH WRISTS.

39. What Was the Employee Doing When the Injury or Illness Occurred? (Be Specific)
EMPLOYEE TRIED TO LIFT A FILE CABINET WHEN HER HAND SLIPPED, CAUSING PAIN/SWELLING TO BOTH WRISTS.

40. Was Accident Caused by Failure of a Machine or Product? ☐ Yes ☒ No

41. Were Mechanical Guards or Other Safeguards Provided? ☐ Yes ☐ No

42. Name machine, Substance or Object Which Directly Injured Employee
FILE CABINET

43. If Mechanical, Specifically What Part?
N/A

44. Name and Addresses of Witnesses
NONE

45. If the Accident Was Caused by Anyone Besides Employee, Give Name and Address
N/A

46. Dependents (Name and Address in Case of Death)
N/A

47. If You Doubt Validity of Claim, State Reason
FORWARD INQUIRY TO: **LEEN ELSEN**

48. Signature of Authorized Employer Representative
SIGNATURE ON FILE

49. Title
DISTRICT ADMIN

50. Date Signed
1 / **15** / **2003**

40049-4-93
DISTRIBUTION: Blue-Workers' Compensation Board
White-Adjusting Company Pink-Employer's File
Yellow and Green-Employee

EMPLOYER: Answer questions 18-50 fully, and
immediately send report. Further instructions on back.
EMPLOYEE: Answer questions 1-17 fully. Carefully read
and follow instruction on front and back of green copy.
VERY IMPORTANT.

S A T I S | DIV CODES | A CODE | B CODE | C CODE | **1**

Form 07-6101 (Rev 9/90)

FIGURE 13-8 Workers' compensation form (notice to employer)

- Special mattresses or recuperative furniture or equipment
- Bills from housekeeper, cook, visiting nurses, or other helpers needed during recuperation.

The client should also document mileage and parking fees for trips to the doctor, hospital, and for any other therapy sessions. The paralegal should follow up to make sure the client is keeping records of this information.

Insurance Coverage and Other Benefits

The trial team will need to know how much of the client's medical and related expenses were paid by insurance policies, workers' compensation benefits, or other sources. The paralegal should also find out if the client is covered by or receiving any assistance from Social Security, Medicare, Medicaid, or any other governmental or private program.

The client should provide the paralegal with copies of any documentation about insurance coverage or possible assistance through governmental agencies. If the client is unable to produce such documentation, it may be necessary for the paralegal to contact the various agencies and request the information. The defendants may also be entitled to some information regarding the insurance payments and government or other benefits, even if such information is not admissible at trial. Depending on your jurisdiction, the fact that some of your bills have been paid may affect the defendant's responsibility to reimburse for expenses.

Previous Claims or Lawsuits of Plaintiff

It is necessary to know about any previous claims or lawsuits in which the client has been involved and how they were resolved. The trial team will determine the information to which the defendant is entitled if defense counsel inquires about this subject matter during discovery. Defendants usually ask for this type of information so as to use it against the plaintiff, to discredit the plaintiff, or to reduce the amount of damages in a lawsuit.

Clients will not always be able or willing to provide all the information concerning prior claims or lawsuits in which they have been involved. Some clients discard legal documents once a legal action is completed. The paralegal may have to visit the court clerk's offices to obtain the relevant documents concerning any past lawsuits.

Practical Application

Some people are "professional plaintiffs"; that is, they sue people for a living for injuries that are contrived or exaggerated. These people are not usually honest with their attorneys. Other clients are just injury-prone and seem to incur more than their share of injuries. A thorough interview and study of current and past medical records often help to determine whether a client's claims ring true. Note that the occasional malingerer is the exception and not the rule!

Previous Injuries to Plaintiff

As a general rule, "one takes the victim (plaintiff) as one finds him." However, it is important to determine if the part of the plaintiff's body that was injured in the accident and is the basis of the current lawsuit was ever injured in the past. It is vital to review medical records carefully to determine whether there are any references to similar injuries or other problems relating to the same part of the body, or whether there is evidence of any preexisting injuries.

For instance, if a plaintiff who has a stiff back from an earlier car accident slips and falls on a slippery floor at the grocery store and reinjures her back, the injured plaintiff may only bring a claim against the grocery store for the injuries and expenses that result from aggravation of the existing condition. There can be no recovery against the grocery store for the stiff back that the plaintiff already had. The plaintiff's claim might be that her back is stiff more often, or that it gives her more pain than she previously experienced. An award against the grocery store for aggravation of an existing condition may be much less than the award for the preexisting stiff-back condition.

In this example, the paralegal should be sure to have all the medical information to evaluate and let trial-team members know that there was more than one injury to the plaintiff's back. The trial team will probably want to follow up with additional questions to the client regarding the previous back problem to ascertain if it is related to the pain attributed to the slip and fall. One's trial team may also want to follow up with the client's doctor.

The Parties' Criminal Histories

Information on the parties' criminal histories is relevant for both defendants and plaintiffs in some cases. The trial team needs to know anything regarding the parties' arrests, convictions, and/or time spent in jail or prison, although this data might not be admissible at trial in your particular case.

Driving Records

Driving records may be particularly relevant in the investigation of an automobile accident, and can also be utilized to determine other information regarding the parties, such as alcohol use. If any party has been ticketed or arrested for an offense such as driving under the influence of alcohol or drugs, the trial team will want to know about it.

Having considered various investigatory techniques, it would be useful to apply these methods to specific types of tort cases. These applications are discussed in § 13.9.

§ 13.9 Investigating Different Types of Tort Cases

Various types of tort cases require specialized methods of investigation. Paralegals and attorneys learn the "right" techniques primarily through experience. This section provides some basic guidelines for investigating some typical tort cases encountered in private law practice.

Automobile Accident Cases

An automobile accident causing injury usually entails a relatively straightforward investigation. The trial team needs to know who and what caused the accident and what damages the plaintiff has suffered. A typical general investigation includes the following steps:

♦ The client is interviewed for information as to how the accident happened, injuries, who was at fault, and any witnesses.

♦ Police accident reports are obtained for information such as:
  ♦ Witness names and addresses
  ♦ The exact location of the accident
  ♦ The disposition of each party to the accident and each vehicle (i.e., what parties were taken to which hospital, what vehicles had to be towed and where they were taken)
  ♦ Injury and property damage to vehicle and contents
  ♦ Any tickets issued by police at the scene
  ♦ Any comments in the report as to fault or factors that contributed to the accident (such as eating, drinking, falling asleep, or other activities).

♦ Photographs should be taken of the vehicle or vehicles and the parties' injuries, if necessary.

♦ Medical records should be ordered and particular attention paid to any tests for alcohol or drugs.

♦ If there is a question regarding a mechanical malfunction, an expert may be called in to inspect the vehicle or vehicles involved.

♦ If there are allegations of dangerous street design or street conditions, additional investigation may be required.

In addition to the preceding, when the trial team represents the defendant, it will be interested in investigating the following:

♦ Names of other possible defendants

♦ Defenses to the plaintiff's claims

♦ Acts of the plaintiff that contributed to the accident

♦ Prior lawsuits by the plaintiff

- Preexisting injuries of the plaintiff
- The plaintiff's prior accidents or claims
- Reputation and standing of the plaintiff's treating physician (who may be relied on by the plaintiff as an expert at trial).

Mechanical Malfunction

If there is a question about possible mechanical malfunction, the trial team probably will find itself going beyond a simple investigation and into the more extensive inquiry necessary in a products liability case. The client should be consulted regarding projected future expenses for which the client would be responsible before the investigation proceeds.

Dangerous Street Conditions

If there are indications of dangerous street conditions, the paralegal should watch for scenarios such as:

- Debris that fell from a truck or other vehicle that might have contributed to the accident
- Vegetation affecting visibility
- A street being repaired or under construction or allegations that lanes were not properly marked, equipment or machinery were left in the street, visibility was obscured, and so on
- A dangerous intersection or design of the street
- A street sign, such as a stop sign or one-way sign, that is obscured or missing
- Possible involvement of a municipality, and whether it is entitled by law to notice of the condition claimed before suit can be brought
- Other accidents at same location.

Construction Sites

If the site of the accident was under construction or repair at the time of the incident, an inquiry as to the conditions may be undertaken. Likewise, if there are allegations of debris on the road, that should be followed up, as any of these scenarios may indicate additional defendants.

Medical Negligence Cases

If a paralegal has a case involving possible medical negligence or malpractice, investigation can be quite complex and costly. Consider a hypothetical, but not unrealistic, example. A patient goes into a hospital to have his appendix removed. The doctor fails to remove a clamp from the patient before suturing him up. One week after being discharged from the hospital, the patient experiences severe pain and a high fever. The patient goes to the emergency room and is admitted for emergency exploratory surgery. The clamp is found and removed. Potential areas of investigation in such a case would include:

- What was the cause of injury or death?
    - Was it a result of medical treatment or lack thereof?
    - Was it a result of negligence on the part of the hospital staff or doctors?
    - Was it a result of something that was done or not done prior to admission to the facility?
    - Did the patient follow prescribed treatment?
- What do the medical records or autopsy records indicate as the cause of injury or death? (See Figures 13-9, 13-10, and 13-11.)
- What was the plaintiff's condition upon arriving at the emergency room?
- What diagnosis had been rendered during the previous hospital admission? (See Figure 13-8 on page 421)
- What types of consent forms and releases for treatment were signed, and who signed them (the victim, his or her guardian, and so forth)?

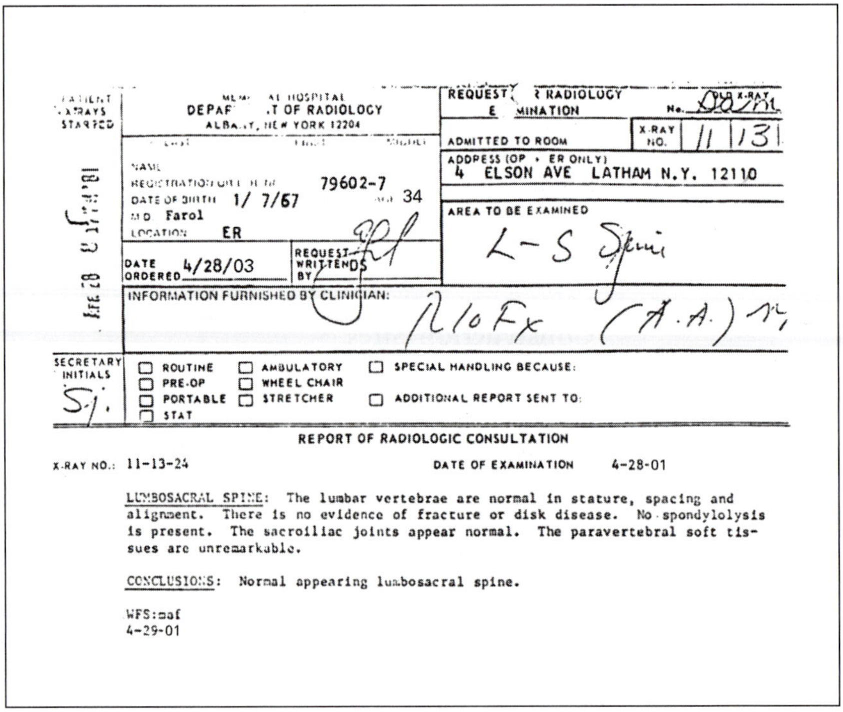
DEPARTMENT OF RADIOLOGY
ALBANY, NEW YORK 12204

REQUEST FOR RADIOLOGY EXAMINATION

ADMITTED TO ROOM | X-RAY NO. 11 13

ADDRESS (OP • ER ONLY) 4 ELSON AVE LATHAM N.Y. 12110

REGISTRATION 79602-7
DATE OF BIRTH 1/ 7/67 34
M.D. Farol
LOCATION ER

AREA TO BE EXAMINED: L-S Spine

DATE ORDERED 4/28/03 | REQUEST WRITTEN BY

INFORMATION FURNISHED BY CLINICIAN:

SECRETARY INITIALS

☐ ROUTINE ☐ AMBULATORY ☐ SPECIAL HANDLING BECAUSE:
☐ PRE-OP ☐ WHEEL CHAIR
☐ PORTABLE ☐ STRETCHER ☐ ADDITIONAL REPORT SENT TO:
☐ STAT

REPORT OF RADIOLOGIC CONSULTATION

X-RAY NO.: 11-13-24 DATE OF EXAMINATION 4-28-01

LUMBOSACRAL SPINE: The lumbar vertebrae are normal in stature, spacing and alignment. There is no evidence of fracture or disk disease. No spondylolysis is present. The sacroiliac joints appear normal. The paravertebral soft tissues are unremarkable.

CONCLUSIONS: Normal appearing lumbosacral spine.

WFS:maf
4-29-01

FIGURE 13-9 Sample medical report (radiology)

Don Acomb, M.D., P.C.
Stan Hoff, M.D., D.M.D., P.C.
65 Western Avenue, Albany, New York 12203
Telephone 438-4400

March 12, 2003

Cathy J. Okrent, Esq.
Washington Square
Box 1501
Albany, New York 12212

Re: Scott Powers
d/a: 5/2/02

Dear Ms. Okrent:

Scott Powers was in the office on March 12, 2003 concerning scars of the right lower leg. According to the history on May 2, 2002 he as apparently attacked by four dogs, receiving bites on the right lower leg. One bite required three sutures and one puncture wound required one suture. The wounds healed without infection.

Examination disclosed a white, soft scar 3 × 1.5 cms. on the lateral part of the mid calf of the right lower leg. This scar is permanent and no treatment is indicated. There are two puncture scars, each measuring 0.6 cms., on the upper and lower lateral leg. These scars are permanent and no treatment is indicated.

If I can be of any further help to you please do not hesitate to let me know.

Sincerely,

_____
DON ACOMB, M.D.

DA: mk

FIGURE 13-10 Sample medical report (doctor's evaluation)

If the initial evaluation indicates a potential case, additional investigation will be warranted. Paralegals will want to find out about any doctors involved, their qualifications and training, and whether they have been the subject of previous lawsuits or complaints. One will also want to find out the same information about the hospital and its personnel.

Obtaining Information About Health Care Providers

Health care facilities, such as hospitals, nursing homes, retirement centers, and rehabilitation hospitals, are overseen by various governmental and

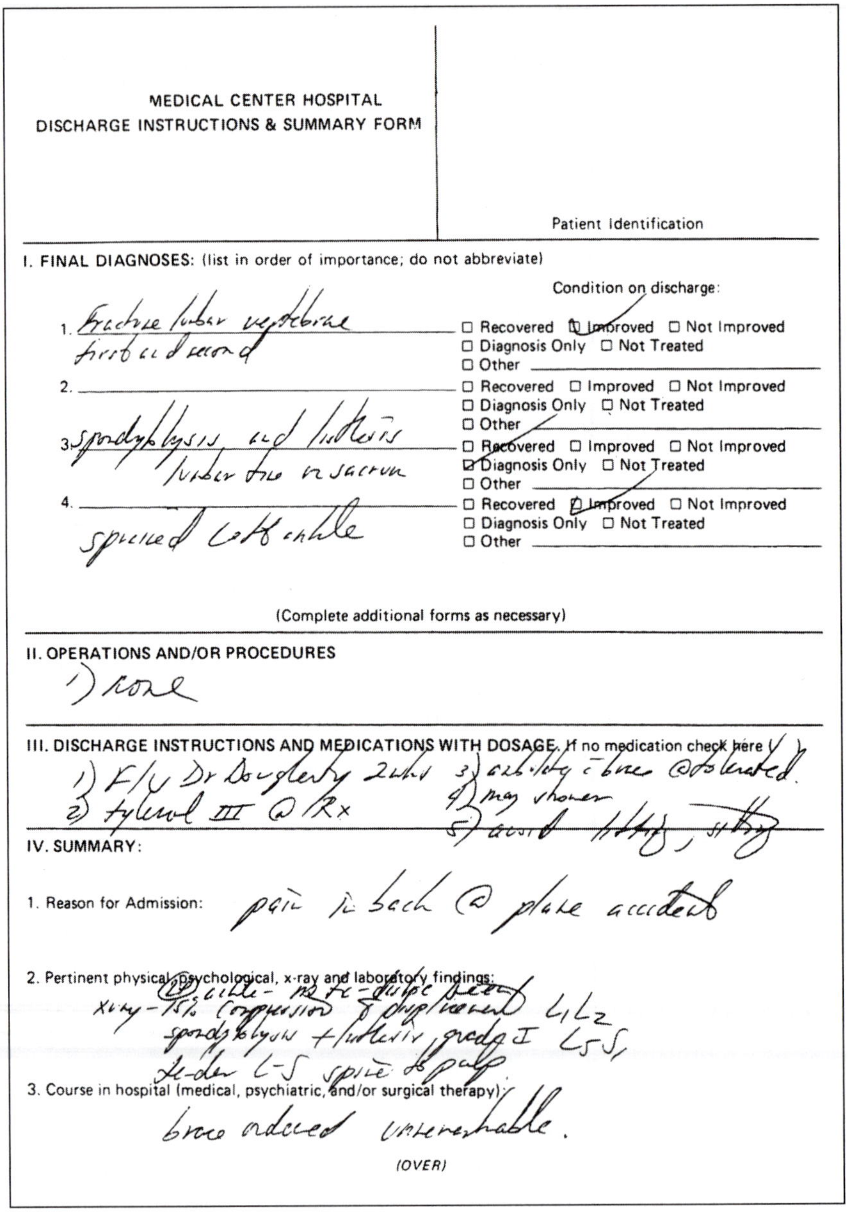

FIGURE 13-11 Sample medical report (discharge form)

private agencies and licensing organizations. For instance, if a paralegal has a case involving someone who contracted a disease from a blood transfusion, he or she should know that all blood banks are overseen by the American Association of Blood Banks. The Association sets out standards and requirements, as well as inspection criteria.

3. Course in hospital, continued:

V. LIMIT OF DISABILITY:

Patient may return to work: ☐ YES ☑ NO

Patient is essentially home bound: ☑ YES ☐ NO

VI. PAP SMEAR INFORMATION FOR FEMALE PATIENTS:

Pap Smear done during this admission ☐ YES ☐ NO ☐ WITHIN LAST 3 YEARS
☐ REFUSED BY PATIENT

VII. PATIENT OR RESPONSIBLE OTHER VERBALIZES, DEMONSTRATES, OR EXHIBITS KNOWLEDGE OF:

Completed by

1. Nature of Illness	☑ YES ☐ NO ☐ N/A	☐ M.D.	☐ RN ☐ Other _____ (Sign & Date)
2. Diet	☐ YES ☐ NO ☑ N/A	☐ M.D.	☐ RN ☐ Other _____ (Sign & Date)
3. Wound care	☐ YES ☐ NO ☑ N/A	☐ M.D.	☐ RN ☐ Other _____ (Sign & Date)
4. Medications	☑ YES ☐ NO ☐ N/A	☐ M.D.	☐ RN ☐ Other _____ (Sign & Date)
5. Special health teaching (colostomy care, casts, diabetic care, etc.)	☑ YES ☐ NO ☐ N/A	☐ M.D.	☐ RN ☐ Other _____ (Sign & Date)
6. Activity	☑ YES ☐ NO ☐ N/A	☐ M.D.	☐ RN ☐ Other _____ (Sign & Date)
7. Follow-up appointments and referrals	☑ YES ☐ NO ☐ N/A	☐ M.D.	☐ RN ☐ Other _____ (Sign & Date)

COMMENTS _____

_____

_____

VIII. SIGNATURE OF PHYSICIAN RESPONSIBLE FOR DISCHARGE OF PATIENT:

_____ M.D. ☐ Intern ☑ Resident
☐ Acting Intern
☐ Fellow ☐ Attending

TO BE COMPLETED BY THE NURSING DIVISION AT THE TIME THE PATIENT LEAVES THE HOSPITAL:

Date ___/__ Time _11:10_ Mode: ☑ Wheelchair ☐ Stretcher ☐ Walked out

Discharge to: ☐ Nursing Home of Extended Care Facility
☑ Home
☐ Other (Specify) _____

Belongings to _____ Accompanied by _____
Signature   ☐ Floor Clerk ☐ Nurse ☐ Other

FIGURE 13-11 Sample medical report (discharge form) (*continued*)

Various specifications and standards for health care providers are set by governmental agencies, professional organizations, and licensing boards. They keep records regarding:

◆ Current addresses

◆ Schools attended and grades earned

◆ Professional credentials

◆ Honors and awards

◆ Continuing education requirements

◆ Licensure status and board certification

◆ Past and present complaints.

Therefore, these organizations are excellent resources for gathering information on defendant doctors, nurses, and other health care professionals. This information can also be utilized to evaluate health care professionals who have been designated as expert witnesses by defendants and those one might want to use as experts. Some states allow access to some of this information on-line.

Practical Application

If the health care professional is a specialist, the paralegal should keep in mind that there are additional qualifications for each specialty area. A separate licensing board or organization typically oversees each specialty. For example, a surgeon might be certified to operate by the American Board of Surgery.

Figure 13-12 shows OSHA Form 301, an injury and illness incident report.

Health Care Facilities That Receive Governmental Funding

If a health care facility receives government funds (such as Medicare), it is inspected by the state health department for compliance with regulations. Such state inspections, along with any compliance and deficiency reports, are public records. As such, they can be obtained for review under the Freedom of Information Act and through discovery. Figure 13-13 on page 432 shows a supervisor's workplace accident investigation report.

Summary

Fact gathering is a significant paralegal role in tort investigations. Paralegals investigate and document the tort scene and interview the client, eyewitnesses, and other persons with pertinent information. Attorneys and law firms often have specialized techniques for conducting investigations. Some use in-house personnel; others hire outside investigative services. Paralegals should customize their investigations to fit the type and size of tort case involved. Details are critical. In part, factual investigations are designed to determine liability and damages. It is important to interview witnesses as soon as possible to obtain the best recollected information. Witnesses explain how the tort occurred according to their observational perspectives.

Defendants are usually determined in-house. It may be difficult to identify or locate potential defendants, especially if they are business entities or transient individuals. One should exercise

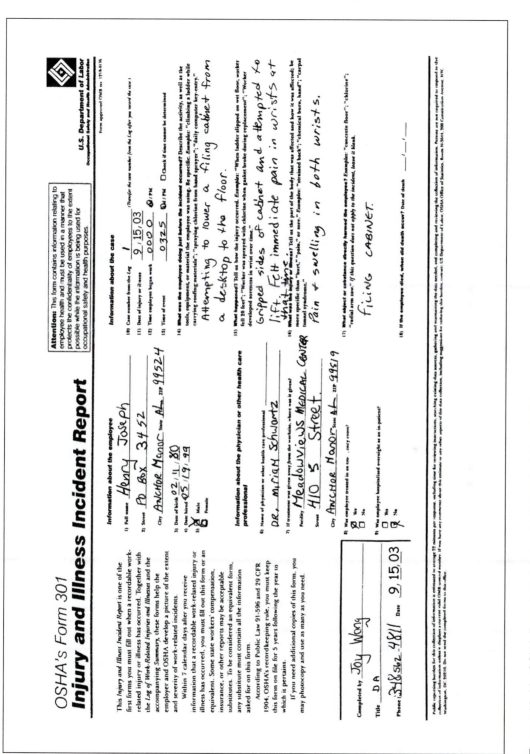

OSHA's *Form 301*

Injury and Illness Incident Report

Attention: This form contains information relating to employee health and must be used in a manner that protects the confidentiality of employees to the extent possible while the information is being used for occupational safety and health purposes.

U.S. Department of Labor
Occupational Safety and Health Administration

Form approved OMB no. 1218-0176

This *Injury and Illness Incident Report* is one of the first forms you must fill out when a recordable work-related injury or illness has occurred. Together with the *Log of Work-Related Injuries and Illnesses* and the accompanying *Summary*, these forms help the employer and OSHA develop a picture of the extent and severity of work-related incidents.

Within 7 calendar days after you receive information that a recordable work-related injury or illness has occurred, you must fill out this form or an equivalent. Some state workers' compensation, insurance, or other reports may be acceptable substitutes. To be considered an equivalent form, any substitute must contain all the information asked for on this form.

According to Public Law 91-596 and 29 CFR 1904, OSHA's recordkeeping rule, you must keep this form on file for 5 years following the year to which it pertains.

If you need additional copies of this form, you may photocopy and use as many as you need.

Information about the employee

1) Full name   Henry Joseph

2) Street   PO Box 3452
City   Anchor Manor   State   AL   ZIP   99524

3) Date of birth   02 / 11 / 80

4) Date hired   05 / 19 / 99

5)   ☒ Male   ☐ Female

Information about the physician or other health care professional

6) Name of physician or other health care professional
Dr. Milian Schwartz

7) If treatment was given away from the worksite, where was it given?
Facility   Meadowview's Medical Center
Street   410 S Street
City   Anchor Manor   State   AL   ZIP   99519

8) Was employee treated in an emergency room?
☒ Yes
☐ No

9) Was employee hospitalized overnight as an in-patient?
☐ Yes
☒ No

Information about the case

10) Case number from the Log   1
(Transfer the case number from the Log after you record the case.)

11) Date of injury or illness   9/15/03

12) Time employee began work   000 0   ☒AM/PM

13) Time of event   0325   ☒AM/PM   ☐ Check if time cannot be determined

14) What was the employee doing just before the incident occurred? Describe the activity, as well as the tools, equipment, or material the employee was using. Be specific. Examples: "climbing a ladder while carrying roofing materials"; "spraying chlorine from hand sprayer"; "daily computer key-entry."

Attempting to lower a filing cabinet from a desktop to the floor.

15) What happened? Tell us how the injury occurred. Examples: "When ladder slipped on wet floor, worker fell 20 feet"; "Worker was sprayed with chlorine when gasket broke during replacement"; "Worker developed soreness in wrist over time."

Gripped sides of cabinet and attempted to lift. Felt immediate pain in wrists at that time.

16) What was the injury or illness? Tell us the part of the body that was affected and how it was affected; be more specific than "hurt," "pain," or sore." Examples: "strained back"; "chemical burn, hand"; "carpal tunnel syndrome."

Pain + swelling in both wrists.

17) What object or substance directly harmed the employee? Examples: "concrete floor"; "chlorine"; "radial arm saw." If this question does not apply to the incident, leave it blank.

Filing cabinet.

18) If the employee died, when did death occur? Date of death   __ / __ / __

Completed by   Joy Wong

Title   DA

Phone   348-562-4811   Date   9/15/03

Public reporting burden for this collection of information is estimated to average 22 minutes per response, including time for reviewing instructions, searching existing data sources, gathering and maintaining the data needed, and completing and reviewing the collection of information. Persons are not required to respond to the collection of information unless it displays a current valid OMB control number. If you have any comments about this estimate or any other aspects of this data collection, including suggestions for reducing this burden, contact: US Department of Labor, OSHA Office of Statistics, Room N-3644, 200 Constitution Avenue, NW, Washington, DC 20210. Do not send the completed forms to this office.

Figure 13-12 OSHA Form 301, injury and illness incident report

SUPERVISOR'S ACCIDENT INVESTIGATION REPORT
Send Completed Report to Risk   within Five (5) days of Date of Injury

Office Name: _Governor's Hospital_   No.: _____ . _____   Date of this Report: _2 · 18 · 03_

EMPLOYEE INFORMATION
Name of Injured (F, MI, L): _Alex A. Lizuski_   SSN: _135-06-9999_   Hire Date: _02 · ___ · 89_
Dept. Name: _Nursing_   Post Held at time of injury: _4 West_   How long at this job: _14 yrs_
Describe injuries sustained by employee: _Laceration / Abrasion Shin Area_

Has the employee lost any work time? ☐ Yes ☒ No   Were they kept overnight in a hospital? ☐ Yes ☒ No
Did the employee receive prompt and appropriate medical care? ☒ Yes ☐ No If no, briefly explain: _____

Treating Physician: _Frances Teika, M.D._
Treating Facility: _Governor's Hospital_
Address: _410 Fifth Street_   Tele: (_203_) _369-1410_

ACCIDENT INFORMATION
Date of Injury: _12 · 18 · 02_   Time of Injury: _4 · 10 ·_   AM/(PM)   ☐ Daylight ☒ Dusk/Dawn ☐ Night
Type of Accident: ☐ Slip, ☐ Fall, ☐ Sprain, ☐ Strain, ☐ Lifting, ☐ Vehicle, ☐ Firearms, ☒ Other, please explain: _Assisting other nurses with a combative patient, hit shin on oak bed rail_
Type of Location (e.g. shopping mall, parking lot, city street, etc.): _Hospital room_
Accident Location: _____ , _____ , ____ , ____
                     Street Address   City   State   ZIP

Relevant Weather Conditions: _____
Type of Lighting at Time of Accident: _____
Client site? ☐ No ☒ Yes Client Name: _Governor's Hospital_
Any witnesses? ☐ No ☒ Yes Witness Names & Contact Info. (e.g. telephone numbers and/or addresses):
Bill Wittier   _518 734-0002_
Victor Roberge   _518 734-0950_

If vehicle related, has the *Auto. Loss Notice* been properly filed? ☐ Yes ☐ No If no, briefly explain: _____

Based upon your investigation, briefly describe what took place (WHO, WHAT, WHEN, WHERE, HOW and WHY): _____
Patient Lavelle Chingere, didn't want to take Medication from a needle, at 4:05 PM, Bpt Hosp, patient became combative, when officer Lix Lizos went to grab his legs, he was pulled into the oak rail and caused laceration / abrasion to Alex A. Lizuski 's shin, left side. This is a pyhic wing, and each case is different

What can be done to avoid a recurrence of this type of accident? _This type of injury just can't be avoided. This is one of two pyhic wings_
What actions have been taken by you or the client to remedy any risk associated with this type of accident? _____

If applicable, has the client been notified of any related hazard or unsafe condition? ☒ Yes ☐ No If no, please explain: _____

If yes, has the condition been corrected? ☐ Yes ☒ No If no, have they committed to remedying the problem? Please explain: _____
as explained above
Investigator's Name: _Jane Leppize, RN_   Title: _Shift Supervisor_
Investigator's Signature: ⊗ _Jane Lupp_
Reviewed by: _____ ⊗ _____   Date: _2 · 18 · 03_

FIGURE 13-13 Supervisor's workplace accident investigation report

extreme caution when naming defendants in lawsuits. The client and/or attorney or law firm could be liable or disciplined for suing the wrong business or person. Potential defendants can be identified in many ways: scrutinizing documents to glean names, addresses, and telephone numbers; making telephone calls to businesses or individuals involved; performing online searches; checking with the secretary of state's corporation or partnership divisions or the county or city offices in which assumed names of businesses are registered; and searching company records and documents. Special difficulties arise with ambulance and fire departments as defendants. These entities are often owned or supervised by local governmental agencies, or they may be volunteer services working under governmental contract. Information concerning licensed or regulated businesses can be obtained through the federal or state regulatory agencies.

Paralegals use photographs, videos, and traditional pencil-and-paper methods of documenting tort scenes. The events in a tort case and their sequence are documented and reconstructed under the same conditions in which the tort originally occurred. Paralegals must know their jurisdiction's evidentiary rules if they are to recognize the types of evidence that will be useful in the tort case. It is important to collect evidence in the proper evidentiary form so that it may be used at trial. Hearsay problems should be anticipated and overcome. Most litigation firms now use computer and video technologies to assist in documenting and reconstructing tort cases.

Local governmental agencies may possess a wealth of information concerning some parties involved in the tort case. Archives contain vital statistics, marriage licenses, property ownership records, police records, and civil suit or criminal records. Newspapers, television, and radio can also provide valuable information about the events that occurred when the tort happened. Databases can also furnish considerable information about the persons or businesses involved in the case.

Paralegals investigate employment and lost wages to help determine the client's damages. Tax, wage, and income records should be obtained. Injury expenses are carefully documented and investigated. It is important to know whether the injured party has received insurance or governmental benefits as a result of the tort. It is also necessary to know whether the plaintiff has previously been involved in claims or lawsuits, as well as preexisting injuries, involving the same factual circumstances as the present tort case. The parties' driving or criminal records may be critical to the current case.

Investigations are tailored to fit the specific aspects of each tort case. Cases involving automobile accidents or medical negligence and health care providers each require specialized questions that paralegals use to gather the information necessary for the trial team to successfully conclude the case.

Key Terms

business directory	hearsay	service of process
discovery	investigation	(process service)
fictitious name		sunshine law

Problems

Assume the following actual cases were actually assigned to you for investigation. As the senior paralegal for the law firm, you performed the preliminary interview of each of the named plaintiffs. Identify what kind of investigation you would conduct and the different sources you would consult to further your investigation. Be sure to consider each of the facts of the case, as well as all the potential defendants.

1. Ms. Santiago was admitted to the Glenwood hospital through the emergency room with severe pain to the abdomen. After an exploratory operation by Dr. Inexperienced, an infected appendix was discovered and removed. Ms. Santiago was released four days later. She continued to have increasingly severe pain and was readmitted to the hospital three weeks later. The same surgeon performed another operative procedure and recovered a surgical sponge left in her during the initial operation and removed it.

2. Suzie Woo is seven months pregnant. While crossing the grounds of the Gentle Breeze Country Club with her friend Dewanna Stevens, she steps on a circular manhole cover, which unbeknownst to her was slightly ajar. The manhole tips open and she falls in the hole, with her stomach preventing her from falling completely down the open pit. Just minutes before, a Quick Rooter Plumbing truck was spotted driving off the grounds of the club.

3. Josh Tyler is walking up the hill on State Street when a car without a driver comes rolling out of a private parking lot, down the street, and pins him against an office building, breaking four of his ribs and his left leg. An ambulance is called by a store employee who sees the accident happen. Josh is taken to the nearest hospital. He later learns that the car recently had been serviced by Jenelle's Auto Repair.

4. Arnold Rubitkowitz is playing bingo at the local Grand Tigers Club fundraiser at the Hotel Luxe. Just when his cards are finally starting to look promising, the five-foot-long fluorescent light fixture drops from the ceiling above his head, rendering him momentarily unconscious. The bingo caller stops the game long enough to summon the local fire department, the police, and the town paramedics, who take Arnold to the local emergency room for treatment.

5. Trevor Vincent is taking a Sunday ride on his motorcycle through a new development by Sherman Oaks Builders in the town of Leewood, Texas. As he approaches a sharp curve in the road, he comes upon some construction debris, is unable to complete the sharp turn, is thrown twenty feet from his motorcycle, lands on his head, and dies. Trevor was not wearing a helmet at the time of the accident.

Review Questions

1. What are the basic components of a tort case investigation? Who conducts these investigations? How are investigations customized? What types of questions are witnesses asked in tort investigations?

2. Why is it important to identify the correct defendant(s) in a tort case? What could happen if incorrect persons or businesses are sued as defendants?

3. How can a client's documents and the telephone help locate potential defendants? Who should a paralegal contact to obtain information about corporations, partnerships, or sole proprietorships that are prospective defendants?

4. What special problems are associated with ambulance and fire departments that are defendants?

5. Who should a paralegal contact to investigate licensed or regulated businesses?

6. How should a paralegal document an accident scene? What conditions should be prevalent when the scene is investigated? What items should be included on the investigation checklist?

7. Why is it important to tort investigations to know the evidentiary rules from one's jurisdiction?

8. How can local governmental agencies, newspapers, television, radio, and computer databases be helpful in researching a tort case?

9. Why are criminal and driving records pertinent to tort investigations? What can this information reveal about the case being investigated?

10. What additional areas should a tort paralegal investigate?

11. What are some of the kinds of information that can be obtained on-line to assist in an investigation?

Project

Divide your class into small groups to investigate the following hypothetical tort cases. Develop question lists, checklists, and other tools that will assist in your work. Group members should role-play the client, witnesses, or other interested persons. This can be done within a group, or groups in class could assume these various roles.

Case #1: *English v. Sidcup College*

Sharon B. English, an audiology and speech pathology student at Sidcup College, slipped and fell down stairs leading from the first floor to the basement of the Student Memorial Union. She suffered substantial physical injury as a result of the fall.

Case #2: *Watermark v. Ootheca Convalescence Center*

Terry D. Watermark is a patient at the Ootheca Convalescence Center, a medical facility devoted to the treatment and rehabilitation of physical injuries. Terry's knees were damaged during a motorcycle accident. During whirlpool treatment, an occupational therapist working for the Rehabilitative Services Corporation, which owned the Center, failed to check the thermostat on the water heating unit affixed to the whirlpool system. Near-boiling water filled the whirlpool, severely scalding Terry's entire body.

Case #3: *Joist v. Mason Dixon Poultry Company*

Samantha K. Joist was driving her automobile along State Highway 144 when a truck, driven by Elliot R. Daniel, ran a stop sign and collided with Samantha's vehicle. Both Elliot and Samantha were injured in the crash. Elliot, who was conscious following the collision, told a paramedic that his brakes had failed suddenly. The truck had the name "Mason Dixon Poultry Company" painted on the sides, along with a telephone number.

Internet Resources

This chapter focuses on tort investigation. To learn more about tort investigation, the following sites can be accessed:

West Legal Directory
http://www.lawoffice.com

Guide to Litigation Law
http://www.hg.org

American Arbitration Association
http://www.adr.org

Federal Rules of Civil Procedure
http://www.law.cornell.edu/rules/frcp

Experts and Consultants
http://www.nocall.org/experts.htm

Agencies that Gather Information Related to Tort Law
http://www.findlaw.com/01topics/22tort/database.html
http://www.statelocal.gov

Kelly Blue Book to Evaluate Property Damage
http://www.kbb.com

Legal Technology
http://www.lawofficecomputing.com

Locate People
http://www.bigfoot.com
http://www.switchboard.com

Annual Reports for Public Companies
http://www.investquest.com

Public Records
http://www.knowx.com

Federation of Insurance and Corporate Counsel
http://www.thefederation.org

Calculation of Damages
http://www.frankenfeld.com/newsletter

For additional resources, visit our Web site at
www.paralegal.delmar.cengage.com

APPENDICES

—————————————⟨◆⟩—————————————

Appendix A   **Confidential Client Information Form**

Appendix B   **Understanding Appellate Court Opinions**

Appendix C   **Supplementary Cases**

Frankel v. Warwick Hotel
Russell v. Archer
Stander v. Orentreich
Summers v. Tice
Cinel v. Connick
Pepsico, Inc. v. Redmond
Roach v. Stern
A&M Records, Inc. v. Napster, Inc.
Jordan v. Town of Pratt
MacPherson v. Buick Motor Company
Greenman v. Yuba Power Products, Inc.
Fishman v. Beach
Girdley v. Coats
Doe v. Cutter Biological

APPENDIX A

〈◆〉

CONFIDENTIAL CLIENT INFORMATION FORM

CONFIDENTIAL CLIENT INFORMATION FORM

This questionnaire is a *confidential* questionnaire for the use of our office only in preparing your claim for personal injuries. The information you furnish us will not be released and will be held strictly confidential. When your claim has been concluded, we will return this questionnaire to you if you wish. Please answer every question fully and accurately because, as your attorneys, we must know all about you and your case. One surprise because of an incorrect or incomplete answer could cause you to lose your case. All of the questions are important even though they may not appear to have anything to do with your case.

Please type or print all answers. Use additional sheets of paper or the reverse side of this form if needed.

Your name: _____

Your address: _____

Your telephone number: _____ Date of accident: _____

Insurance company: _____

Workers' compensation number, if any: _____

Birthplace: _____

Social Security number: _____ Age: _____ Birthdate: _____

Married: _____ Single: _____ Divorced: _____ Separated: _____ Widower: _____ Widow: _____

If divorced, date and place: _____

Names, ages, and addresses of all those (including children) who are dependent upon you for support, and your relationship to each:

Name	Address	Age	Relationship
_____	_____	_____	_____
_____	_____	_____	_____
_____	_____	_____	_____

List the addresses where you have resided during the past ten years and give the period of time at each residence, including dates:

<u>Residence</u>   <u>From</u>   <u>To</u>

_____

_____

_____

Have you ever used any other name? _____ Where? _____

Why?: _____

Are you married at the present time? _____ Date of marriage: _____

Place: _____

WORK BACKGROUND

Present job: _____ Phone: _____

Name and address of employer: _____

_____

Present job title and duties: _____

How long have you worked at this job? _____ Your present pay: $ _____

When you first began working for this employer: _____

List prior employment for past five years:

<u>Name</u>   <u>Address</u>   <u>Date Employed</u>   <u>Job</u>

_____

_____

_____

EDUCATION

How many years did you complete in school? _____ College? _____

Is your spouse employed? _____ Employer's name and address: _____

_____

Wages: $ _____ per _____ Average income entire year for spouse: $ _____

How long employed? _____ Prior employment: _____

Are you living in your employer's household or premises? _____

If related to employer, state relationship: _____

Occupation when injured: _____ Were you doing your regular work? _____

On whose payroll when injured? _____

Wages when injured (per day, per week): _____ Work days per week: _____

Were you a temporary or steady employee? _____

If under 18 years of age, give name and address of your guardian or parent: _____

_____

ACCIDENT

Date of the injury (hour): _____

Date you were forced to leave work because of your injury (hour): _____

Place where injury was sustained (no., street, city or town): _____

_____

Were you on employer's premises? _____ Was injury caused by another person? _____

Name of other person: _____

Who is he/she employed by? _____

Have you claimed or received settlement for this injury? _____ From whom? _____

_____

Name and address of eyewitnesses: _____

_____

_____

When did you first report your injury? _____

To whom did you first report your injury? _____

Have you returned to work? _____ If so, what date? _____

Describe your injury and how the accident happened: _____

_____

_____

MEDICAL HISTORY BEFORE ACCIDENT

Were you hospitalized at any time before the accident in this case? _____ If so, list below all hospitalizations:

Date	Hospital	Doctor	Duration	Nature of Illness

Have you had any physical examinations before this accident? If so, list all physical examinations for five years before the accident:

Date	Place	Name of Doctor	Purpose

Have you had any accidents or injuries before this accident? _____ If so, list below every such accident or injury, whether there was a claim for damages or not:

Date	Place	Nature of Accident or Injury	Treated By

Have you had any illnesses or diseases before this accident? _____ If so, list every such illness or disease suffered in the five years before this accident:

Date	Nature of Illness	Duration	Treated By

Have you had any chronic health problems? _____ If so, list them: _____

Did you use any drugs regularly before the accident? _____ If so, list the type and reason why you used them: _____

Have you ever had any insurance of any kind declined or cancelled? _____ If so, give reason: ____

Have you ever had any broken bones? _____ If so, give date and circumstances: _____

List below what normal activities, including sports, hobbies, or other activities, you enjoyed before this accident: _____

STATEMENTS MADE

Have you told any police officer, investigator, insurance adjustor, or any other person about the accident? _____

Have you given any written statement to any person about the accident? _____ If so, answer the following:

Name of person to whom statement was given: _____

Date given: _____ If written, do you have a copy? _____

Persons present at time: _____ Did you sign the statement? _____

Please give us any statement you know the employer made about the accident, or that you understand he/she may have made: _____

When and where made: _____

Name and address of person who heard it: _____

DAMAGES FROM ACCIDENT

State in full detail, all injuries you received as a result of this accident: _____

_____

State your physical condition—scars, deformities, headaches, pains, etc.—due to injuries received in this accident: _____

_____

Have you missed any time from work as a result of your injury? _____ If so, list the inclusive dates you were unable to work: From: _____   To: _____

From: _____   To: _____

Did you lose wages for the periods of time missed from work due to this accident _____ If so, state the total wages lost to date and the dates: _____

Have you had any increases or decreases in your pay since the accident? _____ If so, explain:

_____

List all hospitals in which you were examined or treated, or to which you were admitted as a patient as a result of the injuries sustained in the accident and the dates:

Hospital	Address	Dates

List the full name, address, and telephone number of each physician or surgeon who has examined or treated you for your injuries as a result of the accident:

Name	Address	Telephone No.

Have you used any of the following in connection with the treatment?

Back or neck brace? _____   Dates: _____

Crutches? _____   Dates: _____

Traction? _____   Dates: _____

Physiotherapy? _____   Dates: _____

Other? _____   Dates: _____

List here all of your usual employment activities that you have *NOT* been able to perform, or can perform only with difficulty, since the accident: _____

_____

Time lost from school (if you are a pupil): _____

Please summarize your out-of-pocket expenses, and if you have not previously given us the name and address, indicate to whom they are owed, as well as the amounts and whether they have been paid.

_____
_____
_____
_____

CONCLUSION

In completing this questionnaire, have you thought of any information for which we have not asked that might be of some assistance to us in serving you? _____ If so, please state it here, no matter how silly, trivial, or embarrassing it may seem. _____

_____
_____
_____
_____

Dated this _____ day of _____ 20 _____.

I have read the above statement and the statements contained therein are true and correct.

_____
Client

APPENDIX B

<(◆)>

UNDERSTANDING APPELLATE COURT OPINIONS

Legal analysis consists of understanding appellate court opinions and applying rules of law to different factual situations. This section addresses legal analysis, a critical aspect of legal study.

Briefing Cases

Many of the chapters in this book include reprinted portions of appellate court opinions to illustrate various tort principles. At first glance, court decisions may appear garbled or unfocused. A structured formula applied to each case helps organize the ideas that the courts express. There are several such methods, but the most popular is explained here.

Structured Analysis

A structured analysis breaks an opinion into several components: facts, procedural history, issues on appeal, rationale, and ruling(s). This approach represents the standard analytical framework used by law school and paralegal students.

Facts From the court opinion, the reader gleans the *facts* that underlie or are necessary to the appellate court's final determination of the case. These are sometimes called the *legally significant facts*. Many facts in the case provide mere background information; these are called *background facts*. Although background facts are not critical to the court's decision, they must be noted to comprehend the complete circumstances involved in the litigation. Sometimes appellate opinions include irrelevant facts that have no real bearing on the outcome of the appeal.

Procedural History The *procedural history*, or *judicial history* as it is sometimes called, is the appellate court's summary of the previous events in the lawsuit: who sued whom, what legal claims were involved, and (most importantly) how the trial court decided the case (if a bench trial) or in whose favor the jury returned its verdict. Procedural history may include a summary of a lower appellate court's decision rendered before the case was appealed to the court that wrote the opinion being studied. Procedural information is critical to grasp the importance of the appellate court's ruling.

Issues   The *issues* include the questions appealed from the trial court's judgment. Every appeal has at least one issue being reviewed by the appellate court, although more often several issues are involved. Issues are normally phrased in terms of a question: Did the trial court err in admitting certain evidence? Given the facts proven during trial, did the defendant commit a certain tort against the plaintiff?

Rationale   The *rationale* is the appellate court's reasoning behind its ruling. It is the process through which the court applies the rules of law to the facts of the case. This application is accomplished by linking a series of arguments that appear to lead to a single logical conclusion (which, conveniently, happens to be the court's decision). Consider the following example. Suppose a state statute requires owners of agricultural vehicles used to haul grain to obtain a special commercial license. Charles sells his old twin-axle grain truck to Donny, who plans to use it in a furniture delivery business. Donny purchases ordinary truck license plates. Has Donny violated the statute? In its rationale, an appellate court would first explain the statutory language (i.e., rule of law) and then apply it to the facts of the case. Thus, although Donny bought a vehicle formerly used to haul grain, its present function is entirely nonagricultural (i.e., conveying furniture). Because the truck is not being used to carry grain, Donny would not be required to purchase the special licenses and thus has not violated the statute.

Ruling   The *ruling* is the appellate court's decision in the case. This decree is directed toward the trial (or lower appellate) court's ruling. If the appellate court agrees that the trial court was correct in deciding the issue on appeal, then the appellate court *affirms* the trial court's judgment. If the appellate court disagrees with the trial court's determination of the appealed issue, then the appellate court *reverses* or *vacates* the trial court's decree. Often reversal or vacation is accompanied by a *remand*, or return, of the case to the trial court with instructions from the appellate court. These instructions may be simply that judgment should be entered for the plaintiff or the defendant (depending, of course, upon which side the appellate court thinks should prevail), or they may include directions that certain factual questions be retried by the trial court.

Briefing an Appellate Court Opinion

As mentioned previously, law school and paralegal students most often use this briefing formula to analyze appellate court opinions. To illustrate how this is done in practice, an actual appellate court opinion has been reproduced here, followed by a suggested case brief that summarizes the elements of the opinion using the briefing formula. To assist in reading opinions reprinted in this book, certain tangential matters and terminology are summarized or explained in brackets: "[ ]." Any parts of the original opinion that have been omitted are indicated in bracketed comments or by bracketed ellipses: "[…]."

Edwards v. Terryville Meat Co.

577 N.Y.S.2d 477 (App. Div. 1991)
N.Y. Supreme Court, Appellate Division
December 23, 1991
Before MANGANO, P.J., and KUNZEMAN, EIBER and BALLETTA, JJ.

MEMORANDUM BY THE COURT.

In a negligence action to recover damages for personal injuries, the plaintiffs appeal […] from […] an order and judgment […] of the Supreme Court, Suffolk County (Cannavo, J.), entered September 11, 1989, as granted the defendant's motion for summary judgment dismissing the complaint […].

ORDERED that the order and judgment entered September 11, 1989, is affirmed […].

In this slip-and-fall case, it was incumbent upon the plaintiffs to come forth with evidence showing that the defendant had either created the allegedly dangerous condition or that it had actual or constructive notice of the condition (see, *Eddy v. Tops Friendly Markets*, 91 A.D.2d 1203, 459 N.Y.S.2d 196, *aff'd*, 59 N.Y.2d 692, 463 N.Y.S. 2d 437, 450 N.E.2d 243[1983]). To constitute constructive notice, a defect must be visible and apparent and it must exist for a sufficient length of time prior to the accident to permit defendant's employees to discover and remedy it" (*Gordon v. American Museum of Natural History*, 67 N.Y.2d 836, 837, 501 N.Y.S. 2d 646, 492 N.E.2d 774 [1986]). The injured plaintiff was in the defendant's store for only about 10 minutes before she allegedly slipped and fell on an unknown milky-colored substance which she concededly did not see until after she fell. There is no evidence that the defendant caused the substance to be on the floor, nor is there sufficient evidence to establish that the defendant had either actual or constructive notice of the substance [citations omitted]. Accordingly, the Supreme Court properly granted the defendant's motion for summary judgment.

A Suggested Case Brief

Citation: *Edwards v. Terryville Meat Co.*, 577 N.Y.S.2d 477 (N.Y. App. Div. 1991).

Facts: Injured plaintiff was in defendant's store 10 minutes when she slipped and fell on unknown milky substance on floor. Plaintiff did not see substance until after falling. No evidence that defendant caused substance to be on floor.

Procedural History: Injured plaintiff and spouse sued defendant for negligence. Supreme Court of Suffolk County granted defendant's motion for summary judgment dismissing plaintiffs' complaint.

Issue: Did trial court err in granting defendant's motion for summary judgment?

(*Implied Issue*) Did plaintiffs present sufficient evidence to establish defendant's liability for negligently causing plaintiff's injuries?

Rationale: This is a slip-and-fall negligence case. To establish defendant's negligence, plaintiffs must prove either that (1) defendant caused slippery substance to be on floor, or (2) defendant knew (or had constructive notice) that substance was on floor. Constructive notice requires that substance be present on floor for sufficient length of time prior to accident to permit defendant's employees to discover and remedy it. In this case, there was no evidence that defendant had created the hazard that injured plaintiff. Further, there was insufficient evidence that defendant had actual or constructive notice of substance, given the short time (10 minutes) that plaintiff was in store before she slipped and fell. Thus, trial court correctly granted defendant's motion for summary judgment.

Ruling: Appellate Division affirmed supreme court's decision.

APPENDIX C

⟨◆⟩

SUPPLEMENTARY CASES

Frankel v. Warwick Hotel
Russell v. Archer
Stander v. Orentreich
Summers v. Tice
Cinel v. Connick
Pepsico, Inc. v. Redmond
Roach v. Stern
A&M Records, Inc. v. Napster, Inc.
Jordan v. Town of Pratt
MacPherson v. Buick Motor Company
Greenman v. Yuba Power Products, Inc.
Fishman v. Beach
Girdley v. Coats
Doe v. Cutter Biological

FRANKEL v. WARWICK HOTEL
United States District Court, E.D. Pennsylvania
881 F. Supp. 183 (E.D. Pa. 1995)
March 31, 1995
Joyner, District Judge
[See Chapter 1.]

This diversity case, involving a dispute between a father and his son, has been brought before the Court by motion of the defendants, who seek dismissal of the amended complaint pursuant to Fed.R.Civ.P. 12(b)(6). For the reasons that follow, the defendants' motion to dismiss will be granted.

The issue for the Court is whether Plaintiff has stated a claim on which relief can be granted; thus, we must take as true all of the factual allegations made in the amended complaint. *ALA, Inc. v. CCAIR, Inc.*, 29 F.3d 855, 859 (3d Cir.1994). Accordingly, the facts giving rise to this lawsuit are as follows. In the fall of 1989, Plaintiff Adam Frankel accepted a job offer from his father, Defendant William Frankel, to work as a restaurant manager at the Warwick Hotel in Philadelphia. Adam Frankel's status was that of an at-will employee. The elder Mr. Frankel is a partner in the Warwick Hotel and an officer of the Frankel Management Company of Philadelphia, Inc. ... On June 8, 1991, the younger Mr. Frankel married Annika Moriarity, a Roman Catholic. On October 16, 1992, William

Frankel because of his antipathy toward Ms. Moriarity and her religion, informed his son that he would be fired unless he divorced his wife. The son refused to leave his wife, and as a result, he was fired on October 24, 1992.

Adam Frankel's amended complaint, filed against the Warwick Hotel, Frankel Management, and William Frankel, contains four counts. In the first two counts, Adam Frankel alleges that he was wrongfully discharged. The third count is brought against William Frankel under an intentional infliction of emotional distress theory. In the fourth count, Adam Frankel alleges that the defendants are liable under the tort theory of invasion of privacy by intentionally interfering with his marriage. In support of their motion, the defendants assert that the amended complaint must be dismissed because the allegations fail to state a claim upon which relief can be granted.

In considering a motion to dismiss pursuant to Rule 12(b)(6), the complaint's allegations must be construed favorably to the pleader. The court must accept as true all of the plaintiff's factual allegations and draw from them all reasonable inferences. *Schrob v. Catterson,* 948 F.2d 1402, 1405 (3d Cir.1991) (citations omitted). Thus, the court will grant a Rule 12(b)(6) motion only if the non-moving party cannot prevail legally under the set of facts alleged. *Markowitz v. Northeast Land Co.,* 906 F.2d 100, 103 (3d Cir.1990). In deciding this motion, this Court will apply these standards to each of the four counts raised in Adam Frankel's amended complaint.

Under Pennsylvania law, employees may be discharged at any time, for any reason or for no reason at all. As a general rule, there is no common law cause of action against an employer for termination of an at-will employment relationship.

***

Generally, the recognized exceptions concern an employee's discharge after he or she refused to violate the law, *see Woodson v. AMF Leisureland Ctrs., Inc.,* 842 F.2d 699 (3d Cir.1988) (dismissal for refusal to serve liquor to intoxicated person); *McNulty v. Borden, Inc.,* 474 F.Supp. 1111 (E.D. Pa.1979) (dismissal for refusal to

participate in antitrust violations); *Field v. Philadelphia Elec. Co.,* 388 Pa.Super. 400, 565 A.2d 1170 (1989) (employee fired for making statutorily required report to NRC), or an employee's right of political participation, *see Novosel* (dismissal for refusal to participate in political lobbying); *Reuther v. Fowler & Williams Inc.,* 255 Pa.Super. 28, 386 A.2d 119 (1978) (employee fired for absence due to jury duty), or employer conduct in violation of a specific statute, as in *Perks v. Firestone Tire & Rubber Co.,* 611 F.2d 1363 (3d Cir. 1979) (employment terminated for individual's refusal to take polygraph test).

***

Since Adam Frankel concedes that he was an at-will employee, the issue here is whether the case falls within that limited exception allowing recovery for a termination that has violated public policy. The younger Mr. Frankel points to three areas of the law as potential sources of public policy justifying a cause of action, all of which relate to policy favoring family cohesiveness. These sources include the Pennsylvania Divorce Code, 23 Pa.Cons.Stat.Ann. § 3101, *et seq.,* legislative findings supporting the general policy that the family deserves protection and preservation, and the Commonwealth's prevention of testamentary attempts to destroy the family. Adam Frankel's contention that these pronouncements amount to the sort of clearly mandated articulations of public policy which justify the creation of an exception to the at-will doctrine, however, is without merit. Like the provisions relied upon by the *McGonagle* plaintiff, the statements relating to the preservation of the family are too vague to be used as a basis for an exception to the employee-at-will doctrine. Typical of the language relied upon is the policy statement contained in the Pennsylvania Divorce Code, which notes that "the protection and preservation of the family is of paramount public concern." 23 Pa.Cons.Stat.Ann. § 3102(a). As is apparent, the provision does not specifically prohibit or mandate any particular conduct; it is instead a vague and general expression of the legislature's view concerning the importance of family unity. As such, it is an inappropriate basis for the creation of an exception to the general rule, Thus, we hold that the case arising from the facts alleged is governed by the general rule regarding termination of an at-will employee. As a result, we must grant the defendants' motion to dismiss as it relates to the first two counts of the amended complaint.

Pennsylvania courts recognize the tort of intentional infliction of emotional distress, but have been cautious in permitting recovery. *Williams v. Guzzardi,* 875 F.2d 46, 52 (3d Cir. 1989). Thus, in order for a plaintiff to recover under this theory of liability, the defendant must have acted in a manner "so outrageous in character and so extreme in degree as to go beyond all possible bounds of decency and to be regarded as atrocious and utterly intolerable in a civilized society."

To recover, a plaintiff must establish the following four elements: (1) defendant's conduct must be intentional or reckless, (2) the conduct must be extreme and outrageous, (3) it must cause emotional distress, and (4) the emotional distress must be severe. *Williams,* 875 F.2d at 52. Further, under Pennsylvania law, to state such a claim in a situation where the plaintiff has allegedly suffered emotional distress as a result of outrageous conduct directed at the plaintiff, as is the case here, there must be an allegation of physical injury. We further note that such a cause of action rarely lies in the context of the employee-employer relationship. As the Third Circuit has noted, "it is extremely rare to find conduct in the employment context that will rise to the level of outrageousness necessary to provide a basis for recovery for the tort of intentional infliction of emotional distress."

Applying these principles to the instant matter, this Court concludes that the intentional infliction of emotional distress claim must be dismissed. The pertinent conduct is William Frankel's alleged threat to discharge his son unless he divorced his wife. While we do not endorse the elder Mr. Frankel's alleged conduct, we cannot conclude that it was so outrageous as to be "utterly intolerable in a civilized society." Moreover, we note that the younger Mr. Frankel has not alleged that he suffered physical injury,

as is required under Pennsylvania law. Accordingly, plaintiff's claim for damages under the theory of intentional infliction of emotional distress must be dismissed.

An invasion of privacy is actionable under Pennsylvania law, *Harris v. Easton Publishing Co.,* 335 Pa.Super. 141, 483 A.2d 1377, 1383 (1984), and consists of four distinct torts, including (1) intrusion upon seclusion, (2) appropriation of name or likeness, (3) publicity given to one's private life, and (4) publicity placing one in a false light. *Id.* Here, Adam Frankel alleges that the defendants are liable under the intrusion upon seclusion tort. Intrusion upon seclusion occurs when a person "intentionally intrudes, physically or otherwise, upon the solitude or seclusion of another or his private affairs or concerns ... if the intrusion would be highly offensive to the reasonable person." *Borse v. Piece Goods Shop, Inc.,* 963 F.2d 611, 620 (3d Cir. 1992) (quoting Restatement (Second) of Torts § 652B). Further, a defendant will not be liable unless the invasion is substantial. *Id.* at 621. The intrusion may be (1) a physical intrusion into a place where the plaintiff has secluded himself or herself, (2) the use of defendant's senses to oversee or overhear plaintiff's private affairs, (3) or some other form of investigation or examination into plaintiff's private concerns. *Id.; Harris,* 483 A.2d at 1383.

Turning to the instant matter, we conclude that Adam Frankel has failed to state a cause of action for invasion of privacy. As the cases make clear, this tort encompasses the physical or sensory penetration of a person's zone of seclusion in an attempt to collect private information concerning that person's affairs. The facts alleged here, that William Frankel terminated his son's employment because the son refused to divorce his wife, do not amount to the type of harm compensable under this theory. Further, to the extent that the intrusion alleged by Adam Frankel is an intentional interference with his marriage, we note that the Restatement specifically excludes marriage contracts from the tort of intentional interference with contract. *See* Restatement (Second) of Torts § 766 (1977) ("One who intentionally and improperly interferes with the performance of a contract (except a contract to marry) between another and a third person by inducing or otherwise causing the third person not to perform the contract, is subject to liability ...”). Thus, we must conclude that Adam Frankel has failed to state a claim for invasion of privacy in his amended complaint.

For the foregoing reasons, the defendants’ motion to dismiss plaintiff’s amended complaint is granted.

RUSSELL v. ARCHER BUILDING CENTERS, INC.

New York Supreme Court, Appellate Division, Third Department
631 N.Y.S.2d 102 (App. Div. 1995)
September 14, 1995
Crew, Justice

[See Chapter 2.]

Appeal from an order of the Supreme Court (Ingraham, J.), entered December 15, 1994 in Otsego County, which denied defendant’s motion for summary judgment dismissing the complaint.

On March 22, 1993, plaintiff Frances Russell (hereinafter Russell) was shopping with her husband, plaintiff John Russell, in a hardware/lumber store owned by defendant in the City of Oneonta, Otsego County. Plaintiffs sought out the tile display and as Russell stepped back to view a sheet of tile, she tripped over the bottom rail of a steel display rack forming one side of the aisle in which she was standing and broke her wrist. The rack in question, which was designed to hold doors and was only partially filled at the time of the accident, appears to have been the only rack in the area where Russell fell.

Plaintiffs commenced this action alleging that the empty segment of the display rack constituted a hazard to the shopping public and caused Russell’s injury. Defendant answered and after examinations before trial, moved for summary judgment dismissing the complaint contending that the display rack was in open and plain view. Defendant further contended that the rack did not constitute a hidden or concealed danger and that it was not liable for the obvious condition which, with the exercise of reasonable care, was readily observable. Supreme Court, finding an issue of fact as to whether the rack was open and obvious when placed in any location where a customer might back into it to view other merchandise, denied the motion. This appeal by defendant followed.

There must be a reversal. While a landowner who holds property open to the public has a general duty to maintain the property in a reasonably safe condition to prevent foreseeable injuries, this duty extends only to conditions that are not readily observable. There is no duty to warn of conditions that can be readily observed with the normal use of one’s senses.

Searching the record in the light most favorable to plaintiffs, we find no basis for finding an issue of fact as to whether the rack was open and obvious. Here, a photograph of the display rack with its offending bottom rail reveals that the rack did not protrude into the plainly discernible and uncluttered aisle, but rather formed a readily apparent part of the merchandise display area. Had Russell exercised ordinary care, she would have observed the self-evident boundaries of the aisle as she walked down it before stopping immediately adjacent to the rack to examine the tile display. Accordingly, the order should be reversed and summary judgment granted to defendant.

ORDERED that the order is reversed, on the law, with costs, motion granted, summary judgment awarded to defendant and complaint dismissed.

STANDER v. ORENTREICH

Supreme Court, New York County
627 N.Y.S.2d 879 (Sup. Ct. 1995)
May 16, 1995
Sklar, Justice

[See Chapter 2.]

The essential question raised by the present motion and cross motion in this action for medical malpractice and related claims is whether plaintiffs' causes of action are barred by the statute of limitations.

Plaintiff Bella Stander and her husband plaintiff Robert Mason move to dismiss the first affirmative defense of defendant dermatologist, Norman Orentreich, MD, which raises the statute of limitations defense. ...

Plaintiff visited Dr Orentreich in July and August 1979 for treatment of linear scleroderma, a skin condition, on her face. Dr Orentreich recommended injections of liquid silicone as the sole treatment for this condition. Silicone is considered a medical device under FDA regulations, not a drug. Based on his recommendation Stander received two sets of injections into her cheek and forehead. She discontinued treatment because the injections were painful and caused discoloration of the skin.

Stander alleges that she noticed no other adverse reactions until somewhere between February and April 1986 when small pink lumps appeared on her forehead. She had these removed by a different doctor—a plastic surgeon—who initially hypothesized that the lumps resulted from factors unrelated to her 1979 treatment by Dr Orentreich. Shortly thereafter more lumps appeared which she had removed in 1987. After pathology analysis and a conversation in February 1988 with a representative from Dow Corning, the manufacturer of the liquid silicone, Stander suspected that the cause of the painful pink lumps emerging on her forehead was the silicone which defendant injected in 1979.

Plaintiff asserts that after learning the purported cause of the lumps, she also learned that Dr Orentreich had injected her with a nonmedical grade of silicone which was not,

as manufactured, suitable for injection into humans, but which defendant reprocessed to cause it to become medical grade. The parties dispute whether or not the liquid silicone which defendant injected was or was not suitable for that use. Plaintiffs allege that defendant negligently processed or manufactured the purportedly reprocessed silicone.

... Plaintiffs have alleged four causes of action against Dr Orentreich: first, for medical malpractice based on departures from accepted standards of medical care; second, for failure to obtain the plaintiff's informed consent to the treatment administered; third, a derivative action for loss of services, society and consortium suffered by plaintiff's spouse, Robert Mason; and fourth, for injury resulting from defendant's alleged negligent manufacture, processing and administration of the injectable liquid silicone.

The statute of limitations requires an action for medical malpractice to be commenced "within two years and six months of the date of the act, omission or failure complained of. ..." The alleged malpractice occurred in July and August of 1979. Plaintiffs have not alleged that the continuous treatment doctrine applies to toll the statute of limitations. Another exception that can extend the time to commence a medical malpractice action is the "foreign object" exception. The statute, however, specifically excludes chemical compounds from the scope of the exception. Stander alleges that the cause of her injury was liquid silicone injected into her body, which defendant alleges is a chemical compound.

Whether the silicone constitutes a chemical compound within the meaning of the statute, and/or a medical device, plaintiffs cannot invoke the benefit of the foreign object exception. This discovery rule is available to delay the running of the statute of limitations "only in circumstances where a foreign object is negligently 'left' in the patient's body without any intended continuing treatment purpose … ."

Dr Orentreich intentionally injected the silicone into Bella Stander precisely as a treatment designed to ameliorate plaintiff's allegations outside the narrow scope of an exception which the Court of Appeals has consistently refused to broaden. These cases indicate, that the exception as interpreted does not apply. Accordingly, plaintiffs' first cause of action is time barred.

The failure to obtain a patient's informed consent sounds in medical malpractice and is subject to the same two and one half year statute of limitations. Accordingly, plaintiffs' second cause of action for lack of informed consent is also time barred.

… Here, plaintiffs specifically disavow any claim sounding in warranty and strict products liability and assert that the fourth cause of action is premised "on a theory of simple negligence."

"An action to recover for personal injuries or wrongful death against a medical practitioner or a medical facility or hospital may be based *either* on negligence principles or on the more particularized medical malpractice standard." When the duty owing to the plaintiff by the defendant arises from the physician-patient relationship or is substantially related to medical treatment, the breach thereof gives rise to an action sounding in medical malpractice as opposed to simple negligence. Where the issue relating to due care may be easily discernible by a jury on common knowledge, simple negligence rules apply.

Plaintiff's fourth cause of action somewhat inartfully asserts that Dr Orentreich negligently manufactured or processed the silicone into what was supposed to be "medical grade" silicone, and that Dr Orentreich negligently administered it to Bella Stander. To the extent that this claim is based on Dr Orentreich's "administration" of the silicone injections into Stander, plaintiffs are asserting a claim for medical malpractice and accordingly that claim is time barred for the reasons discussed above.

To the extent that plaintiffs are claiming that Dr Orentreich used his skills as a chemist to transform nonmedical grade liquid silicone, which was unacceptable for injection into humans, and attempted chemically to reprocess it into a medical grade silicone, but failed to do so due to his negligence, plaintiffs have alleged an action outside the scope of medical malpractice. Plaintiffs' allegation does not directly bear upon the doctor-patient relationship, or the doctor's instructions to or treatment of plaintiff. Rather than implicating as faulty Dr Orentreich's skills as a medical practitioner, plaintiffs are implicating Dr Orentreich's conduct as a chemist and manufacturer. The expert testimony that might be needed would bear on defendant's conduct in these capacities rather than as a medical doctor treating a patient. Such an allegation is cognizable as an action sounding in simple negligence.

Plaintiffs' claim, that since the fourth cause of action sounds in negligence the statute of limitations set forth in CPLR § 214-c applies, is without merit. CPLR § 214-c does not apply to acts or omissions which occurred before July 1, 1986, and which caused an injury that was discovered or should have been discovered before July 1, 1986 and "an action for which was or would have been barred because the applicable period of limitations had expired prior to such date." … Thus CPLR § 214-c is unavailing.

Plaintiffs also claim that the fourth cause of action is timely under the revival statute. Laws of 1993, chap. 419. "An Act to authorize extension of the statute of limitations for commencing a cause of action for personal injury or death caused by silicone." … This section shall not be applicable to any action for medical malpractice.

This unconsolidated statute was enacted primarily to revive previously time barred causes of action of women injured by silicone breast implants. However, the purpose is broader than to protect only such women. … It was designed "[t]o allow the hundreds of injured people, almost all women, who suffered physical injuries more than four years ago as a result of the implantation of silicone in their bodies, to file lawsuits for those injuries even though their cases are time barred under present law."

***

To the extent that plaintiffs allege a claim of negligent manufacture or processing of silicone, it is distinguishable from other recent similar actions against defendant which resulted in the dismissal of claims for strict products liability, breach of warranty, and negligent administration (i.e., medical malpractice). Accordingly, plaintiffs' fourth cause of action for negligent manufacture or processing of silicone liquid which was ultimately injected into Bella Stander is timely, pursuant to L. 1993, ch. 419.

Loss of consortium is a derivative action dependent upon inter alia a viable cause of action for negligence. Accordingly, because plaintiffs have timely commenced a viable claim for simple negligence in their fourth cause of action, Stander's spouse's derivative cause of action for loss of consortium stated in the third cause of action is also viable.

SUMMERS v. TICE

Supreme Court of California
33 Cal.2d 80, 199 P.2d 1
December 16, 1948
Carter, Justice

[See Chapter 2.]

Each of the two defendants appeals from a judgment against them in an action for personal injuries. Pursuant to stipulation the appeals have been consolidated.

Plaintiff's action was against both defendants for an injury to his right eye and face as the result of being struck by bird shot discharged from a shotgun. The case was tried by the court without a jury and the court found that on November 20, 1945, plaintiff and the two defendants were hunting quail on the open range. Each of the defendants was armed with a 12 gauge shotgun loaded with shells containing 7 1/2 size shot. Prior to going hunting plaintiff discussed the hunting procedure with defendants, indicating that they were to exercise care when shooting and to "keep in line." In the course of hunting plaintiff proceeded up a hill, thus placing the hunters at the points of a triangle. The view of defendants with reference to plaintiff was unobstructed and they knew his location. Defendant Tice flushed a quail which rose in flight to a 10-foot elevation and flew between plaintiff and defendants. Both defendants shot at the quail, shooting in plaintiff's direction. At that time defendants were 75 yards from plaintiff. One shot struck plaintiff in his eye and another in his upper lip. Finally it was found by the court that as the direct result of the shooting by defendants the shots struck plaintiff as above mentioned and that defendants were negligent in so shooting and plaintiff was not contributorily negligent.

First, on the subject of negligence, defendant Simonson contends that the evidence is insufficient to sustain the finding on that score, but he does not point out wherein it is lacking. There is evidence that both defendants, at about the same time or one immediately after the other, shot at a quail and in so doing shot toward plaintiff who was uphill from them, and that they knew his location. That is sufficient from which the trial court could conclude that they acted with respect to plaintiff other than as persons of ordinary prudence. The issue was one of fact for the trial court. See *Rudd v. Byrnes*, 156 Cal. 636, 105 P. 957, 26 L.R.A.N.S. 134, 20 Ann.Cas. 124.

Defendant Tice states in his opening brief, "we have decided not to argue the insufficiency of negligence on the part of defendant Tice." It is true he states in his answer to plaintiff's petition for a hearing in this court that he did not concede this point but he does not argue it. Nothing more need be said on the subject.

Defendant Simonson urges that plaintiff was guilty of contributory negligence and assumed the risk as a matter of law. He cites no authority for the proposition that by going on a hunting party the various hunters assume the risk of negligence on the part of their companions. Such a tenet is not reasonable. It is true that plaintiff suggested that they all "stay in line," presumably abreast, while hunting, and he went uphill at somewhat of a right angle to the hunting line, but he also cautioned that they use care, and defendants knew plaintiff's position. We hold, therefore, that the trial court was justified in finding that he did not assume the risk or act other than as a person of ordinary prudence under the circumstances. See *Anthony v. Hobbie*, 25 Cal.2d 814, 818, 155 P.2d 826; *Rudd v. Byrnes, supra*. None of the cases cited by Simonson are in point.

The problem presented in this case is whether the judgment against both defendants may stand. It is argued by defendants that they are not joint tortfeasors, and thus jointly and severally liable, as they were not acting in concert, and that there is not sufficient evidence to show which defendant was guilty of the negligence which caused the injuries—the shooting by Tice or that by Simonson. Tice argues that there is evidence to show that the shot which struck plaintiff came from Simonson's gun because of admissions allegedly made by him to third persons and no evidence that they came from his gun. Further in connection with the latter contention, the court failed to find on plaintiff's allegation in his complaint that he did not know which one was at fault—did not find which defendant was guilty of the negligence which caused the injuries to plaintiff.

Considering the last argument first, we believe it is clear that the court sufficiently found on the issue that defendants were jointly liable and that thus the negligence of both was the cause of the injury or to that legal effect. It found that both defendants were negligent and "That as a direct and proximate result of the shots fired by defendants, and each of them, a birdshot pellet was caused to and did lodge in plaintiff's right eye and that another birdshot pellet was caused to and did lodge in plaintiff's upper lip." In so doing the court evidently did not give

credence to the admissions of Simonson to third persons that he fired the shots, which it was justified in doing. It thus determined that the negligence of both defendants was the legal cause of the injury—or that both were responsible. Implicit in such finding is the assumption that the court was unable to ascertain whether the shots were from the gun of one defendant or the other or one shot from each of them. The one shot that entered plaintiff's eye was the major factor in assessing damages and that shot could not have come from the gun of both defendants. It was from one or the other only.

It has been held that where a group of persons are on a hunting party, or otherwise engaged in the use of firearms, and two of them are negligent in firing in the direction of a third person who is injured thereby, both of those so firing are liable for the injury suffered by the third person, although the negligence of only one of them could have caused the injury. *Moore v. Foster*, 182 Miss., 180 So. 73; *Oliver v. Miles*, 110 So. 666; 50 A.L.R. 357; *Reyher v. Mayne*, 90 Colo. 856, 10 P.2d 1109; *Benson v. Ross*, 143 Mich. 452, 106 N.W. 1120, 114 Am.St.Rep. 675. The same rule has been applied in criminal cases (*State v. Newberg*, 129 Ore. 564, 278 P. 568, 63 A.L.R. 1225), and both drivers have been held liable for the negligence of one where hey engaged in a racing contest causing an injury to a third person. *Saisa v. Lilja*, 76 F.2d 380. These cases speak of the action of defendants as being in concert as the ground of decision, yet it would seem they are straining that concept and the more reasonable basis appears in *Oliver v. Miles, supra*. There two persons were hunting together. Both shot at some partridges and in so doing shot across the highway injuring plaintiff who was travelling on it. The court stated they were acting in concert and thus both were liable. The court then stated: "We think that ... each is liable for the resulting injury to the boy, although no one can say definitely who actually shot him. To hold otherwise would be to exonerate both from liability, although each was negligent, and the injury resulted from such negligence." 110 So. p. 668. It is said in the Restatement: "For harm resulting to a third person from the tortious conduct of another, a person is liable if he ... (b) knows that the other's conduct constitutes a breach of duty and gives substantial assistance or encouragement to the other so to conduct himself, or (c) gives substantial assistance to the other in accomplishing a tortious result and his own conduct, separately considered, constitutes a breach of duty to the third person." (Restatement of Torts § 876(b) (c).) Under subsection (b) the example is given: "A and B are members of a hunting party. Each of them in the presence of the other shoots across a public road at an animal, this being negligent as to persons on the road. A hits the animal. B's bullet strikes C, a traveler on the road. A is liable to C." (Restatement of Torts § 876 (b), com., illus. 3.) An illustration given under subsection (c) is the same as above except the factor of both defendants shooting is missing and joint liability is not imposed. It is further said that: "If two forces are actively operating, one because of the actor's negligence, the other not because of any misconduct on his part, and each of itself is sufficient to bring about harm to another, the actor's negligence may be held by the jury to be a substantial factor in bringing it about." (Restatement of Torts § 432.) Dean Wigmore has this to say: "When two or more persons by their acts are possibly the sole cause of a harm, or when two or more acts of the same person are possibly the sole cause, and the plaintiff has introduced evidence that the one of the two persons, or the one of the same person's two acts, is culpable, then the defendant has the burden of proving that the other person, or his other act, was the sole cause of the harm. (b) ... The real reason for the rule that each joint tortfeasor is responsible for the whole damage is the practical unfairness of denying the injured person redress simply because he cannot prove how much damage each did, when it is certain that between them they did all; let them be the ones to apportion it among themselves. Since, then, the difficulty of proof is the reason, the rule should apply whenever the harm has plural causes, and not merely when they acted in conscious concert. ..." (Wigmore, *Select Cases on the Law of Torts*, § 153.) Similarly Professor Carpenter has said:

"[Suppose] the case where A and B independently shoot at C and but one bullet touches C's body. In such case, such proof as is ordinarily required that either A or B shot C, of course fails. It is suggested that there should be a relaxation of the proof required of the plaintiff ... where the injury occurs as the result of one where more than one independent force is operating, and it is impossible to determine that the force set in operation by defendant did not in fact constitute a cause of the damage, and where it may have caused the damage, but the plaintiff is unable to establish that it was a cause." (20 Cal.L.Rev. 406.)

When we consider the relative position of the parties and the results that would flow if plaintiff was required to pin the injury on one of the defendants only, a requirement that the burden of proof on that subject be shifted to defendants becomes manifest. They are both wrongdoers—both negligent toward plaintiff. They brought about a situation where the negligence of one of them injured the plaintiff, hence it should rest with them each to absolve himself if he can. The injured party has been placed by defendants in the unfair position of pointing to which defendant caused the harm. If one can escape the other may also and plaintiff is remediless. Ordinarily defendants are in a far better position to offer evidence to determine which one caused the injury. This reasoning has recently found favor in this court. In a quite analogous situation this court held that a patient injured while unconscious on an operating table in a hospital could hold all or any of the persons who had any connection with the operation even though he could not select the particular acts by the particular person which led to his disability. *Ybarra v. Spangard*, 25 Cal.2d 486, 154 P.2d 687, 162 A.L.R. 1258. There the court was considering whether the patient could avail himself of res ipsa loquitur, rather than where the burden of proof lay, yet the effect of the decision is that plaintiff has made out a case when he has produced evidence which gives rise to an inference of negligence which was the proximate cause of the injury. It is up to defendants to explain the cause of the injury. It was there said: "If the doctrine is to continue to serve a useful purpose, we should not forget that 'the particular force and justice of the rule, regarded as a presumption throwing upon the party charged the duty of producing evidence, consists in the circumstance that the chief evidence of the true cause, whether culpable or innocent, is practically accessible to him but inaccessible to the injured person.'" Similarly in the instant case plaintiff is not able to establish which of defendants caused his injury.

The foregoing discussion disposes of the authorities cited by defendants such as *Kraft v. Smith*, 24 Cal.2d 124, 148 P.2d 23, and *Hernandez v. Southern California Gas Co.*, 213 Cal. 384, 2 P.2d 360, stating the general rule that one defendant is not liable for the independent tort of the other defendant, or that ordinarily the plaintiff must show a causal connection between the negligence and the injury. There was an entire lack of such connection in the *Hernandez* case and there were not several negligent defendants, one of whom must have caused the injury.

Defendants rely upon *Christensen v. Los Angeles Electrical Supply Co.*, 112 Cal.App. 629, 297 P. 614, holding that a defendant is not liable where he negligently knocks down with his car a pedestrian and a third person then ran over the prostrate person. That involves the question of intervening cause which we do not have here. Moreover it is out of harmony with the current rule on that subject and was properly questioned in *Hill v. Peres*, 136 Cal.App. 132, 28 P.2d 946 (hearing in this court denied), and must be deemed disapproved. See *Mosley v. Arden Farms Co.*, 26 Cal. 2d 213, 157 P.2d 372, 158 A.L.R. 872; *Sawyer v. Southern California Gas Co.*, 206 Cal. 366, 274 P. 544; 2 Cal.Jur. Ten Yr.Supp. Automobiles, § 349; 19 Cal.Jur. 570–572.

Cases are cited for the proposition that where two or more tortfeasors acting independently of each other cause an injury to plaintiff, they are not joint tortfeasors and plaintiff must establish the portion of the damage caused by each, even though it is impossible to prove the portion of the injury caused by each. See *Slater v. Pacific American Oil Co.*, 212 Cal. 648, 300 P. 31; *Miller v.*

Highland Ditch Co., 87 Cal. 430, 25 P. 550, 22 Am.St.Rep. 254; *People v. Gold Run D&M Co.*, 66 Cal. 138, 4 P. 1152, 56 Am.Rep. 80; *Wade v. Thorsen*, 5 Cal.App.2d 706, 43 P.2d 592; *California Orange Co. v. Riverside P. C. Co.*, 50 Cal.App. 522, 195 P. 694; *City of Oakland v. Pacific Gas & E. Co.*, 47 Cal.App.2d 444, 118 P.2d 328. In view of the foregoing discussion it is apparent that defendants in cases like the present one may be treated as liable on the same basis as joint tortfeasors, and hence the last-cited cases are distinguishable inasmuch as they involve independent tortfeasors.

In addition to that, however, it should be pointed out that the same reasons of policy and justice shift the burden to each of defendants to absolve himself if he can—relieving the wronged person of the duty of apportioning the injury to a particular defendant, apply here where we are concerned with whether plaintiff is required to supply evidence for the apportionment of damages. If defendants are independent tortfeasors and thus each liable for the damage caused by him alone, and, at least, where the matter of apportionment is incapable of proof, the innocent wronged party should not be deprived of his right to redress. The wrongdoers should be left to work out between themselves any apportionment. See *Colonial Ins. Co. v. Industrial Acc. Com.*, 29 Cal.2d 79, 172 P.2d 884. Some of the cited cases refer to the difficulty of apportioning the burden of damages between the independent tortfeasors, and say that where factually a correct division cannot be made, the trier of fact may make it the best it can, which would be more or less a guess, stressing the factor that the wrongdoers are not in a position to complain of uncertainty. *California Orange Co. v. Riverside P. C. Co., supra.*

It is urged that plaintiff now has changed the theory of his case in claiming a concert of action; that he did not plead or prove such concert. From what has been said it is clear that there has been no change in theory. The joint liability, as well as the lack of knowledge as to which defendant was liable, was pleaded and the proof developed the case under either theory. We have seen that for the reasons of policy discussed herein, the case is based upon the legal proposition that, under the circumstances here presented, each defendant is liable for the whole damage whether they are deemed to be acting in concert or independently.

The judgment is affirmed.

CINEL v. CONNICK
United States Court of Appeals, Fifth Circuit
15 F.3d 1338 (5th Cir. 1994)
March 11, 1994
Duhé, Circuit Judge

[See Chapter 5.]

Appellant, Dino Cinel, appeals from the district court's grant of Appellees' motions to dismiss under Federal Rule of Civil Procedure 12(b)(6). We modify and affirm.

Appellant sued numerous state actors and private persons, contending that they conspired together over a period of years to deprive him of his civil rights by making public certain allegedly confidential information gathered during a criminal investigation of him. He also asserts state law claims for negligence, state constitutional violations, and invasion of his privacy.

BACKGROUND

In 1988 Dino Cinel was a Roman Catholic priest at St. Rita's Catholic Church in New Orleans, Louisiana. While Cinel was away, another priest at the rectory where Cinel lived, accidentally discovered a variety of sexually oriented materials in Cinel's room including a homemade video tape of Cinel engaged in homosexual activity, primarily with two young men, Christopher Fontaine and Ronald Tichenor. Church officials turned the materials over to the Orleans Parish District Attorney's Office. Cinel alleges that in exchange for transactional immunity and under a confidentiality agreement, he provided the names and addresses of the other men depicted in the film to the DA's office. Upon verifying that they were consenting adults at the time of their sexual involvement with Cinel, the DA's office decided not to prosecute Cinel.

Cinel further alleges that George Tolar, while an investigator for the DA's office, during the investigation gave the names and addresses of Fontaine and Tichenor, and certain unidentified documents in the DA's file, to Gary Raymond. Raymond was a private investigator working for two lawyers, David Paddison and Darryl Tschirn. Cinel contends that Raymond used the information given him by Tolar to solicit the two men as clients for attorneys. One of the men, Fontaine, represented by Paddison and Tschirn, then sued Cinel and the Church in state court in 1989. The other, Tichenor, represented by the same counsel, sued Cinel in 1991.

In 1990, in connection with the Fontaine state civil suit, the state court, at the request of the Church, issued a subpoena duces tecum directing the DA's office to release the materials found in Cinel's room to the litigants in the Fontaine suit. Pursuant to a consent judgment drafted in response to the subpoena, by an assistant district attorney, Raymond Bigelow, the DA's office released the materials to Paddison and Tschirn as custodians, and Raymond was authorized to make copies of the materials "upon the request of any party to this [the Fontaine] litigation." Cinel alleges in his complaint that the allegedly confidential materials were released "under the pretext of a subpoena and consent judgment." However no facts support that conclusion.

Cinel also alleges that a year later Raymond gave copies of the materials to Richard Angelico, a local television investigative reporter, and that Angelico and his employer, WDSU Television, Inc., broadcast excerpts of the materials. Cinel also contends that in February 1992, Raymond sold some of the materials to Geraldo Rivera and his employer, Tribune Entertainment Company, which broadcast excerpts of the material on the national syndicated television program "Now It Can Be Told." Cinel brought § 1983 claims, together with pendent state law claims, against Harry Connick, the district attorney, Raymond Bigelow, and George Tolar in their individual and official capacities. He also sued Gary Raymond, David Paddison, Darryl Tschirn, Richard Angelico, WDSU Television Inc., Geraldo Rivera, and Tribune Entertainment. After the filing of several motions, the district court granted Appellees' motions to dismiss under Federal Rules of civil Procedure 12(b)(6). Cinel appeals.

***

Appellant asserts claims against all Appellees under 42 U.S.C. § 1983 for a violation of his rights to privacy and due process. To state a cause of action under § 1983, Appellant must allege that some person, acting under state or territorial law, has deprived him of a federal right.

***

... Appellant's allegations involving Tolar's release to Raymond of the names and addresses of the men depicted in the video do not implicate any constitutional privacy interests. The release of this information alone does not involve intimate details of Appellant's life. Thus, these facts alleged by Appellant are insufficient to state a claim for a deprivation of his constitutional right of privacy.

Appellant also fails to state a claim for relief against Tolar, Bigelow, and Connick in their individual and official capacities for the release of the sexually oriented materials found in Cinel's room to the private litigants, the Church and Fontaine, pursuant to a subpoena. Because the Church had viewed the materials before giving them to the DA's office, and Fontaine had participated in making the video, the information disclosed was not private as to these parties. In other words, Appellant cannot claim that his privacy has been invaded when allegedly private materials have been disclosed to those who already know the details of that material. Nonetheless, assuming that Appellant had a privacy interest in some of the materials requested by the subpoena, the government officials had a legitimate interest in complying with a validly issued subpoena. Moreover, the government officials drafted the consent judgment to ensure that Appellant's rights were protected by allowing the material to be copied only for the civil litigants.

Appellant fails to state a claim that the state actors denied him his procedural due process rights by not notifying him of the subpoena duces tecum. Appellant has submitted no legal authority to this Court, and we have found none in our independent research, that creates an affirmative duty of a non-party or a governmental official in possession of documents to notify the owner of the subpoenaed documents. ...

Finally, Appellant does not have any claim under the Due Process Clause for damage to his reputation against any Appellees as a result of the publication of the materials. The Supreme Court held in *Paul v. Davis,* 424 U.S. 693, 712, 96 S.Ct. 1155, 1165, 47 L.Ed.2d 405 (1976), that an interest in reputation alone does not implicate a "liberty" or "property" interest sufficient to invoke due process protection.

The remainder of Appellant's § 1983 claims involve an alleged conspiracy between the state and private actors to publish allegedly privileged information from the DA's file and the sexually oriented materials released under the pretext of a civil subpoena. A private party may be held liable under § 1983 if he or she is a "willful participant in joint activity with the State or its agents." ...

Appellant has failed to allege facts that suggest that Tolar's release of information from the DA's file to Raymond rises to the level of a conspiracy to deprive Appellant of his constitutional rights. Appellant contends that Tolar released the information "for the purpose of aiding and abetting [Raymond, Paddison, and Tschirn] and prejudicing Cinel in the civil litigation." Appellant avers that Raymond, Paddison, and Tschirn used the information "to solicit and procure Fontaine and Tichenor as clients in violation of Rule 7.3 of the Louisiana Rules of Professional Conduct." Perhaps, as Appellant alleges, this was improper client solicitation; however, nothing in his complaint implies or states that these Appellees agreed to undertake a scheme to deprive Appellant of his constitutional rights. A lapse of ethics by the Appellees is insufficient by itself to rise to the level of a conspiracy to deprive Appellant of his federal constitutional or statutory rights. Moreover, the subsequent allegation that Angelico and WDSU published the documents cannot be linked back to a state actor. Nothing in Appellant's complaint intimates that Tolar's intention in releasing the information to Raymond was to make it available for future publication.

Likewise, Appellant has failed to aver facts that suggest an agreement between the state actors and the private actors to publish the materials released pursuant to the subpoena. ... Without an agreement between private and state actors, any possible joint action involving only private parties is not actionable under § 1983.

***

Appellant's only discussion of his negligence claims against Paddison and Tschirn is in his reply brief. An appellant abandons all issues not raised and argued in its *initial* brief on appeal.

***

Appellant alleges that Raymond, Paddison, Tschirn, Angelico, WDSU, Rivera and Tribune invaded his right of privacy under Louisiana Civil Code article 2315. Under Louisiana law, one can be held liable for invasion of privacy for making an "unreasonable disclosure of embarrassing private facts." To recover for this tort, a plaintiff must prove that 1) the defendant publicized information concerning the plaintiff's private life, 2) the publicized matter would be highly offensive to the reasonable person, and 3) the information is not of legitimate public concern. Whether a matter is of public concern is a question of law for the court.

The district court held that the materials were a matter of legitimate public concern. It explained that the material related to Appellant's guilt or innocence of criminal conduct. Also, the material implicated the public's concern with the performance of its elected DA, especially because the DA's decision cannot be reviewed by a court. See State v. Perez, 464 So.2d 737, 744 (La. 1985) (explaining that the district attorney is given absolute discretion in the

institution of criminal charges). Finally, the materials concerned Appellant's activities while an ordained Catholic priest and the Church's response to those activities.

At oral argument, Appellant conceded the newsworthiness of the details surrounding his story. Appellant contends, however, that the broadcast portions of the homemade videotape and allegedly confidential deposition added nothing to this topic and were what constituted the invasion of his privacy. We disagree. The materials broadcast by the Appellees were substantially related to Appellant's story. Perhaps the use of the materials reflected the media's insensitivity, and no doubt Appellant was embarrassed, but we are not prepared to make editorial decisions for the media regarding information directly related to matters of public concern. See e.g., Ross v. Midwest Communications, Inc., 870 F.2d 271, 275 (5th Cir.) ("judges, acting with the benefit of hindsight, must resist the temptation to edit journalists aggressively"), cert. denied, 493 U.S. 935, 110 S.Ct. 326, 107 L.Ed.2d 316 (1989); Neff v. Time, Inc., 406 F.Supp. 858, 860 (W.D.Pa. 1976) (noting that "the courts are not concerned with establishing canons of good taste for the press or the public") (internal quotations omitted); Cape Publications, Inc. v. Bridges, 423 So.2d 426, 427–28 (Fla.Dist.Ct.App. 1982) (concluding that when plaintiff's nude picture was relevant to a story of public interest, there is no invasion of privacy, even though picture may be embarrassing or distressful to the plaintiff), cert. denied, 464 U.S. 893, 104 S.Ct. 239, 78 L.Ed.2d 229 (1983).

Appellant argues that the district court erred in dismissing his complaint without leave to amend. ... Appellant did not ask the district court for leave to amend; his brief to this Court is his first such request. ...

We hereby modify the district court's judgment insofar as it dismisses with prejudice Appellant's claims for due process on the issue of transactional immunity and for fair trial under the state and federal constitutions to dismiss those claims for lack of subject matter jurisdiction. The district court's judgment is affirmed as modified.

MODIFIED IN PART and AFFIRMED.

PEPSICO, INC. v. REDMOND

United States Court of Appeals, Seventh Circuit
54 F.3d 1262 (7th Cir. 1995)
May 11, 1995
Flaum, Circuit Judge

[See Chapter 5.]

Plaintiff PepsiCo, Inc., sought a preliminary injunction against defendants William Redmond and the Quaker Oats Company to prevent Redmond, a former PepsiCo employee, from divulging PepsiCo trade secrets and confidential information in his new job with Quaker and from assuming any duties with Quaker relating to beverage pricing, marketing, and distribution. The district court agreed with PepsiCo and granted the injunction. We now affirm that decision.

The facts of this case lay against a backdrop of fierce beverage-industry competition between Quaker and PepsiCo, especially in "sports drinks" and "new age drinks." Quaker's sports drink, "Gatorade," is the dominant brand in its market niche. PepsiCo introduced its Gatorade rival, "All Sport," in March and April of 1994, but sales of All Sport lag far behind those of Gatorade. Quaker also has the lead in the new-age-drink category. Although PepsiCo has entered the market through joint ventures with the Thomas J. Lipton Company and Ocean Spray Cranberries, Inc., Quaker purchased Snapple Beverage Corp., a large new-age-drink maker, in late 1994. PepsiCo's products have about half of Snapple's market share. ... Meanwhile, PepsiCo and Quaker each face strong competition from Coca Cola Co., which has its own sports drink, "PowerAde," and which introduced its own Snapple-rival, "Fruitopia," in 1994, as well as from independent beverage producers.

William Redmond, Jr., worked for PepsiCo in its Pepsi-Cola North America division ("PCNA") from 1984 to 1994. ...

Redmond's relatively high-level position at PCNA gave him access to inside information and trade secrets. Redmond, like other PepsiCo management employees, had signed a confidentiality agreement with PepsiCo. That agreement stated in relevant part that he

w[ould] not disclose at any time, to anyone other than officers or employees of [PepsiCo], or make use of, confidential information relating to the business of [PepsiCo] ... obtained while in the employ of [PepsiCo], which shall not be generally known or available to the public or recognized as standard practices.

Donald Uzzi, who had left PepsiCo in the beginning of 1994 to become the head of Quaker's Gatorade division, began courting Redmond for Quaker in May, 1994. ...

On November 8, 1994, Uzzi extended Redmond a written offer for the position of Vice President–Field Operations for Gatorade and Redmond accepted.

* * *

On November 10, 1994, Redmond met with Barnes and told her that he had decided to accept the Quaker offer and was resigning from PCNA. Barnes immediately took Redmond to Bensyl, who told Redmond that PepsiCo was considering legal action against him.

* * *

From November 23, 1994, to December 1, 1994, the district court conducted a preliminary injunction hearing on the same matter. At the hearing, PepsiCo offered evidence of a number of trade secrets and confidential information it desired protected and to which Redmond was privy. First, it identified PCNA's "Strategic Plan," an annually revised document that contains PCNA's plans to compete, its financial goals, and its strategies for manufacturing, production, marketing, packaging, and distribution for the coming three years. ...

Second, PepsiCo pointed to PCNA's Annual Operating Plan ("AOP") as a trade secret. The AOP is a national plan for a given year and guides PCNA's financial goals, marketing plans, promotional event calendars, growth expectations, and operational changes in that year.

***

PepsiCo also showed that Redmond had intimate knowledge of PCNA "attack plans" for specific markets. ...

Finally, PepsiCo offered evidence of PCNA trade secrets regarding innovations in its selling and delivery systems. Under this plan, PCNA is testing a new delivery system that could give PCNA an advantage over its competitors in negotiations with retailers over shelf space and merchandising.

***

On December 15, 1994, the district court issued an order enjoining Redmond from assuming his position at Quaker through May, 1995, and permanently from using or disclosing any PCNA trade secrets or confidential information. ...

Both parties agree that the primary issue on appeal is whether the district court correctly concluded that PepsiCo had a reasonable likelihood of success on its various claims for trade secret misappropriation and breach of a confidentiality agreement. ...

The Illinois Trade Secrets Act ("ITSA"), which governs the trade secret issues in this case, provides that a court may enjoin the "actual or threatened misappropriation" of a trade secret. ...

The question of threatened or inevitable misappropriation in this case lies at the heart of a basic tension in trade secret law. Trade secret law serves to protect "standards of commercial morality" and "encourage [] invention and innovation" while maintaining "the public interest in having free and open competition in the manufacture and sale of unpatented goods."

***

PepsiCo presented substantial evidence at the preliminary injunction hearing that Redmond possessed extensive and intimate knowledge about PCNA's strategic goals for 1995 in sports drinks and new age drinks.

***

Thus, when we couple the demonstrated inevitability that Redmond would rely on PCNA trade secrets in his new job at Quaker with the district court's reluctance to believe that Redmond would refrain from disclosing these secrets in his new position (or that Quaker would ensure Redmond did not disclose them), we conclude that the district court correctly decided that PepsiCo demonstrated a likelihood of success on its statutory claim of trade secret misappropriation.

***

[W]e concluded that the district court did not abuse its discretion in granting the preliminary injunction on the issue of trade secret misappropriation,

***

Finally, Redmond and Quaker have contended in the alternative that the injunction issued against them is overbroad.

***

However, the injunction against Redmond's immediate employment at Quaker extends no further than necessary and was well within the district court's discretion.

For the foregoing reasons, we affirm the district court's order enjoining Redmond from assuming his responsibilities at Quaker through May, 1995, and preventing him forever from disclosing PCNA trade secrets and confidential information.

Affirmed.

ROACH v. STERN

Supreme Court, Appellate Division, Second Department, New York
252 A.D.2d 488, 675 N.Y.S.2d 133
Memorandum by the Court

[See Chapter 5.]

In an action, *inter alia*, to recover damages for the intentional infliction of emotional distress, the plaintiffs' appeal from an order of the Supreme Court, Kings County (Huttner, J.), dated January 13, 1997, which granted the motion by the defendants Howard Stern and Infinity Broadcasting, Inc., pursuant to CPLR 3211(a)(7) and 3211(a)(1) to dismiss the complaint.

ORDERED that the order is reversed, with costs, the motion is denied, and the complaint is reinstated.

This lawsuit concerns events that occurred during a radio show hosted by the defendant Howard Stern, which was videotaped and later aired on a cable television station. The participants in the program handled and made crude remarks about the cremated remains of the plaintiffs' sister, Deborah Roach. We conclude that the plaintiffs have sufficiently pleaded a cause of action to recover damages for the intentional infliction of emotional distress and therefore the Supreme Court erred in dismissing their complaint.

The deceased, Deborah Roach, who used the name Debbie Tay, was described in a newspaper article following her death as a topless dance, cable-access TV host, and perennial guest on Howard Stern's radio show. Stern gave her the label "Space Lesbian" based on her stories of encounters with aliens. After Tay's death in April 1995 her sister, the plaintiff Melissa Roach Driscol, had the body cremated and gave a portion of the remains to the defendant Chaunce Hayden, Tay's close friend. Driscol asserted that she did so with the understanding that Hayden would "preserve and honor said remains in an appropriate and private manner".

According to the complaint, sometime in July 1995 Hayden engaged in certain "on air" conversations with Stern during his radio show about Tay's death and the disposition of her remains. Upon learning that Stern had encouraged Hayden to appear on the radio show and to bring Tay's remains with him, her brother, the plaintiff Jeff Roach, telephoned the producer of the show and the manager of the radio station to demand that such conversations cease. Nevertheless, on July 18, 1995, Hayden brought a box containing Tay's cremated remains to the radio station. Thereafter Stern, Hayden, and other participants in the broadcast made comments about the remains while handling various bone fragments. The radio show was videotaped and later broadcast on a national cable television station.

The transcript and videotape of the show, which were made available to the court, corroborate the allegations in the complaint that Stern at one point donned rubber gloves and held up certain bone fragments while he guessed whether they came from Tay's skull or ribs. The on-air discussion included the following:

Voice: What's in the bottom?
C. Hayden: They look like clam shells.
Robin Quivers: Boy, that's wild.
Voice: Dig down. That's not normal, is it?
H. Stern: Chew on it, Chaunce.
R. Quivers: There you go.
Voice: What's it taste like?
Voice: It tastes like Cracker Jacks, maybe there's a prize in the bottom.
R. Quivers: Boy of boy, yeah, you're not kidding Chaunce.
H. Stern: Look at the hunks.
R. Quivers: Wooooooh!
H. Stern: Come here, I'll glue her together, give me that, Robin. Let me see that.
R. Quivers: I'm shaking her bones.
C. Hayden: Shake, rattle and roll.
Voice: Want me to get some Krazy Glue?
H. Stern: Let me see this.
(H. STERN PICKS UP A PIECE)
Voice: It's easy … the leg bone's connected to the …
H. Stern: Look at the size of this! That looks like a piece of her head.
R. Quivers: I don't know, I've never seen an actual skull bone, that looks awfully thick.
Voice: Looks like a potato or something …
C. Hayden: It's not normal.

* * *

H. Stern: Heh! Heh! Heh! Heh! Chaunce, watch your language, huh dude!? Rob, here you want to hold Debbie? C'mon man, you like her.
Voice: Oh man!
R. Quivers: What's wrong with you, Ralph?
Voice: Ralph made this so Chaunce could wear it around his neck.
H. Stern: A big bag.
R. Quivers: Bag.
H. Stern; Hey Chaunce, why don't you wear that plastic bag around your neck? You can carry Debbie with you. It would be a big necklace, look at that. There she is, what do you think

that is though? Let me see if I can piece it together.

Voice: Its gotta be a piece of skull, doesn't it Robin?

R. Quivers: I've never seen how thick the skull is.

H. Stern: Alright, hold it, hold … Ralph hold up this picture of Debbie so I can …

R. Quivers: It's awfully thick.

H. Stern: Alright, let's see, this matches …

C. Hayden: well, she was very thickboned.

Voice: That's gotta be her teeth.

Voice: That's her head, that's a piece of her teeth.

Voice: Here's a temple.

R. Quivers: But it's not rounded, why would you say that …

H. Stern: She had a square jaw. This looks like the breast, oh wait, here's her tooth.

R. Quivers: Why don't you think there are any teeth?

H. Stern: What do you think this is, this looks like her ribs. What do you think this is, Chaunce?

Voice: I say it's a rib. It's a rib. Yeah, it's a rib.

R. Quivers: Yeah, look at that curve.

H. Stern: That's a rib? Oh yeah, wow, she was a piece of ash. Alright, very good. Alright, there you go, very good.

R. Quivers: Man.

Voice: Are there any bigger pieces on the bottom?

The plaintiffs commenced this action against Stern, Infinity Broadcasting, Inc. (hereinafter Infinity), the owner of the radio station, and Hayden, in which they alleged, *inter alia*, that the defendants' conduct caused them severe emotional distress. Stern and Infinity moved to dismiss the complaint pursuant to CPLR 3211(a)(7) and CPLR 3211(a)(1) on the ground that the allegations failed to state a cause of action. The Supreme Court granted the motion and dismissed the complaint.

We agree with the Supreme Court that the allegations in the complaint fail to state a cause of action against the moving defendants to recover damages for interference with or mishandling of a corpse. In general, such a cause of action requires a showing of interference with the right of the next-of-kin to dispose of the body (see., e.g., *Darcy v. Presbyterian Hospital*, 202 N.Y. 259, 95 N.E. 695; *Foley v. Phelps*, 1 App.Div. 551, 37 N.Y.S. 471; *Finley v. Atlantic Transport Co.*, 90 Misc. 480, 153 N.Y.S. 439, *affd.* 172 App.Div. 907, 157 N.Y.S. 1124, *affd.* 220 N.Y. 249, 115 N.E. 715; *Correa v. Maimonides Medical Center*, 165 Misc.2d 614, 629 N.Y.S.2d 673; see

also, *Johnson v. State of New York*, 37 N.Y.2d 378, 382, 372 N.Y.S.2d 638, 334 N.E.2d 590). The moving defendants did not interfere with the plaintiffs' decision to cremate the body and divide the ashes with Hayden.

The Supreme Court further determined that, while the conduct complained of in the complaint was "vulgar and disrespectful", it did not rise to the level of outrageousness necessary to maintain a cause of action to recover damages for the intentional infliction of emotional distress. In order to impose liability for this intentional tort, the conduct complained of must be "'so outrageous in character, and so extreme in degree, as to go beyond all possible bounds of decency, and to be regarded as atrocious, and utterly intolerable in a civilized community'" (*Murphy v. American Home Prods. Corp.*, 58 N.Y.2d 293, 303, 461 N.Y.S.2d 232, 448 N.E.2d 86, quoting Restatement [Second] of Torts § 46[1], comment d; see also, *Howell v. New York Post Co.*, 81 N.Y.2d 115, 122, 596 N.Y.S.2d 350, 612 N.E.2d 699. The element of outrageous conduct is "'rigorous, and difficult to satisfy'", and its purpose is to filter out trivial complaints and assure that the claim of severe emotional distress is genuine (*Howell v. New York Post Co.*, *supra*, at 122, 596, N.Y.S.2d 350, 612 N.E.2d 699, quoting Prosser and Keeton, Torts § 12, at 60–61 [5th ed.]). A court may determine, as a matter of law, that the alleged behavior is not sufficiently outrageous to warrant the imposition of liability (*Howell v. New York Post Co.*, *supra*, at 122, 596 N.Y.S.2d 350, 612 N.E.2d 699).

Upon our review of the allegations in the case at bar, we conclude that the Supreme Court erred in determining that the element of outrageous conduct was not satisfied as a matter of law (see, e.g., *Bunker v. Testa*, 234 A.D.2d 1004, 652 N.Y.S.2d 181; *Flatley v. Hartmann*, 138 A.D.2d 345, 525 N.Y.S.2d 637; *Esposito-Hilder v. SEX Broadcasting*, 171 Misc.2d 286, 654 N.Y.S.2d 259, *affd.* 236 A.D.2d 186, 665 N.Y.S.2d 697). Although the defendants contend that the conduct at issue was not particularly shocking, in light of Stern's reputation for vulgar humor and Tay's actions during her guest appearances on his program, a jury might reasonably conclude that the manner in which Tay's remains were handled, for entertainment purposes and against the express wishes of her family, went beyond the bounds of decent behavior.

We further conclude that the remaining elements necessary to establish a cause of action to recover damages for the intentional infliction of emotional distress (see, *Howell v. New York Post Co., supra*) were also sufficiently pleaded in the complaint.

Accordingly, the appellants' motion to dismiss the complaint is denied.

O'Brien, J.P. and Santucci and Florio, JJ., concur.

Krausman, J., dissents and votes to affirm the order appealed from, with the following memorandum:

The majority decision amply demonstrates that Howard Stern and his cohorts behaved in a manner that some would find inappropriate when Chaunce Hayden came on the show with the decedent's remains. Certainly, many would consider their remarks and conduct in handling the decedent's remains tasteless, offensive, and insensitive to the feelings of the plaintiffs, who lost their sister to a drug overdose at the age of 27. However, I disagree with the majority's view that Stern's actions give rise to a cognizable legal right to recover damages for emotional distress.

At common law, emotional injury was not recognized as an independent basis for the recovery of damages, primarily because of the case with which emotional injury could be "feigned without detection" (*Mitchell v. Rochester Railway Co.*, 151 N.Y. 107, 110, 45 N.E. 354). While modern tort law now permits recovery for emotional distress (see, *Fischer v. Maloney*, 43 N.Y.2d 553, 557, 402, N.Y.S.2d 991, 373 N.E.2d 1215), the historical reluctance to allow damages for purely psychic injury is reflected in the formulation of the tort, which demands a showing that the defendant has engaged in "'extreme and outrageous conduct'" (*Howell v. New York Post Co.*, 81 N.Y.2d 115, 121, 596 N.Y.W.2d 350, 612 N.E.2d 699; quoting Prosser and Keeton, Torts § 12, at 60–61 [5th ed.], with the "intent to cause, or disregard of a substantial possibility of causing, severe emotional distress" (*Howell v. New York Post Co., supra*, at 121, 596 N.Y.S.2d 350, 612 N.E.2d 699).

As the Court of Appeals explained in *Howell v. New York Post Co., supra*, at 121, 596 N.Y.S.2d 350, 612 N.E.2d 699, "the first element—outrageous conduct—serves the dual function of filtering out petty and trivial complaints that do not belong in court, and assuring that plaintiff's claim of severe emotional distress is genuine ... In practice, courts have tended to focus on the outrageousness element, the one most susceptible to determination as a matter of law". Since the requirements of the rule are "rigorous, and difficult to satisfy", the Court of Appeals noted in *Howell v. New York Post Co., supra*, at 122, 596 N.Y.S.2d 350, 612 N.E.2d 699, that every one of the emotional distress claims it had considered had failed because "the alleged conduct was not sufficiently outrageous" (*Howell v. New York Post Co., supra*, at 122, 596 N.Y.S.2d 350, 612 N.E.2d 699). Indeed, "'[l]iability has been found only where the conduct has been so outrageous in character, and so extreme in degree, as to go beyond all possible bounds of decency, and to be regarded as atrocious, and utterly intolerable in a civilized community'" (*Murphy v. American Home Prods. Corp.*, 58 N.Y.2d 293, 303, 461 N.Y.S.2d 232, 448 N.E.2d 86, quoting Restatement [Second] of Torts § 46[1], comment d).

The issue of whether the decedent's brother and sister may recover tort damages cannot be considered in a vacuum, with total disregard for who Debbie Tay was. Debbie Tay rose to fame by spinning outrageous tales of sexual encounters with female aliens on the Howard Stern show, and used the notoriety she had achieved to launch her own cable access show. While the plaintiffs now claim that Stern's conduct following their sister's untimely death caused them extreme emotional distress, the defendants note that on one occasion, the decedent's own mother appeared on the show, describing her daughter as an unusual young woman who was "a lot of fun".

The record also reflects the fact that the plaintiff Melissa Roach Driscol voluntarily gave a portion of her sister's remains to the decedent's close friend, the defendant Chaunce Hayden. Hayden brought the decedent's remains on the air as a memorial to her because "the only happiness Debbie had was the Howard Stern show". Once on the air, Hayden encouraged cast members to examine the remains, believing that since the decedent had so enjoyed Stern's irreverent brand of humor during her lifetime, she "would love this". Although the plaintiffs allege that the show's producer ignored their request to cease discussing the disposition of the remains, there is no indication that Stern or Infinity acted out of a desire to cause the plaintiffs distress. Indeed, at the end of the show, Stern advised Hayden that he should have the decedent's remains properly buried or turned into

ashes, telling him to "remember her in your mind". Closing credits announced that the show was "dedicated in loving memory of Debbie Tay". Considering these circumstances, I would find, as a matter of law, that the conduct of Stern and Infinity was not so extreme and outrageous in nature as to be "utterly intolerable in a civilized community" (*Murphy v. American Home Prods. Corp., supra*, at 303, 461, N.Y.S.2d 232, 448 N.E.2d 86, quoting Restatement [Second] of Torts § 46[1], comment d). [See, 171 Misc.2d 80, 653 N.Y.S.2d 532].

A & M RECORDS, INC. v. NAPSTER, INC.
United States Court of Appeals for the Ninth Circuit
284 F.3d 1091 (9th Cir. 2002)
March 25, 2002
Beezer, Circuit Judge
[See Chapter 6.]

Plaintiffs are engaged in the commercial recording, distribution and sale of copyrighted musical compositions and sound recordings. The complaint alleges that Napster, Inc. ("Napster") is a contributory and vicarious copyright infringer. On July 26, 2000, the district court granted plaintiffs' motion for a preliminary injunction. The injunction was slightly modified by written opinion on August 10, 2000. *A&M Records, Inc. v. Napster, Inc.*, 114 F.Supp. 2d 896 (N.D. Cal. 2000). The district court preliminarily enjoined Napster "from engaging in, or facilitating others in copying, downloading, uploading, transmitting, or distributing plaintiffs' copyrighted musical compositions and sound recordings, protected by either federal or state law, without express permission of the rights owner." *Id.* at 927. Federal Rule of Civil Procedure 65(c) requires successful plaintiffs to post a bond for damages incurred by the enjoined party in the event that the injunction was wrongfully issued. The district court set bond in this case at $5 million.

We entered a temporary stay of the preliminary injunction pending resolution of this appeal. We have jurisdiction pursuant to 28 U.S.C. § 1292(a)(1). We affirm in part, reverse in part and remand.

I

We have examined the papers submitted in support of and in response to the injunction application and it appears that Napster has designed and operates a system which permits the transmission and retention of sound recordings employing digital technology.

In 1987, the Moving Picture Experts Group set a standard file format for the storage of audio recordings in a digital format called MPEG-3, abbreviated as "MP3." Digital MP3 files are created through a process colloquially called "ripping." Ripping software allows a computer owner to copy an audio compact disk ("audio CD") directly onto a computer's hard drive by compressing the audio information on the CD into the MP3 format. The MP3's compressed format allows for rapid transmission of digital audio files from one computer to another by electronic mail or any other file transfer protocol.

Napster facilitates the transmission of MP3 files between and among its users. Through a process commonly called "peer-to-peer" file sharing, Napster allows its users to: (1) make MP3 music files stored on individual computer hard drives available for copying by other Napster users; (2) search for MP3 music files stored on other users' computers; and (3) transfer exact copies of the contents of other users' MP3 files from one computer to another via the Internet. These functions are made possible by Napster's MusicShare software, available free of charge from Napster's Internet site, and Napster's network servers and server-side software. Napster provides technical support for the indexing and searching of MP3 files, as well as for its other functions, including a "chat room," where users can meet to discuss music, and a directory where participating artists can provide information about their music.

A. ACCESSING THE SYSTEM

In order to copy MP3 files through the Napster system, a user must first access Napster's Internet site and download the MusicShare software to his individual computer. See http://www.Napster.com. Once the software is installed, the user can access the Napster system. A first-time user is required to register with the Napster system by creating a "user name" and password.

B. LISTING AVAILABLE FILES

If a registered user wants to list available files stored in his computer's hard drive on Napster for others to access, he must first create a "user library" directory on his computer's hard drive. The user then saves his MP3 files in the library directory, using self-designated file names. He next must log into the Napster system using his user name and password. His MusicShare software then searches his user library and verifies that the available files are properly formatted. If in the correct MP3 format, the names of the MP3 files will be uploaded from the user's computer to the Napster servers. The content

of the MP3 files remains stored in the user's computer. Once uploaded to the Napster servers, the user's MP3 file names are stored in a server-side "library" under the user's name and become part of a "collective directory" of file available for transfer during the time the user is logged onto the Napster system. The collective directory is fluid; it tracks users who are connected in real time, displaying only file names that are immediately accessible.

C. SEARCHING FOR AVAILABLE FILES

Napster allows a user to locate other users' MP3 files in two ways: through Napster's search function and through its "hotlist" function.

Software located on the Napster servers maintains a "search index" of Napster's collective directory. To search the files available from Napster users currently connected to the network servers, the individual user accesses a form in the MusicShare software stored in his computer and enters either the name of a song or an artist as the object of the search. The form is then transmitted to a Napster server and automatically compared to the MP3 file names listed in the server's search index. Napster's server compiles a list of all MP3 file names pulled from the search index which include the same search terms entered on the search form and transmits the list to the searching user. The Napster server does not search the contents of any MP3 file; rather, the search is limited to "a text search of the file names indexed in a particular cluster. Those file names may contain typographical errors or otherwise inaccurate descriptions of the content of the files since they are designated by other users." *Napster*, 114 F.Supp.2d at 906.

To use the "hotlist" function, the Napster user creates a list of other users' names from whom he has obtained MP3 files in the past. When logged onto Napster's servers, the system alerts the user if any user on his list (a "hotlisted user") is also logged onto the system. If so, the user can access an index of all MP3 file names in a particular hotlisted user's library and request a file in the library by selecting the file name. The contents of the hotlisted user's MP3 file are not stored on the Napster system.

D. TRANSFERRING COPIES OF AN MP3 FILE

To transfer a copy of the contents of a requested MP3 file, the Napster server software obtains the Internet address of the requesting user and the Internet address of the "host user" (the user with the available files). See generally *Brookfield Communications, Inc. v. West Coast Entm't Corp.*, 174 F.3d 1036, 1044 (9th Cir. 1999) (describing, in detail, the structure of the Internet). The Napster servers then communicate the host user's Internet address to the requesting user. The requesting user's computer uses this information to establish a connection with the host user and downloads a copy of the contents of the MP3 file from one computer to the other over the Internet, "peer-to-peer." A downloaded MP3 file can be played directly from the user's hard drive using Napster's Music-Share program or other software. The file may also be transferred back onto an audio CD if the user has access to equipment designed for that purpose. In both cases, the quality of the original sound recording is slightly diminished by transfer to the MP3 format.

This architecture is described in some detail to promote an understanding of transmission mechanics as opposed to the content of the transmissions. The content is the subject of our copyright infringement analysis.

II

We review a grant or denial of a preliminary injunction for abuse of discretion. *Gorbach v. Reno*, 219 F.3d 1087, 1091 (9th Cir. 2000)(en banc). Application of erroneous legal principles represents an abuse of discretion by the district court. *Rucker v. Davis*, ___ F.3d ___, 2001 WL 55724, at 4 (9th Cir. Jan. 24, 2001)(en banc). If the district court is claimed to have relied on an erroneous legal premise in reaching its decision to grant or deny a preliminary injunction, we will review the underlying issue of law de novo. *Id.* at 4 (citing *Does 1-5 v. Chandler*, 83 F.3d 1150, 1152 (9th Cir. 1996)). On review, we are required to determine, "whether the court employed the appropriate legal standards governing the issuance of a preliminary injunction and whether the district court correctly apprehended the law with respect to the under-lying issues in the case." *Id.* "As long as the district court got the law right, 'it will not be reversed simply because the appellate court would have arrived at a different result if it had applied the law to the facts of the case.'" *Gregorio T. v. Wilson*, 59 F.3d 1002, 1004 (9th Cir. 1995) (quoting *Sports Form, Inc. v. United Press, Int'l*, 686 F.2d 750, 752 (9th Cir. 1982)).

Preliminary injunctive relief is available to a party who demonstrates either: (1) a combination of probable success on the merits and the possibility of irreparable harm; or (2) that serious questions are raised and the balance of hardships tips in its favor. *Prudential Real Estate Affiliates, Inc. v. PPR Realty, Inc.*, 204 F.3d 867, 874 (9th Cir. 2000). "These two formulations represent two points on a sliding scale in which the required degree of irreparable harm increases as the probability of success decreases." *Id.*

III

Plaintiffs claim Napster users are engaged in the wholesale reproduction and distribution of copyrighted works, all constituting direct infringement. The district court agreed. We note that the district court's conclusion that plaintiffs have presented a prima facie case of direct infringement by Napster users is not presently appealed by Napster.

A. INFRINGEMENT

Plaintiffs must satisfy two requirements to present a prima facie case of direct infringement: (1) they must show ownership of the allegedly infringed material and (2) they must demonstrate that the alleged infringers violate at least one exclusive right granted to copyright holders under 17 U.S.C. § 106. See 17 U.S.C. § 501(a) (infringement occurs when alleged infringer engages in activity listed in § 106); see also *Baxter v. MCA, Inc.*, 812 F.2d 421, 423 (9th Cir. 1987); see, e.g., *S.O.S., Inc. v. Payday, Inc.*, 886 F.2d 1081, 1085 n.3 (9th Cir. 1989) ("The word 'copying' is shorthand for the infringing of any of the copyright owner's five exclusive rights. ..."). Plaintiffs have sufficiently demonstrated ownership. The record supports the district court's determination that "as much as eighty-seven percent of the files available on Napster may be copyrighted and more than seventy percent may be owned or administered by plaintiffs." *Napster*, 114 F.Supp.2d at 911.

The district court further determined that plaintiffs' exclusive rights under § 106 were violated: "here the evidence establishes that a majority of Napster users use the service to download and upload copyrighted music. ... And by doing that, it constitutes—the uses constitute direct infringement of plaintiffs' musical compositions, recordings." *A&M Records, Inc. v. Napster, Inc.*, Nos. 99-5183, 00-0074, 2000 WL 1009483, at (N.D. Cal. July 26, 2000) (transcript of proceedings). The district court also noted that "it is pretty much acknowledged ... by Napster that this is infringement." *Id.* We agree that plaintiffs have shown that Napster users infringe at least two of the copyright holders' exclusive rights: the rights of reproduction, § 106(1); and distribution, § 106(3). Napster users who upload file names to the search index for others to copy violate plaintiffs' distribution rights. Napster users who download files containing copyrighted music violate plaintiffs' reproduction rights.

Napster asserts an affirmative defense to the charge that its users directly infringe plaintiffs' copyrighted musical compositions and sound recordings.

B. FAIR USE

Napster contends that its users do not directly infringe plaintiffs' copyrights because the users are engaged in fair use of the material. See 17 U.S.C. § 107 ("[T]he fair use of a copyrighted work ... is not an infringement of copyright."). Napster identifies three specific alleged fair uses: sampling, where users make temporary copies of a work before purchasing; space-shifting, where users access a sound recording through the Napster system that they already own in audio CD format; and permissive distribution of recordings by both new and established artists.

The district court considered factors listed in 17 U.S.C. § 107, which guide a court's fair use determination. These factors are: (1) the purpose and character of the use; (2) the nature of the copyrighted work; (3) the "amount and substantiality of the portion used" in relation to the work as a whole; and (4) the effect of the use upon the potential market for the work or the value of the work. See 17 U.S.C. § 107. The district court first conducted a general analysis of Napster system uses under § 107, and then applied its reasoning to the alleged fair uses identified by Napster. The district court concluded that Napster users are not fair users. We agree. We first address the court's overall fair use analysis.

1. PURPOSE AND CHARACTER OF THE USE

This factor focuses on whether the new work merely replaces the object of the original creation or instead adds a further purpose or different character. In other words, this factor asks "whether and to what extent the new work is 'transformative.'" See *Campbell v. Acuff-Rose Music, Inc.*, 510 U.S. 569, 579 (1994).

The district court first concluded that downloading MP3 files does not transform the copyrighted work. *Napster*, 114 F.Supp. 2d at 912. This conclusion is supportable. Courts have been reluctant to find fair use when an original work is merely retransmitted in a different medium. See, e.g., *Infinity Broadcast Corp. v. Kirkwood*, 150 F.3d 104, 108 (2d Cir. 1994) (concluding that retransmission of radio broadcast over telephone lines is not transformative); *UMG Recordings, Inc. v. MP3.com, Inc.*, 92 F.Supp. 2d 349, 351 (S.D.N.Y.) (finding that reproduction of audio CD into MP3 format does not "transform" the work), certification denied, 2000 WL 710056 (S.D.N.Y. June 1, 2000) ("Defendant's copyright infringement was clear, and the mere fact that it was clothed in the exotic webbing of the Internet does not disguise its illegality.").

This "purpose and character" element also requires the district court to determine whether the allegedly infringing use is commercial or noncommercial. See *Campbell*, 510 U.S. at 584–85. A commercial use weighs against a finding of fair use but is not conclusive on the issue. *Id.* The district court determined that Napster users engage in commercial use of the copyrighted materials largely because (1) "a host user sending a file cannot be said to engage in a personal use when distributing that file to an anonymous requester" and (2) "Napster users get for free something they would ordinarily have to buy." *Napster*, 114 F.Supp. 2d at 912. The district court's findings are not clearly erroneous.

Direct economic benefit is not required to demonstrate a commercial use. Rather, repeated and exploitative copying of copyrighted works, even if the copies are not offered for sale, may constitute a commercial use. See *Worldwide Church of God v. Philadelphia Church of God*, 227 F.3d 1110, 1118 (9th Cir. 2000) (stating that church that copied religious text for its members "unquestionably profit[ed]" from the unauthorized "distribution and use of [the text] without having to account to the copyright holder"); *American Geophysical Union v. Texaco, Inc.*, 60 F.3d 913, 922 (2d Cir. 1994) (finding that researchers at for-profit laboratory gained indirect economic advantage by photocopying copyrighted scholarly articles). In the record before us, commercial use is demonstrated by a showing that repeated and exploitative unauthorized copies of copyrighted works were made to save the expense of purchasing authorized copies. See *Worldwide Church*, 227 F.3d at 1117–18; *Sega Enters. Ltd. v. MAPHIA*, 857 F.Supp. 679, 687 (N.D. Cal. 1994) (finding commercial use when individuals downloaded copies of video games "to avoid having to buy video game cartridges"); see also *American Geophysical*, 60 F.3d at 922. Plaintiffs made such a showing before the district court.

We also note that the definition of a financially motivated transaction for the purposes of criminal copyright actions includes trading infringing copies of a work for other items, "including the receipt of other copyrighted works." See No Electronic Theft Act ("NET Act"), Pub. L. No. 105–147, 18 U.S.C. § 101 (defining "Financial Gain").

2. THE NATURE OF THE USE

Works that are creative in nature are "closer to the core of intended copyright protection" than are more fact-based works. See *Campbell*, 510 U.S. at 586. The district court determined that plaintiffs' "copyrighted musical compositions and sound recordings are creative in nature ... which cuts against a finding of fair use under the second factor." *Napster*, 114 F.Supp. 2d at 913. We find no error in the district court's conclusion.

3. THE PORTION USED

"While 'wholesale copying does not preclude fair use per se,' copying an entire work 'militates against a finding of fair use.'" *Worldwide Church*, 227 F.3d at 1118 (quoting *Hustler Magazine, Inc. v. Moral Majority, Inc.*, 796 F.2d 1148, 1155 (9th Cir. 1986)). The district court determined that Napster users engage in "wholesale copying" of copyrighted work because file transfer necessarily "involves copying the entirety of the copyrighted work." *Napster*, 114 F.Supp.2d at 913. We agree. We note, however, that under certain circumstances, a court will conclude that a use is fair even when the protected work is copied in its entirety. See, e.g., *Sony Corp. v. Universal City Studios, Inc.*, 464 U.S. 417, 449–50 (1984) (acknowledging that fair use of time-shifting necessarily involved making a full copy of a protected work).

4. EFFECT OF USE ON MARKET

"Fair use, when properly applied, is limited to copying by others which does not materially impair the marketability of the work which is copied." *Harper & Row Publishers, Inc. v. Nation Enters.*, 471 U.S. 539, 566–67 (1985). "[T]he importance of this [fourth] factor will vary, not only with the amount of harm, but also with the relative strength of the showing on the other factors." *Campbell*, 510 U.S. at 591 n.21. The proof required to demonstrate present or future market harm varies with the purpose and character of the use:

> A challenge to a noncommercial use of a copyrighted work requires proof either that the particular use is harmful, or that if it should become widespread, it would adversely affect the potential market for the copyrighted work. ... If the intended use is for commercial gain, that likelihood [of market harm] may be presumed. But if it is for a noncommercial purpose, the likelihood must be demonstrated. *Sony*, 464 U.S. at 451.

Addressing this factor, the district court concluded that Napster harms the market in "at least" two ways: it reduces audio CD sales among college students and it "raises barriers to plaintiffs' entry into the market for the digital downloading of music." *Napster*, 114 F.Supp.2d at 913. The district court relied on evidence plaintiffs submitted to show that Napster use harms the market for their copyrighted musical compositions and sound recordings. In a separate memorandum and order regarding the parties' objections to the expert reports, the district court examined each report, finding some more appropriate and probative than others. *A&M Records, Inc. v. Napster, Inc.*, Nos. 99-5183 & 00-0074, 2000 WL 1170106 (N.D. Cal. August 10, 2000). Notably, plaintiffs' expert, Dr. E. Deborah Jay, conducted a survey (the "Jay Report") using a random sample of college and university students to track their reasons for using Napster and the impact Napster had on their music purchases. *Id.* at 2. The court recognized that the Jay Report focused on just one segment of the Napster user population and found "evidence of lost sales attributable to college use to be probative of irreparable harm for purposes of the preliminary injunction motion." *Id.* at 3.

Plaintiffs also offered a study conducted by Michael Fine, Chief Executive Officer of Soundscan, (the "Fine Report") to determine the effect of online sharing of MP3 files in order to show irreparable harm. Fine found that online file sharing had resulted in a loss of "album" sales within college markets. After reviewing defendant's objections to the Fine Report and expressing some concerns regarding the methodology and findings, the district court refused to exclude the Fine Report insofar as plaintiffs offered it to show irreparable harm. *Id.* at 6.

Plaintiffs' expert Dr. David J. Teece studied several issues ("Teece Report"), including whether plaintiffs had suffered or were likely to suffer harm in their existing and planned businesses due to Napster use. *Id.* Napster objected that the report had not undergone peer review. The district court noted that such reports generally are not subject to such scrutiny and overruled defendant's objections. *Id.*

As for defendant's experts, plaintiffs objected to the report of Dr. Peter S. Fader, in which the expert concluded that Napster is beneficial to the music industry because MP3 music file-sharing stimulates more audio CD sales than it displaces. *Id.* at 7. The district court found problems in Dr. Fader's minimal role in overseeing the administration of the survey and the lack of objective data in his report. The court decided the generality of the report rendered it "of dubious reliability and value." The court did not exclude the report, however, but chose "not to rely on Fader's findings in determining the issues of fair use and irreparable harm." *Id.* at 8.

The district court cited both the Jay and Fine Reports in support of its finding that Napster use harms the market for plaintiffs' copyrighted musical compositions and sound recordings by reducing CD sales among college students. The district court cited the Teece Report to show the harm Napster use caused in raising barriers to plaintiffs' entry into the market for digital downloading of music. *Napster*, 114 F.Supp. 2d at 910. The district court's careful consideration of defendant's objections to these reports and decision to rely on the reports for specific issues demonstrates a proper exercise of discretion in addition to a correct application of the fair use doctrine. Defendant has failed to show any basis for disturbing the district court's findings.

We, therefore, conclude that the district court made sound findings related to Napster's deleterious effect on the present and future digital download market. Moreover, lack of harm to an established market cannot deprive the copyright holder of the right to develop alternative markets for the works. See *L.A. Times v. Free Republic*, 54 U.S.P.Q.2d 1453, 1469–71 (C.D. Cal. 2000) (stating that online market for plaintiff newspapers' articles was harmed because plaintiffs demonstrated that "[defendants] are attempting to exploit the market for viewing their articles online"); see also *UMG Recordings*, 92 F.Supp. 2d at 352 ("Any allegedly positive impact of defendant's activities on plaintiffs' prior market in no way frees defendant to usurp a further market that directly derives from reproduction of the plaintiffs' copyrighted works."). Here, similar to *L.A. Times* and *UMG Recordings*, the record supports the district court's finding that the "record company plaintiffs have already expended considerable funds and effort to commence Internet sales and licensing for digital downloads." 114 F.Supp. 2d at 915. Having digital downloads available for free on the Napster system necessarily harms the copyright holders' attempts to charge for the same downloads.

Judge Patel did not abuse her discretion in reaching the above fair use conclusions, nor were the findings of fact with respect to fair use considerations clearly erroneous. We next address Napster's identified uses of sampling and space-shifting.

5. IDENTIFIED USES

Napster maintains that its identified uses of sampling and space-shifting were wrongly excluded as fair uses by the district court.

A. SAMPLING

Napster contends that its users download MP3 files to "sample" the music in order to decide whether to purchase the recording. Napster argues that the district court: (1) erred in concluding that sampling is a commercial use because it conflated a noncommercial use with a personal use; (2) erred in determining that sampling adversely affects the market for plaintiffs' copyrighted music, a requirement if the use is non-commercial; and (3) erroneously concluded that sampling is not a fair use because it determined that samplers may also engage in other infringing activity.

The district court determined that sampling remains a commercial use even if some users eventually purchase the music. We find no error in the district court's determination.

Plaintiffs have established that they are likely to succeed in proving that even authorized temporary downloading of individual songs for sampling purposes is commercial in nature. See *Napster*, 114 F.Supp.2d at 913. The record supports a finding that free promotional downloads are highly regulated by the record company plaintiffs and that the companies collect royalties for song samples available on retail Internet sites. *Id.* Evidence relied on by the district court demonstrates that the free downloads provided by the record companies consist of thirty-to-sixty second samples or are full songs programmed to "time out," that is, exist only for a short time on the downloader's computer. *Id.* at 913–14. In comparison, Napster users download a full, free and permanent copy of the recording. *Id.* at 914–15. The determination by the district court as to the commercial purpose and character of sampling is not clearly erroneous.

The district court further found that both the market for audio CDs and market for online distribution are adversely affected by Napster's service. As stated in our discussion of the district court's general fair use analysis: the court did not abuse its discretion when it found that, overall, Napster has an adverse impact on the audio CD and digital download markets. Contrary to Napster's assertion that the district court failed to specifically address the market impact of sampling, the district court determined that "[e]ven if the type of sampling supposedly done on Napster were a non-commercial use, plaintiffs have demonstrated a substantial likelihood that it would adversely affect the potential market for their copyrighted works if it became widespread." *Napster*, 114 F.Supp.2d at 914. The record supports the district court's preliminary determinations that: (1) the more music that sampling users download, the less likely they are to eventually purchase the recordings on audio CD; and (2) even if the audio CD market is not harmed, Napster has adverse effects on the developing digital download market.

Napster further argues that the district court erred in rejecting its evidence that the users' downloading of "samples" increases or tends to increase audio CD sales. The district court, however, correctly noted that "any potential enhancement of plaintiffs' sales ... would not tip the fair use analysis conclusively in favor of defendant." *Id.* at 914. We agree that increased sales of copyrighted material attributable to unauthorized use should not deprive the copyright holder of the right to license the material. See *Campbell*, 510 U.S. at 591 n.21 ("Even favorable evidence, without more, is no guarantee of fairness. Judge Leval gives the example of the film producer's appropriation of a composer's previously unknown song that turns the song into a commercial success; the boon to the song does not make the film's simple copying fair."); see also *L.A. Times*, 54 U.S.P.Q.2d at 1471–72. Nor does positive impact in one market, here the audio CD market, deprive the copyright holder of the right to develop identified alternative markets, here the digital download market. See *Id.* at 1469–71.

We find no error in the district court's factual findings or abuse of discretion in the court's conclusion that plaintiffs will likely prevail in establishing that sampling does not constitute a fair use.

B. SPACE-SHIFTING

Napster also maintains that space-shifting is a fair use. Space-shifting occurs when a Napster user downloads MP3 music files in order to listen to music he already owns on audio CD. See *Id.* at 915–16. Napster asserts that we have already held that space-shifting of musical compositions and sound recordings is a fair use. See *Recording Indus. Ass'n of Am. v. Diamond Multimedia Sys., Inc.*, 180 F.3d 1072, 1079 (9th Cir. 1999) ("Rio [a portable MP3 player] merely makes copies in order to render portable, or `space-shift,' those files that already reside on a user's hard drive. ... Such copying is a paradigmatic noncommercial personal use."). See also generally *Sony*, 464 U.S. at 423 (holding that "time-shifting," where a video tape recorder owner records a television show for later viewing, is a fair use).

We conclude that the district court did not err when it refused to apply the "shifting" analyses of *Sony* and *Diamond*. Both *Diamond* and *Sony* are inapposite because the methods of shifting in these cases did not also simultaneously involve distribution of the copyrighted material to the general public; the time or space-shifting of copyrighted material exposed the material only to the original user. In *Diamond*, for example, the copyrighted music was transferred from the user's computer hard drive to the user's portable MP3 player. So too *Sony*, where "the majority of VCR purchasers ... did not distribute taped television broadcasts, but merely enjoyed them at home." *Napster*, 114 F.Supp.2d at 913. Conversely, it is obvious that once a user lists a copy of music he already owns on the Napster system in order to access the music from another location, the song becomes "available to millions of other individuals," not just the original CD owner. See *UMG Recordings*, 92 F.Supp.2d at 351–52 (finding space-shifting of MP3 files not a fair use even when previous ownership is demonstrated before a download is allowed); *cf. Religious Tech. Ctr. v. Lerma*, No. 95-1107A, 1996 WL 633131, at 6 (E.D.Va. Oct. 4, 1996) (suggesting that storing copyrighted material on computer disk for later review is not a fair use).

C. OTHER USES

Permissive reproduction by either independent or established artists is the final fair use claim made by Napster. The district court noted that plaintiffs did not seek to enjoin this and any other noninfringing use of the Napster system, including: chat rooms, message boards and Napster's New Artist Program. *Napster*, 114 F.Supp.2d at 917. Plaintiffs do not challenge these uses on appeal.

We find no error in the district court's determination that plaintiffs will likely succeed in establishing that Napster users do not have a fair use defense. Accordingly, we next address whether Napster is secondarily liable for the direct infringement under two doctrines of copyright law: contributory copyright infringement and vicarious copyright infringement.

IV

We first address plaintiffs' claim that Napster is liable for contributory copyright infringement. Traditionally, "one who, with knowledge of the infringing activity, induces, causes or materially contributes to the infringing conduct of another, may be held liable as a `contributory' infringer." *Gershwin Publ'g Corp. v. Columbia Artists Mgmt., Inc.*, 443 F.2d 1159, 1162 (2d Cir. 1971); see also *Fonovisa, Inc. v. Cherry Auction, Inc.*, 76 F.3d 259, 264 (9th Cir. 1996). Put differently, liability exists if the defendant engages in "personal conduct that encourages or assists the infringement."

Matthew Bender & Co. v. West Publ'g Co., 158 F.3d 693, 706 (2d Cir. 1998).

The district court determined that plaintiffs in all likelihood would establish Napster's liability as a contributory infringer. The district court did not err; Napster, by its conduct, knowingly encourages and assists the infringement of plaintiffs' copyrights.

A. KNOWLEDGE

Contributory liability requires that the secondary infringer "know or have reason to know" of direct infringement. *Cable/Home Communication Corp. Network Prods., Inc.*, 902 F.2d 829, 845 & 846 n.29 (11th Cir. 1990); *Religious Tech. Ctr. v. Netcom On-Line Communication Servs., Inc.*, 907 F.Supp. 1361, 1373–74 (N.D. Cal. 1995) (framing issue as "whether Netcom knew or should have known of" the infringing activities). The district court found that Napster had both actual and constructive knowledge that its users exchanged copyrighted music. The district court also concluded that the law does not require knowledge of "specific acts of infringement" and rejected Napster's contention that because the company cannot distinguish infringing from noninfringing files, it does not "know" of the direct infringement. 114 F.Supp.2d at 917.

It is apparent from the record that Napster has knowledge, both actual and constructive, of direct infringement. Napster claims that it is nevertheless protected from contributory liability by the teaching of *Sony Corp. v. Universal City Studios, Inc.*, 464 U.S. 417 (1984). We disagree. We observe that Napster's actual, specific knowledge of direct infringement renders *Sony's* holding of limited assistance to Napster. We are compelled to make a clear distinction between the architecture of the Napster system and Napster's conduct in relation to the operational capacity of the system.

The *Sony* Court refused to hold the manufacturer and retailers of video tape recorders liable for contributory infringement despite evidence that such machines could be and were used to infringe plaintiffs' copyrighted television shows. Sony stated that if liability "is to be imposed on petitioners in this case, it must rest on the fact that they have sold equipment with constructive knowledge of the fact that their customers may use that equipment to make unauthorized copies of copyrighted material." *Id.* at 439 (emphasis added). The *Sony* Court declined to impute the requisite level of knowledge where the defendants made and sold equipment capable of both infringing and "substantial noninfringing uses." *Id.* at 442 (adopting a modified "staple article of commerce" doctrine from patent law). See also *Universal City Studios, Inc. v. Sony Corp.*, 480 F.Supp. 429, 459 (C.D. Cal. 1979) ("This court agrees with defendants that their knowledge was insufficient to make them contributory infringers."), rev'd, 659 F.2d 963 (9th Cir. 1981), rev'd, 464 U.S. 417 (1984); Alfred C. Yen, Internet Service Provider Liability for Subscriber Copyright Infringement, Enterprise Liability, and the First Amendment, 88 Geo. L.J. 1833, 1874 & 1893 n.210 (2000) (suggesting that, after *Sony*, most Internet service providers lack "the requisite level of knowledge" for the imposition of contributory liability).

We are bound to follow *Sony*, and will not impute the requisite level of knowledge to Napster merely because peer-to-peer file sharing technology may be used to infringe plaintiffs' copyrights. See 464 U.S. at 436 (rejecting argument that merely supplying the "'means' to accomplish an infringing activity" leads to imposition of liability). We depart from the reasoning of the district court that Napster failed to demonstrate that its system is capable of commercially significant noninfringing uses. See *Napster*, 114 F.Supp.2d at 916, 917–18. The district court improperly confined the use analysis to current uses, ignoring the system's capabilities. See generally *Sony*, 464 U.S. at 442–43 (framing inquiry as whether the video tape recorder is "capable of commercially significant noninfringing uses"). Consequently, the district court placed undue weight on the proportion of current infringing use as compared to current and future noninfringing use. See generally *Vault Corp. v. Quaid Software Ltd.*, 847 F.2d 255, 264–67 (5th Cir. 1997) (single noninfringing use implicated *Sony*). Nonetheless, whether we might arrive at a different result is not the issue here. See *Sports Form, Inc. v. United Press Int'l*,

Inc., 686 F.2d 750, 752 (9th Cir. 1982). The instant appeal occurs at an early point in the proceedings and "the fully developed factual record may be materially different from that initially before the district court. ..." *Id.* at 753. Regardless of the number of Napster's infringing versus noninfringing uses, the evidentiary record here supported the district court's finding that plaintiffs would likely prevail in establishing that Napster knew or had reason to know of its users' infringement of plaintiffs' copyrights.

This analysis is similar to that of *Religious Technology Center v. Netcom On-Line Communication Services, Inc.*, which suggests that in an online context, evidence of actual knowledge of specific acts of infringement is required to hold a computer system operator liable for contributory copyright infringement. 907 F.Supp. at 1371. Netcom considered the potential contributory copyright liability of a computer bulletin board operator whose system supported the posting of infringing material. *Id.* at 1374. The court, in denying Netcom's motion for summary judgment of noninfringement and plaintiff's motion for judgment on the pleadings, found that a disputed issue of fact existed as to whether the operator had sufficient knowledge of infringing activity. *Id.* at 1374–75.

The court determined that for the operator to have sufficient knowledge, the copyright holder must "provide the necessary documentation to show there is likely infringement." 907 F.Supp. at 1374; *cf. Cubby, Inc. v. Compuserve, Inc.*, 776 F. Supp. 135, 141 (S.D.N.Y. 1991) (recognizing that online service provider does not and cannot examine every hyperlink for potentially defamatory material). If such documentation was provided, the court reasoned that Netcom would be liable for contributory infringement because its failure to remove the material "and thereby stop an infringing copy from being distributed worldwide constitutes substantial participation" in distribution of copyrighted material. *Id.*

We agree that if a computer system operator learns of specific infringing material available on his system and fails to purge such material from the system, the operator knows of and contributes to direct infringement. See *Netcom*, 907

F.Supp. at 1374. Conversely, absent any specific information which identifies infringing activity, a computer system operator cannot be liable for contributory infringement merely because the structure of the system allows for the exchange of copyrighted material. See *Sony*, 464 U.S. at 436, 442–43. To enjoin simply because a computer network allows for infringing use would, in our opinion, violate *Sony* and potentially restrict activity unrelated to infringing use.

We nevertheless conclude that sufficient knowledge exists to impose contributory liability when linked to demonstrated infringing use of the Napster system. See *Napster*, 114 F.Supp.2d at 919 ("Religious Technology Center would not mandate a determination that Napster, Inc. lacks the knowledge requisite to contributory infringement."). The record supports the district court's finding that Napster has actual knowledge that specific infringing material is available using its system, that it could block access to the system by suppliers of the infringing material, and that it failed to remove the material. See *Napster*, 114 F.Supp.2d at 918, 920–21.

B. MATERIAL CONTRIBUTION

Under the facts as found by the district court, Napster materially contributes to the infringing activity. Relying on *Fonovisa*, the district court concluded that "[w]ithout the support services defendant provides, Napster users could not find and download the music they want with the ease of which defendant boasts." *Napster*, 114 F.Supp.2d at 919–20 ("Napster is an integrated service designed to enable users to locate and download MP3 music files."). We agree that Napster provides "the site and facilities" for direct infringement. See *Fonovisa*, 76 F.3d at 264; *cf. Netcom*, 907 F.Supp. at 1372 ("Netcom will be liable for contributory infringement since its failure to cancel [a user's] infringing message and thereby stop an infringing copy from being distributed worldwide constitutes substantial participation."). The district court correctly applied the reasoning in *Fonovisa*, and properly found that Napster materially contributes to direct infringement.

We affirm the district court's conclusion that plaintiffs have demonstrated a likelihood of success on the merits of the contributory copyright infringement claim. We will address the scope of the injunction in part VIII of this opinion.

V

We turn to the question whether Napster engages in vicarious copyright infringement. Vicarious copyright liability is an "outgrowth" of respondeat superior. *Fonovisa*, 76 F.3d at 262. In the context of copyright law, vicarious liability extends beyond an employer/employee relationship to cases in which a defendant "has the right and ability to supervise the infringing activity and also has a direct financial interest in such activities." *Id.* (quoting *Gershwin*, 443 F.2d at 1162); see also *Polygram Int'l Publ'g, Inc. v. Nevada/TIG, Inc.*, 855 F.Supp. 1314, 1325–26 (D. Mass. 1994) (describing vicarious liability as a form of risk allocation).

Before moving into this discussion, we note that Sony's "staple article of commerce" analysis has no application to Napster's potential liability for vicarious copyright infringement. See *Sony*, 464 U.S. at 434–435; see generally 3 Melville B. Nimmer & David Nimmer, Nimmer On Copyright 12.04[A][2] & [A][2][b] (2000) (confining Sony to contributory infringement analysis: "Contributory infringement itself is of two types—personal conduct that forms part of or furthers the infringement and contribution of machinery or goods that provide the means to infringe"). 617 PLI/Pat 455, 528 (Sept. 2, 2000) (indicating that the "staple article of commerce" doctrine "provides a defense only to contributory infringement, not to vicarious infringement"). The issues of Sony's liability under the "doctrines of `direct infringement' and 'vicarious liability'" were not before the Supreme Court, although the Court recognized that the "lines between direct infringement, contributory infringement, and vicarious liability are not clearly drawn." *Id.* at 435 n.17. Consequently, when the *Sony* Court used the term "vicarious liability," it did so broadly and outside of a technical analysis of the doctrine of vicarious copyright infringement. *Id.* at 435 ("[V]icarious liability is imposed in virtually all areas of the law, and the concept of contributory infringement is merely a species of the broader problem of identifying the circumstances in which it is just to hold one individual accountable for the actions of another."); see also *Black's Law Dictionary* 927 (7th ed. 1999) (defining "vicarious liability" in a manner similar to the definition used in *Sony*).

A. FINANCIAL BENEFIT

The district court determined that plaintiffs had demonstrated they would likely succeed in establishing that Napster has a direct financial interest in the infringing activity. *Napster*, 114 F.Supp.2d at 921–22. We agree. Financial benefit exists where the availability of infringing material "acts as a 'draw' for customers." *Fonovisa*, 76 F.3d at 263–64 (stating that financial benefit may be shown "where infringing performances enhance the attractiveness of a venue"). Ample evidence supports the district court's finding that Napster's future revenue is directly dependent upon "increases in userbase." More users register with the Napster system as the "quality and quantity of available music increases." 114 F.Supp.2d at 902. We conclude that the district court did not err in determining that Napster financially benefits from the availability of protected works on its system.

B. SUPERVISION

The district court determined that Napster has the right and ability to supervise its users' conduct. *Napster*, 114 F.Supp.2d at 920–21 (finding that Napster's representations to the court regarding "its improved methods of blocking users about whom rights holders complain ... is tantamount to an admission that defendant can, and sometimes does, police its service"). We agree in part.

The ability to block infringers' access to a particular environment for any reason whatsoever is evidence of the right and ability to supervise. See *Fonovisa*, 76 F.3d at 262 ("Cherry Auction had the right to terminate vendors for any reason whatsoever and through that right had the ability to control the activities of vendors on the premises."); *cf. Netcom*, 907 F.Supp. at 1375–76 (indicating that plaintiff raised a genuine issue of fact regarding ability to supervise by presenting evidence that an electronic bulletin board service can suspend subscriber's accounts). Here, plaintiffs have demonstrated that Napster retains the right to control access to its system. Napster has an express reservation of rights policy, stating on its website that it expressly reserves the "right to refuse service and terminate accounts in [its] discretion, including, but not limited to, if Napster believes that user conduct violates applicable law … or for any reason in Napster's sole discretion, with or without cause."

To escape imposition of vicarious liability, the reserved right to police must be exercised to its fullest extent. Turning a blind eye to detectable acts of infringement for the sake of profit gives rise to liability. See, e.g., *Fonovisa*, 76 F.3d at 261 ("There is no dispute for the purposes of this appeal that Cherry Auction and its operators were aware that vendors in their swap meets were selling counterfeit recordings."); see also *Gershwin*, 443 F.2d at 1161–62 (citing *Shapiro, Bernstein & Co. v. H.L. Greene Co.*, 316 F.2d 304 (2d Cir. 1963), for the proposition that "failure to police the conduct of the primary infringer" leads to imposition of vicarious liability for copyright infringement).

The district court correctly determined that Napster had the right and ability to police its system and failed to exercise that right to prevent the exchange of copyrighted material. The district court, however, failed to recognize that the boundaries of the premises that Napster "controls and patrols" are limited. See, e.g., *Fonovisa*, 76 F.2d at 262–63 (in addition to having the right to exclude vendors, defendant "controlled and patrolled" the premises); see also *Polygram*, 855 F.Supp. at 1328–29 (in addition to having the contractual right to remove exhibitors, trade show operator reserved the right to police during the show and had its "employees walk the aisles to ensure 'rules compliance'"). Put differently, Napster's reserved "right and ability" to police is cabined by the system's current architecture. As shown by the record, the Napster system does not "read" the content of indexed files, other than to check that they are in the proper MP3 format.

Napster, however, has the ability to locate infringing material listed on its search indices, and the right to terminate users' access to the system. The file name indices, therefore, are within the "premises" that Napster has the ability to police. We recognize that the files are user-named and may not match copyrighted material exactly (for example, the artist or song could be spelled wrong). For Napster to function effectively, however, file names must reasonably or roughly correspond to the material contained in the files, otherwise no user could ever locate any desired music. As a practical matter, Napster, its users and the record company plaintiffs have equal access to infringing material by employing Napster's "search function."

Our review of the record requires us to accept the district court's conclusion that plaintiffs have demonstrated a likelihood of success on the merits of the vicarious copyright infringement claim. Napster's failure to police the system's "premises," combined with a showing that Napster financially benefits from the continuing availability of infringing files on its system, leads to the imposition of vicarious liability. We address the scope of the injunction in part VIII of this opinion.

VI

We next address whether Napster has asserted defenses which would preclude the entry of a preliminary injunction. Napster alleges that two statutes insulate it from liability. First, Napster asserts that its users engage in actions protected by § 1008 of the Audio Home Recording Act of 1992, 17 U.S.C. § 1008. Second, Napster argues that its liability for contributory and vicarious infringement is limited by the Digital Millennium Copyright Act, 17 U.S.C. § 512. We address the application of each statute in turn.

A. AUDIO HOME RECORDING ACT

The statute states in part:

No action may be brought under this title alleging infringement of copyright based on the manufacture, importation, or distribution of a digital audio recording device, a digital audio recording medium, an analog recording device, or an analog recording medium, or based on the noncommercial use by a consumer of such a device or medium for making digital musical recordings or analog musical recordings. 17 U.S.C. § 1008.

Napster contends that MP3 file exchange is the type of "noncommercial use" protected from infringement actions by the statute. Napster asserts it cannot be secondarily liable for users' nonactionable exchange of copyrighted musical recordings.

The district court rejected Napster's argument, stating that the Audio Home Recording Act is "irrelevant" to the action because: (1) plaintiffs did not bring claims under the Audio Home Recording Act; and (2) the Audio Home Recording Act does not cover the downloading of MP3 files. *Napster*, 114 F.Supp.2d at 916 n.19.

We agree with the district court that the Audio Home Recording Act does not cover the downloading of MP3 files to computer hard drives. First, "[u]nder the plain meaning of the Act's definition of digital audio recording devices, computers (and their hard drives) are not digital audio recording devices because their 'primary purpose' is not to make digital audio copied recordings." *Recording Indus. Ass'n of Am. v. Diamond Multimedia Sys., Inc.*, 180 F.3d 1072, 1078 (9th Cir. 1999). Second, notwithstanding Napster's claim that computers are "digital audio recording devices," computers do not make "digital music recordings" as defined by the Audio Home Recording Act. *Id.* at 1077 (citing S.Rep. 102–294) ("There are simply no grounds in either the plain language of the definition or in the legislative history for interpreting the term 'digital musical recording' to include songs fixed on computer hard drives.").

B. DIGITAL MILLENNIUM COPYRIGHT ACT

Napster also interposes a statutory limitation on liability by asserting the protections of the "safe harbor" from copyright infringement suits for "Internet service providers" contained in the Digital Millennium Copyright Act, 17 U.S.C. § 512. See *Napster*, 114 F.Supp.2d at 919 n.24. The district court did not give this statutory limitation any weight favoring a denial of temporary injunctive relief. The court concluded that Napster "has failed to persuade this court that subsection 512(d) shelters contributory infringers." *Id.*

We need not accept a blanket conclusion that § 512 of the Digital Millennium Copyright Act will never protect secondary infringers. See S.Rep. 105–190, at 40 (1998) ("The limitations in subsections (a) through (d) protect qualifying service providers from liability for all monetary relief for direct, vicarious, and contributory infringement."), reprinted in Melville B. Nimmer & David Nimmer, Nimmer on Copyright: Congressional Committee Reports on the Digital Millennium Copyright Act and Concurrent Amendments (2000); see also Charles S. Wright, Actual Versus Legal Control: Reading Vicarious Liability for Copyright Infringement Into the Digital Millennium Copyright Act of 1998, 75 Wash.L.Rev. 1005, 1028–31 (July 2000) ("[T]he committee reports leave no doubt that Congress intended to provide some relief from vicarious liability").

We do not agree that Napster's potential liability for contributory and vicarious infringement renders the Digital Millennium Copyright Act inapplicable per se. We instead recognize that this issue will be more fully developed at trial. At this stage of the litigation, plaintiffs raise serious questions regarding Napster's ability to obtain shelter under § 512, and plaintiffs also demonstrate that the balance of hardships tips in their favor. See *Prudential Real Estate*, 204 F.3d at 874; see also *Micro Star v. Formgen, Inc.* 154 F.3d 1107, 1109 (9th Cir. 1998) ("A party seeking a preliminary injunction must show ... 'that serious questions going to the merits were raised and the balance of hardships tips sharply in its favor.'").

Plaintiffs have raised and continue to raise significant questions under this statute, including: (1) whether Napster is an Internet service provider as defined by 17 U.S.C. § 512(d); (2) whether copyright owners must give a service provider "official" notice of infringing activity in order for it to have knowledge or awareness of infringing activity on its system; and (3) whether Napster complies with § 512(i), which requires a service provider to timely establish a detailed copyright compliance policy. See *A&M Records, Inc. v. Napster, Inc.*, No. 99-05183, 2000 WL 573136 (N.D. Cal. May 12, 2000) (denying summary judgment to Napster under a different subsection of the Digital Millennium Copyright Act, § 512(a)).

The district court considered ample evidence to support its determination that the balance of hardships tips in plaintiffs' favor:

> Any destruction of Napster, Inc. by a preliminary injunction is speculative compared to the statistical evidence of massive, unauthorized downloading and uploading of plaintiffs' copyrighted works—as many as 10,000 files per second by defendant's own admission. See Kessler Dec. P 29. The court has every reason to believe that, without a preliminary injunction, these numbers will mushroom as Napster users, and newcomers attracted by the publicity, scramble to obtain as much free music as possible before trial. 114 F.Supp.2d at 926.

VII

Napster contends that even if the district court's preliminary determinations that it is liable for facilitating copyright infringement are correct, the district court improperly rejected valid affirmative defenses of waiver, implied license and copyright misuse. We address the defenses in turn.

A. WAIVER

"Waiver is the intentional relinquishment of a known right with knowledge of its existence and the intent to relinquish it." *United States v. King Features Entm't, Inc.*, 843 F.2d 394, 399 (9th Cir. 1988). In copyright, waiver or abandonment of copyright "occurs only if there is an intent by the copyright proprietor to surrender rights in his work." 4 Melville B. Nimmer & David Nimmer, Nimmer On Copyright P 13.06 (2000); see also *Micro Star v. Formgen, Inc.*, 154 F.3d 1107, 1114 (9th Cir. 1998) (discussing abandonment).

Napster argues that the district court erred in not finding that plaintiffs knowingly provided consumers with technology designed to copy and distribute MP3 files over the Internet and, thus, waived any legal authority to exercise exclusive control over creation and distribution of MP3 files. The district court, however, was not convinced "that the record companies created the monster that is now devouring their intellectual property rights." *Napster*, 114 F.Supp.2d at 924. We find no error in the district court's finding that "in hastening the proliferation of MP3

files, plaintiffs did [nothing] more than seek partners for their commercial downloading ventures and develop music players for files they planned to sell over the Internet." *Id.*.

B. IMPLIED LICENSE

Napster also argues that plaintiffs granted the company an implied license by encouraging MP3 file exchange over the Internet. Courts have found implied licenses only in "narrow" circumstances where one party "created a work at [the other's] request and handed it over, intending that [the other] copy and distribute it." *Smith-Kline Beecham Consumer Healthcare, L.P. v. Watson Pharms., Inc.*, 211 F.3d 21, 25 (2d Cir. 2000) (quoting *Effects Assocs., Inc. v. Cohen*, 908 F.2d 555, 558 (9th Cir. 1990)), cert. denied, 121 S.Ct. 173 (2000). The district court observed that no evidence exists to support this defense: "indeed, the RIAA gave defendant express notice that it objected to the availability of its members' copyrighted music on Napster." *Napster*, 114 F.Supp.2d at 924–25. The record supports this conclusion.

C. MISUSE

The defense of copyright misuse forbids a copyright holder from "secur[ing] an exclusive right or limited monopoly not granted by the Copyright Office." *Lasercomb Am., Inc. v. Reynolds*, 911 F.2d 970, 977–79 (4th Cir. 1990), quoted in *Practice Mgmt. Info. Corp. v. American Med. Ass'n*, 121 F.3d 516, 520 (9th Cir.), amended by 133 F.3d 1140 (9th Cir. 1997). Napster alleges that online distribution is not within the copyright monopoly. According to Napster, plaintiffs have colluded to "use their copyrights to extend their control to online distributions."

We find no error in the district court's preliminary rejection of this affirmative defense. The misuse defense prevents copyright holders from leveraging their limited monopoly to allow them control of areas outside the monopoly. See *Lasercomb*, 911 F.2d at 976–77; see also *Religious Tech. Ctr. v. Lerma*, No. 95-1107A, 1996 WL 633131, at *11 (E.D. Va. Oct. 4, 1996) (listing circumstances which indicate improper leverage). There is no evidence here that plaintiffs seek to control areas outside of their grant of monopoly. Rather, plaintiffs seek to control reproduction and distribution of their copyrighted works, exclusive rights of copyright holders. 17 U.S.C. § 106; see also, e.g., *UMG Recordings*, 92 F.Supp.2d at 351 ("A [copyright holder's] 'exclusive' rights, derived from the Constitution and the Copyright Act, include the right, within broad limits, to curb the development of such a derivative market by refusing to license a copyrighted work or by doing so only on terms the copyright owner finds acceptable."). That the copyrighted works are transmitted in another medium—MP3 format rather than audio CD—has no bearing on our analysis. See *Id.* at 351 (finding that reproduction of audio CD into MP3 format does not "transform" the work).

VIII

The district court correctly recognized that a preliminary injunction against Napster's participation in copyright infringement is not only warranted but required. We believe, however, that the scope of the injunction needs modification in light of our opinion. Specifically, we reiterate that contributory liability may potentially be imposed only to the extent that Napster: (1) receives reasonable knowledge of specific infringing files with copyrighted musical compositions and sound recordings; (2) knows or should know that such files are available on the Napster system; and (3) fails to act to prevent viral distribution of the works. See *Netcom*, 907 F.Supp. at 1374–75. The mere existence of the Napster system, absent actual notice and Napster's demonstrated failure to remove the offending material, is insufficient to impose contributory liability. See *Sony*, 464 U.S. at 442–43.

Conversely, Napster may be vicariously liable when it fails to affirmatively use its ability to patrol its system and preclude access to potentially infringing files listed in its search index. Napster has both the ability to use its search function to identify infringing musical recordings and the right to bar participation of users who engage in the transmission of infringing files.

The preliminary injunction which we stayed is overbroad because it places on Napster the entire burden of ensuring that no "copying, downloading, uploading, transmitting, or distributing"

of plaintiffs' works occur on the system. As stated, we place the burden on plaintiffs to provide notice to Napster of copyrighted works and files containing such works available on the Napster system before Napster has the duty to disable access to the offending content. Napster, however, also bears the burden of policing the system within the limits of the system. Here, we recognize that this is not an exact science in that the files are user named. In crafting the injunction on remand, the district court should recognize that Napster's system does not currently appear to allow Napster access to users' MP3 files.

Based on our decision to remand, Napster's additional arguments on appeal going to the scope of the injunction need not be addressed. We, however, briefly address Napster's First Amendment argument so that it is not reasserted on remand. Napster contends that the present injunction violates the First Amendment because it is broader than necessary. The company asserts two distinct free speech rights: (1) its right to publish a "directory" (here, the search index) and (2) its users' right to exchange information. We note that First Amendment concerns in copyright are allayed by the presence of the fair use doctrine. See 17 U.S.C. § 107; see generally *Nihon Keizai Shimbun v. Comline Business Data, Inc.*, 166 F.3d 65, 74 (2d Cir. 1999); *Netcom*, 923 F.Supp. at 1258 (stating that the Copyright Act balances First Amendment concerns with the rights of copyright holders). There was a preliminary determination here that Napster users are not fair users. Uses of copyrighted material that are not fair uses are rightfully enjoined. See *Dr. Seuss Enters. v. Penguin Books USA, Inc.*, 109 F.3d 1394, 1403 (9th Cir. 1997) (rejecting defendants' claim that injunction would constitute a prior restraint in violation of the First Amendment).

IX

We address Napster's remaining arguments: (1) that the court erred in setting a $5 million bond, and (2) that the district court should have imposed a constructive royalty payment structure in lieu of an injunction.

A. BOND

Napster argues that the $5 million bond is insufficient because the company's value is between $1.5 and $2 billion. We review objections to the amount of a bond for abuse of discretion. *Walczak v. EPL Prolong, Inc.*, 198 F.3d 725 (9th Cir. 1999).

We are reluctant to dramatically raise bond amounts on appeal. See *GoTo.com, Inc. v. The Walt Disney Co.*, 202 F.3d 1199, 1211 (9th Cir. 2000); see also Fed.R.Civ.P. 65(c). The district court considered competing evidence of Napster's value and the deleterious effect that any injunction would have upon the Napster system. We cannot say that Judge Patel abused her discretion when she fixed the penal sum required for the bond.

B. ROYALTIES

Napster contends that the district court should have imposed a monetary penalty by way of a compulsory royalty in place of an injunction. We are asked to do what the district court refused.

Napster tells us that "where great public injury would be worked by an injunction, the courts might ... award damages or a continuing royalty instead of an injunction in such special circumstances." *Abend v. MCA, Inc.*, 863 F.2d 1465, 1479 (9th Cir. 1988) (quoting 3 Melville B. Nimmer & David Nimmer, Nimmer On Copyright §S 14.06[B] (1988)), aff'd, 495 U.S. 207 (1990). We are at a total loss to find any "special circumstances" simply because this case requires us to apply well-established doctrines of copyright law to a new technology. Neither do we agree with Napster that an injunction would cause "great public injury." Further, we narrowly construe any suggestion that compulsory royalties are appropriate in this context because Congress has arguably limited the application of compulsory royalties to specific circumstances, none of which are present here. See 17 U.S.C. § 115.

The Copyright Act provides for various sanctions for infringers. See, e.g., 17 U.S.C. §§ 502 (injunctions); 504 (damages); and 506 (criminal penalties); see also 18 U.S.C. § 2319A (criminal penalties for the unauthorized fixation of and trafficking in sound recordings and music videos of live musical performances). These statutory sanctions represent a more than adequate legislative solution to the problem created by copyright infringement.

Imposing a compulsory royalty payment schedule would give Napster an "easy out" of this case. If such royalties were imposed, Napster would avoid penalties for any future violation of an injunction, statutory copyright damages and any possible criminal penalties for continuing infringement. The royalty structure would also grant Napster the luxury of either choosing to continue and pay royalties or shut down. On the other hand, the wronged parties would be forced to do business with a company that profits from the wrongful use of intellectual properties. Plaintiffs would lose the power to control their intellectual property: they could not make a business decision not to license their property to Napster, and, in the event they planned to do business with Napster, compulsory royalties would take away the copyright holders' ability to negotiate the terms of any contractual arrangement.

X

We affirm in part, reverse in part and remand.

We direct that the preliminary injunction fashioned by the district court prior to this appeal shall remain stayed until it is modified by the district court to conform to the requirements of this opinion. We order a partial remand of this case on the date of the filing of this opinion for the limited purpose of permitting the district court to proceed with the settlement and entry of the modified preliminary injunction.

Even though the preliminary injunction requires modification, appellees have substantially and primarily prevailed on appeal. Appellees shall recover their statutory costs on appeal. See Fed.R.App.P. 39(a)(4) ("[i]f a judgment is affirmed in part, reversed in part, modified, or vacated, costs are taxed only as the court orders.").

AFFIRMED IN PART, REVERSED IN PART AND REMANDED.

[Also see appeal at 284 F.3d 1091 (2002)]

JORDAN v. TOWN OF PRATT

United States District Court, S.D. West Virginia
886 F. Supp. 555 (S.D. W. Va. 1995)
May 24, 1995
Haden, Chief Judge

[See Chapter 7.]

Charles Jordan contends Mark March, a police officer for the Town of Pratt, West virginia, violated his civil rights by arresting him June 21, 1993 on a charge of impersonating a police officer. He contends he "was employed as [sic] by the Air National Guard ... to function as a military police officer one weekend per month, two weeks of the year and any other occasions when [he] was on active duty, and [he] served as a police/security guard for the Adjutant General of West Virginia the remainder of [his] employment." He asserts March and defendant Williams came to his home on June 19, 1993 in response to a complaint concerning a neighbor's dog. Mr. Jordan contends March inquired where he was employed, and when informed Jordan was employed by the Air National Guard, March began "rudely interrogating" him, accused him of lying, and unsuccessfully attempted to take his badge. Mr. Jordan further contends March informed him he was going to check his credentials as a police officer and if he determined they were not legitimate, he would return and arrest Jordan. Mr. Jordan asserts March telephoned a Lieutenant Colonel Johnson of the Air National Guard to determine whether Jordan was a police officer and Johnson informed March that Jordan was a police officer.

Mr. Jordan contends that despite knowing Jordan was a police officer, Officer March, with the approval of Chief of Police Williams, swore out a false complaint and warrant for Jordan's arrest on a charge of impersonating a police officer. Thereafter, Officer March arrested Jordan. Jordan spent approximately four hours in custody. The charge was dropped six weeks later.

The Court must examine whether defendants are protected from suit by the doctrine of qualified immunity. In *Wiley v. Doory,* 14 F.3d 993, 995 (4th Cir. 1994) our Court of Appeals discussed generally the application of qualified immunity as follows:

> Qualified immunity shields a governmental official from liability for civil monetary damages if the officer's 'conduct does not violate clearly established statutory or constitutional rights of which a reasonable person would have known." "In determining whether the specific right allegedly violated was 'clearly established,' the proper focus is not upon the right at its most general or abstract level, but at the level of its application to the specific conduct being challenged." Moreover, "the manner in which this [clearly established] right applies to the actions of the official must also be apparent." As such, if there is a 'legitimate question' as to whether an official's conduct constitutes a constitutional violation, the official is entitled to qualified immunity.

The test for determining whether qualified immunity is available for a particular defendant is an objectively reasonable one. *Shaw v. Stroud,* 13 F.3d 791, 801 (4th Cir.), *cert. denied,* ___ U.S. ___ , 115 S.Ct. 67, 130 L.Ed.2d 24, *and cert. denied,* ___ U.S. ___, 115 S.Ct. 68, 130 L.Ed.2d 24 (1994). Describing application of the "objectively reasonable" qualified immunity test to actions of police officers, our Court of Appeals has observed:

> "[O]fficers are entitled to qualified immunity when they rely on standard operating procedures, if that reliance is reasonable. A police officer is entitled to prevail on an assertion of qualified immunity if a reasonalbe officer possessing the same information would have believed his conduct was lawful."

"[T]he basic purpose of qualified immunity ... is to spare individual officials the burdens and uncertainties of standing trial in those instances where their conduct would strike an objective observer as falling within the range of reasonable judgment. ... '[T]he determination whether a reasonable person in the officer's position would have known that his conduct would violate the right at issue must be made ... in light of any exigencies of time and circumstance that reasonably may have affected the officer's perception.'"

The express purpose of the test of objective reasonableness is to accord "police officers latitude in exercising what are inescapably discretionary functions replete with close judgment calls." ... Moreover, "[b]ecause qualified immunity is designed to shield officers not only from liability but from the burdens of litigation, its establishment at the pleading or summary judgment stage has been specifically encouraged."

***

The right in issue is the Fourth Amendment right "not to be arrested except upon probably cause to believe" Jordan had violated West Virginia's law against impersonating a law enforcement officer pursuant to *W.Va. Code* § 61-1-9 (1990). In order to defeat the motion for summary judgment, Jordan bears the burden of presenting sufficient evidence supporting his contention he was arrested without probable cause.

***

The offense contours are thus straightforward: whenever one falsely represents himself to be a law enforcement officer with the intent to deceive another, that person has violated the statute. The parties dispute whether Jordan's particular employment met the definition of law enforcement officer.

Jordan contends he was clearly a law enforcement officer under the statute because he was commissioned as a police officer for the adjutant general of West Virginia. ...

Defendants argue, in essence, that Jordan's position as security guard with the West Virginia National Guard does not qualify as a law enforcement officer for the purposes of *W.Va. Code* § 61-1-9. The legal question for the Court is whether it was clearly established at the time of the incident that a security guard with the West virginia National Guard qualifies as a law

enforcement officer for the purposes of *W.Va. Code* § 61-1-9.

... It is not incumbent for this Court to determine definitively whether adjutant general security guards are the law enforcement officers referred to in § 61-1-9 because it appears, even if they are, such was not clearly established or known at the time of Mr. Jordan's arrest. ... Moreover, although they are "deemed to have met all the requirements for certification as a law enforcement officer," they are not deemed to be law enforcement officers as that term is used in *W.Va. Code* § 61-1-9. Their status appears to be more accurately described as that of quasi-law enforcement officers. Therefore, the Court concludes the law was not *clearly* established that Mr. Jordan's employment as an adjutant general's security guard constituted employment as a law enforcement officer, as that term is used in § 61-1-9.

Defendants have presented evidence Officer March received a complaint from a neighbor of Mr. Jordan who asserted Mr. Jordan had represented himself to be a police officer with authority in the Town of Pratt. Although Jordan challenges the sum of the facts asserted by the neighbor, it is undisputed Officer March relied upon those facts in seeking a warrant for the arrest. Based upon those facts known to Officer March, the Court concludes a prudent police officer of reasonable caution could determine appropriately Mr. Jordan was in violation of the statute. The complaint information supports a finding of probable cause to make the arrest.

Because the Court determines probable cause existed to make the arrest, Defendants' motion for summary judgment on Mr. Jordan's § 1983 claim is GRANTED.

... Because Mr. Jordan failed to do more than assert bald allegations of state law violations, those state law claims will be dismissed and summary judgment on those issues will be GRANTED in favor of Defendants.

Mrs. Jordan has asserted a claim of invasion of privacy under West Virginia state law. She contends, "[a]s a result of his position as Chief of Police, Defendant Williams came into information regarding the sexual assault of the daughter of the Plaintiff," and he "intentionally and negligently failed to keep this information confidential as required by state law and the dictates of his position, and did communicate the same in order to embarrass Plaintiff[.]" Defendants contend Mrs. Jordan has not established sufficiently an invasion of privacy claim. The Court agrees.

***

By her deposition testimony Mrs. Jordan stated Chief Williams told his daughter of the assault incident involving Mrs. Jordan's daughter in order to ascertain whether his own daughter had been similarly victimized. According to Mrs. Jordan, Chief Williams was concerned for his daughter because the two girls were playmates. Significantly, Mrs. Jordan stated she could understand Chief Williams concern. In such a situation, it is apparent to the Court Chief Williams conversation with his daughter was not unreasonable, although perhaps a poor exercise in judgment. Therefore, defendants' motion for summary judgment in regard to Mrs. Jordan's invasion of privacy claim is GRANTED.

Based upon the foregoing, Defendants' motion for summary judgment is GRANTED, and this action is dismissed.

MACPHERSON v. BUICK MOTOR COMPANY
Court of Appeals of New York
217 N.Y. 382
January 24, 1916
Cardozo, Justice
[See Chapter 9.]

The defendant is a manufacturer of automobiles. It sold an automobile to a retail dealer. The retail dealer resold to the plaintiff. While, the plaintiff was in the car, it suddenly collapsed. He was thrown out and injured. One of the wheels was made of defective wood, and its spokes crumbled into fragments. The wheel was not made by the defendant; it was bought from another manufacturer. There is evidence, however, that its defects could have been discovered by reasonable inspection, and that an inspection was omitted. There is no claim that the defendant knew of the defect and willfully concealed it. The case, in other words, is not brought within the rule of *Kuelling v. Lean Mfg. Co.* (183 N.Y. 78) The charge is one, not of fraud, but of negligence. The question to be determined is whether the defendant owed a duty of care and vigilance to any one but the immediate purchaser.

The foundations of this branch of the law, at least in this state, were laid in *Thomas v. Winchester* (6 N.Y. 397). A poison was falsely labeled. The sale was made to a druggist, who in turn sold to a customer. The customer recovered damages from the seller who affixed the label. The defendant's negligence, it was said, "put human life in imminent danger." A poison falsely labeled is likely to injure any one who gets it. Because the danger is to be foreseen, there is a duty to avoid the injury. Cases were cited by way of illustration in which manufacturers were not subject any duty irrespective of contract. The distinction was said to be that their conduct, though negligent, was not likely to result in injury to any one except the purchaser. We are not required to say whether the chance of injury was always so remote as the distinction assumes. Some of the illustrations might be rejected to-day. The principle of the distinction is for present purposes the important thing.

Thomas v. Winchester became quickly a landmark of the law. In the application of its principle there may at times have been uncertainty or even error. There has never in this state been doubt or disavowal of the principle itself. The chief cases are well known, yet to recall some of them will be helpful. *Loop v. Litchfield* (42 N.Y.

351) is the earliest. It was the case of a defect in a small balance wheel used on a circular saw. The manufacturer pointed out the defect to the buyer, who wished a cheap article and was ready to assume the risk. The risk can hardly have been an imminent one, for the wheel lasted five years before it broke. In the meanwhile the buyer had made a lease of the machinery. It was held that the manufacturer was not answerable to the lessee. *Loop v. Litchfield* was followed in *Losee v. Clute* (51 N.Y. 494), the case of the explosion of a steam boiler. That decision has been criticized (*Thompson on Negligence*, 233; *Shearman & Redfield on Negligence* [6th ed.] § 117); but it must be confined to its special facts. It was put upon the ground that the risk of injury was too remote. The buyer in that case had not only accepted the boiler, but had tested it. The manufacturer knew that his own test was not the final one. The finality of the test has a bearing on the measure of diligence owing to persons other than the purchaser (Beven, *Negligence* [3d ed.], pp. 50, 51, 54; Wharton, *Negligence* [2d ed.] § 134).

These early cases suggest a narrow construction of the rule. Later cases, however, evince a more liberal spirit. First in importance is *Devlin v. Smith* (89 N.Y. 470). The defendant, a contractor, built a scaffold for a painter. The painter's servants were injured. The contractor was held liable. He knew that the scaffold, if improperly constructed, was a most dangerous trap. He knew that it was to be used by the workmen. He was building it for that very purpose. Building it for their use, he owed them a duty, irrespective of his contract with their master, to build it with care.

From *Devlin v. Smith* we pass over intermediate cases and turn to the latest case in this court in which *Thomas v. Winchester* was followed. That case is *Statler v. Ray Mfg. Co.* (195 N.Y. 478, 480). The defendant manufactured a large coffee urn. It was installed in a restaurant. When heated, the urn exploded and injured the plaintiff. We held that the manufacturer was liable. We said that the urn "was of such a character inherently that, when applied to the purposes for which it was designed, it was liable to become a

source of great danger to many people if not carefully and properly constructed."

It may be that *Devlin v. Smith* and *Statler v. Ray Mfg. Co.* have extended the rule of *Thomas v. Winchester*. If so, this court is committed to the extension. The defendant argues that things imminently danger to life are poisons, explosives, deadly weapons—things whose normal function it is to injure or destroy. Whatever the rule in *Thomas v. Winchester* may once have been, it has no longer that restricted meaning. A scaffold (*Devlin v. Smith, supra*) is not inherently a destructive instrument. It becomes destructive only if imperfectly constructed. A large coffee urn (*Statler v. Ray .Mfg. Co., supra*) may have within itself, if negligently made, the potency of danger, yet no one thinks of it as an implement whose normal function is destruction. What is true of the coffee urn is equally true of bottles of aerated water (*Torgeson v. Schultz*, 192 N.Y. 156). We have mentioned only cases in this court. But the rule has received a like extension in our courts of intermediate appeal. In *Burke v. Ireland* (26 App.Div., 487), in an opinion by CULLEN, J., it was applied to a builder who constructed a defective building; in *Kahner v. Otis Elevator Co.* (96 App.Div. 169) to the manufacturer of an elevator; in *Davies v. Pelham Hod Elevating Co.* (65 Hun, 573; affirmed in this court without opinion, 146 N.Y. 363) to a contractor who furnished a defective rope with knowledge of the purpose for which the rope was to be used. We are not required at this time either to approve or to disapprove the application of the rule that was made in these cases. It is enough that they help to characterize the trend of judicial thought.

Devlin v. Smith was decided in 1882. A year later, a very similar case came before the Court of Appeal in England (*Heaven v. Pender*, L.R. [11 Q.B.D.] 503). We find in the opinion of Brett, M.R., afterwards Lord Esher, (p. 510), the same conception of a duty irrespective of contract imposed upon the manufacturer by the law itself: "Whenever one person supplies goods, or machinery, or the like, for the purpose of their being used by another person under such circumstances that every one of ordinary sense would, if he thought, recognize at once that unless he used ordinary care and skill with regard to the condition of the thing supplied or the mode of supplying it, there will be danger of injury to the person or property of him for whose use the thing is supplied, and who is to use it, a duty arises to use ordinary care and skill as to the condition or manner of supplying such thing." He then points out that for a neglect of such ordinary care or skill whereby injury happens, the appropriate remedy is an action for negligence. The right to enforce this liability is not to be confined to the buyer. The right he says extends to the persons or class of persons for whose use the thing is supplied. It is enough that the goods "would in all probability be used at once ... before a reasonable opportunity for discovering any defect which might exist," and that the thing supplied is of such a nature "that a neglect of ordinary care or skill as to its condition or the manner of supplying it would probably cause danger to the person or property of the person for whose use it was supplied, and who was about to use it." On the other hand, he would exclude a case "in which the goods are supplied under circumstances in which it would be a chance by whom they would be used or whether they would be used or not, or whether they would be used before there would probably be means of observing any defect," or where the goods are of such a nature that "a want of care or skill as to their condition or the manner of supplying them would not probably produce danger of injury to person or property." What was said by Lord Esher in that case did not command the full assent of his associates. His opinion has been criticized "as requiring every man to take affirmative precautions to protect his neighbors as well as to refrain from injuring them" (Bohlen, *Affirmative Obligations in the Law of Torts*, 44 Am.LawReg. [N.S.] 341). It may not be an accurate exposition of the law of England. Perhaps it may need some qualification even in our own state. Like most attempts at comprehensive definition, it may involve errors of inclusion and of exclusion. But its tests and standards, at least in their underlying principles, with whatever qualification may be called for

they are applied to varying conditions, are the tests and standards of our law.

We hold, then, that the principle of *Thomas v. Winchester* is not limited to poisons, explosives, and things of like nature, to things which in their normal operation are implements of destruction. If the nature of a thing is such that it is reasonably certain to place life and limb in peril when negligently made, it is then a thing of danger. Its nature gives warning of the consequence to be expected. If to the element of danger there is added knowledge that the thing will be used by persons other than the purchaser, and used without new tests, then, irrespective of contract, the manufacturer of this thing of danger is under a duty to make it carefully. That is as far as we need to go for the decision of this case. There must be knowledge of a danger, not merely possible but probable. It is possible to use almost anything in a way that will make it dangerous if defective. That is not enough to charge the manufacturer with a duty independent of his contract. Whether a given thing is dangerous may be sometimes a question for the court and sometimes a question for the jury. There must also be knowledge that in the usual course of events the danger will be shared by others than the buyer. Such knowledge may often be inferred from the nature of the transaction. But it is possible that even knowledge of the danger and of the use will not always be enough. The proximity or remoteness of the relation is a factor to be considered. We are dealing now with the liability of the manufacturer of the finished product who puts it on the market to be used without inspection by his customers. If he is negligent, where danger is to be foreseen, a liability will follow. We are not required at this time to say that it is legitimate to go back of the manufacturer of the finished product and hold the manufacturers of the component parts. To make their negligence a cause of imminent danger, an independent cause must often intervene; the manufacturer of the finished product must also fail in *his* duty of inspection. It may be that in those circumstances the negligence of the earlier members of the series is too remote to constitute, as to the ultimate user, an actionable wrong. (*Bevin on Negligence* [3d ed.] 50, 51, 54; *Wharton on Negligence* [2d ed.] § 134; *Leeds v. N. Y. Tel. Co.*, 178 N.Y. 118; *Sweet v. Perkins*, 196 N.Y. 482; *Hayes v. Hyde Park*, 153 Mass. 514, 516). We leave that question open. We shall have to deal with it when it arises. The difficulty which it suggests is not present in this case. There is here no break in the chain of cause and effect. In such circumstances, the presence of a known danger, attendant upon a known use, makes vigilance a duty. We have put aside the notion that the duty to safeguard life and limb, whenever consequences of negligence may be foreseen, grows out of contract and nothing else. We have put the source of obligation where it ought to be. We have put its source in the law.

From this survey of the decisions, there thus emerges a definition of the duty of a manufacturer which enables us to measure this defendant's liability. Beyond all question, the nature of an automobile gives warning of probable danger if its construction is defective. This automobile was designed to go fifty miles an hour. Unless its wheels were sound and strong, injury was almost certain. It was as much a thing of danger as a defective engine for a railroad. The defendant knew the danger. It knew also that the car would be used by persons other than the buyer. This was apparent from its size; there were seats for three persons. It was apparent also from the fact that the buyer was a dealer in cars, who bought to resell. The maker of this car supplied it for the use of purchasers from the dealer as plainly as the contractor in *Devlin v. Smith* supplied the scaffold for use by the servants of the owner. The dealer was indeed the one person of whom it might be said with some approach to certainty that by him the car would not be used. Yet the defendant would have us say that he was the one person whom it was under a legal duty to protect. The law does not lead us to so inconsequent a conclusion. Precedents drawn from the days of travel by stage coach do not fit the conditions of travel today. The principle that the danger must be imminent does not change, but the things subject to the principle do change. They are whatever the developing civilization require them to be.

In reaching this conclusion, we do not ignore the decisions to the contrary in other jurisdictions. It was held in *Cadillac M. C. Co. v. Johnson* (221 Fed.Rep. 801) that an automobile is not within the rule of *Thomas v. Winchester*. There was, however a vigorous dissent. Opposed to that decision is one of the Court of Appeals in Kentucky (*Olds Motor Works v. Shaffer*, 145 Ky. 616). The earlier cases are summarized by Judge Sanborn in *Huset v. J.I. Case Threshing Machine Co.* (120 Fed.Rep. 865). Some of them, at first sight inconsistent with our conclusion, may be reconciled upon the ground that the negligence was too remote, and that another cause had intervened. But even when they cannot be reconciled the difference is rather in the application of the principle than in the principle itself. Judge Sanborn says, for example, that the contractor who builds a bridge, or the manufacturer who builds a car, cannot ordinarily foresee injury to other persons than the owner as the probable result (120 Fed.Rep. 865 at 867). We take a different view. We think that injury to others is to be foreseen not merely as a possible but an almost inevitable result. (See the trenchant criticism in *Bohlen*, *supra*, at p. 351). Indeed, Judge Sanborn concedes that his view is not to be reconciled with our decision in *Devlin v. Smith* (*supra*). The doctrine of that decision has now become the settled law of this state and we have no desire to depart from it.

In England the limits of the rule are still unsettled. *Winterbottom v. Wright* (10 M. & W. 109) is often cited. The defendant undertook to provide a mail coach to carry the mail bags. The coach broke down from a latent defect in its construction. The defendant, however, was not the manufacturer. The court held that he was not liable for injuries to a passenger. The case was decided on a demurrer to the declaration. Lord Esher points out in *Heaven v. Pender* (*supra*, at 513) the form of the declaration was subject to criticism. It did not fairly suggest the existence of a duty aside from the special contract which was the plaintiff's main reliance. (See the criticism of *Winterbottom v. Wright* in *Bohlen*, *supra*, at 281, 283). At all events, in *Heaven v. Pender* (*supra*) the defendant, a dock owner, who put up a staging outside a ship, was held liable to the servants of the shipowner. In *Elliott v. Hall* (15 Q.B.D. 315) the defendant sent out a defective truck laden with goods which he had sold. The buyer's servants unloaded it, and were injured because of the defects. It was held that the defendant was under a duty "not to be guilty of negligence with regard to the state and condition of the truck." There seems to have been a return to the doctrine of *Winterbottom v. Wright* in *Earl v. Lubbock* (L.R. [1905] 1 K.B. 253). In that case, however, as in the earlier one, the defendant was not the manufacturer. He had merely made a contract to keep the van in repair. A later case (*White v. Steadman*, L.R. [1913], 3 K.B. 340, 348) emphasizes that element. A livery stable keeper who sent out a vicious horse, was held liable not merely to his customer but also to another occupant of the carriage, and *Thomas v. Winchester* was cited and followed (*White v. Steadman, supra*, at 348, 349). It was again cited and followed in *Dominion Natural Gas Co. v. Collins* (L.R. [1909] A.C. 640, 646). From these cases a consistent principle is with difficulty extracted. The English courts, however, agree with ours in holding that one who invites another to make use of an appliance is bound to the exercise of reasonable care (*Caledonian Ry. Co. v. Mulholland*, L.R. [1898] A.C. 216, 227; *Indermaur v. Dames*, L.R. [1 C. P.] 274). That at bottom is the underlying principle of *Devlin v. Smith*. The contractor who builds the scaffold invites the owner's workmen to use it. The manufacturer who sells the automobile to the retail dealer invites the dealer's customers to use it. The invitation is addressed in the one case to determinate persons and in the other to an indeterminate class, but in each case it is equally plain and in each its consequences must the same.

There is nothing anomalous in a rule which imposes upon A who has contracted with B a duty to C and D and others according as he knows or does not know that the subject-matter of the contract is intended for their use. We may find an analogy in the law which measures the liability of landlords. If A leases to B a tumble-down house he is not liable, in the absence of

fraud, to B's guests who enter it and are injured. This is because B is then under the duty to repair it, the lessor has the right to suppose that he will fulfill that duty, and if he omits to do so, his guests must look to him (*Bohlen, supra*, at 276). But if A leases a building to be used by the lessee at once as a place of public entertainment, the rule is different. There injury to persons other than the lessee is to be foreseen, and foresight of the consequences involves the creation of a duty (*Junkermann v. Tilyou R. Co.*, 213 N.Y. 404, and cases there cited).

In this view of the defendant's liability there is nothing inconsistent with the theory of liability with which the case was tried. It is true that the court told the jury that "an automobile is not an inherently dangerous vehicle." The meaning however, is made plain by the text. The meaning is that danger is not to be expected when the vehicle is well constructed. The court left it to the jury to say whether the defendant ought to have foreseen that the car, if negligently constructed, would become "imminently dangerous." Subtle distinctions are drawn by the defendant between things inherently dangerous and things imminently dangerous, but the case does not turn upon these verbal niceties. If danger was to be expected as reasonably certain, there was a duty of vigilance, and this whether you call the danger inherent or imminent. In varying forms that thought was put before the jury. We do not say that the court would not have been justified in ruling as a matter of law that the car was a dangerous thing. If there was any error, it was none of which the defendant can complain.

We think the defendant was not absolved from a duty of inspection because it bought the wheels from a reputable manufacturer. It was not merely a dealer in automobiles. It was a manufacturer of automobiles. It was responsible for the finished product. It was not at liberty to put the finished product on the market without subjecting the component parts to ordinary and simple tests (*Richmond & Danville R. R. Co. v. Elliott*, 149 U.S. 266, 272). Under the charge of the trial judge nothing more was required of it. The obligation to inspect must vary with the nature of the thing to be inspected. The more probable the danger, the greater the need of caution. There is little analogy between this case and *Carlson v. Phoenix Bridge. Co.* (132 N.Y. 273) where the defendant bought a tool for a servant's use. The making of tools was not the business in which the master was engaged. Reliance on the skill of the manufacturer was proper and almost inevitable. But that is not the defendant's situation. Both by its relation to the work and by the nature of its business it is charged with a stricter duty.

Other rulings complained of have been considered but no error his been found in them.

The judgment should be affirmed with costs.

Bartlett, Justice dissenting

The plaintiff was injured in consequence of the collapse of a wheel of an automobile manufactured by the defendant corporation which sold it to a firm of automobile dealers in Schenectady, who in turn sold the car to the plaintiff. The wheel was purchased by the Buick Motor Company ready made, from the Imperial Wheel Company of Flint, Michigan, a reputable manufacturer of automobile wheels which had furnished the defendant with eighty thousand wheels, none of which had proved to be made of defective wood prior to the accident in the present case. The defendant relied upon the wheel manufacturer to make all necessary tests as to the strength of the material therein and made no such tests itself. The present suit is an action for negligence brought by the subvendee of the motor car against the manufacturer as the original vendor. The evidence warranted a finding by the jury that the wheel which collapsed was defective when it left the hands of the defendant. The automobile was being prudently operated at the time of the accident and was moving at a speed of only eight miles an hour. There was no allegation or proof of any actual knowledge of the defect on the part of the defendant or any suggestion that any element of fraud or deceit or misrepresentation entered into the sale.

The theory upon which the case was submitted to the jury by the learned judge who presided at the trial was that, although an automobile is not an inherently dangerous vehicle, it may become such if equipped with a weak wheel; and that if the motor car in question when it was put upon the market was in itself inherently dangerous by reason of its being equipped with a weak wheel, the defendant was chargeable with a knowledge of the defect so far as it might be discovered by a reasonable inspection and the application of reasonable tests. This liability, it was further held, was not limited to the original vendee, but extended to a subvendee like the plaintiff, who was not a party to the original contract of sale.

I think that these rulings, which have been approved by the Appellate Division, extend the liability of the vendor of a manufactured article further than any case which has yet received the sanction of this court. It has heretofore been held in this state that the liability of the vendor of a manufactured article for negligence arising out of the existence of defects therein does not extend to strangers injured in consequence of such defects but is confined to the immediate vendee. The exceptions to this general rule which have thus far been recognized in New York are cases in which the article sold was of such a character that danger to life or limb was involved in the ordinary use thereof; in other words where the article sold was inherently dangerous. As has already been pointed out the learned trial judge instructed the jury that an automobile is not an inherently dangerous vehicle.

The late Chief Justice Cooley of Michigan, one of the most learned and accurate of American law writers states the general rule thus: "The general rule is that a contractor, manufacturer, vendor or furnisher of any article is not liable to third parties who have no contractual relations with him for negligence in the construction, manufacture or sale of such article." (2 *Cooley on Torts*: [3d ed.], 1486).

The leading English authority in support of this rule, to which all the later cases on the same subject refer, is *Winterbottom v. Wright* (10 Meeson & Welsby 109), which was an action by the driver of a stage coach against a contractor who had agreed with the postmaster-general to provide and keep the vehicle in repair for the purpose of conveying the royal mail over a prescribed route. The coach broke down and upset, injuring the driver, who sought to recover against the contractor on account of its defective construction. The Court of Exchequer denied him any right of recovery on the ground that there was no privity of contract between the parties, the agreement having been made with the postmaster-general alone. "If the plaintiff can sue," said Lord Abinger, the Chief Baron, "every passenger or even any person passing along the road, who was injured by the upsetting of the coach, might bring a similar action. Unless we confine the operation of such contracts as this to the parties who enter into them, the most absurd and outrageous consequences, to which I can see no limit, would ensue."

The doctrine of that decision was recognized as the law of this state by the leading New York case of *Thomas v. Winchester* (6 N.Y. 397, 408) which, however, involved an exception to the general rule. There the defendant, who was a dealer in medicines, sold to a druggist a quantity of belladonna, which is a deadly poison, negligently labeled as extract of dandelion. The druggist in good faith used the poison in filling a prescription calling for the harmless dandelion extract and the plaintiff for whom the prescription was put up was poisoned by the belladonna. This court held that the original vendor was liable for the injuries suffered by the patient. Chief Judge Ruggles, who delivered the opinion of the court, distinguished between an act of negligence imminently dangerous to the lives of others and one that is not so, saying: "If A. build a wagon and sell it to B. who sells it to C. and C. hires it to D., who in consequence of the gross negligence of A. in building the wagon is overturned and injured, D. cannot recover damages against A., the builder. A's obligation to build the wagon faithfully arises solely out of his contract with B. The public have nothing to do with it. ... So, for the same reason, if a horse be defectively shod by a smith and a person hiring the horse from the owner is thrown and injured in consequence of the smith's negligence in shoeing; the smith is not liable for the injury."

In *Torgeson v. Schultz* (192 N.Y. 156, 159) the defendant was the vendor of bottles of aerated water which were charged under high pressure and likely to explode unless used with precaution when exposed to sudden changes of temperature. The plaintiff, who was a servant of the purchaser, was injured by the explosion of one of these bottles. There was evidence tending to show that it had not been properly tested in order to insure users against such accidents. We held that the defendant corporation was liable notwithstanding the absence of any contract relation between it and the plaintiff "under the doctrine of *Thomas v. Winchester, supra*, and similar cases based upon the duty of the vendor of an article dangerous in its nature or likely to become so in the course of the ordinary usage to be contemplated by the vendor either to exercise due care to warn users of the danger or to take reasonable care to prevent the article sold from proving dangerous when subjected only to customary usage." The character of the exception to the general rule limiting liability for negligence to the original parties to the contract of sale was still more clearly stated by Judge Hiscock, writing for the court in *Statler v. Ray Manufacturing Co.* (195 N.Y. 478, 482), where he said that "in the case of an article of an inherently dangerous nature, a manufacturer may become liable for a negligent construction which, when added to the inherent character of the appliance, makes it imminently dangerous, and causes or contributes to the resulting injury not necessarily incident to the use of such in article if properly constructed, but naturally following from a defective construction." In that case the injuries were inflicted by the explosion of a battery of steam-driven coffee urns constituting an appliance liable to become dangerous in the course of ordinary usage.

The case of *Devlin v. Smith* (89 N.Y. 470) is cited as an authority in conflict with the view that the liability of the manufacturer and vendors extends to third parties only when the article manufactured and sold is inherently dangerous. In that case the builder of a scaffold ninety feet high which was erected for the purpose of enabling painters to stand upon it, was held to be liable to the administratrix of a painter who fell therefrom and was killed, being at the time in the employ of the person for whom the scaffold was built. It is said that the scaffold if property constructed was not inherently dangerous; and hence that this decision affirms the existence of liability in the case of an article not dangerous in itself but made so only in consequence of negligent construction. Whatever logical force there may be in this view it seems to me clear from the language of Judge Rapallo, who wrote the opinion of the court, that the scaffold was deemed to be an inherently dangerous structure; and that the case was decided as it was because the court entertained that view. Otherwise he would hardly have said, as he did, that the circumstances seemed to bring the case fairly within the principle of *Thomas v. Winchester.*

I do not see how we can uphold the judgment in the present case without overruling what has been so often said by this court and other courts of like authority in reference to the absence of any liability for negligence on the part of the original vendor of an ordinary carriage to any one except his immediate vendee. The absence of such liability was the very point actually decided in the English case of *Winterbottom v. Wright, supra*, and the illustration quoted from the opinion of Chief Judge Ruggles in *Thomas v. Winchester, supra*, assumes that the law on the subject was so plain that the statement would be accepted almost as a matter of course. In the case at bar the defective wheel on an automobile moving only eight miles an hour was not any more dangerous to the occupants of the car than a similarly defective wheel would be to the occupants of a carriage drawn by a horse at the same speed; and yet unless the courts have been all wrong on this question up to the present time there would be no liability to strangers to the original sale in the case of the horse-drawn carriage.

The rule upon which, in my judgment, the determination of this case depends, and the recognized principle thereto, were discussed by Circuit Judge Sanborn of the United States Circuit Court of Appeals in the Eighth Circuit, in *Huset v. J.I. Case Threshing Machine Co.* (120

Fed.Rep. 865) in an opinion which reviews all the leading American and English decisions on the subject up to the time when it was rendered (1903). I have already discussed the leading New York cases, but as to the rest I feel that I can add nothing to the learning of that opinion or the cogency of its reasoning. I have examined the cases to which Judge Sanborn refers, but if I were to discuss them at length I should be forced merely to paraphrase his language, as a study of the authorities he cites has led me to the same conclusion; and the repetition of what has already been so well said would contribute nothing to the advantage of the bench, the bar or the individual litigants whose case is before us.

A few cases decided since his opinion was written however may be noticed. In *Earl v. Lubbock* (L.R. 1905 [1 K.B.Div.] 253) the Court of Appeal in 1904 considered and approved the propositions of law laid down by the Court of Exchequer in *Winterbottom v. Wright* (*supra*), declaring that the decision in that case, since the year 1842, has stood the test of repeated discussion. The master of the rolls approved the principles laid down by Lord Abinger as based upon sound reasoning; and all the members of the court agreed that his decision was a controlling authority which must be followed. That the Federal courts still adhere to the general rule as I have stated it appears by the decision of the Circuit Court of Appeals in the Second Circuit in March 1915, in the case of *Cadillac Motor Car Co. v. Johnson* (221 Fed.Rep. 801). That case, like this, was an action by a subvendee against a manufacturer of automobiles for negligence in failing to discover that one of its wheels was defective, the court holding that such an action could not be maintained. It is true there was a dissenting opinion in that case, but it was based chiefly upon the proposition that rules applicable to stage coaches are archaic when applied to automobiles and that if the law did not afford a remedy to strangers to the contract the law should be changed. If this be true, the change should be effected by the legislature and not by the courts. A perusal of the opinion in that case and in the *Huset* case will disclose how uniformly the courts throughout this country have adhered to the rule and how consistently they have refused to broaden the scope of the exceptions. I think we I should adhere to it in the case at bar and, therefore, I vote for a reversal of this judgment.

Hiscock, Chase and Cuddeback, JJ., concur with Cardozo, J., and Hogan, J., concurs in result; Willard Bartlett, Ch. J., reads dissenting opinion; Pound, J., not voting.

Judgment affirmed.

GREENMAN v. YUBA POWER PRODUCTS, INC.
59 Cal.2d 57
Traynor, Justice
[See Chapter 9.]

Plaintiff brought this action for damages against the retailer and the manufacturer of a Shopsmith, a combination power tool that could be used as a saw, drill, and wood lathe. He saw a Shopsmith demonstrated by the retailer and studied a brochure prepared by the manufacturer. He decided he wanted a Shopsmith for his home workshop, and his wife bought and gave him one for Christmas in 1955. In 1957 he bought the necessary attachments to use the Shopsmith as a lathe for turning a large piece of wood he wished to make into a chalice. After he had worked on the piece of wood several times without difficulty, it suddenly flew out of the machine and struck him on the forehead, inflicting serious injuries. About 10-1/2 months later, he gave the retailer and the manufacturer written notice of claimed breaches of warranties and filed a complaint against them alleging such breaches and negligence.

After a trial before a jury, the court ruled that there was no evidence that the retailer was negligent or had breached any express warranty and that the manufacturer was not liable for the breach of any implied warranty. Accordingly, it submitted to the jury only the cause of action alleging breach of implied warranties against the retailer and the causes of action alleging negligence and breach of express warranties against the manufacturer. The jury returned a verdict for the retailer against plaintiff and for plaintiff against the manufacturer in the amount of $65,000. The trial court denied the manufacturer's motion for a new trial and entered judgment on the verdict. The manufacturer and

plaintiff appeal. Plaintiff seeks a reversal of the part of the judgment in favor of the retailer, however, only in the event that the part of the judgment against the manufacturer is reversed.

Plaintiff introduced substantial evidence that his injuries were caused by defective design and construction of the Shopsmith. His expert witnesses testified that inadequate set screws were used to hold parts of the machine together so that normal vibration caused the tailstock of the lathe to move away from the piece of wood being turned permitting it to fly out of the lathe. They also testified that there were other more positive ways of fastening the parts of the machine together, the use of which would have prevented the accident. The jury could therefore reasonably have concluded that the manufacturer negligently constructed the Shopsmith. The jury could also reasonably have concluded that statements in the manufacturer's brochure were untrue, that they constituted express warranties, and that plaintiff's injuries were caused by their breach.

The manufacturer contends, however, that plaintiff did not give it notice of breach of warranty within a reasonable time and that therefore his cause of action for breach of warranty is barred by § 1769 of the Civil Code. Since it cannot be determined whether the verdict against it was based on the negligence or warranty cause of action or both, the manufacturer concludes that the error in presenting the warranty cause of action to the jury was prejudicial.

Section 1769 of the Civil Code provides: "In the absence of express or implied agreement of the parties, acceptance of the goods by the buyer shall not discharge the seller from liability in damages or other legal remedy for breach of any promise or warranty in the contract to sell or the sale. But, if, after acceptance of the goods, the buyer fails to give notice to the seller of the breach of any promise or warranty within a reasonable time after the buyer knows, or ought to know of such breach, the seller shall not be liable therefor."

Like other provisions of the Uniform Sales Act (Civ.Code, §§ 1721–1800), § 1769 deals with the rights of the parties to a contract of sale or a sale. It does not provide that notice must be given of the breach of a warranty that arises independently of a contract of sale between common-law decisions that have recognized them in a variety of situations. (See *Gagne v. Bertran*, 43 Cal.2d 481, 486–487 [275 P.2d 15], and authorities cited; *Peterson v. Lamb Rubber Co.*, 54 Cal.2d 339, 348 [5 Cal.Rptr. 863, 353 P.2d 575]; *Klein v. Duchess Sandwich Co., Ltd.*, 14 Cal.2d 272, 276–283 [93 P.2d 799]; *Burr v. Sherwin Williams Co.*, 42 Cal.2d 682, 695–696 [268 P.2d 1041]; *Souza & McCue Constr. Co., Inc. v. Superior Court*, 57 Cal.2d 508, 510–511 [20 Cal.Rptr. 634, 370 P.2d 338].) It is true that in many of these situations the court has invoked the sales act definitions of warranties (Civ.Code, §§ 1732, 1735) in defining the defendant's liability, but it has done so, not because the statutes so required, but because they provided appropriate standards for the court to adopt under the circumstances presented. (See *Clinkscales v. Carver*, 22 Cal.2d 72, 75 [136 P.2d 777]; *Dana v. Sutton Motor Sales*, 56 Cal.2d 284, 287 [14 Cal.Rptr. 649, 363 P.2d 881].) The notice requirements of section 1769, however, it not an appropriate one for the court to adopt in actions by injured consumers against manufacturers with whom they have not dealt. (*La Hue v. Coca-Cola Bottling, Inc.*, 50 Wn.2d 645 [314 P.2d 421, 422]; *Chapman v. Brown*, 198 F.Supp. 78, 85, affd. *Brown v. Chapman*, 304 F.2d 149.) "As between the immediate parties to the sale [the notice requirement] is a sound commercial rule, designed to protect the seller against unduly delayed claims for damages. As applied to personal injuries, and notice to a remote seller, it becomes a booby-trap for the unwary. The injured consumer is seldom 'steeped in the business practice which justifies the rule,' [James, *Product Liability*, 34 Texas L.Rev. 44, 192, 197] and at least until he has had legal advice it will not occur to him to give notice to one with whom he has had no dealings." (Prosser, *Strict Liability to the Consumer*, 69 Yale L.J. 1099, 1130, footnotes omitted.) It is true that in *Jones v. Burgermeister Brewing Corp.*, 198 Cal.App.2d 198, 202–203 [18 Cal.Rptr. 311]; *Perry v. Thrifty Drug Co.*, 186 Cal.App.2d 410, 411 [9 Cal.Rptr. 50]. *Arata v. Tonegato*, 152 Cal.App.2d 837, 841 [314 P.2d 130], and *Maecherlein v. Sealy Mattress Co.*, 145 Cal.App.2d 275, 278 [302 P.2d 331], the court assumed that notice of breach of warranty must be given in an action by a consumer against a manufacturer. Since in those cases, however, the court did not consider the question whether a distinction exists between a warranty based on a contract between the parties and one imposed on a manufacturer not in privity with the consumer, the decisions are not authority for rejecting the rule of the *La Hue* and *Chapman* cases, *supra*. (*Peterson v. Lamb Rubber Co.*, 54 Cal.2d 339, 343 [5 Cal.Rptr. 863, 353 P.2d 575]; *People v. Banks*, 53 Cal.2d 370, 389 [1 Cal.Rptr. 669, 348 P.2d 102]. We conclude, therefore, that even if plaintiff did not give timely notice of breach of warranty to the manufacturer, his cause of action based on the representations contained in the brochure was not barred.

Moreover, to impose strict liability on the manufacturer under the circumstances of this case, it was not necessary for plaintiff to establish an express warranty as defined in § 1732 of the Civil Code. A manufacturer is strictly liable in tort when an article he places on the market, knowing that it is to be used without inspection for defects, proves to have a defect that causes injury to a human being. Recognized first in the case of unwholesome food products, such liability had now been extended to a variety of other products that create as great or greater hazards if defective. (*Peterson v. Lamb Rubber Co.*, 54 Cal.2d 339, 347 [5 Cal.Rptr. 863, 353 P.2d 575] [grinding wheel]; *Vallis v. Canada Dry Ginger Ale, Inc.*, 190 Cal.App.2d 35, 42–44 [11 Cal.Rptr.

823] [bottle]; *Jones v. Bergermeister Brewing Corp.*, 198 Cal.App.2d 198, 204 [18 Cal.Rptr. 311] [bottle]; *Gottsdanker v. Cutter Laboratories*, 182 Cal.App.2d 602, 607 [6 Cal.Rptr. 320] [vaccine]; *McQuaide v. Bridgeport Brass Co.*, 190 F.Supp. 252, 254 [insect spray]; *Bowles v. Zimmer Manufacturing Co.*, 277 F.2d 868, 875 [surgical pin]; *Thompson v. Reedman*, 199 F.Supp. 120, 121 [automobile]; *Chapman v. Brown*, 198 F.Supp. 78, 118, 119, affd. *Brown v Chapman*, 304 F.2d 149 [skirt]; *B.F. Goodrich Co. v. Hammond*, 269 F.2d 501, 504 [automobile tire]; *Markovich. v. McKesson & Robbins, Inc.*, 106, Ohio App. 265 [149 N.E.2d 181, 186–188] [home permanent]; *Graham v. Bottenfield's, Inc.* 176 Kan. 68 [269 P.2d 413, 418] [hair dye]; *General Motors Corp. v. Dodson*, 47 Tenn.App. 438 [338 S.W.2d 655, 661] [automobile]; *Henningsen v. Bloomfield Motors, Inc.*, 32 N.J. 358 [161 A.2d 69, 76–84, 75 A.L.R. 2d 1] [automobile]; *Hinton v. Republic Aviation Corp.*, 180 F.Supp. 31, 33 [airplane].)

Although in these cases strict liability has usually been based on the theory of an express or implied warranty running from the manufacturer to the plaintiff, the abandonment of the requirement of a contract between them, the recognition that the liability is not assumed by agreement but imposed by law (*see e.g., Graham v. Bottenfield's, Inc.*, 176 Kan. 68 [269 P.2d 413, 418]; *Rogers v. Toni Home Permanent Co.*, 167 Ohio St. 244 [147 N.E.2d 612, 614, 75 A.L.R. 2d 103]; *Decker & Sons v. Capps*, 139 Tx. 609, 617 [164 S.W.2d 828, 142 A.L.R. 1479]), and the refusal to permit the manufacturer to define the scope of its own responsibility for defective products (*Henningsen v. Bloomfield Motors, Inc.*, 32 N.J. 358 [161 A.2d 69 84–96, 75 A.L.R. 2d 1]; *General Motors Corp. v Dodson*, 47 Tenn. App. 438 [338 S.W.2d 655, 658–661]; *State Farm Mut. Auto Ins. Co. v. Anderson-Weber, Inc.*, 252 Iowa 1289 [110 N.W.2d 449, 455–456]; *Pabon v. Hackensack Auto Sales, Inc.* 63 N.J.Super. 476 [164 A.2d 773, 778]; *Linn v. Radio Center Delicatessen*, 169 Misc. 879 [6 N.Y.S.2d 110, 112]) make clear that the liability is not one governed by the law of contract warranties but by the law of strict liability in tort. Accordingly, rules

defining and governing warranties that were developed to meet the needs of commercial transactions cannot properly be invoked to govern the manufacturer's liability to those injured by its defective products unless those rules also serve the purposes for which such liability is imposed.

We need not recanvass the reasons for imposing strict liability on the manufacturer. They have been fully articulated in the cases cited above. (See 2 Harper and James, *Torts*, §§ 28. 15–28.16, pp. 1569–1574; Prosser, *Strict Liability to the Consumer*, 69 Yale L.J. 1099; *Escola v. Coca Cola Bottling Co.*, 24 Cal.2d 453, 461 [150 P.2d 436], concurring opinion.) The purpose of such liability is to insure that the costs of injuries resulting from defective products are borne by the manufacturers that put such products on the market rather than by the injured persons who are powerless to protect themselves. Sales warranties serve this purpose fitfully at best. (See Prosser, *Strict Liability to the Consumer*, 69 Yale L.J. 1099, 1124–1134.) In the present case, for example, plaintiff was able to plead and prove an express warranty only because he read and relied on the representations of the Shopsmith's ruggedness contained in the manufacturer's brochure. Implicit in the machine's presence on the market, however, was a representation that it would safely do the jobs for which it was built. Under the circumstances, it should not be controlling whether plaintiff selected the machine because of the statements in the brochure, or because of the machine's own appearance of excellence that belied the defect lurking beneath the surface, or because he merely assumed that it would safely do the jobs it was built to do. It should not be controlling whether the details of the sales from manufacturer to retailer and from retailer to plaintiff's wife were such that one or more of the implied warranties of the sales act arose. (Civ.Code § 1735;) "The remedies of injured consumers ought not to be made to depend upon the intricacies of the law of sales." (*Ketterer v. Armour & Co.*, 200 F. 322, 323; *Klein v. Duchess Sandwich Co., Ltd.*, 14 Cal.2d 272, 282 [93 P.2d 799]). To establish the manufacturer's liability it was sufficient that plaintiff proved that he was injured while using the Shopsmith in a way it was intended to be used as a result of a defect in design and manufacture of which plaintiff was not aware that made the Shopsmith unsafe for its intended use.

The manufacturer contends that the trial court erred in refusing to give three instructions requested by it. It appears from the record, however, that the substance of two of the requested instructions was adequately covered by the instructions given and that the third instruction was not supported by the evidence.

The judgment is affirmed.

FISHMAN v. BEACH
New York Supreme Court, Appellate Division, Third Department
625 N.Y.S.2d 730 (App. Div. 1995)
April 27, 1995
Peters, Justice

[See Chapter 10.]

Appeal from an order of the Supreme Court (Teresi, J.), entered June 29, 1994 in Albany County, which denied a motion by defendant HAJ Entertainment Inc. for summary judgment dismissing the complaint against it.

This action arises as a result of personal injuries sustained by plaintiff after he left a restaurant/bar owned by defendant HAJ Entertainment Inc., doing business as Quintessence (hereinafter Quintessence), on the evening of May 18, 1991. Plaintiff contends that after a verbal confrontation with defendant Christopher Beach and his companion on or about the outdoor steps of Quintessence, plaintiff and Beach became involved in a altercation occurring approximately 60 to 100 feet from the entrance to the restaurant/bar. During such altercation, plaintiff contends that he was caused to enter Madison Avenue and was struck by a car driven by defendant Gino M. Masciotra.

Plaintiff thereafter commenced the instant action against Beach, Masciotra and Quintessence alleging, *inter alia,* a violation of General Obligations Law § 11-101 (the Dram Shop Act) and common-law negligence. Supreme Court denied the motion of Quintessence for summary judgment seeking dismissal of all claims against it.

To sustain a claim under the Dram Shop Act, plaintiff must establish that the vendor unlawfully sold alcohol to an intoxicated person. At the time of the instant accident, an unlawful sale was defined as the sale of alcohol to a "visibly intoxicated person." Hence, on a motion for summary judgment, Quintessence bore the initial burden of establishing entitlement to judgment as a matter of law and, once satisfied, the burden thereby shifted to plaintiff to produce evidentiary proof in admissible form to establish the existence of a triable issue of fact.

In support of the instant motion, Quintessence offered the deposition transcript of its bartender to establish that there was a policy in existence at the time which dictated the procedures to be followed when a patron was either becoming intoxicated or was already intoxicated. The bartender testified that he was not aware of any incidents which occurred in Quintessence on the night of May 17, 1991 or during the early morning hours of May 18, 1991. He further testified that no complaints regarding the presence of an intoxicated person on Quintessence's premises were brought to the attention of himself or other staff employed by Quintessence. Quintessence further annexed the deposition testimony of both David Dolowich and Cynthia Mardowitz, patrons accompanying Beach, which indicated that Beach was not acting visibly intoxicated at any time during that evening. Portions of plaintiff's deposition testimony further indicated that plaintiff did not encounter Beach until he left the restaurant. We find that such evidence clearly satisfied Quintessence's initial burden on the motion for summary judgment.

In opposition thereto, plaintiff set forth his own affidavit detailing that Beach was in a visibly intoxicated condition while standing on the outdoor steps of Quintessence and annexed portions of the deposition transcript of Dolowich, which indicated that Beach was present at Quintessence for approximately 1-1/2 hours during which time he consumed between four and five alcoholic beverages. Plaintiff further submitted an affidavit by a neurologist, Sheldon Staunton, who opined that based upon an affidavit of service describing Beach to be approximately 5 feet 8 inches tall, weighing approximately 145 pounds, his consumption of four or five alcoholic beverages within this undisputed time period would result in actual intoxication.

Viewed in the light most favorable to plaintiff, we find that in the absence of any testimony from Beach, plaintiff has sustained his burden of establishing the existence of a triable issue of fact as to whether Beach was intoxicated at the time of the altercation and if so, whether he had been served alcoholic beverages at Quintessence while he was in a "visibly intoxicated" condition. Accordingly, we reject the contentions raised by Quintessence that on this motion for summary judgment, plaintiff was required to present direct evidence on the actual amount of alcohol consumed by Beach and that one of its employees had to have actually observed Beach to be in a "visibly intoxicated" condition when served with such beverages.

As to the cause of action alleging common-law negligence, we reverse. While clearly Quintessence had a duty to act in a reasonable manner to control the conduct of persons on its premises such as to prevent harm to its patrons, "[d]efendant's duty * * * was limited to conduct on its premises which it had the opportunity to control and of which it was reasonably aware."

The evidence submitted by both parties established that there was no incident which arose while the parties were inside of the premises and, therefore, defendants' duty to control the conduct of Beach was limited only to that conduct of which it was reasonably aware. The facts show that while there was a verbal exchange on the outdoor steps of such premises while music played inside, the record does not reflect that a doorman was stationed there at that time or that Quintessence personnel were informed of any need for assistance. Moreover, the physical altercation which ultimately resulted in plaintiff's injuries indisputably occurred no less than 60 to 100 feet from such premises in a city street. We therefore find that Quintessence cannot be held to a duty "to control the conduct of patrons in consuming alcoholic beverages * * * beyond the area where supervision and control may reasonably be exercised." Accordingly, we dismiss plaintiff's common-law negligence cause of action against Quintessence.

ORDERED that the order is modified, on the law, without costs, by reversing so much thereof as denied the motion by defendant HAJ Entertainment Inc. for summary judgment on the common-law negligence claim; motion granted to that extent, summary judgment awarded to said defendant and the common-law negligence claim is dismissed; and, as so modified, affirmed.

GIRDLEY v. COATS

Supreme Court of Missouri
825 S.W.2d 295 (Mo. 1992)
February 25, 1992
Benton, Judge

[See Chapter 10.]

Plaintiffs, Karen and Jeffrey Girdley, filed a four-count petition against Stephen H. Coats, D.O., and Stephen H. Coats, D.O., Inc., for a negligently performed bilateral tubal ligation. Count III of the Girdleys' petition sought "the reasonable cost of raising and educating the child" because of the negligence of Dr. Coats. Count IV sought the same expenses based on a breach of contract theory. The trial court dismissed Counts III and IV and pursuant to Rule 74.01(b) determined that the order was final for purposes of appeal.

On appeal, the Court of Appeals, Southern District, reversed and remanded the decision of the trial judge with directions to deny the motion to dismiss Counts III and IV. Transfer was granted by this Court. The judgment of the trial judge dismissing Counts III and IV is affirmed.

In reviewing the dismissal, an appellate court assumes all pleaded facts to be true and makes every favorable inference in favor of plaintiffs that may reasonably be drawn from those facts; if any ground is shown that would entitle the plaintiff to relief, the dismissal is improper.

Plaintiffs allege they were unable to afford the expense of any more children. Mrs. Girdley thus consulted with Dr. Coats who recommended bilateral tubal ligation. On March 24, 1988, she underwent surgery and was informed by Dr. Coats that he had ligated the right fallopian tube but that her left ovary and corresponding fallopian tube were congenitally absent. After the sterilization procedure, Dr. Coats advised that she was sterile with no risk of conception. On April 29, 1989, Mrs. Girdley delivered the couple's third child.

Various causes of action arise involving the birth of a child. Although some confusion exists, a consensus has developed labeling the various actions: (1) "wrongful conception" or "wrongful pregnancy"—a medical malpractice action brought by the parents of a child born after a physician negligently performed a sterilization procedure; (2) "wrongful birth"—a claim brought by parents of a child born with defects; and (c) "wrongful life"—a claim brought by the child suffering from such defects. *Wilson v. Kuenzi,* 751 S.W.2d 741, 743 (Mo. banc 1988), *cert. denied,*

488 U.S. 893, 109 S.Ct. 229, 102 L.Ed.2d 219 (1989), declines to recognize causes of action for wrongful birth and wrongful life in this state.

In Missouri, the cause of action for the tort of wrongful conception was specifically recognized in *Miller v. Duhart,* 637 S.W.2d 183 (Mo.App. 1982), which noted that such an action has strong support in the law and is "merely a descriptive label for a form of malpractice." Traditionally, Missouri does not analyze malpractice in terms of contract law.

Clearly, there is a legally cognizable cause of action. However, the parties are sharply divided as to the appropriate measure of damages. The issue may be framed: If a negligently performed sterilization procedure results in the birth of a healthy child, may the plaintiff recover the expenses of raising and educating that child?

Numerous courts have wrestled with this issue, advancing several theories of recovery, along with a plethora of supporting reasons.

A review of the cases establishes that there are four possibilities: (1) no recovery rule; (2) full recovery rule; (3) limited damages rule; and (4) benefits rule. An overwhelming majority of jurisdictions had adopted the limited damages rule whereby recovery of the expenses of raising and educating a child is denied as an element of damages.

Contrary to this majority position, appellants urge that Missouri adopt the full recovery rule claiming that such a rule would protect a constitutional right not to procreate and would allegedly promote sound social policies. Further, appellants assert that the full recovery rule is more in keeping with traditional tort principles. Appellants' position enjoys support in, at most, only three jurisdictions. *Custodio v. Bauer,* 251 Cal. App. 2d 303, 59 Cal. Rptr 463 (1967); *Marciniak v. Lundborg,* 153 Wis. 2d 59, 450 N.W.2d 243 (1990); *Lovelace Medical Center v. Mendez,* 111 N.M. 336, 805 P.2d 603 (1991) (emphasizing that wrongful conception invaded the family's financial security).

Several courts have persuasively articulated the various rationales supporting the limited damages rule—most being variations on themes of public policy. The Kansas Supreme Court concluded that a parent cannot be damaged by the birth of a healthy child:

> As a matter of public policy, the birth of a normal and healthy child does not constitute a legal harm for which damages are recoverable. We recognize wrongful death actions because of the great value we place on human life. ... The birth of a normal, healthy child may be one of the consequences of a negligently performed sterilization, but we hold that it is not a legal wrong for which damages should or may be awarded. *Byrd v. Wesley Medical Center,* 699 P.2d at 468.

The Arkansas Supreme Court reasoned:

> We are persuaded for several reasons to follow those courts which have declined to grant damages for the expense of raising a child. It is a question which meddles with the concept of life and the stability of the family unit. Litigation cannot answer every question; every question cannot be answered in terms of dollars and cents. We are also convinced that the damage to the child will be significant; that being an unwanted or "emotional bastard," who will some day learn that its parents did not want it and, in fact, went to court to force someone else to pay for its raising, will be harmful to that child. It will undermine society's need for a strong and healthy family relationship. We have not become so sophisticated a society to dismiss that emotional trauma as nonsense. *Wilbur v. Kerr,* 628 S.W.2d at 571.

The Illinois Supreme Court analyzed the issues:

> One can, of course, in mechanical logic reach a different conclusion, but only on the ground that human life and the state of parenthood are compensable losses. In a proper hierarchy of values the benefit of life should not be outweighed by the expense of supporting it. Respect for life and the rights proceeding from it are at the heart of our legal system and, broader still, our civilization. *Cockrum v. Baumgartner,* 69 Ill. Dec. at 172, 447 N.E.2d at 389.

Though arguing that the full recovery rule is a natural extension of general principles of tort law, appellants necessarily ignore some of those general principles. The issue of mitigation of damages demonstrates the fallacy of applying strict tort principles in cases where the alleged injury is the birth of a normal, healthy child. It is generally recognized that one injured by the tort of another is required to mitigate damages. *Phegley v. Graham,* 358 Mo. 551, 215 S.W.2d

499, 505 (1948). In the case of a pregnancy caused by a negligent sterilization procedure, either adoption or abortion would clearly mitigate the expense of raising the child. These options illustrate the difficulty in applying strict tort principles to damages from wrongful conception.

> Yet courts recognizing this cause of action have rejected the argument that parents should choose among the various methods of mitigation ...

Speculative results are not a proper element of damages. The costs of child rearing—and especially education—are necessarily speculative. Who can divine, soon after birth, whether the child will be a financial boon or burden to the parents, what level of education will be required or what unique expenses could arise? These determinations are beyond the scope of probative proof. Likewise, an attempt to quantify the expense of raising a child and offsetting that expense by the "benefits" conferred on the family is neither workable nor desirable.

> Perhaps the costs of rearing and educating the child could be determined through use of actuarial tables or similar economic information. But whether these costs are outweighed by the emotional benefits which will be conferred by that child cannot be calculated. The child may turn out to be loving, obedient and attentive, or hostile, unruly and callous. The child may grow up to be President of the United States, or to be an infamous criminal. In short, it is impossible to tell, at an early stage in the child's life, whether its parents have sustained a net loss or net gain.

Judge Turnage's eloquent dissent proposes the "benefits rule," offsetting the "pecuniary and non-pecuniary" benefits to parents from having the child *against* the costs of rearing a child. However, Restatement (Second) of Torts § 920 cmt. b (1977) provides:

> Damages resulting from an invasion of one interest are not diminished by showing that another interest has been benefited.

The dissent thus demonstrates that principles of tort law cannot strictly be applied to this issue.

To the extent that general tort principles militate against application of the full recovery rule, appellants shift into a policy analysis. This Court declines the invitation to waft between strict application of tort principles and application of public policy, in order to achieve the result of shifting the responsibility of supporting a child from its parents to a third party.

The question remains which specific damages are recoverable. Although the issue of damages was not directly before the court in *Miller v. Duhart,* the court of appeals summarized the type of damages:

> As a form of malpractice, "wrongful conception" gives rise to compensatory damages that are measurable. Such damages might include prenatal and postnatal medical expenses, the mother's pain and suffering during the pregnancy and delivery, loss of consortium, and the cost of a second, corrective sterilization procedure. *Miller v. Duhart,* 637 S.W.2d at 188.

The measure of damages in a wrongful conception case shall not include the expenses of raising and educating a healthy, normal child. However, in addition to the damages listed in *Miller v. Duhart,* plaintiffs are entitled to recover, subject to appropriate proof, emotional distress, loss of wages, pain and suffering associated with the second corrective procedure, and any permanent impairment suffered by the parents as a result of the pregnancy, the delivery, or the second corrective procedure.

The judgment of the trial court is affirmed.

***

WILLIAM E. TURNAGE, Special Judge, concurring in part and dissenting in part.

I concur in the holding that there is a cause of action for a so-called "wrongful conception" or "wrongful pregnancy." To me these terms are complete misnomers because I believe the cause of action to be simply one of medical malpractice which happens to involve the birth of a child.

I respectfully dissent from the holding that the cost of rearing a healthy child born as the result of a physician's malpractice in the performance of a sterilization procedure is not recoverable. ... I believe this case is about medical malpractice and whether or not an exception will be carved out to exonerate physicians from liability for the bulk of the damages which flow from malpractice in performing sterilization procedures.

The principal reason given by the states which deny recovery for the costs of rearing a healthy child is the fact that society places such a high value on human life that the birth of a healthy child cannot be a legal wrong for which damages may be recovered. ...

In *Jones v. Malinowski,* 299 Md. 257, 473 A.2d 429, 435[3] (1984), the court answered the above argument in two ways. The court stated:

> To adopt such a policy and rule of law would be to subject a physician to liability for the direct, foreseeable and natural consequences of all negligently performed operations except those involving sterilization—a result, we think, completely at odds with reason. That the public policy of Maryland may foster the development and preservation of the family relationship does not, in our view, compel the adoption of a per se rule denying recovery by parents of child rearing costs from the physician whose negligence has caused their expenditure. In other words, it is not to disparage the value of human life and the societal need for harmonious family units to protect the parents' choice not to have children by recognizing child rearing costs as a compensable element of damages in negligent sterilization cases.

In *University of Arizona Health Sciences Center v. Superior Court,* 136 Ariz. 579, 584, 667 P.2d 1294, 1299 (1983), the court stated that even though a family can adjust to the birth of an unplanned child it must be recognized that there are cases where such birth can cause emotional or economic problems to the parents. In Note, *Judicial Limitations on Damages Recoverable for the Wrongful Birth of a Healthy Infant,* 68 Va.L.Rev. 1311, 1316–17 (1982), the author considered this argument and stated:

> Although they may well have realized that they would love a child if one were born to them, they may also have realized that their affection would not provide the money to feed the child or the time for the working mother to resume her interrupted career. To disallow the parents' recovery because they love their child is to leave uncompensated the significant emotional and economic harms that may accompany a wrongful birth. In a family of limited means, the application of an overriding-benefit theory injures the child as well as the parents, since the exclusion of all damages denies the family a fund from which to provide for the unplanned child.

***

To award damages to the parents for the rearing of an unplanned child does not disparage the worth of the child or indicate a disregard on the part of the court for the worth of a human being. The awarding of such damages is simply the recognition that in today's world it is costly to rear a child and, in fact, the presence of an unplanned child in a family of limited means or in a family with a working mother can prove to be a disruptive factor which will damage the family unit if the child does not bring with it some financial help.

The majority does not suggest, nor is there reason that it should, that the decision of the Girdleys for the wife to undergo a sterilization procedure was in any way illegal or improper. Having elected to undergo a proper procedure to limit the size of their family, this court should not ignore the reality of the hardship which the arrival of an unplanned child can create. To do so is simply to take a "head in the sand" approach to the problem.

***

No one could argue persuasively that it would be reasonable to require a mother to undergo an abortion or place her child for adoption in order to minimize the damages which could be assessed against the negligent physician who performed the sterilization on her. This rule has no application in the manner suggested by the majority.

The majority holds that the costs of child rearing are speculative. It should first be noted that this court by Rule 88.01 has adopted Civil Procedure Form No. 14 for the amount of child support to be awarded in actions involving child support. Courts have long awarded reasonable amounts necessary for the support of children.

DOE v. CUTTER BIOLOGICAL, A DIVISION OF MILES, INC.
United States District Court, D. Idaho
852 F. Supp. 909 (D. Idaho 1994)
May 12, 1994
Ryan, Senior District Judge
[See Chapter 11.]

Plaintiff John Doe is a hemophiliac. Because of his condition, John Doe received a clotting agent known as Factor VIII which facilitates the clotting of blood in hemophiliacs. In December of 1991, John Doe tested positive for the HIV virus.

On October 30, 1992, John Doe commenced this federal action naming those providers of Factor VIII products which were administered to him by the Pocatello Regional Medical Center between 1979 and 1985. At this juncture, the named defendants include: Miles Inc. (Miles), and Armour Pharmaceutical Corporation (Armour).

[T]his court respectfully requested the Idaho Supreme Court to exercise its discretionary authority under Idaho Appellate Rule 12.1(c) to accept and decide the following questions:

> Assuming plaintiff is able to prove that more than one defendant breached a duty of care to the plaintiff, would Idaho allow recovery when it is not possible for plaintiff to prove which defendant caused plaintiff's injury; and, if so, under what theory?

***

Based on traditional theories of causation under Idaho law and John Doe's admitted inability to prove which dose of Factor VIII caused him to contact the HIV virus and, ultimately, to develop AIDS, defendants filed motions for summary judgment as to the issue of causation. ...

In support of their position, defendants note the absence of judicial decisions on the issue of alternative liability and, from a legislative standpoint, emphasize the advent of tort reform, the limitations placed on the common law doctrine of joint and several liability under Idaho Code §§ 6-803(3)-(7) … .

***

As stated earlier, the concept of alternate liability was first developed in the case of *Summers v. Tice,* 33 Cal.2d 80, 199 P.2d 1 (1948). In *Summers,* the plaintiff was injured while hunting quail with the two defendants. Both defendants carried identical shotguns and ammunition. During the hunt, defendants shot simultaneously at the same bird, and plaintiff was struck by bird shot from one of the defendants' guns. Both defendants were found to have acted negligently, but it could not be determined which of them had fired the shot that injured the plaintiff. The California court held that the burden of proof should be shifted to the defendants on the issue of causation. In justifying such a shift, the court said that the defendants were "both wrongdoers; both negligent toward plaintiff. They brought about a situation where the negligence of one of them injured the plaintiff, hence it should rest with them each to absolve himself if he can."

In the absence of any direct pronouncement by the Idaho Supreme Court on the issue of alternate liability, plaintiff relies heavily on the decision of *Hackworth,* wherein the Idaho Supreme Court included the *Summers* case in a string of citations. From this, plaintiff contends that the Idaho Supreme Court would find "one or more of the following alternative theories of liability … applicable to the question of causation in this case: (a) Alternative liability, Section 433B(3), Restatement (Second) of Torts; (b) Market share liability; (c) Enterprise liability; and/or (d) Concert of action, Section 876 of the Restatement (Second) of Torts."

Mere citation to *Summers* certainly does not compel the conclusion that the Idaho Supreme Court would adopt *any* theory of alternative liability. And, had the Idaho Supreme Court expressly adopted the holding from *Summers* in a case where a plaintiff was unable to prove which of two or more negligent defendants caused his injury, such would not compel the conclusion that any or all of the alternative theories of liability should be applied to the suppliers of the Factor VIII concentrates in this case.

On the contrary, unlike the defendants in *Summers,* Miles and Armour point out that their actions in providing Factor VIII concentrates to the plaintiff were not identical and that such actions were certainly not simultaneous in time. Also, when it comes to determining which dose of Factor VIII caused plaintiff's infliction with the HIV virus, Miles and Armour contend that they have no better access to information—which would assist in that determination—than the plaintiff.

In Idaho, and under the circumstances herein, this court finds the viability of the theory of alternate liability originated in *Summers* to be questionable. At this point, … the court finds it useful to discuss each of the other three theories of alternative liability advanced by the plaintiff.

The concept of market share liability was first developed by the California Supreme Court in *Sindell v. Abbott Laboratories,* to address unique causation problems raised by diethylstilbesterol (DES) litigation. In *Sindell,* the plaintiff alleged that she was injured by DES which her mother ingested while pregnant with the plaintiff. Although the plaintiff could not identify the manufacturer responsible for making the DES taken by her mother, the court held that if the plaintiff joined the manufacturers of a substantial share of the DES that her mother might have taken, the burden of proof would shift to the defendants to prove that they could not have supplied the DES which caused the plaintiff's injuries. The court ruled further that each defendant failing to make such a showing would be held liable for the proportion of the judgment represented by its share of the drug market.

In *Sindell,* to support application of the market share theory of liability, the California Supreme Court emphasized two factors—neither of which apply in the case at bar.

First, the court determined that DES was fungible or interchangeable because all DES companies produced the drug from an identical formula. In fact, DES was usually manufactured as a "generic" drug without regard to the actual manufacturer. Thus, each DES manufacturer's product posed the same risk of harm to its users.

Factor VIII concentrates are not akin to DES. On the contrary, as summarized in another proceeding:

> Unlike DES, Factor VIII is not a generic, fungible drug. Each processor prepares its Factor VIII concentrate by its own proprietary processes using plasma collected from its own sources. Each firm's Factor VIII concentrate is clearly distinguishable by brand name, package color, lot number, and number of units of Factor VIII per vial; each firm's Factor VIII concentrate is separately licensed by the Food and Drug Administration. There is no evidence that all Factor VIII products caused or were equally capable of causing HIV infection. Thus, *the risk posed by the different brands of Factor VIII is not identical.*

In other words, one of the bases for the *Sindell* court applying the market share theory of liability was that *each* DES pill was inherently dangerous and potentially harmful, whereas, in this case, it cannot be said that the Factor VIII concentrates at issue were inherently harmful. Rather, such concentrates would only have been harmful if particular plasma donors had been infected with the HIV virus.

The second factor which contributed to the *Sindell* court's application of the market share theory of liability was that the DES product could not be traced to any specific producer. Unlike DES, however, with Factor VIII, it would have been possible—had plaintiff kept such records—to identify the source and lot number for each dose of Factor VIII used by the plaintiff and provided by Defendant Miles, as opposed to Defendant Armour.

In summary, while the market share theory of liability may have been appropriate to apply in the context of DES litigation, *even if* the Idaho Supreme Court had ever sanctioned the use of such a theory—and it has not—it is not clear that the market share theory should be applied to the context of Factor VIII litigation.

As summarized by the New York Court of Appeals:

"Enterprise liability," *also joint and several,* derives from the opinion in *Hall v. Dupont de Nemours & Co.* In that case, plaintiffs were unable to identify the manufacturers of allegedly unsafe blasting caps for the simple reason that the caps had been obliterated by explosion. Since the six defendants in that case did, however, comprise virtually the entire American blasting cap industry and since it appeared that their blasting caps were *manufactured to meet industry-wide safety standards set by their own trade association,* the court held that *defendants could be liable for the joint control of the risk of accidental explosion.*

This court is not aware of any case in which the enterprise theory has been applied to manufacturers of Factor VIII concentrates. ...

Unlike members of the blasting caps industry in *Hall* who were found to have exercised joint control of the risks involved in that case, the actions of Miles and Armour in producing Factor VIII concentrates were closely controlled and/or regulated by the FDA. ...

"[T]he concert of action theory derives from a criminal law concept ... . 'If plaintiffs can establish that all defendants acted tortiously pursuant to a common design, they will all be held liable for the entire result.'"

... Idaho Code § 6-803(3) essentially abolished joint and several liability in Idaho. Thus, it does not appear that the concert of action theory of alternative liability would be viable in Idaho.

***

Prior to 1987, Idaho's Supreme Court adhered to the common law rule of joint and several liability, as it recognized:

[E]ach tortfeasor whose negligence is a proximate cause of an *indivisible* injury should remain individually liable for *all* compensable damages attributable to that injury. Such is the underlying basis for the rule of joint and several liability.

***

However, in 1987, the Idaho legislature enacted Idaho Code § 6-803(3), which limited the doctrine of joint and several liability, and thereby *superseded all previous Idaho court decisions.*

***

Thus, given the recognition that the theory of alternative liability set forth in *Summers v. Tice* involves joint and several liability, and given that the Idaho Supreme Court fully acknowledges that the Idaho legislature abolished joint and several liability when it enacted Idaho Code § 6-803(3), existing Idaho law precludes the endorsement of alternative liability theories.

In addition to the operation of Idaho Code § 6-803(3), which limits the operation of joint and several liability in Idaho, the plain language of Idaho's blood shield statute expressly precludes providers of "blood products" or "blood derivatives" from being held liable for anything other than their own negligence. In the face of this clear statement of public policy by Idaho's legislature, it is difficult to imagine how any theory of alternative liability could be endorsed in this type of case.

***

Because plaintiff concedes that "at trial it will be difficult, if not impossible, to determine which of the Defendants processed the Factor VIII which caused [him] to be stricken with AIDS," defendants, motions for summary judgment on the issue of causation are well taken and must be granted.

***

In addition to precluding recovery based on implied warranties, blood shield statutes also preclude actions based on strict liability in tort.

***

... Notwithstanding the possibility for change in Idaho's statute, as currently worded, and under the circumstances in this case, the Idaho blood shield statute does not permit an action based on strict liability or implied warranties against suppliers of Factor VIII concentrates such as Miles and Armour. Rather, against these defendants Idaho Code § 39-3702 only permits actions based on negligence.

***

Neither the Idaho legislature nor the highest court of this state has declared that, without proof of causation, a plaintiff, such as John Doe, should be able to recover against providers of Factor VIII concentrates, such as Miles and Armour. Accordingly, to avoid summary judgment on his negligence claims, plaintiff contends that this court "should *predict* which alternate theory of causation the Idaho Supreme Court would adopt in this case." This court is not empowered to make such a prediction.

***

Thus, it is this conclusion that plaintiff's motion for partial summary judgment requesting the adoption of one or more alternative liability theories should be denied; that defendants' motions for summary judgment on the issue of causation should be granted; and that plaintiff's attempt to assert products liability claims based on strict liability or implied warranties of merchantability and fitness for a particular purpose should be denied.

GLOSSARY

A

abatement Reduction or decrease ... [or] complete elimination.

abnormally dangerous (ultrahazardous) instrumentalities† Activities or objects that are, by their very nature, extremely hazardous to persons or property. These are relevant to strict (absolute) liability cases.

absolute (strict) liability The legal responsibility for damage or injury, even if you are not at fault or negligent.

abuse of process Using the legal system unfairly; for example, prosecuting a person for writing a "bad check" simply to put on pressure to pay.

alternate dispute resolution Ways to resolve a legal problem without a court decision; for example, arbitration, mediation, minitrial, rent-a-judge, summary trial, etc.

answer The first pleading by the defendant in a lawsuit. This pleading responds to the charges and demands of the plaintiff's complaint. The defendant may deny the plaintiff's charges, may present new facts to defeat them, or may show why the plaintiff's facts are legally invalid.

apprehension Fear.

appropriation Taking something wrongfully.

arbitration Resolution of a dispute by a person (other than a judge) whose decision is binding. This person is called an *arbitrator*. Submission of the dispute for decision is often the result of an agreement (an *arbitration clause*) in a contract. If arbitration is required by law, it is called *compulsory arbitration*.

assault An intentional threat, show of force, or movement that could reasonably make a person feel in danger of physical attack or harmful physical contact.

assembly defect† A theory in products liability concerning whether a defective product is unreasonably dangerous. Errors in production manufacture or assembly may render a product unreasonably hazardous despite safe design.

assumption of risk Knowingly and willingly exposing yourself (or your property) to the possibility of harm. In most states, a person who assumes a risk of harm cannot win a negligence lawsuit against the person responsible for the harm. ...

attachment Formally seizing property (or a person) in order to bring it under control of the court. This is usually done by getting a court order to have a law enforcement officer take control of the property.

attractive nuisance doctrine (attraction theory) A legal principle, used in some states, that if a person keeps dangerous property in a way that children might be attracted to it and be able to get at it, then that person is responsible even if the children are trespassing or at fault when they get hurt.

attractive nuisance† Any item that is dangerous to young children but that is so interesting and alluring as to attract them to the location at which it is kept.

B

bad faith Dishonesty or other failure to deal fairly with another person.

battery An intentional, unconsented to, physical contact by one person (or an object controlled by that person) with another person.

breach of warranty† The violation of either an express or implied warranty.

burden of rejoinder† The defendant's burden of proof to refute the plaintiff's evidence in a lawsuit.

business directory† A listing of corporations and other business organizations by name, geographic location, product or service, brand name, advertising, and other subject headings.

C

castle doctrine The principle (now greatly restricted) that you can use any force necessary to protect your own home or its inhabitants from attack. Also called *dwelling defense doctrine*.

cause-in-fact† Cause of injury in negligence cases. If the tortfeasor's actions resulted in the victim's injuries, then the tortfeasor was the cause-in-fact of the victim's harm.

chattel Item of personal property. Any property other than land.

class action A lawsuit brought for yourself and other persons in the same situation. To bring a *class action* you must convince the court that there are too many persons in the class (group) to make them all individually a part of a lawsuit and that your interests are the same as theirs, so that you can adequately represent their needs.

coming and going rule† Rule used when employees commit torts while coming to or going from work. In respondeat superior cases, this rule helps decide whether an employee's actions fall outside the scope of employment.

coming to the nuisance defense† A defense to private nuisance lawsuits that may be used successfully when a plaintiff owns or uses land at a location in which the alleged nuisance activity was previously occurring. The plaintiff is said to have "come to the nuisance" and thus cannot recover against the defendant.

commercial disparagement† An intentional tort that occurs when a tortfeasor communicates false statements to third parties about a person's goods, services, or business enterprise. The tortfeasor must intend to harm the victim's ability to use goods, furnish services, or conduct business. There are three categories: disparagement of goods, disparagement of services, and disparagement of business.

common law 1. Either all caselaw or the caselaw that is made by judges in the absence of relevant statutes. 2. The legal system that originated in England and is composed of caselaw and statutes that grow and change, influenced by ever-changing custom and tradition.

common use principle† Doctrine in strict liability cases that defines abnormally dangerous activities and substances as those not commonly undertaken or used in everyday life.

community 1. Neighborhood, locality, etc. A vague term that can include very large or very small areas. 2. A group with common interests. 3. Shared.

comparative negligence A legal rule, used in many states, by which the amount of "fault" on each side of an accident is measured and the side with less fault is given damages according to the difference between the magnitude of each side's fault.

compensatory damages Damages awarded for the actual loss suffered by a plaintiff.

complainant 1. A person who makes an official complaint. 2. A person who starts a lawsuit.

complaint The first main paper filed in a civil lawsuit. It includes, among other things, a statement of the wrong or harm done to the plaintiff by the defendant, a request for specific help from the court, and an explanation why the court has the power to do what the plaintiff wants.

consent Voluntary and active agreement.

consortium[†] The rights and duties of both husband and wife, resulting from marriage. They include companionship, love, affection, assistance, cooperation, and sexual relations.

consumer contemplation test[†] A theory in products liability concerning faulty product design that makes a product unreasonably dangerous. If a reasonable person would not have anticipated the danger created by the fault in the product, then the product is unreasonably dangerous.

contempt 1. An act that obstructs a court's work or lessens the dignity of the court. ... 2. A willful disobeying of a judge's command or official court order.

contribution 1. The sharing of payment for a debt (or judgment) among persons who are all liable for the debt. 2. The right of a person who has paid an entire debt (or judgment) to get back a fair share of the payment from another person who is also responsible for the debt.

contributory negligence Negligent (careless) conduct by a person who was harmed by another person's negligence; a plaintiff's failure to be careful that is a part of the cause of his or her injury when the defendant's failure to be careful is also part of the cause.

control[†] The power or authority to direct or oversee.

conversion Any act that deprives an owner of property without that owner's permission and without just cause.

culpability factoring (liability apportionment)[†] A defense to negligence. When the plaintiff's negligence contributed to his or her injuries, comparative negligence calculates the percentage of the defendant's and the plaintiff's negligence and adjusts the plaintiff's damages according to the numbers. The trier-of-fact decides the percentages.

D

damages Money that a court orders paid to a person who has suffered damage (a loss or harm) by the person who caused the injury.

danger/utility test[†] A theory in products liability design that makes a product unreasonably dangerous. Under this test, a product is unreasonably dangerous if the danger created by its design outweighs the benefits derived from its use.

deep pocket The one person (or organization) among many possible defendants best able to pay a judgment. ... This is the one a plaintiff is most likely to sue.

defamation Transmission to others of false statements that harm the reputation, business, or property rights of a person. Spoken defamation is *slander* and written defamation is *libel*.

defamation by computer[†] An intentional tort that occurs when the tortfeasor includes false information about a person's credit or credit rating in a computer database. This false information must be communicated to third parties and must injure the victim's ability to obtain credit.

defense 1. The sum of the facts, law, and arguments presented by the side against whom legal action is brought. 2. Any counter-argument or counter-force.

defense of persons† A defense to the intentional torts of assault, battery, and false imprisonment. Its elements include the use of reasonable force to defend or protect a third party from injury when the third party is threatened by an attacking force.

defense of property† A defense to the intentional torts of assault and battery. Its elements include the use of reasonable force to protect property from damage or dispossession when another person, called the *invader*, attempts to injure or wrongfully take possession of the property.

discovery 1. The formal and informal exchange of information between sides in a lawsuit. … 2. Finding out something previously unknown. …

dispossession† Wrongfully taking away a person's property by force, trick, or misuse of the law.

dominion Legal ownership plus full actual control over something.

domitae naturae† (Latin) "Domesticated nature." Tame, domestic animals.

due (reasonable) care That degree of care a person of ordinary prudence (the so-called *reasonable person*) would exercise in similar circumstances.

duty 1. An obligation to obey a law. 2. A legal obligation to another person, who has a corresponding right. 3. Any obligation, whether legal, moral, or ethical.

E

ejectment The name for an old type of lawsuit to get back land taken away wrongfully.

emotional distress Mental anguish. Non-physical harm that may be compensated for by damages in some types of lawsuits. *Mental anguish* may be as limited as the immediate mental feelings during an injury or as broad as prolonged grief, shame, humiliation, despair, etc.

entry The act of entering [as upon real property].

equitable relief (remedy)† A remedy available in equity; generally non-monetary relief.

exclusive right of possession† A land owner's right to use his or her property without interference from other persons.

exclusive right† A right granted to no one else.

execution sale† A public sale held by a sheriff or other public official of property seized under a writ of execution.

F

false imprisonment An unlawful restraint or deprivation of a person's liberty, usually by a public official.

false light in the public eye† One type of the intentional tort of invasion of privacy. Occurs when the tortfeasor publicly attributes to another individual spurious opinions, statements, or actions.

family relationships rule† Doctrine used in negligent infliction of emotional distress cases. Under this rule, a bystander may recover damages if he or she witnesses the tortfeasor injuring one or more of the bystander's relatives.

fee standard† A test courts use in applying the governmental/proprietary distinction. If a governmental agency assesses a fee for an activity, the activity is considered proprietary; if not, it is considered governmental.

ferae naturae (Latin) "Of wild nature." Naturally wild animals.

fictitious name† A trade or assumed name used by corporations for the purpose of conducting business.

foreseeability† The notion that a specific action, under particular circumstances, would produce an anticipated result. In negligence law, if it were reasonably foreseeable that the plaintiff would be harmed by the defendant's actions, then the scope of duty includes the plaintiff. Foreseeability of injury is another aspect of negligence theory, which falls within proximate cause. Foreseeability is defined in terms of reasonableness.

foreseeable plaintiffs theory† A theory used in analyzing negligence cases. Under this theory, if it were reasonably foreseeable that the injured victim would be harmed as a consequence of the tortfeasor's actions, then the tortfeasor's scope of duty includes the victim. This victim is said to be a *foreseeable plaintiff.* Unforeseeable plaintiffs fall outside the defendant's scope of duty because their injuries could not have been reasonably anticipated as a result of the defendant's conduct. The theory is also used in products liability analysis.

fraud (deceit) Any kind of trickery used to cheat another of money or property.

frolic and detour rule† Conduct of an employee that falls outside of the scope of employment that is purely for the benefit of said employee. An employer is not responsible for the negligence of an employee on a "frolic of his/her own."

G

governmental function(s) An action performed for the general public good by a governmental agency … or by a private organization closely tied to the government. … These functions are state actions subject to the due process of law and equal protection clauses of the Constitution. If performed by a government agency, they are usually free from tort lawsuits unless the suits involve constitutional issues or are otherwise authorized by statute.

gross negligence† Recklessly or willfully acting with a deliberate indifference to the affect the action will have on others.

H

hearsay A statement about what someone else said (or wrote or otherwise communicated).

hot (fresh) pursuit The right of a person who has had property taken to use reasonable force to get it back after a chase that takes place immediately after it was taken.

I

imminent danger exception† A nineteenth- and early twentieth-century exception to the privity of contract requirement in defective product cases.

immunity An exemption from a legally imposed duty, freedom from a duty, or freedom from a penalty.

impact rule The rule (used today in very few states) that damages for emotional distress cannot be had in a negligence lawsuit unless there is some physical contact or impact.

implead Bring into a lawsuit. For example, if A sues B and B sues C in the same lawsuit, B *impleads* C, and the process is *impleader.*

independent contractor A person who contracts with an "employer" to do a particular piece of work by his or her own methods and under his or her own control.

informed consent A person's agreement to allow something to happen (such as surgery) that is based on a full disclosure or full knowledge of the facts needed to make the decision intelligently.

injunction A judge's order to a person to do or to refrain from doing a particular thing.

intent The resolve or purpose to use a particular means to reach a particular result. *Intent* usually explains *how* a person wants to do something and *what* that person wants to get done, while *motive* usually explains *why*.

intentional infliction of emotional distress† An intentional tort that occurs when the tortfeasor's outrageous conduct, which is intended to cause severe emotional anguish in the victim, actually causes the victim such emotional suffering as a result of the tortfeasor's actions.

intentional injury (tort)† An injury *designed* to injure a person or that person's property as opposed to an injury caused by negligence or resulting from an accident.

invasion of privacy Publicizing someone's private affairs that are of no legitimate public concern; using a person for publicity without permission; eavesdropping; or violation of the right to be left alone.

investigation† A systematic examination, especially an official inquiry.

invitee A person who is at a place by invitation.

J

joint and several liability† When two or more persons who jointly commit a tort can be held liable both together and individually.

judge The person who runs a courtroom, decides all legal questions, and sometimes decides entire cases by also deciding factual questions.

L

last clear chance doctrine The legal principle that a person injured in (or having property harmed by) an accident may win damages even when negligent if the person causing the damage, while also negligent, could have avoided the accident after discovering the danger and if the person injured could not have. This rule is not accepted in every state and, where accepted, has many different forms (and names).

libel Written defamation. Publicly communicated, false written statements that injure a person's reputation, business, or property rights. To libel certain public figures, the written statement must also be written with at least a "reckless disregard" for whether the statement is true or false.

licensee A person who is on property with permission, but without any enticement by the owner and with no financial advantage to the owner; often called a *mere, bare,* or *naked licensee* as opposed to an *invitee* in negligence law.

loss of consortium† The loss of one of a spouse's duties. If such loss results from a tort, damages are sometimes given to one spouse to compensate for this loss of consortium.

M

maintenance defect† A theory in products liability concerning whether a defective product is unreasonably dangerous. If a seller fails to maintain a product properly, and the product later causes injury to the ultimate user, then the product was unreasonably dangerous.

malice 1. Ill will. 2. Intentionally harming someone; having no moral or legal justification for harming someone. 3. In defamation law, with knowledge of falsity or with reckless disregard for whether or not something is false.

malicious prosecution A tort committed by bringing charges against someone in order to harm that person and with no legal justification for doing it.

mandamus (Latin) "We command." A *writ of mandamus* is a court order that directs a public official or government department to do something. It may be sent to the executive branch, the legislative branch, or a lower court.

mass tort[†] When large groups of people are injured as a result of a single tortious act. A mass tort typically involves thousands of claimants, years of litigation, and millions of dollars in attorneys' fees and costs. Generally, a smaller number of defendants are involved.

mediation Outside help in settling a dispute. The person who does this is called a *mediator*. This is different from arbitration in that a mediator can only persuade, not force, people into a settlement.

minitrial Alternative dispute resolution by a panel of executives from two companies engaged in a complex dispute. A neutral moderator helps the two sides sort out factual and legal issues to reach a voluntary settlement.

minor A person who is under the age of full legal rights and duties.

misrepresentation 1. *Innocent misrepresentation* is a false statement that is not known to be false. 2. *Negligent misrepresentation* is a false statement made when you should have known better. 3. *Fraudulent misrepresentation* is a false statement known to be false and meant to be misleading.

mistake An unintentional error or act.

mixed nuisance A nuisance that is both public and private.

motive The reason why a person does something.

N

necessary force[†] That degree of force reasonably perceived as required to repel an attack or resist confinement. It is an aspect of self-defense.

necessity Anything from an irresistible force or compulsion to an important, but not required action. *Necessity* often refers to a situation that requires an action that would otherwise be illegal or expose a person to tort liability.

negligence The failure to exercise a reasonable amount of care in a situation that causes harm to someone or something. It can involve doing something carelessly or failing to do something that should have been done. Negligence can vary in seriousness from gross (recklessness or willfulness), through *ordinary* (failing to act as a reasonably careful person would), to *slight* (not much).

negligence per se[†] Negligence that cannot be debated due to a law that establishes a duty of care that the defendant has violated, thus causing injury to another.

negligent infliction of emotional distress[†] Outrageous conduct by the tortfeasor that the tortfeasor reasonably should have anticipated would produce significant and reasonably foreseeable emotional injury to the victim. By his or her actions, the tortfeasor must breach the duty of reasonable care, and the victim must be a reasonably foreseeable plaintiff.

nominal damages[†] Small or symbolic damages awarded in situations in which no actual damages have occurred, or the right has not been proven even though a right has been violated in an intentional tort action.

nuisance 1. Anything that annoys or disturbs unreasonably, hurts a person's use of his or her property, or violates the public health, safety, or decency. 2. Use of land that does anything in definition no. 1

nuisance per se[†] That which is considered a nuisance at all times and no matter the circumstances, regardless of location or surroundings.

O

occupier[†] An individual who does not own but who uses real estate, including tenants (lessees).

P

permanent injunction[†] Abatement orders instructing a defendant to permanently stop doing a nuisance activity. Usually issued after a full hearing.

physical manifestations rule[†] Doctrine applied in negligent infliction of emotional distress cases. Under this rule, the plaintiff may recover damages if physical symptoms accompanied his or her mental anguish.

police power The government's right and power to set up and enforce laws to provide for the safety, health, and general welfare of the people.

post-trial procedures[†] The procedures that occur after a trial, such as an appeal or the steps that must be taken in order to collect on an award.

preponderance of the evidence The greater weight of the evidence, not as to *quantity* (in number of witnesses or facts) but as to *quality* (believability and greater weight of important facts proved). This is a standard of proof generally used in civil lawsuits. It is not as high a standard as *clear and convincing evidence* or *beyond a reasonable doubt*.

pretrial procedures[†] Any procedure that immediately precedes trial; for example, the settlement conference.

prima facie case A case that will be won unless the other side comes forward with evidence to disprove it.

private nuisance A tort that requires a showing of special harm to you or your property and allows the recovery of damages for the harm as well as an injunction.

privilege 1. An advantage; a right to preferential treatment. 2. An exemption from a duty others like you must perform. 3. The right to speak or write defamatory words because the law allows them in certain circumstances. 4. A basic right, such as *privileges and immunities*. 5. A special advantage, as opposed to a right; an advantage that can be taken away. 6. As a defense against an intentional tort, *privilege* is a legal justification to engage in otherwise tortious conduct in order to accomplish a compelling social goal.

privity of contract[†] A legal relationship that exists between parties to a contract. In some cases privity must exist in order for an individual to make a claim against another.

probable cause[†] A reasonable belief that the accused is guilty of the alleged crime.

process A court's ordering a defendant to show up in court or risk losing a lawsuit; a summons.

process serving[†] The method by which a defendant in a lawsuit is notified that the plaintiff has filed suit against the defendant. Also called *service of process*. Governmental officials engaged in process serving are generally immune from intentional tort liability.

product manufacturer[†] The maker of a product that, if defective, gives rise to product liability.

product(s) liability The responsibility of manufacturers (and sometimes sellers) of goods to pay for harm to purchasers (and sometimes other users and even bystanders) caused by a defective product.

professional community standard of care[†] The standard of reasonable care used in negligence cases involving defendants with special skills and knowledge.

proprietary actions[†] Certain business-like activities performed by governmental bodies (usually local government) that are usually associated with the private sector. These can be performed at the discretion of the governmental body and are not given immunity from tort liability.

prosecutor 1. A public official who represents the government's case against a person accused of a crime and who asks the court to convict that person. 2. The private individual who accuses a person of a crime is sometimes called the *private prosecutor.*

proximate cause The "legal cause" of an accident or other injury (which may have several actual causes). The proximate cause of an injury is not necessarily the closest thing in time or space to the injury and not necessarily the event that set things in motion because proximate cause is a legal, not a physical concept.

public disclosure of private facts† One type of the intentional tort of invasion of privacy. Occurs when the tortfeasor communicates purely private information about a person to the public without permission, and a reasonable person would find this disclosure extremely objectionable.

public nuisance† Activity by the tortfeasor that unreasonably and substantially interferes with the public's use and enjoyment of legal rights common to the public.

publication Making public. ... In the law of defamation, *publication* usually means communicating defamatory information to a person other than the person defamed.

punitive (exemplary) damages Extra money [over and above compensatory damages] given to a plaintiff to punish the defendant and to keep a particularly bad act from happening again.

purchaser† One who acquires property through the purchase of said property.

R

reasonable force† Force that is reasonable, limited to that which is necessary to dispel the attacking force for self-defense.

reasonable person standard† A means of determining negligence based on what a reasonable person would have done in the same or similar circumstances. Basically, it is a measurement of the failure to do that which a person of ordinary intelligence and judgment would have done in the same circumstances.

reckless infliction of emotional distress† An intentional tort that occurs when the tortfeasor's outrageous conduct causes the victim to suffer severe mental anguish. Intent to produce the emotional suffering is not necessary. Instead, it is sufficient that the tortfeasor knew, or reasonably should have known, that his or her misbehavior would produce emotional distress. Often with this tort, the tortfeasor's conduct is wanton, with no apparent regard for the victim's suffering.

recusation (recusal) The process by which a judge is disqualified (or disqualifies himself or herself) from hearing a lawsuit because of prejudice or because the judge is interested in the outcome.

remedy The means by which a right is enforced or satisfaction is gained for a harm done. The means by which a violation of rights is prevented, redressed, or compensated.

rent-a-judge Alternative dispute resolution in which two sides in a dispute choose a person to decide the dispute. The two sides may agree to make the procedure informal or formally similar to a real trial, and they may agree to make the decision advisory only or binding and enforceable.

replevin A legal action to get back property wrongfully held by another person.

res ipsa loquitur (Latin) "The thing speaks for itself." A rebuttable presumption (a conclusion that can be changed if contrary evidence is introduced) that a person is negligent if the thing causing an accident was in his or her control only, and if that type of accident does not usually happen without negligence.

respondeat superior (Latin) "Let the master answer." Describes the principle that an employer is responsible for most harm caused by an employee acting within the scope of employment. In such a case, the employer is said to have vicarious liability.

retailer† One who makes retail sales of goods.

rightful repossession† A defense to trespass to land, trespass to chattel, conversion, assault, and battery. Its elements include the use of reasonable force to retake possession of personal property of which the owner has been wrongfully disposed, or to which the owner has been wrongfully denied possession. Efforts to retake the chattel must be made promptly after the original dispossession (or denial of possession) occurs.

S

scope of duty† In negligence law, defined in terms of those individuals who might foreseeably be injured as a result of the tortfeasor's actions. This is called *reasonableness of foreseeability*. The scope of duty includes all those foreseeable plaintiffs who could have been hurt because of the tortfeasor's conduct. This is called *foreseeability of the victim*.

scope of employment The range of actions within which an employee is considered to be doing work for the employer.

self-defense Physical force used against a person who is threatening physical force or using physical force. This is a right if your own family, property, or body is in danger,

but sometimes only if the danger was not provoked. Also, deadly force may (usually) only be used against deadly force.

seller† One who sells property, either their own or through contract with the actual owner.

sensibilities† In nuisance law, ways in which people's physical and emotional sense are affected.

sensory perception rule† Doctrine used in negligent infliction of emotional distress cases. Under this rule, a bystander may recover damages if he or she witnesses a tortfeasor injuring another person, so long as the bystander perceives the event directly through his or her own senses.

service of process The delivery (or its legal equivalent, such as publication in a newspaper in some cases) of a legal paper, such as a writ, by an authorized person in a way that meets certain formal requirements.

sheriff's sale A sale [of property] held by a sheriff to pay a court judgment against the owner of the property.

slander Oral defamation. The speaking of false words that injure another person's reputation, business, or property rights.

slander of title† Occurs when a tortfeasor makes false statements about an individual's ownership of property.

sovereign (governmental) immunity The government's freedom from being sued. In many cases, the United States government has waived immunity by a statute such as the Federal Tort Claims Act.

statutes of limitations Laws that set a maximum amount of time after something happens for it to be taken to court, such as a "three-year statute" for lawsuits based on a contract, or a "six-year statute" for a criminal prosecution.

strict (absolute) liability The legal responsibility for damage or injury, even if you are not at fault or negligent.

substantial factor analysis† A test for indirect causation in negligence cases. The tortfeasor is liable for injuries to the victim when the tortfeasor's conduct was a substantial factor in producing the harm.

summary jury trial Alternative dispute resolution in which the judge orders the two sides in a complex case to present their most important facts to a small jury, with admission of evidence either agreed to or decided by the jury in advance. The two sides may agree in advance to be bound by the verdict or may interview the jurors and use the results to negotiate a settlement.

sunshine law A law requiring open meetings of government agencies or allowing (or assisting) public access to government records.

survival statutes A state law that allows a lawsuit to be brought by a relative for a person who just died. The lawsuit is based on the cause of action that the dead person would have had.

T

"taking the victim as you find him" A theory in negligence cases that states that the victim's injuries were reasonably foreseeable even if the tortfeasor was unaware of the victim's peculiar physical, health, or other pre-existing conditions. In effect, the tortfeasor takes the victim as the tortfeasor finds him, and thus proximately causes the harm.

temporary restraining order (TRO) A judge's order to a person to not take a certain action during the period prior to a full hearing on the rightness of the action.

tender years† Minors; usually those under the age of seven.

tort A civil (as opposed to a criminal) wrong, other than a breach of contract. For an act to be a tort, there must be: a legal duty owed by one person to another, a breach (breaking) of that duty, and harm done as a direct result of the action. Examples of torts are negligence, battery, and libel.

tortfeasor A person who commits a tort.

toxic tort actions† Actions involving toxic chemicals, pollution, hazardous waste disposal and transportation, and other environmentally sensitive issues. This litigation applies many tort theories, including trespass to land, negligence, absolute liability for ultrahazardous substances, products liability, and nuisance.

transferred intent In tort law, the principle that if a person intended to hit another but hits a third person instead, he or she legally *intended* to hit the third person. This "legal fiction" sometimes allows the third person to sue the hitter for an intentional tort.

trespass A wrongful entry onto another person's property.

trespass to chattel† Occurs when the tortfeasor intentionally deprives or interferes with the chattel owner's possession or exclusive use of personal property. The tortfeasor's possession or interference must be unauthorized, which means that the owner cannot have consented.

trial The process of deciding a case (giving evidence, making arguments, deciding by a judge and jury, etc.). It occurs if the dispute is not revoked by pleadings, pretrial motions, or settlement. A trial usually takes place in open court, and may be followed by a judgment, an appeal, etc.

U

ultimate user† In products liability law, a person who is injured by a defective product.

It must have been reasonably foreseeable that the injured party would use the defective product.

unforeseeable plaintiffs[†] Persons whose injuries the tortfeasor could not reasonably have anticipated as a result of the tortfeasor's actions.

unreasonable intrusion[†] One type of the intentional tort of invasion of privacy. Occurs when the tortfeasor engages in an excessive and highly offensive invasion upon another person's seclusion or solitude.

V

vicarious liability Legal responsibility for the acts of another person because of some special relationship with that person; for example, the liability of an employer for certain acts of an employee.

vicious propensity rule[†] Doctrine in absolute liability cases involving domestic animals. Normally owners are not strictly liable for injuries caused by their domestic animals. However, if the animals display vicious propensities and hurt someone or their property, then the owner is absolutely liable. Vicious propensities are proven by past episodes of the animal's nasty behavior.

W

warranty Any promise (or a presumed promise, called an *implied warranty*) that certain facts are true. ... In consumer law, ... any obligations imposed by law on a seller that benefit a buyer; for example, the warranty that goods are merchantable and the warranty that goods sold as fit for a particular purpose are fit for that purpose.

wholesaler[†] One who sells goods wholesale, rather than retail.

wrongful birth[†] The birth of a child having serious defects that results from a doctor's failure to provide proper information (to advise, diagnose, or test properly). Can be the basis for a wrongful birth action.

wrongful death statutes [Statutes that allow] a lawsuit [to be] brought by the dependants of a dead person against the person who caused the death. Damages will be given to compensate the dependants for their loss if the killing was negligent or willful.

Z

zone of danger rule The rule in some states that a plaintiff must be in danger of physical harm, and frightened by the danger, to collect damages for the negligent infliction of emotional distress that results from seeing another person injured by the plaintiff.

INDEX

A

A&M Records, Inc. v. Napster, Inc., 205–207
ABA *Formal Opinion 280*, 378
Abatement, 337
Abnormally dangerous (ultrahazardous)
    instrumentalities, 263
Abnormally dangerous activities, 264–272, 282
    strict liability for, 268
    absolute liability for, 275
Absolute defenses, truth and privilege as, 162
Absolute (strict) liability, 4, 262–263. *See also*
    Strict liability
    elements of, 275
    mislabeled as negligence *per se*, 85–86
    public policy objectives and, 263
Absolute immunity, of children, 362
Abuse of process, 146–147, 148, 149, 169
    elements of, 150
    example of, 150
Accident reconstruction, 412–413
    video and computer technologies in, 416
Accident reports, sample, 404–405, 414–415, 432
Accident scenes, documenting, 412–416
Accountability, 5 6
Acquittal, malicious prosecution and, 146
Acting in concert, 33
Action, reasonably necessary, 244
Activities, abnormally dangerous, 264–272
Actual cause of injury, 31
Actual malice, 153–154
Ad coelum doctrine, 179, 180
Adger v. Dillard Department Stores, 32
Administrative agencies, paralegal representation
    before, 375
Agent, in vicarious liability, 73
Airspace, encroachment upon, 179, 180
Akron Bar Assn. v. Green, 389
Alaska, defense of property case in, 225–227, 249, 251
Alternate dispute resolution, 12
Ambulance services, as defendants, 409, 433
American Bar Association (ABA). *See also* ABA
    Formal Opinion 280
    Code and Model Rules, 380–381
    Code of Professional Responsibility, 380, 381
    Model Rules of Professional Conduct, 378, 392
American Jurisprudence 2d, 34–36
American Law Reports series, 330
Analytical approach, three-tier, 61
Animal absolute liability cases, defenses in, 277–279
Animal owners, liability of, 276–281. *See also*
    Companion animals; Domestic animals
Answer, 11
Anticybersquatting Consumer Protection Act
    (ACPA), 212
"Applicable Statute" case, 252–254
Application, in legal analysis, 7, 9
Appreciable confinement, 126
Apprehension, freedom from, 114
Appropriation, 151, 169
    invasion of privacy by, 159, 160
Arbitration, 12
Arbitration clause, 12
Arbitrator, 12
Arizona
    contributory negligence in, 97–98
    trespass to chattel in, 192–194
Arrest
    by warrant, 246, 248, 256
    warrantless, 250–252, 256
"Asbestos in the Air" case, 268–271
Assault, 3–4, 45, 113 116, 169
    elements of, 122
    examples of, 115–116
Assembly defect, 298
Assumption of risk, 99–104, 108
    in animal absolute liability cases, 278
    as a complete defense, 101
    elements of, 104
    examples of, 103–104, 311–312
    products liability and, 308–309, 313, 315
    proof of, 101
Attachment, 246, 247
Attacking force, countering, 222
Attorneys

duty to disclose, 377–379
enforceable regulations against, 380
malpractice claims against, 406
Attraction theory, 62–66, 73, 77
Attractive nuisance doctrine, 62–66, 73, 87
Automobile accident cases, investigating, 424–425,
433

B

Babits v. Vassar Brothers Hospital, et al., 51
Bad faith, 314–315
Bad check lists, 209
Balancing test, 266
Barber v. Pittsburgh Corning Corp., 120
Bare licensee, 66
"Bashful Bad Boy" case, 132–133
Battery, 3, 45, 116–122, 169
    elements of, 122
    examples of, 121
Benefits, investigating, 422
Benefits analysis, 266
Bennett v. Stanley, 63 64
Berman case, 350
Birth, wrongful, 347–351
"Bite-Worse-Than-Bark" case, 279–280
Blood bank information, 428
Boutte v. Nissan Motor Corp., 291–293
Breach of warranty, 314
Brigance v. Velvet Dove Restaurant, Inc., 21–22, 85
Brown v. Hearst Corp., 165–168
Buckley case, 80–81
"Bulldozing Legal Process" case, 147–149
Bump v. Barnett, 384
Burden of rejoinder, 49, 53, 54
Burden of production, 49
Burden of proof, 49, 53
"Burning Candle" case, 42–44
Burt v. Beautiful Savior Lutheran Church, 177–179
Business. *See also* Businesses
    false statements about, 201
    intent to harm ability to conduct, 203
Business directories, 407, 412
Businesses, investigating licensed or regulated, 411,
    433
Business invitees, 67
Business organizational records, 407
But-for causation, 34
"But-for" test, 35–36, 37

C

California
    commercial use of identity in, 152–154
    consent in, 235–236

negligent infliction law in, 81–83
products liability in, 288
California Code of Judicial Ethics, 391
Captives, consent to confinement and, 125
Carroll v. W.R. Grace & Co., 345–346
Carter v. Thurston, 231
Case resolution, 12 13
Castle doctrine, 222
Causation, 37. *See also* Law of causation
    courts and, 34–36
    as a critical component of negligence, 31
    example of, 36–37
    of injury, 30–37
Causation analysis, *American Jurisprudence 2d* on,
    34–36
Causation in fact, 35
Cause-in-fact, 31, 34, 54
Cereghino v. Boeing Co., 266–267
Chattel, 188 189. *See also* Property
    exercising dominion and control over, 195
    intent to deprive and convert to own use, 196
    intent to deprive of or interfere with, 191
    intermeddling with, 193
    lack of consent to use or possess, 196–197
    physical possession of, 195–196
    trespass to, 188v194
    trifling interference with, 191–194
    unauthorized interference with use of, 189
    unauthorized possession of, 189
Children. *See also* Minors
    immunity of, 362–365
    trespass by, 73
"Children of tender years" immunity, 362–365, 368
Citizens, warrantless arrest by, 250–252
City of Whitefish v. Karen Sparks, 384
Civil actions, 10–12
    torts as, 112
Civil rights actions, 248, 359
Claims, investigating previous, 422
Class action notice, 274
Class actions, 273, 282
Client confidences
    paralegal disclosure of, 388–389
    protecting, 376
Client representation, by nonattorneys, 382–385
Client interview techniques, 402
Clutter, excessive, 322–323
Coming and going rule, 74, 76
"Coming to the nuisance" defense, 326–327,
    332–333, 351, 352
Commercial disparagement, 200, 201–203, 215
    communication (publication) to third parties of,
    203
    elements of, 212
    example of, 211

Commercial speech, 153
Commercial transactions, impediment to, 183
Common law, 3
    contributory negligence and, 94
    negligent infliction of emotional distress and, 78
Common legal rights, use and enjoyment of, 331
Common use principle, 265
Communication (publication) to third parties, of
        commercial disparagement, 203
Community, 161, 169
    harm to reputation in, 160, 161
Community standards, 321, 324
Companion animals, value of, 190
Comparative negligence, 95–99, 108, 178
    in animal absolute liability cases, 278
    criticism of, 96
    elements of, 99
    products liability and, 307
Comparative negligence defense, 98–99
Compensatory damages, 46–47
Competency, paralegal, 376
Complainant, 145
Complaint, 10
Complete defense, 101
Comprehensive Environmental Response,
        Compensation
        and Liability Act (CERCLA), 188
Compulsory arbitration, 12
Computer, defamation by, 210–211
Computerized credit reporting, 204
Computerized databases, as information resources,
        418
Computer technologies, use of, 416
Conclusion, in legal analysis, 7, 9
Conduct
    "extreme and outrageous," 138
    outrageous, 130 131, 139
    minimum standards of, 6
Confidences
    disclosure of, 388 389
    protecting, 376
Confinement, 122
    appreciable, 126
    consent to, 125
    force necessary to prevent, 222–223
    intent and, 125–126
    time period of, 126
Connecticut Worker's Compensation Act, 367
Consent, 233–237, 255
    in animal absolute liability cases, 278
    battery and, 117
    to confinement, 125
    elements of, 237
    example of, 237
    implied, 234–235

informed, 233–234, 255
    trespass and, 175, 176
    to use or possess chattel, 196–197
Consequential damages, 46
Consortium, 344, 352
Construction sites, investigating, 425
Consumer contemplation test, 297–298
Consumer information, disclosure of, 208–209
Contact
    force necessary to prevent, 222–223
    harmful or offensive, 117
    imminent threat of, 114
    physical, 117
Contempt of court, 338, 352
Continuing nuisances, 325–326
"Continuous Representation" case, 105–106
Contract, privity of, 289, 295, 315
Contract law warranties, comparison of products
        liability to, 314, 315
Contribution, 34
Contributory liability, 207
Contributory negligence, 70–71, 93–94, 108
    in animal absolute liability cases, 278
    common law rule of, 94
    products liability and, 307, 313, 315
Control, 276, 282
Conversion, 194–199, 214
    as a crime, 198–199
    elements of, 195, 199
    examples of, 199
Conviction, good-faith, 237, 238
Copyright infringement, 205–207
Corporations, obtaining information about, 407–408
Counter-claims, 11
"Country Club Nuisance" case, 324–326
Court of Claims, 358
"Crazy Trucker" case, 114v115
Credit information, invasion of privacy and, 208–209
Credit reporting, computerized, 204
Crime
    conversion as, 198–199
    versus tort, 113
Criminal acts, information resources regarding, 418
Criminal histories, investigating, 423
Criminal prosecution
    groundless, 145
    threatening, 385
Crop destruction, 322
Csizmadia v. Town of Webb, 341–343
Cuevas v. Royal D'Iberville Hotel, 85
Culpability, 5–6
Culpability factoring (liability apportionment),
        95–96
Cybersquatting, 212–214

D

Damage, deprivation of chattel via, 195–196
Damages, 19, 45–48, 54, 337. *See also* Money
    damages
  consequential, 46
  economic and non-economic, 46–47
  general, 46
  for injury resulting from trespass, 178–179
  investigations concerning, 433
  for medical care, 348–350
  nominal, 47, 176
  special, 46
  punitive (exemplary), 47
  in wrongful birth actions, 347
  in wrongful death actions, 352
  in wrongful life actions, 348–350
Damnum absque injuria, 328
Danger, full appreciation of, 100–101
"Dangerous instrumentality" doctrine, 64
Dangerous street conditions, investigating, 425
Danger/utility test, 298
Databases, as information resources, 418
Daubert v. Merrell Dow Pharmaceuticals, Inc., 268,
    270, 291–292
Deadly force, 222
  in defense of property, 225
Deadly traps, in defense of property, 225
Dean & a. v. MacDonald, 102–103
Death, wrongful, 343–347, 352
"Death-Before-Litigation" case, 345–346
Deceit, 140–145
Deception, tortfeasor's profit from, 141
Decker v. Princeton Packet, Inc., 80–81, 162–164
Deep pocket, 294
Defamation, 160–168, 169. *See also* Defamation by
    computer
  per se, 163–164
  truth as a defense against, 166–167
Defamation by computer, 200, 204
  example of, 210–211
  elements of, 212
Defamatory statements, 161, 163
Defendants
  ambulance services and fire departments as, 409
  caution in naming, 406
  determining, 403–412, 430–433
  locating, 403–412
  superior proof position of, 52
Defendant search, sample, 411–412
Defendant's exclusive control, res ipsa loquitur
    and, 50
Defense, complete, 101. *See also* Defenses
Defense of others, in animal absolute liability
    cases, 278–279
Defense of persons, 224–228, 255

  elements of, 224, 228
Defense of property, 224–228, 255
  as a defense, 193
  elements of, 225, 228
  example of, 227–228
Defenses, 220. *See also* Intentional tort defenses;
    Self-defense
Defenses to negligence, Internet resources
    concerning, 110
"Defiant Trucker" case, 225–227, 249, 251
Delahanty v. Hinckley, 271–272, 305
Deodands, 263
Depositions, 11
Deprivation of possession, 199
  extent of, 195
  methods of, 195–196
Deprivation of use, 193
Destruction
  of crops, 322
  deprivation of chattel via, 195–196
  of injured party remedy, 183
Details, investigating, 398
Deterrence, 6
Deuschle v. Jobe, 132–133
Dillon v. Legg, 81, 82, 83
Disabilities, matching skills with, 25
Discharge form, sample, 428–429
Discovery, 11
  using to locate defendants, 403
Disease, causation of, 268–271
Disparagement
  of business, goods, or services, 201
  commercial, 200, 201–203
Dispossession, 189, 191, 192–193
  wrongful, 230
Doctor's evaluation, sample, 427
Documentation, visual 412, 413
Documents
  admissible form for, 413
  hearsay, 415–416
  obtaining, 406
  studying, 403–405
Doe v. Cutter Biological, 369
Dog-bite statutes, 279
Doing business as (d/b/a) certificate, 409
Domain names, infringing, 212–214
Domestic animals, 277, 280, 282
Dominion, 276, 282
Domitae naturae, 276, 277, 281, 282
"Door-to-Door Solicitation" case, 333–334
Douglas v. Gibson, 29–30
Driver information, 418
  investigating, 423
  request for, 419
"Drunken Duty" case, 21–22

Due (reasonable) care, 20
Dust emissions, 323
Duty, 20 22. *See also* Scope of duty
    products liability and, 301–302
Duty of care, 19
    to oneself, 93–94
Dwelling defense doctrine, 222
Dykeman v. Englebrecht, 97–98

E

Earnings potential, lost, 344
Economic damages, 46–47
Egede-Nissen v. Crystal Mountain, Inc., 70–72
Ejectment, 225
Emotional distress
    determining, 131
    elements of, 139
    infliction of, 130–139
    intentional infliction of, 130, 138
    negligent infliction of, 60, 78–83, 88
    reckless infliction of, 135
    property damage and, 190–191
Employees, 74
Employer/employee relationships, vicarious
        liability and, 87
Employers, 74
    immunity of, 366
Employment
    investigating, 420, 433
    liability and, 74, 76, 77–78
Entry
    lawful, 175
    unauthorized, 175
Environmental Protection Agency (EPA), civil
        lawsuits by, 188
Environmental statutes, 188
Epidemiology, 269–270. *See also* Causation of disease
Equitable relief (remedies), 337, 341, 352
"Errant Lot Line" case, 202–203
Error (act), unintentional, 237–240
Escape, false imprisonment and, 126
Escola v. Coca Cola Bottling Co., 290
Estiverne v. Sak's Fifth Avenue, 208–209
Ethics. *See also* Paralegal ethics
    opinions concerning, 389
    role of, 372
Evidence
    preponderance of, 49
    quality of, 49
Evidentiary form, proper, 413 415, 433
Evidentiary rules, jurisdictional, 413, 433
Excavations, unwanted, 323
Exclusive right, 176
Exclusive right of possession, 176
"Exclusive Workers' Compensation" case, 366–367

Execution sales, 246, 247, 249
Exemplary damages, 47
Expenses, injury-related, 420–422
Express assumption of risk, 101
Expressed consent, 117
Express invitation, 68
Express threats of force, 125
Express warranty, tort recovery under, 296, 297
External forces, necessity and, 244
"Extreme and outrageous" conduct, 138

F

Fact gathering, 430
Factual cause of injury, 31
Factual distinctions, 8
Failure to warn seller or manufacturer, 299
Fair Credit Reporting Act (FCRA), 204, 208
"Fair report" privilege, 166, 167
Fair use defense, 206, 207
"Faked Financing" case, 141–144
False arrest, 192 194
False imprisonment, 120, 122–129, 169
    examples of, 129
    reasonable means of escape and, 126
False information
    about credit rating, 204
    knowledge of, 141
False light in the public eye, 158–159, 160, 169
"False light" invasion of privacy, 166, 168
False representation, 143
False statements, 141
    communication (publication) to third parties,
        201, 215
    about goods, services, or business, 201
    regarding property ownership, 200
"False Still" case, 152–154
Family relationships rule, 81, 82, 83
Family immunity, 365, 368
Fault, absolute (strict) liability and, 262–263, 282
Federal Tort Claims Act, 356, 357
Federal Trade Commission (FTA), on bad checks,
        209
Federal Rules of Appellate Procedure, 209
Fee standard, 358
Ferae naturae, 276, 281, 282, 335
Fictitious name, 409
Fidelity Mortgage Co. v. Cook, 141–144
Field v. Philadelphia Electric Co., 118–120
Fire departments, as defendants, 409, 433
Flooding, 322
Force. *See also* Necessary force
    countering, 222
    express or implied threats of, 125
    reasonable, 222, 223, 224, 225, 249
Foreseeability, 20, 22–23, 88

full appreciation of danger and, 100 101
  of injury, 37–38
  negligence and, 364
Foreseeable plaintiffs theory, 23, 282, 283
  products liability and, 302–303
  scope of duty of, 24
Fraud, 140–145, 169
  example of, 144
Fraudulent misrepresentation, 140
"Free-Falling Flight Attendant" case, 70–72
"Free-Roaming Feline" case, 230–232
Freiburger v. Fry, 202
Fresh pursuit, 229
Frivolous litigation, 149–150, 169
Frolic and detour rule, 75, 77
Frye v. United States, 292
Full appreciation of danger, 100 101

G

General damages, 46
Genetic counseling, wrongful birth and, 347
Goals, socially desirable, 240–241
Good-faith conviction, 237, 238
Goods
  false statements about, 201
  intent to harm ability to use, 203
Goodwill, 201
Government
  actions against public nuisance by, 351–352
  functions of, 357–358
  immunity of, 356–358, 368
  as plaintiff, 331
  as sovereign, 357
Governmental agencies
  as information resources, 416, 433
  request for information to, 409–410
  special notice requirements for, 409
  tort liability for, 357
Governmental officials, tort immunity for, 359–361
Governmental/proprietary distinction, 357
  difficulty with and elimination of, 358
Government Web sites, 407
Greene County Board of Education v. Bailey, 197–198
Greenman v. Yuba Power Products, Inc., 288, 290
Griggs v. BIC Corp., 301
Gross negligence, 19, 47
Ground vibrations, as a nuisance, 322
Groundless criminal prosecution, 145
Groups, allocating losses among, 6–7
Guardian ad litem, 350
Gun manufacturers, liability of, 272

H

Hampton v. Hammons, 84

Harassment, in a hostile work environment, 137–138
Harm, under trespass law, 176. *See also* More
  substantial harm
Harmful contact, 117
Hazard-benefit balancing test, 266
Hazardous Materials Transportation Act, 188
Hazardous waste. *See* Toxic tort actions
Health care facilities, state inspection
  information concerning, 430
Health care providers
  investigating, 427–430, 433
  standards for, 429–430
Health hazards, 323–324
  from private nuisances, 351
Health laws, violating, 352
Hearsay, problems related to, 415–416
Higgins v. E.I. Dupont de Nemours & Co., 309–311
Hittle v. Scripto-Tokai Corp., 378
Hoffman, H., 210
Hoffman v. Capital Cities/ABC, Incorporated,
  152–154
Hossler v. Hammel, 202–203
Hostile work environment harassment, 137–138
Hot (fresh) pursuit, 229
"Humiliated Newspaper Lady" case, 133v135
Hypothetical problems, analyzing, 7–8

I

Identity, commercial use of, 152–154
Illness incident report, 431
Imminent danger exception, 290
Imminent threat of contact, 114
Immoral activities, 352
Immunity, 356. *See also* Tort immunities
  of children, 362–365
  public officer's, 246–250
  rationale for, 359–360
  spousal, 365, 368
  statutory, 271, 273–275
  tender-years, 362–365, 368
Immunity defense, 360–361
Immunity doctrine, exceptions to, 359
Impact rule, 78–79, 83
Impleader, process of, 93
Impleading, 93
Implicit invitation, 68
Implied assumption of risk, 101
Implied consent, 117, 234–235
Implied intent, 185
Implied threats of force, 125
Implied warranty, tort recovery under, 296, 297
Inaccurate information, belief based upon, 237, 238
Inappropriate use, ultrahazardous activities and, 265
Incidental injury, nuisance and, 328
Independent contractors, 75, 77, 87

vicarious liability for, 75–76
Indiana Tort Claims Act (ITCA), 361
Individuals, allocating losses among, 6–7
Information. *See also* Inaccurate information;
    Information resources
  about corporations, 407–408
  about health care providers, 427–430
Information resources, public and private sector,
    416–419
Informed consent, 233–234, 255
"Infringing Song" case, 204–207
Injunctions, 337–338, 352
Injured party remedy, destruction of, 183
Injuries to property, 174–217. *See also* Property
  conversion, 194–199
  slander of title, commercial disparagement, and
    defamation by computer, 200–214
  toxic tort actions, 181–188
  trespass to chattel, 188–194
  trespass to land, 174–180
Injury. *See also* Personal injury; Substantial injury
  causation of, 19, 30–37
  facts and circumstances surrounding, 397
  force necessary to prevent, 222–223
  foreseeability of, 37–38
  to innocent party, 141
  intentional, 3, 112
  from malicious prosecution, 146
Injury and illness incident report, 431
Injury-related expenses, investigating, 420–422
Innocent misrepresentation, 140
In re Joint Eastern & Southern Districts Asbestos
    Litigation, 268–271
Insurance, absolute liability as, 263
Insurance coverage, investigating, 422
Integrity, paralegal, 376. *See also* Paralegal ethics
Intent, 112–113, 240
  for assault and battery, 235–236
  battery and, 117–118
  implied, 185
  negligence and, 3
  transferred, 118
Intentional acts, 112–113, 131
"Intentional Cyber Squatter" case, 212–214
Intentional infliction of emotional distress, 130,
    138, 168, 169
  elements and examples of, 139
Intentional injury (tort), 3, 112. *See also*
    Intentional torts; Intentional tort defenses
Intentional interference, 176
Intentional tort defenses, 220–259
  absolute immunity of children for, 362
  consent, 221, 233–237
  defense of persons or property, 220, 224–228
  Internet resources related to, 259

mistake, 221, 237–240
necessity, 221, 243–246
privilege, 221, 240–243
public officer's immunity for legal process
    enforcement, 221, 246–250
rightful repossession, 220, 228–233
self-defense, 220, 221–224
statutes of limitations, 221, 252–254
warrantless arrest by law enforcement officials
    or citizens, 221, 250–252
workers' compensation, 221, 254–255
Intentional torts, 112–172. *See also* Intentional
    tort defenses; Intentional torts to property
  assault and battery, 113–122
  false imprisonment, 122–129
  fraud and misrepresentation, 140–145
  infliction of emotional distress, 130–139
  Internet resources concerning, 172
  invasion of privacy, 151–160
  libel and slander, 160–168
  malicious prosecution and abuse of process,
    145–150
Intentional torts to property, 174–217
  conversion, 194–199
  Internet resources related to, 217
  slander of title, commercial disparagement, and
    defamation by computer, 200–214
  toxic tort actions, 181–188
  trespass to chattel, 188–194
  trespass to land, 174–180
Intent to confine, 125–126
Intent to deprive, 196
Intent to harm, disparagement of goods and, 203
Interference
  intentional, 176
  unreasonable and substantial, 321
Internet resources
  for defenses to negligence, 110
  for intentional tort defenses, 259
  for intentional torts and injuries to persons, 172
  for intentional torts to property, 217
  for investigation, 406–407
  for learning about torts, 16
  for negligence, 57
  for paralegal ethics, 394
  for products liability, 318
  for special negligence actions, 90
  for special tort actions, 354
  for strict liability, 285
  for tort immunities, 370
  for tort investigation, 435–436
Interrogatories, 11
Interview techniques
  client, 402
  witness, 398–402

Intimidation tactics, 324
Intoxication, consent and, 234
Intrusion, unreasonable, 151–152, 159, 160
"Intrusion on Hog Heaven" case, 327–329
Invader, defense of property against, 225
Invasion of privacy, 151–160, 169, 208–209
    example of, 159
    elements of, 160
Investigation, 397. *See also* Tort investigation
    areas for, 420–423
    of automobile accident cases, 424–425
    customizing, 398
    of health care providers, 427–430
    of medical negligence cases, 425–427
Investigative services, 430
Investigators, types of, 397
Invitation
    implicit and express, 68
    limited areas of, 68–70
Invitees, 67, 87
    land owner's highest duty of reasonable care
        toward, 68
    status of, 61
    tort relief for, 69–70
    versus licensees, 68
IRAC analytical framework, 7–8, 9

J

Jackson v. City of Biloxi, 44
Jacobs v. City of Jacksonville, 332, 333–334
Johnson v. Valu Food, Inc., 123–124
Joint and several liability, 33–34
Jones v. Clinton, 136
Judges
    immunity from tort liability, 246, 248–249, 359,
        368
    recusal of, 390–392
Judicial trends, modern, 61
Jurco v. State, 225–227, 249, 251
Jurisdictions, evidentiary rules for, 413
Jurors, reasonable person decisions by, 24–25
Jury trial, summary, 13
Justice courts, paralegal representation in, 375
Justifiable reliance, 143

K

King, as sovereign, 357
King's writs, 5
Knight v. Jewett, 235–236
Knoller v. City and County of San Francisco, 279,
    390–392
Known risk, voluntary assumption of, 100
Koepnick v. Sears, Roebuck & Co., 191–194
Koester v. VCA Animal Hospital, 189–191

L

Lack of consent, to use or possess chattel, 196–197
Land. *See also* Land owners
    physical effects on, 322–323
    sanctity of, 179
    trespass to, 174–180
    victim's status on, 61
Land owner cases, traditional negligence theory
        in, 70
Land owners. *See also* Property ownership
    duty of reasonable care toward licensees, 66–67
    exclusive right of possession by, 176–177
    highest duty of reasonable care toward invitees,
        68
    liability of, 87
    negligence liability of, 73
    reasonable care standards for, 61
    "zero duty" toward trespassers of, 62
Lanham Act, 153
Last clear chance doctrine, 94
"Late Diagnosis" case, 27
Law, rules of, 7, 8
Law enforcement officials, warrantless arrest by,
        250–252, 256
Law of causation, 40. *See also* Causation
Lawful entry, 175
Lawsuits, investigating previous, 422
Lawyer ethics codes, inclusion of paralegals in, 377
Lawyers, ethical conduct for, 381
Legal actions, limitations of, 104, 252
Legal analysis, issues in, 7, 9
Legal assistants, NALA Model Standards and
        Guidelines for Utilization of, 373–374. *See*
also Paralegals
Legal cause, 37. *See also* Proximate causes
Legal ethics, role of, 372. *See also* Paralegal ethics
Legal process enforcement, public officer's
        immunity for, 246–250
Legal proceedings, misuse of, 146–147
Legal rights, use and enjoyment of, 331
Legislators, immunity from tort liability, 359, 368
Leo v. Kerr-McGee, 182–184
Lewis v. Fowler, 198
Liability, 46. *See also* Absolute (strict)
        liability; Strict liability
    for abnormally dangerous activities, 264–272
    apportionment of, 95–96
    joint and several, 33–34
    products, 4, 6
    proximate cause and, 281–282
    scope of employment and, 74, 76, 77–78
    for trespass, 178
    vicarious, 73–78
Libel, 160, 169
    elements of, 168

example of, 164–165
nature of the statement in, 160
Licensed businesses, investigating, 411
Licensees, 66, 67, 87
land owner's duty of reasonable care toward, 66–67, 73
versus invitees, 68
Licensee status, 61
Liens, improper, 146–147
Limitations of actions, 104, 252
Lineberry v. State Farm Fire & Casualty Co., 156–158
Litigation, frivolous, 149–150, 169
"Living Dead" case, 162–164
Local governmental agencies, as information resources, 416
Losses, allocating among individuals or groups, 6–7
Loss of consortium, 344
Lost lifetime earnings potential, 344
Lost wages, investigating, 420, 433
Lousiana State Bar Assn. v. Edwins, 389

M

MacPherson v. Buick Motor Co., 290
Maintenance defect, in products liability, 298–299
Malice, 145–146
actual, 153–154
Malicious prosecution, 145–150, 169
elements of, 150
example of, 149–150
recovery for, 146
Malicious statements, 202
Malpractice, 25–28, 54, 352. *See also* Medical malpractice
Malpractice insurance, 105
Mandamus order, 337
Manufacturers, failure to warn by, 299
Marengo Cave Co. v. Ross, 179
Marrs v. Marriott Corp., 154–155
Marshall v. Ranne, 280
Martin v. Heffelfinger, 360–361
Mass torts, 273–275, 282
Master, 74–75
"McDonald's Coffee" case, 48
McDonald's Game class action notice, 274
Means of escape, false imprisonment and, 126
Mechanical malfunction, investigating, 425
Mechanic's liens, improper, 146–147
Media, negligence on the part of, 167
Mediation, 12
Mediator, 12
Medical expenses, damages for, 348–350
Medical malpractice, 26 28
state statutes of limitations for, 107
Medical treatment, negligent, 252–254
Medical negligence cases, investigating, 425–427,

433
Medical reports, sample, 426–427, 428–429
Mens rea, 240
Mental anguish, 130. *See also* Emotional distress
Mental retardation, consent and, 234
Mere licensee, 66
Mezrah v. Bevis, 27
Minimum standards of conduct, 6
Minitrial, 12 13
"Minor Imprisonment" case, 123–124
Minors. *See also* Children entries
immunity of, 362–365
negligent failure to control, 363–365
Misconduct
paralegal, 379
wanton, 135
Misrepresentation, 140–145, 169
examples of, 144–145
Missouri v. Jenkins, 389
Mistake, 237–240, 255–256
elements of, 240
example of, 239
Mitchell v. Globe International Publishing, Inc., 133–134
Mixed nuisances, 321, 332, 352
elements of, 336
Mobile tort, 199
Money, conversion claims concerning, 197–198
Money damages, 337, 341, 352
Montana, wrongful death action in, 345–346
More substantial harm, thwarting, 243–244
"More-Than-Touch Football Game" case, 235–236
Moscatello v. University of Medicine and Dentistry of New Jersey, 348–350
Motive, 240–241
Motor vehicle consent statutes, 87
Motor vehicle vicarious liability, 76, 77–78
Musical compositions, copyright infringement of, 205–207

N

Naked (mere, bare) licensee, 66
NALA rules, legal effect of, 377
"Napster" case, 204–207
National Association of Legal Assistants (NALA), list of permissible paralegal activities by, 377. *See also* NALA rules
National Association of Legal Assistants (NALA) Ethics Code and Guidelines, 372–379, 392
National Oceanic and Atmospheric Administration (NOAA), 417
National Federation of Paralegal Associations (NFPA) Code and Model Rules, 379–380, 392
Necessary force, 222–223
Necessity, 241, 243–246

elements of, 246
example of, 246
Negligence, 3, 18–57. *See also* Negligence
defenses; Negligence *per se*; Special
negligence actions
accountability for, 77–78
in animal absolute liability cases, 278
causation of injury and, 30–37
comparative, 95–99, 108, 178, 278, 307
contributory, 70 71, 93–94, 108, 278, 307, 313,
315
damages and, 45–48
defined, 18–19, 40–41
duty and reasonable care standard and, 20–30
elements of, 19–20
gross, 19, 47
handling reports about, 410
immunity of children from, 362–363
Internet resources related to, 57
ordinary, 19
percentages of, 95–96
presumption of, 50
in products liability, 295, 307
proving, 48–53
proximate cause and, 37–45
slight, 19
state statutes of limitations for, 107
statute violation and, 53
tort recovery in, 296
Negligence defenses, 92–110
assumption of risk, 99–104
comparative negligence, 95–99
contributory negligence and last clear chance,
93–94
statutes of limitations, 104–107
use of, 92–93
Negligence per se, 84–87, 88
absolute liability mislabeled as, 85–86
class of persons protected by, 85
elements of, 87
examples of, 86–87
toxic torts as, 86–87
Negligence theory
in land owner cases, 70
traditional, 73
Negligent acts (omissions), 19
Negligent infliction law, California approach to,
81–83
Negligent infliction of emotional distress, 78–83, 88
elements of, 83
Negligent misrepresentation, 140
Neighboring uses, unwanted associations with, 324,
351
Newspapers, as sources of information, 417
News reports, as sources of information, 417

New torts, creation of, 209–210
"1983" action, 248, 359
Noise, excessive, 323
Nominal damages, 47, 176
Nonattorneys, client representation by, 382–385
Non-economic damages, 46–47
Noor v. Continental Casualty Co., 27
Notice to employer, 421
"Not-So-Bright Light" case, 301–302, 377–379
"Not-So-Gut-Wrenching Conflict" case, 191–194
Noxious odors, 323
"Nuisance Lake" case, 185–188
"Nuisance Pool" case, 63–64
Nuisances, 320 330. *See also* Nuisances *per se*;
Private nuisances; Public nuisances
continuing, 325–326
elements of, 187
mixed, 321, 332, 352
permanent, 325
remedies for, 336–343
Nuisances *per se*, 332
elements of, 336
examples of, 335
"Nuked Plaintiff" case, 118–120

O

Obituaries, false, 163–164
Obscene gestures, 160
Occupiers, 60–61
negligence liability of, 73
Odors, noxious, 323
Offensive contact, 117
preventing, 222–223
Offensive force, countering, 222
Offensiveness, personal nature of, 324
Officers, tort immunity for, 359–361
Ohio Casualty Insurance Co. v. Todd, 21–22, 84–85
Omissions, negligent, 19
Ordinary negligence, 19
OSHA injury and illness incident report, 431
Outrageous conduct, 130–131, 139
"Overzealous Store Security Officer" case, 126–129
Owners, of land, 61. *See also* Land owners
Ownership, false statements regarding, 200
Owner's use of property, intent to hinder or
damage, 200–201

P

Palsgraf v. Long Island Railroad, 39–41
Paralegal activities, NALA list of permissible, 377
Paralegal ethics, 372–394
American Bar Association (ABA) Code and Model
Rules for, 380 385

hypothetical problems concerning, 385–389
information concerning, 389–392
Internet resources related to, 394
National Association of Legal Assistants (NALA)
 Ethics Code and Guidelines for, 372–379, 392
National Federation of Paralegal Associations
 (NPPA) Code and Model Rules for, 379–380
Paralegals. *See also* Personal injury paralegals
 avoiding the appearance of impropriety by, 376
 client confidences and, 376
 independent legal judgment by, 376
 integrity and competency of, 376
 investigations by, 397, 430
 lay representation in justice or small claims
  courts by, 375
 negligence by, 387
 representation before administrative agencies
  by, 375
 restricted duties of, 372–374
 sanctioning of, 379
 supervised duties of, 375–376
 unauthorized practice of law by, 386, 387–388
 unethical conduct by, 385–389
"Parental Control" case, 363–365
Partner names, *obtaining*, 409
Partnerships, obtaining information about, 408–409
Pecuniary benefit test, 358
Pennsylvania Ethics Handbook, 378
Pennsylvania Rule of Professional Conduct, 378
Percentage of negligence, 95–96
Perez v. Southern Pacific Transport Co., 61
Permanent injunctions, 338, 352
Permanent nuisances, 325
Per se, 161–162, 336
Personal injury, 112 172. *See also* Personal injury
 litigation
 assault and battery, 113–122
 false imprisonment, 122–129
 fraud and misrepresentation, 140–145
 infliction of emotional distress, 130–139
 intentional torts, 112–113
 invasion of privacy, 151–160
 libel and slander, 160–168
 malicious prosecution and abuse of process,
  145–150
Personal injury litigation, 396
 Internet resources concerning, 172
 misuse of, 146
Personal injury paralegals
 interview techniques for, 402
 tasks of, 396
"Personal-Property Pet" case, 189–191
Persons
 defense of, 224–228, 255
 protecting, 5–6

Pets, as personal property, 189–191
Photography, invasion of privacy by, 159
Physical barriers, as a method of false
 imprisonment, 124–125
Physical contact, 117. *See also* Contact
Physical manifestations rule, 79, 83
Physical proximity, in negligent infliction law, 82
Pierce v. Finerty, 231
Plaintiffs
 previous injuries to, 423
 "professional," 422
Police
 liability of, 359
 power of, 331
Police accident report, sample, 404–405
Policy. *See* Public policy
Pollicino v. Roemer and Featherstonehaugh P.C.,
 105–106
"Polluting Toll Booth" case, 338–341
Pollution, 322. *See also* Toxic tort actions
Possession, 214
 deprivation of, 195–196
 exclusive right of, 176–177
 interference with, 185
 unauthorized, 189
 wrongful denial of, 229–230
Post-trial procedures, 12
Pote v. Jarrell, 147–149
Powers v. Palacios, 279–280
Premises liability, 60–73, 87. *See also* Licensees
Preponderance of the evidence, 49
"Presidential Passion" case, 136
Presumption of negligence, 50
Pretrial procedures, 11
Prima facie case, 49
 of sexual harassment, 137
Principal, in vicarious liability, 73
Principal/agent relationship, employment and,
 73–74
Prior v. White, 333–334
Privacy, invasion of, 151–160
Private nuisances, 187, 320, 321, 351
 elements of, 330
 examples of, 321–324, 329–330
Private prosecutor, 248
Private facts, public disclosure of, 156–158, 160
Private sector resources, 416–419
Privilege, 240–243, 256, 356
 as an absolute defense, 162
 elements of, 243
 example of, 242–243
 exceptions to, 359
 less injurious alternatives and, 241
 similarity to other defenses, 241–242
Privity of contract, 289, 315

in products liability, 295
Probable cause, 145
Procanik case, 349, 350
Process, 246, 247
    abuse of, 146–147, 148, 149
Process enforcement defense, 246–250, 256
    elements of, 250
Process serving, 246, 247
    to partnerships, 409
Product defects, 315. *See also* Products liability
    ignoring, 308
Product design, faulty, 297–298
Product distribution chain, 294
Product instructions/warnings, failure to follow, 309
Product maintenance, 315
    improper, 298–299, 308
Product manufacture/assembly, error in, 298
Product manufacturer, 293
Product misuse, 313, 315
    by ultimate user, 307
Products. *See also* Products liability
    misuse of, 309–311, 313
    unreasonably dangerous, 296–299
Products liability, 4, 6, 184, 288–318
    bad faith and, 314–315
    business requirement for, 299
    comparison to contract law warranties, 314
    defenses to, 306–313
    elements of, 295–306
    examples of, 303–304
    Internet resources related to, 318
    parties involved in, 293–294
    substantially unchanged condition requirement for, 299–300
    theory and history of, 288–293
Products liability formula, 295
Professional community standard of care, 25
Professional conduct, incompetent and improper, 386
Professional malpractice, 25–28
"Professional plaintiffs," 422
Professional responsibility, ABA code of, 381
Proof
    burden of, 49
    in negligence cases, 48–53
Property. *See also* Chattel; Deprivation of possession; Injuries to property
    conversion of, 7
    damage to or destruction of, 190–191, 195–196
    defense of, 224–228, 255
    emotional injury and, 190–191
    intent to hinder or damage owner's use of, 200–201
    protecting, 5–6
    retaking possession of, 229

Property ownership. *See also* Land owners
    communication (publication) of false statements concerning, 201
    false statements regarding, 200
Proper use requirement, products liability and, 300
Proprietary actions, tort liability for, 357–358
Prosecution, malicious, 145–150
Prosecutors, immunity of, 246, 248–249
Prosser, William L., 209–210
Proximate causes, 35, 37–45, 54, 281–282, 283
    examples of, 45, 303–304
    products liability and, 300
    scope of duty and, 38–42
Publication, 160, 161
    of false statements, 200, 201
Public business records, 407–408
Public disclosure of private facts, 156–158, 160, 169
Public figures, defamation and, 161
Public health laws, violating, 352
Public nuisance *per se*, 332
Public nuisances, 187–188, 320–321, 331–354, 351–352
    elements of, 336
    examples of, 335
    types of, 331–332
Public officers
    immunity for legal process enforcement, 246–250
    immunity of, 368
    tort immunity for, 359–361
Public policy
    products liability and, 289
    statutory immunity and, 271
    strict liability and, 263
Public sector resources, 416–419
Pulliam v. Allen, 360
Punitive (exemplary) damages, 47
Purchasers, 294
"Purloined Purse" case, 197–198

Q

Quality of evidence, standard of proof and, 49
"Quarter-Sized Puddle" case, 32
Quid pro quo sexual harassment, 137

R

Radiology report, sample, 426
Radio news reports, as sources of information, 417
Ramirez case, 183–184
Real property, defense of, 225. *See also* Injuries to property; Property
Reasonable apprehension, 114
Reasonable care, 18–19
    in abnormally dangerous activities, 264–265
Reasonable care duty, 20

strict liability and, 282, 283
Reasonable care standard, 20–30
  defined, 23–25
  for land owners, 61
Reasonable community standard, 321
Reasonable force, 222, 223, 224, 225, 249, 255
Reasonable man. *See* Reasonable person
Reasonable means of escape, false imprisonment
    and, 126
Reasonableness
  of foreseeability, 20
  negligence and, 19
Reasonableness test, outrageous conduct and,
    130–131
Reasonable person, 20
Reasonable person test (standard), 23–25, 26, 117,
    351
  nuisances and, 321
Reasonable plaintiffs theory, 54
Reasonably necessary action, 244
Reckless infliction of emotional distress, 135, 169
  elements of, 139
"Recusal" case, 390
Regulated businesses, investigating, 411
"Rejected Check" case, 208–209
Remedies, 352
  for nuisances, 336–337
Rent-a-judge, 13
Replevin, 246, 247–248
Repossession
  prompt efforts at, 229
  rightful, 228–233
Reputation, harm to in the community, 160, 161
Research, via telephone, 406
Res ipsa loquitur, 49–52, 53, 54
  example of, 52
Resources, public and private sector, 416–419. *See
    also* Internet resources
Respondeat superior, 74–76, 87
Restatement of Torts, 238
Restatement (Second) of Torts, 238–239, 271,
    272, 273
  on animal owner's liability, 280
  on child trespass, 64–65
  on dangerous activities liability, 264, 272,
    275, 282
  on dispossession, 192–193
  on mistake, 239
  on necessity, 245
  on privilege, 241–242
  on property reclamation, 231
  on strict products liability, 290, 296, 297,
    299, 302, 304, 305, 306
  on trespass to chattel, 193
Restatement (Second) rule, 264–266, 296

Restatements of the Law, 238
Restraining order, temporary, 338
"Restraint" case, 29–30
Retailers, 293, 294
"Return of the Living Dead" case, 80–81
Rightful repossession, 228–233, 255
  elements of, 233
  example of, 232–233
"Right to be let alone," 151
Riparian law, 322
Risk. *See also* Known risk
  assumption of, 99–104, 278, 308
  of substantial harm, 264, 282
Robinson v. Health Midwest Development Group,
    252–254
Rogers v. T.J.X. Cos., 127–129
Rosenberg v. Packerland Packing Co., 114–115
Rowland v. Christian, 61
Rule 11 sanctions, 208, 209
Rules of law, 7, 8
*Russell Corporation v. Sullivan et al. Avondale
    Mills, Inc.*, 185–188

S

Safety devices, removal of, 307
Sampson v. Zimmerman, 42–44
"Saturday Night Special" case, 271–272, 305
"Scale that Shook Tort Law" case, 39–41
Schroeder case, 350
Scienter, 143
Scientific evidence, sufficiency of, 268
Scope of duty, 20–30
  proximate cause and, 38–42
  of reasonable care and foreseeable plaintiffs
    theory, 24
  victim's status on land and, 61
Scope of employment, liability within and outside,
    74, 76, 77–78
*Second Restatement. See Restatement (Second) of
    Torts* entries
Secretaries of state offices, 407
  sample requests to, 408
Self-defense, 221–224, 255
  in animal absolute liability cases, 278–279
  elements of, 221, 224
  example of, 223
Sellers, 293
  failure to warn by, 299
Sensibilities, offending, 323–324
Sensory perception rule, 81, 82, 83
Servant, 74–75
Service of process, 10, 246, 247
  to partnerships, 409
  trespass and, 175
Services

false statements about, 201
intent to harm ability to supply, 203
Seven-year-old rule, 368
Sexual advances, 135
Sexual harassment, 136–139
quid pro quo, 137
Shehyn v. United States, 230–232
Sheriff's sales, 247
Sherk v. Indiana Waste Systems, Inc., 327–329
Shields v. Zuccarini, 212 214
Silvester v. Spring Valley Country Club, 325–326
Skills, matching with disabilities, 25
Slander, 160, 169. *See also* Slander *per se*
elements of, 168
example of, 164
nature of the statement in, 160
Slander of title, 200–201, 202–203, 215
elements of, 212
Slander *per se*, 161–162
"Sleeping Driver" case, 291–293
Slight negligence, 19
Small claims courts, paralegal representation in, 375
Smith v. Scripto-Tokai Corp., 301–302, 377–379
Smoke emissions, 323
Social conduct, minimum standards of, 6
Socially desirable goals, 240–241
"Social utility claim," 272, 305
Soil pollution, 322
Sole proprietor names, obtaining, 409
Sovereign immunity, 356–358, 368
modern applications of, 357
Sparks v. Johnson, 382–385
Special damages, 46
from nuisances, 187
Special duty, based upon special relationship, 28–30
Special negligence actions, 60–90
Internet resources related to, 90
negligence *per se*, 84–87
negligent infliction of emotional distress, 78–83
premises liability, 60–73
vicarious liability, 73–78
Special relationship, special duty based upon, 28–30
Special tort actions, 320–354
Internet resources related to, 354
nuisances, 320–330
public nuisances, 331–336
remedies for nuisances, 336–343
survival and wrongful death statutes, 343–347
wrongful birth, 347–351
Speech, commercial, 153
"Speedway Release" case, 102–103
Spousal immunity, 365, 368
Standard of care, 25
State ex rel. Freison v. Isner, 383–384
State inspection information, obtaining, 430

State-of-the-art discoverability test, 298
States, suits against, 358
State statutes of limitations, 107
Statutes
environmental, 188
violation of, 53, 55
Statutes of limitations, 108, 252–254, 256
as defenses to negligence, 104–107
nuisances and, 325–326
sample, 107
"Statutory Hangover" case, 84–85, 341–343
Statutory immunity, 271
example of, 273–275
Stevens, G., 210
Street conditions, investigating, 425
Strict liability, 4, 262–263, 315
for abnormally dangerous activities, 264–272
animal owners and, 276–281
duty of reasonable care and, 282, 283
example of, 280–281
historical development of, 263
Internet resources related to, 285
limitations to, 263
mass torts and, 273–275
proximate cause and, 281–282
public policy objectives and, 263
scope of, 281–282
tort recovery under, 296, 297
Strict products liability, 288
Stuyvesant v. Wilcox, 231
Sua sponte, 272
"Substantial damage," from nuisances, 187
Substantial factor analysis, 31–33, 34
Substantial factor test, 36
Substantial harm, high risk of, 264, 282
Substantially unchanged condition requirement, 299–300
Sufficiency, of scientific evidence, 268
Summary jury trial, 13
Summers v. Tice, 33
Sunshine laws, 409
Supervisor's workplace accident investigation report, 432
Survival statutes, 343–347, 352

T

"Taking the victim as you find him," 42
Taylor v. Chubb, 389
Technical trespass, 176
Telephone, as a research tool, 406
Telephone calls, incessant, 324
Television, as a source of information, 417
Temperatures, excessive, 323
Temporary injunctions, 338, 352

Temporary restraining orders (TROs), 338, 352
Tender-years immunity, 362–365, 368
Ten Hopen v. Walker, 190
Tennessee v. Garner, 359
Theft, 198
Third parties, defamation and, 161
Thomas v. Winchester, 289–290
Three-tier land owner standards, 61
Three-year statute of limitations, 107
Title, slander of, 200–201
Tort analysis, 8 9
Tort defenses, 92
Tortfeasors, 2, 3, 6
    multiple, 33–34
    profit from deception by, 141
Tort handbook, 210
Tort immunities, 356–370
    children of tender years, 362–365
    governmental (sovereign), 356–358
    Internet resources related to, 369
    public officers, 359–361
    spousal/family, 365
    workers' compensation, 366–367
Tort investigation, 396–436
    areas for, 420–423
    defendant determination and location, 403–412
    goals of, 398
    importance of, 397–398
    Internet resources related to, 435–436
    public and private sector resources and, 416–419
    scene documentation, 412–416
    of various types of tort cases, 424–430
    witness interview, 398–402
Tort law, 13–14
    categories of, 3
    development of, 209–210
    history of, 4–5
    modern, 5
    public policy objectives in, 5–7
    sources of, 3
"Tort Liability for Defamation by Computer"
    (Stevens & Hoffman), 210
Tort problems, solving, 8–10
Tort recovery, elements of, 296, 297
Torts. *See also* Intentional torts; Mass torts; New
    torts; Special tort actions; Tort defenses
    defined, 2–3
    intentional, 3–4
    Internet resources related to, 16
    toxic, 86–87, 320
    unique elements of, 4
    versus crimes, 113
Tort scenes, documenting, 412–416, 430, 433
"Toxic Fire Paint" case, 309–311
Toxic Substances Control Act, 188

Toxic tort actions, 181–188, 214, 264
"Toxic Tort" case, 181–184
Toxic tort nuisances, 323–324
Toxic torts, 320
    as negligence *per se*, 86–87
Toxic trespass, 185–188
    elements of, 185
Toxic waste seepage, 185
Traditional negligence theory, in land owner
    cases, 70
Transferred intent doctrine, 118, 223
Trespass, 4, 45, 174. *See also* Trespass to
    chattel; Trespass to land
    above and below land, 179–180
    compensation for injury resulting from, 178–179
    defense of property against, 225
    duty of reasonable care and, 65, 67
Trespassers, 87
    land owner duty to, 73
    land owner "zero duty" toward, 62
    status of, 61
Trespassing children, 62–66
    land owner duty to, 73
Trespass to chattel, 188–194, 214
    elements of, 194
Trespass to land, 174–180, 214
    elements of, 194
    examples of, 180
Trial, 11
Trier-of-fact, 24–25
Trover lawsuits, 194–195, 198
Truth
    as an absolute defense, 162, 169
    as a defense, 243
    as a defense against defamation, 166–167
"Truthful Video Camera" case, 154–155
Two-year statute of limitations, 107

U

Ultimate users, 294, 313, 315
    product misuse by, 307
Ultrahazardous activities, 264, 282
"Ultrahazardous Activity" case, 266–267
Ultrahazardous instrumentalities, 263
Unauthorized entry, 175
"Unauthorized Practice" case, 382–385
"Un-Easy Rider" case, 97–98
"Unexpected Burn" case, 51
Unforeseeable injuries, 38
Unforeseeable plaintiffs, 23
"Unhappy Probationer" case, 360–361
"Unholy Waters" case, 177–179
Uniform Commercial Code (UCC), 314
Uniform Contribution Among Tortfeasors Act of
    1984, 97–98

Unintentional error (act), 237–240
United States Environmental Protection Agency v. The Port Authority of New York and New Jersey, 338–341
Unreasonable and substantial interference, 321
Unreasonable intrusion, 151–152, 160, 169
  example of, 159
Unreasonably dangerous products, 296–299
Unwanted associations, 324
Unwanted excavations, 323
Use and enjoyment, 321
Used car sales, fraud or misrepresentation in, 144–145

V

Vicarious liability, 60, 73–78, 87
  for independent contractors, 75–76
  motor vehicle, 76, 77–78
Vicious propensity rule, 277, 282–283
  example of, 280–281
Victim, foreseeability of, 20
Video cameras, 154–155, 156–158
Video news footage, 417
Video technologies, use of, 416
"Viewing Room Covered by the Umbrella" case, 156–158
Visual documentation, 412–413
Volition, consent and, 234
Voluntary acceptance, consent and, 234
Voluntary agreement, 255
Voluntary assumption of known risk, 100
Vorvis v. Southern New England Telephone Co., 366–367

W

Wages, investigating, 420
Warnings, product, 309
Warrant, arrest by, 246, 248, 256
Warranties, 289
  breach of, 314
  tort recovery under, 296, 297
Warrantless arrest, 250–252, 256
  defenses to, 250
  example of, 251
Water pollution, 322
Weather statistics, 417
Web sites, researching, 406–407. *See also* Internet resources
Wells v. Hickman, 363–365
Wholesalers, 293
Wild animals, 276, 280, 282
Wildlife ownership, 276–277
Winterbottom v. Wright, 289
Witnesses, interview techniques and questions for,

398–402, 430
Witness statement, sample, 399–401
"Woodchipper Murderer" case, 165–168
Workers' compensation, 254–255, 256
  employee suits and, 366–367, 368
Workers' compensation form, 421
Workplace accident investigation report, 432
Writing, defamation via, 160
Writ of mandamus, 337
Writ of "trespass," 178
Wrongful birth actions, 347–351, 352
  elements of, 351
Wrongful death actions
  damages in, 344
  defenses in, 344
  examples of, 346
  plaintiffs in, 343
  typical facts in, 343
Wrongful death statutes, 343–347, 352
  elements of, 347
Wrongful dispossession, 230
Wrongful life actions, 320, 348–350
  example of, 351
"Wrongful Life and Birth Pregnancy" case, 348–350

Z

Zone of danger, 38, 54, 88
Zone of danger rule, 79, 83